What's New in This Edition

Teach Yourself Database Programming with Visual Basic 5 in 21 Days, Second Edition, teaches you all the techniques necessary to build a complete database solution. In this edition, we have concentrated on improving on our Visual Basic 4 efforts. You'll find the following new features/improvements in this edition:

☐ All exercises and code examples take advantage of new Visual Basic 5 features.

☐ All coding is for 32-bit application development. All references to 16-bit code have been removed.

☐ The text now includes code and examples for creating your own data-bound custom controls for data validation and indexed list retrieval. You'll also find ActiveX DLLs to handle data form generating, data graphing, error trapping, and security management.

☐ All BAS module library routines have been converted to Active X DLLs and OLE Servers.

☐ Two entirely new chapters have been added. One covers the Remote Data Controls and Remote Data Objects. The other new chapter shows you how to use the replication features of Microsoft Jet databases.

☐ Coverage has been added for Crystal Reports Pro version 4.5.

☐ The SQL-VB utility has been improved. This handy scripting utility can now be called as an OLE Server from any other VBA-compliant application, including Microsoft Office tools. SQL-VB5 can also manage data in all Microsoft Jet-supported database formats, including ODBC data connections.

☐ The chapter on Visual Basic Database Objects has been totally revamped, including coverage of the new Microsoft Jet 3.5 data-access object library and the new ODBCDirect options for the standard data control.

Teach Yourself DATABASE PROGRAMMING WITH VISUAL BASIC® 5

in 21 Days, Second Edition

Teach Yourself

DATABASE
PROGRAMMING
WITH
VISUAL BASIC® 5
in 21 Days

Michael C. Amundsen
Curtis L. Smith

SAMS
PUBLISHING

201 West 103rd Street
Indianapolis, Indiana 46290

This edition is dedicated to all our past, present, and future readers. Thanks for your continued support.—Mike Amundsen

To Chris—Curtis Smith

Copyright © 1997 by Sams Publishing

SECOND EDITION

International Standard Book Number: 0-672-31018-X

Library of Congress Catalog Card Number: 96-71197

2000   99   98   4   3

Interpretation of the printing code: the rightmost double-digit number is the year of the book's printing; the rightmost single-digit, the number of the book's printing. For example, a printing code of 97-1 shows that the first printing of the book occurred in 1997.

Composed in AGaramond and MCPdigital by Macmillan Computer Publishing

Printed in the United States of America

Trademarks

Publisher and President   Richard K. Swadley
Publishing Manager   Greg Wiegand
Director of Editorial Services   Cindy Morrow
Director of Marketing   Kelli S. Spencer
Assistant Marketing Managers   Kristina Perry, Rachel Wolfe

Acquisitions Editor
Sharon Cox

Development Editor
Richard Alvey

Software Development Specialist
Brad Myers

Production Editor
Mary Ann Faughnan

Indexer
Bruce Clingaman

Technical Reviewer
Greg Guntle

Editorial Coordinator
Katie Wise

Technical Edit Coordinator
Lynette Quinn

Resource Coordinator
Deborah Frisby

Editorial Assistants
Carol Ackerman
Andi Richter
Rhonda Tinch-Mize

Cover Designer
Tim Amrhein

Book Designer
Gary Adair

Copy Writer
Peter Fuller

Production Team Supervisors
Brad Chinn
Charlotte Clapp

Production
Jennifer Dierdorff
Brice Gosnell
Ayanna Lacey
Paula Lowell
Ryan Rader
Becky Stutzman
Colleen Williams

Overview

Contents

Acknowledgments

There are a number of people to thank this time around. First, of course are the thousands of kind people who read our first edition. We were lucky enough to receive many comments from readers. Many of your suggestions and requests have been added to this second edition.

We'd also like to thank all of those colleagues and clients who have become test subjects for our theories and sample projects. Even though some of you were not really "willing subjects," your support and encouragement were invaluable in allowing us to continue to experiment with Visual Basic in the real world instead of at some isolated test terminal.

Finally, the folks at Sams Publishing continued to provide invaluable assistance and support as we worked through this new edition. So many people work on a book that trying to name even a few only serves to point out many uncredited others. If this book reads well, looks good on paper, and covers the topics most requested, that is due in large part to the good work of the people at Sams. Any typos, errors, and omissions that remain exist despite their tremendous efforts.

About the Authors

Mike Amundsen

Mike Amundsen works as an IS Consulting and Training Specialist for Design-Synergy Corporation, a consulting and project management firm specializing in information technology services. He travels the U.S. and Europe teaching and consulting on Windows development topics.

Mike's other book projects include authoring the *MAPI, SAPI, and TAPI Developer's Guide* published by Sams Publishing, and contributing to Sams Publishing's *Visual Basic 4 Unleashed* and Sams' *VB4 Developer's Guide*. Mike is a contributing editor for Cobb's *Inside Visual Basic for Windows* newsletter and regularly contributes to Cobb's *Access Developer's Journal, Inside Microsoft Access*, and *Microsoft Office Developer's Journal*. His work has also been published in *Visual Basic Programmer's Journal* magazine and *VB Tech* magazine.

When he's not busy writing or traveling to client sites, Mike spends time with his family at his home in Kentucky. You can reach Mike at his CompuServe address—102461,1267 or at MikeAmundsen@msn.com on the Internet.

Curtis Smith

Curtis Smith has been working in the computer industry for many years. He has a financial background, which helps to bring a practical real-world flair to *Teach Yourself Database Programming with Visual Basic 5 in 21 Days*. Curtis has worked in the federal government, and in the banking, transportation, and pharmaceutical industries. He has significant experience implementing financial, project management, inventory, and maintenance software applications. Curtis currently holds an MBA from Miami University (Oxford, Ohio), and is a Certified Public Accountant in the state of Ohio.

Tell Us What You Think!

As a reader, you are the most important critic and commentator of our books. We value your opinion and want to know what we're doing right, what we could do better, what areas you'd like to see us publish in, and any other words of wisdom you're willing to pass our way. You can help us make strong books that meet your needs and give you the computer guidance you require.

Do you have access to CompuServe or the World Wide Web? Then check out our CompuServe forum by typing GO SAMS at any prompt. If you prefer the World Wide Web, check out our site at http://www.mcp.com.

 **NOTE**
> If you have a technical question about this book, call the technical support line at 317-581-3833.

As the publishing manager of the group that created this book, I welcome your comments. You can fax, e-mail, or write me directly to let me know what you did or didn't like about this book—as well as what we can do to make our books stronger. Here's the information:

Fax: 317-581-4669

E-mail: programming_mgr@sams.samspublishing.com

Mail: Greg Wiegand
          Sams Publishing
          201 W. 103rd Street
          Indianapolis, IN 46290

Introduction

Welcome to Database Programming in Visual Basic 5

Welcome to *Teach Yourself Database Programming with Visual Basic 5 in 21 Days, Second Edition.* You cover a lot of ground in the next 21 lessons—from developing fully functional input screens with fewer than 10 lines of Visual Basic code and writing Visual Basic code libraries, to handling complex user security and auditing in multiuser applications, to creating online help files for your Visual Basic programs, and much more. Whether you are a power user, a business professional, a database guru, or a Visual Basic programmer, you'll find something in this book to help you improve your Visual Basic and database skills.

Each week you focus on a different aspect of database programming with Visual Basic. In Week 1, you learn about issues related to building simple database applications using the extensive collection of data controls available with Visual Basic. In Week 2, you concentrate on techniques for creating database applications using Visual Basic code. In Week 3, you study advanced topics such as SQL data definition and manipulation language, and issues for multiuser applications such as locking schemes, database integrity, and application-level security. You also learn techniques for creating ODBC-enabled Visual Basic applications.

Database Design Skills

This book helps you develop your database design skills, too. Each week covers at least one topic on database design. Day 2 covers Visual Basic database data types, and Day 7 covers the use of the Visdata program to create and manage databases. Day 8 teaches you to use SQL SELECT statements to organize existing data into usable datasets. On Days 13 and 15, you learn advanced SQL data definition and manipulation techniques, and on Day 16 you learn the five rules of data normalization.

ActiveX DLLs and Custom Controls

Throughout the book, we show you how to develop DLLs and custom controls that you can reuse in all your future Visual Basic programs. This includes components for input validation, error trapping, report printing, graphing data, creating input forms, user log in/log out, program security features, audit trails, and the ODBC API. All of these components can be added to existing and future Visual Basic programs with very little, if any, modification. After you build these libraries, you can modify them to fit your specific needs, and even add new libraries of your own.

Who Should Read This Book

This book is designed to help you improve your database programming skills using Visual Basic. You do not have to be a Visual Basic coding guru to use this book. If you are a power user who wants to learn how to put together simple, solid data entry forms using Visual Basic, you'll get a lot from this book. If you have some Visual Basic experience and want to take the next step into serious database programming, you'll find a great deal of valuable information here, too. Finally, if you are a professional programmer, you can take many of the techniques and code libraries described here and apply them to your current projects.

What You Need to Use This Book

Most of the code examples in this book were built using Microsoft Visual Basic 5, Professional Edition (the Remote Data Control and Remote Data Objects can only be used with the Enterprise edition of Visual Basic 5). Most of the examples work using Visual Basic 4, Professional Edition but some do not. Version 5 of Visual Basic has several new features not available with version 4. If you are using Visual Basic 4, you can still get a great deal out of this book, but we strongly encourage you to upgrade to Visual Basic 5. There are lots of new features in Visual Basic 5 and you'll be glad you upgraded.

If you have Visual Basic 5 Enterprise Edition, you can take advantage of some new features not available in the Professional Edition, but this is not a necessity. It also helps if you have Microsoft Word, which is used in the lesson on building help files.

Visual Basic 5 is only available in a 32-bit version. That means you need to run Visual Basic (and its completed projects) under Windows 95 or Windows NT.

Quick Course Summary

Here is a brief rundown of what you accomplish each week.

Week 1: Data Controls and Microsoft Jet Databases

In the first week, you learn about the relational database model, how to use the Visual Basic database objects to access and update existing databases, and how to use the Visdata program to create and maintain databases. You also learn how to design and code data entry forms (including use of the Visual Basic bound data controls), and how to create input validation routines at the keystroke, field, and form levels. Lastly, you learn how to use the Visual Basic Crystal Reports Pro report writer to design simple reports, and how to use the Crystal Reports control to run those reports from within your Visual Basic programs.

When you complete the work for Week 1, you will be able to build Microsoft Jet databases, create solid data entry forms that include input validation routines, and produce printed reports of your data.

Week 2: Programming with the Microsoft Jet Database Engine

Week 2 concentrates on topics that are of value to developers in the standalone and workgroup environments. We cover a wide variety of topics, including:

- ☐ How to use the Structured Query Language (SQL) to extract data from existing databases.
- ☐ What the Microsoft Jet engine is, and how you can use Visual Basic code to create and maintain data access objects.
- ☐ How to create data entry forms with Visual Basic code.
- ☐ How to use the Microsoft graph control to create graphs and charts of your data.
- ☐ How to use data-bound list boxes, data-bound combo boxes, and data-bound grids to create advanced data entry forms.
- ☐ How to make applications more solid with error trapping.

When you complete the chapters for Week 2, you will be able to build advanced database structures using the SQL language, and create complex data entry forms using Visual Basic code, including bound lists and grids, and error-handling routines.

Week 3: Advanced Database Programming with SQL and ODBC

In the third and final week, we cover several very important topics. This week's work focuses on the database issues you encounter when you develop database applications for multiple users and/or multiple sites. You learn advanced SQL language for manipulating records within existing databases (DML). You also learn the five rules of data normalization and how applying those rules can improve the speed, accuracy, and integrity of your databases.

We cover Visual Basic database locking schemes for the database, table, and page levels. We also explain the advantages and limitations of adding cascading updates and deletes to your database relationship definitions. You learn how to use the Visual Basic keywords `BeginTrans`, `CommitTrans`, and `Rollback` to improve database integrity and processing speed during mass updates.

We show you how to write data entry forms that use the Remote Data Control, Remote Data Objects, and ODBC API calls to link directly with the ODBC interface to access data in registered ODBC data sources. You also learn how to install the ODBC Administrator and create new ODBC data sources for your ODBC-enabled Visual Basic programs.

We review application-level security schemes such as user login and log out, program-level access rights, and audit trails to keep track of critical application operations.

You also learn how to use the Microsoft Replication Manager to establish and maintain database replication schemes to protect and update your mission-critical distributed data.

When you finish the final week of the course, you will be able to use advanced SQL statements to create and maintain databases. You will also be able to build solid multiuser applications that include database locking schemes, cascades, and transactions; ODBC API interfaces; application security and audit features; and you will be able to manage distributed data through replication.

The Appendixes

There is additional material in the Appendixes, too. There's a detailed explanation of the SQL-VB5 Interpreter used throughout the book (including the source code) and a complete chapter on writing your own online help files for your Visual Basic applications.

What's Not Covered in This Book

Although there is a lot of good stuff in this book, there are some important topics we don't cover in these pages. For example, we don't talk in detail about Visual Basic coding in general. If you are new to Visual Basic, you might want to review the book *Teach Yourself Visual Basic in 21 Days*. This is an excellent introduction to Visual Basic.

Although we discuss issues such as connecting to back-end databases such as SQL Server and Oracle, we do not cover the specifics of these systems. We focus on techniques you need for connecting your Visual Basic applications to remote databases, and not on how to operate remote databases.

We also do not cover any third-party controls or add-ins for Visual Basic 4. That isn't because we don't think they are useful. There are literally hundreds of new and existing third-party products for Visual Basic, and many of them are very good. We have included samples and demo versions of some of those third-party products on the accompanying CD-ROM. However, because we wanted the book to be as accessible as possible to all our readers, we use only those controls or add-in products that are included in the Visual Basic 5 Professional Edition.

What's on the CD-ROM?

In the back of this book, there is a CD-ROM that contains lots of Visual Basic code, sample and demonstration programs, and handy utilities. Following is a brief description of the contents of the CD. Refer to the installation directions on the last page of the book for details on how to install and run these programs.

Chapter Projects and Examples

All examples and exercises mentioned in this book are stored in the TYSDBVB directory of the CD-ROM. You can copy these files directly to your workstation hard disk or enter them from the listings in the book.

Visual Basic Code Libraries, DLLs, and Custom Controls

All reusable code libraries mentioned in the text are also included on the CD. If you want to save yourself some typing, you can simply add these libraries to your Visual Basic projects. You can also copy these libraries to your workstation hard drive and modify them for your own use.

Recommended Files

Besides the contents of the CD, we recommend you pick up the following product on your own:

☐ MS Windows 95 Help Authoring Kit: This is Microsoft Corporation's Help authoring kit, which includes all the tools you need to convert Microsoft Word formatted documents into compiled help files for your Visual Basic application. You can obtain this from Microsoft press or find a freeware version of it (called What6) from the Microsoft site at

```
http://www.microsoft.com/kb/softlib/mslfiles/what6.exe
```

SQL-VB5 Interpreter

The \SQLVB5 directory contains the executables and the source code for the SQL-VB5 Interpreter program. This program is covered in Appendix A. The SQL-VB5 program reads ASCII text files containing valid SQL scripts. The SQL-VB5 Interpreter can be used to create, modify, update, and delete Microsoft Jet-format databases. A number of new features have been added to SQL-VB5 including the ability to handle non-Jet data formats and the new OLE Automation wrapper to allow you to call SQL-VB5 from other VBA-compliant programs.

Shareware and Demos

The CD-ROM also contains various shareware and demo versions of third-party software. We encourage you to test these software tools and, if you like what you find, support the software authors by purchasing a licensed copy of the programs you find useful.

Online Resources

We encourage you to keep in touch with us electronically. You can visit our Web site at www.amundsen.com/tysdbvb and e-mail us at MikeAmundsen@msn.com and Curtis_Smith@fuse.net. Additional information on our Web site and other valuable Visual Basic online resources can be found in the resource.htm file on the CD-ROM.

Week

1

At a Glance

This week, you learn the skills you need to create a simple database that contains a master record table, and you design and implement a complete data entry form, including input validation routines. You also design and implement a simple list report that you can call from within your Visual Basic application.

Day 1: You learn basic controls and write a complete Visual Basic database data entry application using no more than three lines of Visual Basic code.

Day 2: You learn the basics of relational database theory, including databases, data tables, and fields. You also learn the database data types recognized by Visual Basic and how to use them in your Visual Basic applications.

Day 3: You learn what the Visual Basic database objects are and how to use them to read and write data tables.

Day 4: You learn how to design and build quality data entry forms using Visual Basic-bound data controls. You also learn how to design forms that conform to the Windows 95 style specifications.

Day 5: You learn the fundamentals of input validation for data entry forms. You learn how to write keyboard filters and field-level and form-level validation routines. You also create your first Visual Basic custom control when you build the Vtext control that contains validation routines you can use in any Visual Basic application.

Day 6: You learn how to use the Crystal Reports Pro report writer that ships with Visual Basic 5 to create and run quality reports from your databases.

You also create a generic Report Print form that prints any report definition created with Crystal Reports. This generic form can be added to any Visual Basic program.

Day 7: You use the Visual Data Manager (Visdata) to perform database operations to create and maintain your applications. This includes designing databases, building tables, and creating SQL statements.

Day 1

Your First Database Program in Visual Basic 5

This chapter is for readers who have never created database applications using Visual Basic. Those who already know how to use the Visual Basic data control and the bound controls to make simple data entry programs might want to skip this chapter and move on to Day 2, "Creating Databases."

Your project today is to create a completely functional data entry program using Visual Basic. The program you create will be able to access data tables within an existing database; it will also allow users to add, edit, and delete records.

Sound like a lot for one day? Not really. You will be amazed at how quickly you can put together database programs. Much of the drudgery commonly associated with writing data entry programs (screen layout, cursor control, input editing, and so on) is automatically handled using just a few of Visual Basic's input controls. In addition, with Visual Basic's data controls it's easy to add the capability to read and write database tables, too.

So let's get started!

Starting Your New Visual Basic Project

If you already have Visual Basic up and running on your PC, select File | New Project to create a new project. If you haven't started Visual Basic yet, start it now. Select Standard EXE and click OK in the dialog that appears. Now you're ready to create the data entry screen.

Adding the Database Control

The first thing you need to do for the database program is open up the database and select the data table you want to access. To do this, double-click the data control in the Visual Basic toolbox (see Figure 1.1). This places a data control in the center of the form. When this is done, the form is ready to open a data table. At this point, your screen should look something like the one in Figure 1.1.

Figure 1.1.

*The data control as it
appears when first
added to your form.*

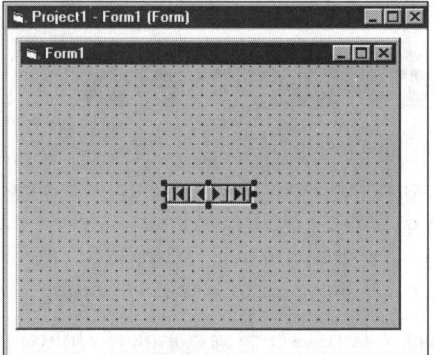

TIP

Are you not sure which of those icons in the toolbox is the data control? You can press F1 while the toolbox window is highlighted to display a help screen describing each of the Visual Basic tools. This screen shows the tool icon and points to additional help, listing the properties, events, and methods available for each of the controls. You

can get help on a particular control in the toolbox by clicking the icon and pressing F1 to activate Visual Basic help.

Tool Tips are also available in Visual Basic 5. Simply rest the mouse pointer on any icon to view a pop-up description of that item. This option can be toggled on and off by selecting Tools | Options, choosing the General tab, and then checking the Show ToolTips checkbox.

Next you need to set a few of the control's properties to indicate the database and data table you want to access.

Setting the DatabaseName and RecordSource Properties

You must first set the following two properties when linking a data control to a database:

DatabaseName   Selected database

RecordSource   Selected data table in the database

The BOOKS5.MDB database will be used in the exercise that follows. This database can be found in the TYSDBVB5\Source\Data directory on the CD that shipped with this book.

TIP   If you do not see the Properties dialog box, press F4 or select View | Properties Window from the menu, or click the properties icon on the Visual Basic toolbar at the top of the screen.

To set the DatabaseName of the data control, first select the data control by single-clicking the control (the data control will already be selected if you did not click anywhere else on the form after you double-clicked the data control in the Toolbox). This forces the data control properties to appear in the Visual Basic Properties dialog box. Locate the DatabaseName property (properties are listed in either alphabetical or categorical order, depending upon the tab you select in the Properties box), and click the property name. When you do this, three small dots (. . .), the properties ellipsis button, appear to the right of the data entry box. Clicking the ellipsis button brings up the Windows standard File | Open dialog box. You should now be able to select the BOOKS5.MDB file from the list of available database files (\\TYSDBVB5\SOURCE\DATA\BOOKS5.MDB). Your screen should look something like the one in Figure 1.2.

Figure 1.2.

*Using the Visual Basic
File | Open dialog box
to set the
DatabaseName
property.*

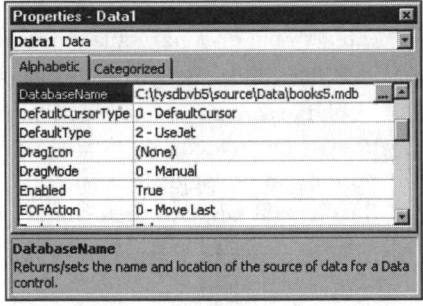

When you have located the BOOKS5.MDB file and selected OK, Visual Basic inserts the complete drive, path, and filename of the database file into the input area, linking the database and your program together. Always double-check this property to make sure that you correctly selected the desired database.

> **NOTE**
>
> People often use the words *database* and *data table* interchangeably. Throughout this book, *data table* is used to refer to a single table of data and *database* is used to refer to a collection of related tables. For example, the Titles table and the Publishers table are two *data tables* in the BOOKS5 *database*.

Now that you know what database you will use, you must select the data table within that database that you want to access by setting the RecordSource property of the data control. You can do this by locating the RecordSource property in the Properties window, single-clicking the property, and then single-clicking the small down arrow to the right of the property input box. This brings up a list of all the tables in the BOOKS5.MDB database, as shown in Figure 1.3. For the first database program, you will use the Titles data table in the BOOKS5.MDB database.

Figure 1.3.

*Setting the
RecordSource property
to the Titles table.*

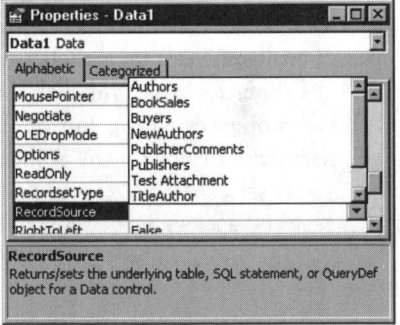

To select the Titles table from this list, simply click on it. Visual Basic automatically inserts the table name into the RecordSource property in the Properties window.

Setting the Caption and Name Properties

You need to set two other data control properties in the project. These two properties are not required, but setting them is a good programming practice because it improves the readability of the programming code. Here are the optional properties:

Caption   Displayed name of the data control

Name   Program name of the data control

Setting the Caption property of the data control sets the text that displays between the record selection arrows on the data control. (Please note that you will need to expand the width of the data control to read this text.) It is a good habit to set this to a value that makes sense to the user.

Setting the Name property of the data control sets the text that will be used by the Visual Basic programmer. This is never seen by the user, but you should set the Name to something similar to the Caption to make it easier to relate the two when working on your program.

For your program, set the Caption property of the data control to Titles and the Name property of the data control to datTitles. Now that you've added the Caption property, use the mouse to stretch the data control so that you can see the complete caption. Your form should look like the one in Figure 1.4.

Figure 1.4.

A data control stretched to show the Caption property.

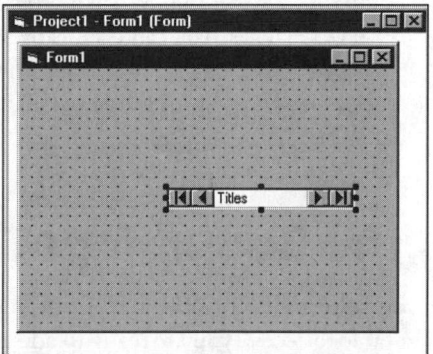

NOTE   The name of the data control (datTitles) might seem unusual. It is, however, a logical name if you remove the first three letters, *dat*. This prefix is added to designate this object as a data control. The three-character-prefix naming convention is Microsoft's suggested nomenclature for Visual Basic 5 and is used throughout this book.

Use the search phrase "Object Naming Conventions" in the Visual Basic 5 Books Online to find a complete listing of the suggested object prefixes.

Saving Your Project

Now is a good time to save your work up to this point. To save this project, select File | Save Project from the main menu. When prompted for a filename for the form, enter DATCNTRL.FRM. You will then be prompted for a filename for the project. Enter DATCNTRL.VBP.

It's always a good idea to save your work often.

NOTE   This, and all other projects that you complete from this book, can be found on the CD included with this book.

TIP   One way to make sure you keep an up-to-date copy of your project saved on disk is to set the "When a program starts:" environment variable to Save Changes. You can do this by selecting Tools | Options... and choosing the Environment tab. Then select either the Save Changes option or the Prompt to Save Changes option.

Adding the Bound Input Controls

Now that you've successfully linked the form to a database with the data control and selected a data table to access, you are ready to add input controls to the form. Visual Basic 5 supplies you with input controls that can be directly bound (connected) to the data table you want to access. All you need to do is place several input controls on the form and assign them to an existing data control.

NOTE

> Associating a control on a form to a field in a data table is referred to as *binding a control*. When they are assigned to a data source, these controls are called *bound input controls*.

Let's add the first bound input control to the Titles table input form. Place an input control on the form by double-clicking the textbox control in the Visual Basic 5 toolbox. This inserts a textbox control directly in the center of the form. When the control is on the form, you can use the mouse to move and resize it in any way you choose. You could add additional input controls by double-clicking the textbox button in the toolbox as many times as you like. Set the Name property of this control to txtTitle. Add a label to describe this control by double-clicking the Label control. Set the label's Name property to lblTitle, and the Caption property to Title. Refer to Figure 1.1 if you have any problems finding a particular Visual Basic control.

TIP

> When double-clicking controls onto a form, each instance of the control is loaded in the center of the form. When you add several controls in this manner, each control is loaded in exactly the same place on the form, like a stack of pancakes. It looks as though you still only have one, but they're all there! You can view each of the controls you loaded on your form by using the mouse to drag and drop the top-most control to another portion of the form.

Setting the DataSource and DataField Properties

You must set two textbox properties in order for the textbox control to interact with the data control. These are the two required properties:

DataSource   Name of the data control

DataField   Name of the field in the table

A relationship is established between a field (the DataField property) in a table (the DataSource property) and a bound control when you set these two properties. When this is done, all data display and data entry in this input control is linked directly to the data table/field you selected.

Setting the DataSource property of the textbox control binds the input control to the data control. To set the textbox DataSource property, first select the textbox control (click it once), and then click the DataSource property in the Property window. By clicking this property's down arrow, you can see a list of all the data controls currently active on this form. You have only added one data control to this form, so you see only one name in the list (see Figure 1.5). Set the DataSource value to datTitles by clicking the word datTitles in the drop-down list box.

Figure 1.5.

Setting the DataSource property of a bound textbox.

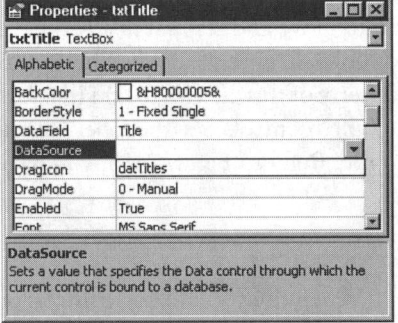

The second required property for a bound input control is the DataField property. Setting this property binds a specific field in the data table to the input control. Set the DataField property of the current input control by single-clicking the DataField property in the Property window and then single-clicking the down arrow to the right of the property. You now see a list of all the fields that are defined for the data table that you selected in the DataSource property (see Figure 1.6). Click the Title field to set the DataField property for this control.

Figure 1.6.

Selecting the DataField property of the bound textbox control.

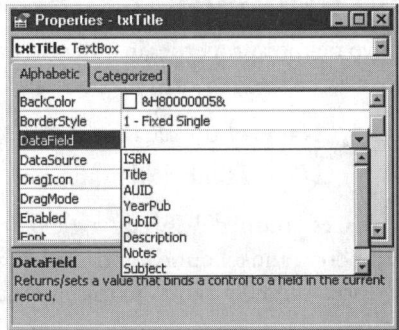

1

1

Now that you have the general idea, finish up the data entry form by adding bound input controls for the remaining fields in the Title data table. Refer to Table 1.1 for details.

While you're at it, add Label controls to the left of the textbox controls and set their Caption properties to the values shown in Table 1.2. Size and align the controls on the form, too. Also, size the form by selecting its borders and dragging to a desired shape. Your form should look something like the one in Figure 1.7 when you're done.

Table 1.1. The Input Control DataSource and DataField properties for the Titles form.

Textbox	DataSource	DataField
txtISBN	datTitles	ISBN
txtTitle	datTitles	Title
txtYearPub	datTitles	YearPub
txtPubID	datTitles	PubID
txtDescription	datTitles	Description
txtNotes	datTitles	Notes
txtSubject	datTitles	Subject
txtComments	datTitles	Comments

Table 1.2. The Label Control Caption properties for the Titles form.

Label	Caption
lblISBN	ISBN
lblTitle	Title
lblYearPub	Year Published
lblPubID	Publisher ID
lblDescription	Description
lblNotes	Notes
lblSubject	Subject
lblComments	Comments

Figure 1.7.

The completed data entry form for Titles.

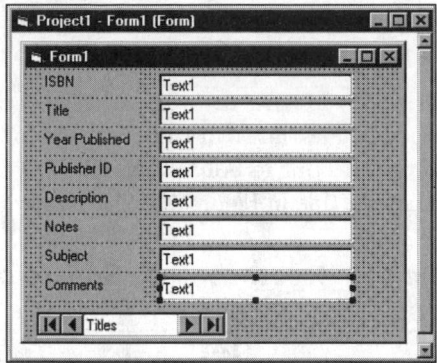

You can now run the program and see the data control in action. Select Run | Start (or press F5) to compile and run your program. You can walk through the data table by clicking the left and right arrows on the data control at the bottom of the form. The left-most arrow (the one with the bar on it) moves you to the first record in the data table. The right-most arrow (which also has a bar) moves you to the last record in the data table. The other two arrows simply move you through the data table one record at a time.

You can make any changes permanent to the data table by moving to a different record in the table. Try this by changing the data in the Title input control, moving the record pointer to the next record, and then moving the pointer back to the record you just edited. You will see that the new value was saved to the data table.

Now let's include the capability to add new records to the data table and to delete existing records from the data table.

Adding the New and Delete Command Buttons

Up to this point, you have not written a single line of Visual Basic code. However, in order to add the capability to insert new records and delete existing records, you have to write a grand total of two lines of Visual Basic code: one line for the add record function, and one line for the delete record function.

The first step in the process is to add two command buttons labeled Add and Delete to the form. Refer to Table 1.3 and Figure 1.8 for details on adding the command buttons to your form.

Table 1.3. Command Button properties for the Title form.

Name	Caption
cmdAdd	&Add
cmdDelete	&Delete

NOTE

Adding an ampersand (&) to the Caption of a command button causes the letter immediately following the ampersand to be underlined. The underlined letter (also known as a *shortcut key* or *hot key*) serves as a prompt to the user to indicate that it can be pressed in conjunction with the Ctrl key to execute the procedure that the button contains.

Figure 1.8.

The form layout after adding the Add and Delete command buttons.

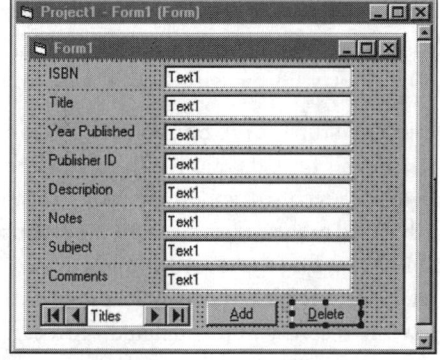

Double-click the Add button to bring up the Visual Basic code window to add code behind the Add command button. You see the subroutine header and footer already entered for you. All you need to do is add a single line of Visual Basic code between them.

```
Private Sub cmdAdd_Click()
    datTitles.Recordset.AddNew  ' add a new record to the table
End Sub
```

NOTE

Visual Basic automatically creates the Sub_End Sub routines for each new procedure you create. When you are performing the exercises in this book, insert the code only between these two lines (in other words, don't repeat the Sub_End Sub statements, or your code will not work properly).

Now open the code window behind the Delete button and add this Visual Basic code:

```
Private Sub cmdDelete_Click()
   datTitles.Recordset.Delete  ' delete the current record
End Sub
```

Runtime and Design Time Properties

RecordSet is a *runtime only* property of the data control. This property is a reference to the underlying data table defined in the *design time* RecordSource property. The RecordSet can refer to an existing table in the database or a virtual table, such as a Visual Basic Dynaset or Snapshot. This is covered in more depth on Day 3, "Visual Basic Database Objects." For now, think of the RecordSet property as a runtime version of the RecordSource property you set when you designed the form.

In the two preceding code snippets, you used the Visual Basic methods `AddNew` and `Delete`. You will learn more about these and other Visual Basic methods in the lesson on Day 4, "Creating Data Entry Forms with Bound Controls."

Save the project and run the program again. You can now click the Add button and see a blank set of input controls for data entry. Fill them all with some data (refer to Figure 1.9 for an example of a new record), and then move to another record in the table. The data is automatically saved to the data table. You can also use the Delete button to remove any record from the table. First, find the record you just added (it's the last record in the table), and then click the Delete button. Now move to the previous record in the table and try to move forward again to view the record you just deleted. You can't. It's not there!

NOTE

When you entered data into this form, you may have noticed that the tab sequence didn't follow a logical progression. This happened because you added the txtTitles control first, but placed the txtISBN control in the first position on the form. Visual Basic defines the tab order of controls in the sequence they are placed on the form.

To correct this problem quickly, select the last control you want in your tab sequence (in this case, the Exit button) and enter 0 in its TabIndex property. Next, select the second-to-last control in the tab sequence (the Delete button) and enter 0 in its TabIndex property. Continue to set all the TabIndex values to zero for all controls in your tab sequence by moving backward through the form. Complete the process by setting the TabIndex value of the txtISBN control to 0.

> The TabIndex property of a control is incremented by 1 each time a lower value is entered in another control. Therefore, by setting the TabIndex property of the txtISBN control to 0, you reset the value of the TabIndex property of txtTitle to 1, txtYearPub to 2, and so on.

Figure 1.9.

Example data filling in blank fields after clicking the Add button.

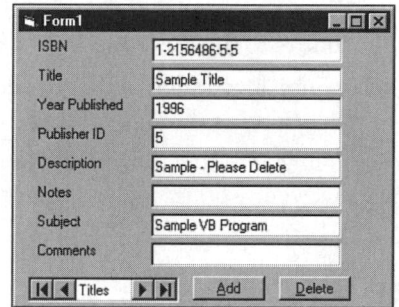

If you didn't enter data into the data entry form that you created in this exercise in quite the same way as Figure 1.9 (for example, you incorrectly entered characters in the Year field, which only accepts numbers), you might have received an error message from Visual Basic 5 saying that you have invalid data in one of the fields. This is supposed to happen! Visual Basic 5 (more precisely, the Microsoft JET Engine) verifies all data entries to ensure that the correct data type is entered in each field. Input validation routines, a means of restricting data entry even further, are covered in depth on Day 5, "Input Validation," and error trapping is reviewed in the lesson on Day 14, "Error Handling in Visual Basic 5.0." You can skip over these messages for now.

Summary

In today's lesson you learned the following:

☐ You learned how to use the data control to bind a form to a database and data table by setting the DatabaseName and DataSource properties.

☐ You learned how to use the textbox bound input control to bind an input box on the form to a data table and data field by setting the DataSource and DataField properties.

☐ You learned how to combine standard command buttons and the AddNew and Delete methods to provide add record and delete record functionality to a data entry form.

Quiz

1. What are the two properties of the data control that must be set when you link a form to an existing database and data table?

2. What property must you set if you want the data control to display the name of the data table in the window between the record pointer arrows?

3. What are the two properties of the textbox control that must be set when you bind the input control to the data control on a form?

4. How many lines of code does it take to add a delete record function to a Visual Basic form when using the data control?

5. What environment setting can you use to make sure that Visual Basic will automatically save your work each time you attempt to run a program in design mode?

Exercises

1. Add the caption "The Titles Program" to the data entry form created in this chapter.

2. Place an additional command button labeled Exit on the data entry form. Add code behind this command button to end the program when it is clicked.

3. Modify the Add button to move the cursor to the first input control (txtISBN) on the data entry form. (Hint: search for SetFocus in the Visual Basic online help.)

Day 2

Creating Databases

In today's lesson, you learn a working definition of a *relational database,* as well as the basic elements of a database, including *data table, data record,* and *data field.* You also learn the importance of establishing and maintaining *data relationships.* These are some of the key elements to developing quality databases for your applications.

You also learn Visual Basic *database field types,* including their names, storage sizes, and common uses. Along the way, you create a programming project that explores the limits, possibilities, and common uses of Visual Basic database field types.

Relational Databases

Before looking at the individual components of relational databases, let's first establish a simple definition. For the purposes of this book, a relational database is defined as *a collection of data that indicates relation among data elements;* or, to put it even more directly, a relational database is *a collection of related data.*

In order to build a collection of related data, you need three key building blocks. These building blocks are (from smallest to largest)

- ☐ Data fields (sometimes called *data columns*)
- ☐ Data records (also known as *data rows*)
- ☐ Data tables

Let's look at each of these elements in more depth.

Data Fields

The first building block in a relational database is the *data field.* The data field contains the smallest element of data that you can store in a database, and each field contains only one data element. For example, if you want to store the name of a customer, you must create a data field somewhere in the database and also give that field a name, such as CustomerName. If you want to store the current account balance of a customer, you must create another field, possibly calling it AccountBalance. All the fields you create are stored in a single database (see Figure 2.1).

Figure 2.1.

Examples of data fields in a database.

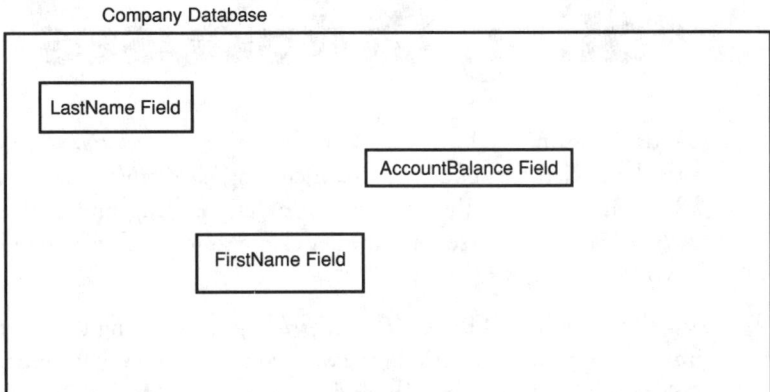

Company Database

LastName Field

AccountBalance Field

FirstName Field

NOTE

In formal database theory, a data field is often referred to as a *data column.* Throughout this book, the phrases *data field* and *data column* are used interchangeably.

Although it is possible to store more than one data element in a single field (such as first and last name), it is not good database practice to do so. In fact, storing more than one data element in a field can lead to problems when you or other users try to retrieve or update data.

2

This concept seems simple in theory, but it's not so easy in practice. The CustomerName field discussed earlier is a good example. Assume that you have a database that contains a list of your customers by name, and you need to sort the list by last name. How would this be done? Can you assume that each CustomerName data field contains a last name? Do some contain only a first name? Possibly some contain both first and last names—but in what order (*last name, first name* or *first name, last name*)? When you look at this situation, you discover that you're actually storing *two* data elements in the CustomerName field (first name and last name). For this reason, many databases contain not just the CustomerName data field, but data fields for LastName and FirstName.

When you begin constructing your database, spend time thinking about the various ways you (and your users) need to retrieve useful data. The quality and usefulness of your database rests on the integrity of its smallest element—the data field.

Data Records

Data records are a collection of related data fields. To use the example started earlier, a Customer Record could contain the fields LastName, FirstName, and AccountBalance. All three fields describe a single customer in the database.

NOTE   Formal database theory refers to a data record as a *data row*. Both *data record* and *data row* are used interchangeably throughout this book.

A single data record contains only one copy of each defined data field. For example, a single data record cannot contain more than one LastName data field. Figure 2.2 shows the Company Database with a Customer Record defined. The Customer Record (row) contains three fields (columns).

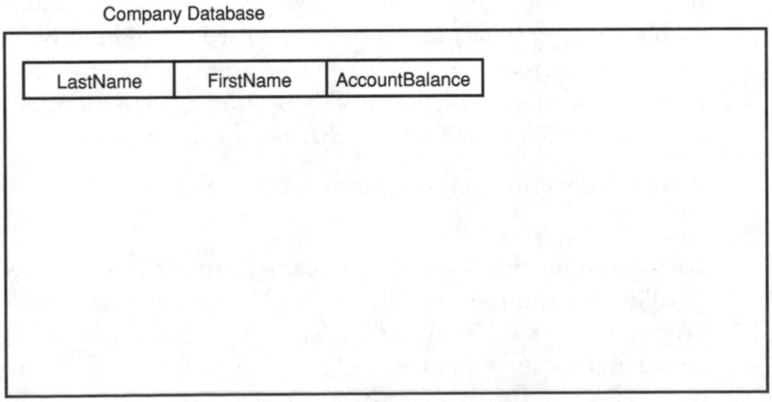

Figure 2.2.

An example of a data record in a database.

Company Database

LastName	FirstName	AccountBalance

Data Table Rows and Columns

By combining data fields and data records, you create the most common element of relational databases—the data table. This element contains multiple data records, and each data record contains multiple data fields (see Figure 2.3).

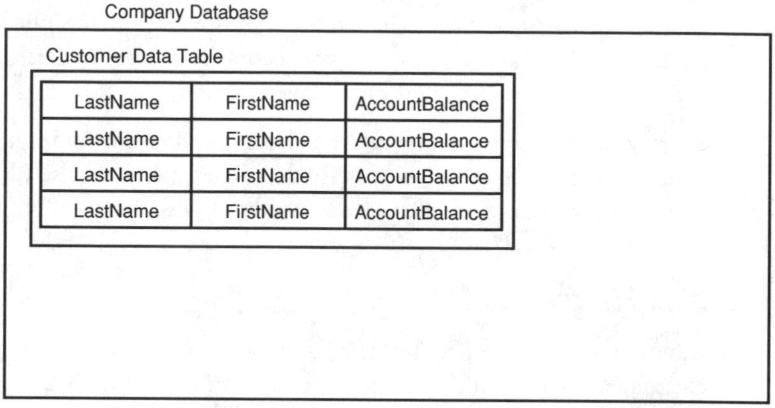

Figure 2.3.

An example of a data table in a database.

Company Database

Customer Data Table		
LastName	FirstName	AccountBalance
LastName	FirstName	AccountBalance
LastName	FirstName	AccountBalance
LastName	FirstName	AccountBalance

Just as each data record contains related data fields (LastName, FirstName, and AccountBalance), each data table contains related records. Data tables have meaningful names (Customer Table or Invoice Table, for example) in the same way that data fields have meaningful names (LastName, FirstName, AccountBalance, and so on). These names help you and other users to remember the contents of the elements (table elements and field elements).

Database Relationships

Just as a data record can contain several related data fields, a database can contain several related tables. Using relationships is a very efficient way to store complex data. For example, a table storing customer names could be related to another table storing the names of items the customer has bought, which could be related in turn to a table storing the names of all the items you have to sell. By establishing meaningful relationships between data tables, you can create flexible data structures that are easy to maintain.

You establish relationships between data tables by using *pointer* or *qualifier fields* in your data table.

You use qualifier fields to point to records in other tables that have additional information. Qualifier fields usually describe what's known as *one-to-one* relationships. A good example of a one-to-one relationship is the relationship between a single customer record and a single record in the shipping address table (see Figure 2.4).

2

Figure 2.4.

An example of a one-to-one relationship between tables.

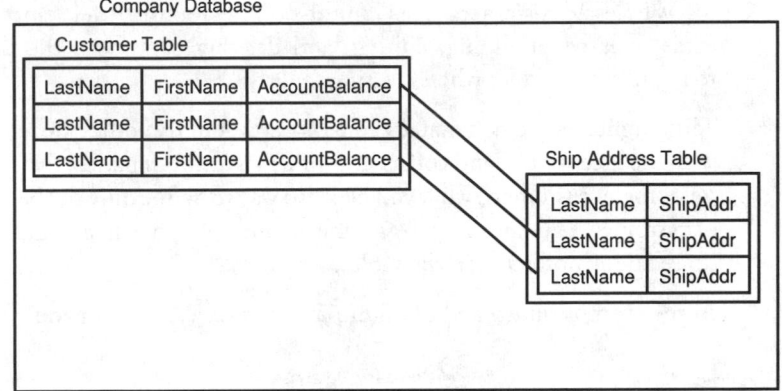

You use pointer fields to point to one or more records in other tables that have related information. Pointer fields usually describe what are known as *one-to-many* relationships. A good example of a one-to-many relationship is the relationship between a single customer master record and several outstanding customer orders (see Figure 2.5).

Figure 2.5.

An example of a one-to-many relationship between tables.

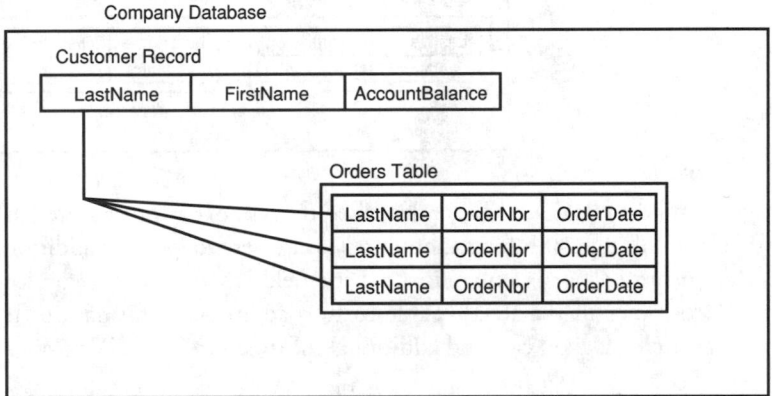

One-to-One Relationships

One-to-one relationships are used to link records in a master table (such as the Customer Table) to a *single* related record in another table.

For example, assume you have two types of customers in your Company Database: retail and wholesale. Retail customers get paid commissions on sales, so you need to add a Commission field to the Customers table. Wholesale customers, however, purchase their products at a discount, so you also need to add a Discount field to the Customers table. Now your database users have to remember that, for Retail customers, the Discount field must be left empty, and for Wholesale customers, the Commission field must be left empty. You must remember these rules when adding, editing, and deleting data from the database, and you must remember these rules when creating reports.

This might seem to be a manageable task now, but try adding dozens more data fields (along with the exceptions), and you have quite a mess on your hands! Instead of establishing all data fields for all customers, what you need is a way to define only the fields you need for each type of customer. You can do this by setting up multiple tables in a single database and then setting up relationships between the tables.

In the example illustrated in Figure 2.6, you have added an additional data field: Type.

Figure 2.6.

Using a qualifier field to establish a one-to-one relationship.

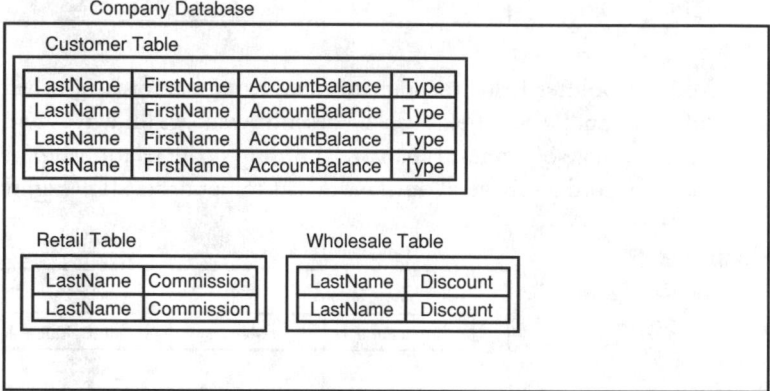

This data field *qualifies*, or describes, the type of customer stored in this data record. You can use this type of information to tell you where to look for additional information about the customer. For example, if the Type field is set to Retail, you know you can look for the customer in the Retail Table to find additional information. If the Type field is set to Wholesale, you can find additional information in the Wholesale Table.

By creating the RecordType field, you can establish a one-to-one relationship between records in the Customer Table and the Retail and Wholesale Tables.

One-to-Many Relationships

One-to-many relationships are used to link records in a master table (such as the Customer Table) to multiple records in another table.

For example, you can keep track of several orders for each customer in your database. If you were not creating a relational database, you would probably add a data field to your customer table called Order. This would contain the last order placed by this customer. But what if you needed to keep track of more than one outstanding order? Would you add two, four, or six more order fields? You can see the problem.

Instead, you can add an additional table (the Orders Table) that can contain as many outstanding orders for a single customer as you need. After you create the Orders Table, you can establish a relationship between the Customer Table and the Orders Table using the LastName field (refer back to Figure 2.4). The LastName field is used as a pointer into the Orders Table to locate all the orders for this customer.

You can use many different approaches to establish relationships between tables. They are usually established through a *key field*. Key fields are covered in depth in the next section.

Key Fields

Usually, at least one data field in each data table acts as a key field for the table. Key fields in relational databases are used to define and maintain database integrity and to establish relationships between data tables. You create keys in your data table by designating one (field) or more in your table as either a *primary key* or a *foreign key*. A data table can have only one primary key, but it can have several foreign keys. The primary key is used to control the order in which the data is displayed. The foreign key is used to relate fields to fields in other (foreign) tables in the database.

NOTE

Key fields are sometimes referred to as *index fields* or *indexes*. Both "key fields" and "index fields" are used interchangeably throughout the book. It is important to note that in most PC databases (Xbase, Paradox, Btreive, and so forth), indexes are used only to speed processing of large files and play only a minor role in maintaining table relationships. The Visual Basic database model (.mdb files) and other true relational database models use key fields to establish database integrity rules as well as to speed database search and retrieval.

As mentioned earlier, a data table can have only one primary key. The primary key is used to define a unique record in the data table. In the Customer table, the LastName field is the primary key field for the data table. This means that no two records in that table can have exactly the same value in the LastName fields (see Figure 2.7). Any attempt to add more than one record with an identical primary key would result in a database error.

Figure 2.7.

*The LastName field is
the primary key field
of the Customer table.*

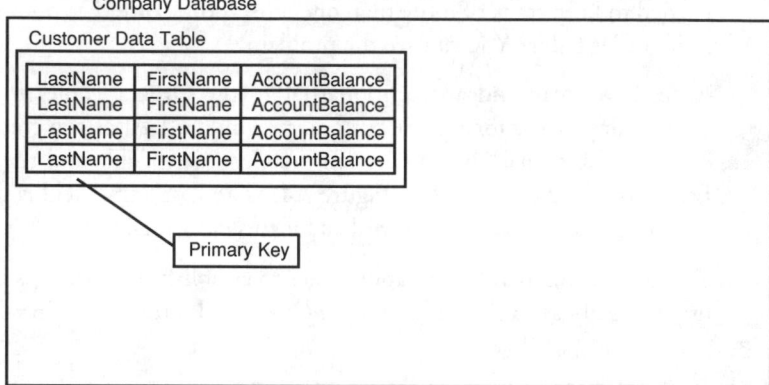

TIP

> The main role of the primary key is to maintain the internal integrity of
> a data table. For this reason, no two records in a data table can have the
> same primary key value. Many companies with large customer bases use
> Social Security numbers or area codes and telephone numbers, because
> they know they are likely to have more than one customer with the
> same name. In these cases, the SSN or phone number would be the
> primary key field.

A data table can have more than one foreign key. It can also have no foreign key at all. In the
Orders Table, the LastName field would be defined as a foreign key field. This means that
it is a nonunique field in this data table that points to a key field in an external (foreign) table.
Any attempt to add to the Orders table a record that contains a value in the LastName field,
which does not also exist in a LastName field in the Customer Table, would result in a
database error. For example, if the Customer table contains three records (Smith, Amundsen,
and Jones), and you try to add a record to the Orders Table by filling the LastName field of
the Orders Table with Paxton, you get a database error. By creating foreign key fields in a
table, you build data integrity into your database. This is called referential integrity.

TIP

> The main role of a foreign key is to define and maintain relationships
> between data tables in a database. For this reason, foreign key fields are
> not unique in the data table in which they exist.

NOTE Database integrity and foreign keys are covered in depth on Day 16, "Database Normalization," and Day 17, "Multiuser Considerations."

Now that you've worked through the basics of database elements in general, let's look at specific characteristics of Visual Basic data fields.

Visual Basic Database Field Types

Visual Basic stores values in the data table in data fields. Visual Basic recognizes 14 different data field types that you can use to store values. Each data field type has unique qualities that make it especially suitable for storing different types of data. Some are used to store images, the results of checkbox fields, currency amounts, calendar dates, and various sizes of numeric values. Table 2.1 lists the 14 database field types recognized by Visual Basic.

The first column contains the Visual Basic data field type name. This is the name you use when you create data tables using the Visual Data Manager from the Toolbar. You learn about using this tool in Day 7, "Using the Visdata Program."

The second column shows the number of bytes of storage taken by the various data field types. If the size column is set to "V," the length is variable and is determined by you at design time or by the program at runtime.

The third column in the table shows the equivalent Visual Basic data type for the associated database field type. This column tells you what Visual Basic data type you can use to update the database field.

Table 2.1. Visual Basic data field types.

Data Field Type	Size	VBType	Comments
BINARY	V	(none)	Limited to 255 bytes
BOOLEAN	1	Boolean	Stores 0 or -1 only
BYTE	1	Integer	Stores 0 to 255 only
COUNTER	8	Long	Auto-incrementing Long type
CURRENCY	8	Currency	15 places to left of decimal, 4 to right
DATETIME	8	Date/Time	Date stored on the left of decimal point, time stored on the right
DOUBLE	8	Double	

continues

Table 2.1. continued

Data Field Type	Size	VBType	Comments
GUID	16	(none)	Used to store Globally Unique Identifiers
INTEGER	2	Integer	
LONG	8	Long	
LONGBINARY	V	(none)	Used for OLE objects
MEMO	V	String	Length varies up to 1.2 gigabytes
SINGLE	4	Single	
TEXT	V	String	Length limited to 255

NOTE

It is important to understand the difference between the Visual Basic *data field types* and the Visual Basic *data types*. The data field types are those recognized as valid data types within data tables. The data types are those types recognized by Visual Basic when defining variables within a program. For example, you can store the value 3 in a BYTE field in a data table, but you store that same value in an Integer field in a Visual Basic program variable.

Even though it is true that Visual Basic allows programmers to create database applications that can read and write data in several different data formats, all database formats do not recognize all data field types. For example, xBase data fields do not recognize a CURRENCY data field type. Before developing cross data-engine applications, you need to know exactly what data field types are needed and how they are to be mapped to various data formats. The various data formats are covered in Day 9, "Visual Basic and the Microsoft Jet Engine."

A number of things in Table 2.1 deserve additional comment:

☐ LONGBINARY data fields are for storing images and OLE objects. Visual Basic has no corresponding internal data type that maps directly to the LONGBINARY data field types. This information is usually stored as character data in Visual Basic. For example, a bitmap image would be stored in a LONGBINARY data table field, but it would be stored as a string variable in a Visual Basic program. Double-clicking a data-bound LONGBINARY field automatically invokes the local application that is registered to handle the stored OLE object.

☐ The BOOLEAN data field type is commonly used to store the results of a bound checkbox input control. It stores only a -1 (True) or 0 (False). For example, if you enter 13 into the input box, Visual Basic stores -1 in the data field. To make matters trickier, Visual Basic does not report an error when a number other than 0 or -1 is entered. You should be careful when using the BOOLEAN data type because any number other than 0 entered into a BOOLEAN data field is converted into -1.

☐ The BYTE data field type only accepts input ranging from -0 to 255. Any other values (including negative numbers) result in a runtime error (error number 524) when you attempt to update the data record.

WARNING

This behavior is changed from Visual Basic 4.0. In the past, Microsoft Jet would automatically convert the invalid value to a byte value and not report an error. For example, if you enter the value 255 (stored as FF in hexadecimal), Visual Basic stores 255 in the data field. If you enter 260 (stored as 0104 in hexadecimal—it takes two bytes!), Visual Basic stores a decimal 4 in the data field because the right-most byte is set to hexadecimal 04.

☐ The COUNTER data field type is a special case. This is an auto-incrementing, read-only data field. Any attempt to write a value to this data field results in a Visual Basic error. Visual Basic keeps track of the integer value to place in this field; it cannot be altered through the input controls or through explicit programming directives. The COUNTER field is often used as a unique primary key field in sequential processing operations.

☐ MEMO and TEXT data field types both accept any character data as valid input. MEMO data fields are built with a default length of 0 (zero). The physical length of a MEMO field is controlled by the total number of characters of data stored in the field. The length of a TEXT field must be declared when the data field is created. The Visual Data Manager that ships with Visual Basic allows the TEXT field to have a length of 1 to 255 bytes.

☐ GUID data field types are used to store a special type of 128-bit number—the Globally Unique Identifier. This value is used to identify ActiveX components, SQL Server remote procedures, Microsoft Jet replication IDs, and other objects that require a unique identifier. For more on Microsoft Jet replication, see Day 20, "Database Replication."

Building the Visual Basic 5 Field Data Types Project

The following project illustrates how different Visual Basic data field types store user input. You also see how Visual Basic responds to input that is out of range for the various data field types.

1. Begin by creating a new Visual Basic project (select File | New Project). Using Table 2.2 and Figure 2.8 as guides, populate the Visual Basic form.

WARNING

Notice that you are creating a set of four buttons with the same name, but different Index property values. This is a *control array*. Control arrays offer an excellent way to simplify Visual Basic coding. However, they behave a bit differently than non-arrayed controls. It is important that you build the controls exactly as described in this table.

Figure 2.8.

The form for the Visual Basic data field types project.

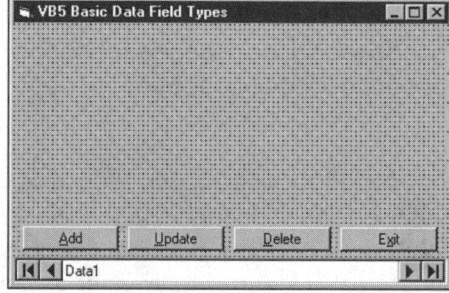

Table 2.2. Controls for the Visual Basic data field types project.

Control	Property	Setting
Project	Name	prjFieldTypes
Form	Name	frmFieldTypes
	Caption	VB5 Basic Data Field Types
CommandButton	Name	cmdBtn
	Caption	&Add
	Height	300
	Index	0
	Width	1200

Control	Property	Setting
CommandButton	Name	cmdBtn
	Caption	&Add
	Height	300
	Index	0
	Width	1200
CommandButton	Name	cmdBtn
	Caption	&Update
	Height	300
	Index	1
	Width	1200
CommandButton	Name	cmdBtn
	Caption	&Delete
	Height	300
	Index	2
	Width	1200
CommandButton	Name	cmdBtn
	Caption	E&xit
	Height	300
	Index	3
	Width	1200
DataControl	Name	datFieldTypes
	DatabaseName	FIELDTYPES.MDB (include correct path)
	RecordSource	FieldTypes

2. Now add the code behind the command button array. Double-click the Add
   button (or any other button in the array) to bring up the code window. Enter the
   code from Listing 2.1 into the cmdBtn_Click event.

TYPE **Listing 2.1. Code for the cmdBtn_Click event.**

```
Private Sub cmdBtn_Click(Index As Integer)
    '
    ' handle button selections
    '
```

continues

Listing 2.1. continued

```
        On Error GoTo LocalError
        '
        Select Case Index
            Case 0 ' add
                datFieldTypes.Recordset.AddNew
            Case 1 ' update
                datFieldTypes.UpdateRecord
                datFieldTypes.Recordset.Bookmark =
                ➥datFieldTypes.Recordset.LastModified
            Case 2 ' delete
                datFieldTypes.Recordset.Delete
                datFieldTypes.Recordset.MovePrevious
            Case 3 ' exit
                Unload Me
        End Select
        Exit Sub
        '
LocalError:
        MsgBox Err.Description, vbCritical, Err.Number
        '
End Sub
```

There may be several things in this code segment that are new to you. First, different lines of code are executed based on the button that is pushed by the user. This is indicated by the Index parameter that is passed to the Click event. Second, some error-handling code has been added to make it easy for you to experiment with the data form. You learn more about error-handling in Day 14, "Error Handling in Visual Basic 5.0." Don't worry if this code segment looks a bit confusing. For now, just go ahead and enter the code that is shown here.

Now is a good time to save the project. Save the form as FieldTypes.frm and the project as FieldTypes.vbp. Run the project just to make sure that you have entered all the code correctly up to this point. If you get error messages from Visual Basic, refer back to Table 2.2 and the preceding code lines to correct the problem.

Testing the BOOLEAN Data Type

Now you can add a text box input control and a label to this form. Set the caption of the label to Boolean:. Set the DataSource property of the text box to datFieldTypes and the DataField property to BooleanField. Set the Text property to blank. Refer to Figure 2.9 for placement and sizing.

Figure 2.9.

Adding the
BOOLEAN data type
input control.

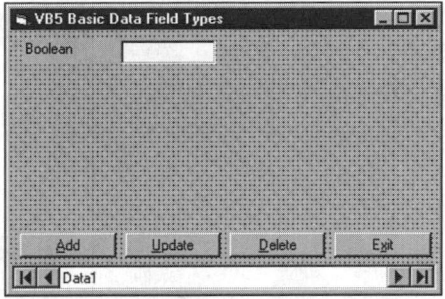

Now run the program. If this is the first time you've run the program, you should see an empty field. Press the Add button to create a new record and then press the Update button to save that record. You see that the first value in the input box is a 0, the default value for BOOLEAN fields. Enter the number 13 in the text box and click the Update button. This forces the data control to save the input field to the data table and update the display. What happened to the 13? It was converted to -1. Any value other than 0, when entered into a BOOLEAN data type field, is converted to -1.

Testing the BYTE Data Type

Now let's add a label and input control for the BYTE data type field. Instead of picking additional controls from the Toolbox Window and typing in property settings, Visual Basic allows you to copy existing controls. Copying controls saves time, reduces typing errors, and helps to keep the size and shape of the controls on your form consistent.

To copy controls, use the mouse pointer, with the left mouse button depressed, to create a dotted-line box around both the label control and the text box control already on your form (in this case, the label Boolean and its text box). When you release the left mouse button, you see that both controls have been marked as selected. Now click Edit | Copy to copy the selected controls to the Clipboard. Use Edit | Paste to copy the controls from the Clipboard back onto your form.

At this point, Visual Basic asks you whether you want to create a Control Array. Say yes, both times. You then see the two controls appear at the top left of the form. Use your mouse to position them on the form (see Figure 2.10).

Figure 2.10.

Copying controls on a form.

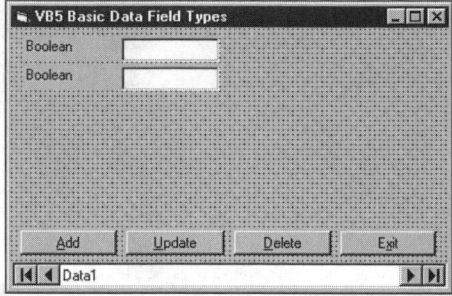

 **TIP**   The Textbox and Label controls on this form are part of a control array. Because using control arrays reduces the total number of distinct controls on your forms, they reduce the amount of Windows resources your program uses. You can copy controls as many times as you like—even across forms and projects!

You just created duplicates of the BOOLEAN input control. All you need to do now is change the label caption to Byte and the text box DataField property to ByteField, and you have two new controls on your form with minimal typing. Your form should look like the one in Figure 2.11.

Figure 2.11.

Adding the BYTE data type to your form.

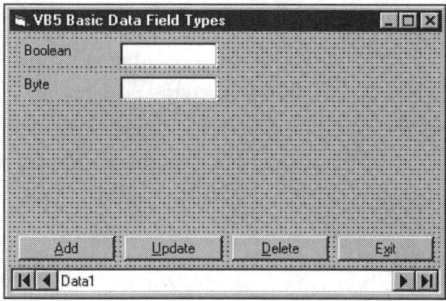

Save and run the program. This time, after pressing the Add button, enter the value 256 into the Byte input control and press the Update button. You see that when Visual Basic attempts to store the value to the data table, a runtime error is reported. Byte data fields can only accept positive values between 0 and 255. Trying to save any other value in this data field causes the Microsoft Jet data engine to report an error to Visual Basic.

Testing the CURRENCY Data Type

Copy the label and text box control again using the mouse to select the controls to be copied, and the Copy and Paste commands from the Edit menu. Change the label Caption property to Currency and the text box DataField property to CurrencyField. Refer to Figure 2.12 for spacing and sizing of the controls.

Figure 2.12.

Adding the CURRENCY data type to the form.

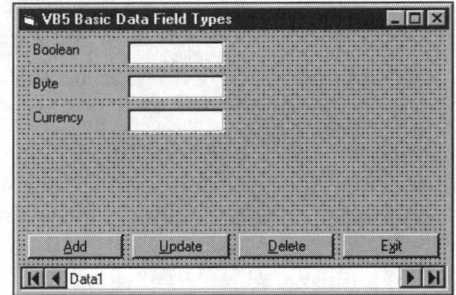

Save and run the program and test the CURRENCY data type text box. Press the Add button; enter the value 1.00001; force Visual Basic to save the value to the data table (press the Update button) and see what happens. Try entering 1.23456. When storing values to the CURRENCY data type field, Visual Basic stores only four places to the right of the decimal. If the number is larger than four decimal places to the right, Visual Basic rounds the value before storing it in the data field. Also, you notice that Visual Basic does not add a dollar sign ($) to the display of CURRENCY type data fields.

Testing the DATETIME Data Type

The Visual Basic DATETIME data type field is one of the most powerful data types. Visual Basic performs extensive edit checks on values entered in the DATETIME data type field. Using DATETIME data type fields can save a lot of coding when you need to make sure valid dates are entered by users.

Create a new set of label and text box controls by copying the label and text box controls again. Change the label caption property to DateTime and the text box DataField property to DateTimeField. Your form should look like the one in Figure 2.13.

Save and run the program. Try entering 12/32/95. As you can see, Visual Basic gives you an error message whenever you enter an invalid date. Now enter 1/1/0 into the Date text box. Notice that Visual Basic formats the date for you.

Figure 2.13.

Adding the DATETIME data type to the form.

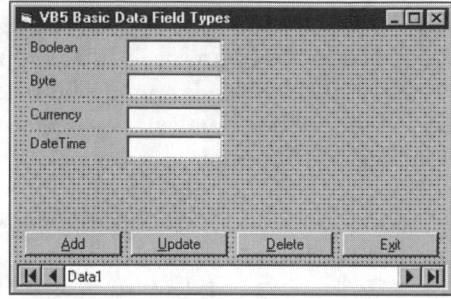

How does Visual Basic decide what date format to use? The date format used comes from the settings in the Windows 95 Control Panel Regional Settings applet. While you have this program running, experiment by calling up the Windows 95 Regional Settings applet. (From the task bar, select Start | Settings | Control Panel, and then select Regional Settings.) Change the date format settings, and return to your Visual Basic program to see the results.

TIP

The Visual Basic DATETIME data type should always be used to store date values. If you install your program in Europe, where the common date display format is *DD-MM-YY* instead of the common U.S. format of *MM-DD-YY*, your program will work without a problem. If you store dates as strings in the format *MM/DD/YY* or as numeric values in the format *YYMMDD*, your program will not be able to compute or display dates correctly across international boundaries.

Testing the COUNTER Data Type

Now let's test a very special database field type—the COUNTER data type. This data type is automatically set by Visual Basic each time you add a new record to the data table. The COUNTER data type makes an excellent unique primary key field because Visual Basic is able to create and store more than a billion unique values in the COUNTER field without duplication.

NOTE

Actually, the Counter data type is not a true database field type. Instead, the Counter data type is a Long data field with its Attribute property set to AutoIncrField. You won't find the Counter data type listed in the documentation, but you will see references to auto-incrementing fields and see a "Counter" type as an option when you build data fields with the Visual Data Manager.

Copy another label/text box control set onto the form. Change the label caption property to Counter and the text box DataField property to AutoIncrField. See Figure 2.14 for guidance in positioning and sizing the control.

Figure 2.14.

Adding the COUNTER data type to the form.

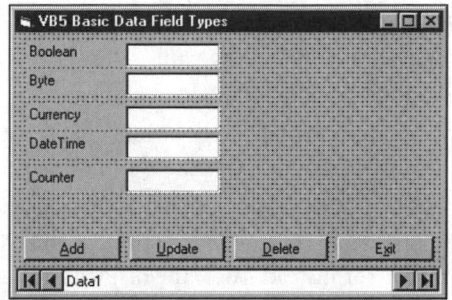

Now save and run the program one more time. Notice that the COUNTER data type already has a value in it, even though you have not entered data into the field. Visual Basic sets the value of COUNTER fields; users do not. Add a new record to the table by pressing the Add button. You see a new value in the COUNTER input control. Visual Basic uses the next available number in sequence. Visual Basic is also able to ensure unique numbers in a multiuser setting. If you have three people running the same program adding records to this table, they will all receive unique values in the Counter text box.

WARNING

You should never attempt to edit the value in the COUNTER text box! If Visual Basic determines that the counter value has been changed, it displays a Visual Basic error message, and you cannot save the record. Even if you reset the value in the COUNTER data field back to its original value, Visual Basic refuses to save the record.

Additional Visual Basic Data Types

The rest of the Visual Basic data types (INTEGER, SINGLE, DOUBLE, TEXT, MEMO, BINARY, LONGBINARY, and GUID) are rather unspectacular when placed on a form. The following are some notes on the various Visual Basic data types that you should keep in mind when you are designing your data tables.

☐ Visual Basic returns an error if you enter more than the maximum number of characters into a TEXT data field.

☐ The LONGBINARY data field is used to store graphic image data and allows any alphanumeric data to be entered and saved. The storage of graphic data is covered later in the book (see Day 11, "Displaying Your Data with Graphs").

☐ Check the Visual Basic online help under Visual Basic Data Types for additional information on the high and low ranges for DOUBLE, INTEGER, and SINGLE data fields.

☐ BOOLEAN data fields allow you to enter values other than 0 or -1 without reporting an error. Notice that Visual Basic alters the data you entered into these data fields without telling you!

☐ The CURRENCY data field stores only the first four places to the right of the decimal. If you enter values beyond the fourth decimal place, Visual Basic rounds the value to four decimal places and gives you no message.

☐ The DATETIME data field has some interesting behavior. Visual Basic does not let you store an invalid date or time in the data field; you receive a "Type mismatch" error instead. Also, the display format for the dates and times is determined by the settings you choose in the Windows Control Panel (through the International icon). In fact, when valid data is stored in a DATETIME data field, you can change the display format (say from 12-hour time display to 24-hour time display), and the next time you view that data record, it reflects the changes made through the Control Panel.

☐ The GUID data field type is used to store special 128-bit numbers called Globally Unique Identifiers.

☐ The BINARY data field type allows from 0 to 255 bytes of data storage and has only limited uses. If you are using the Visual Data Manager, you see a "Binary" field type—this is actually the LONGBINARY field.

☐ The MEMO and LONGBINARY data field types are known as "large value" data fields since they can hold up to 1.2 gigabytes of data in a single field. If you are working with large data fields, you need to move data between your program and the data table using the GetChunk and AppendChunk methods. You learn more about these methods on Day 9.

☐ The Visual Basic 5 documentation describes several other data field types recognized by Microsoft Jet (Big Integer, Char, Decimal, Float, Numeric, Time, TimeStamp, and VarBinary). However, these other data field types cannot be created using the Visual Data Manager or using Visual Basic code. These additional data field types may be returned by data tables built using other database tools, including Microsoft SQL Server or other back-end databases.

2

Summary

Today you learned the following about relational databases:

- ☐ A relational database is a collection of related data.
- ☐ The three key building blocks of relational databases are data fields, data records, and data tables.
- ☐ The two types of database relationships are one-to-one, which uses qualifier fields, and one-to-many, which uses pointer fields.
- ☐ There are two types of key (or index) fields: primary key and foreign key.

You also learned the 14 basic data field types recognized by Microsoft Jet and Visual Basic. You constructed a data entry form that allows you to test the way Visual Basic behaves when attempting to store data entered into the various data field types.

Quiz

1. What are the three main building blocks for relational databases?
2. What is the smallest building block in a relational database?
3. A data record is a collection of related _____.
4. What is the main role of a primary key in a data table?
5. Can a data table have more than one foreign key defined?
6. List all the possible values that can be stored in a BOOLEAN data field.
7. What is the highest value that can be stored in a BYTE data field?
8. What happens when you attempt to edit a COUNTER data field?
9. How many places to the right of the decimal can be stored in a CURRENCY data field?
10. What Windows Control Panel Applet determines the display format of DATE data fields?

Exercises

Answer questions 1, 2, and 3 based on the data in this table:

SSN	Last	First	Age	City	St	Comments
123-45-6789	Smith	Mark	17	Austin	TX	Trans. from New York.
456-79-1258	Smith	Ron	21	New York	NY	Born in Wyoming.
987-65-8764	Johnson	Curt	68	Chicago	IL	Plays golf on Wed.

1. How many records are in the previous data table?
2. Which field should you select as the primary key?
3. Identify each data field, its Data Field Type, and its VISUAL BASIC Type.
4. Modify the Visual Basic Data Field Types example from this lesson by creating a checkbox and placing the results in the existing BOOLEAN textbox.

Day 3

Visual Basic Database Objects

In the previous day's lesson, you learned how to create simple data entry forms using some of the data-bound controls and the various data field types. Today you learn about the programmatic data objects of Visual Basic 5.0. Data objects are used within a Visual Basic program to manipulate databases, as well as the data tables and indexes within the database. The data objects are the representations (in program code) of the physical database, data tables, fields, indexes, and so on. Throughout today's lesson, you create small Visual Basic programs that illustrate the special features of each data object.

Every Visual Basic program that accesses data tables uses data objects. Even if you are only using the data-aware controls (for example, the data control and bound input controls) and are not writing programming code, you are still using Visual Basic data objects.

The primary data object used in Visual Basic programs is the Recordset object. This is the object that holds the collection of data records used in your Visual Basic programs. There are three different types of Recordset objects. They are

- Dynaset-type Recordset object
- Table-type Recordset object
- Snapshot-type Recordset object

Any one of these Recordset objects can be used to gain access to an existing data table in a database. However, they each have unique properties and behave differently at times. Today you learn how these three types of Recordset data objects differ and when it is best to use these objects in your programs.

NOTE

In previous versions of Visual Basic, the Recordset object types were available as unique data objects (Dynaset, Table, and Snapshot). These objects can still be used when working with the older (version 2.5) data access object model, but it is not recommended. All data access object models now support the Recordset object types and that is the object you should use in all new Visual Basic programs.

You also learn about another data object today: the Database object. You can use the Database object to get information about the connected database. In this lesson, you learn about the general properties and behaviors of the Database object of the data control and how you can use them in your programs.

NOTE

You learn more about the Database object in Day 9 "Visual Basic and the Microsoft Jet Engine."

Dataset-Oriented Versus Data Record-Oriented

Before you learn about Visual Basic data objects, you should first learn some basics of how Visual Basic operates on databases in general. When you understand how Visual Basic looks at databases, you can better create programs that meet your needs.

The database model behind the Microsoft Access database and other SQL-oriented databases is quite different from the database model behind traditional PC databases such as FoxPro, dBASE, and Paradox. Traditional PC databases are *record-oriented* database systems. Structured Query Language (SQL) databases are *dataset-oriented* systems. Understanding the difference between record-oriented processing and dataset-oriented processing is the key to understanding how to optimize database programs in Visual Basic.

In record-oriented systems, you perform database operations one record at a time. The most common programming construct in record-oriented systems is the loop. The following pseudocode example shows how to increase the price field of an inventory table in a record-oriented database:

```
ReadLoop:
    If EndOf File
        Goto EndLoop
    Else
Read Record
        If Record.SalesRegion = 'Northeast' Then
            Price=Price*1.10
            Write Record
        End If
    EndIf
Goto ReadLoop
EndLoop:
End Program
```

Processing in record-oriented systems usually involves creating a routine that reads a single data record, processes it, and returns to read another record until the job is completed. PC databases use indexes to speed the process of locating records in data tables. Indexes also help speed processing by allowing PC databases to access the data in sorted order (by LastName, by AccountBalance, and so on).

In data-oriented systems, such as Microsoft Access, you perform database operations one set at a time, not one record at a time. The most common programming construct in set-oriented systems is the SQL statement. Instead of using program code to loop through single records, SQL databases can perform operations on entire tables from just one SQL statement. The following pseudocode example shows how you would update the price field in the same inventory file in a dataset-oriented database:

```
UPDATE Inventory SET Price=Price*1.10 WHERE Inventory.SalesRegion = 'Northeast'
```

The UPDATE SQL command behaves with SQL databases much like keywords behave with your Visual Basic programs. In this case, UPDATE tells the database that it wants to update an entire table (the Inventory table). The SET SQL command changes the value of a data field (in this case, the Price data field). The WHERE command is used to perform a logical comparison of the SalesRegion field to the value Northeast. As you can see, in dataset-oriented databases, you create a single statement that selects only the records you need to perform a database operation. After you identify the dataset, you apply the operation to all records in the set. In dataset systems, indexes are used to maintain database integrity more than to speed the location of specific records.

Visual Basic and Data Objects

Visual Basic database objects are dataset-oriented. Visual Basic programs generally perform better when data operations are done with a dataset than when data operations are done on single records. Some Visual Basic objects work well when performing record-oriented operations; most do not. The Visual Basic table-type Recordset object is very good at performing record-oriented processing. The Visual Basic Dynaset- and snapshot-type Recordset objects do not perform well on record-oriented processes.

A common mistake made by database programmers new to Visual Basic is to create programs that assume a record-oriented database model. These programmers are usually frustrated by Visual Basic's slow performance on large data tables and its slow response time when attempting to locate a specific record. Visual Basic's sluggishness is usually due to improper use of Visual Basic data objects—most often because programmers are opening entire data tables when they only need a small subset of the data in order to perform the required tasks.

Dataset Size Affects Program Performance

Unlike record-oriented systems, the size of the dataset you create affects the speed at which Visual Basic programs operate. As a data table grows, your program's processing speed can deteriorate. In heavily transaction-oriented applications, such as accounting systems, a dataset can grow quickly and cripple your application's ability to process information. If you are working in a network environment where the machine requesting data and the machine storing the data are separated, sending large datasets over the wire can affect not only your application, but all applications running on the network. For this reason, it is important to keep the size of the datasets as small as possible. This does not mean you have to limit the number of records in your data tables! You can use Visual Basic data objects to select the data you need from the table instead.

For example, you might have a data table that contains thousands of accounting transactions. If you want to modify the payment records in the data table, you can create a data object that contains all of the records (quite a big set), or you can tell Visual Basic to select only the payment records (a smaller set). Or, if you know that you only need to modify payment records that have been added to the system in the last three days, you can create an even smaller dataset: The smaller the dataset, the faster your program can process the data. Visual Basic data objects give you the power to create datasets that are the proper size for your needs.

The Dynaset-Type Recordset Data Object

The Visual Basic Dynaset-type Recordset data object is the most frequently used data object in Visual Basic programs. It is used to dynamically gain access to part or all of an existing data table in a database, hence the name *Dynaset*. When you set the DatabaseName and RecordSource properties of a Visual Basic data control, you are actually creating a Visual Basic Dynaset-type Recordset. You can also create a Dynaset-type Recordset by using the CreateDynaset method of the Database object.

When you create a Visual Basic Dynaset-type Recordset, you do not create a new physical table in the database. A Dynaset exists as a *virtual* data table. This virtual table usually contains a subset of the records in a real data table, but it can contain the complete set. Because creating a Dynaset does not create a new physical table, Dynasets do not add to the size of the database. However, creating Dynasets does take up space in RAM on the machine that creates the set (the one that is running the program). Depending on the number of records in the Dynaset, temporary disk space can also be used on the machine requesting the dataset.

Strengths of the Dynaset-Type Recordset Object

There are several reasons to use Dynasets when you access data. In general, Dynasets require less memory than other data objects and provide the most update options, including the capability to create additional data objects from existing Dynasets. Dynasets are the default data objects for the Visual Basic data control, and they are the only updatable data object you can use for databases connected through Microsoft's Open Database Connectivity (ODBC) model. The following sections provide more details of the strengths of the Dynaset data object.

Dynasets Are Really Key Sets

Visual Basic Dynasets use relatively little workstation memory, even for large datasets. When you create a Dynaset, Visual Basic performs several steps. First, Visual Basic selects the records you requested. Then, it creates temporary index keys to each of these records and sends the complete set of keys to your workstation along with enough records to fill out any bound controls (text boxes and/or grid controls) that appear on your on-screen form. This process is illustrated in Figure 3.1.

Figure 3.1.

Dynasets contain key sets that point to the actual data.

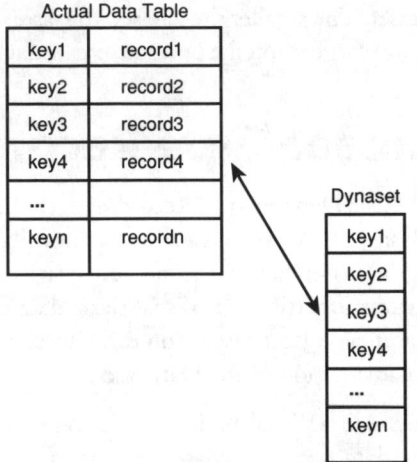

 **NOTE**

The actual data request engine used by Visual Basic is called the Microsoft Jet data engine. In pure SQL systems, all requests for data result in a set of data records. Data requests to the Microsoft Jet engine result in a set of keys that point to the data records. By returning keys instead of data records, Microsoft Jet engine is able to limit network traffic and speed database performance.

The set of keys is stored in RAM and—if the set is too large to store in RAM alone—in a temporary file on a local disk drive. As you scroll through the dataset, Visual Basic retrieves actual records as needed from the physical table used to create the Dynaset. If you have a single text box on the form, Visual Basic retrieves the data from the table one record at a time. If you have a grid of data or a loop that collects several records from the table in succession, a small set of the records in the dataset is retrieved by Visual Basic. Visual Basic also caches records at the workstation to reduce requests to the physical data table, which speeds performance.

If the Dynaset is very large, you might end up with a key set so large that it requires more RAM and temporary disk space than the local machine can handle. In that case, you receive an error message from Visual Basic. For this reason, it is important that you use care in creating your criteria for populating the dataset. The smaller the dataset, the smaller the key set.

Dynasets Are Dynamic

Even though Dynasets are virtual tables in memory created from physical tables, they are not static copies of the data table. After you create a Dynaset, if anyone else alters the underlying data table by modifying, adding, or deleting records, you see the changes in your Dynaset as soon as you refresh the Dynaset. Refreshing the Dynaset can be done using the `Refresh` method. You can also refresh the Dynasets by moving the record pointer using the arrow keys of the data control or using the `MoveFirst`, `MoveNext`, `MovePrevious`, and `MoveLast` methods. Moving the pointer refreshes only the records you read, not the entire Dynaset.

Although the dynamic aspect of Dynasets is very effective in maintaining up-to-date views of the underlying data table, Dynasets also have some limitations and drawbacks. For example, if another user deletes a record that you currently have in your Dynaset and you attempt to move to that record, Visual Basic reports an error.

Dynasets Can Be Created from More than One Table

A Dynaset can be created using more than one table in the database. You can create a single view that contains selected records from several tables, update the view, and therefore update all the underlying tables of the data at one time. This is a very powerful aspect of a Visual Basic Dynaset data object. Using Visual Basic Dynasets, you can create virtual tables that make it easy to create simple data entry screens and display graphs and reports that show specialized selections of data.

Use Dynasets to Create Other Dynasets or Snapshots

Often in Visual Basic programs, you need to create a secondary dataset based on user input. The Dynaset data object is the only data object from which you can create another Dynaset.

You can create additional Dynasets by using the `Clone` method or the `CreateDynaset` method. When you clone a Dynaset, you create an exact duplicate of the Dynaset. You can use this duplicate to perform look-ups or to reorder the records for a display. Cloned Dynasets take up slightly less room than the original Dynaset.

Let's put together a short code sample that explores Dynasets. You do this all in Visual Basic code, too, instead of using the Visual Basic data control.

First start a new Visual Basic 5.0 Standard EXE project. Be sure to add a reference to the Microsoft DAO 3.5 Object Library before you begin coding. To do this, Select Project | References from the Main menu (see Figure 3.2).

3

Figure 3.2.

*Adding the Microsoft
DAO 3.5 Reference to
a Visual Basic Project.*

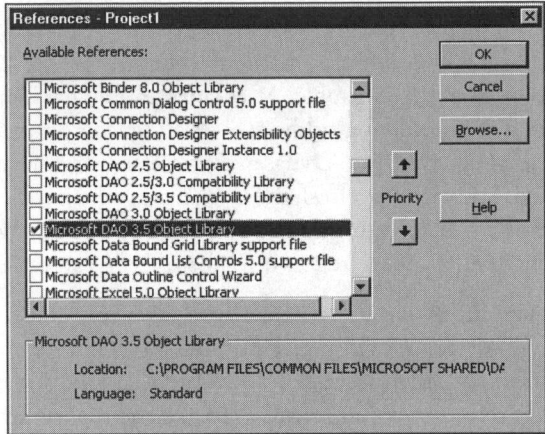

Now double-click the form to open the code window to the Form_Load event. You write the entire example in this procedure.

When you open a Dynaset using Visual Basic code instead of using the data control, you must create two Visual Basic objects: a Database object and a Recordset object. Listing 3.1 shows how you create the objects in Visual Basic code.

Listing 3.1. Creating a Database object and a Recordset object.

```
Private Sub Form_Load()
    '
    ' creating Dynaset-type recordsets
    '
    Dim db As Database ' the database object
    Dim rs As Recordset ' the recordset object
    '
End Sub
```

You must initialize these objects with values before they can access data. This process is similar to setting the properties of the data control. To initialize the values, you first create two variables that correspond to the DatabaseName and RecordSource properties of the Visual Basic data control. The code sample in Listing 3.2 shows how it is done.

TIP   The code sample in Listing 3.2 uses the App.Path Visual Basic keywords. You can use the Path method of the App object to determine
the drive letter and directory from which the program was launched. In

most projects throughout this book, you find the databases are stored in the same directory as the sample projects. By using the `App.Path` method as part of the database name, you always point to the correct drive and directory for the required file.

TYPE **Listing 3.2. Declaring database and data table variables.**

```
Private Sub Form_Load()
    '
    ' creating Dynaset-type recordsets
    '
    Dim db As Database ' the database object
    Dim rs As Recordset ' the recordset object
    '
    ' create local variables
    Dim strDBName As String
    Dim strRSName As String
    '
    ' initialize the variables
    strDBName = App.Path & "\..\data\books5.mdb"
    strRSName = "Titles"
    '
End Sub
```

TIP

Notice that you created two string variables, and both variable names start with the letters "str", which stand for *string type*. This is the prefix of the variable name. The prefix of the name tells you what type of data is stored in the variable. This is common programming practice. Adhering to a strict naming convention makes it easier to read and maintain your programs.

Before you continue with the chapter, save this form as DYNASETS.FRM and save the project as DYNASETS.VBP.

Now that you have created the data objects, created variables to hold database properties, and initialized those variables with the proper values, you are ready to actually open the database and create the Dynaset-type Recordset. The code in Listing 3.3 shows how to do this using Visual Basic code.

Listing 3.3. Opening the database and creating the Dynaset.

TYPE

```
Private Sub Form_Load()
    '
    ' creating dynaset-type recordsets
    '
    Dim db As Database ' the database object
    Dim rs As Recordset ' the recordset object
    '
    ' create local variables
    Dim strDBName As String
    Dim strRSName As String
    '
    ' initialize the variables
    strDBName = App.Path & "\..\data\books5.mdb"
    strRSName = "Titles"
    '
    ' create the objects
    Set db = DBEngine.OpenDatabase(strDBName)
    Set rs = db.OpenRecordset(strRSName, dbOpenDynaset)
    '
End Sub
```

There are two added lines in Listing 3.3. The first added line opens the BOOKS5.MDB database and sets the Visual Basic database object db to point to the database. This gives your Visual Basic program a direct link to the selected database.

TIP

Note that this database object was created using the OpenDatabase method of the DBEngine object. The DBEngine is covered in greater detail on Day 9.

Now you can use the db data object to represent the open database in all other Visual Basic code in this program. The second line creates a Dynaset-type Recordset object that contains all the records in the Titles table. The Visual Basic rs object is set to point to this set of records. Notice that the OpenRecordset method is applied to the db Database object.

TIP

Notice that these last two lines of code use the Set keyword. This Visual Basic keyword is used to initialize all programming objects. You might think that you could perform the same task using the following code line:

```
Rs = db.OpenRecordSet(strRSName,dbOpenRecordset)
```

> However, this does not work. In Visual Basic, all objects must be
> created using the Set keyword.

The code in Listing 3.3 is all that you need to open an existing Microsoft Access database and create a Dynaset-type Recordset ready for update. However, for this project, you want to see a bit more. Let's add some code that tells you how many records are in the Titles data table.

You need one more variable to hold the record count. You also use the MoveLast method to move the record pointer to the last record in the Recordset. This forces Visual Basic to touch every record in the collection, and therefore gives you an accurate count of the total number of records in the table. You get the count by reading the RecordCount property of the Recordset. When you have all that, you display a Visual Basic message box that tells you how many records are in the Recordset. Listing 3.4 contains the code to add.

TYPE **Listing 3.4. Counting the records in a Dynaset.**

```
Private Sub Form_Load()
    '
    ' creating dynaset-type recordsets
    '
    Dim db As Database ' the database object
    Dim rs As Recordset ' the recordset object
    '
    ' create local variables
    Dim strDBName As String
    Dim strRSName As String
    Dim intRecs As Integer
    '
    ' initialize the variables
    strDBName = App.Path & "\..\data\books5.mdb"
    strRSName = "Titles"
    '
    ' create the objects
    Set db = DBEngine.OpenDatabase(strDBName)
    Set rs = db.OpenRecordset(strRSName, dbOpenDynaset)
    '
    ' count the records in the collection
    rs.MoveLast ' move to end of list to force a count
    intRecs = rs.RecordCount ' get count
    MsgBox strRSName & " :" & CStr(intRecs), vbInformation, "Total Records in
Set"
    '
End Sub
```

Save the form (DYNASETS.FRM) and project (DYNASETS.VBP) again and run the program. You see a message box telling you how many records are in the Recordset. Figure 3.3 shows the results of a typical run.

Figure 3.3.

*Displaying the
RecordCount of a
Recordset.*

You can use the OpenRecordset command on an existing Recordset to create a smaller subset of the data. This is often done when the user is allowed to create a record selection criterion. If the dataset returned is too large, the user is allowed to further qualify the search by creating additional criteria to apply to the dataset.

Let's modify DYNASETS.VBP to create a smaller Dynaset-type Recordset from the existing Recordset. You need to create a new Recordset object and a new variable called strFilter to hold the criteria for selecting records. The code in Listing 3.5 shows how to add the object and variable to the existing DYNASETS.VBP project.

TYPE

Listing 3.5. Adding a new Recordset object and string variable.

```
Private Sub Form_Load()
    '
    ' creating dynaset-type recordsets
    '
    Dim db As Database ' the database object
    Dim rs As Recordset ' the recordset object
    Dim rs2 As Recordset ' <<< add another recordset object
    '
    ' create local variables
    Dim strDBName As String
    Dim strRSName As String
    Dim intRecs As Integer
    Dim strFilter As String ' <<< add filter
    '
    ' initialize the variables
    strDBName = App.Path & "\..\data\books5.mdb"
    strRSName = "Titles"
    strFilter = "YearPub>1990" ' <<< set filter
    '
    ' create the objects
    Set db = DBEngine.OpenDatabase(strDBName)
    Set rs = db.OpenRecordset(strRSName, dbOpenDynaset)
    '
    ' count the records in the collection
    rs.MoveLast ' move to end of list to force a count
```

3

```
    intRecs = rs.RecordCount ' get count
    MsgBox strRSName & " :" & CStr(intRecs), vbInformation, "Total Records in
Set"
    '
End Sub
```

Now that you have the object and the variable (marked with <<< in Listing 3.5), you can add code that creates a new Recordset. First you set the Filter property of the existing Recordset using the variable you just created. Then you create the new Recordset from the old one. See the last two lines of the code in Listing 3.6.

TYPE **Listing 3.6. Using the Filter property to create a Recordset.**

```
Private Sub Form_Load()
    '
    ' creating dynaset-type recordsets
    '
    Dim db As Database ' the database object
    Dim rs As Recordset ' the recordset object
    Dim rs2 As Recordset ' another recordset
    '
    ' create local variables
    Dim strDBName As String
    Dim strRSName As String
    Dim intRecs As Integer
    Dim strFilter As String
    '
    ' initialize the variables
    strDBName = App.Path & "\..\data\books5.mdb"
    strRSName = "Titles"
    strFilter = "YearPub>1990"
    '
    ' create the objects
    Set db = DBEngine.OpenDatabase(strDBName)
    Set rs = db.OpenRecordset(strRSName, dbOpenDynaset)
    '
    ' count the records in the collection
    rs.MoveLast ' move to end of list to force a count
    intRecs = rs.RecordCount ' get count
    MsgBox strRSName & " :" & CStr(intRecs), vbInformation, "Total Records in
Set"
    '
    ' create filtered collection
    rs.Filter = strFilter
    Set rs2 = rs.OpenRecordset
    '
End Sub
```

Now that you've created the new Recordset from the old one, you can get a count of the selected records. You can add the same code you used earlier: Move to the end of the Recordset, get the RecordCount, and show it in a message box. Listing 3.7 shows the completed program.

Listing 3.7. Displaying the record count of the filtered

TYPE **Recordset.**

```
Private Sub Form_Load()
'
    ' creating dynaset-type recordsets
    '
    Dim db As Database ' the database object
    Dim rs As Recordset ' the recordset object
    Dim rs2 As Recordset ' another recordset
    Dim rs3 As Recordset ' for cloning
    '
    ' create local variables
    Dim strDBName As String
    Dim strRSName As String
    Dim intRecs As Integer
    Dim strFilter As String
    '
    ' initialize the variables
    strDBName = App.Path & "\..\..\data\books5.mdb"
    strRSName = "Titles"
    strFilter = "YearPub>1990"
    '
    ' create the objects
    Set db = DBEngine.OpenDatabase(strDBName)
    Set rs = db.OpenRecordset(strRSName, dbOpenDynaset)
    '
    ' count the records in the collection
    rs.MoveLast ' move to end of list to force a count
    intRecs = rs.RecordCount ' get count
    MsgBox strRSName & " :" & CStr(intRecs), vbInformation, "Total Records in
Set"
    '
    ' create filtered collection
    rs.Filter = strFilter
    Set rs2 = rs.OpenRecordset
    '
    ' count the records in the collection
    rs2.MoveLast ' move to end of list to force a count
    intRecs = rs2.RecordCount ' get count
    MsgBox strFilter & " :" & CStr(intRecs), vbInformation, "Total Records in
Set"
    ' exit program
    End
    '
End Sub
```

Save and run the code to check the results (see Figure 3.4). Notice that the first record count (the full dataset) is larger than the second record count (the filtered dataset).

3

Figure 3.4.

Display RecordCount
of the Filtered
Recordset.

It is also important to notice that the second Recordset object was created *from* the first Recordset object. This a very powerful feature of Visual Basic. When you want to get a smaller dataset, you don't have to reload the data from the database; you can use an existing Recordset as the source for a new dataset.

TIP

Creating subsets of a Recordset in this manner can sometimes be slower than simply creating a new Recordset from the database itself. The exception to this rule is when your database is stored at a distant server. In cases where your source data is far away and possibly available only over a slow network connection, using the Filter property to create subsets of data can be faster.

Now let's make one more series of changes to DYNASETS.VBP that illustrate the Clone method for Recordsets. Cloning a Recordset makes a duplicate of the set. Add another data object (rs3), and add the Clone Recordset program code in Listing 3.8.

TYPE   **Listing 3.8. Cloning a new Recordset.**

```
Private Sub Form_Load()
    '
    ' creating dynaset-type recordsets
    '
    Dim db As Database ' the database object
    Dim rs As Recordset ' the recordset object
    Dim rs2 As Recordset ' another recordset
    Dim rs3 As Recordset ' for cloning
    '
    ' create local variables
    Dim strDBName As String
    Dim strRSName As String
    Dim intRecs As Integer
    Dim strFilter As String
    '
    ' initialize the variables
    strDBName = App.Path & "\..\data\books5.mdb"
    strRSName = "Titles"
    strFilter = "YearPub>1990"
    '
```

continues

Listing 3.8. continued

```
    ' create the objects
    Set db = DBEngine.OpenDatabase(strDBName)
    Set rs = db.OpenRecordset(strRSName, dbOpenDynaset)
    '
    ' count the records in the collection
    rs.MoveLast ' move to end of list to force a count
    intRecs = rs.RecordCount ' get count
    MsgBox strRSName & " :" & CStr(intRecs), vbInformation, "Total Records in
Set"
    '
    ' create filtered collection
    rs.Filter = strFilter
    Set rs2 = rs.OpenRecordset
    '
    ' count the records in the collection
    rs2.MoveLast ' move to end of list to force a count
    intRecs = rs2.RecordCount ' get count
    MsgBox strFilter & " :" & CStr(intRecs), vbInformation, "Total Records in
Set"
    '
    ' clone the recordset
    Set rs3 = rs.Clone ' clone it
    rs3.MoveLast ' move to end
    intRecs = rs3.RecordCount ' get count
    MsgBox "Cloned Recordset: " & CStr(intRecs), vbInformation, "Total Records
in Set"
    '
End Sub
```

Notice that all you have to do to clone a Recordset is to use the Clone method to load a new Recordset object variable. When you run the program this time, you see that the Recordset created using the Clone method contains the same number of records as its parent.

Dynasets Can Use Bookmarks, Filters, and Sorts

Dynaset-type Recordsets can use the Bookmark, Filter, and Sort properties to reorder data for display (Sort) or create a subset of the Recordset (Filter). Using the Visual Basic Find method on a Recordset forces Visual Basic to start at the first record in the collection and read each one until a match is found. Once the selected record is found, your user may want to return to the record that was displayed before the search began. That's what Visual Basic Bookmarks do. They remember where you were.

When you search for a record in the dataset using one of the Find methods, you should set Bookmarks before your search to remember where you started. This is especially handy if your Find criteria results in a null record. When a FindFirst method fails to locate the desired record, the record pointer is set to the first record in the collection. If you have saved the bookmark before starting the search, you can reset the Visual Basic Bookmark and return the user to the place from which the search started.

Let's build a quick project to demonstrate the use of Bookmarks. Use the information in Table 3.1 to create a small form with a data control, two bound input controls, two label controls, and a single command button.

Table 3.1. Controls for BOOKMARKS.FRM.

Control	Property	Setting
VB.Form	Name	FrmBookMarks
	Caption	"Bookmark Demonstration"
	ClientHeight	1320
	ClientLeft	60
	ClientTop	345
	ClientWidth	4605
	StartUpPosition	2 'CenterScreen
VB.CommandButton	Name	CmdSaveBookmark
	Caption	"&Save Bookmark"
	Height	300
	Left	2760
	Top	180
	Width	1695
VB.Data	Name	DtaBookMarks
	Align	2 'Align Bottom
	Caption	"Data1"
	Connect	"Access"
	DatabaseName	C:\TYSDBVB5\SOURCE\DATA\BOOKS5.MDB
	RecordsetType	1 'Dynaset
	RecordSource	"Authors"
VB.TextBox	Name	TxtName
	DataField	"Name"
	DataSource	"dtaBookMarks"
	Height	300
	Left	1440
	Top	600
	Width	3015

continues

Table 3.1. continued

Control	Property	Setting
VB.TextBox	Name	TxtAUID
	DataField	"AUID"
	DataSource	"dtaBookMarks"
	Height	300
	Left	1440
	Top	180
	Width	1215
VB.Label	Name	LblName
	BorderStyle	1 'Fixed Single
	Caption	"Author Name"
	Height	300
	Left	120
	Top	600
	Width	1215
VB.Label	Name	LblAUID
	BorderStyle	1 'Fixed Single
	Caption	"Author ID"
	Height	300
	Left	120
	Top	180
	Width	1215

Refer to Figure 3.5 as a guide for sizing and locating the controls on the form.

Figure 3.5.

*Laying out the
Bookmark Demon-
stration form.*

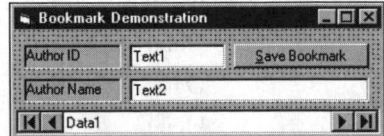

When you have completed the form layout, add the following code behind the command
button. The code in Listing 3.9 is a toggle routine that saves the current place in the table by
reading (and storing) the Bookmark, or restores the previous place in the table by reading (and
updating) the Bookmark.

Listing 3.9. Coding the `cmdSaveBookmarks_Click` **event for**
BOOKMARKS.VBP.

```
Private Sub cmdSaveBookmark_Click()
    '
    ' show how bookmarks work
    '
    Static blnFlag As Boolean
    Static strBookmark As String
    '
    If blnFlag = False Then
        '
        ' flip flag and set caption
        blnFlag = True
        cmdSaveBookmark.Caption = "&Restore Bookmark"
        '
        ' save bookmark for later
        strBookmark = dtaBookMarks.Recordset.Bookmark
        MsgBox "Bookmark Saved", vbInformation
    Else
        '
        ' flip flag and set caption
        blnFlag = False
        cmdSaveBookmark.Caption = "&Save Bookmark"
        '
        ' restore saved bookmark
        dtaBookMarks.Recordset.Bookmark = strBookmark
    End If
    '
End Sub
```

TIP

Listing 3.9 uses two Static variables. Static variables keep their value even after the procedure ends. Using Static variables in your program is an excellent way to keep track of flag values even after procedures or functions exit. The only other way to make sure that variables maintain their value after exit from a routine is to place them in the declaration area of the form. The problem with placing them at the form-level declaration is that they now can be altered by routines in other procedures or functions on the same form. Declaring Static variables within the procedures in which they are used follows good programming practice by limiting the scope of the variable.

Save the form as BOOKMARKS.FRM and the project as BOOKMARKS.VBP, and then run the program. The program opens the BOOKS5.MDB file, creates a Dynaset-type Recordset of all the records in the Authors data table, and presents the first record on the form. Note that the command button caption says Save Bookmark. Click the command button to create a Bookmark that points to this record of the collection. The caption changes to Restore Bookmark. Now use the arrow buttons on the data control to move to another record on the form. Click the command button. You see that the record pointer has been returned to the first record in the collection. This is because the Recordset Bookmark property was reset to the value you stored earlier.

Dynasets and ODBC

If you are accessing data from an ODBC (Open Database Connectivity) data source, the only Visual Basic data object you can use to update the underlying data table is a Dynaset-type Recordset. You learn more about ODBC connected databases on Day 19, "ODBC Data Access Via the ODBC API."

Limitations of the Dynaset-Type Recordset Data Object

Although the Dynaset is an excellent data object, it has a few drawbacks that must be considered. Chief among these is that Dynasets do not allow you to specify an existing index, and you cannot use the Visual Basic Seek method to quickly locate a single record in the Dynaset. Also, errors can occur when displaying records in a Dynaset if the records in the underlying data table have been altered or deleted by another user.

Dynaset Access and Seek Limitations

Dynasets cannot make use of Index objects that exist in a database because the Index is built to control the entire data table and not just a subset of the data. Because Dynasets could be subsets of the data table, the Index is useless. Also, because you cannot specify an Index object for a Dynaset, you cannot use the Visual Basic Seek method on a Dynaset.

These are only minor limitations. If you have defined an Index in the underlying table with the Primary flag turned on, the Visual Basic data engine uses the primary key index when creating the Dynaset. This usually puts the Dynaset in optimal order. Even though you cannot use the Seek method on a Dynaset, you can use the FindFirst, FindNext, FindPrevious, and FindLast methods. Even though they are not true index searches, they are fast enough for operations on small- to medium-sized Dynasets. You learn more about Seek, Find, and Move in Day 10, "Creating Database Programs with Visual Basic Code."

3

Dynamic Membership-Related Errors

If your program opens a database and creates a Dynaset from an underlying table while another user has also opened the same database and created a Dynaset based on the same underlying data table, it is possible that both users will attempt to edit the same data record. If both users edit the same record and both attempt to save the record back to the underlying table, the second person who attempts to save the record receives a Visual Basic error.

When the second person tries to save the record, Visual Basic discovers that the original record in the underlying data table has been altered. In order to maintain database integrity, Visual Basic does not allow the second person to update the table.

When to Use the Dynaset-Type Recordset Data Object

The Dynaset object should be used in most database programs you write. In most cases, the Visual Basic Dynaset data object is the most effective data access object to use. It offers you a way to create a dynamic, updatable subset of data records in one or more data tables. The Dynaset object is the default object created by the bound data control and is the only updatable data object you can use to access ODBC data sources.

The Dynaset is not a good data object to use when you need to do a great deal of record-oriented processing on large datasets, such as index look-ups on large transaction files. If you have a Visual Basic program that uses Dynasets and is showing slow database performance, look for places where you can limit the size of Dynasets by narrowing the selection criteria.

The Table-Type Recordset Data Object

The Visual Basic Table-type Recordset data object is the data object that gives you access to the physical data table, sometimes referred to as the *base table*. You can use the Table object to directly open the table defined by Data Manager (or some other database definition tool). The chief advantage of using the Table object is that you can specify search indexes and use the Visual Basic Seek method. Like Dynasets, Tables take a limited amount of local workstation memory.

Table-type Recordset data objects also give you instant information on the state of the data table. This is important in a multiuser environment. As soon as a user adds or deletes a record from the table, all other users who have the data table open as a Visual Basic Table object also see the changes.

Visual Basic Table objects have their drawbacks, too. You cannot use a Select statement to initialize a Table object, and you cannot combine data tables to create unique views of the database when you create Table objects.

You cannot use Bookmarks, create Filters, or sort the table. Furthermore, you cannot use the Table data object to access ODBC data sources. Only Dynasets and Snapshots can be used with ODBC data sources.

Strengths of the Table-type Recordset Data Object

The real strength of Table objects is that you can specify Index objects to use when searching for specific records in the table. Table objects also use limited workstation memory and offer instant updates whenever that data in the table changes.

Data Pointers and Instant Membership Notification

Like Dynasets, Table objects use limited workstation memory because Visual Basic caches pointers to the actual records at the workstation instead of loading all the records into workstation memory. This gives your programs the fastest access speed of all the data objects when you are searching for a single record.

Unlike Dynasets and Snapshots, Table objects are not subsets of the data table. They contain all the records in the table at all times. As soon as a new record is added to the data table, the record is available to the Table object. Also, as soon as a user deletes a record from the table, the Table object is updated to reflect the deletion.

Table-Type Recordset Objects, Indexes, and the Seek Method

The Visual Basic Table-type Recordset data object enables you to specify an index to apply to the data table. You can use indexes to order the data table for displays and reports and to speed searches using the Seek method.

The following project (TBSEEK.VBP) demonstrates the use of Visual Basic Table-type Recordset objects, indexes, and the Seek method. It opens the Titles table of the BOOKS5.MDB database and gives you the ability to select one of three indexes. When the index is selected, the program loads the records from the table into a list box. When you click the Search button, you are prompted to enter a search value to use in the Seek method on the table.

Use the information in Table 4.2 to build a new Standard EXE project that demonstrates the use of Visual Basic Table objects, indexes, and the Seek method.

Table 3.2. Controls for the TBSEEK.VBP **project.**

Control	Property	Setting
VB.Form	Name	frmTbSeek
	Caption	"Table Index and Seek Demonstration"
	ClientHeight	2895
	ClientLeft	60
	ClientTop	345
	ClientWidth	6540
	StartUpPosition	3 'Windows Default
VB.CommandButton	Name	cmdExit
	Caption	"E&xit"
	Height	300
	Left	5220
	Top	2520
	Width	1200
VB.CommandButton	Name	cmdSeek
	Caption	"&Seek"
	Height	300
	Left	3900
	Top	2520
	Width	1200
VB.CommandButton	Name	cmdPublisher
	Caption	"&Publisher"
	Height	300
	Left	2640
	Top	2520
	Width	1200
VB.CommandButton	Name	CmdISBN
	Caption	"&ISBN"
	Height	300
	Left	1380
	Top	2520
	Width	1200

3

continues

Table 3.2. continued

Control	Property	Setting
VB.CommandButton	Name	CmdTitle
	Caption	"&Title"
	Height	300
	Left	120
	Top	2520
	Width	1200
VB.ListBox	Name	LstRecordset
	Height	2040
	Left	120
	Top	360
	Width	6255
VB.Label	Name	LblIndex
	BorderStyle	1 'Fixed Single
	Height	255
	Left	120
	Top	60
	Width	6255

Refer to Figure 3.6 as a guide for placement and positioning of the controls listed in Table 3.2.

Figure 3.6.

Laying out the TbSeek form.

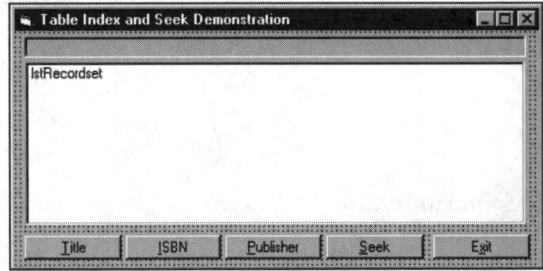

Because you again create data objects in Visual Basic code in this exercise, you need to load the Microsoft DAO 3.5 Object Library for this project.

After you have placed the controls on the form and sized them, you need to place the code from Listing 3.10 in the declaration section of the form. This code declares several variables that you use throughout the form.

TYPE **Listing 3.10. Declaration code for the TBSEEK.VBP project.**

```
Option Explicit
'
' form-level variables
'
Dim db As Database
Dim rs As Recordset
'
Dim strDBName As String
Dim strRSName As String
Dim strIndex As String
Dim strField As String
```

Place the code from Listing 3.11 in the Form_Load event of the form. This code opens the BOOKS.MDB database and opens the Titles table.

TYPE **Listing 3.11. Coding the Form_Load routine of TBSEEK.VBP.**

```
Private Sub Form_Load()
    '
    ' set vars
    strDBName = App.Path & "\..\..\Data\Books5.mdb"
    strRSName = "Titles"
    '
    ' open database and table
    Set db = DBEngine.OpenDatabase(strDBName)
    Set rs = db.OpenRecordset(strRSName, dbOpenTable)
    '
End Sub
```

Place the procedure shown in Listing 3.12 in the declaration section. This is the procedure that sets the table index and loads the list box in the proper order.

TYPE **Listing 3.12. Coding the LoadList routine of TBSEEK.VBP.**

```
Public Sub LoadList()
    '
    ' load data collection into list box
    '
```

continues

Listing 3.12. continued

```
        Dim strLine As String
        lstRecordset.Clear
        '
        rs.Index = strIndex
        rs.MoveFirst
        '
        On Error Resume Next ' in case we get null fields
        '
        Do While Not rs.EOF
            strLine = rs.Fields("Title")
            strLine = strLine & " ¦ " & CStr(rs.Fields("YearPub"))
            strLine = strLine & " ¦ " & CStr(rs.Fields("ISBN"))
            strLine = strLine & " ¦ " & CStr(rs.Fields("PubID"))
            lstRecordset.AddItem strLine
            rs.MoveNext
        Loop
        '
        lblIndex.Caption = "Titles Table - Indexed by [" & strField & "]"
        '
End Sub
```

The `LoadList` procedure is an example of a way to load a Visual Basic list box with data from a table. The routine first clears out the list box. Then the Index property of the table object is set (based on the user's input) and moves to the first record in the table.

Now the fun starts. The `Do While..Loop` construct reads each record in the table and creates a single line of text (`strLine`) that contains each of the fields separated by a single space. Notice that you need to use the `CStr()` function to convert the numeric fields in the data table (`YearPub`, `ISBN`, and `Pub_ID`) into string values before you can add them to `strLine`. After the line is built, the `strLine` is added to the list box using the `lstRecordset.AddNew` method. After the line is added to the list box, the record pointer is advanced using the `rs.MoveNext` method. This goes on until there are no more records in the table.

The following three code segments go behind the appropriate command button to set the indexes. They set values for selecting the index, setting the display, and calling the routine to load the list box.

Place this code in the `cmdTitle_Click` event:

```
Private Sub cmdTitle_Click()
    '
    ' set for Title index
    '
    strIndex = "Title"
    strField = "Title"
    LoadList
    '
End Sub
```

Place this code in the cmdISBN_Click event:

```
Private Sub cmdISBN_Click()
    '
    ' set for ISBN index
    '
    strIndex = "PrimaryKey"
    strField = "ISBN"
    LoadList
    '
End Sub
```

Place this code in the cmdPublisher_Click event:

```
Private Sub cmdPublisher_Click()
    '
    ' set for PubID index
    '
    strIndex = "PubID"
    strField = "PubID"
    LoadList
    '
End Sub
```

The Seek routine shown in Listing 3.13 calls an input box to prompt the user for a search value, performs the seek, and reports the results of the search. The routine first checks to see whether the user has filled the list box by selecting an index. If the list box contains data, the routine calls the Visual Basic InputBox function to get user input, and then invokes the Seek method of the table object. If the record is *not* found, you see a Seek Failed message. If you entered a record that is on file, you see a Record Found message.

TYPE **Listing 3.13. Coding the Seek routine for TBSEEK.VBP.**

```
Private Sub cmdSeek_Click()
    '
    ' perform table seek
    '
    Dim strSeek As String
    '
    If lstRecordset.ListCount = 0 Then
        MsgBox "Select an Index First!", vbExclamation, "Missing Index"
    Else
        strSeek = InputBox("Enter a Seek value for " & strField)
        rs.Seek "=", strSeek
        If rs.NoMatch = True Then
            MsgBox strSeek & " not in table", vbCritical, "Seek Failed"
        Else
            MsgBox rs.Fields("Title"), vbInformation, "Record Found"
        End If
    End If
    '
End Sub
```

Of course, every project should have an Exit button. Enter the following line for the Exit button:

```
Private Sub cmdExit_Click()
    '
    ' end program
    '
    rs.Close
    db.Close
    Set rs = Nothing
    Set db = Nothing
    Unload Me
    '
End Sub
```

When you have completed the coding, save the form as TBSEEK.FRM and the project as TBSEEK.VBP, and then run the program. Click the Title, ISBN, or Publisher buttons to set the index and load the list box. Note that each time you select a different button, the list is loaded in a different order. After the list is loaded, click the Seek button to perform an indexed search on the data table. If you enter a value that is in the index, the program reports the title of the book in a message box; otherwise, you see an error message. See Figure 3.7 for an example.

Figure 3.7.

*Testing the TbSeek
Demonstration
Project.*

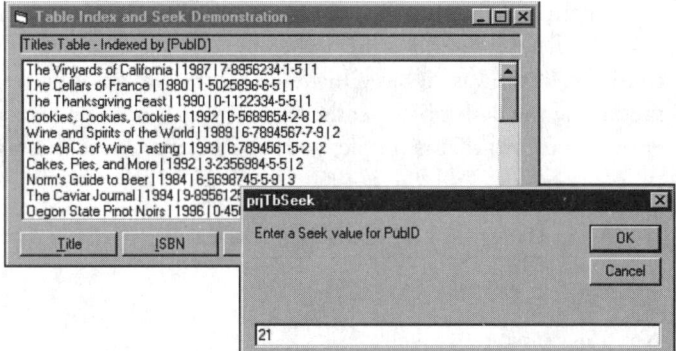

Limitations of the Table-Type Recordset Data Object

Even though the Visual Basic Table-type Recordset object provides the fastest search speed of any of the data objects, it also has certain drawbacks. You cannot sort a table; you can't use the Table object when accessing ODBC data sources; and you can't use the Visual Basic data control to access a Table object.

Tables Cannot Use Bookmarks, Sorts, or Filters

Unlike Dynasets and Snapshots, Visual Basic Table objects cannot be sorted, filtered, or have Bookmarks set. Instead of sorting the data, you can use Index objects to establish the order of the data in the table. If you need to filter the table (usually because it is a large table), you need to create a Dynaset or Snapshot that contains a subset of the data in the table.

Table objects can't use Bookmarks, so you can't mark your place in a table, move around, and then return to the location using Visual Basic Bookmarks. You can, however, save the table index value instead. The table must have an index declared, and you must know the fields used in the declared index. You can get this information from the Design form of Data Manager, or you can get it at runtime by reading the Index.Name and Index.Fields properties of the Table object. Refer to the section on the Database data object for an example of how to read the Index.Name and Index.Fields properties of a data table.

ODBC Data Source Limitations

If you plan to do any work with ODBC data sources, you have to forget using the Visual Basic Table object. It does not matter whether the ODBC source is a SQL Server data source or a spreadsheet on your local workstation. You cannot define a Table object to access the data. You must use a Dynaset or Snapshot object for ODBC data requests.

The reason for this limitation is that the ODBC driver gives Visual Basic access to virtually any type of data. There is no requirement that the data source comply with the Visual Basic data engine data table format. Because the Table object is designed specifically to provide direct access to Visual Basic data tables, it can only be used to access a data table that exists as data table in a Microsoft Access database.

When to Use the Table-Type Recordset Data Object

The Visual Basic Table-type Recordset object is the best choice when you need to provide speedy searches of large data tables. As long as you do not need to access ODBC data sources, and you do not need to get a set of data for processing, the Table object is an excellent choice.

If, however, you need to process sets of data instead of single records, the Table object does not work as easily or as quickly as a Dynaset or Snapshot object.

The Snapshot-Type Recordset Data Object

Visual Basic Snapshot-type Recordset objects are almost identical to Dynaset-type Recordsets in behavior and properties. However, there are two major differences between Snapshot objects and Dynaset objects. These two differences are the most important aspects of Snapshots.

☐ Snapshots are stored entirely in workstation memory.
☐ Snapshots are read-only and nonupdatable objects.

Instead of reviewing strengths and limitations of the Snapshot data object, let's look at these two properties of Snapshots in depth.

Snapshot-Type Recordset Storage

You need to consider several things when using Snapshot data objects. For example, unlike Visual Basic Dynasets, Snapshot objects are stored entirely at the workstation. If you create a Snapshot that contains 500 data records, all 500 records are sent from the data table directly to your workstation and loaded into RAM memory. If the workstation does not have enough RAM available, the records are stored in a temporary file on a local disk drive.

Because all the requested records are loaded on the local machine, initial requests for data can take longer with Snapshots than with Dynasets. However, when the data records are retrieved and stored locally, subsequent access to records within the Snapshot object is faster than with the Dynaset object. Also, because all records must be stored locally, you must be careful not to request too large a dataset; you might quickly run out of local RAM or disk space.

Snapshots are static views of the underlying data tables. If you request a set of data records in a Snapshot object, and then someone deletes several records from the underlying data table, the Snapshot dataset does *not* reflect the changes in the underlying table. The only way you can learn about the changes in the underlying data tables is to create a new Snapshot by making a new request.

Snapshot-Type Recordsets Are Read-Only Data Objects

Visual Basic Snapshots are read-only data objects. You cannot use Snapshots to update data tables. You can only use them to view data. This is because Snapshots are actually a copy of the data records created at your local workstation.

The project in Listing 3.14 illustrates the static aspect of Snapshot data objects compared to the dynamic aspect of Dynaset and Table data objects. Start a new Standard EXE project. There are no controls in this project, so be sure to add the Microsoft DAO 3.5 Object Library to access the data objects.

The entire source code is listed. Enter it into a single form and save it as SNAPSHOTS.FRM and SNAPSHOTS.VBP.

Listing 3.14. Comparing Snapshot-type and Dynaset-type Recordsets.

```
Option Explicit
'
' form level variables
'
```

```
        Dim db As Database
        Dim rsDynaset As Recordset
        Dim rsSnapshot As Recordset
        Dim rsTable As Recordset
        '
        Dim strDBName As String
        Dim strRSName As String
        Dim varRecords As Variant
        Dim intReturned As Integer
        Dim intColumns As Integer

        Private Sub Form_Activate()
            '
            ' main control routine
            '
            strDBName = App.Path & "\..\..\Data\books5.mdb"
            strRSName = "Titles"
            OpenFiles
            '
            ' show title
            Me.Cls
            Me.Print "Comparing Recordset Types (Dynaset, Snapshot, & Table)"
            Me.Print
            '
            ' show first compare
            Me.Print ">First Pass"
            CountRecs rsDynaset, "Dynaset"
            CountRecs rsSnapshot, "Snapshot"
            CountRecs rsTable, "Table"
            Me.Print
            '
            ' save rec, delete it, count
            SaveDynasetRec
            DeleteDynasetRec
            Me.Print ">After Dynaset Delete"
            CountRecs rsDynaset, "Dynaset"
            CountRecs rsSnapshot, "Snapshot"
            CountRecs rsTable, "Table"
            Me.Print
            '
            ' restore rec and count
            RestoreDynasetRec
            Me.Print ">After Dynaset Restore"
            CountRecs rsDynaset, "Dynaset"
            CountRecs rsSnapshot, "Snapshot"
            CountRecs rsTable, "Table"
            Me.Print
            '
        End Sub

        Public Sub OpenFiles()
            '
            ' open database and
            ' populate objects
            '
```

continues

Listing 3.14. continued

```
        Set db = DBEngine.OpenDatabase(strDBName)
        '
        With db
            Set rsDynaset = .OpenRecordset(strRSName, dbOpenDynaset)
            Set rsSnapshot = .OpenRecordset(strRSName, dbOpenSnapshot)
            Set rsTable = .OpenRecordset(strRSName, dbOpenTable)
        End With
        '
    End Sub

    Public Sub CountRecs(rsTemp As Recordset, strType As String)
        '
        ' count records in the object
        '
        Dim intCount As Integer
        '
        With rsTemp
            .MoveFirst
            .MoveLast
            intCount = .RecordCount
        End With
        '
        Me.Print vbTab, "Total for " & strType & ":"; intCount
        '
    End Sub

    Public Sub SaveDynasetRec()
        '
        ' save a single record
        '
        With rsDynaset
            .MoveFirst
            varRecords = .GetRows(1)
        End With
        '
    End Sub

    Public Sub DeleteDynasetRec()
        '
        ' remove first record in the collection
        '
        With rsDynaset
            .MoveFirst
            .Delete
        End With
        '
    End Sub

    Public Sub RestoreDynasetRec()
        '
        ' add saved rec back in
        '
        Dim intLoop As Integer
        '
```

3

```
    With rsDynaset
        .AddNew
        For intLoop = 0 To UBound(varRecords, 1)
            .Fields(intLoop).Value = varRecords(intLoop, 0)
        Next
        .Update
    End With
    '
End Sub
```

Although there is not a lot of code in this example, there are a few things worth pointing out. First, you see extensive use of the With..End With construct in Listing 3.14. This construct was introduced in Visual Basic 4.0 and is very useful when working with Visual Basic objects. Using the With..End With construct is faster than naming the same objects several times in code.

Also, notice the use of the GetRows method of the Recordset. This method fills a variant data variable with the contents of one or more records from the Recordset. This is a very efficient way to read several records into memory without using the slower For..Next loops.

When you run the SNAPSHOTS.VBP program, you see three record count reports. The first report occurs right after the data objects are created. The second count report occurs after a record has been removed from the Dynaset object. The last count report occurs after the record has been restored to the Dynaset object. Note that both the Table and the Dynaset objects reflect the changes in the data table, but the Snapshot does not (see Figure 3.8).

Figure 3.8.

Comparing Dynasets, Snapshots, and Tables.

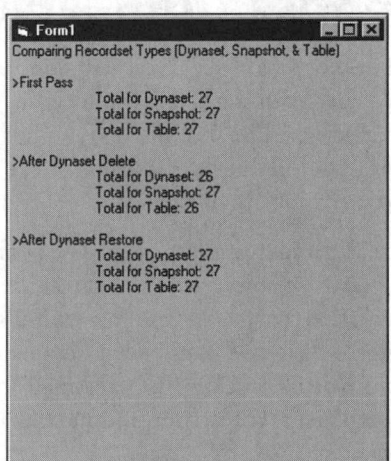

When to Use the Snapshot Data Object

Visual Basic Snapshot-type Recordset objects work best if you have a small set of data that you need to access frequently. For example, if you have a list of valid input values for a particular field stored in a control table, you can load these valid values into a Snapshot and refer to that dataset each time you need to verify user input.

If the dataset is not too large, Snapshots are very good for use in creating calculated reports or graphic displays. It is usually a good idea to create a static dataset for use in calculating reports. This way, any changes in the dataset that might occur in a multiuser environment from the time you start the report to the time you end it will not confuse any calculations done by the report.

 **TIP**

> It's a good idea to keep your Snapshots to less then 64KB in size. You can estimate the eventual size of your Snapshots by calculating the number of bytes in an average data record and estimating the average number of records you can expect in your Snapshot. You can refer to Day 2, "Creating Databases," for information on the size of Visual Basic data types.

The Database Data Objects

The Database object of a Visual Basic data control allows you access to all the properties and methods associated with the database underlying the data control. By using the related data objects, TableDefs, Fields, and Indexes, you can get information about all the tables in the database, all the indexes in the database, and all the fields in each table. Also, you can get additional information about the field types and index parameters.

The Database data object is most useful when you are developing generic database routines. Because the Database object gives you access to all the field names and properties, you can use this information to write generic data table display and update routines instead of having to write routines that have hard-coded field names and data types. TableDefs objects are covered in more detail on Day 10, "Creating Database Programs with Visual Basic Code". For now, though, let's write a short routine that lists all the tables, fields, and indexes in the BOOKS5.MDB database.

First, start a new Standard EXE project in Visual Basic 5 and load the Microsoft Jet DAO 3.5 Object Library. Use the information in Table 3.3 to set the form property settings and place the data control on the form.

Table 3.3. The controls for the 04ABC1.MAK project.

Control	Property	Setting
Form	Caption	Database Objects Demo
	WindowState	Maximize
DataControl	Alignment	Align Bottom
	DatabaseName	"BOOKS5.MDB"
	RecordSource	Authors

Be sure to place the data control at the very bottom of the form. It is only there to give you access to the various database properties that you print on the form itself. Enter the program code in Listing 3.15 in the Form_Activate event.

TYPE **Listing 3.15. Listing Database objects.**

```
Private Sub Form_Activate()
    '
    ' show high-level database objects
    '
    Dim tb As TableDef
    Dim fl As Field
    Dim ix As Index

    Data1.DatabaseName = App.Path & "\..\..\data\books5.mdb"
    Data1.Refresh
    '
    For Each tb In Data1.Database.TableDefs
        Me.Print "Table Info:"
        Print " "; tb.Name
        For Each fl In tb.Fields
            Print " -"; fl.Name
        Next
        MsgBox "Press OK to continue"
        Me.Cls
    Next
    '
    On Error Resume Next ' in case there's no index
    '
    For Each tb In Data1.Database.TableDefs
        Me.Print "Index Info:"
        Print " "; tb.Name
        For Each ix In tb.Indexes
            Print " -"; ix.Name;
            Print "[";
            Print ix.Fields;
            Print "]"
```

continues

Listing 3.15. continued

```
        Next
        MsgBox "Press OK to continue"
        Me.Cls
    Next
    '
End Sub
```

After you enter the code, save the form as DATABASE.FRM and the project as DATABASE.VBP, and then run the program. You see a list on the screen showing the table name, a list of all the fields in the table, and a dialog box. Click the dialog box to continue to the next table. After clicking OK through the table listing, you see a list of each index defined for each table, which you can also click through one at a time. Your two screens should look something like the one in Figure 3.9 for tables and the one in Figure 3.10 for indexes.

Figure 3.9.

List of fields in the Publishers table in BOOKS5.MDB.

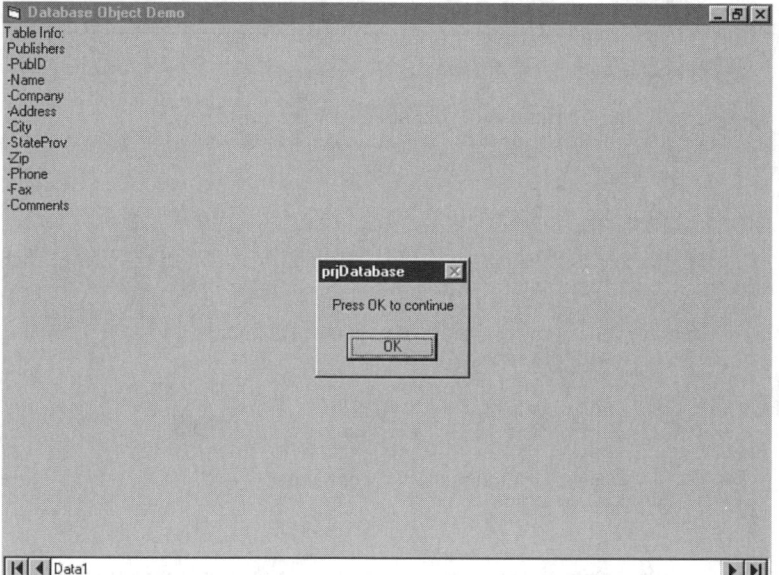

NOTE

As you click through the database tables, you see several tables that start with "MSYS." These are system tables used by the Microsoft Jet database engine and are not used for data storage or retrieval. You should also notice that each Index object consists of a unique name and one or more fields (displayed in brackets). You do not see a data table

associated with the index because the Microsoft Jet engine does not store that information in a manner you can easily see (it's actually in one of those "MSYS" tables!).

Figure 3.10.

List of indexes for the Titles table in BOOKS5.MDB.

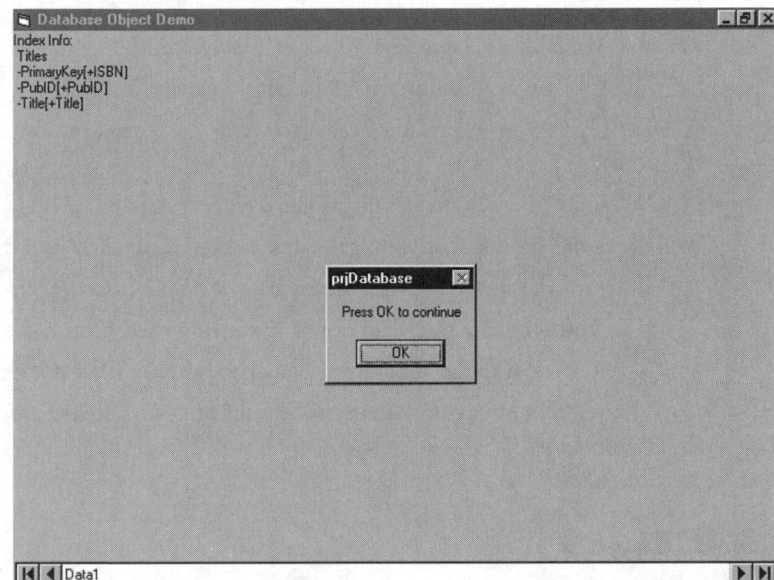

Summary

In today's lesson, you learned that there are three main types of Visual Basic Recordset data objects:

☐ Table-type objects: These are used when you have a large dataset and need to do frequent searches to locate a single record. You can use the Visual Basic Seek method and use Visual Basic Indexes with the Table object.

☐ Dynaset-type objects: These are used in most cases when you need read and write access to datasets. The Dynaset uses little workstation memory and allows you to create virtual tables by combining fields from different tables in the same database. The Dynaset is the only data object that allows you to read and write to ODBC data sources.

☐ Snapshot-type objects: These are used when you need fast read-only access to datasets. Snapshot objects are stored in workstation memory, so they should be kept small. Snapshots are good for storing validation lists at the workstation or for small reports.

You also learned about another data object—the Database object. You can use the Database object to get a list of tables in the database, a list of indexes associated with the tables, and a list of fields in each of the tables.

Quiz

1. Are Visual Basic Database objects dataset-oriented or record-oriented?
2. What is the most common Visual Basic data object?
3. Do Dynasets use a relatively large amount or small amount of workstation RAM? Why?
4. What are the weaknesses of using a Dynaset object?
5. What are the main advantages of using the Table data object?
6. Do you use the `Refresh` method with the Table data object?
7. Can you open a Table data object by setting the properties of a data control?
8. What is the difference between a Snapshot and a Dynaset data object?
9. Which data object do you use to extract table and field names from a database definition?

Exercises

1. What type of Recordset data object would you use—Dynaset, Table, or Snapshot—to create an attachment to an ODBC data source that you would like to update periodically? Why?

   Write the code to open this type of data object. Assume that the database name is `C:\DATA\ACCTPAY.MDB`, with your desired table named Vendors.

2. Given the same data source as in Exercise 1, write the code to open a data object to be used in the generation of a report. (Assume the RAM memory is adequate on the machine running the program.)

3. Given the same data source as in Exercise 1, write the code that opens the data object so that you can access the data often in a multiuser environment to search for single records.

Day 4

Creating Data Entry Forms with Bound Controls

Today's lesson is a review of all the bound data controls that are shipped with Visual Basic Professional. You'll review the special properties, events, and methods that relate to database programming, and you'll create short examples to illustrate how each of the bound controls can be used in your database programs.

You'll also review general rules for designing quality forms for Windows programs, covering alignment, font selection, control placement and spacing, and color choices.

Finally, you'll create a short project that establishes customizable color schemes for your application. This project will show you how to use the Windows Control Panel Color applet to set colors for your applications.

What Are Bound Data Controls?

Before you get into the details of listing the properties, events, and methods of Visual Basic bound data controls, let's review what a bound control is and why it's so useful.

Bound data controls are the same as any other Visual Basic control objects, except that they have been given additional properties, events, and methods that allow you to "bind" them directly to one or more data tables. This binding makes it easy to create data-aware input and display objects that you can use to perform data input and display with very little program code. Using bound controls simplifies your programming chores a great deal. Most bound controls automatically handle the various chores related to processing data entry and display for databases. The bound controls make it easy to write Visual Basic programs that handle all (or nearly all) of the following processes:

☐ Loading data from the database into a Visual Basic data object

☐ Selecting the data record(s) requested by the user

☐ Loading form controls with values in the requested record(s)

☐ Trapping simple user input errors

☐ Enforcing database integrity rules

☐ Updating the data object with modified data from the form controls

You do not need to use bound data controls in your database programs. In fact, as you will see in the lessons next week, there are times when it is better to use unbound controls in your programs. However, when you use unbound controls, you need to take responsibility for handling all the processes outlined in the preceding list. Although this is not an insurmountable task, it's a good idea to take advantage of the power of bound data controls whenever possible. Using the prebuilt and tested bound controls helps you create solid, functional database entry forms in a short period of time.

The Data Control

The Visual Basic data control is the control used to gain access to database tables. The data control allows you to establish a link to a single Dynaset data object in a database. You can have more than one data control in your program and more than one data control on a single form.

Like all Visual Basic controls, there are properties, events, and methods associated with the data control. Because this book is on databases, this lesson will focus on the properties, events, and methods that are important in dealing with database activity. In the process, you will build a small program that illustrates these database-related aspects of the Visual Basic data control.

Data Control Properties

There are five data control properties that deserve special attention:

- ☐ DatabaseName
- ☐ Exclusive
- ☐ Options
- ☐ ReadOnly
- ☐ RecordSource

There is a sixth data control property that is used only for data access: the Connect property. The Connect property is used when you are accessing non-Microsoft Access databases. You'll learn more about using the Connect property in the lesson on Day 9.

Setting DatabaseName and RecordSource Properties

The DatabaseName and RecordSource properties were discussed in Day 3. The DatabaseName property contains the name of the database you want to access. In Microsoft Access databases, this would be the complete drive, path, and filename of the Microsoft Access database file. For example, to connect to the BOOKS5.MDB Microsoft Access database located in the C:\DATA directory, you would set the DatabaseName property to C:\DATA\BOOKS5.MDB. You can do this through the Property box at design time or through Visual Basic code at runtime.

Let's start a project to illustrate the data control properties, events, and methods. Load Visual Basic and start a new project. Drop a data control on a blank form. For this project, let's accept the default data control name property of Data1.

In Day 3, you set the DatabaseName and RecordSource properties at design time using the Visual Basic properties window. Visual Basic allows you to set most control properties at runtime (that is, while the program is running). The advantage of setting properties at runtime is that you can build programs that allow users to decide what database and data table they want to access. For this project, you'll set these properties at runtime using Visual Basic code.

NOTE

Design time refers to the time when you are designing your Visual Basic application. *Runtime* refers to the time when your finished application is running.

You will set these data control values in a separate procedure, called OpenDB. To create a new procedure in Visual Basic, double-click anywhere on the form in order to bring up a Visual Basic code window. Now select Add Procedure… from the Visual Basic Tools menu. You'll see a dialog box that asks you for the name of the procedure (see Figure 4.1).

Figure 4.1.

Creating a new Visual Basic procedure.

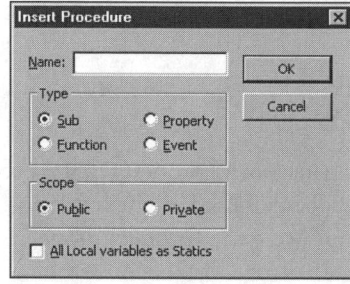

Enter OpenDB. Make sure the radio button for Sub is selected and then click OK. You now see the new Visual Basic procedure header and footer, ready for you to enter your program code.

The following procedure sets the DatabaseName property of the data control on the current form. Please note where we have entered the location of the BOOKS5.MDB file. You may need to substitute a different path if you installed the database elsewhere on your system.

NOTE

If you install your data files in the same directory as your program files, you can use the App.Path command to identify the data file location. App.Path can be used as part of the database name to identify the database location without having to know the name of the directory in which it is stored. The Path property of the App object returns the drive and directory in which the project has been stored.

This methodology is useful when building applications that will be distributed across an organization, or to multiple organizations. App.Path allows you to utilize setup programs that let the user select the directory in which to install the program files. Your data files will be found as long as they are stored with the program files.

As an illustration, if we had installed our BOOKS5.MDB file in the same directory as we saved the current project, we could substitute:

```
cDBName = App.Path + "\books5.mdb"
```

for the line:

```
cDBName = "c:\tysdbvb5\source\data\books5.mdb"
```

This would allow us to move and store our programs in any directory without having to worry about changing the pointer to our database.

Place the following code in the general declarations section of your form:

```
Public Sub OpenDB()
   Dim cDBName As String     ' declare a string variable
   '
   cDBName = "c:\tysdbvb5\source\data\books5.mdb" ' point to database
   '
   Data1.DatabaseName = cDBName ' set database property
   '
   Data1.Refresh ' update data control properties
End Sub
```

TIP

When you enter Visual Basic program code, Visual Basic looks for typing errors automatically. Each time you press the Enter key, Visual Basic scans the line, capitalizes Visual Basic reserved words (if everything has been typed correctly), adds spaces between the equal signs, and so on. When you enter code, don't try to capitalize or space properly; let Visual Basic do it for you. That way, if you finish a line and press the Enter key and then notice that Visual Basic has not "edited" for you, you'll know that there is probably something on that line that Visual Basic didn't understand. Now you'll catch your typing errors as you code!

The last line in the procedure forces the data control to update all the new properties that have been set in the routine. Any time you use Visual Basic code to change data control properties, you must invoke the `Refresh` method to update the data control. This is just one of the data control methods. Other data control methods are discussed throughout today's lesson.

> **TIP**
>
> Notice that in the code example you declare a variable, set the variable to a value, and then set the data control property with the variable. This could all be done in a single line of code. Here's an example:
>
> ```
> Data1.DatabaseName= C:\TYSDBVB5\SOURCE\DATA\BOOKS5.MDB"
> ```
>
> By declaring variables and using those variables to set properties, you'll create a program that is easier to understand and modify in the future.

When you set the DatabaseName property, you are telling Visual Basic the *database* you are using. However, at this point, Visual Basic does not know what *data table* you want to use with the data control. Use the RecordSource property to indicate the data table you want to access.

Now, modify the OpenDB procedure you created earlier by adding code that sets the RecordSource property of the data control to access the Authors data table. Be sure to declare a variable, initialize it to the correct table, and then use the variable to set the data control property. When you are finished, your procedure should look like the one shown in the following code example:

```
Public Sub OpenDB()
    Dim cDBName As String    ' declare a string variable
    Dim cTblName As String   ' declare a string variable
    '
    cDBName = "c:\tysdbvb5\source\data\books5.mdb" ' point to database
    cTblName = "Authors" ' point to authors table
    '
    Data1.DatabaseName = cDBName ' set database property
    Data1.RecordSource = cTblName ' set recordsource property
    '
    Data1.Refresh ' update data control properties
End Sub
```

Before you get too far into the project, you should save your work. Save the form as BNDCTRL1.FRM and the project as BNDCTRL.VBP.

Setting the ReadOnly and Exclusive Properties

There are two more data control properties that you'll need to set in this example: ReadOnly and Exclusive. The ReadOnly and Exclusive properties are Boolean (True/False) properties that you can use to limit access to the database. When you set the Exclusive property to True, you are opening the database for *your* use only. In other words, no one else can open the database (or any of the tables in the database) while you have it open. This is handy when you want to perform major updates or changes to the database and do not want anyone else in the file at the same time.

For the example, you'll open the database for exclusive use. Modify the OpenDB procedure so that it sets the Exclusive property to True. Your code should look like the following code:

```
Public Sub OpenDB()
    Dim cDBName As String    ' declare a string variable
    Dim cTblName As String   ' declare a string variable
    Dim bExclusive As Boolean ' declare true/false var
    '
    cDBName = "c:\tysdbvb5\source\data\books5.mdb" ' point to database
cTblName = "Authors" ' point to authors table
    bExclusive = True ' set to exclusive open
    '
    Data1.DatabaseName = cDBName ' set database property
    Data1.RecordSource = cTblName ' set recordsource property
    Data1.Exclusive = bExclusive
    '
    Data1.Refresh ' update data control properties
End Sub
```

WARNING

When you open the database with Exclusive set to True, no other programs that access the database can be run without errors until you close the database. Use the Exclusive property sparingly!

The ReadOnly property opens the database with read rights only. You will not be allowed to make any changes, additions, or deletions in any table while you have the database open in read-only mode. This is handy when you are using the data for creating a report or for display purposes only. (Read-only mode is faster, too.)

NOTE

Don't confuse the Exclusive property and the ReadOnly property; they are not the same! The Exclusive property makes sure that *no one else* can access the database while you have it open. The ReadOnly property makes sure that *your program* cannot update the database while you have it open. The Exclusive property affects everyone who wants to access the database. The ReadOnly property affects only the person running your program.

Again, for this example, you'll open the file as read-only. Make changes to the OpenDB procedure to include variables that set the ReadOnly property to True. When you are done, your code should look something like the following code:

```
Public Sub OpenDB()
    Dim cDBName As String    ' declare a string variable
    Dim cTblName As String   ' declare a string variable
```

```
    Dim bExclusive As Boolean ' declare true/false var
    Dim bReadOnly As Boolean ' declare true/false var

    cDBName = "c:\tysdbvb5\source\data\books5.mdb" ' point to database
    cTblName = "Authors" ' point to authors table
    bExclusive = True ' set to exclusive open
    bReadOnly = True ' set to read only
    '
    Data1.DatabaseName = cDBName ' set database property
    Data1.RecordSource = cTblName ' set recordsource property
    Data1.Exclusive = bExclusive
    Data1.ReadOnly = bReadOnly
    '
    Data1.Refresh ' update data control properties
End Sub
```

Now, save your work before entering more Visual Basic code.

Setting the Options Property

All the properties you have set in the previous code relate to the database that Visual Basic is accessing. The Options property of the Visual Basic data control allows you to establish the properties of the Dynaset opened in the RecordSource property of the data control. There are several options that can be set in the Options property of the data control. In today's lesson, you will learn about the three most commonly used options.

Here are the three Options values for the data control that is covered today:

- ☐ dbDenyWrite
- ☐ dbReadOnly
- ☐ dbAppendOnly

These three options are actually Visual Basic constants that are predefined in the language. They are like Visual Basic variables, except that they have a single, set value that cannot be changed. Table 4.1 shows the three constants and their numeric values.

Table 4.1. Dynaset option values.

Dynaset Option	Numeric Value
dbDenyWrite	1
dbReadOnly	4
dbAppendOnly	8

Setting the dbDenyWrite option prevents other users from changing the data in the Dynaset while you have it open (similar to the Exclusive database property). The dbReadOnly option prevents you from changing the data in the Dynaset (similar to the ReadOnly database property). The dbAppendOnly option lets you add new data to the Dynaset but does not let you modify or delete existing records.

Setting the dbReadOnly option speeds processing of the Dynaset and is handy for generating displays or reports. The dbDenyWrite option is useful when you want to make major changes to the Dynaset and want to prevent other users from accessing the records in the Dynaset until you are done making your changes. Using the dbAppendOnly option lets you create data entry routines that limit user rights to adding records without deleting or modifying existing ones.

Now you'll add the code that sets the Options property of the data control. You'll notice that you do not have a property for each of the three options. How do you set them individually? You do this by adding up the constants and placing the result in the Options property of the data control.

For example, if you want to open the Dynaset for only appending new records, set the Options property of the data control to dbAppendOnly. If you want to open the Dynaset to deny everyone the right to update the database and to allow read-only access for the current user, set the Options property to dbDenyWrite + dbReadOnly.

For now, set the data control options to DenyWrite and ReadOnly. When you are done, your procedure should look like this:

```
Public Sub OpenDB()
    Dim cDBName As String      ' declare a string variable
    Dim cTblName As String     ' declare a string variable
    Dim bExclusive As Boolean ' declare true/false var
    Dim bReadOnly As Boolean ' declare true/false var
    '
    cDBName = "c:\tysdbvb5\source\data\books5.mdb" ' point to database
    cTblName = "Authors" ' point to authors table
    bExclusive = True ' set to exclusive open
    bReadOnly = True ' set to read only
    '
    Data1.DatabaseName = cDBName ' set database property
    Data1.RecordSource = cTblName ' set recordsource property
    Data1.Exclusive = bExclusive
    Data1.Options = dbDenyWrite + dbReadOnly
    Data1.ReadOnly = bReadOnly
    '
    Data1.Refresh ' update data control properties
End Sub
```

4

You have now completed the procedure for opening the BOOKS5.MDB database and creating a Dynaset from the Authors table. The database and the Dynaset will be opened exclusively for read-only access. Only one thing is missing. You must first make sure the OpenDB procedure is executed! Place the following code line in the Form_Load procedure:

```
Sub Form_Load ()
    OpenDB ' open the database, set dynaset
End Sub
```

Now save the project and run the program. If you get an error report, review the code examples and then make the necessary changes before going on to the next section, where you'll add a few more routines that illustrate how data control methods work.

Data Control Methods

Most Visual Basic controls have associated methods. Each method can be thought of as a function or process that you can tell the program to run. The Visual Basic data control has several methods, but only three are database related. Here's a list of them:

- [ ] Refresh
- [ ] UpdateControls
- [ ] UpdateRecord

You have used the Refresh method in today's example already. This method is used any time you change any of the properties of the data control. Using the Refresh method updates the data control and forces it to rebuild the Dynaset. This refresh updates not only the behaviors and properties of the Dynaset but also the records in the set. If records are added to the table by another user after your program has created its Dynaset, invoking the Refresh method will make sure your Dynaset contains the most recent records.

The UpdateControls method is used to update any bound input controls. Invoking the UpdateControls method is the same as reading the current record and putting the values in the fields of the data table into the input controls on a form. This happens automatically each time you press the arrow buttons on the data control. But you can force the update to occur any time during the data entry process. It's especially handy if you want to undo user changes to a data record.

Now, add a single field to the form and test the UpdateControls method. Add a text box control to the form and set the DataSource property to Data1. You'll set the DataField property using Visual Basic code in a moment; leave it blank for now. Refer to Figure 4.2 for positioning and sizing the control.

4

Figure 4.2.

*Adding the bound text
box control.*

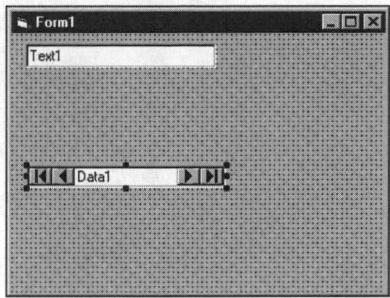

Now add the following new procedure (BindControls) to your form. Remember, to insert a procedure you need to use the Add Procedure... command from the Tools menu after you have double-clicked the form. This new procedure links the text box to the field in the Dynaset using the DataField property of the text box.

```
Public Sub BindControls()
   Dim cField1 As String
   '
   cField1 = "Name"
   '
   Text1.DataField = cField1
End Sub
```

Now, add the BindControls procedure to the Form_Load event to make sure it gets called when the program starts. Your Form_Load event should look like this:

```
Sub Form_Load ()
   OpenDB ' open the database, set dynaset
   BindControls ' link controls to data fields
End Sub
```

You need to add a command button to the form to activate the UpdateControls method. Place a single command button on the form and set its Name property to cmdRestore and its caption to &Restore. Also, add the following code line behind the cmdRestore_Click event:

```
Private Sub cmdRestore_Click()
   data1.UpdateControls ' restore textbox values
End Sub
```

Your form should look like the one shown in Figure 4.3.

Now save and run the project. When the first record comes up, edit the field. Change the name or add additional information to the field. Before you click an arrow button, press the Restore button. You'll see that the data in the textbox reverts to the value initially read into it when you first started the program.

4

Figure 4.3.

Adding a Restore button to the form.

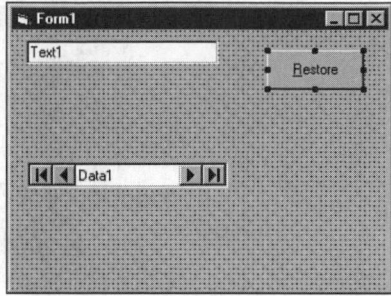

Now, add a button that invokes the UpdateRecord method. The UpdateRecord method tells Visual Basic to save the values of the bound input controls (the textbox in this project) to the Dynaset. Refer to Figure 4.4 for sizing and positioning the button.

Figure 4.4.

Adding the Update button to the form.

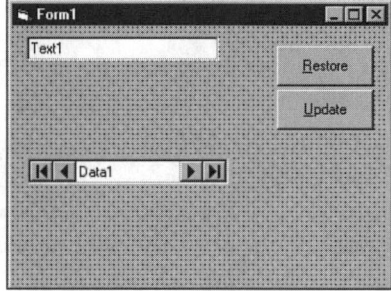

Using the UpdateRecord method updates the Dynaset without moving the record pointer. Now, add a command button to the form, set its Name property to cmdUpdate and its Caption property to &Update, and then place the following code line behind the button in the cmdUpdate_Click event:

```
Private Sub cmdUpdate_Click()
    data1.UpdateRecord 'write controls to dynaset
End Sub
```

NOTE

It is important to remember the difference between the UpdateControls method and the UpdateRecord method. The UpdateControls method reads from the data object and writes to the form controls. It updates the controls. The UpdateRecord method reads from the form controls and writes to the data object. It updates the record.

Save and run the project again. This time, after you edit the text box, click the Update button. Now, move the record pointer forward to the next record and then back to the record you edited. What do you see? The record was not updated! Remember, in the OpenDB procedure you set the ReadOnly property of the database to True and turned on the ReadOnly value of the Options property. Now modify the OpenDB procedure and change the ReadOnly property to False and drop the dbReadOnly and dbDenyWrite constants from the Options property by setting the Options property to 0.

When you rerun the program, you can now edit the text box, restore the old value with the Restore button, or save the new value with the Update button. You can also save the new value by moving the record pointer.

This last behavior of the data control can cause some problems. What if you changed a field and didn't want to save the changes, but instead of clicking the Restore button, you moved to the next record? You would change the database and never know it! In the next section, you'll use one of the data control's events to help you avoid just such a situation.

Data Control Events

All Microsoft Windows programs contain events. These events occur each time the computer senses that a user clicks a button or passes the mouse over an object on the form, or when any other process occurs. When an event takes place, the Windows operating system sends a message that tells all processes currently running that something has happened. Windows programs can then "listen" for messages and act, based on their programming code, when the right message comes along.

In Visual Basic, you can create program code that executes each time a specific event occurs. There are three data control events that relate to database functions:

- ☐ `Reposition`
- ☐ `Validate`
- ☐ `Error`

The `Reposition` event occurs each time the data control moves to a new position in the Dynaset. The `Validate` event occurs each time a data control leaves the current record. The `Error` event occurs each time a database error occurs when the arrow buttons on the data control are used to move the record pointer. Visual Basic automatically creates procedure headers and footers for all the events associated with a control. When you place a data control on your form, Visual Basic creates the procedures `Data1_Reposition`, `Data1_Validate`, and `Data1_Error`.

Now, add some code to the project that will tell you when an event occurs. First, you need to get a message box to pop up each time you reposition the record pointer using the arrow buttons on the data control. To do this, place the following code in the Data1_Reposition event:

```
Private Sub Data1_Reposition()
    MsgBox "Repositioning the pointer..."
End Sub
```

Next, to get a message box to pop up each time you leave a record using the data control's arrow buttons, place the following code in the Data1_Validate event:

```
Private Sub Data1_Validate(Action As Integer, Save As Integer)
    MsgBox "Validating Data..."
End Sub
```

Now save and run the project. You'll notice that the message from the Reposition event is the first thing you see after the program begins. This is because the pointer is positioned on the first record in the Dynaset when the Dynaset is first created. (See Figure 4.5.)

Figure 4.5.

The Reposition *event at the start of the program.*

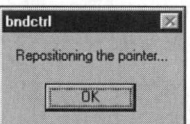

After you click the OK button in the message box, you'll see the Visual Basic form with the data control. Click one of the arrow buttons. You'll see that the message from the Validate event pops up. This message is sent before Visual Basic leaves the current record. (See Figure 4.6.)

Figure 4.6.

The Validate *event message.*

After you click the OK button in the message box, you'll see the message from the Reposition event again. This is the event message sent when Visual Basic reads the next record.

You might have noticed that the header for the Validate event contains two parameters: Action and Save. These two parameters can be used to learn more about what action is currently being attempted on the data control and can give you control over whether the user should be allowed to save the new data to the Dynaset. These parameters are set by Visual Basic while the program is running. You can read the values in these parameters at any time

during the program. For now, you'll explore the Action parameter. The next set of code adds a routine to the `Validate` step that pops up a message box each time the arrow buttons of a data control are clicked.

Just like the Options property constants, Visual Basic also provides a set of predefined constants for all the possible Action values reported in the `Validate` event. Although these constants are handy, they are not very useful to users of your programs. The following code example shows you how to translate those constants into a friendly message using a string array. Add the following line to the general declarations section of the form.

```
Option Explicit
Dim VldMsg(4) As String ' declare message array
```

Now add the following procedure, which loads a set of messages into the array you declared previously. These messages are displayed each time the corresponding action occurs in the `Validate` event. Notice that you are using the predefined Visual Basic constants.

```
Public Sub MakeVldMsgArray()
    VldMsg(vbDataActionMoveFirst) = "MoveFirst"
    VldMsg(vbDataActionMovePrevious) = "MovePrevious"
    VldMsg(vbDataActionMoveNext) = "MoveNext"
    VldMsg(vbDataActionMoveLast) = "MoveLast"
End Sub
```

Update the `Form_Load` event to call the `MakeVldMsgArray` procedure. You can see that `MakeVldMsgArray` has been added at the start of the event. Here's the code:

```
Private Sub Form_Load()
    MakeVldMsgArray ' create message array
    OpenDB ' open the database, set dynaset
    BindControls ' link controls to data fields
End Sub
```

Now you need to add the one bit of code that will be executed each time the `Validate` event occurs. This code displays a simple message each time you click the arrow buttons of the data control. The actual message is determined by the Action value that Visual Basic passes to the `Validate` event. The Action value is, of course, determined by the arrow button on the data control that you click while the program is running.

Now you have to replace the "Validating data" message that you entered in the previous example. Here's the new code:

```
Private Sub Data1_Validate(Action As Integer, Save As Integer)
    MsgBox VldMsg(Action) ' message based on user action
End Sub
```

Save and run the program to see a message box that tells you what you probably already know! There are several other actions that can occur during the `Validate` event. You'll explore these actions on Day 5.

For the rest of the project, comment out the `Validate` event code and the `Reposition` event code. Now you'll concentrate on adding additional Visual Basic bound controls to the project.

The Bound Text Control and the Bound Label Control

There are no database-related methods or events associated with the bound text control or bound label control. And there are only two properties of the bound text control and the bound label control that are database related:

☐ DataSource

☐ DataField

The DataSource property is the name of the data control that maintains the link between the data table and the text or label control. The DataField property identifies the actual field in the data control Dynaset to which the text box or label control is bound. You cannot set the DataSource property at runtime—it's a design time-only property. You can, however, set the DataField property at either runtime or design time.

Bound text controls give you the ability to add input fields to your data forms that automatically link to the Dynaset defined in the data control. Bound label controls are handy when you want to display information without letting users update it. You've already added a bound text control to the project, so now add a bound label control, too.

You'll add the label control to display the AuID (the author ID) field of the Authors table. This will give users the chance to see the author ID but not update it. Add a label control to the form, and set its DataSource property to Data1. Also, set the BorderStyle property to Fixed Single to make it look similar to a text box control. Refer to Figure 4.7 for positioning and placement.

Figure 4.7.

Adding the bound label control.

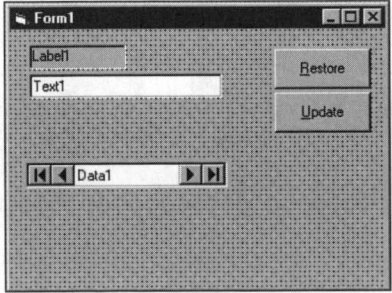

4

Now update the `BindControls` procedure to set the DataField property of the label control. Your code should look like this:

```
Public Sub BindControls ()
   Dim cField1 As String
   Dim cField2 As String
   '
   cField1 = "Name"
   cField2 = "AuID"
   '
   Text1.DataField = cField1
   Label1.DataField = cField2
End Sub
```

Now save and run the project. You'll see that the label control contains the values stored in the AuID field of the Dynaset. As you move through the Dynaset using the arrow buttons, the label control is updated just as the text control is updated.

The Bound Checkbox Control

The bound checkbox control is basically the same as the text control. It has no special database-related events or methods and has the same two database-related properties: DataSource and DataField. The difference between the text box control and the checkbox control is in how the data is displayed on the form and saved in the Dynaset.

Checkboxes are linked to Boolean data type fields. You'll remember that these fields can only hold -1 or 0. Checkboxes do not display -1 or 0. They display an empty box (0) or a checked box (-1). By clicking the display of the checkbox, you can actually update the Boolean value of the bound Dynaset field.

Using Figure 4.8 as a guide, add a checkbox control to the form. Set its DataSource property to Data1 and its Caption property to Under Contract. You do not need to set the DataField property at this time. This will be done by modifying the BindControls procedure.

Figure 4.8.

Adding the bound checkbox control.

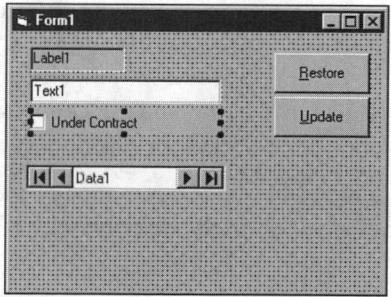

Now, update the `BindControls` procedure to link the checkbox control to the Contracted field in the Authors table. When you are done, your `BindControls` procedure should look like this:

```
Public Sub BindControls ()
    Dim cField1 As String
    Dim cField2 As String
    Dim cField3 As String
    '
    cField1 = "Name"
    cField2 = "AuID"
    cField3 = "Contracted"
    '
    Text1.DataField = cField1
    Label1.DataField = cField2
    Check1.DataField = cField3
End Sub
```

Save and run the project. You will see that some checkboxes are turned on, and some are turned off. You now have a bound checkbox control!

The Bound OLE Control

The Visual Basic OLE control has no database-related events or methods and only two database-related properties:

☐ DataSource

☐ DataField

Like the bound checkbox control, the OLE control has unique behaviors regarding displaying bound data. The OLE control is used to display OLE objects that are stored in an MDB file by Microsoft Access. This control cannot be used to display binary pictures saved directly to an MDB file by an application other than Access.

Now, let's add an OLE control to the form and bind it to a field in the Authors table. Drop an OLE control on the form and select the Cancel button in the Insert Object dialog box when you are prompted for the Object Type. Now, set the OLE control's DataSource property to Data1, and its SizeMode property to 1 – Stretch. Refer to Figure 4.9 for control sizing and placement. We will bind this control to the Cover field with Visual Basic code in the following section, so, leave the DataField property empty.

After you add the control to the form, update the `BindControls` procedure to bind the OLE control to the Cover field in the Authors table. When you're done, the procedure should look like this:

```
Public Sub BindControls ()
    Dim cField1 As String
    Dim cField2 As String
```

```
        Dim cField3 As String
        Dim cField4 As String
        '
        cField1 = "Name"
        cField2 = "AuID"
        cField3 = "Contracted"
        cField4 = "Cover"
        '
        Text1.DataField = cField1
        Label1.DataField = cField2
        Check1.DataField = cField3
        OLE1.DataField = cField4
End Sub
```

Figure 4.9.

*Adding the bound
OLE control.*

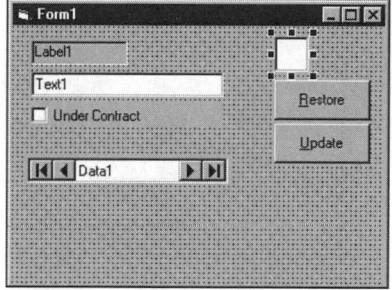

Save and run the project. You'll now see icons displayed in the top-right corner of the form (only for the first few records). These icons are stored in the binary data type field of the database. Note that you don't have to do any fancy "loading" of the picture into the OLE control, because the data control binding handles all that for you!

When you run your completed project, it should look like the one shown in Figure 4.10.

Figure 4.10.

The completed project.

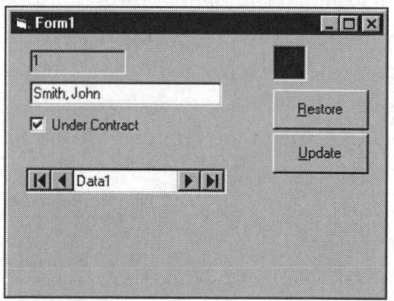

You have just completed a form that contains bound controls for handling text, numeric, Boolean, and OLE object data types stored in a database.

General Rules for Designing Quality Forms

Now that you know how to use the Visual Basic data controls, it's time to learn about form design. Microsoft encourages developers to adhere to a general set of guidelines when designing the look and feel of their programs. In this project, you'll focus on the layout and design of quality forms. We will define guidelines for the following aspects of form design:

☐ Control placement and spacing
☐ Label alignment
☐ Standard fonts
☐ Use of colors

The guidelines set here will be used throughout the remainder of the projects in this book.

NOTE The style guidelines used in this book adhere to the look and feel of Microsoft Windows 95. Even if you are still using Windows 3.1 or Windows for Workgroups, we encourage you to adopt the Windows 95 layout standards because many of the people using your programs may already be running Windows 95 on their PCs.

Guidelines for Win95-Style Forms

There are a few general guidelines for developing Win95-style forms. The primary areas to consider are listed in Table 4.2. This table describes the standard measurements Microsoft recommends for form controls. It also contains recommended spacing for these controls. Refer to Figure 4.11 when reading this section. This figure shows an example of a data entry form that is built using the Windows 95 standards described in this section.

Figure 4.11.

A Win95-style input form.

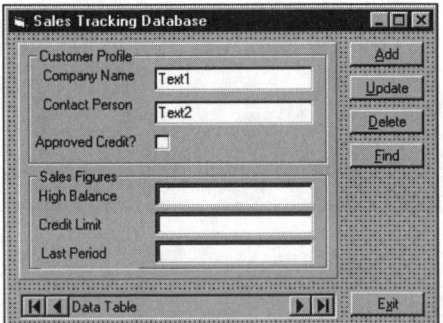

The Default Form Color

When you first start your form, set its BackColor property to light gray. Set the BackStyle property for labels to Transparent so that the background color can show through. For controls that do not have a BackStyle property (such as checkbox controls and radio button controls), set the BackColor property to light gray. The gray tones are easier to read in varied light. Using gray tones also reduces the chance that a user who experiences color-blindness will have difficulty with your input screens.

Using the SSPanel Control to Lift Input Areas Off the Page

Use the SSPanel control to create a palette on which to place all display and input controls. Do not place buttons or the data control on the palette unless they act as part of the input dialog box (see Figure 4.11). Use only one palette per form. The palette is not the same as a frame around a set of controls. The palette is used to raise the set of controls up from the page. This makes it easy for the user to see that these controls are grouped together and that they deserve attention.

The SSPanel is a Sheridan 3D control. It may not appear in your toolbox when you first start Visual Basic 5. To add it, right click the Toolbox and select Components.... Now enter a check next to Sheridan 3D Controls. If you do not see the words Sheridan 3D Controls, then click the Browse button and find the file for them—THREED32.OCX.

The Default Font

Use 8-point sans serif, regular (not bold) as the default font for all controls. If you want to use larger type in a title, for example, do so sparingly. Keep in mind that the default font is a proportionally spaced font. The space taken up by the letter W is greater than the space taken up by the letter j. This can lead to difficulty aligning numbers and columnar data. If you are doing a lot of displays and lists that include numeric amounts or other values that should line up, you should consider using a monospaced font such as Courier or FixedSys.

Input Areas and Display Areas

Use the color white to indicate areas where the user can perform input. If the field is for display purposes only, set it to gray (or to the form color if it is not gray). This means that all labels should appear in the same color as the form background (such as gray labels for gray forms). Also, make all display-only areas appear recessed on the palette. All text boxes that are active for input should appear white. This makes the action areas of your form stand out to the user. By keeping to the standard of white for input controls and gray (or form-colored) for display-only controls, users will not be so quick to attempt to edit a read-only control.

Using the Frame Controls to Group Related Information

When placing controls on a form, you should group related items together by enclosing them within a frame control. This frame control is sometimes called a *group box* because it boxes in a group of related controls. The frame caption is optional, but it is recommended. Using the frame control to group related items helps the user to quickly understand the relationship between fields on the form.

Alignment of Controls on the Form

All controls should be left-justified on the form. Show a clean line from top to bottom. This makes it easy to read down a list of fields quickly. Try to avoid multicolumn labels. If you must have more than one column of labels and input controls, be sure to left-align the second column, too.

Standard Sizing and Spacing for Controls

All controls should have standard height, spacing, and width where appropriate. Microsoft publishes its Win95 spacing standards in pixels or DLU (dialog units). Because Visual Basic controls work in twips instead of pixels, you need to know that one pixel equals 15 twips. Table 4.2 shows the recommended spacing and sizing for various controls on a form. Use these as a guide when creating your forms.

Table 4.2. Control spacing and sizing.

Form Control	Size/Spacing
Control height	300 twips
Command button width	1200 twips
Vertical spacing between controls	60 twips for related items 90 twips for unrelated items
Border widths (top, bottom, and side)	120 twips

Notice that the height of all controls is the same. This makes it easy to align controls on a form regardless of their type (command buttons, textboxes, checkboxes, and so on). The recommended spacing between controls seems quite wide when you first begin designing forms with these standards. However, you'll find that once you get the hang of these numbers, you'll be able to put together very clean-looking forms in a short amount of time.

4

Colors

Color standards for Win95 are quite simple—use gray! Although Microsoft recommends the gray tones for all forms, the color settings are one of the most commonly customized GUI properties in Windows programs. In this section you will learn two ways you can approach adding color to your applications: system colors and custom colors.

First, put together a simple form using Table 4.3 and Figure 4.12 as a guide. Remember that you are building a Win95-style form! You won't spend time linking the input controls to a data control right now—just concentrate on building the form and adding color-switching capabilities.

 **TIP**

Here are a few suggestions to help you build the form:

☐ Before you begin placing controls on the form, set the Grid Height and Grid Width properties on the General Tab in the Tools | Options menu item to 60 each. This will give you a smaller grid to work with and will make it easier to place controls on the form.

☐ Place the SSPanel you will use for your palette on the form first. Then place all other controls directly on the palette. Do not place controls on the palette by double-clicking the tool in the tools window or by using the Copy command. Click the control icon once and then paint the control on the palette with the mouse. This sets the control as a "child" of the palette. Now, any time you move the palette, the controls will move along with it.

☐ Place the bound command buttons on the palette one after the other without setting any properties. When you want to set the command button properties, click one of the command buttons and then hold the Shift key while you click each of the other three. Now you can use the properties window to set values for all four of the controls at once. Set the command button's FontBold, Height, and Width properties this way to save time.

☐ You can easily set border widths if you remember that the grid dots appear every 60 twips on the form. All border widths should be set at 120 twips. This Microsoft standard makes it easy to distinguish separate controls and keeps a nice border around the form and around palettes and frames. Because border widths should be set at 120 twips, make sure that you can see two grid dots between the edge of the form and the edge of any other control (panel, command button, and so on).

☐ Remember that controls should be separated from each other by at least 90 twips. The value of 90 twips is an odd value when compared to the 60 twips between items and the 120 twips between borders. This odd spacing causes the user to break up the sections of the form a bit. This makes it easy for the user to see the separation between controls. When placing controls in a vertical line, use the Top property to determine where the control appears on the form. Because each control is 330 twips in height and the controls must be 90 twips apart, add 420 twips (330 + 90) to the Top value to determine where the next control should appear underneath.

Figure 4.12.

The color-switching project.

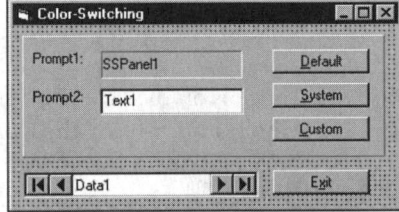

Table 4.3. Controls for the Color-Switching project.

Control	Property	Setting
Form	Caption	Color-Switching
	Name	frmColor
SSPanel	Caption	(set to blank)
	Name	pnlPalette
Text box	Name	txtOneLine
	FontBold	False
	Height	300
	Width	1800
SSPanel	Name	pnlDisplayOnly
	FontBold	False

Control	Property	Setting
	Height	300
	Width	1800
	Caption	SSPanel1
	BevelInner	1 – Inset
	BorderWidth	1
	Alignment	1 – LeftMiddle
Label	Caption	Prompt1:
	FontBold	False
	BackStyle	2 – Transparent
Label	Caption	Prompt2:
	FontBold	False
	BackStyle	2 – Transparent
Data Control	Caption	Data
	FontBold	False
	Height	300
	Width	1800
Command Button	Name	cmdDefault
	Caption	&Default
	FontBold	False
	Height	300
	Width	1200
Command Button	Name	cmdSystem
	Caption	&System
	FontBold	False
	Heigth	300
	Width	1200
Command Button	Name	cmdCustom
	Caption	&Custom
	FontBold	False
	Height	300
	Width	1200

continues

Table 4.3. continued

Control	Property	Setting
Command Button	Name	cmdExit
	Caption	E&xit
	FontBold	False
	Height	300
	Width	1200

Save the form as COLORS.FRM and the project as COLORS.VBP. You have built a form that has three command buttons: Default, System, and Custom. You'll add code to the project that makes each of these buttons change the color scheme of the form. First, you'll add the code that sets the colors to the Win95 default: light gray.

Standard Colors

First, create a Visual Basic constant to represent the hex value for light gray, white, and black. Here's the code:

```
Option Explicit
'
' constant for colors
Const LIGHT_GRAY = &HC0C0C0
Const WHITE = &HFFFFFF
Const BLACK = &H0
```

Next, add a new procedure, SetColors, that sets the colors of the form. Because you'll be using this code to set more than one color scheme, add a parameter called nSet to the procedure header. You only have one set right now, but you'll add others soon. The following code sets the BackColor property of the form and data control to light gray:

```
Sub SetColors (nSet As Integer)
    '
    ' set to default colors
    If nSet = 0 Then
        pnlDisplayOnly.BackColor = LIGHT_GRAY
        pnlPalette.BackColor = LIGHT_GRAY
        frmColor.BackColor = LIGHT_GRAY
        Data1.BackColor = LIGHT_GRAY
        '
        txtOneLine.BackColor = WHITE
        txtOneLine.ForeColor = BLACK
    End If
End Sub
```

4

Finally, add a single line of code to the Default command button to execute the SetColors procedure.

```
Sub cmdDefault_Click ()
    SetColors 0
End Sub
```

Save and run the project. You'll now see that the background for the form and the data control are set to light gray when you click the Default button. The form now meets the default color standards for Win95 forms.

Custom Colors

You may want to set your own customized colors for your form. The following code will do just that. Suppose you want the background to appear in red and the text to appear in blue.

First, add the constants for blue and red to your declaration section:

```
Option Explicit
'
' constant for colors
Const LIGHT_GRAY = &HC0C0C0
Const WHITE = &HFFFFFF
Const BLACK = &H0
Const BLUE = &H800000
Const RED = &H80
```

Next, modify the SetColors procedure to include your new colors. Notice that you now need to set both the ForeColor and the BackColor properties of all the controls along with the BackColor of the form itself. This time, you'll set the colors to the custom set if the parameter is set to 1. Here's the code:

```
Sub SetColors (nSet As Integer)
    '
    ' set to default colors
    If nSet = 0 Then
        pnlDisplayOnly.BackColor = LIGHT_GRAY
        pnlPalette.BackColor = LIGHT_GRAY
        frmColor.BackColor = LIGHT_GRAY
        Data1.BackColor = LIGHT_GRAY
        '
        txtOneLine.BackColor = WHITE
        txtOneLine.ForeColor = BLACK
    End If
    '
    ' set to custom colors
    If nSet = 1 Then
        pnlDisplayOnly.BackColor = RED
        pnlPalette.BackColor = RED
        frmColor.BackColor = RED
        Data1.BackColor = RED
        '
```

4

```
            txtOneLine.BackColor = WHITE
            txtOneLine.ForeColor = BLUE
      End If
End Sub
```

Now, add the following code to the Custom button:

```
Sub cmdCustom_Click ()
    SetColors 1
End Sub
```

Save and run the program to see the results. Not such a good color scheme, you say? Well, some may like your custom setting; some may want to keep the default setting. Now you can select the scheme you want with a click of the mouse!

System Colors

As you can see in the previous code example, some color schemes can be less than perfect. Many programmers add routines to allow users to customize the color scheme to their own taste. The easiest way to do this is to let Windows set the color scheme for you. The code example that follows uses the color scheme selected through the Windows 95 Display applet. This is an excellent way to give your users the power to customize their application color without writing a lot of Visual Basic code.

There are several Windows constants for the system colors that are set by the Control Panel program. For this example, you'll use only three. The following code shows a modified declaration section with the Windows system color constants added:

```
Option Explicit
'
' constant for colors
Const LIGHT_GRAY = &HC0C0C0
Const WHITE = &HFFFFFF
Const BLACK = &H0
Const BLUE = &H800000
Const RED = &H80
'
' windows system color values
Const WINDOW_BACKGROUND = &H80000005      ' Window background.
Const WINDOW_TEXT = &H80000008            ' Text in windows.
Const APPLICATION_WORKSPACE = &H8000000C ' Background color of MDI apps
```

Next, you'll add code to the SetColors routine that sets the colors to the Windows system colors.

```
Sub SetColors (nSet As Integer)
    '
    ' set to default colors
    If nSet = 0 Then
       pnlDisplayOnly.BackColor = LIGHT_GRAY
       pnlPalette.BackColor = LIGHT_GRAY
```

```
        frmColor.BackColor = LIGHT_GRAY
        Data1.BackColor = LIGHT_GRAY
        '
        txtOneLine.BackColor = WHITE
        txtOneLine.ForeColor = BLACK
    End If
    '
    ' set to custom colors
    If nSet = 1 Then
        pnlDisplayOnly.BackColor = RED
        pnlPalette.BackColor = RED
        frmColor.BackColor = RED
        Data1.BackColor = RED
        '
        txtOneLine.BackColor = WHITE
        txtOneLine.ForeColor = BLUE
    End If
    '
    ' set to system colors
    If nSet = 2 Then
        pnlDisplayOnly.BackColor = APPLICATION_WORKSPACE
        pnlPalette.BackColor = APPLICATION_WORKSPACE
        frmColor.BackColor = APPLICATION_WORKSPACE
        Data1.BackColor = APPLICATION_WORKSPACE
        '
        txtOneLine.BackColor = WINDOW_BACKGROUND
        txtOneLine.ForeColor = WINDOW_TEXT
    End If
End Sub
```

Finally, add this line of code to the System button to activate the system color scheme:

```
Sub cmdSystem_Click ()
    SetColors 2
End Sub
```

Save and run the program. When you click the System button, you'll see the color scheme you selected in the Control Panel as the color scheme for this application. Now, while the program is still running, start the Control Panel application and select a new color scheme for Windows. Your Visual Basic program instantly changes its own color scheme!

Summary

Today you have learned the following about creating data entry forms with Visual Basic bound data controls.

The Visual Basic data control has five database-related properties. Three refer to the *database* and two refer to the *Dynaset*.

☐ The database properties of the Visual Basic data control are DatabaseName, which is used to select the database to access; Exclusive, which is used to prevent other users from opening the database; and ReadOnly, which is used to prevent your program from modifying the data in the database.

☐ The Dynaset properties of the Visual Basic data control are Recordsource, which is used to select the data table within the database; and Options, which is used to set ReadOnly, DenyWrite, and AppendOnly properties to the Dynaset.

The Visual Basic data control has three database-related methods:

☐ Refresh updates the data control after setting properties.

☐ UpdateControls reads values from the fields in the Dynaset and writes those values to the related form controls.

☐ UpdateRecord reads values from the form controls and writes those values to the related fields in the Dynaset.

The Visual Basic data control has three database-related events:

☐ Reposition occurs each time the record pointer is moved to a new record in the Dynaset.

☐ Validate occurs each time the record pointer leaves the current record in the Dynaset.

☐ Error occurs each time a database error occurs.

The Visual Basic bound form controls can be used to link form input and display controls to data fields in the database.

☐ The bound textbox control is used for data entry on character and numeric data table fields.

☐ The bound label control is used for display-only character and numeric data table fields.

☐ The bound checkbox control is used for data entry on the Boolean data type field.

☐ The bound OLE control is used to display OLE objects stored directly in an MDB file by Microsoft Access.

☐ The Three-D panel control behaves the same as the label control; the Three-D checkbox control behaves the same as a standard checkbox control.

You have also learned the following general rules for creating Visual Basic forms in the Windows 95 style:

☐ The default color is light gray for backgrounds.

☐ The SSPanel control is used to create a palette on which to place all other controls.

☐ The default font is 8-point sans serif, nonbold.

☐ Input areas should have a white background, and display areas should have a light gray background. Also, display areas should be recessed into the input palette.

☐ Frame controls are used to group related items on a form.

☐ All controls, including field prompts, should be left justified. Field prompts should be written in mixed case and followed by a semicolon.

☐ The standard spacing and sizing of common controls should be as follows:

The control height is 300 twips.

The command button width is 1200 twips.

The vertical spacing between controls is 60 twips for related items and 90 twips for unrelated items.

The border widths (top, bottom, and side) should be 120 twips.

Finally, you learned how to write code that sets control colors to the Windows 95 default colors, how to create your own custom color scheme, and how to link your control colors to the color scheme selected with the Windows Control Panel Color applet.

Quiz

1. How do you establish a database name for a data control using Visual Basic code?

2. What property do you set to define a table in Visual Basic code?

3. What is the main difference between the `UpdateControls` and the `UpdateRecord` methods?

4. What two values can a bound checkbox produce?

5. What property do you use to bind a control to a field in a table?

6. What is the standard form color for Windows 95 applications? What is the standard color of the input areas? What is the standard color of display-only text? How are labels aligned?

Exercises

1. Write Visual Basic code to set the properties to open a database (named `STUDENTS.MDB`) for a data control named Data1.

2. Modify the code you wrote in the first exercise and set the properties to open a table (Addresses) in `STUDENTS.MDB`.

3. Modify the code you wrote in the second exercise by binding controls to the data fields in the Addresses table. Include fields for StudentID (which you should declare as cField1), Address (cField2), City (cField3), State (cField4), and Zip (cField5).

Day 5

Input Validation

Today you learn about one of the most important aspects of database programming—*input validation*. Validating user input *before* it is written to the database can improve the quality of the data stored in your tables. Good validation schemes can also make your program user friendly and, in many cases, can increase the speed at which users can enter valid data.

We cover several specific topics on input validation, including the following:

☐ Field-level validation versus form-level validation

☐ How to speed data entry by filtering keyboard input

☐ How to use input masks to give users hints when entering data

☐ How to limit user choices and speed input with validation lists

☐ How to handle required field inputs in Windows forms

☐ How to handle conditional field input validation in Windows forms

After you learn how to develop input validation routines, you build a set of validation custom controls. These custom controls handle seven valuable validation routines that you can use in your projects throughout the book. You can also use these custom controls in any project you build in the future.

Also, today is the day you build the main data entry form for the MASTER.MDB database. You use this database and data entry form in several chapters of the book. You use all the techniques you've learned this week, including the use of bound data controls and input validation to build a solid data entry form.

Before you get into the details of how to perform input validation, let's first talk about what input validation is and why it is so important to good database application design.

What Is Input Validation?

Input validation is the process of checking the data entered by the user *before* that data is saved to the database. Input validation is a proactive process—it happens while data is being entered. Input validation is not the same thing as error trapping. Error trapping is a reactive process—it happens after the data has been entered. This is an important point. Input validation should be used to prevent errors. If you have good input validation schemes, you have fewer errors to trap! You learn more about the reactive process on Day 14, "Error Handling in Visual Basic 5."

Input validation can be used to give users guides on how to enter valid data. The best example of this kind of input validation is the use of a validation list. A validation list is a list of valid inputs for a field. If the user has only a limited number of possible valid choices for an input field, there is much less chance of a data entry error occurring. Good validation schemes give the user a list of valid input from which to choose while performing data entry.

Input validation can automatically edit data as the user enters it, instead of telling the user to fix invalid entries. For example, if the data entered in a field must be in all capital letters, the program should automatically convert lowercase characters to uppercase instead of waiting while the user enters mixed case, and then reporting an error and forcing the user to reenter the data.

Input validation reaches beyond the individual keystroke and field. It is also important to validate data at the form level. Input validation schemes should make sure that all required fields on a form are completed properly. If you have several fields that must be filled with valid data before the record can be saved to the database, you must have a method for checking those fields before you allow the user to attempt to save the record.

Conditional input fields must be validated, too. A conditional field is slightly different from a required field. Conditional fields usually occur when a user has checked a Yes/No box and

then must enter additional data to complete the process. For example, if the user indicates on a form that the customer requests all products to be shipped instead of picked up, input validation should make sure that valid data has been entered into the shipping address fields. Another example of conditional field validation is when entering a value in one field requires that the value in another field be within a certain range. For example, if the customer's credit limit is above $50,000, you must enter a valid credit-worthiness code of 5 or above. In this case, the two fields must be checked against one another and verified before the user can save the record to the database.

As you can see from the preceding examples, input validation is more than just making sure the data entered in a field is correct. Input validation should be viewed as a set of rules to ensure that quality data is entered into the system. Before you begin writing your data entry forms, you should spend time developing a comprehensive set of validation rules. Once you develop these rules, you are ready to start creating your data entry form.

Common Input Validation Rules

Almost every field in your database requires some type of input validation. Before you design your form, put together a list of all the fields you need on the form and answer the following questions for each input field:

- ☐ Must data be entered in the field? (Is it a required field?)
- ☐ What characters are valid/invalid for this field? (Numeric input only, capital letters only, no spaces allowed, and so on.)
- ☐ For numeric fields, is there a high/low range limit? (Must be greater than zero and less than 1000, can't be less than 100, and so on.)
- ☐ Is there a list of valid values for this field? (Can user enter only Retail, Wholesale, or Other; Name must already be in the Customer table, and so on.)
- ☐ Is this a conditional field? (If users enter Yes in field A, they must enter something in field C.)

Even though each data entry form is unique, you can use some general guidelines when putting together input validation schemes.

- ☐ If possible, limit keystrokes to valid values only. For example, if the field must be numeric, don't allow the user to enter character values. If spaces are not allowed, make sure the space bar is disabled. Help the user by limiting the kinds of data that can be entered into the field.
- ☐ Limit input choices with lists. If there is a limited set of valid inputs for a field, give the user a pick list or set of radio buttons to choose from.

5

☐ Inform the user of range limits. If a field has a high or low range limit, tell the user what the limits are.

☐ Point out required fields on a form. Mark required fields with a leading asterisk (*) or some other appropriate character. Possibly change the background color of required fields.

☐ Group conditional fields together on the form. If entering Yes in one field means that several other fields must be completed, put the additional fields close to the Yes/No field to help the user. Keep conditional fields of this type disabled until the Yes/No flag has been set. This helps the user see that new fields must be entered.

Field-Level Validation

The first level of validation is at the field level. This is the place where you can make sure the user is entering the right characters in the field, entering the data into the field in the proper format, and entering a valid value based on a list of possible choices.

For the rest of this section, you will be building a sample application that illustrates the various input validation methods this chapter covers. If you haven't done so already, start up Visual Basic 5 and create a new Standard EXE project. Set the caption of the form to Input Validation and the Name of the form to frmValidation. Set the project Name property to Validation and save the form as VALIDATION.FRM; save the project as VALIDATION.VBP.

Filtering Keyboard Input

One of the easiest ways to perform input validation is to filter keyboard input. Filtering keyboard input requires capturing the keystrokes of the user *before* they appear on the screen and filtering out the keystrokes you do not want to appear in the input controls. You can filter invalid or undesirable keystrokes by creating a beep for the user each time an invalid key is pressed (for example, a beep each time a letter is pressed in a numeric field). You can also convert the invalid key to a valid one (for example, change lower case to upper case). Or you can simply ignore the keystroke completely and prevent the invalid values from ever appearing in the input control.

 **TIP**

Keep in mind that not all your potential users may be able to hear an audible beep and could become confused at the inability to input data. Windows 95 has several useful Accessibility Options that you may want to review, including the use of message boxes for hearing-impaired users.

5

For the first keyboard filtering example, you set up a textbox control that accepts only numerals zero through nine. First, add a label control and a textbox control to the form. Set the caption property of the label control to Numbers. Set the Name property of the textbox control to txtNumber and set the text property to blank. Your form should resemble the one in Figure 5.1.

Figure 5.1.
Adding the Numbers input control.

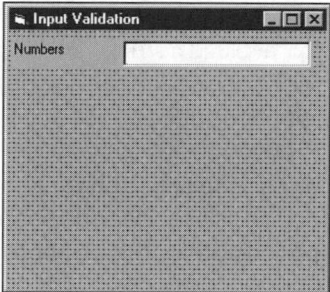

Save and run the program. You can enter any type of data in the textbox that you wish— numbers, letters, spaces, and so on. Now you add a small bit of code that filters out all but the numerals zero through nine. You do this by using the textbox control KeyPress event.

The KeyPress event occurs each time a user presses a key while the field has the focus. Each time a key is pressed while the cursor is in the textbox control, the ASCII value of the key is sent to the KeyPress event where you can evaluate it and act accordingly.

NOTE

Each key on the keyboard has an ASCII (American Standard Code for Information Interchange) numeric value. Your Visual Basic 5 documentation has a list of the ASCII codes for each key on the keyboard.

In this example, you want to ignore any keystroke that is not a 0, 1, 2, 3, 4, 5, 6, 7, 8, or 9. To do this, you need to add a small bit of code (see Listing 5.1) to the KeyPress event of the txtNumbers textbox.

TYPE   **Listing 5.1. Limiting data entry in the Keypress event.**

```
Private Sub txtNumber_KeyPress(KeyAscii As Integer)

    Dim strValid As String

    strValid = "0123456789"
```

continues

Listing 5.1. continued

```
    If InStr(strValid, Chr(KeyAscii)) = 0 Then
        KeyAscii = 0
    End If
    '
End Sub
```

In Listing 5.1, you declared a string variable that holds the list of valid keys. The next line loads the string with the valid keys for this field, and the next line checks to see whether the key pressed is in the string of valid keys. It does this by converting the numeric value passed by Visual Basic 5 in the KeyAscii parameter (the ASCII value of the key pressed) into a readable character using the Visual Basic 5 Chr function and searching for the result in the list of valid keys in the cValid string. If the key pressed is not in the cValid string, the keystroke is set to 0. Setting the keystroke to 0 is telling Visual Basic 5 to pretend nothing was ever typed!

Now save and run the program. No matter what keys you type, only the numerals 0 through 9 appear in the textbox. You have filtered out everything but numerals. You may also notice that keystrokes, such as the backspace and delete keys, no longer work! You've told Visual Basic 5 to ignore them. You can fix that by adding a statement that checks to see whether the keystroke is a control code. Control codes are used in Visual Basic 5 to indicate that the key the user pressed was not a printable character but a keyboard control character. Common control characters are the Escape key, the Return key, the Backspace key, and so on.

You can also add any other characters to the validity list if you like. For example, you probably want to be able to enter a minus sign, a plus sign, and a decimal point in this number field. To do this, all you need to do is add those three characters to the cValid string. Your program code should now look like Listing 5.2.

TYPE **Listing 5.2. The KeyPress event with control characters.**

```
Private Sub txtNumber_KeyPress(KeyAscii As Integer)
    '
    Dim strValid As String
    '
    strValid = "0123456789+-."
    '
    If KeyAscii > 26 Then ' if it's not a control code
        If InStr(strValid, Chr(KeyAscii)) = 0 Then
            KeyAscii = 0
        End If
    End If
    '
End Sub
```

Notice that in Listing 5.2, you first tested to see whether the key pressed was greater than 26. ASCII code 26 is the last Visual Basic 4 control code. The routine in Listing 5.2 now skips over filtering of control codes. When you save and run the program, you can pass the plus, minus, and decimal point characters into the textbox, too.

Now let's create validation code that accepts only uppercase characters. This is a bit trickier. Instead of ignoring lowercase input, you convert it to upper case, and then pass it through to the textbox.

First add another label and textbox control. Set the label caption to Uppercase. Set the Name property of the textbox to txtUpper and set the text property to blank. Your form should look like the one in Figure 5.2.

Figure 5.2.

Adding the Uppercase control and conversion to the form.

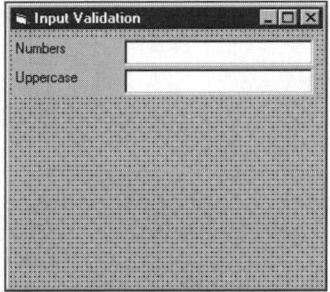

The code needed for the txtUpper KeyPress event is in Listing 5.3. Even though there's only one line of code in this routine, there's a lot going on. This line of code (reading from the inside function outward) first coverts the Keyascii value into a printable character, converts that character to upper case, and then converts the character back to an ASCII numeric value. Notice that instead of setting the Visual Basic 5 KeyAscii parameter to zero (discarding it), this routine converts it to an uppercase value. This works no matter what key is pressed.

TYPE **Listing 5.3. The KeyPress event to force letters to uppercase.**

```
Private Sub txtUpper_KeyPress(KeyAscii As Integer)
    '
    KeyAscii = Asc(UCase(Chr(KeyAscii))) ' change to uppercase
    '
End Sub
```

When you save and run the program, you see that any letter key you enter converts to an uppercase letter and passes through to the textbox.

The two types of keyboard filters illustrated here (discard or convert) can be combined to form a powerful input validation tool. Let's create a validation example that allows only uppercase letters A through Z, or numerals 0 through 9—no spaces or any other characters.

First add a new label/textbox control pair. Set the label caption property to Combined. Set the textbox Name property to txtCombined and the text property to blank. Refer to Figure 5.3 for positioning and sizing information.

Figure 5.3.

Adding the Combined control to the form.

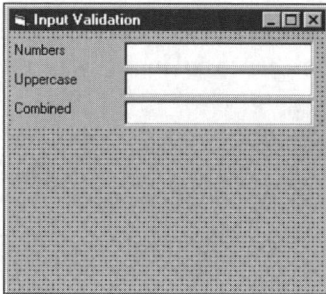

Listing 5.4 shows how to combine a check against a valid list and a conversion of keystrokes into a single input validation.

TYPE   **Listing 5.4. A single `KeyPress` event to check for valid entry and force uppercase.**

```
Private Sub txtCombined_KeyPress(KeyAscii As Integer)
    '
    Dim strValid As String
    '
    strValid = "0123456789ABCDEFGHIJKLMNOPQRSTUVWXYZ"
    '
    KeyAscii = Asc(UCase(Chr(KeyAscii)))
    '
    If KeyAscii > 26 Then
        If InStr(strValid, Chr(KeyAscii)) = 0 Then
            KeyAscii = 0
        End If
    End If
    '
End Sub
```

5

Input Masking

It is very common to have fields on your form that require special input formats. Examples of special formats would be telephone numbers, Social Security numbers, hour/minute time entry, and so on. Visual Basic 5 ships with a bound data control that handles special input and display formatting—the MaskedEdit control. The MaskedEdit control works like the standard Visual Basic 5 textbox control, with a few added properties that make it a powerful tool for your input validation arsenal.

Let's add a phone number input field to the form. Add a new label to the form and set its caption property to Phone. Now add a MaskedEdit control to the form. Set its Name property to mskPhone, the Mask property to (###) ###-#### and the PromptInclude property to False.

TIP

It is essential that you set the PromptInclude property to False when using the MaskedEdit control as a bound control. If the PromptInclude property is set to True, you get a database error each time you add a new record to the table or attempt to save or read a record that has a null value in the data field linked to the MaskedEdit bound control.

Your form should resemble Figure 5.4.

Figure 5.4.

Adding the MaskedEdit Phone control to the form.

You do not need to add any additional filtering to the control because the MaskedEdit control makes sure that only digits are entered and that the input is limited to 10 digits formatted as a standard U.S. phone number.

Save and run the program. You can see that when the control is initialized, the phone number mask is displayed. When the MaskedEdit control receives the focus, a series of underlines appear as an input guide for the user. The underlines disappear when control is given to an object other than the MaskedEdit control.

NOTE

The formatting characters of the MaskedEdit control are *not* saved to the database field when the PromptInclude property is set to False. This means that in the previous example, only the phone number digits would be saved to the data table, not the parentheses or the dash.

The Visual Basic 5 MaskedEdit control offers an extensive set of input masking tools. It ships with several input masks predefined, including dollar amounts, U.S. phone numbers, and several date and time formats. To view these formats, select the MaskedEdit control, click the right (alternate) mouse button, and select Properties from the menu that appears. You find the formats on the General tab.

You can also create custom input format masks for inventory part numbers, e-mail addresses, and so on. Although we won't cover all the possibilities here, there is one other MaskedEdit format option that you illustrate on your form in this lesson because it is very useful when displaying dollar amounts.

The MaskedEdit control gives you the power to add a *display* mask in addition to an *input* mask. Up to this point, you have been using the input mask capabilities of the MaskedEdit control. Now let's add a control that shows the display capabilities, too.

Add another label control and another MaskedEdit control to the form. Set the label caption property to Dollars. Set the MaskedEdit control Name property to mskDollars and the format property to `$#,##0.00;($#,##0.00)`.

TIP

The MaskedEdit display property actually has three parts, each separated by the semicolon (;). Part one determines how positive values are displayed. Part two determines how negative values are displayed. Part three determines how zero values are displayed.

This property affects the display of the data, not the input, so you do not see any input guides when you set the format property or when you save and run the program. Your form should look like the one in Figure 5.5.

Figure 5.5.

*Adding the Dollar
control to the form.*

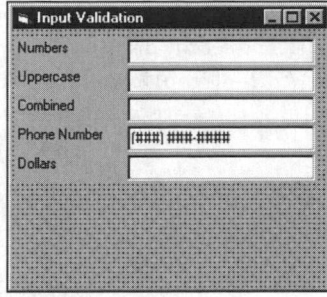

Now run the program and enter a numeric value in the Dollars textbox. When you leave the textbox to go to another control, you see the MaskedEdit control format the display of the amount you entered. Your screen should resemble Figure 5.6. Please note that two decimal places always appear to the right of the decimal.

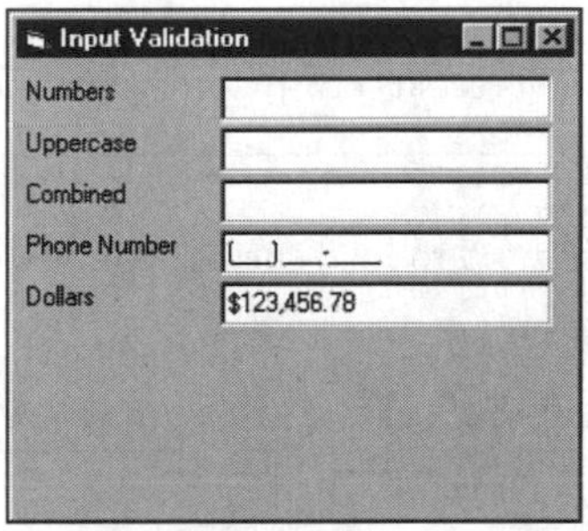

Figure 5.6.

*The display results of
the MaskedEdit
control.*

Validation Lists

One of the most common field-level input validation routines is the use of a validation list. The list contains a set of possible inputs for the field—usually displayed in a list box or a drop-down list control. Instead of having to guess at a valid value, the user can simply scan the list and click on the proper choice. Validation lists require a bit more programming to use, but the rewards far exceed the effort. Using validation lists virtually guarantees that you will not have a data entry error occur on the input field.

Before you can use a validation list for input validation, you must first have a list. It is usually a good idea to load any validation lists you need for a form at the time you load the form. This means that validation lists should be loaded in the Form_Load event. Let's add some code to your project that loads a drop-down list box with a list of possible customer types.

First add another label and a drop-down combo box control to the form. Set the label caption to Customer Type, and set the drop-down combo box Name property to cboCustType and the Style property to 2—DropDown List. Your form should look like the one in Figure 5.7.

Figure 5.7.

*Adding the
DropDown List
control to the form.*

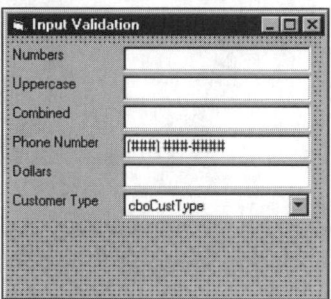

 **NOTE**

> You can't change the height of the combo box control in Visual Basic 5. It is set at 315 twips and cannot be updated.

Now add Listing 5.5 to load the list box with valid values.

TYPE **Listing 5.5. The `Form_Load` event to load a list box.**

```
Sub Form_Load ()
    '
    ' load dropdown list box
    cboCustType.AddItem "Retail"
    cboCustType.AddItem "Wholesale"
    cboCustType.AddItem "Distributor"
    cboCustType.AddItem "Other"
End Sub
```

In Listing 5.5, you are adding values directly to the list using program code. Each `AddItem` method adds an additional valid selection to the list. You could also load the control with values from a data table. This would give you a more dynamic list of valid values. For now, stick to the direct load example here; later in this book, you add validation lists loaded from data tables.

Now save and run the program. You can now click the down arrow of the drop-down list box and see the list of valid values. Now the user can't help but pick a correct item for the input field.

Notice that when you first start the form, the combo box shows an empty value. This indicates no selection has been made. You can add some code to your form that selects a default item from the list, too. Add the following line of code to the Form_Load event:

```
cboCustType.ListIndex = 0 ' set default value
```

Now when the form starts, you see the first value in the list has already been selected.

Up to this point, you have been developing methods for handling field-level validation. The next step is to add validation routines at the form level.

Form-Level Validation

Form-level validation is an essential part of designing a good validation scheme for your form. Although many input errors can be caught and corrected at the field level, there are several validation steps that can only be performed well at the form level.

Although field-level validation is performed at the time a key is pressed or at the time a field loses focus, form-level validation is performed at the time the user presses Enter, or clicks the OK or Save button. These are validations that are done after the user has entered all fields, but *before* any attempt is made to store the values to a data table.

Form-level validation can be divided into three groups:

☐ Independent content validation

☐ Required field validation

☐ Dependent field validation

Let's look at each type of form-level validation.

Independent Content Validation—High/Low Ranges

A common form-level validation routine is one that checks the upper and lower values of a numeric entry and makes sure the value is within the high/low range. This is very useful on all types of forms that have dollar amounts or unit count minimum and maximum values.

NOTE   Although it might seem that this kind of validation should be done at the field level, it is better to perform it at the form level. If a user enters a value that is not within the acceptable range, the field that contains the invalid data must be given focus so that the user can correct the entry. Setting the control's focus is best done outside of any other control's GotFocus or LostFocus event. Also, because a user can use the mouse to skip over any field on the form, placing independent content validation routines within the controls' events means that users may skip important validation steps in the process.

To set up the form-level validation, first add a single command button to the form. Set its Name property to cmdOK and its caption property to &OK. Now add another label/textbox pair to the form. Set the label caption to High/Low. Set the textbox Name property to txtHighLow and the text property to blank. Refer to Figure 5.8 for sizing and placement information.

Figure 5.8.

Adding the High/Low control and OK button to the form.

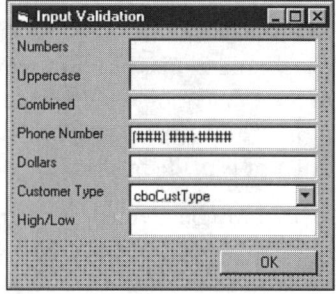

Next add Listing 5.6 to the cmdOK_click event.

Listing 5.6. The form-level validation routine to check for values in a range.

`TYPE`

```
Private Sub cmdOK_Click()
    '
    Dim intHigh As Integer
    Dim intLow As Integer
    Dim strHighLowMsg As String
    '
    intHigh = 100
    intLow = 1
    strHighLowMsg = "High/Low field must contain a value between " & _
        CStr(intLow) & " and " & CStr(intHigh)
    '
    If Val(txtHighLow) < intLow Or Val(txtHighLow) > intHigh Then
        MsgBox strHighLowMsg
        txtHighLow.SetFocus
    End If
    '
End Sub
```

5

The code in Listing 5.6 establishes the integer variables for the high and low in the range, sets them to 100 and 1 respectively, and then checks the value entered into the txtHighLow text control. If the value is out of the allowed range, a message is displayed, and the input cursor is moved back to the field that contains the invalid data. Notice that the message not only tells the user that the data is invalid, it also tells the user what values are acceptable. If the data entered is within range, the program exits normally.

Now save and run the program. If you skip to the OK button without entering data or enter data outside the allowed range, you see the validation message.

Independent Content Validation—Min/Max Field Lengths

Another common form-level validation step is to make sure that character strings meet the minimum or maximum length requirements. This is done in the same way numeric values are checked for high and low ranges.

Let's add input validation to ensure that the Uppercase textbox you placed on the form earlier is no longer than 10 characters, and at least 3 characters in length. You just need to add the code in Listing 5.7 to the cmdOK_click event that checks the txtUpper field for length.

TYPE | **Listing 5.7. The form-level validation routine to check the length of fields and a valid range of values.**

```
Private Sub cmdOK_Click()
    '
    Dim intHigh As Integer
    Dim intLow As Integer
    Dim strHighLowMsg As String
    '
    Dim intMinLen As Integer
    Dim intMaxLen As Integer
    Dim strMinMaxMsg As String
    '
    Dim blnOK As Boolean
    '
    intHigh = 100
    intLow = 1
    strHighLowMsg = "High/Low field must contain a value between " & _
        CStr(intLow) & " and " & CStr(intHigh)
    '
    intMinLen = 3
    intMaxLen = 10
    strMinMaxMsg = "Upper field must be between " & _
        CStr(intMinLen) & " and " & CStr(intMaxLen) & " long."
    '
```

continues

5

Listing 5.7. continued

```
        blnOK = False
        '
        ' check high/low field
        If Val(txtHighLow) < intLow Or Val(txtHighLow) > intHigh Then
            MsgBox strHighLowMsg
            blnOK = False
            txtHighLow.SetFocus
        End If
        '
        ' check upper field
        If Len(txtUpper) < intMinLen Or Len(txtUpper) > intMaxLen Then
            MsgBox strMinMaxMsg
            blnOK = False
            txtUpper.SetFocus
        End If
        '
        ' set if all passed
        If blnOK = True Then
            Unload Me
        End If
        '
End Sub
```

In Listing 5.7, you added variables for the minimum and maximum length of the entry field, a new message variable, and a flag variable to show that all validation steps passed. Notice that you changed the structure of the validation steps from a simple If_Then_Else to a series of If_Then routines. If the validation does not pass, a flag is set to make sure the form does not unload.

Save and run the form to test the validation rule. You see that now both form-level validation rules must be met before the form unloads.

NOTE

> The txtUpper field has both field-level and form-level validation rules applied to it. The field-level routine executes when data is entered into the field. The form-level validation routine executes when this data record is saved. It is perfectly acceptable, and sometimes recommended, to have both field-level and form-level validation for the same control.

Required Fields

Almost every form has at least one field that is required input. Some forms may have several. Checking for required input fields is done at the form level. Let's add code at the cmdOK_click event that makes sure that users fill out the Combined field every time.

All you need to do is validate that the txtCombined field contains valid data. Listing 5.8 shows how this is done.

TYPE

Listing 5.8. The form-level validation routine to check for required fields.

```
Private Sub cmdOK_Click()
'
    Dim intHigh As Integer
    Dim intLow As Integer
    Dim strHighLowMsg As String
'
    Dim intMinLen As Integer
    Dim intMaxLen As Integer
    Dim strMinMaxMsg As String
'
    Dim blnOK As Boolean
'
    intHigh = 100
    intLow = 1
    strHighLowMsg = "High/Low field must contain a value between " & _
        CStr(intLow) & " and " & CStr(intHigh)
'
    intMinLen = 3
    intMaxLen = 10
    strMinMaxMsg = "Upper field must be between " & _
        CStr(intMinLen) & " and " & CStr(intMaxLen) & " long."
'
    blnOK = False
'
    ' check high/low field
    If Val(txtHighLow) < intLow Or Val(txtHighLow) > intHigh Then
        MsgBox strHighLowMsg
        blnOK = False
        txtHighLow.SetFocus
    End If
'
    ' check upper field
    If Len(txtUpper) < intMinLen Or Len(txtUpper) > intMaxLen Then
        MsgBox strMinMaxMsg
```

continues

5

Listing 5.8. continued

```
        blnOK = False
        txtUpper.SetFocus
    End If
    '
    ' check the combined field
    If Len(Trim(txtCombined)) = 0 Then
        MsgBox "Combined field is a required field"
        blnOK = False
        txtCombined.SetFocus
    End If
    '
    ' set if all passed
    If blnOK = True Then
        Unload Me
    End If
    '
End Sub
```

The only change you made is to check the length of the string in the txtCombined textbox. If the result is zero, an error message is displayed. Notice the use of the Trim function to remove any trailing or leading spaces from the txtCombined string. This makes sure that users who enter blank spaces into the field do not get past the validation step.

Conditional Fields

There are times when entering a value in one field of the form means that other fields on the form must also contain valid data. Fields of this type are called *conditional fields*. A good example of conditional field validation can be found in an order tracking system. For example, when a user enters Yes in the Ship to Site? field, he or she must then enter a valid value in the Shipping Address field. The Shipping Address field is a conditional field because its validation is based on the condition of the Ship to Site? field.

Now add a conditional validation to the project. Make the field CustType conditional to the field Upper. In other words, if the Upper field contains data, the CustType field must contain data. See Listing 5.9 for an example of how to do this.

TYPE   **Listing 5.9. The form-level conditional validation routine.**

```
Private Sub cmdOK_Click()
    '
    Dim intHigh As Integer
    Dim intLow As Integer
    Dim strHighLowMsg As String
    '
```

```
    Dim intMinLen As Integer
    Dim intMaxLen As Integer
    Dim strMinMaxMsg As String
    '
    Dim blnOK As Boolean
    '
    intHigh = 100
    intLow = 1
    strHighLowMsg = "High/Low field must contain a value between " & _
        CStr(intLow) & " and " & CStr(intHigh)
    '
    intMinLen = 3
    intMaxLen = 10
    strMinMaxMsg = "Upper field must be between " & _
        CStr(intMinLen) & " and " & CStr(intMaxLen) & " long."
    '
    blnOK = False
    '
    ' check high/low field
    If Val(txtHighLow) < intLow Or Val(txtHighLow) > intHigh Then
        MsgBox strHighLowMsg
        blnOK = False
        txtHighLow.SetFocus
    End If
    '
    ' check upper field
    If Len(txtUpper) < intMinLen Or Len(txtUpper) > intMaxLen Then
        MsgBox strMinMaxMsg
        blnOK = False
        txtUpper.SetFocus
    End If
    '
    ' check the combined field
    If Len(Trim(txtCombined)) = 0 Then
        MsgBox "Combined field is a required field"
        blnOK = False
        txtCombined.SetFocus
    End If
    '
    ' check conditoinal upper/custtype fields
    If Len(Trim(txtUpper)) <> 0 And Len(Trim(cboCustType)) = 0 Then
        MsgBox "If Upper field conains data then " & _
            "the Customer Type field must also contain data"
        blnOK = False
        cboCustType.SetFocus
    End If
    '
    ' set if all passed
    If blnOK = True Then
        Unload Me
    End If
    '
End Sub
```

5

Save and run the program. Now you must enter valid data in both fields before the form unloads. You have probably also found out that each time you click the OK button, all the form-level validation steps are performed. It is good programming practice to deliver all the validation results to the user at once. It can be very frustrating to fill out a form, receive an error message, and then fix the message, only to receive another one, and another one, and so on.

Creating Your Own Validation Custom Control

The input validation routines you created today cover most of the situations you are likely to encounter when designing data entry forms. In fact, after you design one or two of these forms, you begin to see that you are writing the same validation code over and over again. Instead of repeatedly writing the same code, or even constantly performing cut, copy, and paste operations, Microsoft Visual Basic 5 gives you the power to create your own custom controls that have new properties and methods for input validation. Once you build these new controls, they can be used in all your data entry programs.

Creating a Custom Control

In this section you get a crash course on creating custom controls using Visual Basic 5.

NOTE

There are a lot of possibilities and considerations when creating custom controls. In this section, you get only the basics. You can find excellent examples of how to create your own custom controls and associated property pages in the Visual Basic 5 online documentation. Look up "Controls" in the Online Books Index to see a list of topics related to using Visual Basic 5 to create custom controls.

The first step in creating a custom control is to open a Visual Basic 5 UserControl code module. This module is a bit like the standard Visual Basic BAS (pronounced *bass*, like the fish) modules and like the Class modules introduced in Visual Basic 4. Using the UserControl module allows you to create properties, methods, and events for your custom control. Once you complete the control code, you can compile the object into an ActiveX control (sometimes called an *OCX control*) that can be used in any ActiveX-compliant developer tool. You can use this control in Visual Basic (versions 4 and 5), C++, Access, and, in most cases, Microsoft Internet Explorer.

To create a new custom control, select File | New Project from the main menu and then select ActiveX Control from the list of default templates (see Figure 5.9).

Figure 5.9.

Opening a Visual Basic BAS module.

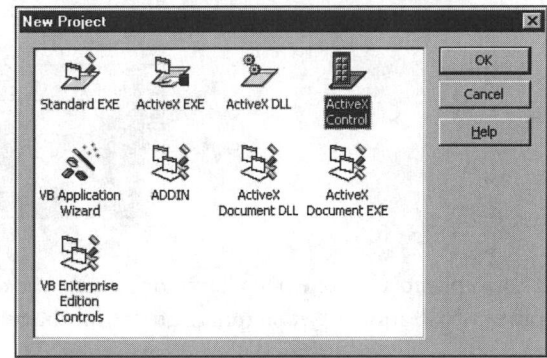

Set the Name property of the UserControl module to VText (validated textbox) and set the project name to CustomValidation. Create a new directory for this project called CustomValidation. Save the UserControl file as VTEXT.CTL and the project as CUSTOMERVALIDATION.VBP. This is the framework for creating your custom validation control.

Creating a custom control is really easy. You need to build four primary sets of routines for a custom control:

☐ Properties

☐ Methods

☐ Events

☐ Maintenance routines

Although the first three types of code routines are fairly obvious, the fourth, maintenance routines, are new. When you create an ActiveX control, you need to write code that manages the setting and retrieving of property values during both design time and runtime. To do this, you need to write a few short routines to keep track of all the property settings for your control. You learn how to code each of these types of routines as you build your validation textbox.

Laying Out the Control and Building the Maintenance Routines

For this example, you only need one visual control on your custom control—the TextBox control. Place a single TextBox control on your UserControl form. Don't worry about its size or placement. You set all that up in code. After you add the TextBox control to the UserControl form space, it should look like the UserControl in Figure 5.10

Figure 5.10.

Adding the TextBox control to the UserControl form space.

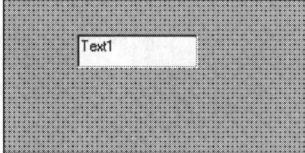

The next step is to add code that allows for resizing the control (at design time or runtime), and some initialization code that runs the first time the control is added to a Visual Basic form. First, add the code in Listing 5.10 to your project. This handles resizing of the control.

TYPE   **Listing 5.10. Adding code to the `UserControl_Resize` event.**

```
Private Sub UserControl_Resize()
    '
    ' make textbox fill the control space
    '
    With Text1
        .Left = 1
        .Top = 1
        .Height = UserControl.Height
        .Width = UserControl.Width
    End With
    '
End Sub
```

Now, each time the user resizes the control, the textbox stretches to fill the space.

Next you need to add a few lines of code to the `InitProperties` event. This code sets the default size of the control when it is placed on a form. Enter the code from Listing 5.11 into the `UserControl_InitProperties` event.

Listing 5.11. Adding code to the `UserControl_InitProperties` event.

`TYPE`

```
Private Sub UserControl_InitProperties()
    '
    With UserControl
        .Width = 1200
        .Height = 300
    End With
    '
    Text1.Text = UserControl.Name
    '
End Sub
```

Along with the `Resize` and `InitProperties` events, there are two other very important events that you must populate with code. These are the `ReadProperties` and `WriteProperties` events of the UserControl. These two events are used to keep track of design-time property settings. When you set properties during design time, Visual Basic must have a way to store them so that the runtime version of Visual Basic knows what they are.

Because we haven't defined any custom properties to remember, you won't be coding these two events until a bit later in the chapter. However, it is important that you remember to code the `Read` and `Write` property routines for each custom property you define for your control. If you fail to do this, you won't be able to access any of the design-time property values once your Visual Basic program starts running.

Now that the maintenance steps have been addressed, it's time to add some functionality to the new control.

Coding the KeyFilter Validations for the Custom Control

The first validation routine to add to the custom control is the key press filter routines. In this example control, you add key press filters for upper case, digits, and numeric data. These routines work very much like the key press routines you coded in the first part of this chapter. You need to create a few properties, some default values, and a couple of events to handle key press validation. Listing 5.12 shows the declarations for the key press routines. Add this code to the general declaration section of your UserControl module.

5

Listing 5.12. Adding the KeyFilter declarations to the VText control.

```
' ----------------------------------------------
' KeyFilter values
'
' Event list
Public Event NumericError(KeyAscii)
Public Event DigitsError(KeyAscii)
'Default Property Values:
Const m_def_UpperCase = 0
Const m_def_Digits = 0
Const m_def_Numeric = 0
'Property Variables:
Dim m_UpperCase As Boolean
Dim m_Digits As Boolean
Dim m_Numeric As Boolean
Dim m_Text As String
```

The code in Listing 5.12 establishes two events that fire messages back to your Visual Basic program if an invalid key is pressed. This code also defines local storage for three Boolean properties and one string property. The three Boolean properties also have a default value defined. You add the new Public properties in just a moment.

First, add some code to the InitProperties event to set the default values for these new properties. The code in Listing 5.13 shows the modified UserControl_InitProperties event.

Listing 5.13. Adding KeyFilter defaults to the InitProperties event.

```
Private Sub UserControl_InitProperties()
    '
    ' initialize control values
    '
    With UserControl
        .Width = 1200
        .Height = 300
    End With
    '
    Text1.Text = UserControl.Name
    '
    ' KeyFilter properties
    m_UpperCase = m_def_UpperCase
    m_Digits = m_def_Digits
    m_Numeric = m_def_Numeric
    '
End Sub
```

Now it's time to create the new properties to match the local storage variables. To create properties for your control, select Tools | Add Procedure from the main menu. This brings up the dialog box you use to add all your properties, methods, and events. Enter UpperCase as the name, select the Property and Public radio buttons, and then press OK (see Figure 5.11).

Figure 5.11.

Adding a new property to the VText control.

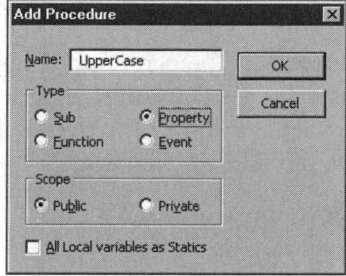

Notice that Visual Basic has created two special functions in your UserControl module. The `Property Get` routine is used to allow others to "get" the value of your published property. The `Property Let` routine is used to "let" others send you a value to store in the property. For this chapter, you create all your custom control properties this way.

TIP

Visual Basic 5 ships with an ActiveX Control Wizard that helps you create all the properties, methods, and events for your control. Although you'll not be using this wizard in this chapter, you can learn more about this and other aspects of creating custom controls by using the search word "controls" in the Visual Basic Book Online documents.

5

You need to modify these default routines to match your published properties. The code in Listing 5.14 shows you how to code the `Let` and `Get` routines for the UpperCase property.

TYPE

Listing 5.14. Coding the `Let` and `Get` routines for the UpperCase property.

```
Public Property Get UpperCase() As Boolean
    UpperCase = m_UpperCase
End Property

Public Property Let UpperCase(ByVal New_UpperCase As Boolean)
    m_UpperCase = New_UpperCase
    PropertyChanged "UpperCase"
End Property
```

The code in Listing 5.14 is typical of property-handling routines. The main job of these routines is to transfer values between the control and its "host" program. Note the use of the `PropertyChanged` method. This method informs Visual Basic that the property has been updated and forces Visual Basic to update the design-time properties Window and fire off the event needed to update the stored properties.

You need to declare Public properties for the Digits and Numeric storage values. Use the same process you used for the UpperCase property. Select Tools | Add Procedure; enter the property name (for example, Digits); select the Property and Public option buttons, and then press Enter. Do this for both the Digits and Numeric properties.

Listing 5.15 shows the code to add to the Digits property Let and Get routines.

TYPE **Listing 5.15. Coding the Digits property Let and Get routines.**

```
Public Property Get Digits() As Boolean
    Digits = m_Digits
End Property

Public Property Let Digits(ByVal New_Digits As Boolean)
    m_Digits = New_Digits
    PropertyChanged "Digits"
End Property
```

After adding the Digits code, add the code from Listing 5.16 to the Numeric property Let and Get routines.

TYPE **Listing 5.16. Coding the Numeric property Let and Get routines.**

```
Public Property Get Numeric() As Boolean
    Numeric = m_Numeric
End Property

Public Property Let Numeric(ByVal New_Numeric As Boolean)
    m_Numeric = New_Numeric
    PropertyChanged "Numeric"
End Property
```

There is one final property you need to create—the Text property. Unlike the three other properties, which are unique to this control, the Text property is "mapped" to the Text property of the TextBox control that appears as part of the VText control. Even though the Text property exists for the TextBox, you must publish the Text property for the VText control before users can access any data in the Text1.Text control. After using Tools | Add

Procedure to create the Public property Text, enter the code from Listing 5.17 into the corresponding Let and Get routines for the Text property.

Listing 5.17. Coding the Text property Let and Get routines.

```
Public Property Get Text() As Variant
    Text = Text1.Text
End Property

Public Property Let Text(ByVal vNewValue As Variant)
    Text1.Text = vNewValue
End Property
```

Finally, you need to set the attributes of this property so that it can be used within database forms. Select Tools | Procedure Attributes to bring up the attributes dialog.

Select the Text property, select the Advanced button, and place a check mark in all the Data Bindings fields at the bottom of the form. This adds the DataField and DataSource properties to the VText control (see Figure 5.12).

Figure 5.12.

Setting the Data Bindings of a custom property.

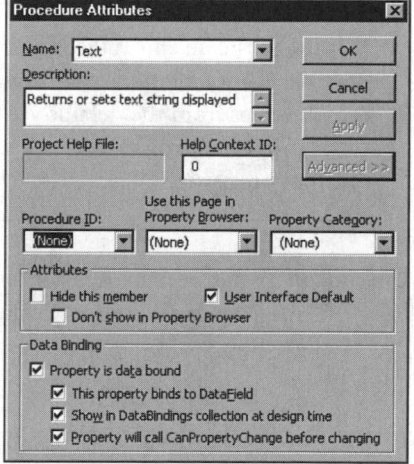

There is one more set of routines you need to code before your property handling is complete. You need to add code to the WriteProperties and ReadProperties events of the UserControl. This code is executed each time the control moves from design time to runtime. Listing 5.18 shows the code for the WriteProperties event. Add this to your UserControl modules.

Listing 5.18. Coding the `WriteProperties` event of the VText control.

```
Private Sub UserControl_WriteProperties(PropBag As PropertyBag)
    '
    ' save design-time property values
    '
    With PropBag
        Call .WriteProperty("UpperCase", m_UpperCase, m_def_UpperCase)
        Call .WriteProperty("Digits", m_Digits, m_def_Digits)
        Call .WriteProperty("Numeric", m_Numeric, m_def_Numeric)
        '
        Call .WriteProperty("Text", Text1.Text, UserControl.Name)
    End With
    '
End Sub
```

All read and write operations are performed using the PropBag ("Property Bag") object. This object contains the correct settings for all the properties at any given time. Notice that the `WriteProperty` method of the PropBag object takes three parameters: property name, current value, and default value. The default value is used if the current value is set to null.

TIP

Although the default value is an optional parameter for the `WriteProperty` method, you should use it. Values are saved only if they are different from the default value. If you include default values for all your properties, you can reduce the size of the file needed to store your custom properties.

Next, add the code in Listing 5.19 to the `UserControl_ReadProperties` event. This ensures that Visual Basic runtime loads the property values stored by in the `WriteProperties` event by Visual Basic design time.

TYPE

Listing 5.19. Coding the `ReadProperties` event for the VText control.

```
Private Sub UserControl_ReadProperties(PropBag As PropertyBag)
    '
    ' read design-time property values
    '
    With PropBag
        m_UpperCase = .ReadProperty("UpperCase", m_def_UpperCase)
        m_Digits = .ReadProperty("Digits", m_def_Digits)
        m_Numeric = .ReadProperty("Numeric", m_def_Numeric)
        '
        Text1.Text = .ReadProperty("Text", UserControl.Name)
```

5

```
    End With
    '
End Sub
```

The `ReadProperty` method uses two parameters (property name and default value) and returns a value. This return value should be placed in the local storage variable for the Public property.

Now that all the properties are built, you need to add the code that actually validates user input. For this control, you create a single Public method that checks all three key press validation rules. Select Tools | Add Procedure and enter KeyValidate as the name. Select the Function and Public option buttons before pressing the OK button. Now add the code from Listing 5.20 to the project.

TYPE **Listing 5.20. Coding the `KeyValidate` method.**

```
Private Function KeyValidate(intKeyValue As Integer) As Integer
    '
    ' check value against rules
    '
    Dim strNumeric As String
    Dim strDigits As String
    '
    strNumeric = "0123456789+-."
    strDigits = "0123456789"
    '
    ' convert to uppercase
    If m_UpperCase = True Then
        intKeyValue = Asc(UCase(Chr(intKeyValue)))
    End If
    '
    ' check for digits
    If m_Digits = True Then
        If InStr(strDigits, Chr(intKeyValue)) = 0 Then
            intKeyValue = 0
            RaiseEvent DigitsError(intKeyValue)
        End If
    End If
    '
    ' check for numerics
    If m_Numeric = True Then
        If InStr(strNumeric, Chr(intKeyValue)) = 0 Then
            intKeyValue = 0
            RaiseEvent NumericError(intKeyValue)
        End If
    End If
    '
    KeyValidate = intKeyValue
    '
End Function
```

5

The code in Listing 5.20 combines code from several of the KeyPress events you coded in the first part of this chapter. The only real difference is the use of the RaiseEvent keyword. This keyword is used to send a message back to the host program using this control. In this case, the messages are sent if an invalid key has been entered. Along with the message, the invalid key's ASCII value is returned. You see this event when you test the control a bit later in this chapter. After adding the KeyValidate routine, you need to add some code to the project to call KeyValidate each time a key is pressed. Listing 5.21 shows the code to add to the Text1_KeyPress event.

TYPE | **Listing 5.21. Coding the** Text1_KeyPress **event.**

```
Private Sub Text1_KeyPress(KeyAscii As Integer)
    '
    KeyAscii = KeyValidate(KeyAscii)
    '
End Sub
```

This code should look familiar. Now, each time the user presses a key in the textbox, the KeyValidate function is called. If the key press is invalid, an error event message is fired off to the host program.

That's all the coding you need to do to create a custom control that filters key presses. Save the UserControl module (VTEXT.CTL) and the project file (CUSTOMVALIDATION.VBP) and close all the windows associated with this project. You should now see a new control appear in the toolbox. This is your new custom control. You use it in a test form to make sure you've built all the code correctly.

Testing the KeyFilter Options of the VText Control

To test the new control, you need to add a new project to this project group. Select File | Add Project and select the Standard EXE project template from the New Project tab. Locate the new VText control in your toolbox and add it to the blank form (see Figure 5.13).

Figure 5.13.
Adding the VText control to a blank form.

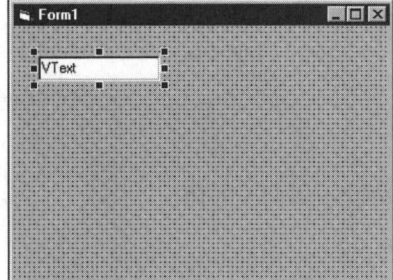

Set the Name property of the new control to vtxUpper, the UpperCase property to True, and the Text property to "". Save the form as TEXT.FRM and the project as TEST.VBP and run the project. When you type in the textbox, all your input is converted to uppercase (see Figure 5.14).

Figure 5.14.

Testing the VText control's UpperCase option.

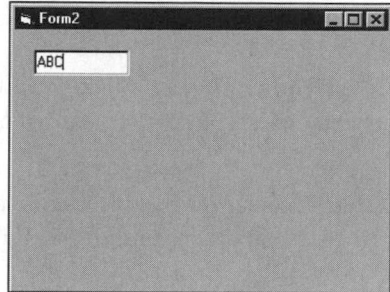

Now add two more VText controls to the form. Set the Name property of one to vtxDigits, the Digits property to True, and the Text property to "". For the other control, set the name property to vtxNumeric, the Numeric property to True, and the Text property to "". You can also add three labels to the form as shown in Figure 5.15.

Figure 5.15.

Laying out the Test form.

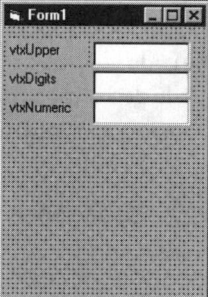

After laying out the form, you can add two lines of code to the project. These lines of code display a message box each time the user presses an invalid key inside each of the VText controls. Add the code in Listing 5.22 to the project.

TYPE   **Listing 5.22. Coding the error events for VText.**

```
Private Sub vtxDigits_DigitsError(KeyAscii As Variant)

    MsgBox "Enter Digits only! '0123456789'"

End Sub
```

continues

Listing 5.22. continued

```
Private Sub vtxNumeric_NumericError(KeyAscii As Variant)
    '
    MsgBox "Enter Numeric data only! '0123456789.+-'"
    '
End Sub
```

Now save and run the test project. When you attempt to enter invalid data in the vtxDigits or the vtxNumeric boxes, you see the message box reminding you of the valid keystrokes for that control.

That ends the crash course on creating custom controls. The next three sections show you how to add other validation options to your VText control.

Adding Range-Checking Options to the VText Control

One of the other validation options you can add to the VText control is range checking. By adding min and max properties and a property to toggle the range checking on or off, along with a single validation method and an error event, you can expand the power of the VText control considerably.

Listing 5.23 shows the code you need to add to the general declaration section of the VText UserControl. These code declarations define the events, methods, and properties needed to add range checking to your custom control.

TYPE **Listing 5.23. Declaring range-checking properties, events, and methods.**

```
' ------------------------------------------------
' CheckRange values
'
' event list
Public Event InRangeError(vValue)
' Properties
Dim m_CheckRange As Boolean
Dim m_HighValue As Variant
Dim m_LowValue As Variant
' Default Values
Const m_def_CheckRange = 0
Const m_def_LowValue = 0
Const m_def_HighValue = 0
```

5

Next you need to use the Tools | Add Procedures dialog to create three new properties. Make CheckRange a Boolean Public property. Then make HighValue and LowValue Variant Public properties.

TIP

> You might think that HighValue and LowValue should be declared numeric types, that is, Integer or Long. However, this may not be the best idea. Although Integers or Longs might be OK, what if you declare the property as Integer and want to set it to a number greater than 33000? Although a Long data type could accept the higher number, what if you wanted to set the property from within a code segment using an integer variable? Using a Variant data type and performing type checking gives you the greatest degree of flexibility.

The code in Listing 5.24 shows you how to populate the Property Let and Get routines for the three new properties.

TYPE   **Listing 5.24. Coding the Let and Get property routines.**

```
Public Property Get CheckRange() As Boolean
    CheckRange = m_CheckRange
End Property

Public Property Let CheckRange(ByVal vNewValue As Boolean)
    m_CheckRange = vNewValue
    PropertyChanged "CheckRange"
End Property

Public Property Get LowValue() As Variant
    '
    LowValue = m_LowValue
    '
End Property

Public Property Let LowValue(ByVal vNewValue As Variant)
    '
    If IsNumeric(vNewValue) = False Then
        Error 380 ' invalid property value
    Else
        m_LowValue = vNewValue
        PropertyChanged "LowValue"
    End If
    '
End Property
```

5

continues

Listing 5.24. continued

```
Public Property Get HighValue() As Variant
    '
    HighValue = m_HighValue
    '
End Property

Public Property Let HighValue(ByVal vNewValue As Variant)
    '
    If IsNumeric(vNewValue) = False Then
        Error 380 ' invalid property
    Else
        m_HighValue = vNewValue
        PropertyChanged "HighValue"
    End If
    '
End Property
```

Notice how the HighValue and LowValue Let routines handle the incoming value. First, the parameter is checked to see if it can pass as a numeric value. If not, an error is invoked. If the parameter can be converted into numeric data, the value is stored and the PropertyChanged method is used to mark the item.

WARNING

When reporting an error from within an ActiveX control, it is always better to "raise" an error using the Error keyword than to display a custom message box. Custom message boxes can get in the way of the host program interface at either runtime or design time. However, using the Error method to report an error is handled appropriately by the host development tool.

After adding the new properties to the file, you need to update the InitProperties event to reflect the new default values for the range-checking properties. Listing 5.25 shows how this is done. Add this code to the end of the InitProperties event.

TYPE

Listing 5.25. Adding the range-checking properties to the InitProperties event.

```
    ' InRange properties
    m_CheckRange = m_def_CheckRange
    m_HighValue = m_def_HighValue
    m_LowValue = m_def_LowValue
```

Next you need to update the ReadProperties and WriteProperties events of the UserControl. Listing 5.26 has the modified ReadProperties event. Refer to Listing 5.27 for the most recent changes to the WriteProperties event.

TYPE **Listing 5.26. Modifying the ReadProperties event.**

```
Private Sub UserControl_ReadProperties(PropBag As PropertyBag)
    '
    ' read design-time property values
    '
    With PropBag
        m_UpperCase = .ReadProperty("UpperCase", m_def_UpperCase)
        m_Digits = .ReadProperty("Digits", m_def_Digits)
        m_Numeric = .ReadProperty("Numeric", m_def_Numeric)

        m_CheckRange = .ReadProperty("CheckRange", m_def_CheckRange)
        m_LowValue = .ReadProperty("LowValue", m_def_LowValue)
        m_HighValue = .ReadProperty("HighValue", m_def_HighValue)
        '
        Text1.Text = .ReadProperty("Text", UserControl.Name)
    End With
    '
End Sub
```

TYPE **Listing 5.27. Modifying the WriteProperties event.**

```
Private Sub UserControl_WriteProperties(PropBag As PropertyBag)
    '
    ' save design-time property values
    '
    With PropBag
        Call .WriteProperty("UpperCase", m_UpperCase, m_def_UpperCase)
        Call .WriteProperty("Digits", m_Digits, m_def_Digits)
        Call .WriteProperty("Numeric", m_Numeric, m_def_Numeric)
        '
        Call .WriteProperty("CheckRange", m_CheckRange, m_def_CheckRange)
        Call .WriteProperty("LowValue", m_LowValue, m_def_LowValue)
        Call .WriteProperty("HighValue", m_HighValue, m_def_HighValue)
        '
        Call .WriteProperty("Text", Text1.Text, UserControl.Name)
    End With
    '
End Sub
```

5

Now you need to write the actual range validation routine. Use the Tools | Add Procedure dialog to create a method called InRangeValidate with the Sub and Public options. Add the code from Listing 5.28 to the method.

TYPE   **Listing 5.28. Coding the `InRangeValidate` method.**

```
Public Sub InRangeValidate()
    '
    ' check value within range
    '
    Dim varCheckValue As Variant
    '
    If IsNumeric(Text1.Text) = False Then
        RaiseEvent InRangeError(varCheckValue)
        Exit Sub
    Else
        varCheckValue = Text1.Text
    End If
    '
    If varCheckValue < m_LowValue Or varCheckValue > m_HighValue Then
        RaiseEvent InRangeError(varCheckValue)
    End If
    '
End Sub
```

Notice that the first check is to make sure that the data entry is really numeric data. Then the numeric data is compared to the min and max values set in the properties. If the comparison fails, a new error event is fired off to the host environment.

Finally, to call this routine automatically within the control, place the following code behind the `Lost_Focus` event for the Text1 control:

```
Private Sub Text1_LostFocus()
    '
    If CheckRange = True Then InRangeValidate
    '
End Sub
```

That's it for the range-checking features of the VText control. Save the control (`VTEXT.CTL`) and the project (`CUSTOMVALIDATION.VBP`) before you test your new features.

Testing the InRange Options of the VText Control

Select the TEST project again and add a new vText control to the form along with an OK button (see Figure 5.16).

Now set the following properties on the new VText control:

- ☐ Name   vtxInRange
- ☐ CheckRange   True
- ☐ Digits   True

☐	HighValue	100
☐	LowValue	50
☐	Text	""

Figure 5.16.

Laying out the range-checking controls on the test form.

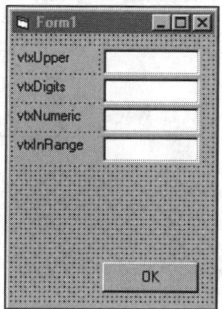

After setting these values, add the code in Listing 5.29 to the test form.

TYPE **Listing 5.29. Adding code to handle the InRange properties.**

```
Private Sub cmdOK_Click()
    If vtxInRange.CheckRange = True Then
        vtxInRange.InRangeValidate
    End If
End Sub

Private Sub vtxInRange_InRangeError(vValue As Variant)
    '
    MsgBox "InRange Error Reported!"
    '
End Sub
```

Notice the addition of the validation code behind the cmdOK button. This is required, even though you added built-in validation within the control itself. Remember that the Lost_Focus event was used to trigger the InRangeValidate routine. What if the user loads the form, enters data in every field but this one and then proceeds by pressing OK? As you may have guessed, nothing happens since the vtxInRange control never received focus. This is the essence of form-level validation.

Save and run the project. You see an error whenever your input range is out of bounds.

Adding CheckSize Options to the VText Control

Another important form-level validation option is to check the length of the input string. You need three new properties: CheckSize (Boolean), MinLength (integer), and MaxLength (integer). The code in Listing 5.30 shows the modifications to the general declaration section of the UserControl.

TYPE **Listing 5.30. Modifying the declaration section of VText.**

```
' ---------------------------------------------
' CheckSize values
'
' event list
Public Event CheckSizeError(vValue)
' Properties
Dim m_CheckSize As Boolean
Dim m_MinLength As Integer
Dim m_MaxLength As Integer
' Default values
Const m_def_CheckSize = 0
Const m_def_MinLength = 0
Const m_def_MaxLength = 0
```

Next, update the InitProperties event to set the default values for these new properties. See Listing 5.31 for code to add to the InitProperties event.

TYPE **Listing 5.31. Modifying the InitProperties event.**

```
'
    ' CheckSize properties
    m_CheckSize = m_def_CheckSize
    m_MinLength = m_def_MinLength
    m_MaxLength = m_def_MaxLength
```

Now, you need to modify the ReadProperties and WriteProperties events for the VText control. Listing 5.32 shows you how to modify the ReadProperties event.

TYPE **Listing 5.32. Modifying the ReadProperties event.**

```
Private Sub UserControl_ReadProperties(PropBag As PropertyBag)
    '
    ' read design-time property values
    '
```

```
    With PropBag
        m_UpperCase = .ReadProperty("UpperCase", m_def_UpperCase)
        m_Digits = .ReadProperty("Digits", m_def_Digits)
        m_Numeric = .ReadProperty("Numeric", m_def_Numeric)
        '
        m_CheckRange = .ReadProperty("CheckRange", m_def_CheckRange)
        m_LowValue = .ReadProperty("LowValue", m_def_LowValue)
        m_HighValue = .ReadProperty("HighValue", m_def_HighValue)
        '
        m_CheckSize = .ReadProperty("CheckSize", m_def_CheckSize)
        m_MinLength = .ReadProperty("MinLength", m_def_MinLength)
        m_MaxLength = .ReadProperty("MaxLength", m_def_MaxLength)
        '
        Text1.Text = .ReadProperty("Text", UserControl.Name)
    End With
    '
End Sub
```

Now refer to Listing 5.33 to update the `WriteProperties` event.

TYPE **Listing 5.33. Modifying the `WriteProperties` event.**

```
Private Sub UserControl_WriteProperties(PropBag As PropertyBag)
    '
    ' save design-time property values
    '
    With PropBag
        Call .WriteProperty("UpperCase", m_UpperCase, m_def_UpperCase)
        Call .WriteProperty("Digits", m_Digits, m_def_Digits)
        Call .WriteProperty("Numeric", m_Numeric, m_def_Numeric)
        '
        Call .WriteProperty("CheckRange", m_CheckRange, m_def_CheckRange)
        Call .WriteProperty("LowValue", m_LowValue, m_def_LowValue)
        Call .WriteProperty("HighValue", m_HighValue, m_def_HighValue)
        '
        Call .WriteProperty("CheckSize", m_CheckSize, m_def_CheckSize)
        Call .WriteProperty("MinLength", m_MinLength, m_def_MinLength)
        Call .WriteProperty("MaxLength", m_MaxLength, m_def_MaxLength)
        '
        Call .WriteProperty("Text", Text1.Text, UserControl.Name)
    End With
    '
End Sub
```

5

Now that you've handled the housekeeping chores for this option, you're ready to code the new properties. Listing 5.34 shows the `Let` and `Get` methods for the three new properties.

Listing 5.34. Coding the Let and Get methods for the CheckSize properties.

TYPE

```
Public Property Get CheckSize() As Boolean
    CheckSize = m_CheckSize
End Property

Public Property Let CheckSize(ByVal vNewValue As Boolean)
    m_CheckSize = vNewValue
    PropertyChanged "CheckSize"
End Property

Public Property Get MinLength() As Variant
    MinLength = m_MinLength
End Property

Public Property Let MinLength(ByVal vNewValue As Variant)
    '
    If IsNumeric(vNewValue) = False Then
        Error 380 ' invalid property
    Else
        m_MinLength = Val(vNewValue)
        PropertyChanged "MinLength"
    End If
    '
End Property

Public Property Get MaxLength() As Variant
    MaxLength = m_MaxLength
End Property

Public Property Let MaxLength(ByVal vNewValue As Variant)
    '
    If IsNumeric(vNewValue) = False Then
        Error 380 ' invalid property
    Else
        m_MaxLength = Val(vNewValue)
        PropertyChanged "MaxLength"
    End If
    '
End Property
```

Notice, again, the use of IsNumeric() and the Error keyword to check for and report invalid property values. After completing the new properties, create a new Public Sub called CheckSizeValidate and enter the code shown in Listing 5.35.

5

TYPE **Listing 5.35. Coding the `CheckSizeValidate` method.**

```
Public Sub CheckSizeValidate()
    '
    ' check for proper size
    '
    Dim varTemp As Variant
    '
    varTemp = Len(Text1.Text)
    '
    If varTemp < m_MinLength Or varTemp > m_MaxLength Then
        RaiseEvent CheckSizeError(varTemp)
    End If
    '
End Sub
```

Finally, because this is a form-level routine, modify the Text1_LostFocus event to match the code shown in Listing 5.36.

TYPE **Listing 5.36. Modifying the `Lost_Focus` event of the TextBox.**

```
Private Sub Text1_LostFocus()
    '
    If CheckRange = True Then InRangeValidate
    If CheckSize = True Then CheckSizeValidate
    '
End Sub
```

Save (and close) the control project before you switch to the TEST project to test the new options.

Testing the CheckSize Options of the VText Control

Now select the TEST.FRM form and add a label and a VText control. Set the label caption to vtxCheckSize. Set the VText control's name to vtxCheckSize. Then set the vtxCheckSize MinLength property to 5 and the MaxLength property to 10. Set the CheckSize property to True and the UpperCase property to True. Finally, set the Text property to "". Refer to Figure 5.17 for the location and size of the controls.

5

Figure 5.17.

Laying out the vtxCheckSize controls.

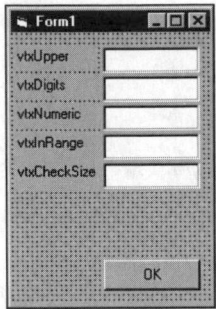

After laying out the controls, add the code in Listing 5.37 to the CheckSizeError event of the vtxCheckSize control.

TYPE   **Listing 5.37. Coding the error message for vtxCheckSize.**

```
Private Sub vtxCheckSize_CheckSizeError(vValue As Variant)
    '
    MsgBox "Invalid Entry Length! [" & CStr(vValue) & "]"
    '
End Sub
```

You should also add code to the cmdOK_Click event to handle validation if the user never loses focus on the vtxCheckSize control. See Listing 5.38 for modifications to the code.

TYPE   **Listing 5.38. Modifying the cmdOK_Click event code.**

```
Private Sub cmdOK_Click()
    '
    If vtxInRange.CheckRange = True Then
        vtxInRange.InRangeValidate
    End If
    '
    If vtxCheckSize.CheckSize = True Then
        vtxCheckSize.CheckSizeValidate
    End If
    '
End Sub
```

Now save and run the TEST project. You see an error message when you enter a value in the vtxCheckSize field that is less than three characters or more than ten characters long.

Adding Required and Conditional Options to the VText Control

You can also add code to mark the data entry field as required or to set conditional requirements on fields. This was illustrated in the first part of the chapter. Listing 5.39 shows the complete general declarations section with the modifications to include the values for the required and conditional options.

Listing 5.39. Modifying general declarations for the Required option.

```
Option Explicit

' -----------------------------------------------
' KeyFilter values
'
' Event list
Public Event NumericError(KeyAscii)
Public Event DigitsError(KeyAscii)
'Default Property Values:
Const m_def_UpperCase = 0
Const m_def_Digits = 0
Const m_def_Numeric = 0
'Property Variables:
Dim m_UpperCase As Boolean
Dim m_Digits As Boolean
Dim m_Numeric As Boolean
Dim m_Text As String


' -----------------------------------------------
' CheckRange values
'
' event list
Public Event InRangeError(vValue)
' Properties
Dim m_CheckRange As Boolean
Dim m_HighValue As Variant
Dim m_LowValue As Variant
' Default Values
Const m_def_CheckRange = 0
Const m_def_LowValue = 0
Const m_def_HighValue = 0


' -----------------------------------------------
' CheckSize values
'
' event list
Public Event CheckSizeError(vValue)
' Properties
```

continues

Listing 5.39. continued

```
Dim m_CheckSize As Boolean
Dim m_MinLength As Integer
Dim m_MaxLength As Integer
' Default values
Const m_def_CheckSize = 0
Const m_def_MinLength = 0
Const m_def_MaxLength = 0

' ---------------------------------------------
' Required values
'
Public Event RequiredError() ' event
Dim m_Required As Boolean ' property
Const m_def_Required = 0 ' default

' ---------------------------------------------
' Conditional values
Public Event ConditionalError(strMsg) ' event
Dim m_CheckConditional As Boolean ' property
Const m_def_CheckConditional = 0 ' default
```

Next comes the InitProperties event. Listing 5.40 shows the entire InitProperties event, including the Required and Conditional values.

TYPE **Listing 5.40. The final `UserControl_InitProperties` event code.**

```
Private Sub UserControl_InitProperties()
    '
    ' initialize control values
    '
    With UserControl
        .Width = 1200
        .Height = 300
    End With
    '
    Text1.Text = UserControl.Name
    '
    ' KeyFilter properties
    m_UpperCase = m_def_UpperCase
    m_Digits = m_def_Digits
    m_Numeric = m_def_Numeric
    '
    ' InRange properties
    m_CheckRange = m_def_CheckRange
    m_HighValue = m_def_HighValue
    m_LowValue = m_def_LowValue
    '
    ' CheckSize properties
    m_CheckSize = m_def_CheckSize
```

```
    m_MinLength = m_def_MinLength
    m_MaxLength = m_def_MaxLength
    '
    ' Required property
    m_Required = m_def_Required
    '
    ' Conditional property
    m_CheckConditional = m_def_CheckConditional
    '
End Sub
```

After updating the InitProperties event, you can add the actual properties Required (Boolean) and CheckConditional (Boolean). Listing 5.41 has the code for the Let and Get methods for these two properties.

TYPE Listing 5.41. Coding the Let and Get methods for the new properties.

```
Public Property Get Required() As Boolean
    Required = m_Required
End Property

Public Property Let Required(ByVal vNewValue As Boolean)
    m_Required = vNewValue
    PropertyChanged "Required"
End Property

Public Property Get CheckConditional() As Boolean
    CheckConditional = m_CheckConditional
End Property

Public Property Let CheckConditional(ByVal vNewValue As Boolean)
    m_CheckConditional = vNewValue
    PropertyChanged "CheckConditional"
End Property
```

After you've coded the property routines, you can update the WriteProperties event. Listing 5.42 shows the complete code for this event.

TYPE Listing 5.42. Complete code for the WriteProperties event of the UserControl.

```
Private Sub UserControl_WriteProperties(PropBag As PropertyBag)
    ' save design-time property values
    '
```

continues

Listing 5.42. continued

```
    With PropBag
        Call .WriteProperty("UpperCase", m_UpperCase, m_def_UpperCase)
        Call .WriteProperty("Digits", m_Digits, m_def_Digits)
        Call .WriteProperty("Numeric", m_Numeric, m_def_Numeric)
        '
        Call .WriteProperty("CheckRange", m_CheckRange, m_def_CheckRange)
        Call .WriteProperty("LowValue", m_LowValue, m_def_LowValue)
        Call .WriteProperty("HighValue", m_HighValue, m_def_HighValue)
        '
        Call .WriteProperty("CheckSize", m_CheckSize, m_def_CheckSize)
        Call .WriteProperty("MinLength", m_MinLength, m_def_MinLength)
        Call .WriteProperty("MaxLength", m_MaxLength, m_def_MaxLength)
        '
        Call .WriteProperty("Required", m_Required, m_def_Required)
        '
        Call .WriteProperty("CheckConditional", m_CheckConditional,
m_def_CheckConditional)
        '
        Call .WriteProperty("Text", Text1.Text, UserControl.Name)
    End With
    '
End Sub
```

Listing 5.43 shows the complete code for the ReadProperties event. Match this to the one in your project.

TYPE   **Listing 5.43. Final version of the ReadProperties event.**

```
Private Sub UserControl_ReadProperties(PropBag As PropertyBag)
    '
    ' read design-time property values
    '
    With PropBag
        m_UpperCase = .ReadProperty("UpperCase", m_def_UpperCase)
        m_Digits = .ReadProperty("Digits", m_def_Digits)
        m_Numeric = .ReadProperty("Numeric", m_def_Numeric)
        '
        m_CheckRange = .ReadProperty("CheckRange", m_def_CheckRange)
        m_LowValue = .ReadProperty("LowValue", m_def_LowValue)
        m_HighValue = .ReadProperty("HighValue", m_def_HighValue)
        '
        m_CheckSize = .ReadProperty("CheckSize", m_def_CheckSize)
        m_MinLength = .ReadProperty("MinLength", m_def_MinLength)
        m_MaxLength = .ReadProperty("MaxLength", m_def_MaxLength)
        '
        m_Required = .ReadProperty("Required", m_def_Required)
        '
```

```
        m_CheckConditional = .ReadProperty("CheckConditional",
m_def_CheckConditional)
        '
        Text1.Text = .ReadProperty("Text", UserControl.Name)
    End With
    '
End Sub
```

After adding the property methods, you need to add the CheckRequired method. Use the Tools | Add Procedure menu option to add a Public Sub called CheckRequired and enter the code from Listing 5.44.

TYPE **Listing 5.44. Coding the CheckRequired method.**

```
Public Sub CheckRequired()
    '
    If m_Required = True And Len(Trim(Text1.Text)) = 0 Then
        RaiseEvent RequiredError
    End If
    '
End Sub
```

Then you can add the Public Sub ConditionalValidate routine and copy the code from Listing 5.45 to your project.

TYPE **Listing 5.45. Coding the ConditionalValidate method.**

```
Public Sub ConditionalValidate(MasterName As String, ChildName As String, _
ChildValue As Variant)
    '
    ' make sure conditional field is also filled in
    '
    Dim strMsg As String
    '
    strMsg = "The [" & MasterName & "] field contains data, " & _
        " the [" & ChildName & "] field must also contain valid data"
    '
    If Len(Trim(ChildValue)) = 0 Then
        RaiseEvent ConditionalError(strMsg)
    End If
    '
End Sub
```

5

This last routine is unique in that it is the only routine that requires parameters to be passed. Because ConditionalValidate is checking the status of more than one control, you need to supply it with the name and contents of the dependent control.

Finally, update the Text1_LostFocus event to match the one shown in Listing 5.46.

TYPE   **Listing 5.46. Updated** Text1_LostFocus **event.**

```
Private Sub Text1_LostFocus()
    '
    If CheckRange = True Then InRangeValidate
    If CheckSize = True Then CheckSizeValidate
    If Required = True Then CheckRequired
    '
End Sub
```

That's the end of the coding for the VText control. Save this control for now while you test one more time.

Testing the Required and Conditional Options of the VText Control

Bring up the TEST.FRM form and add two more VText controls to the form. Set the Name property of one to vtxRequired and of the other to vtxConditional. Add two labels with their captions set to vtxRequired and vtxConditional. For the vtxRequired control, set the CheckRequired property to true. For the vtxConditional control, set CheckConditional to true. Refer to Figure 5.18 for layout details.

Figure 5.18.

Laying out the Required and Conditional options form.

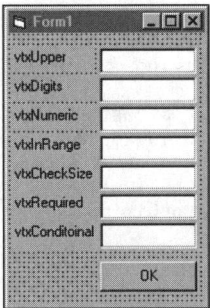

Now add the code shown in Listing 5.47 to each of the error events and the cmdOK_Click events.

> ### Listing 5.47. Adding code for the Required and Conditional
> **TYPE** options.

```
Private Sub cmdOK_Click()
    '
    If vtxInRange.CheckRange = True Then
        vtxInRange.InRangeValidate
    End If
    '
    If vtxCheckSize.CheckSize = True Then
        vtxCheckSize.CheckSizeValidate
    End If
    '
    If vtxConditional.CheckConditional = True Then
        vtxConditional.ConditionalValidate _
            "vtxConditional", "vtxUpper", vtxUpper.Text
    End If
    '
End Sub

Private Sub vtxConditional_ConditionalError(strMsg As Variant)
    '
    MsgBox strMsg
    '
End Sub

Private Sub vtxRequired_RequiredError()
    '
    MsgBox " This is a required field!"
    '
End Sub
```

Notice the use of parameters when calling the ConditionalValidate method. You should also note that the ConditionalValidate method is the only method in this control that must be executed by the user. There is no normal event that forces a conditional input check across multiple data entry fields on a form. Now save and run the project. You should see error messages when you attempt to violate the data entry rules on these controls.

Compiling and Registering the VText Control

Now that you have coded, saved, and tested the VText control, you are ready to create an ActiveX control (or OCX) from the file. Select File | Make OCX from the main menu. You are prompted to confirm the OCX name (keep CUSTOMVALIDATION.OCX) and, after you click OK, Visual Basic 5 creates a complete ActiveX control for your use. You use this control in the next, and final, section when you build the CompanyMaster form.

After creating the OCX, save the project group. This might also be a good time to take a short break before you move on to the last section of the chapter.

Building the CompanyMaster Input Form

Because you learned about data controls and form design in Day 4, "Creating Data Entry Forms with Bound Controls," and developed an ActiveX control to handle input validation in the first part of today's lesson, you are ready to design the first data entry form for the CompanyMaster data table.

Following are the four basic steps to coding data entry forms in Visual Basic 5:

- ☐ Define the basic form.
- ☐ Place input controls and prompts.
- ☐ Add and code command buttons.
- ☐ Code input validation.

You can use these steps in coding any forms for Visual Basic 5. You follow these steps while you construct the CompanyMaster data entry form.

Defining the Basic Form

The first step is to set the size of the data entry form, add the input palette, and add any frames needed. These are the basic components of the form. All other controls are placed upon the palette within the frames you install in this step.

TIP

If you put the palette and frames up first, you can place all other controls as so-called children of the palette and frames. This way, when you move the frame, all controls within that frame also move. The same thing happens when you move the large palette. Creating forms this way makes it easy to make slight adjustments later.

At this time, you also add the data control and the final exit button to the form. Use the information in Table 5.1 and Figure 5.19 as a guide for sizing and placing the basic form components.

Figure 5.19.

*Laying out the basic
form components of
the CompanyMaster
form.*

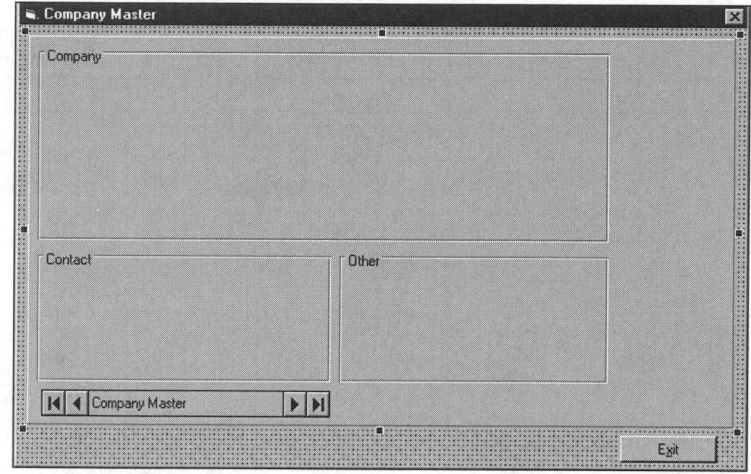

Save your form as MASTER.FRM, and save the project as MASTER.VBP.

Table 5.1. CompanyMaster form components.

Object	Property	Setting
Form	Name	frmMaster
	Border Style	1—Fixed Single
	Caption	Company Master
	Height	5955
	Left	195
	Max Button	False
	Top	330
	Width	9105
	Save Filename	Mast01.FRM
SSPanel	Caption	"" (blank)
	Height	4815
	Left	120
	Top	120
	Width	8715

continues

Table 5.1. continued

Object	Property	Setting
Data Control	BackColor	Light Gray
	Caption	Company Master
	DatabaseName	`C:\TYSDBVB5\DATA\MASTER.MDB`
	Height	330
	Left	300
	RecordSource	Company Master
	Top	4500
	Width	3615
Command Button	Name	cmdExit
	Caption	E&xit
	Height	330
	Left	7500
	Top	5100
	Width	1200
SSFrame	Caption	Company
	Height	2355
	Left	120
	Top	180
	Width	7155
SSFrame	Caption	Contact
	Height	1635
	Left	120
	Top	2640
	Width	3675
SSFrame	Caption	Other
	Height	1635
	Left	3900
	Top	2640
	Width	3375

5

Placement of Input Controls and Prompts

Now you are ready to place the input controls on the form. Each input control has an associated screen prompt. All screen prompts are done using the Visual Basic 5 Label control. You use VTextBox, MaskedEdit, and Check3D controls for input fields. You also use SSPanel3D controls for the read-only display fields.

NOTE

> Do not double-click controls onto the form. Always single-click the control icon in the Tools window, and then use the mouse to paint the control within the proper frame control. This ensures that the controls are children of the frame control and move whenever you move the frame. To play it safe, always select the panel by clicking it prior to selecting a control to place on it.

Because you are using the Win95 design specifications, you need to spend time aligning and sizing controls accordingly. All the information you need to properly size and place the controls is contained in Table 5.2 and Figure 5.20.

Figure 5.20.

Laying out the input controls and prompts.

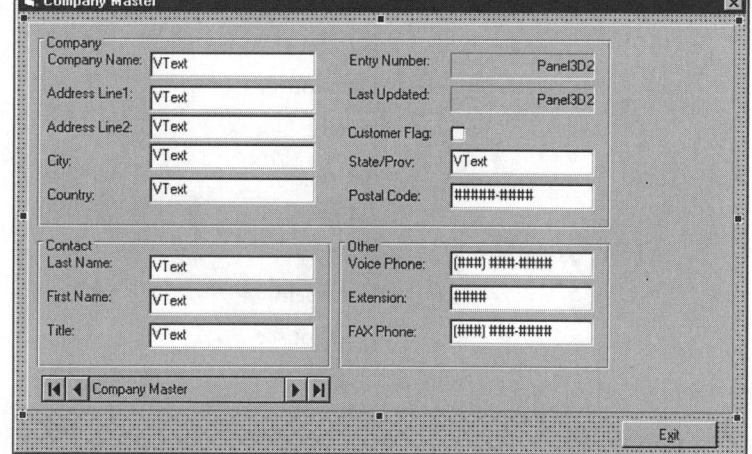

Table 5.2. CompanyMaster input controls and prompts.

Object	Property	Setting
VTextBox	Name	vxtCompanyName
	DataField	CompanyName
	DataSource	Data1
	Height	330
	Left	1380
	Top	240
	Width	2100
VTextBox	Name	vxtAddr1
	DataField	Addr1
	DataSource	Data1
	Height	330
	Left	1380
	Top	660
	Width	2100
VTextBox	Name	vxtAddr2
	DataField	Addr2
	DataSource	Data1
	Height	330
	Left	1380
	Top	1080
VTextBox	Name	vxtCity
	DataField	City
	DataSource	Data1
	Height	330
	Left	1380
	Top	1500
	Width	2100
VTextBox	Name	vxtCountry
	DataField	Country

Object	Property	Setting
	DataSource	Data1
	Height	330
	Left	1380
	Top	1920
	Width	2100
SSPanel3D	Name	pnlEntryNbr
	Alignment	4—Right Just Middle
	BevelOuter	1—Inset
	BorderWidth	1
	DataField	EntryNbr
	DataSource	Data1
	FontBold	False
	Height	330
	Left	5160
	Top	240
	Width	1800
SSPanel3D	Name	pnlLastUpdated
	Alignment	4—Right Just Middle
	BevelOuter	1—Inset
	BorderWidth	1
	DataField	LastUpdated
	DataSource	Data1
	Height	330
	Left	5160
	Top	660
	Width	1800
SSCheck3D	Name	chkCustFlag
	Alignment	1—Right Justify
	Caption	Customer Flag:
	DataField	CustFlag

continues

Table 5.2. continued

Object	Property	Setting
	DataSource	Data1
	Height	330
	Left	3900
	Top	1080
	Width	1455
VTextBox	Name	vxtStateProv
	DataField	StateProv
	DataSource	Data1
	Height	330
	Left	5160
	Top	1500
	Width	1800
MaskEdBox	Name	mskPostCode
	DataField	PostalCode
	DataSource	Data1
	Height	330
	Left	5160
	Mask	#####-####
	PromptInclude	False
	Top	1920
	Width	1800
VTextBox	Name	vxtLastName
	DataField	LastName
	DataSource	Data1
	Height	330
	Left	1380
	Top	240
	Width	2100
VTextBox	Name	vxtFirstName
	DataField	FirstName
	DataSource	Data1

5

Object	Property	Setting
	Height	330
	Left	1380
	Top	660
	Width	2100
VTextBox	Name	vxtTitle
	DataField	Title
	DataSource	Data1
	Height	330
	Left	1380
	Top	1080
	Width	2100
MaskEdBox	Name	mskVoicePhone
	DataField	VoicePhone
	DataSource	Data1
	Height	330
	Left	1380
	Mask	(###) ###-####
	PromptInclude	False
	Top	240
	Width	1800
MaskEdBox	Name	mskExtension
	DataField	Extension
	DataSource	Data1
	Height	330
	Left	1380
	Mask	####
	PromptInclude	False
	Top	660
	Width	1800
MaskEdBox	Name	mskFAXPhone
	DataField	FAXPhone

continues

Table 5.2. continued

Object	Property	Setting
	DataSource	Data1
	Height	330
	Left	1380
	Mask	(###) ###-####
	PromptInclude	False
	Top	1080
	Width	1800
Label	Caption	Company Name:
	BackStyle	0—Transparent
	Height	330
	Left	120
	Top	240
	Width	1200
Label	Caption	Address Line1:
	BackStyle	0—Transparent
	Height	330
	Left	120
	Top	660
	Width	1200
Label	Caption	Address Line2:
	BackStyle	0—Transparent
	Height	330
	Left	120
	Top	1080
	Width	1200
Label	Caption	City:
	BackStyle	0—Transparent
	Height	330
	Left	120
	Top	1500
	Width	1200

Object	Property	Setting
Label	Caption	Country:
	BackStyle	0—Transparent
	Height	330
	Left	120
	Top	1920
	Width	1200
Label	Caption	Entry Number:
	BackStyle	0—Transparent
	Height	330
	Left	3900
	Top	240
	Width	1200
Label	Caption	Last Updated:
	BackStyle	0—Transparent
	Height	330
	Left	3900
	Top	660
	Width	1200
Label	Caption	State/Prov:
	BackStyle	0—Transparent
	Height	330
	Left	3900
	Top	1500
	Width	1200
Label	Caption	Postal Code:
	BackStyle	0—Transparent
	Height	330
	Left	3900
	Top	1920
	Width	1200

5

continues

Table 5.2. continued

Object	Property	Setting
Label	Caption	Last Name:
	BackStyle	0—Transparent
	Height	330
	Left	120
	Top	240
	Width	1200
Label	Caption	First Name:
	BackStyle	0—Transparent
	Height	330
	Left	120
	Top	660
	Width	1200
Label	Caption	Title:
	BackStyle	0—Transparent
	Height	330
	Left	120
	Top	1080
	Width	1200
Label	Caption	Voice Phone:
	BackStyle	0—Transparent
	Height	330
	Left	120
	Top	240
Label	Caption	Extension:
	BackStyle	0—Transparent
	Height	330
	Left	120
	Top	660
	Width	1200

Object	Property	Setting
Label	Caption	FAX Phone:
	BackStyle	0—Transparent
	Height	330
	Left	120
	Top	1080
	Width	1200

NOTE Please note that we have used the U.S. nine-digit ZIP code in this exercise. You might want to modify this mask if you live in a country that has a different ZIP code format.

You need to add one more set of input controls to the form—the Company Logo controls. Refer to Table 5.3 and Figure 5.21 for sizing and placement of the Image control that holds the picture and the associated label control for the prompt. You add code behind the image control in the next section.

Figure 5.21.

Adding the Company Logo controls.

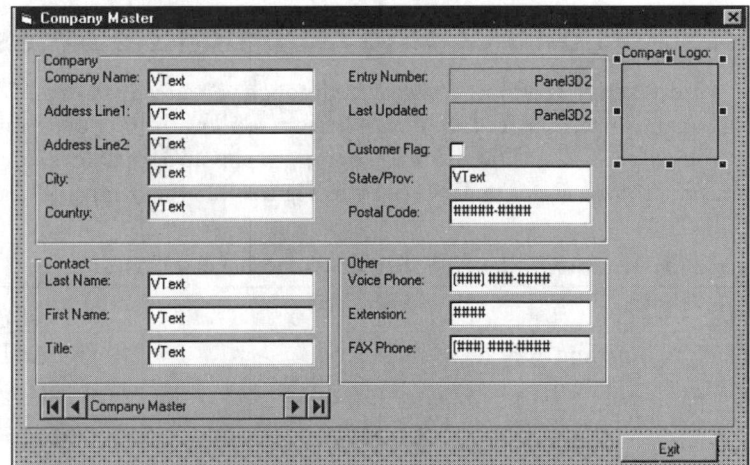

Table 5.3. CompanyMaster Company Logo controls.

Object	Property	Setting
Image	BorderStyle	1—Fixed Single
	DataField	CompanyLogo
	DataSource	Data1
	Height	1200
	Left	7380
	Stretch	-1 True
	Top	360
	Width	1200
Label	Caption	Company Logo:
	BackStyle	0—Transparent
	Height	330
	Left	7380
	Top	120
	Width	1200

Adding and Coding Command Buttons

Next, add the command buttons. Although you already have the Visual Basic 4 data control on the form, you need additional buttons to allow the user to perform adds, deletes, updates, finds, and so on. You also add a button to pop up a small form for adding comments to the data record. Refer to Table 5.4 and Figure 5.22 for sizing and placement information.

Table 5.4. CompanyMaster command buttons.

Object	Property	Setting
CommandButton	Name	cmdAdd
	Caption	&Add
	Height	330
	Left	7380
	Top	1620
	Width	1200

5

Object	Property	Setting
CommandButton	Name	cmdUpdate
	Caption	&Update
	Height	330
	Left	7380
	Top	2040
	Width	1200
CommandButton	Name	cmdRestore
	Caption	&Restore
	Height	330
	Left	7380
	Top	2880
	Width	1200
CommandButton	Name	cmdDelete
	Caption	&Delete
	Height	330
	Left	7380
	Top	3300
	Width	1200
CommandButton	Name	cmdFind
	Caption	&Find
	Height	330
	Left	7380
	Top	3720
	Width	1200
CommandButton	Name	cmdNotes
	Caption	&Notes
	Height	330
	Left	7380
	Top	4140
	Width	1200

5

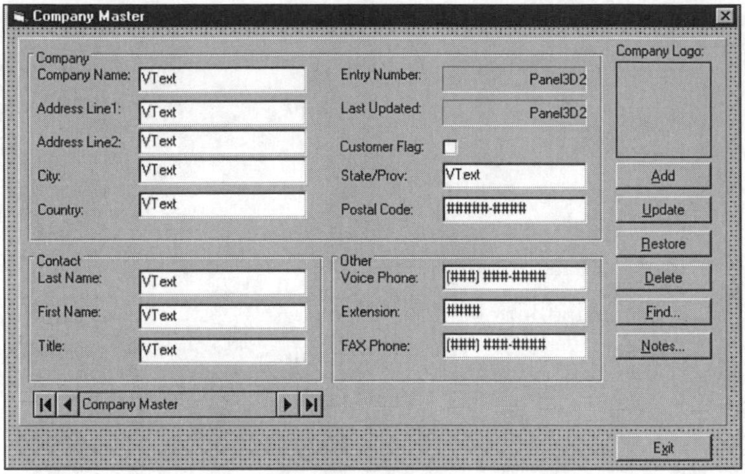

Figure 5.22.
*Adding the
CompanyMaster
command buttons.*

First, add the following line of code in the general declaration section of the form.

```
Dim nAddRec as Integer
```

The following code sections should be placed behind each button. You placed identical code behind other examples earlier this week. Begin with Listing 5.48, which shows the code to enter behind the cmdAdd command button.

TYPE **Listing 5.48. Adding data records.**

```
Private Sub cmdAdd_Click()
    '
    Data1.Recordset.AddNew ' add a new record to table
    nAddRec = True
    '
End Sub
```

Now add the code in Listing 5.49 to the cmdExit button. This code unloads the form when the Exit button is selected.

TYPE **Listing 5.49. Unloading the CompanyMaster form.**

```
Sub cmdExit_Click ()
  Unload Me ' close myself (better than END)
End Sub
```

Now enter the code in Listing 5.50 to the cmdFind_Click event. When executed, this code queries the user to enter an appropriate search string.

TYPE **Listing 5.50. Finding data records.**

```
Private Sub cmdFind_Click()
    '
    Dim nResult As Integer
    Dim cFind As String
    Dim cBookMark As String
    '
    cFind = InputBox("Enter Search String:", "CompanyMaster FIND")
    If Len(cFind) > 0 Then
        cBookMark = Data1.Recordset.Bookmark
        Data1.Recordset.FindFirst cFind
        If Data1.Recordset.NoMatch Then
            MsgBox "Can't Find [" & cFind & "]", vbExclamation, "Find Error"
            Data1.Recordset.Bookmark = cBookMark
        End If
    End If
    '
End Sub
```

The code in Listing 5.51 should be entered into the cmdRestore_Click event to restore the controls to their original value when the cmdRestore command button is selected.

TYPE **Listing 5.51. Restoring the data controls.**

```
Private Sub cmdRestore_Click()
    '
    nAddRec = False
    Data1.UpdateControls ' restore controls from table
    '
End Sub
```

Now enter code to save the data. Use Listing 5.52 as a guide and enter this code into the cmdUpdate_Click event.

TYPE **Listing 5.52. Writing a record.**

```
Private Sub cmdUpdate_Click()
    '
    If nAddRec = False Then
        Data1.Recordset.Edit
    End If
    '
```

continues

Listing 5.52. continued

```
    Data1.Recordset.Update ' write record to table
    '
    nAddRec = False
    '
End Sub
```

Listing 5.53 contains the code that should now be entered into the `cmdDelete_Click` event. This code deletes the displayed record after the user confirms the deletion.

TYPE **Listing 5.53. Deleting a record.**

```
Private Sub cmdDelete_Click()
    '
    Dim nResult As Integer
    '
    ' give user chance to reconsider
    nResult = MsgBox("Are you sure?", 1, "Delete Record")
    If nResult = 1 Then
        Data1.Recordset.Delete
        Data1.Recordset.MoveFirst
    End If
    '
End Sub
```

You need to add code behind the Image control to allow users to update the CompanyLogo field. Users should be able to locate a file on the disk, and then save it to the field. The form then displays the saved image. You can give users access to loading files by adding the Visual Basic 5 CommonDialog control to the form. Select the CommonDialog control from the Tools window and place it at the bottom of the form. It does not really matter where it is placed—the CommonDialog control is invisible at runtime. Once the control is on the form, add the code in Listing 5.54 to the `Image1_DblClick` event.

TYPE **Listing 5.54. Updating the company logo.**

```
Private Sub Image1_DblClick()
    '
    ' set dialog properties
    CMDialog1.Filter = "Bitmap (*.bmp)¦*.bmp¦Metafiles (*.wmf)¦*.wmf¦"
    CMDialog1.DialogTitle = "Load Company Logo"
    '
    ' run dialog box
    CMDialog1.Action = 1
    '
    ' if they picked a file, load it up
```

```
    On Error GoTo PicErr ' in case user picks a bad file
    If Len(CMDialog1.filename) <> 0 Then
        Image1.Picture = LoadPicture(CMDialog1.filename)
    End If
    '
    ' all done, go to exit
    GoTo PicExit
    '
    ' handle bad picture error
PicErr:
    MsgBox "Unable to load selected file.", vbExclamation, "Picture Error"
    Resume Next
    '
    ' final exit of procedure
PicExit:
    '
End Sub
```

The code in Listing 5.54 sets file type and caption properties of the common dialog box, runs the dialog, and then, if a file has been selected, attempts to save it to the image control. You add a little error trapping here in case the user selects an invalid file type.

Adding Input Validation

The last step in creating Visual Basic 5 data entry forms is adding the input validation routines. The following is a list of the input rules you should use when coding the validation routines:

☐ The following fields are required for each form:

CompanyName

Addr1

City

State/Province

☐ The following dependent field rules apply to the form:

If the Addr2 field has data, the Addr1 field must have data.

If the FirstName field has data, the LastName field must have data.

☐ The StateProv field should allow only uppercase data entry.

First, set the UpperCase property of the vxtStateProv control to True. This forces all data input into this control to upper case. You can accomplish most of these validation checks using the Required property of the new VText control. However, you also need to call the conditionalValidate method for the three controls that require conditional input.

5

To start, set the Required property to True for the following controls:

- ☐ CompanyName
- ☐ Addr1
- ☐ City
- ☐ State/Province

Next, you need to add message code in the error event of the required fields. Listing 5.55 shows the code to place in the various events.

TYPE **Listing 5.55. Coding the error messages for the required fields.**

```
Private Sub vxtAddr1_RequiredError()
    '
    MsgBox "This is a required field", vbExclamation, vxtAddr1.DataField
    '
End Sub

Private Sub vxtCity_RequiredError()
    '
    MsgBox "This is a required field", vbExclamation, vxtCity.DataField
    '
End Sub

Private Sub vxtCompanyName_RequiredError()
    '
    MsgBox "This is a required field", vbExclamation, vxtCompanyName.DataField
    '
End Sub

Private Sub vxtStateProv_RequiredError()
    '
    MsgBox "This is a required field", vbExclamation, vxtStateProv.DataField
    '
End Sub
```

Now you need to add the code that checks for conditional input. The best place to put the conditional code is in a single ValidateForm method. This covers all the field- and form-level validation in one pass. Listing 5.56 shows the ValidateForm method for this form. Create a new Sub called ValidateForm and enter the code from listing 5.56.

TYPE **Listing 5.56. Performing validation checks.**

```
Private Sub ValidateForm()
    '
    ' check required fields
    vxtCompanyName.CheckRequired
```

```
    vxtAddr1.CheckRequired
    vxtCity.CheckRequired
    vxtStateProv.CheckRequired
    '
    ' check conditional fields
    vxtAddr2.ConditionalValidate vxtAddr2.DataField, vxtAddr1.DataField,
vxtAddr1.Text
    vxtFirstName.ConditionalValidate vxtFirstName.DataField,
vxtLastName.DataField, vxtLastName.Text
    '
End Sub
```

After you enter this code, you need to add a few lines to the Data1_Validate event. The code in Listing 5.57 calls the validation routine each time the Update button is clicked or the arrow keys are pressed on the data control.

Listing 5.57. Calling validation routines when the Update button is pressed.

TYPE

```
Private Sub Data1_Validate(Action As Integer, Save As Integer)
    '
    ValidateForm
    '
End Sub
```

Summary

Today you learned how to perform input validation on data entry forms. You learned that input validation tasks can be divided into three areas:

☐ Key filtering: Preventing unwanted keyboard input

☐ Field-level validation: Validating input for each field

☐ Form-level Validation: Validating input across several fields

You also learned that you should ask yourself a few basic questions when you are developing validation rules for your form.

☐ Is it a required field?

☐ What characters are valid/invalid for this field? (Numeric input only, capital letters only, no spaces allowed, and so on.)

☐ For numeric fields, is there a high/low range limit? (Must be greater than zero and less than 1000, can't be less than 100, and so on.)

5

☐ Is there a list of valid values for this field? (Can the user enter only Retail, Whole-sale, or Other; Name must already be in the Customer table, and so on.)

☐ Is this a conditional field? (If users enter Yes in field A, then they must enter something in field C.)

You learned how to write keyboard filter validation functions using the Visual Basic 5 KeyPress event. You learned how to write field-level validation functions that check for valid input ranges, input that is part of a list of valid data, and input that is within minimum and maximum length requirements. You also learned how to write validation functions that make sure dependent fields have been filled out properly.

Finally, you learned how to use Visual Basic 5 to create your own custom control that incorporates all the validation techniques you learned in this chapter. You can use this ActiveX control in all your future Visual Basic projects.

You also applied your knowledge of bound data controls, Visual Basic 5 data entry form design, and validation processing to create the data entry form for the CompanyMaster data table.

Quiz

1. What is the difference between input validation and error trapping?

2. What value must you subtract from a lowercase character to get its uppercase ASCII value?

3. What Visual Basic 4 event occurs every time a key is pressed on your keyboard?

4. Do characters in a validation list need to be entered in any particular order?

5. What does the following code mean?

   ```
   If Len(Trim(txtUpper)) <> 0 then
   ```

6. Should conditional field validation be performed at the field level or the form level?

7. When should you load validation lists?

8. What do the three sections of the format property of the MaskedEdit control represent? What character separates these sections?

Exercises

1. Write code to allow entry of only capital letters in a field. The user should be able to enter control codes, but not numbers or symbols.

2. Write the format property for a MaskedEdit control that rounds the entered number to the nearest hundredth, includes commas in all numbers, and places an en dash (–) in front of negative numbers.

3. Write a form-level validation routine that requires that entry be made into a field named txtDate before a record can be saved by pressing a button named cmdOK.

4. Write the code to fill a combo box named cboEmployees with your employees' last names of Smith, Andersen, Jones, and Jackson. What property do you set in the combo box control to sort these names alphabetically?

5

Day 6

Creating Reports with Crystal Reports Pro

Today you'll learn how to create reports that can be called from within your Visual Basic 5 programs. To do this, you'll use Crystal Reports Pro, which ships with Visual Basic 5. You'll learn some basic concepts on how a report writer works, including:

- ☐ The concepts of report headers, detail lines, and footers
- ☐ The three main field types: database, text, and formula

When you have an understanding of the basics, you'll take a quick tour of Crystal Reports Pro to learn how to create list reports. Finally, you'll learn how to use the Crystal Reports Pro Control in Visual Basic 5 programs to run reports directly from your Visual Basic 5 applications.

What Is Crystal Reports Pro?

Crystal Reports Pro is a complete program that helps you define reports, save their definitions to disk, and then run these reports against databases to create final printouts. Crystal Reports Pro has an added feature that lets you run the final reports from within your Visual Basic 5 application using the Crystal Reports Pro control, which ships with Visual Basic 5.

Throughout this day, you'll use Crystal Reports Pro to illustrate concepts and to work out practice examples. Start Crystal Reports Pro now and follow along through the rest of the day. You can start Crystal Reports Pro in one of two ways: from the Visual Basic 5 main menu by selecting Add In | Report Designer, or by selecting the Crystal Reports Pro icon from the Visual Basic 5 program group. If you have not already done so, start Visual Basic 5 and select Report Designer from the Add Ins menu. (See Figure 6.1.)

Figure 6.1.

Starting Crystal Reports Pro from Visual Basic 5.

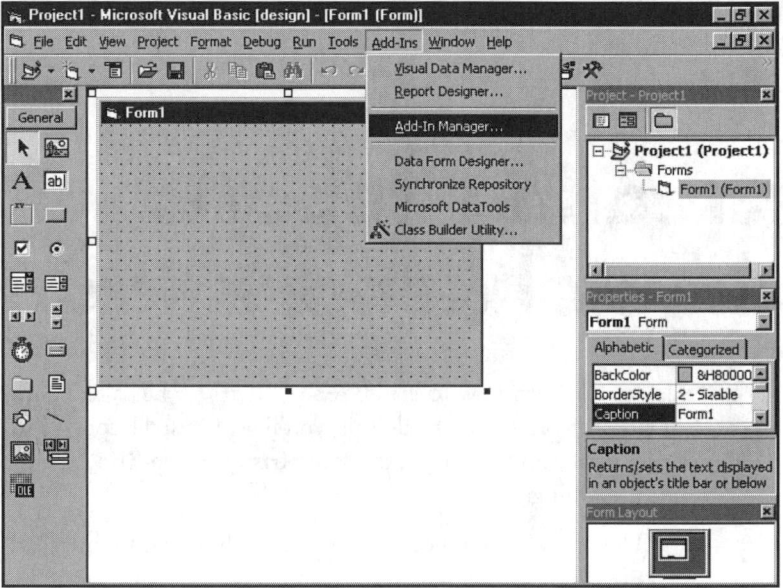

When you start Crystal Reports Pro, you'll see the Crystal Reports Pro greeting dialog box. Press Proceed to Crystal Reports Pro. You'll now see the main Crystal Reports Pro screen (see Figure 6.2). This is where you create, modify, and run your reports.

6

NOTE

You will see the Crystal Reports Pro Registration form the first time you load Crystal Reports Pro. Complete this form and follow its instructions to register your software. After it is completed, you will not see this form again.

Figure 6.2.

The Crystal Reports Pro main screen.

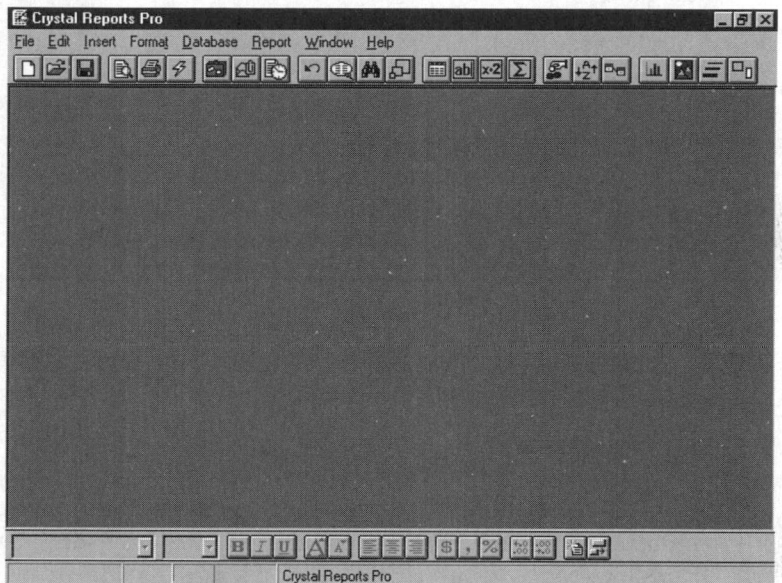

Crystal Reports Pro Bands

Crystal Reports Pro is a *banded report writer*. A banded report writer treats all output as "bands" of data. Each band has its own processes (such as functions it performs) and settings (properties) that you can manipulate in order to create the report layout and behaviors you need. Here are the main bands in Crystal Reports Pro:

- [ ] The header and footer bands
- [ ] The detail band

The header and footer bands contain information that appears at the top and bottom of every page of the report. This could be report titles, page numbers, print date and time, and so on. Every report has a header and a footer band.

The detail band contains the actual print lines. The detail band is the report version of a data table record. You use the report writer to lay out a detail band the same way you use a Visual

Basic 5 form to lay out a data entry screen. Detail bands can have more than one physical line. However, detail bands describe only one logical record.

Crystal Reports Pro Fields

Within each band, you place fields to be displayed. Crystal Reports Pro recognizes three types of fields:

☐ Database fields

☐ Text fields

☐ Formula fields

Database fields are fields taken directly from data tables in the database you open when you first start Crystal Reports Pro. You can load any database format recognized by the Visual Basic 5 database object (for example, Microsoft Access, FoxPro, dBASE), including ODBC data sources. You add fields by selecting them from a list of available fields and placing them in the desired location on the report form.

Text fields are fields that contain explicit text you want to appear on the report form. This text is not stored in a data table. An example of a text field is Print Date. If you want this text to appear at the top of every page, you create a text field that contains it and then you place it in the header band.

Formula fields are fields that are calculated results of either database fields or text fields (or a combination of both). Crystal Reports Pro requires you to declare a formula field name and then allows you to use any existing text field, database field, or other formula field as part of the new formula field. Formula fields can be numeric or character based. For example, if you want to print the value `Expiration Date:` followed by the database field DataTable.Expire, but do not want to have to place two field objects in the detail band, you can create a single formula field, called ExpDate, that contains the following expression:

```
"Expiration Date: "+DataTable.Expire
```

Crystal Reports Pro has several predefined formula fields available, along with a host of functions and operators that you can use to construct complex formulas, including the use of nested `If` statements to test data.

In the following sections, you'll begin a report definition to illustrate how bands and fields are used in Crystal Reports Pro.

NOTE   For the following exercise, please make sure that you have instructed Crystal Reports Pro to utilize the Report Gallery when starting a new report. To do this, Select File | Options..., and then select the New Report tab. The option Use Report Gallery for new reports should be checked.

The Detail Band

If you haven't already done so, start Crystal Reports Pro. Select New... from the File menu and then select Standard from the Create New Report dialog box. Next, click the Data File icon in the Create Report Expert Dialog. Locate and load the CRYSRPT.MDB Microsoft Access database file that ships with this book. It can be found in the ..\\TYSDBVB5\SOURCE\DATA directory. Your screen should look similar to the one shown in Figure 6.3. Click the database and select Add to load the database into the report. Press Done once the database is loaded.

Figure 6.3.

Loading a database with Crystal Reports Pro.

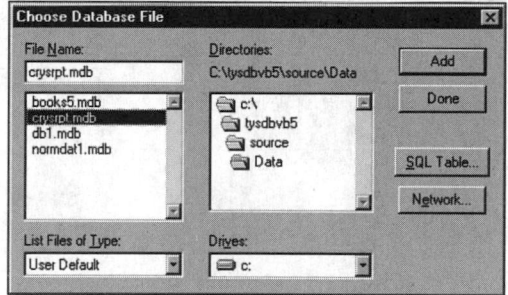

When the database is loaded, Crystal Reports Pro lets you move through the Create Report Expert tabbed dialog to create the report definition. Click the tab labeled 3:Fields to display a list of available tables and fields from the database. (See Figure 6.4.)

First, you'll add a database field to the detail band of the report. Double-click the EntryNbr field in the Database Fields box to add the field to the Report Fields. Now, click the Preview Report button to display the report and then select the Design Tab. Your report form should look like the one shown in Figure 6.5.

6

Figure 6.4.

Displaying fields for your report.

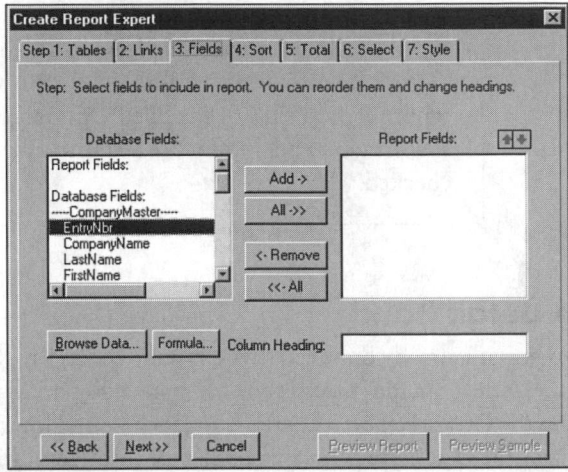

Figure 6.5.

Placing a database field in the detail band.

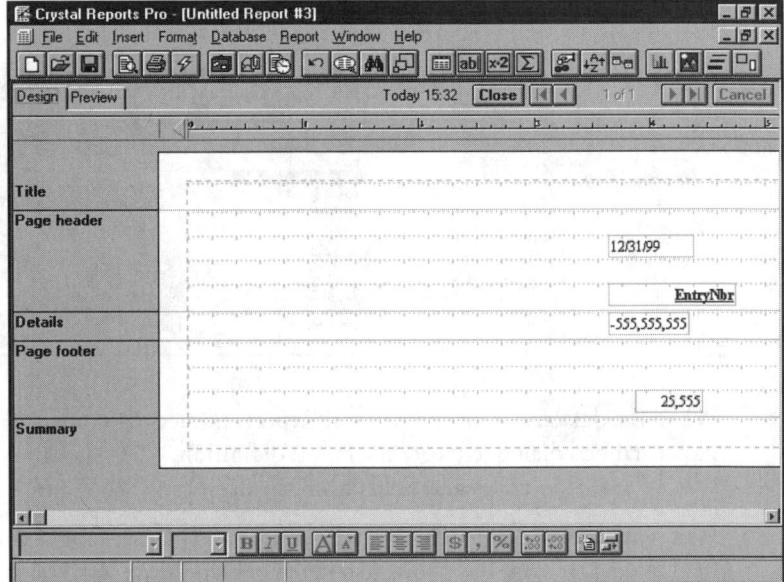

Now you'll add the company name and address to the detail band. But before you do this, expand the detail band to accept more than one line of data. Move the pointer over the solid line that separates the Details band from the Page Footer band. When the cursor turns to a double-sided arrow, press the left mouse button and pull down the detail band line to allow for several lines of data (just a rough guess at the size will do). When you are satisfied that the detail area is large enough, release the mouse button to drop the detail band line. (See Figure 6.6 for a reference.)

Figure 6.6.

Expanding the detail band.

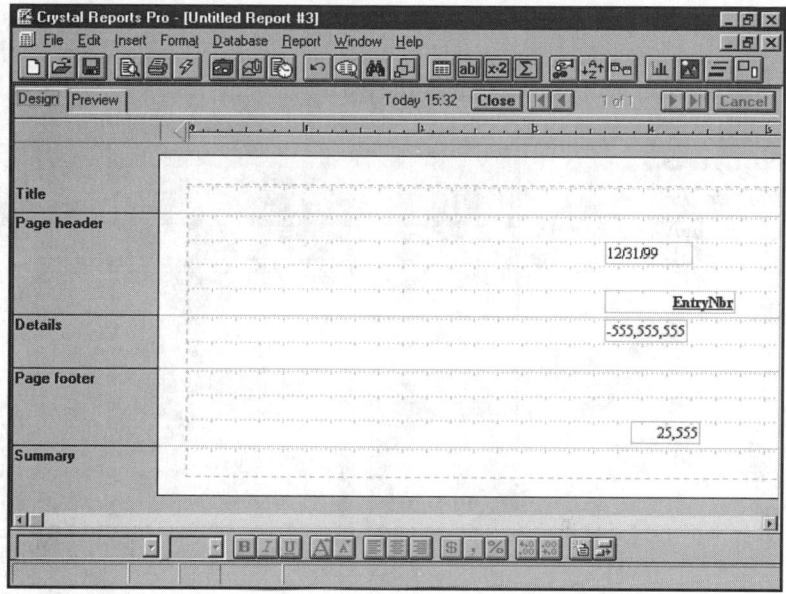

Now, we will add the following fields to the detail area. This can be done by selecting Insert | Database Field… from the Crystal Reports Pro Menu. A list box of tables and fields appears on your screen. Add the field by clicking it and dragging it to the Details band of the report.

 **TIP**

> It is sometimes easier to work with field names than with character holders in the Details Band. The option to view the field names can be selected by choosing File | Options… from the Crystal Reports Pro menu, and then checking the Show Field Names option on the Layout Tab.

- ☐ CompanyName
- ☐ Addr1
- ☐ Addr2
- ☐ City
- ☐ StateProv
- ☐ PostalCode

Place the CompanyName, Addr1, and Addr2 fields under each other and next to the EntryNbr field. Place the City, StateProv, and PostalCode fields together on one line. As you

6

place each field in the detail band, you'll see the field names appear, one on top of another, in the header section. Delete all the field names except CompanyName. See Figure 6.7 for the sizing and placement of the database fields.

Figure 6.7.

Placing the CompanyName and Address fields on the report.

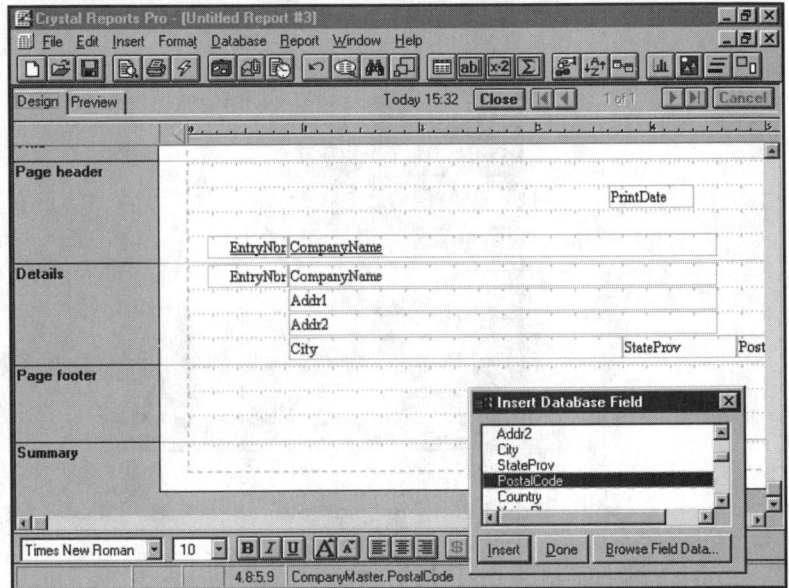

Before going any further, you should save this report definition. Select Save As… from the File menu. Enter COMAST1.RPT as the report name and then click OK to save the report. (See Figure 6.8.)

Figure 6.8.

Saving the report form as COMAST1.RPT.

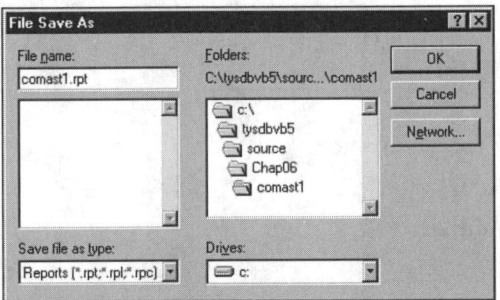

Now run the report to see whether everything is working. Select Print Preview from the File menu. Crystal Reports Pro automatically opens the data table, loads the records, and sends the report to a display window. You should see something like the example in Figure 6.9.

Figure 6.9.

Running the first report to a window.

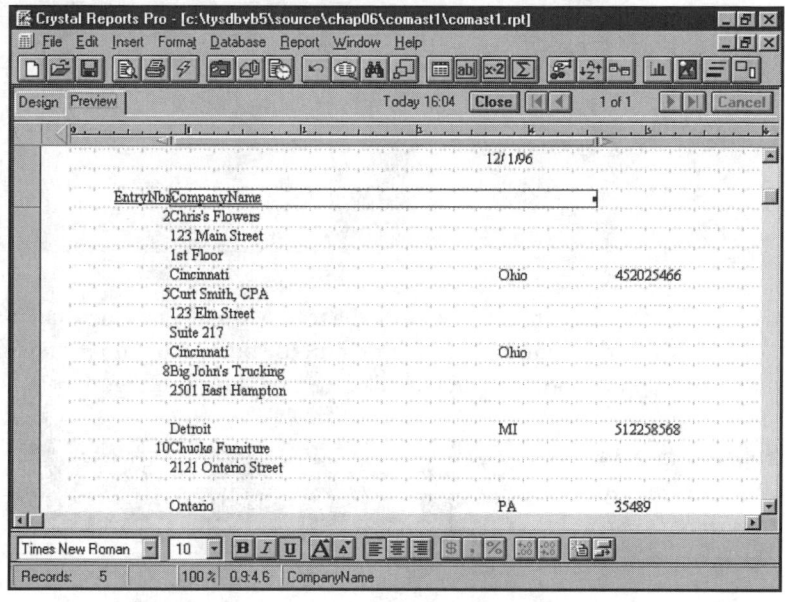

NOTE

To adjust your view of the report, you can zoom in and out by selecting Report | Zoom. You can also select between landscape and portrait orientation by selecting File | Printer Setup, and then selecting the desired orientation.

Notice that you can use this window to scroll up and down the page, to "walk" through the pages of the report, to zoom in and out, and to send the report to the default printer. These options are covered in more depth later. For now, select the Design tab to close the preview window.

The Header and Footer Bands

You can add information that appears at the top and bottom of every page by adding fields to the header and footer bands. Now, we will add a report title and date in the header band and a page number in the footer band.

6

You'll need to use a text field to create a report title for the header band. Select Text Field… from the Insert menu. Enter the text Company Master Report in the dialog box. (See Figure 6.10.)

Figure 6.10.

Creating a text field.

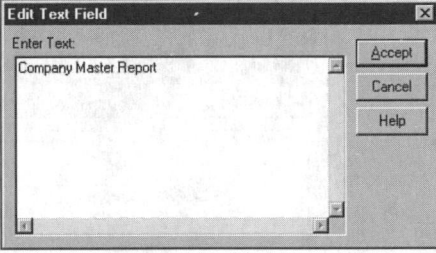

Click the Accept button to store the text. Move the rectangle cursor to the top center of the Page Header band and press the left mouse button to drop the text field on the header band. Your report form should look like the one shown in Figure 6.11.

Figure 6.11.

Dropping the text field in the header band.

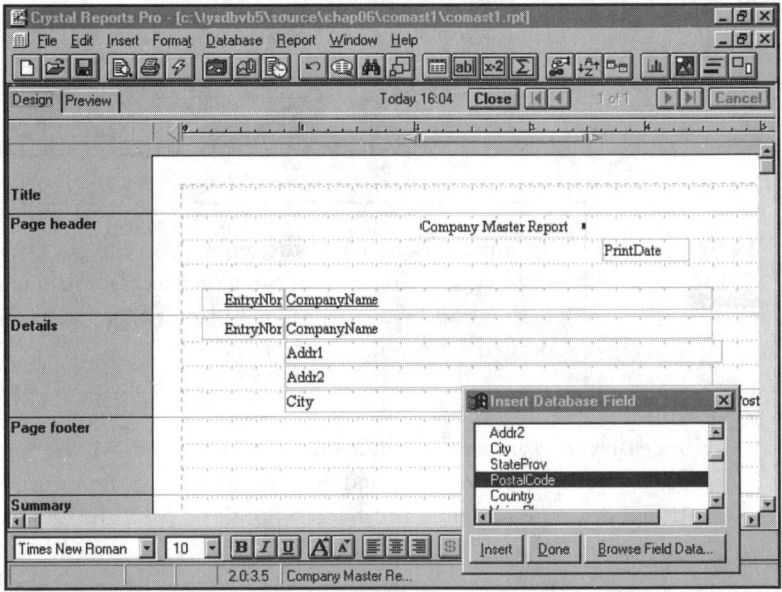

You can also add titles by typing text directly on the report form. This is easier than creating text fields, but it has its drawbacks. Once you type text on the form, you cannot move the text or resize it in any way. If you want to move the field later, you'll have to erase it and re-enter the data in the new location. If you use text fields, as in the preceding example, you can simply select the field and move it or resize it as needed.

To illustrate the process of adding text directly to the report form, move the cursor to the top-left corner of the report form and type Date:. Next, select Special Field | Print Date Field from the Insert menu. Now, move your rectangle cursor to a location near Date: and press the left mouse button to drop the report date onto the form. Your report form should now look like the one shown in Figure 6.12.

Figure 6.12.

Adding direct text and a date field to the report.

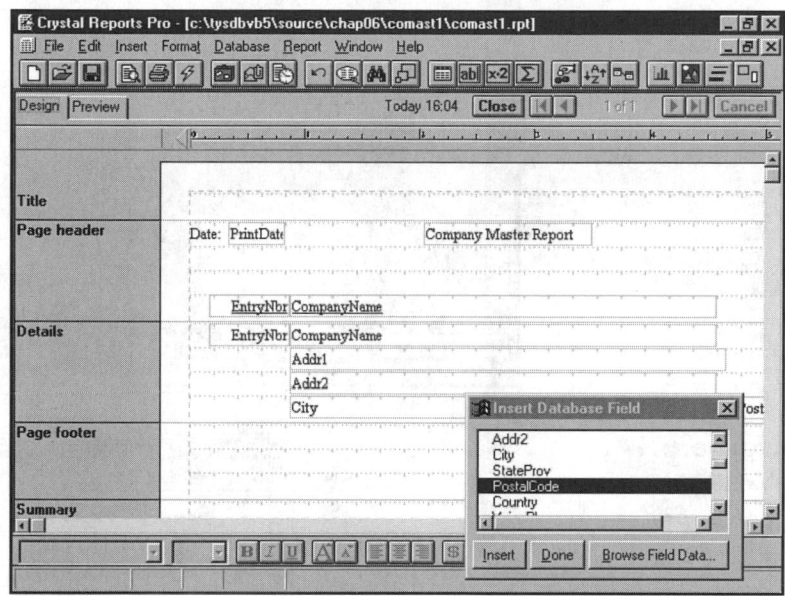

You can also add page numbers to the footer band. This time, create a text field that contains the text Page:. Place this text field at the bottom of the footer band. Select Special Field | Page Number Field from the Insert menu, and then place this field next to the text field. See Figure 6.13 for placement and sizing information.

Save and preview the report by selecting Print Preview from the File menu. You'll see the report title, print date, and page numbers appear on each page of the report.

You need to add one more improvement to your report. Notice how the City, StateProv, and PostalCode fields print very far apart? You need to allow enough space for long city names, but you do not want to see lots of empty space on the form. What you need is a formula field that combines all three fields into a single field that has extra spaces removed.

Select Formula Field... from the Insert menu. In the dialog box, enter CityLine as the name for the formula field. (See Figure 6.14.)

6

Figure 6.13.

Adding page numbers to the report form.

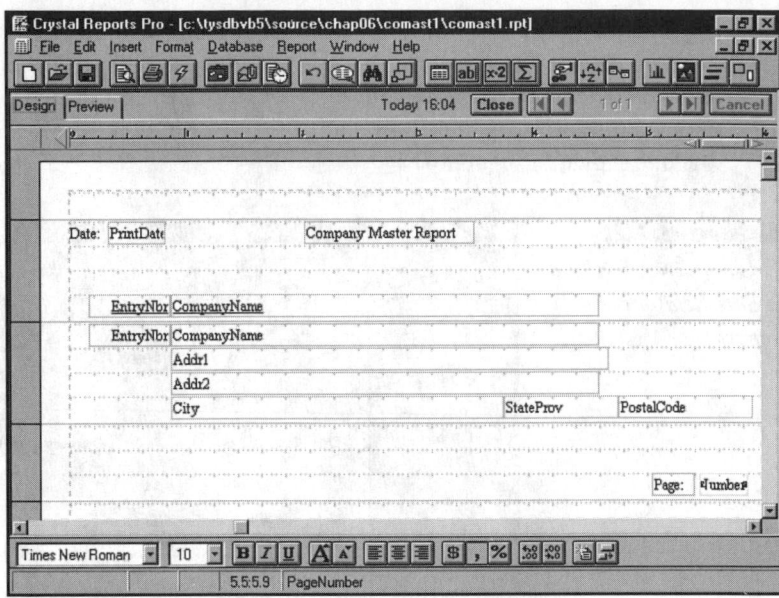

Figure 6.14.

Naming a new formula field.

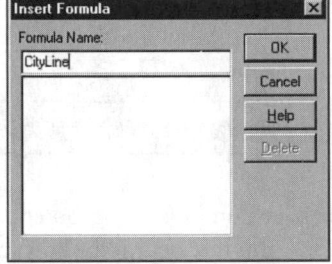

After you click OK, you'll see the formula window. This is where you put together the details of the CityLine formula. You see the following four sections in this window:

☐ Fields: This is a list of available database fields.

☐ Functions: This is a list of available Crystal Reports Pro functions.

☐ Operators: This is a list of arithmetic and logical operators.

☐ Formula Text: This is where you build your formula.

You can type all the information into the Formula Text window, or you can use your mouse to point-and-click items from the Fields, Functions, and Operators windows through most of the formula-building process. The point-and-click method saves time and reduces typing errors.

You need to remove trailing spaces from the right of the fields, so start the formula by double-clicking the `TrimRight()` function from the Functions list. Notice that when you add a function to the Formula Text window, your cursor is positioned ready to insert the required parameters. Because the cursor is already between the two parentheses of the `TrimRight()` function, double-click City from the Fields list. Crystal Reports Pro places the field name (along with the data table name) inside the `TrimRight()` function. (See Figure 6.15.)

Figure 6.15.

Adding the
`TrimRight()`
function and the City
field.

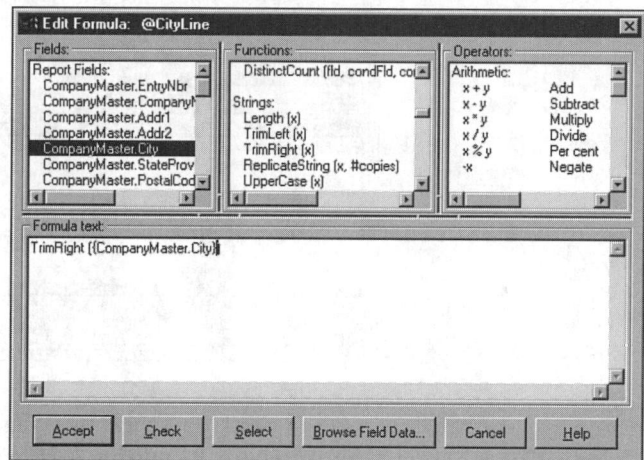

You need to add a similar function that does the same thing to the StateProv database field. First, move the cursor in the Formula text box to the end of the formula string and enter a plus sign (+). Next, add another `TrimRight()` function and insert the StateProv field into the function. Compare your screen to the one shown in Figure 6.16.

Figure 6.16.

Adding the
`TrimRight()`
function and the
StateProv field.

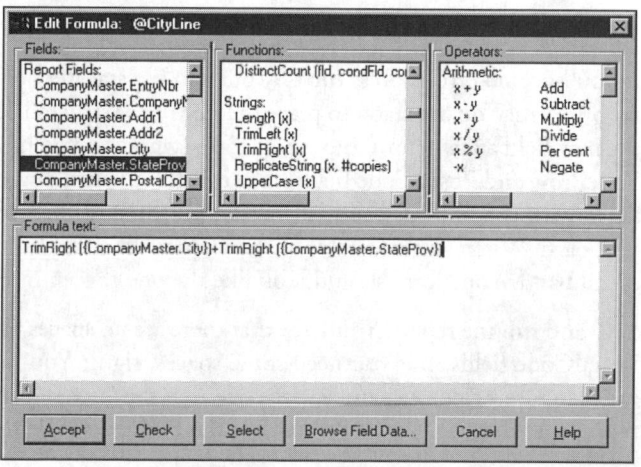

Now you need to add the PostalCode field to the formula. You don't need to trim spaces from the PostalCode field, so just add the plus sign and select the PostalCode field. Your formula should look like the one shown in Figure 6.17.

Figure 6.17.

Adding the PostalCode field to the formula.

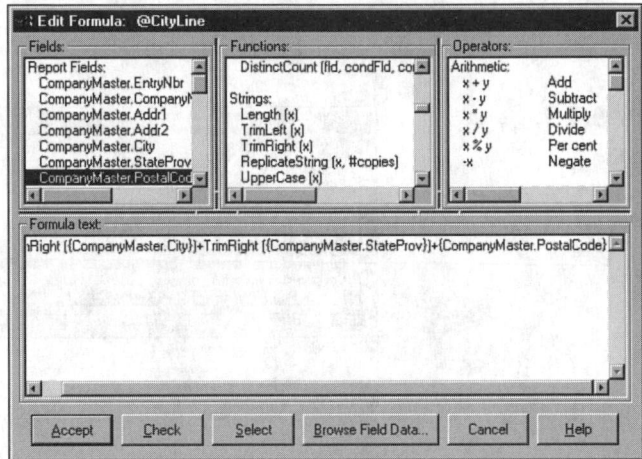

Before you save the field, you can check the syntax by using the Check button. When you click the Check button, Crystal Reports Pro Writer checks the formula for any errors and then reports the results in a message box. (See Figure 6.18.)

Figure 6.18.

Checking the formula.

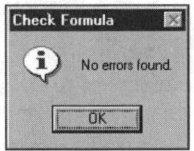

If you have no errors, press the OK button. Crystal Reports Pro Writer returns you to the report form. You are ready to place the newly constructed formula field on the form. Place the new field anywhere on the report form (wherever you have space). Next, delete the City, StateProv, and PostalCode fields from the detail band. You can do this by selecting all three fields with the Shift key and left mouse button and then pressing the Delete key on your keyboard. When all three fields are gone, move the CityLine formula field into place in the detail band. Your form should look like the one shown in Figure 6.19.

Save and run the report. You'll see that there are no spaces between the City, StateProv, and PostalCode fields. But you need some spaces, right? You need to edit the formula field in order to insert a comma and a space between the City and the StateProv fields and to insert two spaces between the StateProv and the PostalCode fields.

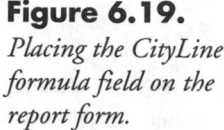

Figure 6.19.

Placing the CityLine formula field on the report form.

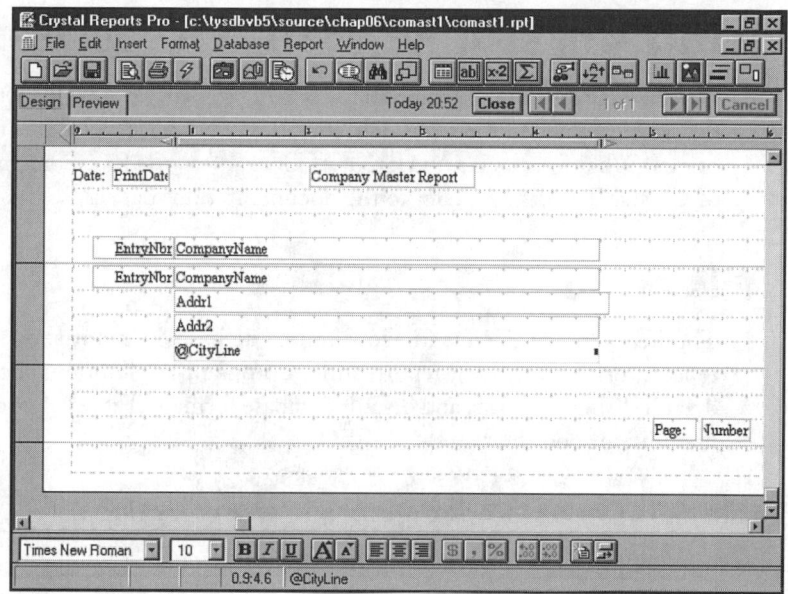

To edit an existing formula field, select the field by clicking it with the mouse. Then, select Formula from the Edit menu. Crystal Reports Pro presents the formula window with the CityLine formula already loaded. Go directly to the Formula text box and make the needed changes to the formula. Your formula should now look like the one shown in Figure 6.20.

Press the Accept button to save the formula; then save and run the report. You now see a much better looking final line on the address.

Figure 6.20.

Editing the CityLine formula.

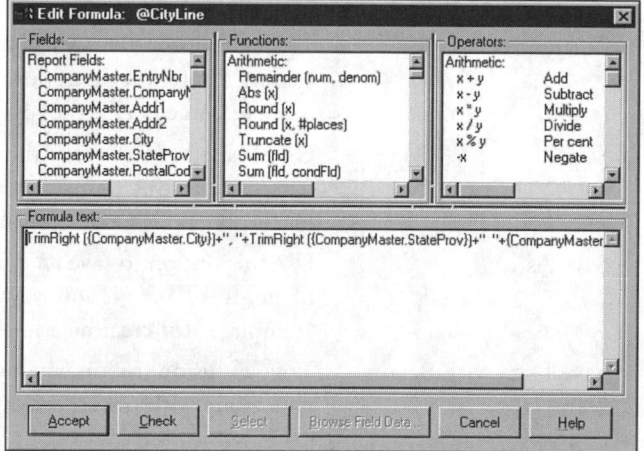

Using Crystal Reports Pro Writer

Crystal Reports Pro is a great tool for putting together simple list reports. It is also excellent for creating a wide variety of labels, including mailing labels, name tags, diskette labels, and others. What follows is a quick tour of Crystal Reports Pro. For a more in-depth treatment of Crystal Reports Pro, refer to the documentation that ships with Visual Basic 5.

File Menu

The items in the File menu allow you to define new reports, open existing reports, save reports, print the current report, and set program-level options such as default directories, default display formats, and default database formats. Table 6.1 contains a summary of the menu items and their uses.

Table 6.1. Crystal Reports Pro File menu options.

Menu option	Description
New...	Use this option to create a brand-new report. The Create Report Expert prompts you to select a database (even if you already have one open) after you select the type of report to create. Once the database is open, you can assemble a basic report by selecting fields from the Fields Tab in the Create Report Expert, or by manually adding fields by selecting Database Fields... from the Insert menu. You can create Cross Tab reports, Mailing Label reports, Summary reports, graphs, Top N reports, and Drill Down reports from the Create New Report dialog.
Open...	This selection prompts you to open an existing Crystal Report Pro report definition (*.RPT). When the definition is open, you can edit the report and save the changes.
Save	Use this selection to save the report definition to the current report name. If no name exists, you are prompted to supply one. The default file extension is .RPT.
Save As...	Use this option to save an existing report under a new name. It is handy if you want to use an existing report as a "template" for creating a new, slightly different report.
Save Data with Report	Toggle this option on when you want to store the report's data along with the report definition.
Close	This selection closes the current report. If you have made changes, you are asked whether you want to save the report definition before it is closed.

Menu option	Description
Print Preview	This selection displays the report on screen for your review.
Print | Preview Sample...	Use this option to generate a sample report. When you select this option, you are prompted to enter the number of records to display. This can be a time-saver, especially if you are generating a report that is ordinarily very long.
Print | Printer...	This selection sends the current report to the attached printer. See the Printer menu for more options.
Print | Export...	This selection allows you to print to a file in numerous formats, including Lotus, Excel, and HTML formats.
Print | Mail...	This option allows you to send the printed report by e-mail.
Print | Report Definition	This selection prints an abstract of the current report. Information is displayed regarding the fields, headers, database, formulas, and other items placed on the report.
Printer Setup...	This selection displays a dialog box of the current printer settings.
Page Margins...	This selection allows you to set the top, bottom, left, and right margins of the report.
Options	Use this item to set program-level defaults for all reports. You can set defaults for the directory to which reports are saved and the directory from which databases are read. You can also set the default database and index formats.
	You can set the default display formats for string, numeric, currency, date, and Boolean data formats. You can also set the default fonts for the header, footer, detail, group, and total bands.
	There are also several preference settings that control how Crystal Reports Pro displays menu bars, fields on a report, and so on.
Report Options...	Use this option to define how the current report handles data fields, indexes, print previews, and print engine error messages.
Exit	This selection exits Crystal Reports Pro. If you have made any changes to any open report definition, you are asked whether you want to save the changes before exiting.

6

Edit Menu

The Edit menu contains the usual Cut, Copy, Paste, and Clear options, plus several other options that allow you to edit formulas, text fields, and summary and group bands, as well as undo changes made to your report. See Table 6.2 for a brief summary of the Edit menu.

Table 6.2. Crystal Reports Pro Edit menu options.

Menu option	Description
Undo	This option allows you to reverse changes made to your report. For example, this option can be used to replace a field you inadvertently delete from the Detail band.
Redo	This function becomes available after the Undo function is performed. It performs the exact same process that was reversed by the Undo feature. This function, in conjunction with the Undo function, is a handy tool for "What if?" kinds of layout questions.
Cut	Use this selection to cut out selected text. This only works for text that is placed directly on the report form. It does not work for any field-type objects (database, text, or formula).
Copy	Use this selection to copy selected text from your report form to the Clipboard. This copies text that was placed directly onto a form and does not work for any field-type objects (database, text, or formula).
Paste	Use this selection to paste text from the Clipboard directly on the report form. This does not place the selected text into database, formula, or text fields.
Paste Special…	This selection allows you to use the Windows Clipboard to copy information from other applications and place the information into your Crystal Report. Objects can either be embedded or linked. If they are linked, changes in the source flow through to your report.
Select Fields	This item allows you to use a "lasso" to draw a rectangle around and select an entire group of objects. You can accomplish the same effect by holding the Shift key as you select objects; however, this process is not as quick.
Formula	Use this option to edit an existing formula field. First, you must select the formula field to edit; then you select this menu item to call up the formula editor.

6

Menu option	Description
Text Field	Use this option to edit an existing text field. First, you must select the text field to edit; then you select this menu item to call up the Text Field edit box.
Summary Field	Use this option to edit an existing summary operation field. First, you must select the summary field to edit; then you select this menu item to call up the Summary Operation dialog box. Summary options include Sum, Average, Min, Max, Count, Variance, and Standard Deviation.
Browse Field Data	Use this option to view a list of all the possible values in a data field. First, you must select the data field on the report form to browse; then you select this menu item to see a list box containing all the unique values for this field. You'll also see field definition information in the upper-left corner of the list box (string type, length 30, and so on). This is handy if you want to review the data behind the form while you are constructing a report.
Show/Hide Sections	This option displays a dialog box that allows you to hide or display different sections of your report. This option is also available by pressing the right mouse button while on a section heading.
Delete Section...	This option is available only when grouping is used in a report. Use this option to delete a grouping that has been added to a report.
Object	This menu item allows you to edit an OLE object that you have embedded in your report. An object must first be selected before you can choose this item. The types of objects within your report appear at the bottom of the Edit menu. Each object type has submenus of actions that can be performed on that type of object.
Links	This menu item allows you to update and change links to objects embedded within your report.
Query...	Use this option to edit a query used to extract data from an SQL data source. This option is only available when you are attached to an SQL data source such as Microsoft SQL Server.
Query Title...	Use this option to modify the title of the query. Again, this option is available only when you are attached to an SQL data source.
Refresh Data...	Use this option to update data used in this report. This option is only available when attached to an SQL data source.

6

Insert Menu

The Insert menu allows you to add database, text, and formula fields to your report definition. You can also add graphic images, lines, and boxes. Crystal Reports Pro gives you shortcuts to add page numbers, record numbers, print date, and group numbers to the report definition. The Insert menu is the menu you use to add new sections, subtotal bands, summary bands, and the report grand total band. Table 6.3 provides a short summary of the Insert menu options.

Table 6.3. Crystal Reports Pro Insert menu options.

Menu option	Description
Database Field	Use this option to select a field from the attached database. You can select any field in any table. You can select the same field more than once.
Text Field	Use this option to create a text field for your report form. After you create the text field, you can manipulate the format, font, and color the same way you can in a database field.
Formula Field	Use this option to create a new formula field or edit an existing formula field. Select this menu item and you see a list box showing all the formula fields defined for this report. If you double-click one of the fields in the list, you see the formula editor with the selected formula loaded, ready for editing. If you type in a new formula name, you see the formula editor ready for you to create a new formula.
Special Field | Page Number Field	Use this option to create a page number field for your Page Number Field report form. This field always reports the current page number.
Special Field | Record Number Field	Use this option to create a record number for your report. This field always reports the current sequential record number in the selected records as sorted by the report. This field does not report the position of the record in the physical table, but the position of the record in the sorted report list.
Special Field | Group Number Field	Use this option to create a group number field to place on Group Number Field reports. This field can be used to report counts of group breaks within the report.

6

Menu option	Description
Special Field | Print Date Field	Use this option to create a Today's Date field to place on your report form. This field reports the date on which the report is printed.
Subtotal	Use this option to create a subtotal band for your report form. First, you must select a numeric field to subtotal. When you create a subtotal field, a new section is created automatically (if it does not already exist). You can select the grouping field to use for each subtotal as well as the sort order of the grouping field.
Grand Total	Use this menu item to create a grand total band on your report form. First, you must select a field to total, and then you select this menu item. You do not have to select a numeric field for the grand total band because the grand total band can report a count as well as a numeric total.
Summary	Use this option to insert fields for counts, sums, averages, minimums, maximums, sample variances, sample standard deviations, population variances, or population standard deviations of selected fields.
Group Section	This option allows you to set the points at which your report will break and total.
Group Name Field...	Use this option to insert a field that contains the text that uniquely identifies each group. This is a good tool to use to place a caption at the beginning of each group. A group must be inserted into the report before this option can be executed.
Line	Use this item to draw lines on your report. After a line has been placed on the report, you can resize it using the mouse pointer. You can set the line thickness, type, and color by double-clicking anywhere on the line to call up a dialog box.
Box	Use this item to place a box anywhere on the report form. You can use the mouse pointer to resize the box. When you double-click the selected box, you'll call up a dialog box that lets you set the border style, thickness, and color. You can also set the fill color of the box.

6

continues

Table 6.3. continued

Menu option	Description
Picture...	Use this item to place a bitmap graphic image on your report. When you select this item you'll be shown the Choose Graphics dialog box, which you use to locate a graphic image file. When you select a file and press OK, Crystal Reports Pro allows you to place and size that image anywhere on the report.
Graph/Chart Expert...	Use this option to invoke a dialog that assists in the creation of a graph that can be placed on the report.
Object...	This option allows you to select and insert an OLE object into your report. You can either embed or link the object.

Format Menu

The Format menu gives you options for changing the font, borders, color, and display format of existing fields. You use this menu to edit the graphic, line, and box objects on your report. You can also set formatting options for existing section bands of your report. Table 6.4 provides a short summary of the Format menu options.

Table 6.4. Crystal Reports Pro Format menu options.

Menu option	Description
Report Style Expert...	The Report Style Expert is a set of pre-defined report style templates that can be assigned to the report. Just select this option from the Format menu and choose the desired style from the list box that appears.
Auto Arrange Report	This option, when invoked, arranges the fields and labels into a neat arrangement.
Font	Use this menu item to edit the font attributes of the selected fields. You must first select one or more fields; then you select this menu item.
Field	Use this menu item to change the display format of the selected field. Different dialog boxes appear depending on the field type selected.
Border and Colors	Use this menu option to set field colors, to set borders around fields, to set the width of the borders, to add shadows to the borders, and so on.

6

Menu option	Description
Change Line Height...	Use this option to adjust the height of the selected row. Please note that this option is disabled when a field or an object is selected.
Line...	Use this menu item to modify the thickness, type, and color of existing line objects on the report form.
Box...	Use this menu item to modify the attributes of a box object already on the report form.
Picture...	Use this option to set the cropping, scaling, sizing, and positioning of a selected picture.
Graph/Chart...	Use this item to modify the sizing, scaling, and positioning of graphic images loaded from the Insert	Graph/Chart menu item. (Refer to Table 6.3.)
Section	Use this menu item to set attributes of all the sections (bands) of the report. There are several attributes that can be set from this dialog box, but not all apply to all objects. They are Hide Section, Print at Bottom of Page, New Page After, New Page Before, Reset Page Number After, Keep Section Together, Suppress Blank Lines, and Format with Multi-Columns.

Database Menu

The Database menu can be used to set and update table links, to add and remove database files, to establish table aliases, to correct naming conflicts, to make sure the data set currently in use by Crystal Reports Pro is updated, and to log on or off ODBC data sources. Table 6.5 provides a short summary of the Database menu options.

Table 6.5. Crystal Reports Pro Database menu options.

Menu option	Description
Visual Linking Expert...	Use this option to view and modify relationships that exist between related tables in the database used in the current report.
Add Database to Report	Use this menu item to add additional database files to your report definition. It is possible to have more than one Microsoft Access database as a source for your report definition.

continues

Table 6.5. continued

Menu option	Description
Remove from Report	Use this menu item to remove a database file from your report definition.
Set Location	This option allows you to set the physical location of the databases being used in your report. This option is extremely helpful if databases are moved or if network mappings vary for the users of your reports.
Set Alias	Use this menu item to establish helpful alias names for the tables in your report. Using meaningful alias names can make it easier to maintain your reports in the future.
Verify Database	Selecting this menu item forces Crystal Reports Pro to refresh all data tables used in the report. This is a one-time action that makes sure you have the most up-to-date data to work with for your report.
Verify on Every Print	This menu item is a toggle on/off option. When the item is toggled on, Crystal Reports Pro performs a refresh each time it runs the report. This is an "automated" version of the Verify Database menu option.
Log On Server…	Use this menu item to attach an ODBC data source to the report definition.
Log Off Server…	Use this menu item to detach an ODBC data source from the report definition.
Show SQL Query…	Use this option to view the SQL query that Crystal Reports Pro is generating and sending to your data source. You can edit the query that is being used by Crystal Reports Pro to extract data from your SQL data source.
Stored Procedures Parameters…	Use this option to review the details of the procedures maintained in your SQL data source.

Report Menu

The Report menu contains all the options for record selection, grouping, and sorting. Also available are options for database refreshing and report defaults. Table 6.6 provides a short summary of the Report menu options.

Table 6.6. Crystal Reports Pro Report menu options.

Menu option	Description
Select Records Expert...	Use this menu item to create record-level selection criteria for your report. You must first select a report field to use as the start of your criteria. You are then prompted to select from a list of criteria that includes >, <, =, as well as other operators.
Edit Selection Formula | Record...	This function is similar to the Select Records menu item. The Formula difference is that this function allows you to work in the Crystal Reports Pro script language in order to write your Pick criteria.
Edit Selection Formula | Group...	This option allows you to set the selection criterion for the groups to appear on this report.
Change Group Expert...	This option makes it easier for you to change how the data is grouped. This allows you to experiment easily with the layout grouping of the current report.
Top N/Sort Group Expert...	Use this option to create reports that extract data based upon a defined percentage. For example, you might use this option to generate a report that selects the top 10% of items sold for the first quarter by your company.
Sort Records...	Use this menu item to establish the sort order of the report. When you select this item, you'll see a sort dialog box that lists all the possible sort fields on the left and shows the selected sort order on the right. You can use more than one report field in the sort criteria. Also, you can indicate an ascending or descending sort at the field level.
Search...	Use this option to find records based upon criteria defined in the dialog displayed by this selection. This option can be used only while in Preview mode. Searched for records are highlighted when located.
Search Again...	Redo the search defined by the Search... menu selection.
Zoom	This option allows you to change the size of the report displayed on the screen.
Refresh Report Data	Crystal Reports Pro automatically retrieves data under only a few circumstances while in print preview mode. Use this option to reload your data if you suspect that it changed since the last time you previewed the report.
Report Title...	Use this option to place a title on the current report.
Set Print Date...	Use this option to toggle between the default system date, or to define a date to appear in the date field of this report.

6

Calling the Report from Within Visual Basic 5

When you have developed and saved your report definition using Crystal Reports Pro, you are ready to modify your Visual Basic 5 program to run the report from within your Visual Basic 5 application. Throughout the rest of this day, you'll be modifying the data entry form you built on Day 5, "Input Validation." If you haven't done so yet, start Visual Basic 5 and load the CompanyMaster data entry program you created on Day 5.

The Crystal Reports Pro Control

It is very easy to run reports defined using Crystal Reports Pro from Visual Basic 5. Crystal Reports Pro for Visual Basic 5 ships with a special control (the Crystal Reports Pro Control) that can be added to any Visual Basic 5 form. Once you drop the control on your form, you only need to set a few properties to get a report printout from your program. The control has several properties that you can alter when setting up or running a report.

First, place the Crystal Reports Pro Control onto the CompanyMaster data entry form. It doesn't matter where you place the control because it's invisible at runtime. Once you have placed the control on the form, set the ReportFileName property to C:\TYSDBVB5\SOURCE\ CHAP06\COMAST1\COMAST1.RPT and the WindowTitle property to Company Master Report. Leave CrystalReport1 as the default name for the control. Next, add a command button to the form. Refer to Figure 6.21 for placement and sizing.

Figure 6.21.

Adding the Print command button.

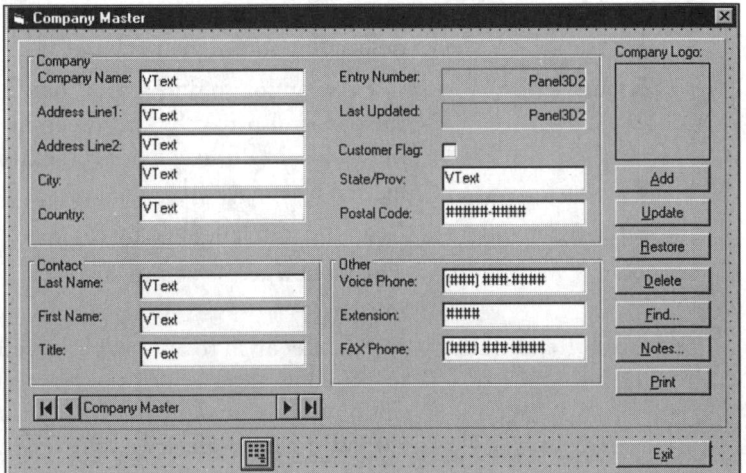

Use the information in Table 6.7 to set the properties of the command button.

Table 6.7. Property settings for the Print command button.

Control	Properties	Settings
Command Button	Name	cmdPrint
	Caption	&Print
	Font	Ms Sans Serif
		Regular, 8 point
	Height	330
	Left	7440
	Top	4080
	Width	1200

Now add the following line of code behind the cmdPrint_Click event (this code line starts Crystal Reports Pro):

```
Private Sub cmdPrint_Click()
    CrystalReport1.Action = 1 'force Crystal Reports Pro to run report
End Sub
```

Now save and run the program. When you click the Print button, Crystal Reports Pro creates the report and sends it to a screen window. You can preview this report in the window and, if you like, use the Print button on the report window toolbar to send the report to the printer. (See Figure 6.22.)

Figure 6.22.

Viewing the report from Visual Basic 5.

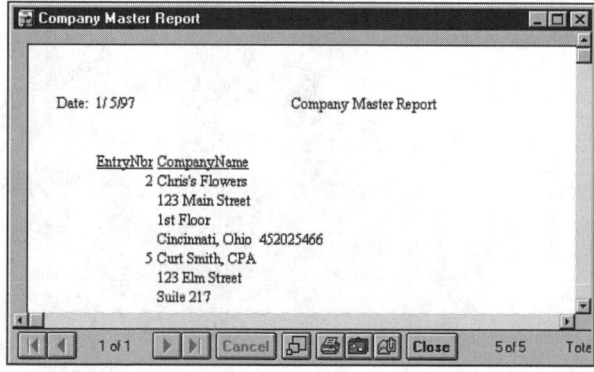

Designing the Print Report Dialog Box

There are a handful of report parameters that you can set using the Crystal Reports Pro Control. Instead of setting them in Visual Basic 5 code, you'll create a simple report dialog box that can be used to set the most common parameters. This dialog box is *portable*, so you can use it in any future Visual Basic 5 program.

Use Figure 6.23 and the information in Table 6.8 to construct a generic Print Report dialog box. Please note that you will be adding text boxes that have their Visible property set to False, meaning that they won't appear at runtime. These controls should simply be placed in a convenient position (such as the open space between the Printer Setup and Exit command buttons).

Figure 6.23.

Building a generic Print Report dialog box.

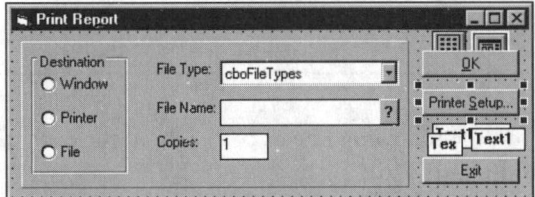

Table 6.8. Control information for the Print Report dialog box.

Control	Property	Setting
Form	Name	frmReport
	BackColor	Light Gray
	Caption	Print Report
	Height	2475
	Width	6540
	Save As	Report.frm
Command Button	Name	cmdOK
	Caption	&OK
	Height	330
	Left	5100
	Top	240
	Width	1200
Command Button	Name	cmdPrnSetup
	Caption	Printer &Setup
	Height	330

Control	Property	Setting
	Left	5100
	Top	720
	Width	1200
Command Button	Name	cmdExit
	Caption	E&xit
	Height	330
	Left	5100
	Top	1560
	Width	1200
SSPanel	BorderWidth	1
	Caption	(blank)
	Height	1815
	Left	120
	Top	120
	Width	4815
Text Box	Name	txtReportName
	Visible	False
Text Box	Name	txtWindowTitle
	Visible	False
Text Box	Name	txtReportDBName
	Visible	False
Common Dialog	Left	5700
	Top	1
Crystal Report	Left	5200
	Top	1
SSFrame	Caption	Destination
	Height	1515
	Left	120
	Top	120
	Width	1200

6

continues

Table 6.8. continued

Control	Property	Setting
SSOption	Name	opt3dDest(0)
	Caption	Window
	Height	330
	Left	120
	Top	240
	Width	1000
SSOption	Name	opt3dDest(1)
	Caption	Printer
	Height	330
	Left	120
	Top	660
	Width	1000
SSOption	Name	opt3dDest(2)
	Caption	File
	Height	330
	Left	120
	Top	1080
	Width	1000
Combo Box	Name	cboFileTypes
	Left	2475
	Style	2 – DropDown
	Top	240
	Width	2220
Text Box	Name	txtFileName
	Height	330
	Left	2475
	Text	(blank)
	Top	720
	Width	1995

6

Control	Property	Setting
Command Button	Name	cmdFileName
	Caption	"?"
	Height	330
	Left	4440
	Top	720
	Width	260
Text Box	Name	txtCopies
	Height	330
	Left	2475
	Text	1
	Top	1140
	Width	600
Label	BackStyle	0 – Transparent
	Caption	File Type:
	Height	330
	Left	1680
	Top	240
	Width	900
Label	BackStyle	0 – Transparent
	Caption	File Name:
	Height	330
	Left	1680
	Top	720
	Width	900
Label	BackStyle	0 – Transparent
	Caption	Copies:
	Height	330
	Left	1680
	Top	1140
	Width	900

6

Adding the Print Report Dialog Box Code

After you have constructed the form, you need to add some code behind the form. First, declare two form-level variables in the declarations section. You'll use these variables to set the properties of the Crystal Reports Pro Control:

```
Option Explicit

Dim cFileName As String
Dim cReportName As String
```

The `LoadFileTypes` procedure loads the various report file types recognized by Crystal Reports Pro into a drop-down combo box. Add this procedure to your project:

```
Private Sub LoadFileTypes ()
    '
    ' load type selections
    cboFileTypes.Clear
    cboFileTypes.AddItem "Record"
    cboFileTypes.AddItem "Tab Separated"
    cboFileTypes.AddItem "Text"
    cboFileTypes.AddItem "DIF"
    cboFileTypes.AddItem "CSV"
    cboFileTypes.AddItem "*RESERVED*"
    cboFileTypes.AddItem "Tab Separated Text"
End Sub
```

The code in the `Form_Activate` event initializes the form caption and the Crystal Reports Pro window caption. It also checks to see that a report name and database name have been passed to the form. This is where you load the combo box, too.

```
Private Sub Form_Activate ()
    '
    ' fix up form caption
    If Len(Trim(Me.txtWindowTitle)) = 0 Then
        Me.txtWindowTitle = "Print Report"
    End If
    Me.Caption = Me.txtWindowTitle
    '
    ' check for passed database name
    If Len(Trim(Me.txtReportDBName)) = 0 Then
        MsgBox "Missing Database Name!"
        Unload Me
    End If
    '
    ' check for passed report name
    If Len(Trim(Me.txtReportName)) = 0 Then
        MsgBox "Missing Report Name!"
        Unload Me
    End If
    '
    ' set default copies
    txtCopies = 1
    '
    LoadFileTypes ' fill drop down list box
End Sub
```

The following code section handles the selection of the report destination. Notice that this code toggles the enabled/disabled properties of the file-related controls. The controls are kept disabled unless the user select the "file" destination option. Here's the code:

```
Private Sub opt3dDest_Click (Index As Integer, Value As Integer)
   Dim nFile As Integer
   '
   ' send report to window
   If opt3dDest(0) = True Then
      CrystalReport1.Destination = 0
      nFile = False
   End If
   '
   ' send report to printer
   If opt3dDest(1) = True Then
      CrystalReport1.Destination = 1
      nFile = False
   End If
   '
   ' send report to file
   If opt3dDest(2) = True Then
      CrystalReport1.Destination = 2
      nFile = True
   End If
   '
   ' enable/disable file controls
   txtFileName.Enabled = nFile
   cboFileTypes.Enabled = nFile
   cmdFileName.Enabled = nFile
End Sub
```

The next section of code calls the Visual Basic 5 common dialog box to allow the user to select a filename as the destination for the report output. Notice the use of the &H2 value in the Flags property. This forces the common dialog box to issue a warning message if the user selects a filename that already exists. Once a valid file is selected, it is loaded into a form-level variable for later use. Here's the code:

```
Private Sub cmdFileName_Click ()
   '
   ' set some parms
   CMDialog1.DialogTitle = "Save Report File Name"
   CMDialog1.Filter = "Text (*.txt)¦*.txt¦"
   CMDialog1.Flags = &H2
   '
   ' run the save as dialog
   CMDialog1.Action = 2
   '
   ' load the selected filename into control
   If Len(CMDialog1.Filename) > 0 Then
      cFileName = CMDialog1.Filename
   End If
   Me.txtFileName = cFileName
End Sub
```

6

You need a bit of code to enable the Print Setup command button. Notice that you set the Flags property to &H40. This forces the common dialog box to display the Printer Setup dialog box. Here's the code:

```
Private Sub cmdPrnSetup_Click ()
   CMDialog1.Flags = &H40 ' force the printers setup dialog box
   CMDialog1.Action = 5 ' run the printer setup
End Sub
```

The code for the OK command button is the most involved of the form. This routine performs input validation, sets final report properties, sets up an error trap, and then runs the Crystal Reports Pro report. The input validation should look familiar. Note that an additional input validation test had to be invented to check the combo box. After the validation pass, a few properties of the report control are set. Afterwards, the report is generated.

The report run is wrapped in an error-trapping routine. Error trapping is covered in greater detail next week. For now, you should note that after the error trap is turned on, the code attempts to erase the output filename, if necessary, and then runs the report. Once the report is done, the error trapping is turned off.

The error routine is simple. It displays a Message box for any error encountered, except for the error that occurs when the user attempts to erase a file that does not exist. Here's the code:

```
Private Sub cmdOK_Click ()
   Dim nOK As Integer ' validation results
   Dim nVldErr As Integer ' validation pass/fail flag
   Dim cMsg As String ' report error string
   Dim cTitle As String ' error title
   '
   ' perform validation
   If CrystalReport1.Destination = 2 Then
      nOK = IsValid(txtFileName, "Save File Name", True)
      If nOK = False Then
         nVldErr = True
      End If
      '
      If cboFileTypes.ListIndex = -1 Then
         MsgBox "Missing Print File Type", 0, "Validation Error"
         cboFileTypes.SetFocus
         nVldErr = True
      End If
   End If
   '
   ' did we find an error?
   If nVldErr = True Then
      GoTo OKExit ' leave now!
   End If

   '
   ' set some final parameters
   CrystalReport1.WindowTitle = txtWindowTitle ' set the window title
```

```
      CrystalReport1.DataFiles(0) = txtReportDBName ' set the database location
      CrystalReport1.ReportFileName = txtReportName ' set the report location
      CrystalReport1.CopiesToPrinter = txtCopies ' set the copies parm
      '
      ' if it's going to a file
      If cboFileTypes.ListIndex <> -1 Then
          CrystalReport1.PrintFileType = cboFileTypes.ListIndex
          CrystalReport1.PrintFileName = txtFileName
      End If
      '
      On Error GoTo ReportErr   ' set error trap
      Kill txtFileName          ' delete file if it's there
      CrystalReport1.Action = 1       ' run report
      On Error GoTo 0           ' turn off error trap
      GoTo OKExit               ' exit sub

  '
  ' report any error you get
  ReportErr:
      If Err <> 53 Then ' skip file not found msg
          '
          ' see if the error is from CRW
          If CrystalReport1.LastErrorNumber <> 0 Then
              cMsg = Str(CrystalReport1.LastErrorNumber)
              cMsg = cMsg + ":" + CrystalReport1.LastErrorString
              cTitle = "Crystal Reports Pro Error"
          Else
              '
              ' error was from VB
              cMsg = Str(Err) + ":" + Error$(Err)
              cTitle = "Visual Basic Error"
          End If
          '
          ' show the error # and text
          MsgBox cMsg, 0, cTitle
      End If
      Resume Next

  '
  ' end of this procedure
  OKExit:
  End Sub
```

Finally, you need a bit of code behind the Exit button:

```
Private Sub cmdExit_Click ()
    Unload Me
End Sub
```

Save the form as REPORT.FRM before you continue. You now need to make a few changes to the code behind the Print button on the CompanyMaster data entry form. You'll get rid of the Crystal Reports Pro Control on the main form because you have one on the Print Report dialog box now. You'll also set two parameters behind the Print button before you call the Print Report dialog box.

> **TIP**
>
> Notice in the following code that you load the form (without showing it), set the values of the form's controls, and then show the form modally. This is a good way to pass parameters between forms—load it, pass them, show it.

```
Private Sub cmdPrint_Click ()
    '
    ' load the next form
    Load frmReport
    '
    ' set values on the next form
    frmReport.txtReportDBName = "c:\tysdbvb5\source\data\Crysrpt.mdb"
    frmReport.txtReportName = "c:\tysdbvb5\source\chap06\comast1\comast1.rpt"
    frmReport.txtWindowTitle = "Company Master Report"    '
    ' show the form modally
    frmReport.Show 1
End Sub
```

Now save and run the project. You should see the Company Master Report dialog box prompting you to set parameters for your print job. (See Figure 6.24.)

Figure 6.24.

Running the Company Master Report dialog box.

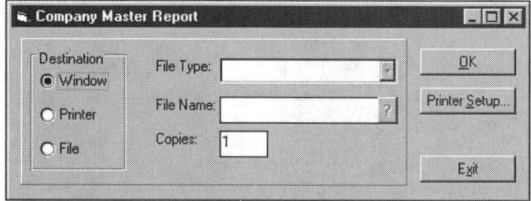

Not only have you finished a report routine for the `CompanyMaster` project you have been working on this week, but you now have the Print Report dialog box, which can be used in any future Visual Basic 5 project that uses the Crystal Reports Pro report writer.

Summary

Today you learned how to use the Crystal Reports Pro report writer to create a simple list report using the data tables you created earlier in the week. You also learned that Crystal Reports Pro is a banded report writer. Here are the main bands in a report:

- ☐ The header and footer bands: These bands appear on every page.
- ☐ The detail band: This band contains the equivalent of a data table record.
- ☐ The section band: This band contains subtotals or groupings of the data.

You also learned that Crystal Reports Pro recognizes three types of fields on the report form:

☐ Database fields: These fields are from attached data tables.

☐ Text fields: These fields are made up of literal text created by the user.

☐ Formula fields: These fields are calculated fields created by the user.

You also learned how to use the Crystal Reports Pro Control to run a report from within your Visual Basic 5 program. Finally, you created the Print Report dialog box, which lets you control the report destination, the file type, and the number of copies printed.

Quiz

1. List and describe each of the three bands in a Crystal Report.
2. To which database types can Crystal Reports Pro attach?
3. How do you insert text directly on a Crystal Reports Pro design form?
4. How do you produce mailing labels in Crystal Reports Pro?
5. In Crystal Reports Pro, can you browse data contained in a database that you are using for a report?
6. How do you insert selection criteria in a Crystal Reports Pro report?
7. How do you join tables in Crystal Reports Pro?

Exercises

1. Write a formula that can be used in Crystal Reports Pro to count the number of records in a list of last names. Assume a field name of NameLast.
2. Write a formula to display a list of vendors that have not supplied their federal tax ID numbers to your accounting manager. This information is stored in a field named EmployerID.
3. Build a Crystal Reports Pro report using the BOOKS5.MDB database that can be found in the TYSDBVB5\SOURCE\DATA directory of the CD that shipped with this book. Before starting, select File | Options, select the New Report tab, and de-select the Use Report Gallery for new reports option. Include the following items in your report:

   ☐ Insert the fields PubID, Publisher, and Comments from the PublisherComments table.

   ☐ Modify the page to print in landscape mode.

6

☐ Insert the Name field from the Publishers table. Make sure that a link exists between the PubID field in the Publisher Comments table to the PubID field in the Publishers table.

☐ Set a descending sort order on the Publishers.Name field.

☐ Insert the report title Comments on Publishers. Format this title with Arial, 14 point bold text.

☐ Insert a grand total record count.

☐ Insert a page number at the bottom right of the page footer.

☐ Insert the current date at the bottom left of the page footer.

☐ Print the report and the report definition when you have finished the layout.

Day **7**

Using the Visdata Program

Today you will learn everything you need to know about using one of the most valuable sample programs that is shipped with Visual Basic 5—the Visdata sample application. You'll learn how to use the Visdata sample application to maintain your database files, including creating and modifying database tables, performing simple data entry on existing tables, and using Visdata to make backup copies of existing databases.

NOTE

This lesson does not cover the source code for Visdata or talk about how Visdata works. You can, however, learn a great deal by bringing the Visdata project up within Visual Basic 5 and studying the modules and forms. Studying Visdata in this manner is an excellent way to learn how to create dynamic data entry forms, handle SQL processing, and link your Visual Basic 5 programs to back-end database servers using ODBC drivers.

Using Visdata to Maintain Databases and Tables

Visdata is an excellent tool for constructing and managing databases for your Visual Basic 5 applications. You can use it to create new databases, add or modify tables and indexes, establish relationships, set user and group access rights, test and store SQL query statements, and perform data entry on existing tables.

Visdata can present dynamic data entry forms in page format or grid layout format. You can add, edit, or delete records in any table using Visdata. You can connect to Microsoft Jet versions 1.1, 2.0, or 3.0 databases, as well as versions of dBASE, FoxPro, and Paradox. You can even access data from Excel spreadsheets, delimited text files and ODBC-connected databases. Visdata is a great tool for building sample tables and entering test data for your Visual Basic 5 applications. It is also a good tool for compacting, repairing, and managing user and group access rights for Microsoft Jet databases.

Visdata allows you to test SQL queries and save them in your Microsoft Jet database as stored queries that you can access from your Visual Basic 5 programs. You can also use Visdata to copy records from one table to another—even to copy whole data tables from one database to another. This capability gives you the power to create backups of selected information from your existing databases.

Finally, you can use Visdata to inspect the properties of Microsoft Jet data objects such as fields, relationships, tables, and indexes. You can learn a great deal about how the Microsoft Jet database engine operates by using Visdata to peek under the hood to see the heart of the Visual Basic 5 data access engine.

7

The Visdata Opening Screen

If you don't already have Visdata running, start it now. You can start Visdata by selecting Visual Data Manager... from the Add-Ins menu. Once started, select File | Open Database... | Microsoft Access..., and then open the BOOKS5.MDB database that shipped with the CD included with this book. Your screen should look like Figure 7.1.

Figure 7.1.

The Visdata main screen.

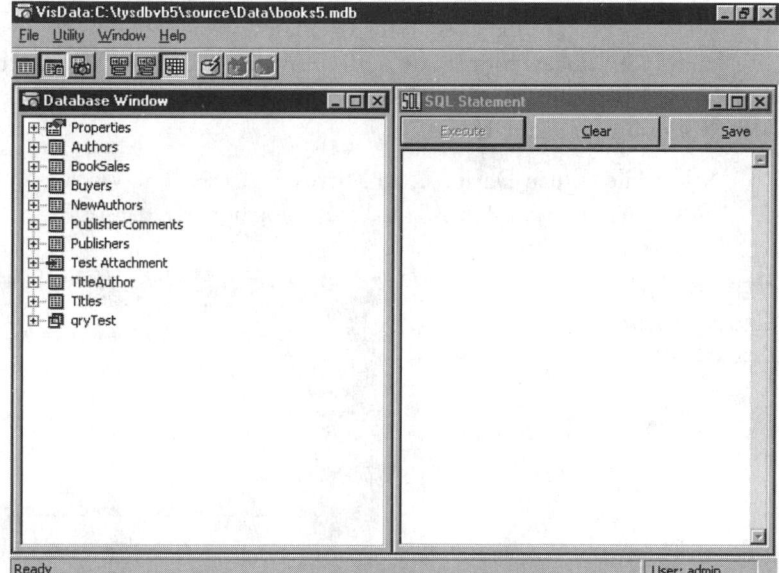

This MDI form is "Data Central" for the Visdata application. All database activity starts from this screen. Four major components of this screen deserve attention:

☐ The Main Menu: This menu gives you access to all the features of Visdata. This menu also expands once you open a database.

☐ The Database Window: This window shows all the properties and table objects present in the database you currently have open.

☐ The SQL Statement Window: This window allows you to write and execute standard SQL statements against the database you currently have open.

☐ The Toolbar: You use this to determine the type of data objects you want to work with.

Now let's go through each of the four components of the Visdata main screen in a bit more depth.

7

The Main Menu

The Visdata Main Menu contains four menu items: File, Utility, Window, and Help. The Utility menu item is enabled once a database is opened.

The Visdata Main Menu gives you access to all the features and options of the program. You'll learn each menu option in depth later, but first, let's explore the File menu options just a bit.

The File | Open Database… option, which we used in the preceding section, allows you to open an existing database. This database can be any one of several formats. The most common database format you'll probably deal with is the Microsoft Jet format (also known as the Microsoft Access database format). For practice, let's use Visdata to open an existing Microsoft Jet database.

Select File | Open Database… | Microsoft Access. The Visdata program presents you with an Open Microsoft Access Database dialog box (see Figure 7.2).

Figure 7.2.

Opening a Microsoft Access database.

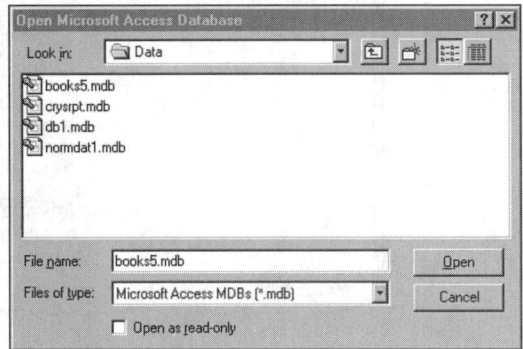

Locate and select the BOOKS5.MDB database that can be found in the \TYSDBVB5\SOURCE\DATA directory on the CD that ships with this book. Click the Open button to load the database. Once the database is loaded, Visdata updates the Database window to show all the primary data access objects in the currently opened database. Your screen should now look something like Figure 7.3.

You can close the database by selecting File | Close from the Visdata main menu.

The Database Window

The Database window shows all the major data access objects in the currently opened database. The Database window is where you go to add new tables to the database and modify the design of one of the current tables. You can also open existing data tables to add records to them. If you click the alternate mouse button within the Database window while you have a table highlighted, you see several other table management options.

Figure 7.3.

Visdata with an open database.

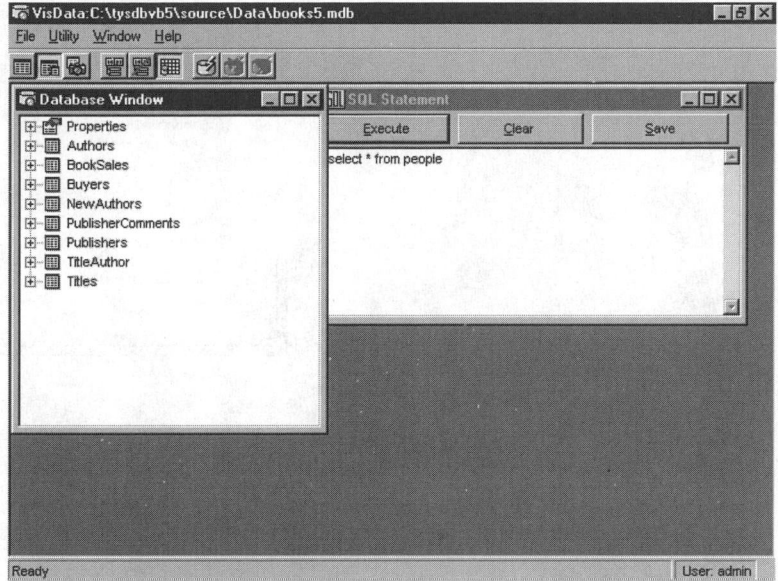

 **NOTE**

We use the term "alternate mouse button" to avoid any confusion between left-handed and right-handed users. If you have your mouse set for left-handed use, the alternate button is the left button; if you have your mouse set for right-handed use, the alternate button is the right button.

Properties

The Properties object shows the various properties of the opened database. With the BOOKS5.MDB database open, click the + sign next to the Properties object. Your screen should look like Figure 7.4.

 **NOTE**

Many of the properties listed on this screen are available only in the Version 3.0 Microsoft Jet MDB format. Don't be alarmed if your screen has several empty fields. You learn more about the difference between the various MDB formats later.

7

Figure 7.4.
Viewing the database
properties.

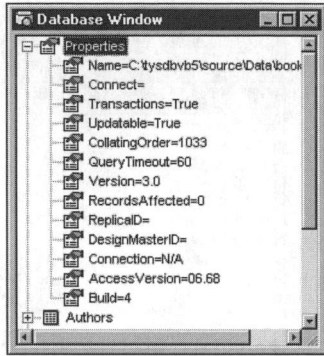

Open

The Open alternate mouse option loads the selected table. It performs the same function as double-clicking the table name.

Design

The dDesign option brings up the table Structure design dialog. You can view, edit, and add fields and indexes from this screen. Try this with a few tables so you can get a feel for the information available in the Design dialog.

Rename

The Rename option allows you to rename the highlighted table without deleting the data. Highlight the Authors table by clicking it once with the primary mouse button. Now click the alternate mouse button to bring up the context menu. Select Rename from the menu and enter MoreAuthors as the new name, and then press Enter. Your screen should look like Figure 7.5 as you rename the Authors table.

Before you continue with the project, change the MoreAuthors table back to Authors using the same technique previously described.

Delete

The Delete option lets you delete the highlighted table and all its contents. To delete a table and all its contents, select the table you want to delete and click the alternate mouse button.

Select the MoreAuthors table and click the alternate mouse button to bring up the context menu. Select Delete from the list. Click Yes at the confirmation dialog message to delete the MoreAuthors table. Your window list refreshes automatically.

Figure 7.5.

Renaming a data table.

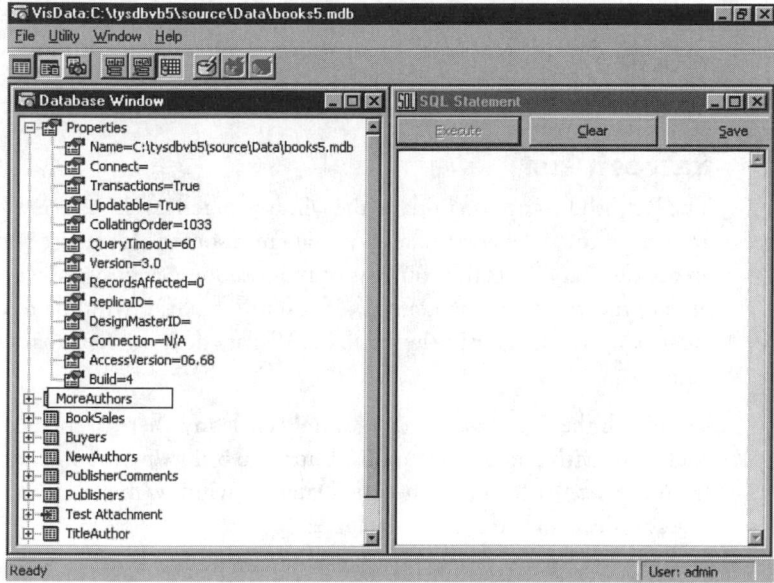

Copy Structure

The Copy Structure… option lets you copy the highlighted table's field layout and design, with or without existing data, to a different database. Select the Authors table and click the alternate mouse button to bring up the context menu. Select Copy Structure… from the menu list, and you see a dialog box like the one in Figure 7.6.

Figure 7.6.

Copying a table.

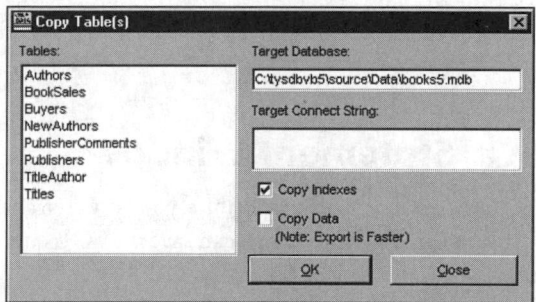

Notice that you can enter a new database name and connect string in the dialog box. This capability means you can copy the structure to an entirely different database. Leave the database name and connect string alone for now. Check the Copy Indexes and Copy Data checkboxes, click on the Authors table in the Table list box, and click OK. You are then prompted for a table name. Enter MoreAuthors and click OK. A message from Visdata

7

appears, telling you that the new table has been created. When you exit the dialog by clicking Close, Visdata refreshes the Window List automatically. You should now see a new table in the list—MoreAuthors.

Refresh List

The Refresh List option updates the window to reflect changes in the data access objects that are part of the database. Usually, Visdata refreshes the Database window each time you take an action that affects the contents of the list. Some actions, however, do not automatically update the window. For example, if you use the SQL window to enter SQL statements to create a new data table in the database, Visdata does not automatically refresh the Database window.

To refresh the Database window, simply click anywhere in the Database window, and then click once with the alternate mouse button to bring up the context menu. Select Refresh List from the list. Visdata refreshes the Database window to reflect the current state of the data access objects in the opened database.

New Table

This option displays the Table Structure dialog, which can be used to construct a new table or index. We work on building new tables in the section entitled "Adding Tables and Indexes to the Database" later in this chapter.

New Query

This option displays the Visdata Query Builder, which can be used to help build SQL statements. We discuss the Query Builder when describing the Utility menu later in this chapter.

The SQL Statement Window

The SQL Statement window enables you to enter and execute standard SQL statements against the opened database. You can save the SQL query for later use in your Visual Basic 5 programs.

Select the SQL Statement window by clicking the top border of the window one time. Now enter the following SQL query into the text window:

```
SELECT * FROM Authors
```

Now, make sure that the Use DBGrid Control on New Form icon, located at the top of the Visdata window, is selected, and then select the Execute button in the SQL Statement

window to run the query. This is not an SQL Passthrough query, so answer No when prompted with this question.

This statement selects all the data in the Authors table and presents it to the screen. Your screen should look like the one in Figure 7.7.

Figure 7.7.

Results of an SQL query.

AUID	Name	DOB	Contracted
1	Smith, John	4/25/62	-1
2	Rodgers, Bill	12/17/45	0
3	Tailor, Mark	12/15/55	-1
4	Thompson, Carol	2/2/69	0
5	Jackson, Sharon	6/25/65	-1
6	Burns, Timothy R.	11/11/66	0
7	Bishop, Diane	12/12/60	0
8	Kennedy, Martin Jr.	7/14/75	0
9	Victor, George	7/15/65	0
10	DeSilvia, Carl	12/31/49	-1
11	Richards, Becky	10/22/63	0
12	Mullaney, Terrance (	4/1/32	0
13	Thompson, James E.	6/30/66	0
14	Valley, Margo	8/14/55	-1
15	Cruis, Jonathon	4/15/50	-1

Right Click for Data Control Properties

NOTE

We will cover SQL SELECT queries in depth in the lesson on Day 8, "Selecting Data with SQL." For now, just remember that you can write, test, and save your SQL queries using the Visdata SQL window.

You can save this query for later use within your Visual Basic 5 programs by first closing the screen that contains the result of your Select query and then clicking on the Save button in the SQL Statement window. Next, supply the query object name qryTest, and click OK in the dialog box that appears (see Figure 7.8). Again, this is not an SQL Passthrough query, so answer No when the SQL Passthrough dialog appears.

Each time you load Visdata, the program remembers the last SQL query you entered in the SQL window. You can click the Clear button to clear out the text in the SQL Statement window.

The Toolbar Buttons

Icons appear on a toolbar near the top of the Visdata main screen. You use these icons to establish the type of data object Visdata uses to access the data and the type of data entry form Visdata uses to present the selected data on the screen. You can also use these icons to assist in making changes to your database, with the option of committing the changes once made or rolling back (undoing) the change.

7

Figure 7.8.
Saving a query.

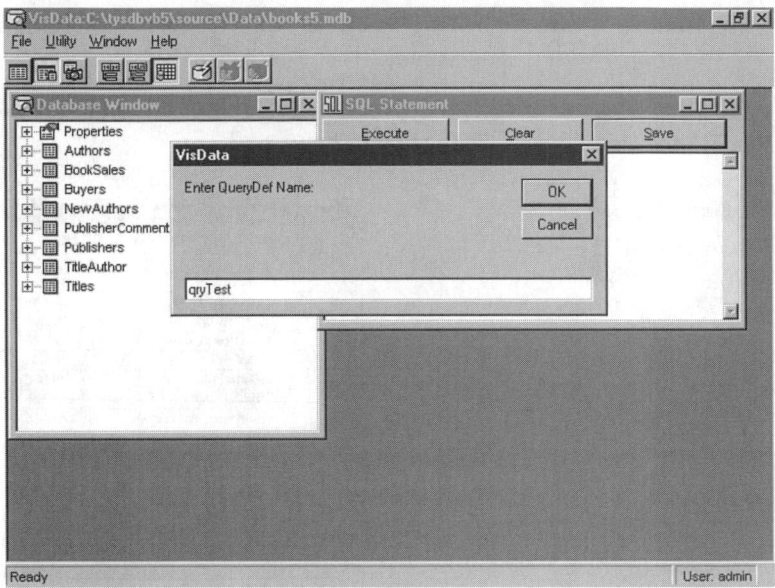

Selecting the Default Data Access Object

The first set of icons controls the type of data access object that Visdata uses to open the data table. The default data access object is the Visual Basic 5 Dynaset, the most flexible Visual Basic 5 data access object. You can use the Dynaset object to create updatable views of more than one table or open an existing table for read/write access.

You can also use the Snapshot data access object to open a read-only view of one or more data tables. Snapshot objects are faster than Dynasets, but require more workstation memory.

Finally, if you only need access to the physical base table in the database, you can select the Table radio button. Tables are fast and require little workstation memory. The disadvantage of the Table data access object is that you cannot use it to combine two or more tables into a single view.

Even though most of the work you do from Visdata is with base tables, you should set this radio button to use the Dynaset data access object. Dynasets are fast enough for almost all Visdata work and they provide the most flexibility when dealing with multitable views.

Selecting the Default Data Form

The second set of icons enables you to select the type of data form you see when you load your data access object. Visual Basic 5 now ships with a very nice data-bound grid tool. This grid automatically loads all the fields in the selected data access object and scrolls data records into

the table as needed. This grid object may be the most useful selection of the three. Click the Use DBGrid Control on New Form icon to make this your default data form.

The other two icons select two versions of a standard data entry form. The first icon, Use Data Control on New Form, loads the records from the data access object one at a time, using the Visual Basic 5 data control tool. The second icon, Don't Use Data Control on New Form, presents a similar form, but without using the Visual Basic 5 data control tool. The advantage of the Data Control form is that it handles BIT and BINARY data type fields better than the No Data Control form. The No Data Control form, however, allows users to press F4 to display the entire contents of a data field whose contents overflow the control's display area. This zooming feature is handy when dealing with large text fields or memo fields.

You can switch the Form Type radio button after each table is opened and displayed, which enables you to open one or more tables using different data forms. Let's open three tables, each using a different data form.

First, select the Use DBGrid Control on New Form icon from the toolbar. Now double-click the Authors table. This action brings up the Authors table in a grid display. Your screen should look like Figure 7.9.

Figure 7.9.

Authors table using the grid data form.

AUID	Name	DOB	Contracted
1	Smith, John	4/25/62	-1
2	Rodgers, Bill	12/17/45	0
3	Tailor, Mark	12/15/55	-1
4	Thompson, Carol	2/2/69	0
5	Jackson, Sharon	6/25/65	-1
6	Burns, Timothy R.	11/11/66	0
7	Bishop, Diane	12/12/60	0
8	Kennedy, Martin Jr.	7/14/75	0
9	Victor, George	7/15/65	0
10	DeSilvia, Carl	12/31/49	-1
11	Richards, Becky	10/22/63	0
12	Mullaney, Terrance (	4/1/32	0
13	Thompson, James E.	6/30/66	0
14	Valley, Margo	8/14/55	-1
15	Cruis, Jonathon	4/15/50	-1

Dynaset:Authors — Refresh | Sort | Filter | Close

Right Click for Data Control Properties

NOTE

Please note that the columns in this view can be resized. Simply select a column divider with your mouse and drag to the desired width.

7

Next, select the Use Data Control on New Form button and double-click the Authors table again. Now you see the same data presented in a standard data entry from. Your screen should now look like Figure 7.10.

Figure 7.10.

Authors table using the Data Control form.

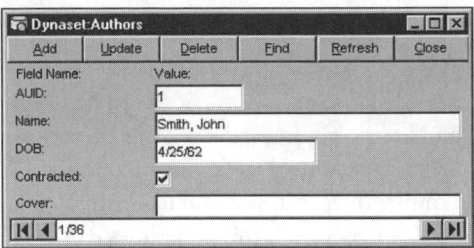

Next, select the Don't Use Data Control on New Form icon and double-click the Authors table a third time. Now, you see the Authors data presented in a slightly different data entry form. Notice the differences in the way the Contracted field appears on the Don't Use Data Control on New Form (as text) form and the Data Control form (checkbox). Figure 7.11 shows a tiled view of the three data forms side by side.

Figure 7.11.

Three data forms side by side.

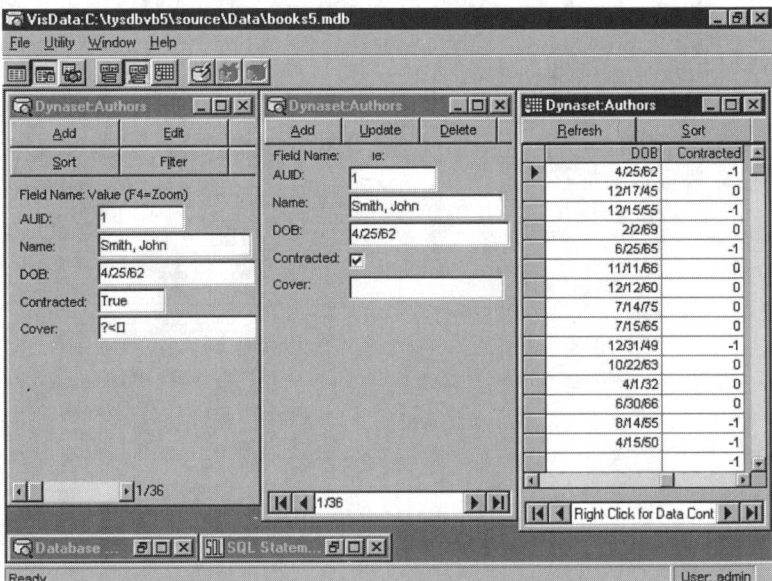

Beginning, Rolling Back, and Committing Transactions

A basic principle in database management is the concept of begin, rollback, and commit transactions. This refers to the theory that changes are temporarily made to the database and reviewed before they are made permanent. If an error occurs as a result of the temporary change, the transaction can be undone, or *rolled back* without causing permanent damage to the underlying data. This is a particularly handy concept when making large changes to multiple data tables. We address this issue in detail in Day 17, "Multiuser Considerations."

To use this concept in Visdata, simply select the Begin a Transaction icon before you make a change to your database. If you like the change, select the Commit current Transaction icon and the change becomes permanent. If you don't like the change, press the Rollback current Transaction icon to undo the changes.

Please note the use of the word "current" in the Commit and Rollback operations. This refers to all changes made since the last time the Begin icon was selected. Transactions cannot be rolled back once they are committed.

Now that you have seen the major components of the Visdata main screen, let's review each of the menu items in greater detail.

The Visdata File Menu

The Visdata File menu contains nine items. You can open, create, and close databases from the file menu, import and export data from and to the open database, log into a designated workspace, and review any errors that have been logged since you started Visdata. You can compact or repair Microsoft Jet databases from the File menu. You also exit the program from the File menu.

If you have used Visdata before, you'll also see a list of the most recently used databases in this menu. You can reload one of those databases by clicking its name in the File menu.

Open Database

Before you can begin working on an existing database, you must first load it using the Open Database… menu option. This menu option enables you to load one of several database formats. Each format has a slightly different set of options in the menu tree. You can load Microsoft Access, dBASE, FoxPro, Paradox, Excel, text files, and ODBC data sources.

NOTE

You can load only one database at a time into Visdata. If you need to work on tables from more than one database, you need to use the Utility | Attachments… menu option to attach the foreign data tables (the tables that are contained within a database other than the one on which you are working) to the database you currently have open. We cover the Attach option later in this lesson.

7

When you select Open Database…, you see several other menu choices. You select one of the secondary items depending on the database format you want to access. The following sections cover each of the secondary menu choices and how you use them to open existing databases.

Microsoft Access

When you select the Microsoft Access… option, Visdata brings up a File Open dialog box and prompts you to select the Microsoft Access database you wish to load (see Figure 7.12).

Figure 7.12.

Loading a Microsoft Access database.

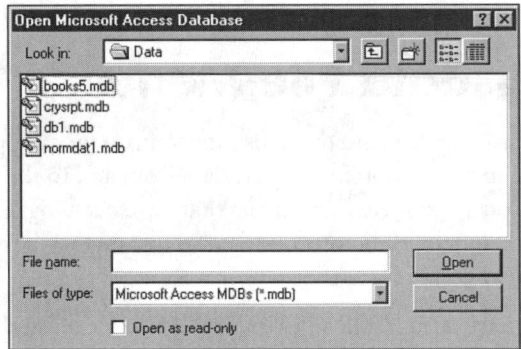

dBASE (III, IV, and 5.0)

You can also use Visdata to load dBASE-format databases. When you select the dBASE menu option, you see an additional menu that asks you to select version III, IV, or 5.0 database format.

WARNING

You must tell Visdata what dBASE format you are loading so that it knows what index files and memo field formats to expect. If you load an incorrect format into Visdata, you do not see an error message right away. You may receive error messages, however, when you attempt to read or write data to the database. These errors may permanently corrupt your database. Be sure you load the FoxPro and dBASE databases using the correct menu option to avoid problems.

When you select the correct format, you see the File Open dialog box prompting you to locate and load a database. After the database is loaded, you see the list of available tables. You also see a message at the bottom of the screen suggesting that you use the Attach option to access the dBASE format data tables (see Figure 7.13).

Figure 7.13.
Viewing a loaded dBASE database.

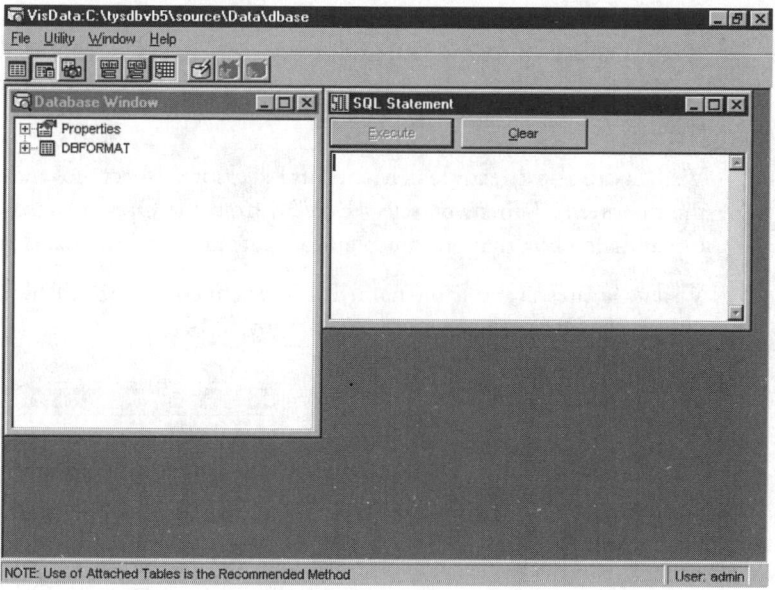

 **TIP**

When you deal with non-Microsoft Jet data formats, you get better performance speed if you access them through the Utility | Attachments... menu option. We cover the Utility | Attachments... menu option later in today's lesson.

FoxPro (2.0, 2.5, 2.6, and 3.0)

Loading the FoxPro format databases works the same as loading the dBASE format databases. When you select FoxPro from the menu, you see an additional menu list that asks you to select the proper database format. When you select the format, you see the File Open dialog prompting you to locate and load the proper database. The same warnings mentioned in the preceding dBASE section apply here. Do not attempt to load a FoxPro 2.6 format database using the FoxPro 2.5 format menu option. Even if the file loads initially without errors, you will probably get unpredictable results and may even corrupt your database.

Paradox (3.x, 4.x, and 5.0)

Opening Paradox files with Visdata works much like opening FoxPro or dBASE format databases. You select the database version you wish to access, and then fill out the File Open dialog box to locate and load the database. The CD that ships with this book contains a

7

Paradox 4.x format database called PDSAMPLE.DB. You can locate and load this file from the \TYSDBVB5\SOURCE\DATA\PARADOX directory.

Excel

Visdata can also directly load Microsoft Excel spreadsheet files and enable you to manipulate their contents. When you select Excel... from the Open Database menu, you see the File Open dialog box that prompts you to locate and load the Excel spreadsheet.

Visdata locates all sheets and named ranges defined in the Excel file and presents them as table objects in the Database window (see Figure 7.14).

Figure 7.14.

Using Visdata to directly load an Excel spreadsheet.

Figure 7.15 shows the sample Excel spreadsheet \TYSDBVB5\SOURCE\DATA\XLDATA\EXSAMPLE.XLS as it appears in Excel. The range name box is opened in the illustration so that you can see how the range names in Excel compare to the table names in Visdata.

Figure 7.16 shows the same Excel file opened using Visdata. In Figure 7.16, the table object Sheet1$ has been opened as a Dynaset object.

WARNING

Visdata opens Excel data files for exclusive use only. If you have an Excel spreadsheet open with Visdata, no other program on your workstation, or any other program on the network, can open the same spreadsheet. If some other program has an Excel spreadsheet open, you cannot open it using Visdata until the other program closes that file.

After you open the Excel file, you can perform all data entry operations on that file including creating new tables and editing data in existing tables in the spreadsheet.

Figure 7.15.

Viewing CH0702.XLS
with Excel.

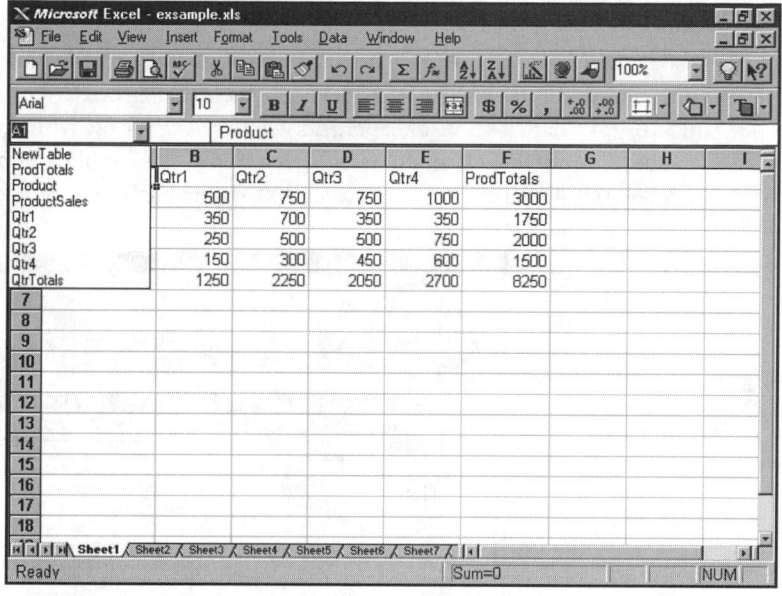

Figure 7.16.

Viewing CH0702.XLS
with Visdata.

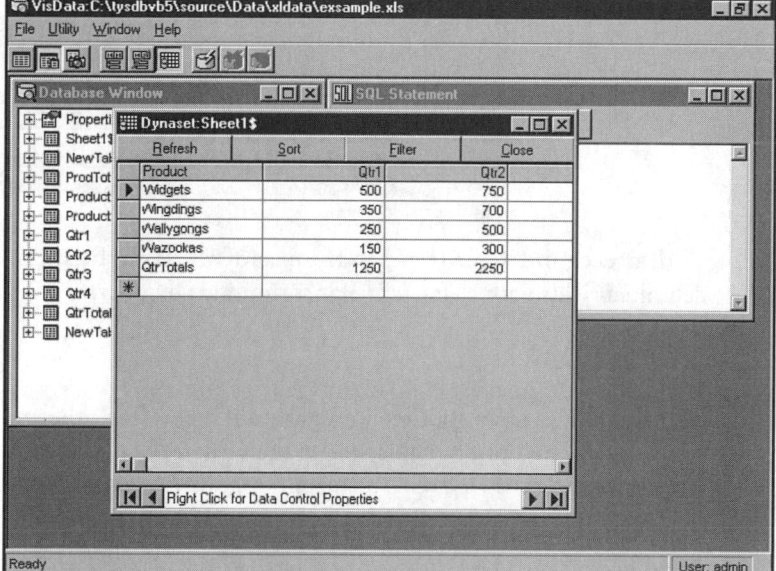

7

Text Files

Visdata can load various standard formats of ASCII text files for read-only access. When you select a file to load (using the File Open dialog box), you actually open the entire directory as a database. Visdata permits you to select any file with a .TXT extension from the Database window and open it as a read-only data table. Figure 7.17 shows the file \TYSDBVB\SOURCE\DATA\TEXT\TXSAMPLE.TXT opened as a read-only data file.

Figure 7.17.

Opening a text file with Visdata.

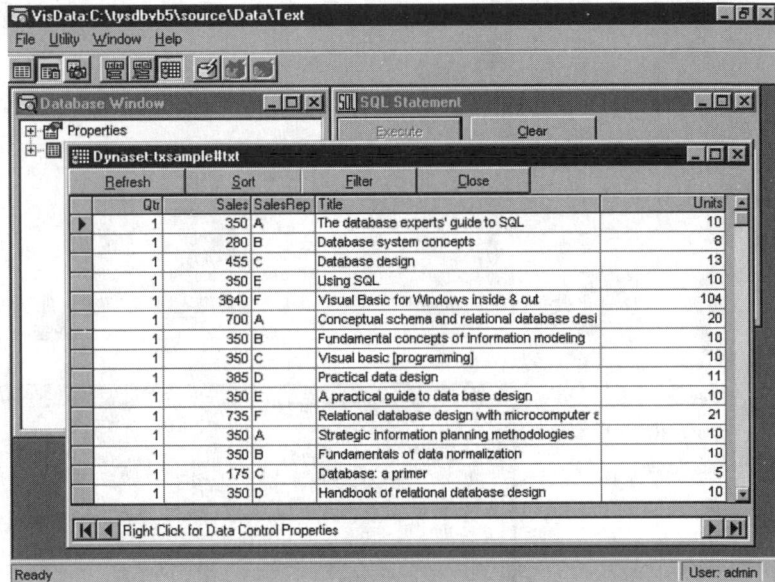

Visdata recognizes several types and formats of ASCII text files. The default format is comma-delimited fields with character fields surrounded by quotes.

ODBC

The ODBC... menu option is slightly different from the previously discussed Open commands. This option enables you to use Visdata to open predefined ODBC data sources. When you select the ODBC... menu option, you see a screen that asks you for the data source type, data source name, user ID, and password for that data source (see Figure 7.18).

After you fill out the ODBC dialog box, Visdata locates and opens the data source and updates the Database window.

Figure 7.18.

Using Visdata to open an ODBC data source.

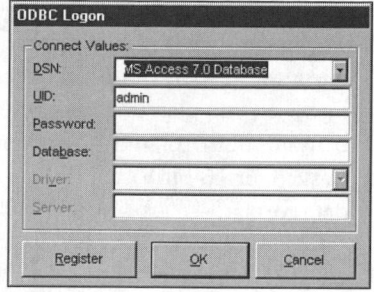

Before you can open an ODBC data source, you must first define that data source using the ODBC program from the Control Panel. You learn about defining and accessing ODBC data sources in depth in Week 3. If you want more information on defining ODBC data sources, you can refer to the help available when you load the ODBC programs from the Control Panel.

New...

The New menu option enables you to use Visdata to create entirely new databases in several formats. This section concentrates on the Microsoft Access database format. Most of the rules for creating Microsoft Jet databases apply equally to non-Microsoft Jet formats. Although the Visdata application can create a non-Microsoft Jet database, you should not use Visdata to create non-Microsoft Jet databases very often. If you need to work in non-Microsoft Jet formats, use the native database engine to create the data files. You can then use Visdata to access and manipulate the non-Microsoft Jet databases.

Access (Version 2.0 and 7.0)

When you select the Microsoft Access menu item, Visdata asks you to select one of two versions of Microsoft Access data format: 2.0 or 7.0. The 2.0 format can be read by all versions of Microsoft Access and by Microsoft Visual Basic versions 4.0 and later. Version 7.0 format databases can only be read by the 32-bit version of Visual Basic 4 and by the 32-bit version of Microsoft Access. The advantage of the older formats is that the data can be read by most versions of the software. The advantage of the version 7.0 format is that it allows for additional database properties that are not available in the older formats.

WARNING

Attempting to read a version 7.0 Microsoft Access database with Access version 2.0 or Visual Basic version 3.0 results in an error that tells you your database is invalid or corrupt. If you know that you will be

7

working only with software that can read version 7.0 files, you should select the version 7.0 format because it provides additional features. If, however, you plan to deploy your database in an environment that contains both 16- and 32-bit versions of the software (you use Visual Basic 3, or 16-bit Visual Basic 4), you should stick with the version 2.0 data format.

After you select a database format from the submenu, Visdata presents you with a dialog box that prompts you to enter a filename for the new database (refer to Figure 7.19).

Figure 7.19.

Creating a new Microsoft Access database.

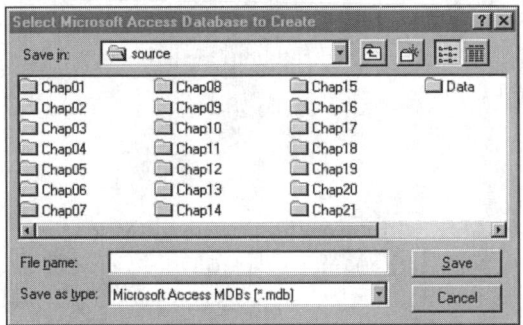

Creating a new database does not automatically create data tables; you must use the New command button in the Database window to create a new table.

dBASE, FoxPro, and Paradox

Creating dBASE, FoxPro, and Paradox format databases is similar to creating Microsoft Access databases. When you select one of these formats, you are prompted to indicate the exact version of the database you want to create. After you select a version, Visdata presents you with a simple dialog box that prompts you to enter a name for the database. This name is not a data file; it is a file directory (called a *folder* in Windows 95). You can include any valid drive designator and directory path you want when you create the database. See Figure 7.20 for an example of creating a FoxPro database directory.

WARNING

Remember that Visdata creates directories (or folders), not data files, when you create dBASE, FoxPro, or Paradox databases. Be sure to use names that make sense as directories or folders.

Figure 7.20.

Creating a FoxPro database directory.

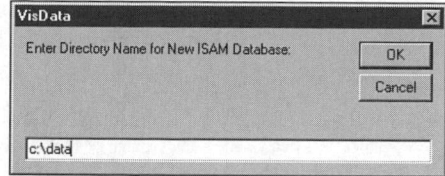

Text

You can use Visdata to create text data files. These files are comma-delimited ASCII text files that you can open for read-only access from Visdata. Even though you can create the database files and tables, you cannot add any data to the tables or create indexes on the data tables. This might be useful if you want to create ASCII text data files for use by other applications.

When you select the text menu option, Visdata prompts you to enter a name for the database. This name is used to create a directory (Windows 95 folder) on the designated drive. You can use any valid device designator and directory path you want when you create the database.

Close Database

The Close Database menu option simply closes the open database. All tables are closed at the same time.

Import/Export...

The Import/Export... function allows you to move data into and out of the currently open database. To bring data in from another database, simply select Import/Export... from the File menu. When this option is selected, you are presented with the dialog shown in Figure 7.21.

Figure 7.21.

The Import/Export dialog.

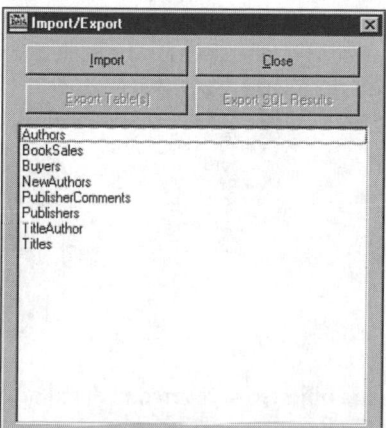

7

Next, select the Import command button. You are requested to select the database format from which to extract data. See Figure 7.22 for details.

Figure 7.22.

The Import Data Format selection.

Select your database format and select OK. You are then presented with a dialog that allows you to select a data table to import from the database you selected in the preceding step. (See Figure 7.23.)

Figure 7.23.

Selecting a table to import.

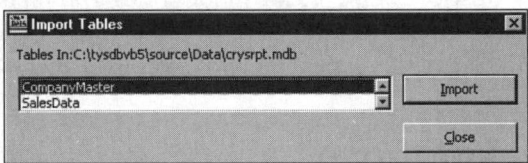

Select the desired table and select the Import button to move the data into the currently open database.

To export data, select Import/Export… from the File menu. Then, select the table from the dialog that appears and press the Export Table(s) button. You are then prompted to select a format and a file to hold the exported data.

Workspace

The Workspace menu item displays a login dialog that allows you to log in to the currently open database as a different user. This is handy if you want to test user IDs and passwords. When you select Workspace from the menu, you see a dialog box that requests a login ID and password (see Figure 7.24).

Figure 7.24.

Viewing the Login dialog.

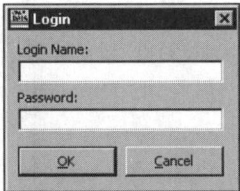

Workspace data objects are covered in detail on Day 10, "Creating Database Programs with Visual Basic Code."

Errors

The Errors menu option shows the last error or set of errors reported to Visdata (see Figure 7.25).

Figure 7.25.

Viewing the errors collection.

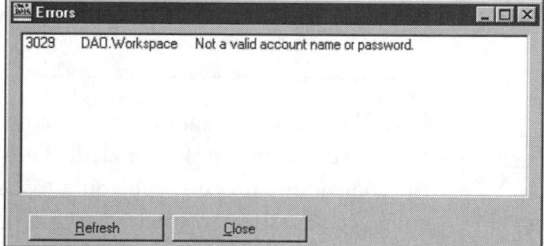

Some data sources return more than one error message per transaction (usually ODBC data sources), which is referred to as the *errors collection*. This menu option lets you review the errors collection in a grid listing. If no errors have been returned, this grid is empty.

TIP

Even if you have had several successful database transactions since your last error, the most recent error remains in this grid display.

Compact MDB...

You can use Visdata to compact existing Jet databases (MDB files). Compacting a database removes empty space in the data file once occupied by records that were deleted. Running the Compact menu option also reorganizes any defined indexes stored in the database.

When you select Compact MDB..., you have to select a database format. If you select 3.0 MDB... from this menu, the database you selected is compacted and stored as a Microsoft Jet version 3.0 database. If you select 2.0 from this menu, the database you select is compacted and stored as a Microsoft Jet version 2.0 database.

NOTE

Although not recommended, you can use the Compact Database menu option to convert older database formats to newer ones, but you cannot use the Compact Database menu option to convert newer formats to older ones. For example, you cannot convert a 3.0 Microsoft Jet database to a 2.0 Microsoft Jet database.

7

When you select the target format, you see a File Open dialog box asking you to select the database you want to compact. The database you select cannot be opened by any other program while it is being compacted. After you select the source database, you have to enter the name of the destination database file. If you select the same name as the source, your current data file is overwritten with the new format. If you select a new database filename, all information is copied from the source database to the target database.

WARNING

Even though Visdata allows you to compact a database file onto itself, this practice is not recommended. If anything happens midway through the compacting process, you could lose some or all of your data. Always compact a database to a new database filename.

Before Visdata compacts your database, you will be asked if you want to encrypt the data. If you say Yes, Visdata copies all data and encrypts the file so that only those who have access to the security files can read the data. We talk more about data encryption on Day 21 "Securing Your Database Applications."

Repair MDB...

If you get a "database corrupt" error when you attempt to open a Microsoft Jet database file, you may need to repair your database. Database files can become damaged due to power surges during read/write operations or due to physical device errors (damaged disk drive plates, and so on). You can repair an existing database by selecting Repair MDB... from the File menu. You then see a File Open dialog box that asks you for the database filename. Once you select the filename, Visdata loads and repairs the database to the best of its capabilities. Unfortunately, you may receive a message saying some of the data could not be recovered.

TIP

Remember to make copies of your database on a regular basis. You should not depend on the Repair routine to recover all your data. If you experience a program crash due to corrupted data, you can always restore the file from the most recent backup.

You should also use the Windows 95 or DOS defragment utility on your hard drive after performing a Compact or Repair function to improve the overall performance of your application.

Exiting Visdata

The Exit item does just what you expect. When you exit Visdata, your current database closes, along with all open database objects. If you have text in the SQL window, it is saved and restored the next time you load Visdata. Visdata also remembers the windows you had open, as well as their sizes and their locations for the next time you load Visdata.

Adding Tables and Indexes to the Database

When you have created a new database, you can add new tables and indexes to the database. You can also add new tables and indexes to existing databases. To illustrate the process of managing database tables using Visdata, let's create a new Microsoft Access (Jet) database, add a new table, add a new index, and then modify the table structure.

Creating the New CH07NEW.MDB Database

If you haven't already done so, load and start Visdata. Select File | New... | Microsoft Access... | Version 7.0 MDB... from the main menu and enter CH07NEW.MDB in the Select Microsoft Access Database to Create dialog box (see Figure 7.26). Click the Save button to create the new database.

Figure 7.26.

Creating
CH07NEW.MDB.

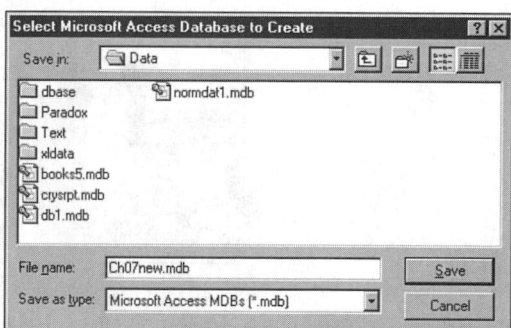

Adding a New Table to the Database

To add a new table to the database, click the alternate mouse button in an open space of the Database window and select New Table to bring up the Table Definition dialog box. Your screen should look like Figure 7.27.

7

Figure 7.27.

Defining a new table.

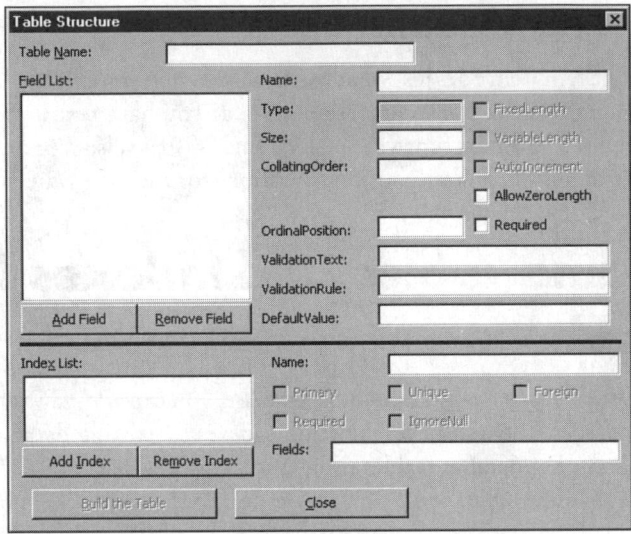

Enter NewTable in the Table Name field at the top of the dialog box. Now you can add fields to the data table. Click the Add Field command button to bring up the Add Field dialog box. Your screen should look like Figure 7.28.

Figure 7.28.

Adding a new field to the table.

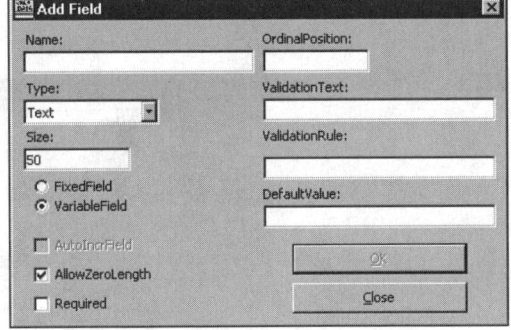

Enter the field name Field1. Set the type to Text and the Size to 10. Notice that you can set default values and validation rules here, as well. We'll cover these properties on Day 9, "Visual Basic and the Microsoft Jet Engine."

After you have entered the information you need to define the field, click the OK button to save the field properties to the database.

Be sure you click the OK button after each field you define. If you just fill out the dialog box and then click the Close button, the information you entered on the form won't be saved to the database.

Now that you have defined Field1, let's define one more field. Enter Field2 as the name, and select Currency as the Field Type. Notice that you cannot set the field size. Only Text type fields allow you to set a field size. Now click the OK button to save this field definition; then exit the field definition dialog by clicking the Close button. The Table Structure dialog box should now show two fields defined. Refer to Figure 7.29 as a guide.

Figure 7.29.

Table Structure with two fields defined.

Editing an Existing Field

When you return to the Table Structure screen, notice that the same set of properties you saw in the Add Field dialog box appears to the right of the Fields list. You can edit some of these values for the field by highlighting the field in the list on the left and editing the dialog values on the right. Make Field2 required by selecting the Required checkbox at the right side of the dialog box.

Building the Table

Before you leave this screen, you must first click the Build Table button to actually create the table in your database. Up to this point, Visdata has stored the data table and index definitions in memory. Clicking the Build the Table button is the step that actually creates the data table.

7

WARNING

If you click the Close button before you click the Build the Table button, you lose all your table definition information. You have to enter all the table definition data again before you can build the new table.

When you add data to an existing data table, you cannot use Visdata to modify the table structure. You must first remove all records from the data table before you can make any modification to the structure. You can, however, add new fields to a table after data has been entered.

Adding a New Index to the Database Using the Design Button

You can add indexes to existing tables by selecting the table, clicking the alternate mouse button, and selecting Design… from the menu that appears. This option brings up the same input form you used to add fields to the database. Now let's add a Primary Key index for the NewTable you just created.

WARNING

Even though Visdata allows you to enter New Index information during the New Tables process, you cannot build a new table and a new index for the same table at one time. Visdata must see the data table that already exists before it can create an index for that table. Use the Design mode of the Table Structure dialog box to add indexes to existing tables.

Click the Add Index command button to bring up the Add Index dialog box. Enter PKNewTable as the index name. Click Field1 in the field list to make that field the source of the Primary Key index. Your screen should look like Figure 7.30.

Be sure to click the OK button to add the index definition to the database. When you have added the index definition, click Close to exit the dialog. Your screen should now look like Figure 7.31.

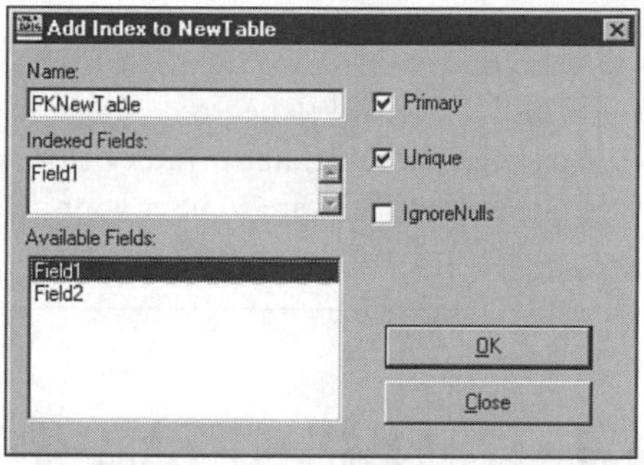

Figure 7.30.

Adding a new index to the database.

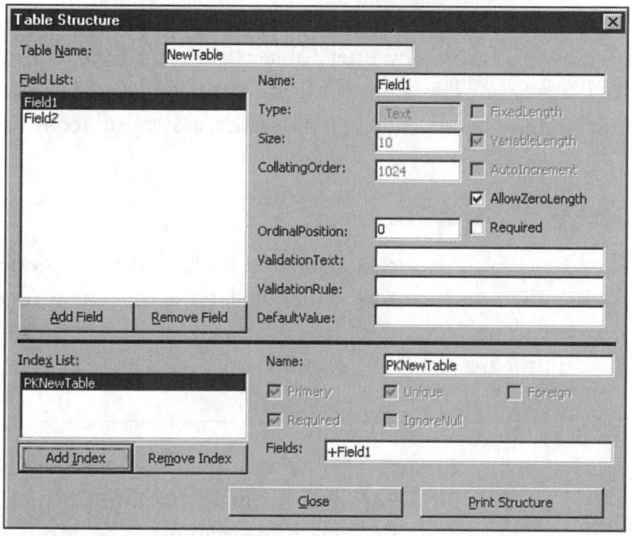

Figure 7.31.

The Table Structure dialog after adding a new index.

Printing the Table Structure

While you are in the Design mode of the Table Structure dialog, you can click the Print Structure button to get a hard-copy printout of the selected table and index objects you have defined. Visdata sends the information directly to the default printer defined for Windows and does not prompt you for any options. Please note that the Print Structure button does not appear when creating a New table; it appears only when you select Design after the table has been created.

TIP

If you want to save the structure to a file, you can use the printer applet in the Control Panel to define a printer as a file, and then set that print device as the default printer before you click the Print Structure button in Visdata. Be sure to reset your default printer after you send your table structures to a disk file.

The Visdata Utility Menu

The Visdata Utility menu contains several options to help you manage your data tables. You can create, test, and save query objects using the Query Builder; build data entry forms with the Data Form Designer; perform global replace routines on existing data tables; define attachments; define security; and define system preferences.

Query Builder...

The Query Builder serves as a good tool for testing queries and then saving them to the database as query objects. You can later access these objects from your Visual Basic 5 programs. The Query Builder enables you to perform complex queries without having to know all the details of SQL syntax.

NOTE

We cover SQL SELECT queries in detail on Day 8, "Selecting Data with SQL." For now, if you are not familiar with SQL statements, just follow along with the example. The important thing to remember is that you can use the Visdata Query Builder to create, test, and store SQL queries.

Let's build a query, test it, and save it in a database. First, make sure you have BOOKS5.MDB open (found in the TYSDBVB5\SOURCE\DATA directory on the CD included with this book), and then select Utility | Query Builder... from the main menu. You see a data entry form ready for your input (see Figure 7.32).

You have several options on this screen. It's easy to get confused if you are not quite sure of what to look for. Instead of going through all the possible options for a query, this example goes step-by-step through a rather simple SELECT query and its results. Table 7.1 shows the values to select and Figure 7.33 shows the completed form. Refer to these items as you build your query.

Figure 7.32.

Using the Query Builder.

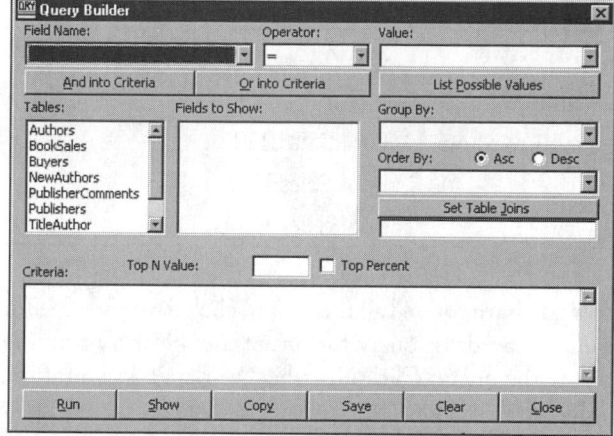

Figure 7.33.

The completed query.

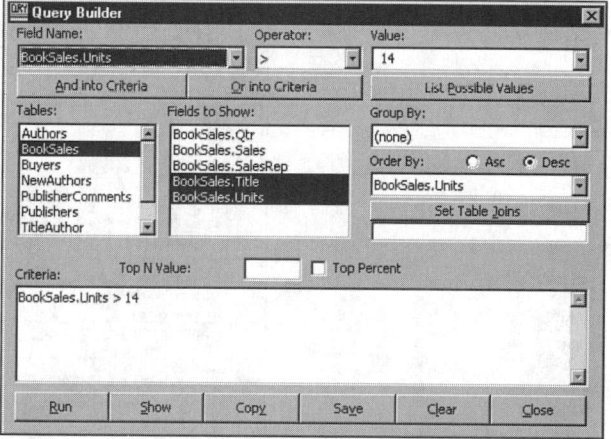

Be sure to set the values in the screen in the order they appear in Table 7.1. After you enter the Field Name, Operator, and Value settings, click the And into Criteria button to force the settings into the Criteria box at the bottom of the window.

Table 7.1. Building a query.

Property	Setting
Tables	BookSales
Field Name	BookSales.Units
Operator	>

continues

7

Table 7.1. continued

Property	Setting
Value	14
Fields to Show	BookSales.Title
	BookSales.Units
Order by	BookSales.Units, Desc

After you have entered all the values, click Save and enter qryTest at the dialog prompt. You have just saved the query for future use. Now try running it. Click Run to get Visdata to execute the query. Click No when Visdata asks you if this is an SQL Passthrough query. Visdata then executes the query and displays the results on your screen, as shown in Figure 7.34.

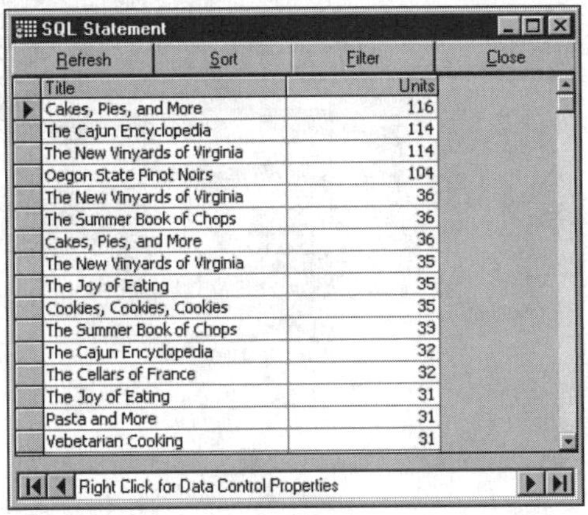

Figure 7.34.

Results of the executed query.

Data Form Designer...

The Data Form Designer builds a data entry form complete with a data control and command buttons for data administration. The form is saved to the currently active Visual Basic project. To demonstrate, let's build a sample form with the Data Form Designer.

First, make sure you have the BOOKS5.MDB (TYSDBVB5\SOURCE\DATA) database open in Visdata. Next, select Data Form Designer... from the Utility Menu. You should see the Data Form Designer dialog (see Figure 7.35).

Figure 7.35.

*The Data Form
Designer.*

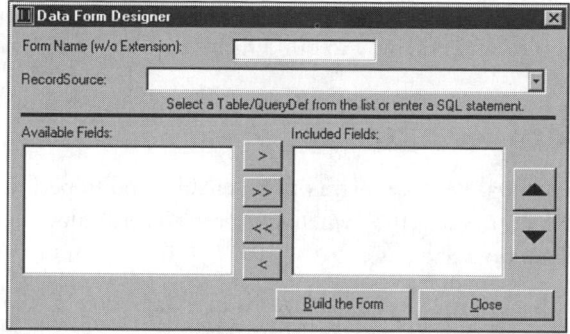

Enter frmAuthors in the Form Name field. Next, select Authors as the RecordSource. Note, when you select Authors, all of the fields within that table appear in the Available Fields list box. Now, click the >> button to move all the fields into the Included Fields list box. Your dialog should look like Figure 7.36.

Figure 7.36.

*The completed
frmAuthors design.*

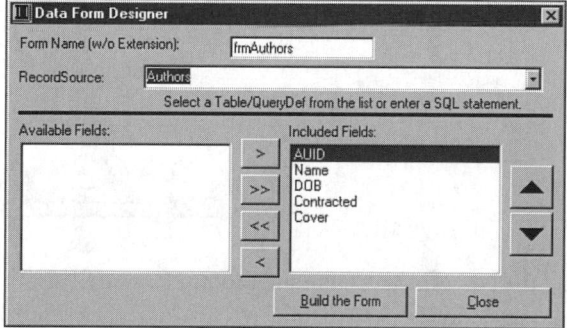

Click the Build the Form button to save the form to the currently active Visual Basic 5 project.

Now, close the Data Form Designer and Visdata and return to your Visual Basic 5 project. Open frmAuthors. You should see a form similar to the one in Figure 7.37.

Figure 7.37.

*The completed
frmAuthors form.*

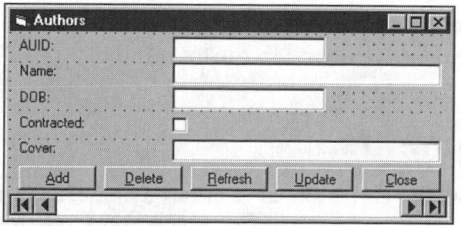

7

Notice how you have all the data fields, as well as a data control and command buttons. This is a quick and easy way to build forms for data entry!

Global Replace...

The Global Replace menu option enables you to perform a mass update of existing tables, which comes in handy when you need to zero values in test data or need to perform mass updates on a database.

For this example, set all the fields in a data table to the same value. Load the BOOKS5.MDB database (TYSDBVB5\SOURCE\DATA), and then select Utility | Global Replace... from the menu. You see the Global Replace dialog box, as shown in Figure 7.38.

Figure 7.38.

Entering a Global Replace command.

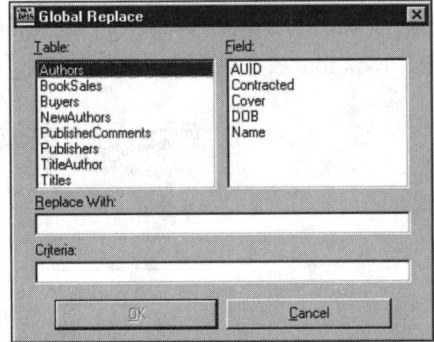

Select the NewAuthors table and the Contracted field. Set the Replace With value to zero and leave the Criteria field blank. When you click the OK button, Visdata resets all the NewAuthors.Contracted fields to zero. You can limit the number of records affected by the Global Replace command by entering an appropriate logical statement in the Criteria box. For example, if you wanted to update only the records that have an Au_ID value of 30, you could enter the following line in the Criteria box:

```
Au_ID=30
```

We cover Criteria more in depth in the lesson on Day 8, and you'll learn more about the global replace command in the lesson on Day 14, "Error Handling in Visual Basic 5.0."

Attachments...

Visdata allows you to attach external database files to an existing Microsoft Access (Jet) format database. When you create an attachment, you actually create a link between your own Microsoft Access database and another database. You don't actually import any data from the

external database into your own MDB. By creating attachments, you can access and manipulate external data files as if they are native Microsoft Access tables. Attached tables appear in the Database window as local table objects in your database, even though they are only links to external data files.

TIP

> Not only is the attachment method convenient, it provides the fastest way to access external data using Visual Basic 5 programs. You can load, index, and display attached external tables faster than you can if you use ODBC or directly open the external data files in their native format.

Now create an attached table in the BOOKS5.MDB database that we used earlier today.

If you like, you can create an attachment to any other Microsoft Jet format database you already have on hand.

First, if you don't have it loaded already, select File | Open Database... from the main menu to load the BOOKS5.MDB (TYSDBVB5\SOURCE\DATA) database. Then select the Utility | Attachments menu option. You will see a grid that shows all the current attachments for this database. Because there are no attachments to this database, this box should be empty. Click the New command button to open the New Attached Table dialog box. Your screen should now look like Figure 7.39.

Figure 7.39.

Adding an attachment to a Microsoft Access database.

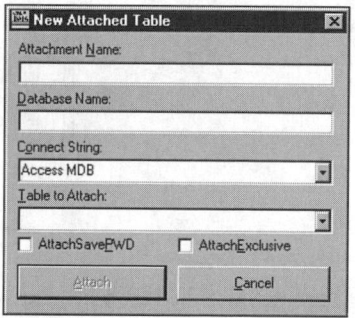

Table 7.2 shows the information you should enter into the Attachment dialog box.

7

Table 7.2. New Attached Table dialog box values.

Dialog Field	Value
Attachment Name	Test Attachment
Database Name	\TYSDBVB5\SOURCE\DATA\CRYSRPT.MDB
Connect String	Access MDB
Table to Attach	CompanyMaster

If you are attaching to a data source that requires a password in the connect string, you could check the AttachSavePWD checkbox to prevent a login dialog each time you open the database. If you want to create an exclusive attachment, you could check the AttachExclusive checkbox. Leave both of these fields blank for now.

After filling out the dialog form, click Attach to commit the attachment. After you close the Attachment dialog box, you see that the grid is updated to show the new attachment you just added to the database. Close the New Attached Tables dialog and the Attachments grid. You now see a new entry in your Database window list. This shows a new table object. Note how the icon for the attachment differs from the other tables' icons. Your screen should look something like the one in Figure 7.40.

Figure 7.40.
An attached table object.

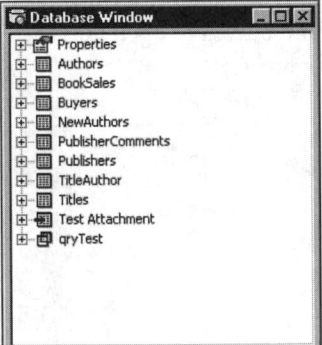

You can now access this attached table just like you would any table you created using Visdata.

Groups/Users...

Selecting Utility | Group/Users... brings up the Groups/Users/Permissions dialog shown in Figure 7.41.

Figure 7.41.

*The Groups/Users/
Permissions dialog.*

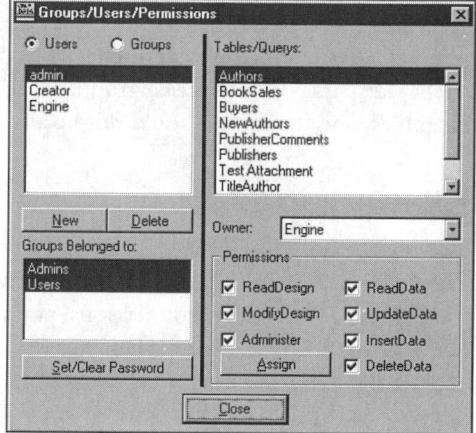

This dialog can be used to set all of the permission rights for users and groups. In order to use this function, you must have a security file (SYSTEM.MD?) to which you belong. This function allows the setting of rights and passwords on a user and on a group level.

SYSTEM.MD?

Use the SYSTEM.MD? menu option to locate and load the SYSTEM.MD? security file. The SYSTEM.MD? file contains information about Microsoft Access file security, including defined users, groups, workspaces, passwords, and data object rights. You must create this file using the Microsoft Access utility WRKGADM.EXE.

The Utility | SYSTEM.MD? menu option presents you with a File Open dialog so that you can locate and load a SYSTEM.MD? file. Once it is loaded, Visdata adds this information to the Registry so that you won't have to reload it in the future.

Preferences

The Preferences menu option lets you customize the way Visdata shows you information. Two toggle settings control the way Visdata displays data, and two parameter settings control the way Visdata performs database logins and queries.

Open Last Database on Startup

When you toggle on the Open Last Database option, Visdata remembers the last database you had open when you last exited Visdata and automatically attempts to open that file the next time you start Visdata.

7

Include System Files

When you toggle on the Include System Files option, you see several tables maintained by Microsoft Jet to keep track of table, user, group, relation, and query definitions. Users cannot access these tables, and the tables should not be altered or removed at any time.

Query Time-Out Value

You can use the Query Time-Out Value menu option to adjust the number of seconds Visdata waits before reporting a time-out error when attempting a query. If you work with slow external data files or ODBC connections, you can adjust this value upward to reduce the number of errors Visdata reports when you run queries.

Login Time-Out Value

You can use the Login Time-Out Value menu option to adjust the number of seconds Visdata waits before reporting a time-out error when attempting to log into a remote data source. Adjust this value upward if you get time-out errors when dealing with slow ODBC or external data sources.

The Visdata Windows and Help Menus

The last two items on the Visdata main menu are the Windows menu and the Help menu. These two items contain the usual options that all good Windows programs have.

The Windows Menu

This menu helps you control how all the child windows are displayed within the main MDI form. You can Cascade, Tile, or Arrange Icons from this menu. You can also force the focus to one of the three default Visdata windows: Database window, SQL window, or MDI form.

The Help Menu

The Help menu gives you access to the Visdata Help file included with your version of Visual Basic 5. You can also view the About box from this menu.

Summary

Today you learned how to use the Visdata sample application to perform all the basic database operations needed to create and maintain databases for your Visual Basic 5 applications.

You learned how to do the following:

- ☐ Open existing databases.
- ☐ Create new databases.
- ☐ Add tables and indexes to existing databases.
- ☐ Attach external data sources to existing Microsoft Access databases.
- ☐ Access data using the three data access objects: Table, Dynaset, and Snapshot.
- ☐ View data on-screen using the three data forms: form view with the data control; form view without the data control; and grid view using the data-bound grid.
- ☐ Build and store SQL queries using the Query Builder.

You learned to use Visdata to perform database utility operations, including the following:

- ☐ Copying tables from one database to another
- ☐ Repairing corrupted Microsoft Access (Jet) databases
- ☐ Compacting and converting versions of Microsoft Jet databases
- ☐ Performing global replace operations on tables

You learned to use Visdata to adjust various system settings that affect how Visual Basic 5 displays data tables and processes local and external database connections and parameters that control how Visual Basic 5 locks records at update time.

Quiz

1. Where can you find a copy of the Visdata source code?
2. How do you copy a table in Visdata?
3. When do you need to Refresh the Tables/Queries window?
4. Can you manipulate spreadsheet data with Visdata?
5. What information can be obtained from the Properties object in the Database window?
6. Why would you compact a database?
7. Can you compact a database onto itself with the File | Compact MDB command?
8. Can you use Visdata to modify a table's structure once data has been entered?
9. Can you save queries in Visdata?
10. In what formats can you export data using the Visdata tool?
11. How would you use Visdata to convert an existing Access 2.0 database into an Access 7.0 format?

7

Exercises

You have been asked to build a database to track entities that purchase from and sell to your organization. Complete the following tasks using Visdata as your development tool.

1. Build a new database and name it Contacts. This database should have a format that can be read by Microsoft Access 7.0.

2. Build a table of customers (tblCustomers). Include the following fields:

Field	Type	Size
ID	Text	10
Name	Text	50
Address1	Text	50
Address2	Text	50
City	Text	50
StateProv	Text	25
Zip	Text	10
Phone	Text	14
Fax	Text	14
Contact	Text	50
Notes	Memo	NA

3. Build a primary key (PKtblCustomers) on the ID field for the tblCustomers table.

4. Print the table structure for tblCustomers.

5. Create and enter five sample records into the tblCustomers table.

6. Because you also need to track those from whom you purchase, copy the structure (no records) from tblCustomers to a new table, tblVendors.

7. Export the data in the tblCustomers table to a text file.

7

Week

1

In Review

In the first week, you learned about the relational database model, how to use the Visual Basic database objects to access and update existing databases, and how to use the Visual Data Manager (Visdata) program to create and maintain databases. You also learned how to design and code data entry forms, including use of the Visual Basic bound data controls, and how to create input validation routines at the keystroke, field, and form levels. Finally, you learned how to use the Visual Basic Crystal Reports Pro report writer to design simple reports, and you learned how to use the CRYSTAL.VBX control to run those reports from within your Visual Basic programs.

Day 1: Your First Database Program in Visual Basic 5

The first day's lesson gave you a crash course in how to build a fully functional data entry form in Visual Basic with minimal programming code. On Day 1, you learned the following:

- ☐ How to use the data control to bind a form to a database and data table by setting the DatabaseName and RecordSource properties

- ☐ How to use the Text box bound input control to bind an input box on the form to a data table and data field by setting the DataSource and DataField properties

- ☐ How to combine standard command buttons and the AddNew and Delete methods to provide Add and Delete record functionality to a data entry form

Day 2: Creating Databases

The lesson on Day 2 concentrated on the fundamentals of relational databases. You learned the following about relational databases:

- ☐ A relational database is a collection of related data.

- ☐ The three key building blocks of relational databases are data fields, data records, and data tables.

- ☐ The two types of database relationships are one-to-one (which uses qualifier fields) and one-to-many (which uses pointer fields).

- ☐ There are two types of key (or index) fields: primary and foreign.

You also learned the 14 basic data field types recognized by Visual Basic 5. You constructed a data entry form that allows you to test the way Visual Basic behaves when attempting to store data entered into the various data field types.

Day 3: Visual Basic Database Objects

In Day 3's lesson, you learned that there are three main types of Visual Basic Recordset data objects:

- ☐ Table-type objects: These are used when you have a large dataset and need to do frequent searches to locate a single record. You can use the Visual Basic Seek method and use Visual Basic Indexes with the Table object.

☐ Dynaset-type objects: These are used in most cases when you need read and write access to datasets. The Dynaset uses little workstation memory and allows you to create virtual tables by combining fields from different tables in the same database. The Dynaset is the only data object that allows you to read and write to ODBC data sources.

☐ Snapshot-type objects: These are used when you need fast read-only access to datasets. Snapshot objects are stored in workstation memory, so they should be kept small. Snapshots are good for storing validation lists at the workstation or for small reports.

You also learned about another data object—the Database object. You can use the Database object to get a list of tables in the database, a list of indexes associated with the tables, and a list of fields in each of the tables.

Day 4: Creating Data Entry Forms with Bound Controls

On Day 4, you learned about creating data entry forms with Visual Basic bound data controls.

You learned that the Visual Basic data control has five database-related properties. Three refer to the database and two refer to the Dynaset.

The Database properties of the Visual Basic data control are

☐ DatabaseName: Used to select the database to access

☐ Exclusive: Used to prevent others from opening the database

☐ ReadOnly: Used to prevent your program from modifying the data in the database

The Dynaset properties of the Visual Basic data control are

☐ RecordSource: Used to select the data table within the database

☐ Options: Used to set ReadOnly, DenyWrite, and AppendOnly properties for the Dynaset

You learned that the Visual Basic data control has three database-related methods:

☐ Refresh: Used to update the data control after setting properties

☐ UpdateControls: Used to read values from the fields in the Dynaset and write those values to the related form controls

☐ UpdateRecord: Used to read values from the form controls and write those values to the related fields in the Dynaset

You learned that the Visual Basic data control has three database-related events:

☐ Reposition: Occurs each time the record pointer is moved to a new record in the Dynaset

☐ Validate: Occurs each time the record pointer leaves the current record in the Dynaset

☐ Error: Occurs each time a database error occurs

You learned how to use Visual Basic-bound form controls to link form input and display controls to data fields in the database.

☐ Bound textbox control: Used for data entry on character and numeric data table fields

☐ Bound label control: Used for display-only character and numeric data table fields

☐ Bound checkbox control: Used for data entry on the BOOLEAN data type field

☐ Bound image control: Used to display images stored in the BINARY data type field

☐ The 3D panel control behaves the same as the label control, and the 3D checkbox control behaves the same as a standard checkbox control

You also learned several general rules for creating Visual Basic forms in the Windows 95 style:

☐ The default color is light gray for backgrounds.

☐ Use the panel3D control to create a palette on which to place all other controls.

☐ The default font is 8-point sans serif, regular.

☐ Input areas should have a background that is white; display areas should have a background that is light gray. Display areas should be recessed into the input palette.

☐ Use frame controls to group related items on a form.

☐ Left-justify all controls, including field prompts. Field prompts should be written in mixed case and followed by a semicolon.

☐ Standard spacing and sizing for common controls are as follows:

    ☐ Control height is 330 twips.

    ☐ Command button width is 1200 twips.

    ☐ Vertical spacing between controls is 90 twips for related items and 210 twips for unrelated items.

    ☐ Border widths (top, bottom, and side) should be 120 twips.

Lastly, you learned how to write code that sets control colors to the Windows 95 default colors, how to create your own custom color scheme, and how to link your control colors to the color scheme selected with the Windows Control Panel color applet.

Day 5: Input Validation

On Day 5, you learned how to perform input validation on data entry forms. You learned that input validation tasks can be divided into three areas:

☐ Key filtering: Preventing unwanted keyboard input

☐ Field-level validation: Validating input for each field

☐ Form-level validation: Validating input across several fields

You also learned that you should ask yourself a few basic questions when you are developing validation rules for your form.

☐ Is it a required field?

☐ What characters are valid/invalid for this field? (Numeric input only, capital letters only, no spaces allowed, and so on.)

☐ For numeric fields, is there a high/low range limit? (Must be greater than zero and less than 1000, can't be less than 100, and so on.)

☐ Is there a list of valid values for this field? (Can the user enter only Retail, Wholesale, or Other; Name must already be in the Customer table, and so on.)

☐ Is this a conditional field? (If users enter Yes in field A, they must enter something in field C.)

You learned how to write keyboard filter validation functions using the Visual Basic 5 KeyPress event. You learned how to write field-level validation functions that check for valid input ranges, input that is part of a list of valid data, and input that is within minimum and maximum length requirements. You also learned how to write validation functions that make sure dependent fields have been filled out properly.

Finally, you learned how to use Visual Basic 5 to create your own custom control that incorporates all the validation techniques you learned in this chapter. You can use this ActiveX control in all your future Visual Basic projects.

You also applied your knowledge of bound data controls, Visual Basic 5 data entry form design, and validation processing to create the data entry form for the CompanyMaster data table.

Day 6: Creating Reports with Crystal Reports Pro

On Day 6, you learned how to use Crystal Reports Pro to create a simple list report using the data tables you created earlier in the week. You also learned that Crystal Reports Pro is a *banded* report writer. These are the main bands in a report:

- ☐ Header and Footer bands appear on every page.
- ☐ Detail bands contain the equivalent of a data table record.
- ☐ Section bands contain subtotals or groupings of the data.

You also learned that Crystal Reports Pro recognizes three types of fields on the report form:

- ☐ Database fields are from attached data tables.
- ☐ Text fields are literal text created by the user.
- ☐ Formula fields are calculated fields created by the user.

You also learned how to use the CRYSTAL.VBX control to run a report from within your Visual Basic program. Finally, you created a generic print report dialog that lets you control the report destination, file type, and number of copies.

Day 7: Using the Visdata Program

You wrapped up your first week of study by learning how to use the Visdata sample application to perform all the basic database operations needed to create and maintain databases for your Visual Basic 5 applications.

You learned how to:

- ☐ Open existing databases
- ☐ Create new databases
- ☐ Add tables and indexes to existing databases
- ☐ Attach external data sources to existing Microsoft Access databases
- ☐ Access data using the three data access objects: Table, Dynaset, and Snapshot
- ☐ View data on-screen using the three data forms: form view with the data control; form view without the data control; and grid view using the data-bound grid
- ☐ Build and store SQL queries using the Query Builder

You learned to use Visdata to perform database utility operations, including:

- ☐ Copying tables from one database to another.
- ☐ Repairing corrupted Microsoft Access (Jet) databases.
- ☐ Compacting and converting versions of Microsoft Jet databases.
- ☐ Performing global replace operations on tables.

You learned to use Visdata to adjust various system settings that affect how Visual Basic 5 displays data tables and processes local and external database connections and parameters that control how Visual Basic 5 locks records at update time.

WEEK 2

At a Glance

In this week, you build upon the skills you developed in Week 1. Emphasis moves to developing skills that you need for application development in a workgroup environment. In addition, you create tools that you use in every Visual Basic database application.

NOTE

> Most of the material covered this week requires the Professional Edition of Visual Basic. However, if you are working with the Learning Edition of Visual Basic, you can still learn a great deal from this week's lessons.

There are lessons on the SQL data definition language, SQL data manipulation language, and Visual Basic Data Access Objects (DAO). Other lessons cover how to use Visual Basic code to create database applications; displaying data with graphics; error trapping; and data-bound lists, combo boxes, and grids.

When you've completed this week's lessons, you will know most of the techniques needed to build solid Visual Basic database applications using Visual Basic code. You'll also have several Visual Basic custom controls that you can use in future Visual Basic projects. Here is more detailed information about this week's lessons:

Day 8: You begin the second week with the first of three days devoted to one of the most important topics in database programming—Structured Query Language (SQL). After learning in general terms what SQL can do for you, you learn the basics of this powerful and simple language. You learn about SQL clauses you can use to select and sort records from your databases. You also learn SQL keywords such as SELECT, ORDER BY, WHERE, DISTINCTROW, TOP N, TOP N PERCENT, and GROUP BY. You also study SQL Aggregate functions (SUM, AVG, and so on), joins, unions, and cross-tab queries.

Day 9: In this lesson, you delve into the database engine that ships with Visual Basic 5—Microsoft Jet. You learn the hierarchical design and use of the Data Access Object (DAO) available to you in your development. The emphasis is on the methods, properties, and events of each object.

Day 10: On Day 10, you temporarily abandon use of the data control in favor of writing Visual Basic code to manage data. You learn the pluses and minuses of this practice. During the lesson, you build an OLE Server library that can be used as the basis for future Visual Basic data entry projects.

Day 11: You get graphical in Day 11. Users can identify trends and deviations in data much more quickly with graphics and charts than they can with raw data. You learn how to use the graph tool that ships with Visual Basic 5 to give your applications a polished, graphical appearance. During the lesson, you construct a graphing control that you can use in all your future Visual Basic projects.

Day 12: In Day 12, you learn about the data-bound list boxes, combo boxes, and grids that ship with Visual Basic 5. You also learn how to use subforms to display data.

Day 13: Day 13 won't be unlucky as you focus on creating databases with the SQL language. In this second day devoted to SQL, you learn how to use SQL Data Manipulation Language (DML) to create and modify databases, tables, relationships and indexes. You'll also work with SQL-VB5, a tool that can read text file scripts developed in any standard text editor or word processor to create and modify databases.

Day 14: The final chapter this week focuses on error trapping. No one intends to release a product with bugs in it, but it does happen. Error trapping manages these bugs, and many other unforeseen kinds of problems. Emphasis is on the different kinds of errors an application can encounter and how to handle each. You also build a reusable error trapping control that can be dropped into any Visual Basic application.

You've got a great deal of information to cover—so, let's begin Week 2!

Day 8

Selecting Data with SQL

Today is your first lesson in Structured Query Language (SQL). SQL is a powerful manipulation language used by Visual Basic and the Microsoft Access Jet database engine as the primary method for accessing the data in your databases. SQL statements fall into two broad categories: data manipulation language statements (DML) and data definition language statements (DDL). The DDL statements enable you to define data tables, indexes, and database relationships. DML statements are used to select, sort, summarize, and calculate the information stored in the data tables.

Today, you will learn about the DML statements. When you complete this lesson, you will be able to use SQL statements to construct database queries that can be retrieved, and you will be able to reorder data in any format recognized by Visual Basic. Because SQL is used in almost all relational database systems (SQL Server, Oracle, Gupta, and so on), you will also be able to apply the knowledge you gain here in almost any other relational database environment you might encounter in the future.

In this lesson, you will learn how to use the SELECT_FROM statement to select data from one or more tables and present that information in a single table for update or review. You will also learn how to limit the data you select to only the records that meet your criteria using the WHERE clause. You'll learn how to easily reorder the data in tables using the ORDER BY clause. You will also learn how to create simple statements that automatically summarize and total the data using the GROUP BY_HAVING clause.

You will learn about typical SQL functions to manipulate numbers and strings. This lesson also covers advanced DML statements such as PARAMETERS, UNIONS, JOINS, and TRANSFORM_PIVOT.

Today, you will create actual SQL queries (and in some cases, store them for later use) using the Visual Basic Visdata program you learned about on Day 7.

What Is SQL?

Before jumping into specific SQL statements and their use, you should understand the definition of SQL and its uses and origins. SQL stands for *Structured Query Language*. It was developed in the 1970s at IBM as a way to provide computer users with a standardized method for selecting data from various database formats. The intent was to build a language that was not based on any existing programming language, but could be used within any programming language as a way to update and query information in databases.

NOTE

The word *SQL* should be pronounced *ess-que-ell* instead of *sequel*. The confusion about the pronunciation of the word stems from the database language's origin. The SQL language is a successor of a language called Sequel developed by IBM in the late 1960s. For this reason, many (especially those familiar with IBM's Sequel language) continued to pronounce the name of the new database language improperly.

SQL statements are just that—statements. Each statement can perform operations on one or more database objects (tables, columns, indexes, and so on). Most SQL statements return results in the form of a set of data records, commonly referred to as a *view*. SQL is not a particularly friendly language. Many programs that use SQL statements hide these statements behind point-and-click dialogs, query-by-example grids, and other user-friendly interfaces. Make no mistake, however, that if the data you are accessing is stored in a relational database, you are using SQL statements, whether you know it or not.

ANSI Standard SQL Versus Microsoft Jet SQL

SQL syntax is determined by a committee that is part of the American National Standards Institute (ANSI). The ANSI-SQL committee is made up of information systems professionals who take on the job of establishing and enforcing standards on the rapidly moving computer-programming industry. Although each computer-programming language and database interface has its own unique version of SQL, nearly everyone has agreed to adhere to the basic standards defined by the ANSI-SQL committee. The most widely used SQL standard is SQL-89. This standard was first promulgated in 1989. An updated set of standards (SQL-92) was developed three years later.

Within each set of SQL standards, there are three levels of compliance. A database product must meet Level I compliance in order to call itself an SQL-compatible product. Levels II and III are optional levels of compliance that products can also attain in order to increase interoperability among database systems.

The Microsoft Jet database engine that is used to process all Visual Basic SQL statements is ANSI SQL-89 Level I compliant. There are very slight differences between ANSI SQL-89 and Microsoft Jet SQL at Level II and Level III. We won't dwell on these differences here. Those who are interested in learning more about ANSI SQL standards and Microsoft Jet compliance can find additional documentation elsewhere. The lessons in this book focus strictly on the Microsoft Jet SQL syntax. Be assured that once you master the concepts covered here, you will be able to use the same skills in almost all SQL-based programming and query tools you encounter.

SQL Basics

Now it's time to start building SQL statements. If you haven't already done so, load the Visual Basic Visdata application you learned about on Day 7. Using Visdata, load the BOOKS5.MDB that is included in the \TYSDBVB5\SOURCE\DATA directory of the CD that ships with this book. You will use this database for most of today's lesson.

NOTE This book shows reserved SQL words in uppercase letters (for example, SELECT). This is not required by Visual Basic, but it is a good programming habit.

The SELECT_FROM **Statement**

In this section, you will learn about the most commonly used SQL statement, the SELECT_FROM statement. The SELECT_FROM statement lets you pick records from one or more tables in a database. The results of a SELECT_FROM statement are returned as a *view*. This view is a subset of the source data. In Visual Basic, the view can be returned as a Recordset, Table, Dynaset, or Snapshot. Because today's lesson focuses on getting results you can display, views will be returned as Visual Basic Snapshot data objects.

In its simplest form, a SELECT_FROM statement contains two parts:

☐ A list of one or more table columns to select;

☐ A list of one or more tables that contain the requested columns.

NOTE | Standard SQL syntax uses the word *column* to describe a field and *row* to describe a record. This book uses the term *field* interchangeably with *column* and *record* interchangeably with *row*.

A simple example of a valid SQL statement is

```
SELECT AUID FROM Authors
```

This SQL statement tells the Microsoft Jet database engine to return a data object that contains the AUID from the Authors table. Enter this SQL statement into the Visdata SQL window and click the Execute button to see the returned result set. Your screen should look similar to the one in Figure 8.1.

Figure 8.1.

The result set from the first SELECT *statement.*

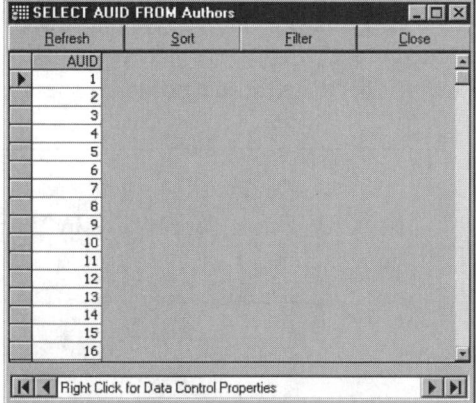

As you can see from the result set, the SELECT_FROM statement returns all the rows in the table. Whether the table contains 10 or 10,000 records, you can get a complete result set with just one SELECT_FROM statement. This is quite handy, but it can also be quite dangerous. If the result of your SELECT_FROM statement contains too many records, you can slow down the network, possibly run out of memory on your local workstation, and eventually lock up your PC. Later in this lesson, you will learn how to use the WHERE clause to limit the size of your view to only those records you need.

To return all the columns from a table, you can list each column in the SELECT statement. This works if you have only a few columns in the table. However, if you have several columns, it can become quite tedious. There is a shortcut. To automatically list all columns in the table in your result set, instead of typing column names, you can type the asterisk (*). The asterisk tells SQL to return all columns in the requested table. The SELECT statement to display all columns of the Author table would look like this:

```
SELECT * FROM Authors
```

Enter the preceding SELECT statement into the Visdata SQL window and review the results. Your screen should look like the one in Figure 8.2.

Figure 8.2.

*The results of the SELECT * query.*

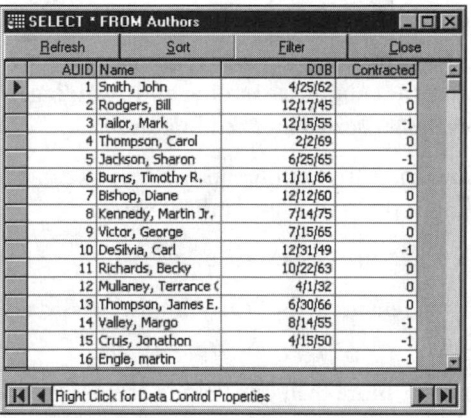

Notice that even though you listed no fields in your SELECT statement, all fields were returned in the result set. This is very useful when you want to display a data table but do not know the names of all the columns. As long as you know a valid table name, you can use the SELECT_FROM statement to display the entire table.

The order in which you list columns in the SELECT_FROM statement controls the order in which they are displayed in the result set. Figure 8.3 shows the results of the following SELECT_FROM statement:

```
SELECT Name, AUID FROM Authors
```

Figure 8.3.

Using the
SELECT_FROM
*statement to change
column display order.*

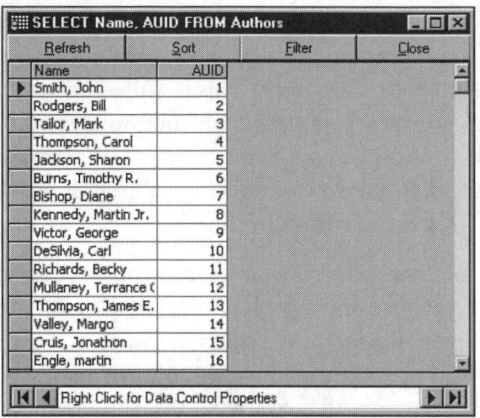

The ORDER BY Clause

When you use the SELECT_FROM statement, the records returned in the result set are returned in the order in which they were found in the underlying table. But what if you wanted to display the results of your SELECT_FROM statement in a specialized sorted order? You can use the ORDER BY clause to do just that.

Placing ASC or DESC after each field in the ORDER BY clause indicates the order in which you want to sort the column, ascending or descending. If no order is supplied, SQL assumes that you want the set sorted in ascending order.

The following SQL example shows how you can display the records in the Authors table in descending sorted order, by Author Name.

```
SELECT * FROM AUTHORS ORDER BY Name DESC
```

Enter this statement in the SQL window of Visdata and execute it. Compare your results to Figure 8.4.

You can enter more than one field in the ORDER BY clause. SQL will create a result set that reflects the aggregate sort of the ORDER BY clause. Using Visual Basic Visdata, enter and execute the following SELECT_FROM statement. Compare your results to those in Figure 8.5.

```
SELECT StateProv, City FROM Publishers ORDER BY StateProv DESC, City ASC
```

Notice in the example shown in Figure 8.5 that you have combined the ability to alter the row order of the data in the result set with the ability to alter the column order of the data in the result set. These are powerful tools. Now that you know how to use SQL to display complete, single-data tables, you can learn how to limit the result set to only those records you need.

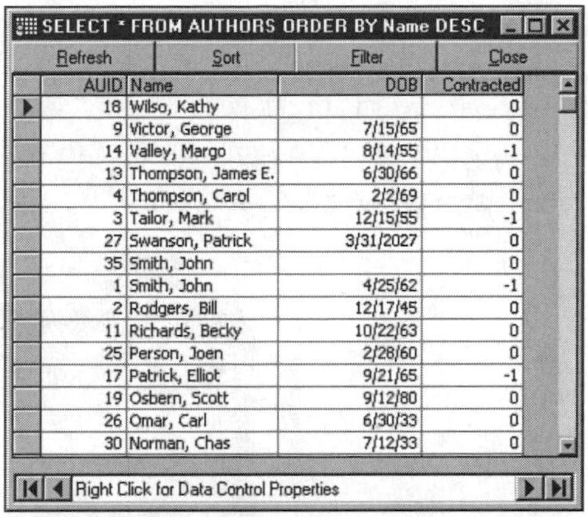

Figure 8.4.

The results of the descending ORDER BY clause.

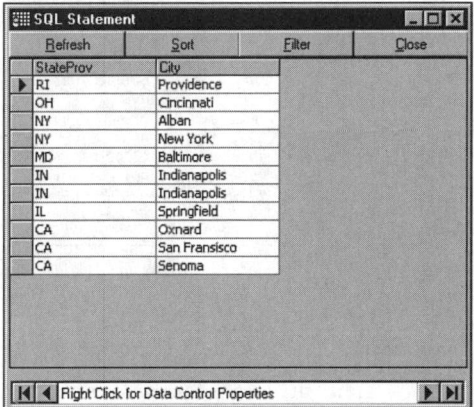

Figure 8.5.

Results of multiple-column ORDER BY clause.

The WHERE Clause

One of the most powerful aspects of the SELECT_FROM statement is its capability to control the content of the result set using the WHERE clause. There are two ways to use the WHERE clause to control the content of the result set:

☐ Use WHERE to limit the contents of a result set.

☐ Use WHERE to link two or more tables in a single result set.

Using WHERE to Limit the Result Set

The WHERE clause enables you to perform logical comparisons on data in any column in the data table. In its simplest form, the WHERE clause consists of the following:

```
WHERE column = value
```

In this line, `column` represents the name of the column in the requested data table, and `value` represents a literal value such as NY or Smith. It is important to know that the WHERE clause is always preceded by a SELECT_FROM statement. Use Visdata to enter and execute the following SQL statement, and compare your results to those in Figure 8.6.

```
SELECT Name, StateProv FROM Publishers
    WHERE StateProv = 'CA'
```

Figure 8.6.

The results of a simple WHERE *clause SQL query.*

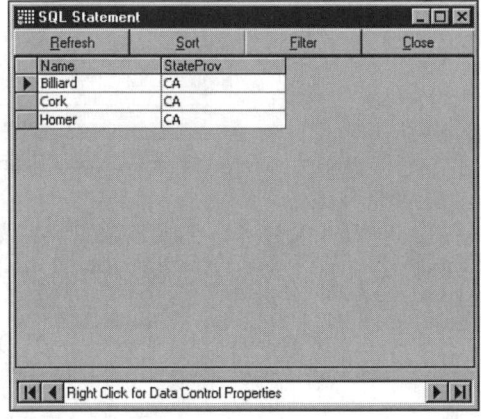

TIP

This book uses single quotation marks (') around string literals within SQL statements. Visual Basic SQL accepts both single and double quotation marks within SQL. Because you will often be building SQL statements in Visual Basic code, using single quotation marks within SQL statements makes it easier to construct and maintain SQL statements as Visual Basic strings.

The previous SQL statement returns a *subset* of the data in the result set. That is, the resulting view does not contain all of the rows of the Publishers table. Only those rows that have columns meeting the WHERE clause criteria are returned in the result set.

You can link WHERE clauses using the AND and OR operators. Enter and execute the following SQL statement, and compare your results to Figure 8.7.

```
SELECT Name, StateProv, City FROM Publishers
    WHERE StateProv = 'CA' AND City <> 'Senoma'
```

Figure 8.7.

The results of a complex WHERE *clause.*

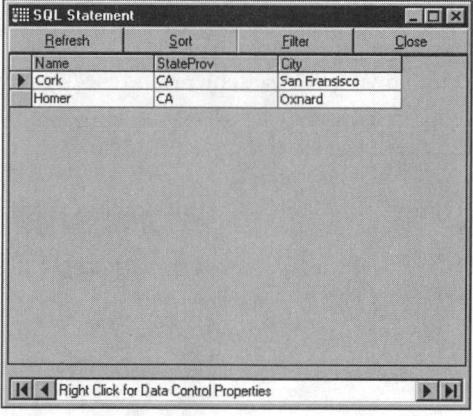

You can use several AND and OR operators to link valid logical comparisons together to form a single WHERE clause. You can also use more than just =, <>, >, <, <=, and >= logical comparisons. Visual Basic SQL supports the use of BETWEEN_AND, IN, and LIKE comparisons. The following SQL statement illustrates the use of BETWEEN_AND in a WHERE clause. Check your results against those shown in Figure 8.8.

```
SELECT PubID, Name, StateProv, City FROM Publishers
   WHERE PubID BETWEEN 10 AND 15
```

Figure 8.8.

Using BETWEEN_AND *in a* WHERE *clause.*

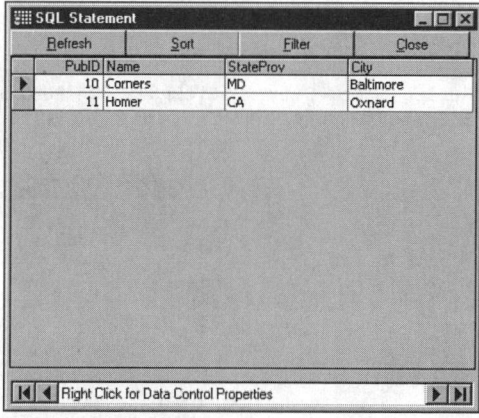

The result set contains only rows that have a PubID value between 10 and 15. Notice that the values listed in the BETWEEN_AND clause (10 and 15) are included in the result set.

You can also use SQL to return a result set that contains rows that match a set of noncontiguous data. For example, if you wanted a list of all the publishers in the states of

New York, California, and Alaska, you could use the IN keyword followed by the desired values, separated by commas, within parenthesis, as part of the WHERE clause. Enter and execute the following SQL statement, and check your results against those shown in Figure 8.9.

```
SELECT PubID, Name, City, StateProv FROM Publishers
    WHERE StateProv IN ('NY','CA','RI')
```

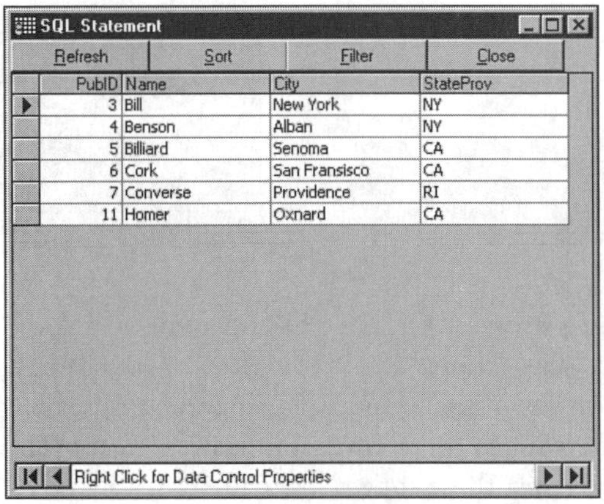

Figure 8.9.

Using the IN keyword in the WHERE clause.

You can also use the LIKE function to return all rows whose columns' contents are similar to the literals passed in the function. For example, to return all rows with a StateProv column that has the letter A in any position, you would use the following SQL SELECT_FROM statement (see Figure 8.10 for results):

```
SELECT PubID, Name, City, StateProv FROM Publishers
    WHERE StateProv LIKE('*I*')
```

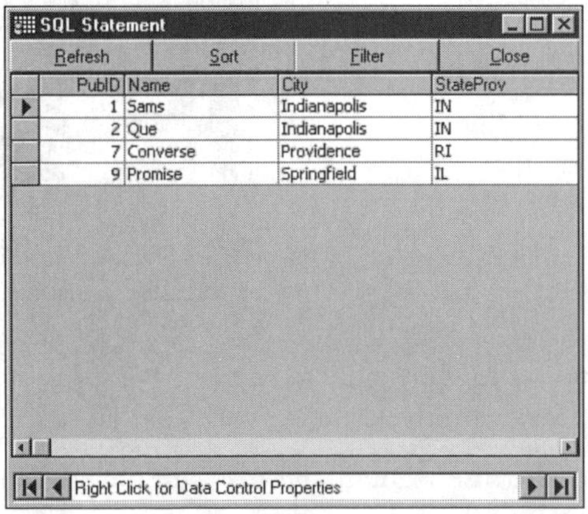

Figure 8.10.

Using the LIKE function in a WHERE clause.

The LIKE function is a very powerful tool. It is covered in more depth in a later section of today's lesson, "SQL Aggregate Functions."

Using WHERE to Link Two or More Tables in a Result Set

You can use the WHERE clause to compare columns from different tables. In doing so, you can set up criteria that can link two or more tables in a single result set. The syntax for this form of the WHERE clause is

```
SELECT table1.columnA, table2.columnA FROM table1, table2
WHERE table1.columnA = table2.columnA
```

table1 and table2 are different data tables in the same database. columnA represents a single column in each of the tables. Use Visdata to enter and execute the following SQL statement. Compare your result set to the one in Figure 8.11.

```
SELECT Titles.Title, Publishers.Name
   FROM Publishers, Titles
   WHERE Publishers.PubID =Titles.PubID
```

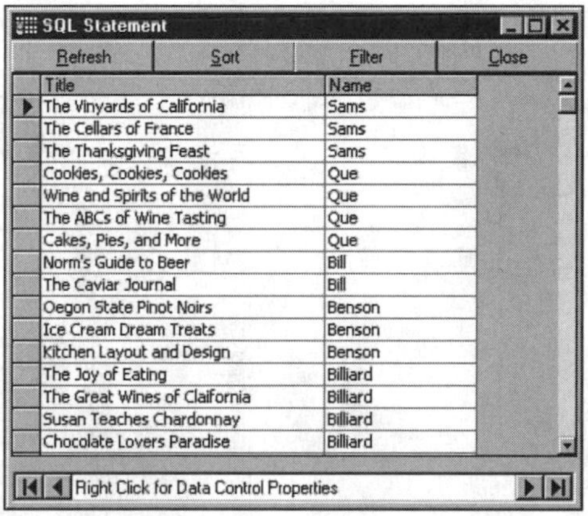

Figure 8.11.

Using the WHERE clause to link two tables in a single result set.

Title	Name
The Vinyards of California	Sams
The Cellars of France	Sams
The Thanksgiving Feast	Sams
Cookies, Cookies, Cookies	Que
Wine and Spirits of the World	Que
The ABCs of Wine Tasting	Que
Cakes, Pies, and More	Que
Norm's Guide to Beer	Bill
The Caviar Journal	Bill
Oegon State Pinot Noirs	Benson
Ice Cream Dream Treats	Benson
Kitchen Layout and Design	Benson
The Joy of Eating	Billiard
The Great Wines of Claifornia	Billiard
Susan Teaches Chardonnay	Billiard
Chocolate Lovers Paradise	Billiard

The preceding SQL statement creates a result set that displays the book title and publisher's name. This is accomplished using the WHERE clause to tell SQL to select only those rows where the PubID values in each table match up. Keep in mind that this is done without any programming code, special indexing, or sorting commands. SQL handles all those tasks for you. Also, there are a few new items in this SQL statement that bear further review.

This is the first SQL statement you have encountered today that lists columns from two different tables. When selecting columns from more than one table, it is good programming practice to precede the column name with the table name and join the two with the period (.). As long as the column name is unique among all columns in the tables from which you are selecting, SQL does not require you to use the table.column syntax. But it is a good habit to do so, especially when you are building SQL statements in Visual Basic code.

You should also notice that the WHERE clause comparison columns (Publishers.PubID and Titles.PubID) were not included in the SELECT portion of the statement. You do not have to include the column in the SELECT portion of the statement to use it in the WHERE portion of the statement, as long as the column already exists in the underlying table.

Combining tables using the WHERE clause always returns a nonupdateable result set. You cannot update the columns in a view created in this manner. If you want to link tables together and also be able to update the underlying tables for that view, you need to use the JOIN clause, which is covered later today.

You can combine the link-type and limit-type versions of the WHERE clause in a single SQL SELECT_FROM statement. Execute the following statement and compare your results to those in Figure 8.12.

```
SELECT Titles.PubID,Titles.Title,Publishers.Name
   FROM Titles, Publishers
   WHERE Titles.PubID = Publishers.PubID
      AND Publishers.PubID BETWEEN 5 AND 10
```

Figure 8.12.

Combining link-type and limit-type WHERE clauses.

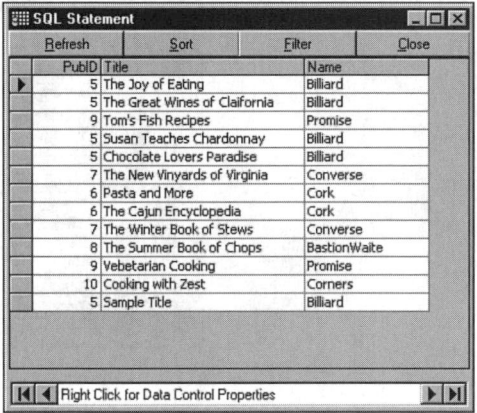

The preceding SQL statement selects only those records in which the PubID columns match *and* the PubID values are between 5 and 10.

You can use the WHERE clause to link more than two data tables. The linking column for table1 and table2 does not have to be the same column for table2 and table3. Execute the following statement and review your results against those in Figure 8.13.

```
SELECT Titles.PubID,Titles.Title,Publishers.Name,Authors.Name
   FROM Titles, Publishers,Authors
   WHERE Titles.PubID = Publishers.PubID
      AND Titles.AUID = Authors.AUID
```

Figure 8.13.
Using the WHERE *clause to link three tables.*

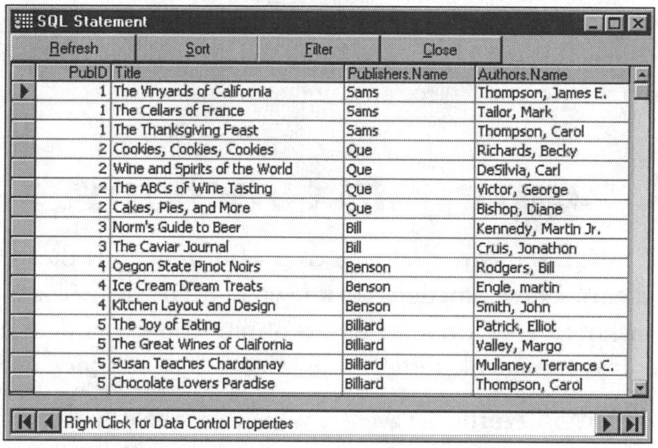

PubID	Title	Publishers.Name	Authors.Name
1	The Vinyards of California	Sams	Thompson, James E.
1	The Cellars of France	Sams	Tailor, Mark
1	The Thanksgiving Feast	Sams	Thompson, Carol
2	Cookies, Cookies, Cookies	Que	Richards, Becky
2	Wine and Spirits of the World	Que	DeSilvia, Carl
2	The ABCs of Wine Tasting	Que	Victor, George
2	Cakes, Pies, and More	Que	Bishop, Diane
3	Norm's Guide to Beer	Bill	Kennedy, Martin Jr.
3	The Caviar Journal	Bill	Cruis, Jonathon
4	Oegon State Pinot Noirs	Benson	Rodgers, Bill
4	Ice Cream Dream Treats	Benson	Engle, martin
4	Kitchen Layout and Design	Benson	Smith, John
5	The Joy of Eating	Billiard	Patrick, Elliot
5	The Great Wines of Claifornia	Billiard	Valley, Margo
5	Susan Teaches Chardonnay	Billiard	Mullaney, Terrance C.
5	Chocolate Lovers Paradise	Billiard	Thompson, Carol

In the previous example, the Publishers table and the Titles table are linked using the PubID column. The Titles table and the Authors table are linked using the AUID field. When the link is made, the selected columns are displayed in the result set.

You might have noticed that SQL assigns column names to the result sets. There are times when these assigned names can be misleading or incomplete. You can use the `AS` keyword to rename the columns in the result set. The following SQL statement is one example of using the `AS` keyword in the `SELECT` statement to rename the column headers of the result set. This renaming does not affect the original column names in the underlying tables. Execute the following SQL statement and compare your results to those in Figure 8.14.

```
SELECT Titles.PubID AS PubCode,    Titles.Title AS BookTitle,
   Publishers.Name AS PubName,
   Authors.Name AS AuthorName
   FROM Titles, Publishers,Authors
   WHERE Titles.PubID = Publishers.PubID
      AND Titles.AUID = Authors.AUID
```

Figure 8.14.
Using the AS *keyword to rename columns in the result set.*

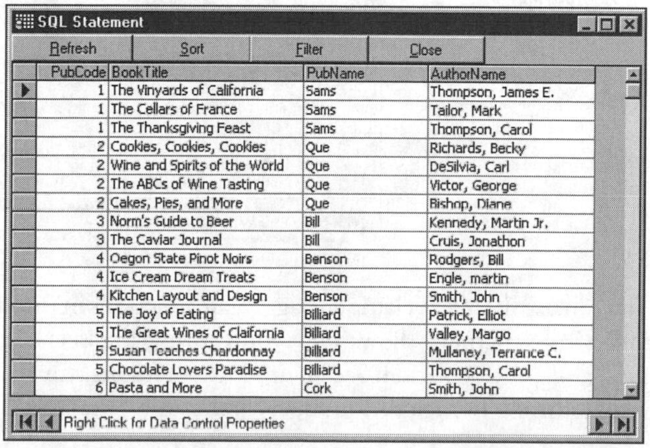

PubCode	BookTitle	PubName	AuthorName
1	The Vinyards of California	Sams	Thompson, James E.
1	The Cellars of France	Sams	Tailor, Mark
1	The Thanksgiving Feast	Sams	Thompson, Carol
2	Cookies, Cookies, Cookies	Que	Richards, Becky
2	Wine and Spirits of the World	Que	DeSilvia, Carl
2	The ABCs of Wine Tasting	Que	Victor, George
2	Cakes, Pies, and More	Que	Bishop, Diane
3	Norm's Guide to Beer	Bill	Kennedy, Martin Jr.
3	The Caviar Journal	Bill	Cruis, Jonathon
4	Oegon State Pinot Noirs	Benson	Rodgers, Bill
4	Ice Cream Dream Treats	Benson	Engle, martin
4	Kitchen Layout and Design	Benson	Smith, John
5	The Joy of Eating	Billiard	Patrick, Elliot
5	The Great Wines of Claifornia	Billiard	Valley, Margo
5	Susan Teaches Chardonnay	Billiard	Mullaney, Terrance C.
5	Chocolate Lovers Paradise	Billiard	Thompson, Carol
6	Pasta and More	Cork	Smith, John

Now that you know how to use the SELECT_FROM statement to select the desired rows and columns from data tables, read about how to use SQL functions to calculate and manipulate data within your selected columns and rows.

SQL Aggregate Functions

The SQL standards define a core set of functions that are present in all SQL-compliant systems. These functions are known as *aggregate functions*. Aggregate functions are used to quickly return computed results of numeric data stored in a column. The SQL aggregate functions available through the Microsoft Access Jet database engine are

- ☐ AVG: Returns the average value of all the values in a column.
- ☐ COUNT: Returns the number of columns and is usually used to determine the total rows in a view. COUNT is the only standard SQL aggregate function that can be applied to a non-numeric column.
- ☐ SUM: Returns the total of all the values in a column.
- ☐ MAX: Returns the highest of all the values in a column.
- ☐ MIN: Returns the lowest of all the values in a column.

The following SQL statement illustrates all five of the SQL aggregate functions. Enter and execute this statement, and check your results against Figure 8.15.

```
SELECT COUNT(Units) AS UnitCount,
    AVG(Units) AS UnitAvg,
    SUM(Units) AS UnitSum,
    MIN(Units) AS UnitMin,
    MAX(Units) AS UnitMax
    FROM BookSales
```

Figure 8.15.

Using SQL aggregate functions.

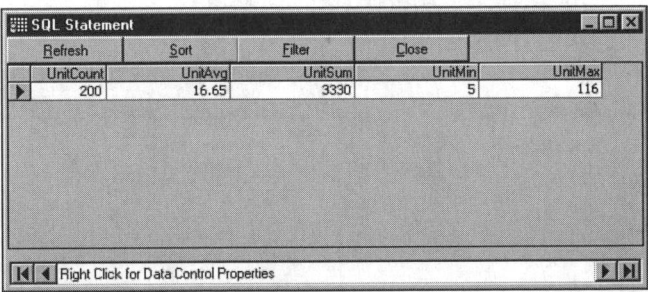

You can use the WHERE clause and aggregate functions in the same SELECT_FROM statement. The following statement shows how you can use the WHERE clause to limit rows included in the aggregate calculation. See Figure 8.16 for results. Compare these numbers to those in the view returned in the previous query (refer to Figure 8.15).

```
SELECT COUNT(Units) AS UnitCount,
    AVG(Units) AS UnitAvg,
    SUM(Units) AS UnitSum,
    MIN(Units) AS UnitMin,
    MAX(Units) AS UnitMax
    FROM BookSales
    WHERE Qtr = 1
```

Figure 8.16.

Using the WHERE *clause to limit the scope of aggregate functions.*

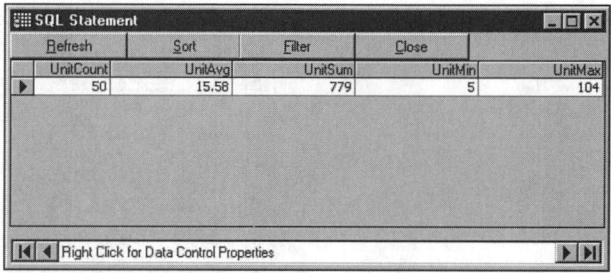

Using Visual Basic Functions in a SELECT Statement

When you call the Microsoft Access Jet database engine from within a Visual Basic program, you can use any valid Visual Basic functions as part of the SQL statement. For example, if you want to create a result set with a column that holds only the first three characters of a field in the underlying table, you could use the Visual Basic Left$ function as part of your column list in the SELECT_FROM statement, in the following line (see Figure 8.17):

```
SELECT Left$(Name,3), Name
    FROM Authors
```

Figure 8.17.

Using Visual Basic functions in an SQL statement.

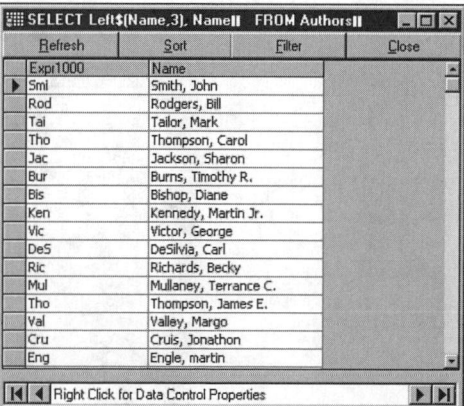

You can also use Visual Basic syntax to combine several data table columns into a single column in the result set. Enter and execute the following example and compare your results to Figure 8.18.

```
SELECT Name, City+", "+StateProv+"  "+Zip AS ADDRESS
    FROM Publishers
```

Figure 8.18.

Using Visual Basic syntax to combine columns.

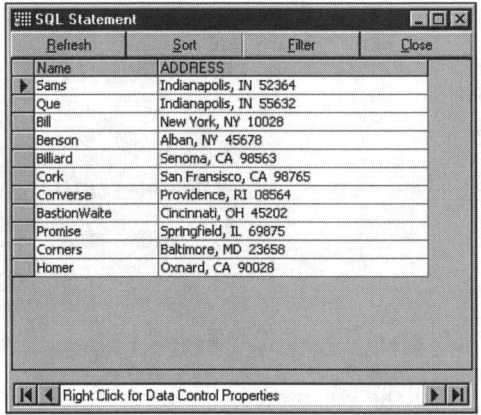

You can also use Visual Basic functions as part of the WHERE clause in an SQL statement. The following example (Figure 8.19) returns only rows that have the letter *a* as the second character in the Name column.

```
SELECT Name FROM Publishers
    WHERE Mid$(Name,2,1)="a"
```

Figure 8.19.

Using Visual Basic functions in an SQL WHERE *clause.*

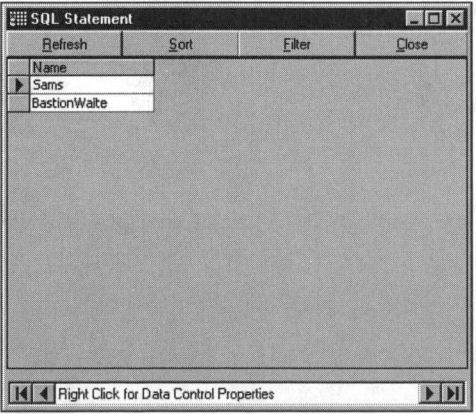

Even though using familiar Visual Basic functions and syntax is very handy, it has its drawbacks. Chief among them is the fact that after you create an SQL statement that uses

Visual Basic–specific portions, your code is no longer portable. If you ever move the SQL statements to another database engine (such as SQL Server), you must remove the Visual Basic–specific portions of the SQL statements and replace them with something else that will work with the database engine you are using. This will not be an issue if you plan to stick with the Microsoft Access Jet engine for all your database access.

Another possible drawback that you'll encounter if you use Visual Basic–specific syntax in your SQL statements is that of speed. Extensive use of Visual Basic–specific code within SQL statements results in a slight performance hit. The speed difference is minor, but it should be considered.

It is better to use as few Visual Basic–specific functions in your SQL statements as possible. You will not limit the portability of your code, and you will not suffer from unduly slow processing of the SQL statements.

NOTE

You can't use user-defined functions within your SQL statements when you use the Microsoft Access Jet database engine from within Visual Basic. You can only use the built-in SQL functions and the predefined Visual Basic functions.

More SQL DML Statements

Now that you know how to create basic SQL SELECT_FROM statements and you know how to use the built-in SQL functions, return to the basic SELECT_FROM statement and add a few more enhancements to your SQL tool kit.

The DISTINCT and DISTINCTROW Clauses

There are times when you select data from a table that has more than one occurrence of the rows you are trying to collect. For example, you want to get a list of all the customers that have at least one order on file in the Orders table. The problem is that some customers have several orders in the table. You don't want to see those names appear more than once in your result set. You can use the DISTINCT keyword to make sure that you do not get duplicates of the same customer in your result set.

Enter and execute the following statement. As a test, execute the same SQL statement without the DISTINCT clause and compare the result sets. Refer to Figure 8.20 as an example.

```
SELECT DISTINCT AUID FROM Titles
   ORDER BY AUID
```

Figure 8.20.

Using the DISTINCT *keyword to remove duplicates from a result set.*

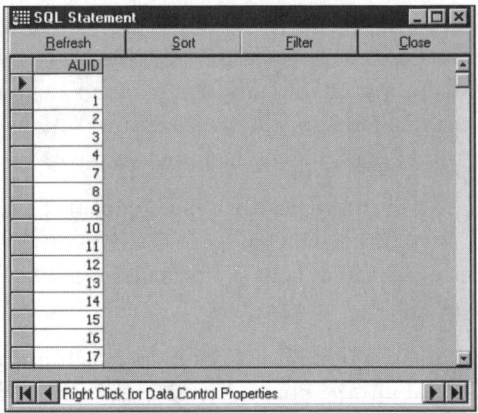

If you include more than one column in the SELECT list, all columns are used to evaluate the uniqueness of the row. Execute and compare the result sets of the following two SQL statements. Refer to Figure 8.21 as a guide.

```
SELECT DISTINCT Title
    FROM BookSales

SELECT DISTINCT Title, Units
    FROM BookSales
```

Figure 8.21.

Using DISTINCT *on multiple columns.*

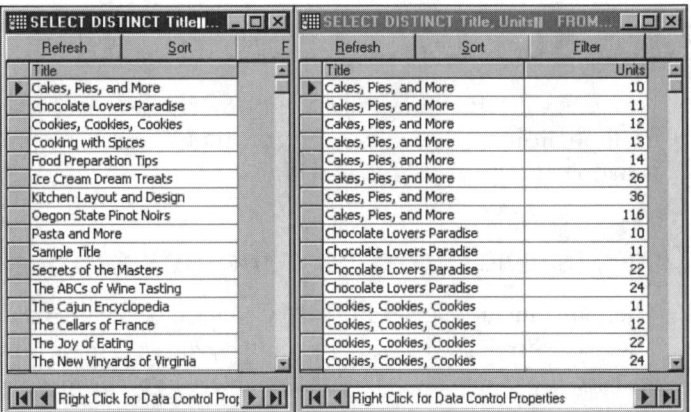

Notice that the first SQL statement returns a single record for each Title in the data table. The second SQL statement returns more records for each Title because there are distinct Units values for each Title.

There are also times when you want to collect data on all rows that are distinct in any of the fields. Instead of using the DISTINCT keyword and listing all the fields in the table, you can

use the DISTINCTROW keyword. The following SQL statement (see Figure 8.22) uses DISTINCTROW to return the same records as the SQL statement in the previous example.

```
SELECT DISTINCTROW *
    FROM BookSales
    ORDER BY Title
```

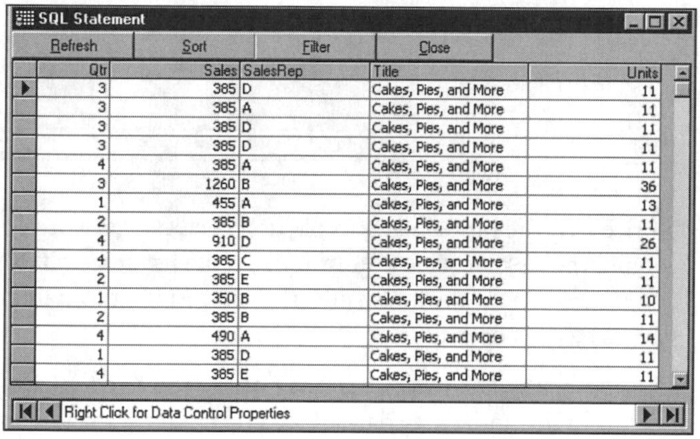

Figure 8.22.

Using DISTINCTROW *in an SQL statement.*

Both the DISTINCT and DISTINCTROW keywords enable you to limit the contents of the result set based on the uniqueness of one or more columns in the data table. In the next section, you'll learn how you can limit the contents of the result set to the records with the highest numeric values in selected columns.

The TOP n and TOP n PERCENT Clauses

You can use the TOP n or TOP n PERCENT SQL keywords to limit the number of records in your result set. Suppose you want to get a list of the five top-selling books in a data table. You can use the TOP n clause to get just that. TOP n returns the first *n* number of records. If you have two records of the same value, SQL returns both records. For the previous example, if the fifth and sixth records were both equal, the result set would contain six records, not just five.

When you use the TOP clause, you must also use the ORDER BY clause to make sure that your result set is sorted. If you do not use the ORDER BY clause, you receive an arbitrary set of records because SQL first executes the ORDER BY clause and then selects the TOP n records you requested. Without the ORDER BY clause, it is quite likely that you will not get the results you intended. If a WHERE clause is present, SQL performs the WHERE clause, the ORDER BY clause, and then the TOP n clause. As you can see, failure to use the ORDER BY clause most certainly returns garbage in your result set (see Figure 8.23).

```
SELECT TOP 5 * FROM BookSales
    ORDER BY Sales DESC
```

Figure 8.23.

Using TOP n *to limit the result set.*

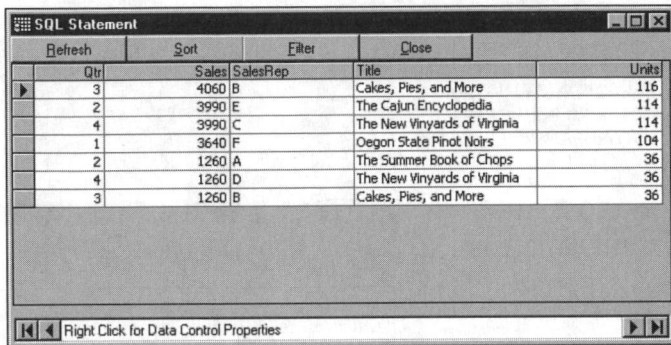

Notice that the preceding example uses the DESC keyword in the ORDER BY clause. Whether you use the DESC or ASC ORDER BY format, the result set still contains the first *n* records in the table (based on the sort). Also note that the result set contains more than five records, because several records have the same Sales value.

The TOP n PERCENT version returns not the top five records, but the top five percent of the records in the underlying data table. The results of the following SQL statement (see Figure 8.24) contain several more records than the result set shown previously.

```
SELECT TOP 5 PERCENT * FROM BookSales
    ORDER BY Sales
```

Figure 8.24.

Using
TOP n PERCENT
to limit the result set.

Qtr	Sales	SalesRep	Title	Units
1	175	C	Food Preparation Tips	5
2	175	C	Training New Chefs	5
3	175	E	Pasta and More	5
4	175	F	The New Vinyards of Virginia	5
1	280	B	Secrets of the Masters	8
4	280	F	The ABCs of Wine Tasting	8
3	280	E	Kitchen Layout and Design	8
2	280	B	Oegon State Pinot Noirs	8
1	350	F	Cooking with Spices	10
1	350	A	The Cajun Encyclopedia	10
1	350	C	Chocolate Lovers Paradise	10
1	350	D	Oegon State Pinot Noirs	10
1	350	F	Pasta and More	10
1	350	C	Training New Chefs	10
1	350	A	Oegon State Pinot Noirs	10
1	350	D	Chocolate Lovers Paradise	10

The GROUP BY_HAVING Clause

One of the more powerful SQL clauses is the GROUP BY_HAVING clause. This clause lets you use the SQL aggregate functions discussed earlier today to easily create result sets that contain a list of subtotals of the underlying data table. For example, you might want to be able to create a data set that contains a list of Titles and the total Units sold, by Title. The following SQL statement (see Figure 8.25) can do that:

```
SELECT Title, SUM(Units) AS UnitsSold
   FROM BookSales
   GROUP BY Title
```

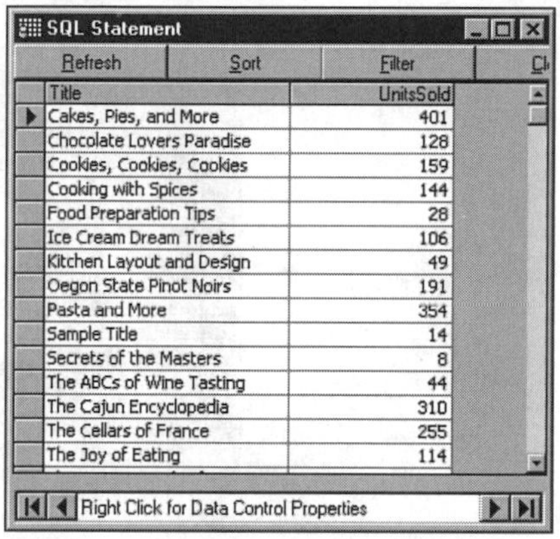

Figure 8.25.

Using GROUP BY *to create subtotals.*

The GROUP BY clause requires that all numeric columns in the SELECT column list be a part of an SQL aggregate function (SUM, AVG, MIN, MAX, and COUNT). Also, you cannot use the * as part of the SELECT column list when you use the GROUP BY clause.

What if you wanted to get a list of all the book titles that sold more than 100 units for the year? The first thought would be to use a WHERE clause:

```
SELECT Titles, SUM(Units) AS UnitsSold
   WHERE Sum(Units) > 100
   GROUP BY Units
```

However, if you try to run this SQL statement, you discover that SQL does not allow aggregate functions within the WHERE clause. You really want to use a WHERE clause *after* the aggregate function has created a resulting column. In plain English, the query needs to perform the following steps:

☐ Add up all the units.

☐ Write the results to a temporary table.

☐ Display only those rows in the temporary table that have a unit total greater than 100.

Luckily, you don't have to actually write all this in a series of SQL statements. You can get the same results by adding the HAVING keyword to the GROUP BY clause. The HAVING clause acts the same as the WHERE clause, except that the HAVING clause acts upon the resulting columns created by the GROUP BY clause, not the underlying columns. The following SQL statement (see Figure 8.26) returns only the Titles that have sold more than 100 units in the last year:

```
SELECT Title, SUM(Units) AS UnitsSold
    FROM BookSales
    GROUP BY Title HAVING SUM(Units)>100
```

Figure 8.26.

Using the HAVING
clause with
GROUP BY.

SQL Statement			
Refresh	Sort	Filter	Close
Title		UnitsSold	
▶ Cakes, Pies, and More		401	
Chocolate Lovers Paradise		128	
Cookies, Cookies, Cookies		159	
Cooking with Spices		144	
Ice Cream Dream Treats		106	
Oegon State Pinot Noirs		191	
Pasta and More		354	
The Cajun Encyclopedia		310	
The Cellars of France		255	
The Joy of Eating		114	
The New Vinyards of Virginia		443	
The Summer Book of Chops		246	
Training New Chefs		168	
Vegetarian Cooking		158	
◄ ◄ Right Click for Data Control Properties			► ►

The columns used in the HAVING clause do not have to be the same columns listed in the SELECT clause. The contents of the HAVING clause follow the same rules as those for the contents of the WHERE clause. You can use logical operators AND, OR, and NOT, and you can include VB-specific functions as part of the HAVING clause. The following SQL statement (see Figure 8.27) returns sales in dollars for all titles that have more than 100 units sold and whose titles have the letter *a* as the second letter in the title:

```
SELECT Title, SUM(Sales) AS SalesAmt
    FROM BookSales
    GROUP BY Title
    HAVING SUM(Units)>100 AND Mid$(Title,2,1)="a"
```

Figure 8.27.

Using a complex
HAVING *clause.*

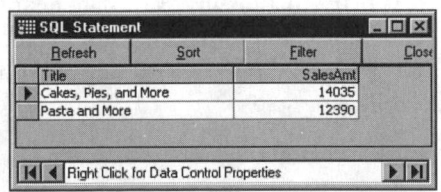

SQL Statement			
Refresh	Sort	Filter	Close
Title		SalesAmt	
▶ Cakes, Pies, and More		14035	
Pasta and More		12390	
◄ ◄ Right Click for Data Control Properties			► ►

8

SQL JOINs

The JOIN clause is a very powerful optional SQL clause. Remember when you learned how to link two tables together using WHERE table1.column1 = table2.column1? The only problem with using the WHERE clause is that the result set is not updateable. What if you need to create an updateable result set that contains columns from more than one table? You use JOIN.

There are three types of JOIN clauses in Microsoft Access Jet SQL:

- ☐ INNER JOIN
- ☐ LEFT JOIN
- ☐ RIGHT JOIN

The following sections describe each form of JOIN and how it is used in your programs.

The INNER JOIN

The INNER JOIN can be used to create a result set that contains only those records that have an exact match in both tables. Enter and execute the following SQL statement (see Figure 8.28):

```
SELECT PublisherComments.Comments,
    Publishers.Name, Publishers.StateProv
    FROM PublisherComments INNER JOIN Publishers
    ON PublisherComments.PubID = Publishers.PubID
```

Figure 8.28.

Using the INNER JOIN SQL clause.

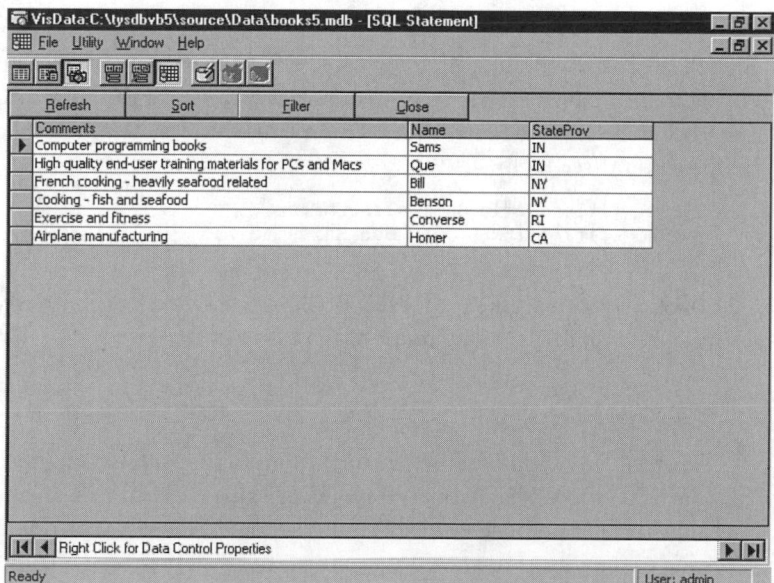

NOTE

> PublisherComments was used as the name for the table used in the preceding example. When creating a Microsoft Access database, we could easily have named the table "Publisher Comments" (note the space), in which case, we would have had to enclose the table name in brackets in the preceding query, like so:
>
> ```
> [Publisher Comments]
> ```
>
> This is a good time to point out that it is a bad idea to use embedded spaces as table names. Not only do you need to include brackets around the name in a query, but also the Wizard available to up-size Access data files to Microsoft SQL Server does not work successfully on tables with spaces embedded in their names.

The preceding SQL statement returns all the records from the Publisher table that have a PubID that matches a PubID in the [Publisher Comments] table. This type of JOIN returns all the records that reside within both tables—thus, an INNER JOIN.

This is handy if you have two tables that you know are not perfectly matched against a single column and you want to create a result set that contains only those rows that match on both sides. The INNER JOIN also works well when you have a parent table (such as a CustomerTable) and a child table (such as a ShipAddressTable) with a one-to-one relationship. Using an INNER JOIN, you can quickly create a list of all CustomerTable records that have a corresponding ShipAddressTable record on file.

INNER JOINs work best when you create a JOIN on a column that is unique in both tables. If you use a table that has more than one occurrence of the JOIN column, you'll get a row for each occurrence in the result set. This might be undesirable. The following example illustrates the point (see Figure 8.29):

```
SELECT Titles.Title,BookSales.Units
   FROM Titles INNER JOIN BookSales
   ON Titles.Title = BookSales.Title
```

In the previous example, the table BookSales has numerous entries for each title (one for each quarter recorded), so the result of the INNER JOIN returns each Title multiple times.

The LEFT JOIN

The LEFT JOIN is one of the two outer joins in the SQL syntax. Although INNER JOIN returns only those rows that have corresponding values in both tables, the outer joins return all the records from one side of the join, whether or not there is a corresponding match on the other side of the join. The LEFT JOIN clause returns all the records from the first table on the list (the left-most table) and any records on the right side of the table that have a matching column value. Figure 8.30 shows the same SQL query that was shown in Figure 8.28.

```
SELECT Publishers.Name,PublisherComments.Comments
  FROM Publishers LEFT JOIN PublisherComments
  ON Publishers.PubID = PublisherComments.PubID
```

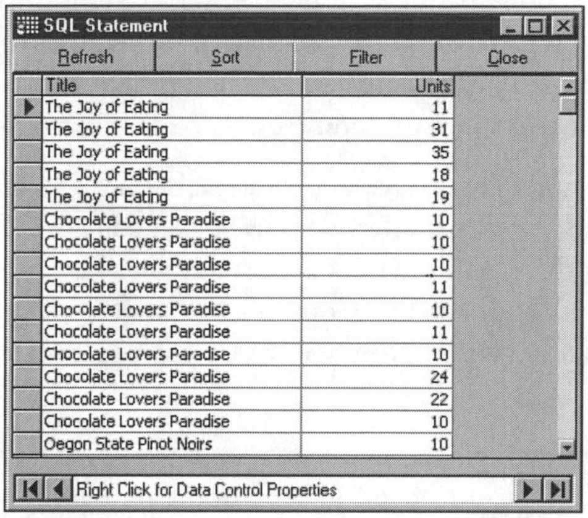

Figure 8.29.

Using an INNER
JOIN *on a non-unique column.*

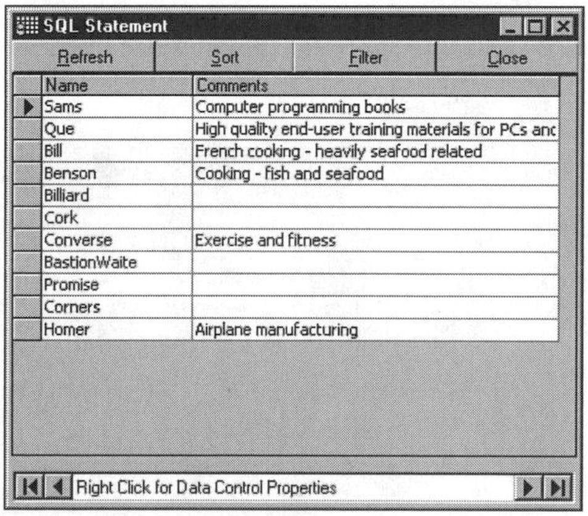

Figure 8.30.

Using the LEFT JOIN
clause.

Notice that the result set has blank comments in several places. The LEFT JOIN is handy when you want a list of all the records in the master table and any records in the dependent table that are on file.

The RIGHT JOIN

The RIGHT JOIN works the same as the LEFT JOIN except that the result set is based on the second (right-hand) table in the JOIN statement. You can use the RIGHT JOIN in the same manner you would use the LEFT JOIN.

UNION **Queries**

Another powerful SQL clause is the UNION clause. This SQL keyword lets you create a union between two tables or SQL queries that contain similar, but unrelated, data. A UNION query is handy when you want to collate information from two queries into a single result set. Because UNION queries return nonupdateable result sets, they are good for producing on-screen displays, reports, and base data for generating graphs and charts.

For example, if you have a customer table and a vendor table, you might want to get a list of all vendors and customers who live in the state of Ohio. You could write an SQL statement to select the rows from the Customers table. Then write an SQL statement to select the rows from the Vendors table. Combine the two SQL statements into a single SQL phrase using the UNION keyword. Now you can get a single result set that contains the results of both queries.

In the following SQL statement (see Figure 8.31), you are creating a result set that contains all Publishers and Buyers located in the state of New York.

```
SELECT Name, City, StateProv, Zip FROM Publishers WHERE StateProv='NY'
    UNION
SELECT Name, City, StateProv, Zip FROM Buyers WHERE StateProv='NY'
    ORDER BY Zip
```

Figure 8.31.

An example of a
UNION *query.*

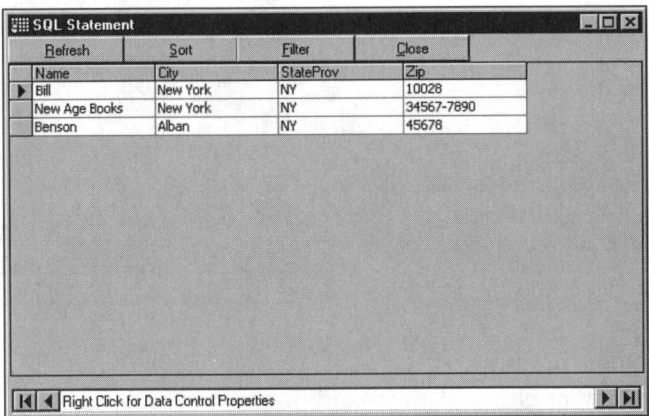

A note of caution when using the UNION query. To keep the same number of data columns, SQL does a data type override to insert results into columns that are not the same data types. The UNION query uses the column names of the first SQL query in the statement and creates a result set that displays the data even if data types must be altered to do so.

Each portion of the UNION query must have the same *number* of columns. If the first query results in six displayable columns, the query on the other side of the UNION statement must also result in six columns. If there is not an equal number of columns on each side of a UNION query, you receive an SQL error message.

You can also use UNION queries on the same table. The following SQL statement (see Figure 8.32) shows how you can use SQL to return the top-selling titles and the bottom-selling titles in the same result set:

```
SELECT SUM(Sales) AS TotSales,Title FROM BookSales
    GROUP BY Title HAVING SUM(Sales)>4000
UNION
    SELECT SUM(Sales) AS TotSales,Title FROM BookSales
    GROUP BY Title HAVING SUM(Sales)<1000
ORDER BY TotSales
```

Figure 8.32.

Using UNION *on the same data table.*

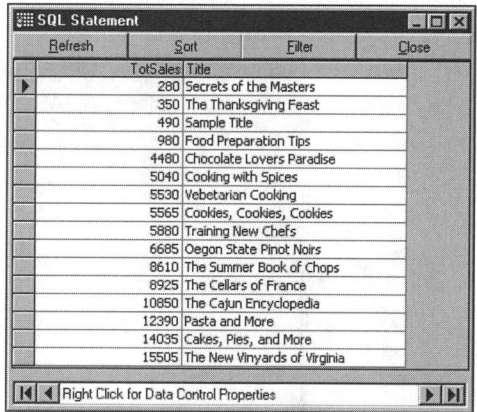

You can use Visual Basic stored queries (QueryDefs) as replacements for the complete SQL statement on either side of a UNION keyword. You can also link several SQL queries together with successive UNION keywords.

Crosstab Queries with TRANSFORM_PIVOT

The last SQL statement covered today is the TRANSFORM_PIVOT statement. This is a very powerful SQL tool that enables you to create result sets that contain summarized data in a form known as a *crosstab query*. Instead of trying to explain a crosstab query, let's look at a sample problem.

Suppose you have a data table that contains information on book titles and sales by quarter (sound familiar?). You have been asked to produce a view set that lists each book title down the left side and each quarter across the top with the sales figures for each quarter to the right of the book title. The only problem is that your data table has a single record for each quarter for each book. For example, if book A has sales in three quarters this year, you have three rows in your data table. If book B has sales for four quarters, you have four rows, and so on. How can you produce a view that lists the quarters as columns instead of as rows?

You can accomplish this with a complicated set of subsequent SQL statements that produces temporary views, merges them together, and so on. Thanks to the folks who invented the Microsoft Access Jet database engine, however, you can use the TRANSFORM_PIVOT statement instead. You can produce the entire result set in one SQL statement using TRANSFORM_PIVOT. The following SQL statement shows how this can be done. See Figure 8.33 for a sample result set.

```
TRANSFORM SUM(BookSales.Sales)
    SELECT Title FROM BookSales
    GROUP BY Title
PIVOT BookSales.Qtr
```

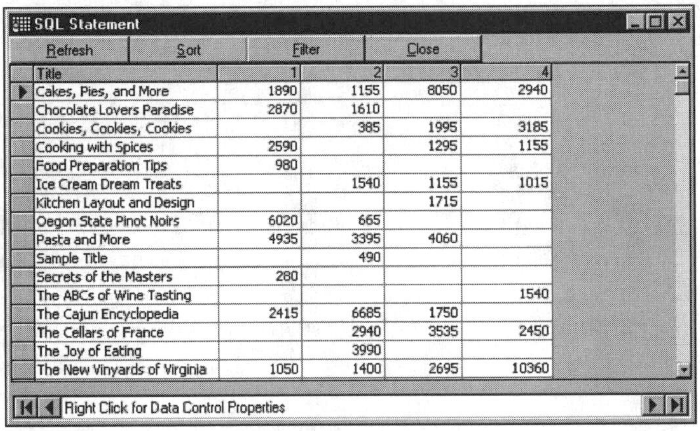

Figure 8.33.

The TRANSFORM_PIVOT *example.*

Title	1	2	3	4
Cakes, Pies, and More	1890	1155	8050	2940
Chocolate Lovers Paradise	2870	1610		
Cookies, Cookies, Cookies		385	1995	3185
Cooking with Spices	2590		1295	1155
Food Preparation Tips	980			
Ice Cream Dream Treats		1540	1155	1015
Kitchen Layout and Design			1715	
Oegon State Pinot Noirs	6020	665		
Pasta and More	4935	3395	4060	
Sample Title		490		
Secrets of the Masters	280			
The ABCs of Wine Tasting				1540
The Cajun Encyclopedia	2415	6685	1750	
The Cellars of France		2940	3535	2450
The Joy of Eating		3990		
The New Vinyards of Virginia	1050	1400	2695	10360

Right Click for Data Control Properties

Notice the form of the TRANSFORM_PIVOT statement. It starts with the TRANSFORM keyword, not the SELECT keyword. Notice that a single SQL aggregate function immediately follows the TRANSFORM keyword. This is required, even if no real totaling will be performed. After the TRANSFORM aggregate function clause, you have the standard SELECT_FROM clause. Notice that the preceding example did not include the Booksales.Sales column in the SELECT statement because it will be produced by the TRANSFORM_PIVOT clause automatically. The GROUP BY clause is required in order to tell SQL how to treat the successive rows that will be handled for each BookSales.Title. Finally, add the PIVOT keyword, followed by the column that you want to use, as the set of headers that follow out to the right of the GROUP BY clause.

TRANSFORM_PIVOT uses the data in the PIVOT column as column headers in the result set. You will have as many columns in your result set as you have unique values in your PIVOT

8

column. This is important to understand. Using columns that contain a limited set of data (such as months of the year) produces valuable result sets. However, using a column that contains unique data (such as the CustomerID column) produces a result set with an unpredictable number of columns.

The nice thing about TRANSFORM_PIVOT is that it is easy to produce several different views of the same data by just changing the PIVOT column. For example, what if you wanted to see the book sales results by BookSales.SaleRep instead of by BookSales.Qtr? All you have to do is change the PIVOT field. See the following code example and Figure 8.34.

```
TRANSFORM SUM(BookSales.Sales)
    SELECT Title FROM BookSales
    GROUP BY Title
PIVOT BookSales.SalesRep
```

Figure 8.34.

Changing the PIVOT field.

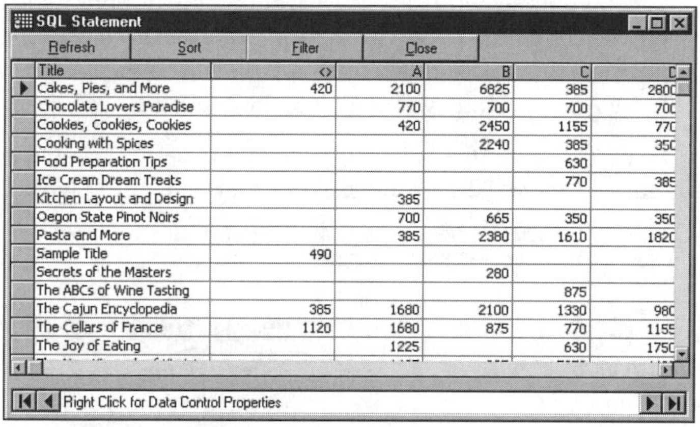

Title	<>	A	B	C	C
Cakes, Pies, and More	420	2100	6825	385	2800
Chocolate Lovers Paradise		770	700	700	700
Cookies, Cookies, Cookies		420	2450	1155	770
Cooking with Spices			2240	385	350
Food Preparation Tips				630	
Ice Cream Dream Treats				770	385
Kitchen Layout and Design		385			
Oegon State Pinot Noirs		700	665	350	350
Pasta and More		385	2380	1610	1820
Sample Title	490				
Secrets of the Masters			280		
The ABCs of Wine Tasting				875	
The Cajun Encyclopedia	385	1680	2100	1330	980
The Cellars of France	1120	1680	875	770	1155
The Joy of Eating		1225		630	1750

Notice, in Figure 8.34, that you can see a column with the header <>. When Microsoft Access Jet ran the SQL statement, it discovered some records that had no value in the BookSales.SaleRep column. SQL automatically created a new column (<>) to hold these records and make sure they were not left out of the result set.

Even though TRANSFORM_PIVOT is a powerful SQL tool, there is one drawback to its widespread use in your programs. The TRANSFORM_PIVOT clause is not an ANSI-SQL clause. Microsoft added this clause as an extension of the ANSI-SQL command set. If you use it in your programs, you will not be able to port your SQL statements to other back-end databases that do not support the TRANSFORM_PIVOT SQL clause. Despite this drawback, you will find TRANSFORM_PIVOT a very valuable SQL tool when it comes to producing result sets for summary reports, data graphs, and charts.

Nested SELECT Queries

Visual Basic 5 allows for the use of nested SELECT queries. These are often referred to as SQL subqueries and are literally queries contained within queries. Nested SELECT queries can prove to be useful when you want to perform a query based upon the results of another query.

To demonstrate the use of a SQL subquery, let's start Visdata and open the SUBQRY.MDB database that can be found in the \\TYSDBVB5\SOURCE\DATA directory of the CD that shipped with this book. This database contains a sample listing of authors, publishers, and book sales activity (notice that this database is very similar to the BOOKS5.MDB database) for a fictitious publisher. Our goal in this exercise is to extract the phone numbers of all the authors who sold more than 500 books in the first quarter.

As you examine the table structure of this database in Visdata, you notice the BookSales table contains the sales records by quarter, but the phone number is contained in the Authors table. We therefore need to query the BookSales table to find all the authors who sold more than 500 books in the first quarter, and then use that result set to find the writers' phone numbers in the Authors table. We need to build a nested SELECT query.

To do this, enter the following code into the SQL Statement window of Visdata. Execute your statement. The result set should look similar to Figure 8.35.

```
SELECT * FROM Authors WHERE AUID IN (SELECT AUID
FROM Booksales WHERE Sales>500 AND Qtr=1)
```

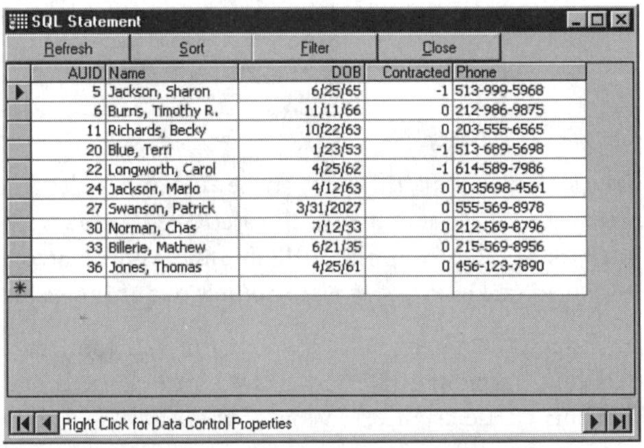

Figure 8.35.

The results of an SQL subquery.

An SQL subquery has three main components—the comparison, the expression, and the SQL statement. The comparison in our example is the SELECT FROM Authors query. The expression is the IN keyword. The SQL statement is the SELECT statement within the parentheses.

NOTE

> The SQL statement on which you base the comparison statement must be a SELECT statement. This statement must also be enclosed in parentheses and is referred to as a subquery.

In the exercise, the SELECT statement contained within the parentheses (the sqlstatement, or subquery) is executed first to determine which authors sold more than 500 books in the first quarter. The SELECT statement outside of the parentheses (the main query) is then executed upon the result set created by the subquery. The IN keyword instructs the SELECT FROM Authors statement to take only those records that were extracted by the subquery.

Other keywords that can be used in the expression include ANY and ALL. Also, numeric expression such as > and < can be used in conjunction with the keyword to make comparisons.

For example, if you use the syntax > ANY in comparing the main query with the subquery (WHERE AUID > ANY), your result set displays all records from the main query that have a value greater than any value extracted from the subquery. Using > ALL (WHERE AUID > All) extracts only those records that are greater in value than every record extracted by the subquery.

Without the ability to use nested SQL statements, the preceding exercise would have required you to perform a JOIN on the two tables, or build a table to store the subqueries result set, and then execute the main query on the table. The use of nested SQL SELECT statements can be a great time saver.

Summary

Today you learned how to create basic SQL statements that select data from existing tables. You learned that the most fundamental form of the SQL statement is the SELECT_FROM clause. This clause is used to select one or more columns from a table and display the results of that statement in a result set, or view.

You also learned about the optional clauses that you can add to the SELECT_FROM clause:

☐ The WHERE clause: Used to limit the rows in the result set using logical comparisons (for example, WHERE Table.Name = "SMITH") and to link two tables in a single, nonupdateable, view (for example, WHERE Table1.Name = Table2.Name).

☐ The ORDER BY clause: Used to control the order in which the result set is displayed (for example, ORDER BY Name ASC).

☐ The GROUP BY clause: Used to create a subtotal result set based on a break column (for example, GROUP BY Name).

☐ The HAVING clause: Used only with the GROUP BY clause, the HAVING clause acts as a WHERE clause for the GROUP BY subtotal clause (for example, GROUP BY Name HAVING SUM(SalesTotal)>1000).

☐ The INNER JOIN clause: Used to join two tables together into a single, updateable result set. The INNER JOIN returns rows that have a corresponding match in both tables.

☐ The LEFT JOIN and RIGHT JOIN clauses: Used to join two tables into a single, updateable result set. The LEFT JOIN includes all records from the first (left-hand) table and all rows from the second table that have a corresponding match. The RIGHT JOIN works in reverse.

☐ The UNION clause: Used to combine two or more complete SQL queries into a single result set (for example, SELECT * FROM Table1 UNION SELECT * FROM Table2).

☐ The TRANSFORM_PIVOT clause: Used to create a crosstab query as a result set (for example, TRANSFORM SUM(MonthlySales) FROM SalesTable GROUP BY Product PIVOT Month).

You also learned about additional SQL keywords that you can use to control the contents of the result set:

☐ BETWEEN_AND logical operators

☐ DISTINCT and DISTINCTROW

☐ AS to rename columns in the result set

☐ TOP n and TOP n PERCENT

☐ The SQL aggregate functions AVG, COUNT, MAX, MIN, and SUM

Finally, you learned about the SQL subquery, and how to nest SELECT statements to extract data from a table based upon the results of another SELECT statement.

Quiz

1. What does SQL stand for? How is SQL pronounced?
2. What SQL statement enables you to select data from table fields?
3. What wildcard character do you use in a SELECT_FROM statement to include all fields of a table in your result?
4. What clause do you use in an SQL statement to sort the displayed data?
5. Identify two functions that a WHERE clause performs in an SQL statement?
6. How do you rename the column headings in an SQL statement?
7. What are SQL aggregate functions? List the SQL aggregate functions available through the Microsoft Access Jet database engine.

8

8. What are the drawbacks of using Visual Basic functions in SQL statements?

9. What is the difference between the DISTINCT and DISTINCTROW SQL clauses?

10. What clause should you always use with the TOP n or TOP n PERCENT clause?

11. What are the three join types available in Microsoft Jet SQL? Briefly explain how each is used.

12. When would you use a UNION query?

Exercises

As a corporate MIS staff member, you are given the task of assisting the Accounting Department in extracting data from its accounts payable and accounts receivable systems. As part of your analysis, you determine that these systems possess the following data tables and fields:

CustomerMaster

CustomerID
Name
Address
City
State
Zip
Phone
CustomerType

CustomerType

CustomerType
Description

OpenInvoice

InvoiceNo
CustomerID
Date
Description
Amount

Suppliers

SupplierID
Name
Address

continues

Suppliers

City
State
Zip
Phone

Use this information to answer the questions that follow:

1. Write an SQL statement to list all of the customers. Include their IDs, names, addresses, phone numbers, and customer types.

2. Display all of the information in the Open Invoice table, but display CustomerID as Account.

3. Display the same information requested in Exercise 2, but sort the data by customer and then by invoice number within each customer.

4. Display all suppliers that can be found within New York City. Display their IDs, names, addresses, and phone numbers.

5. Display the Customer types, names, and addresses for all customers with a customer type of ABC.

6. Select and display customer IDs and names for customer names beginning with AME.

7. Display the CustomerID and Name of all customers who have an open invoice. Sort your information by CustomerID.

8. Select and display the five largest outstanding invoices.

9. Display a listing of names and phone numbers of all customers and vendors who reside in Ohio.

Day 9

Visual Basic and the Microsoft Jet Engine

Today you'll learn the details of the heart of the Visual Basic database system—Microsoft Jet, the part of Visual Basic that handles all database operations. Whether you are reading a Microsoft Access-format database, accessing a FoxPro file, or connecting to a back-end database server using ODBC, Microsoft Jet is there. You can also use Visual Basic to create a link between an existing Microsoft Jet database and data in non-Microsoft Jet databases. This process of attaching external data sources provides an excellent way to gain the advantages of the Microsoft Jet data access object layer without having to convert existing data to Microsoft Jet format.

Today you will learn about several object collections that exist in Visual Basic Microsoft Jet databases, including the new ODBCDirect objects available in the Microsoft Jet 3.5 data engine. The objects covered in this chapter include the following:

- ☐ The DBEngine object
- ☐ The Workspace object

- [ ] The Database object
- [ ] The TableDef object
- [ ] The Field object
- [ ] The Index object
- [ ] The Relation object
- [ ] The Connection object
- [ ] The Recordset object

Throughout this lesson, you will build a single Visual Basic project that illustrates the various data access objects you learn about today. You can apply the Visual Basic coding techniques you learn today in future Visual Basic database projects.

What Is the Microsoft Jet Database Engine?

The idea behind Microsoft Jet is that you can use one interface to access multiple types of data. Microsoft designed Microsoft Jet to present a consistent interface to the user regardless of the type of data the user is working with. Consequently, you can use the same Microsoft Jet functions that you use to access an ASCII text file or Microsoft Excel spreadsheet to also perform data operations on Microsoft Access databases.

The Microsoft Jet engine is not a single program; it is a set of routines that work together. The Microsoft Jet engine talks to a set of translation routines. These routines convert your Microsoft Jet request into a request that the target database can understand. Translation routines exist for Microsoft Access databases and for non-Microsoft Access ISAM files such as dBASE, FoxPro, Paradox, and so on. A translation set even exists to handle ODBC data sources using the Microsoft Jet interface. In theory, you could access any data file format through the Microsoft Jet engine, as long as some set of translation routines is made available to the engine.

 **NOTE**

> The detailed inner workings of the Microsoft Jet engine go beyond the scope of this book. If you want to learn more about how the Microsoft Jet interface works, you can obtain copies of several white papers Microsoft has released on the topic of Microsoft Jet and the data access object layer. You can get these papers through various online sources and through the Microsoft Developers Network CDs.

Advantages of Microsoft Jet over the Data Control Object

So far, you have learned to use the data control object to perform database administrative tasks. The data-access objects (DAOs) addressed in this chapter perform all of the services that the data control does, as well as many more. The data-access objects give you complete control over database management.

If possible, use the data control object to manage your data. It is much easier to use because many of the administrative functions are handled for you. You can always add DAO in your code to work with the data control object.

Microsoft Jet Data Objects

Microsoft Jet is organized into a set of data-access objects. Each of the objects has collections, properties, and methods:

- [ ] Collections: Data-access objects that contain the same type of objects.
- [ ] Properties: The data contained within an object (control button, form, and so on) that defines its characteristics. You *set* an object's properties.
- [ ] Methods: The procedures that can be performed on an object. You *invoke* a method.

The Microsoft Jet data access objects exist in a hierarchy, which means that a top-down relationship exists between the objects. You learn the various Microsoft Jet data-access objects in the order they reside in the hierarchy. As you push deeper into the object hierarchy, you move toward more specific data objects. For example, the first data object in the hierarchy is the DBEngine data-access object. All other data-access objects exist underneath the DBEngine data-access objects.

 **NOTE** Throughout the rest of this chapter you will see the phrases "data-access objects" and "data objects." They both refer to the data-access object layer of the Microsoft Jet engine.

If you do not already have Visual Basic up and running, start it now and begin a new Standard EXE project. Make sure that your system can reference the Microsoft Jet 3.5 Data Access Object Library.

WARNING

If you don't have a reference to the data-access object layer in your project, you cannot access any of the features of the Microsoft Jet database engine.

If you can't tell whether your reference to the data access object is activated, select Project | References... from the Visual Basic main menu. Use Figure 9.1 as a reference.

Figure 9.1.

Reviewing the data-access object reference.

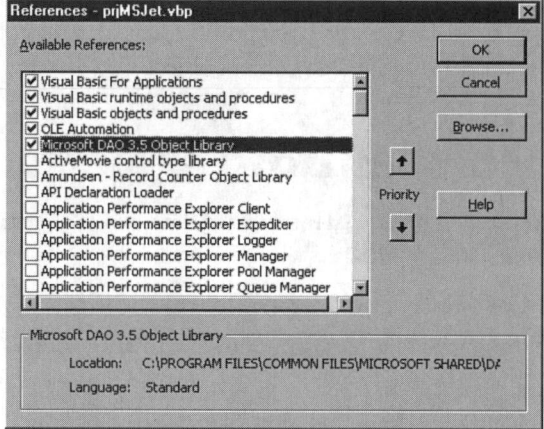

Throughout this chapter you'll be using the Microsoft Jet 3.5 data engine. This is the most recent version of the data engine available. You can use older versions of the data engine to maintain compatibility with earlier Visual Basic projects, but it is recommended that you use Microsoft Jet 3.5 for all future projects.

The DBEngine Data Object

The DBEngine data object is the default data object for all access to the database operations under Visual Basic. Even if you do not explicitly use the DBEngine object, your program is still accessing all other data objects by way of the DBEngine object because it is invoked by default when Visual Basic begins any database work.

TIP

Even though Visual Basic does not require that you explicitly use the DBEngine data object, you should use the object in all your future Visual Basic projects to ensure maximum compatibility with any future versions of Visual Basic.

The DBEngine Object Collections

The DBEngine object contains three different object collections. Each of these collections in turn contains other data-access objects. To put it another way, the DBEngine is the top level of the DAO hierarchy, and it contains the following collections:

☐ Workspaces: A collection of all the defined Workspace objects. The next section of this chapter covers Workspace objects. The Workspace collection is the default collection for the DBEngine object.

☐ Errors: A collection of the most recent database-related errors encountered in this session. Error objects are covered later in this chapter.

☐ Properties: A collection of all the properties of the DBEngine object.

The DBEngine Object Properties

Like all Visual Basic objects, you can list the properties of the object by accessing the Properties collection. Let's write a short bit of code to list (enumerate) all the properties of the DBEngine data access object.

Before coding the DBEngine routines, you need to add a support routine to your form. This routine makes it easier to read the output of the rest of the routines in this chapter. Create a new function called ShowType and enter the code from Listing 9.1.

TYPE **Listing 9.1. Creating the ShowType support routine.**

```
Public Function ShowType(varTypeCode As Variant) As String
    '
    ' return friendly name of variable type
    '
    Dim strReturn As String
    '
    Select Case varTypeCode
        Case vbEmpty
            strReturn = "Empty"
        Case vbNull
            strReturn = "Null"
        Case vbInteger
            strReturn = "Integer"
        Case vbLong
            strReturn = "Long"
        Case vbSingle
            strReturn = "Single"
        Case vbDouble
            strReturn = "Double"
        Case vbCurrency
            strReturn = "Currency"
```

continues

Listing 9.1. continued

```
        Case vbDate
            strReturn = "Date"
        Case vbString
            strReturn = "String"
        Case vbObject
            strReturn = "Object"
        Case vbError
            strReturn = "Error"
        Case vbBoolean
            strReturn = "Boolean"
        Case vbVariant
            strReturn = "Variant"
        Case vbDataObject
            strReturn = "dao"
        Case vbDecimal
            strReturn = "Decimal"
        Case vbByte
            strReturn = "Byte"
        Case vbArray
            strReturn = "Array"
        Case Else
            strReturn = "[" & CStr(varTypeCode) & "]"
    End Select
    '
    ShowType = strReturn
    '
End Function
```

Now you're ready to start DAO programming!

First, add a single button to the bottom of the current form. Set its Name property to cmdDBEngine and its Caption property to DBEngine. Now double-click the button to bring up the cmdDBEngine_Click event window and enter the code shown in Listing 9.2.

TYPE   **Listing 9.2. Coding the cmdDBEngine_Click event.**

```
Private Sub cmdDBEngine_Click()
    '
    ' show engine properties
    '
    On Error GoTo LocalErr
    '
    Dim objItem As Object
    Dim strMsg As String
    '
    strMsg = ""
    For Each objItem In DBEngine.Properties
        strMsg = strMsg & objItem.Name
        strMsg = strMsg & " = "
        strMsg = strMsg & objItem.Value
        strMsg = strMsg & " {"
```

9

```
        strMsg = strMsg & ShowType(objItem.Type) & "}"
        strMsg = strMsg & vbCrLf
    Next
    '
    MsgBox strMsg, vbInformation, "DBEngine"
    Exit Sub
    '
LocalErr:
    strMsg = strMsg & "<err>"
    Resume Next
End Sub
```

In Listing 9.2, you first tell Visual Basic to ignore any errors it might receive while enumerating the DBEngine properties. Then you declare an object variable to hold the properties of the DBEngine object and a string variable to hold the constructed display message. You then use the Visual Basic 5 For..Each loop to list each of the properties of the DBEngine object and build a display message string.

Save the form as FRMMSJET.FRM and the project as PRJMSJET.VBP. When you run the project, you see a single button at the bottom of the form. Click that button to force Visual Basic to enumerate the properties of the DBEngine data-access object. Your screen should look like Figure 9.2.

Figure 9.2.

The enumerated
DBEngine properties.

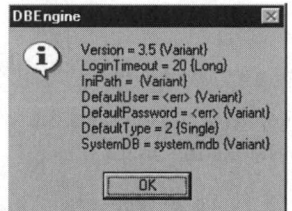

Setting the DBEngine Properties

You can set the properties of the DBEngine object in your program, too. For example, you can use the IniPath property to point to a special ISAM driver needed to process the related database:

```
DBEngine.IniPath = _"HKEY_LOCAL_MACHINE\SOFTWARE\Microsoft\Jet\3.5\
ISAM Formats\FoxPro 3.0"
```

NOTE   In Microsoft Jet 2.5, the IniPath property actually points to an INI file in the <WINDOWS> folder on the workstation. In Microsoft Jet 3.0 and 3.5, the IniPath property is used to point to a location in the workstation's System Registry.

The DefaultUser and DefaultPassword properties are covered when you learn about the Workspace data-access object.

The DBEngine Object Methods

We'll cover six of the Visual Basic methods that are associated with the DBEngine data-access object:

- ☐ `RepairDatabase` is used to fix corrupted Microsoft Jet database files.
- ☐ `CompactDatabase` is used to clean up, and also convert, existing Microsoft Jet databases.
- ☐ `RegisterDatabase` is used to create a link between an external data source and an existing Microsoft Jet database.
- ☐ `Idle` is used to force Visual Basic to pause processing while the DBEngine updates the contents of any existing data access objects.
- ☐ `SetOption` is used to modify one or more of the Microsoft Jet Registry settings at runtime.
- ☐ `CreateWorkspace` is used to establish a workspace for accessing one or more databases. You'll learn about this method in the section on Workspace objects later in this chapter.

Using the `RepairDatabase` Method

You can use the `RepairDatabase` method to fix corrupted Microsoft Jet database files. The default syntax to invoke this method is

```
DBEngine.RepairDatabase databasename
```

Add another command button to the current project. Place it at the bottom of the screen. Set its Name property to cmdDBRepair and its Caption property to DBRepair. Add a CommonDialog control to the form and then enter the code in Listing 9.3.

TYPE   **Listing 9.3. Coding the `cmdDBRepair_Click` event.**

```
Private Sub cmdDBRepair_Click()
    '
    ' fix a corrupted db
    '
    Dim strDBName As String
    '
    CommonDialog1.ShowOpen
    strDBName = CommonDialog1.filename
    '
    If strDBName <> "" Then
```

```
        DBEngine.RepairDatabase strDBName
        MsgBox strDBName & " Repaired"
    End If
    '
End Sub
```

The code in Listing 9.3 declares a local variable for the database name and then prompts the user to enter the name of a database to repair. After checking to make sure a database name was entered, the code executes the RepairDatabase method and reports the results.

Save and run the program. When you click the Repair button, locate and select the DBREPAIR.MDB database (see Figure 9.3).

Figure 9.3.

Entering a database to repair.

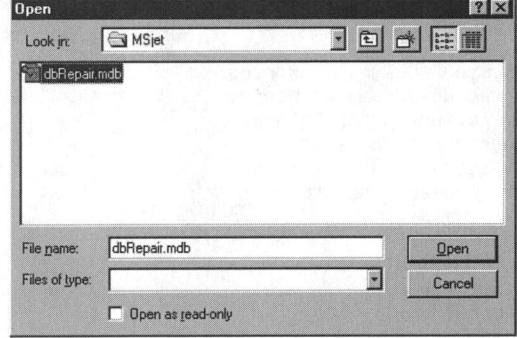

The repair method executes and the final message box appears.

WARNING

The RepairDatabase method overwrites the existing file with the repaired database file. You should make a backup copy of your database files before you execute the RepairDatabase method.

Using the CompactDatabase Method

The CompactDatabase method cleans out empty space in Microsoft Jet databases and performs general optimization chores that improve access speed. You can also use the CompactDatabase method to convert older versions of Microsoft Jet databases to newer versions.

The syntax for this method is

```
DBEngine.CompactDatabase oldDatabase, NewDatabase, locale, options
```

In this line, `oldDatabase` is the name (including path) of the database to be compacted; `NewDatabase` is the name (including path) of the new, compacted database; and `locale` is the language in which the data is written. Options can be added to encrypt or decrypt a database, as well as to change versions. Multiple options must be joined with the plus (+) sign.

Add another button to the `PRJMSJET.VBP` project. Set its Name property to cmdDBCompact and its Caption property to &DBCompact. Enter the code in Listing 9.4 into the `cmdDBCompact_Click` event window. This code compacts any Microsoft Jet database.

TYPE **Listing 9.4. Coding the `cmdDBCompact_Click` event.**

```
Private Sub cmdDBCompact_Click()
    '
    ' compact/convert an MS db
    '
    Dim strOldDBName As String
    Dim strNewDBName As String
    Dim intEncrypt As Integer
    Dim strVersion As String
    Dim intVersion As Integer
    Dim strHeader As String
    '
DBCompactStart:
    '
    ' init vars
    strOldDBName = ""
    strNewDBName = ""
    strVersion = ""
    strHeader = "Compact Database Example"
    '
    ' get db to read
    CommonDialog1.DialogTitle = "Open Database to Convert"
    CommonDialog1.Filter = "MS Jet ¦ *.mdb"
    CommonDialog1.ShowOpen
    strOldDBName = CommonDialog1.filename
    '
    If Trim(strOldDBName) = "" Then Exit Sub
    '
    ' get new name to write
    CommonDialog1.DialogTitle = "Open Database to Write"
    CommonDialog1.Filter = "MS Jet ¦ *.mdb"
    CommonDialog1.filename = "TDP_Fixed.mdb"
    CommonDialog1.ShowOpen
    strNewDBName = CommonDialog1.filename
    '
    If Trim(strNewDBName) = "" Then GoTo DBCompactStart
    '
    ' get target version (must be same or higher!)
dbVersion:
    intVersion = 0
```

```
        strVersion = InputBox("Enter target version" & vbCrLf & "1.1, 2.0, 2.5,
    ➥3.0, 3.5", strHeader)
        MsgBox strVersion
        Select Case Trim(strVersion)
            Case "1.1"
                intVersion = dbVersion11
            Case "2.0"
                intVersion = dbVersion20
            Case "2.5"
                intVersion = dbVersion20
            Case "3.0"
                intVersion = dbVersion30
            Case "3.5"
                intVersion = dbVersion30
            Case Else
                MsgBox "Invalid version!", vbCritical, "Version Error"
                GoTo dbVersion
        End Select
        '
        ' encryption check
        intEncrypt = MsgBox("Encrypt this Database?", vbInformation + vbYesNo,
    strHeader)
        If intEncrypt = vbYes Then
            intEncrypt = dbEncrypt
        Else
            intEncrypt = dbDecrypt
        End If
        '
        ' now try to do it!
        DBEngine.CompactDatabase strOldDBName, strNewDBName, dbLangGeneral,
    intVersion + intEncrypt
        MsgBox "Process Completed"
        '
    End Sub
```

The code in Listing 9.4 declares its local variables and then prompts the user to enter the database file to compact or convert. If no filename is entered, the routine skips to the exit. If a filename is entered, the user is prompted to enter a target filename. If no name is entered, the program returns to try the whole thing again. After getting the filename, the user is prompted to supply the target MSJH version number. The value entered is checked and the user is returned to the input box if an invalid option was entered. Finally, the user is asked whether the database should be encrypted. After that, the CompactDatabase method is invoked.

Save your work and execute this program. You are prompted to enter the name of the database to compact. Enter the path and name for DBREPAIR.MDB. You then must enter a database to compact to. You can just accept the filename suggested to you. Next, enter the version. Answer Yes when you are prompted with the encryption question. The new database is now compacted and saved.

> If you plan to run your database application using any 16-bit data tool, you'll need to store the database in the Microsoft Jet 2.5 version. Only Microsoft Jet 2.5 can run on both 32- and 16-bit platforms.

Using the `RegisterDatabase` Method

The `RegisterDatabase` method enables you to register an ODBC data source for Microsoft Jet access. The Visual Basic documentation encourages programmers to rely on the Windows Control Panel ODBC Setup utility rather than using the `RegisterDatabase` method. If, however, you want to perform the ODBC registration process within your Visual Basic program, you can use the `RegisterDatabase` method to do so.

The easiest way to provide ODBC registration capabilities in your program is to supply a limited number of parameters and force Windows to present the ODBC registration dialog for you—a fairly easy task. For this example, add a new command button to the bottom of the form. Set its Name property to cmdDBRegister and its Caption property to DBRegister. Add the code in Listing 9.5.

TYPE **Listing 9.5. Coding a `DBRegistration` routine.**

```
Private Sub cmdDBRegister_Click()
    '
    ' invoke ODBC registration
    '
    On Error Resume Next
    '
    Dim strDSN As String
    Dim strDriver As String
    Dim blnQuiet As Boolean
    Dim strAttrib As String
    Dim strDelim As String
    '
    strDelim = Chr(0)
    strDSN = "TDPSample"
    strDriver = "SQL Server"
    blnQuiet = False
    strAttrib = "SERVER=\\SQLSERVER2" & strDelim
    strAttrib = strAttrib & "DATABASE=ProductionData" & strDelim
    strAttrib = strAttrib & "DESCRIPTION=Sample ODBC Registration" & strDelim
    '
    DBEngine.RegisterDatabase strDSN, strDriver, blnQuiet, strAttrib

End Sub
```

The preceding code first tells Visual Basic to ignore any reported errors, and then it supplies a set of parameters for creating an ODBC data source. The parameters for the RegisterDatabase method are

☐ SourceName: The name that will be used as the database name for the OpenDatabase method.

☐ DriverName: The name of an ODBC driver installed and available on your workstation.

☐ SilentFlag: Setting this to False forces Windows to present the ODBC registration dialog box. If it is set to True, Windows attempts to register the ODBC data source without prompting the user with the ODBC registration dialog box.

☐ AttributeList: A list of attribute settings for the ODBC source. Examples of attributes include any server device name, database name, and any other parameters required by the back-end database server.

WARNING

> The Microsoft Visual Basic documentation tells you to create an Attributes list with each attribute separated by a CR-LF pair. This is *not* correct. You should delimit each attribute entry with a CHR(0) in order for the RegisterDatabase routine to work properly.

Save and run the project. When you click the DBRegister button, you see the Windows ODBC Registration dialog box appear with some of the parameters already entered. You can complete the information and click OK to register the ODBC data source on your system. Refer to Figure 9.4 as an example.

Figure 9.4.

Registering an ODBC data source.

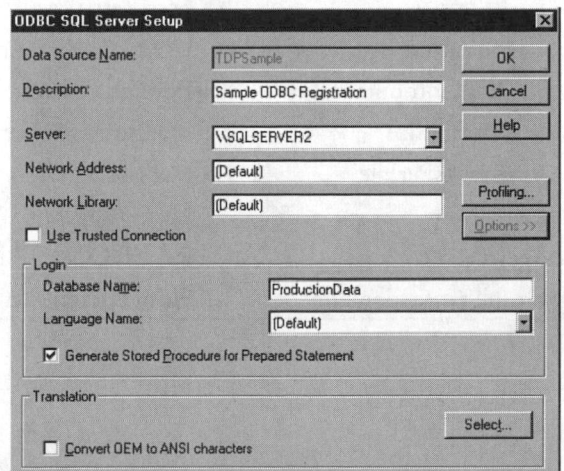

Completing an ODBC registration inserts data into the `HKEY_USERS\DEFAULT\ODBC\ODBC.INI` section of the Windows Registry on 32-bit systems. The data is added to the `ODBC.INI` file in the `<WINDOWS>` folder on 16-bit systems. You can add features to the earlier `cmdDBRegister_Click` example by prompting the user to enter the `SourceName` and `DriverName`. You could also fill out all values within the program and set the `SilentFlag` to `True`. In this way, you could use the routine to install new ODBC connections for Visual Basic applications without requiring the user to know anything at all about ODBC or Microsoft Jet.

WARNING

> Failure to register an ODBC data source properly can result in un-expected errors and possible loss of data. Be sure to test your `RegisterDatabase` routines completely before using them on live data.

The `SetOption` Method

The `SetOption` method of the DBEngine object allows you to override performance values in the Registry at runtime. You can use this option to perform runtime tuning of the Microsoft Jet engine. Table 9.1 shows the values you can adjust using the `SetOption` method.

Table 9.1. Tuning values for the `SetOption` method of the DBEngine.

Constant	Description
dbPageTimeout	PageTimeout key
dbSharedAsyncDelay	SharedAsyncDelay key
dbExclusiveAsyncDelay	ExclusiveAsyncDelay key
dbLockRetry	LockRetry key
dbUserCommitSync	UserCommitSync key
dbImplicitCommitSync	ImplicitCommitSync key
dbMaxBufferSize	MaxBufferSize key
dbMaxLocksPerFile	MaxLocksPerFile key
dbLockDelay	LockDelay key
dbRecycleLVs	RecycleLVs key
dbFlushTransactionTimeout	FlushTransactionTimeout key

For example, to adjust the value of the LockRetry setting, you could use the following code:

```
DBEngine.SetOption dbLockRetry = dbLockRetry * 1.5
```

Any changes made to the Registry settings are in effect only as long as your program is running. They are not saved to the Windows Registry.

The `Idle` Method

The `Idle` method forces Visual Basic to pause while the DBEngine catches up on any changes that have been made to all the open data-access objects. This method becomes useful when you have a lot of database traffic or a lot of data-access objects in a single program. The syntax is simple:

```
DBEngine.Idle
```

The Workspace Data Object

The Workspace data object identifies a database session for a user. Workspaces are created each time you open a database using Microsoft Jet. You can explicitly create Workspace objects to manage database transactions for users and to provide a level of security during a database session. Even if you do not explicitly create a Workspace object, Visual Basic 5.0 creates a default Workspace each time you begin database operations.

NOTE

> Although you can create Workspace data objects, you can't save them. Workspace objects are temporary. They cease to exist as soon as your program stops running or as soon as you close your last data access object.

The Workspace object contains three collections, two properties, and eight methods. The Workspaces collection contains one property (Count) and one method (Refresh). The Workspaces collection enables you to access multiple Workspace objects. The Workspace object enables you to access the properties, collections, and methods of the named Workspace object.

The Workspace Object Collections

The Workspace data-access object contains three object collections:

☐ Databases: A collection of all the Database objects opened for this Workspace object. This is the default collection.

☐ Groups: A collection of all the defined Group objects that have access to this Workspace.

☐ Users: A collection of all the defined User objects that have access to this Workspace.

NOTE You can only access the Group and User objects if the Microsoft Jet security is activated. You can only activate Microsoft Jet security through Microsoft Access. Although Visual Basic cannot *initiate* database security, you can manage the security features using Visual Basic 5.0. Security features are covered on Day 21, "Securing Your Database Applications."

The Workspace Object Properties

Three Workspace object properties exist: the workspace name, the workspace user name, and the Isolate ODBC Trans property. The Isolate ODBC Trans property can be used to control the number of ODBC connections used during the database session.

NOTE ODBC connections are covered in depth in Week 3 of this book. For now, just remember that you can control the number of connections used by the session by altering the Isolate ODBC Trans property of the Workspace object.

When you begin a database operation, Visual Basic 5.0 creates a default workspace with the name #Default Workspace # and the user name admin. Let's add some code to the CH1001.VBP project to enumerate the default Workspace properties.

Add a new button to the form. Set its Name property to cmdWorkspaces and its Caption property to &Workspaces. Enter the code in Listing 9.6 into the cmdWorkspaces_Click code window.

TYPE **Listing 9.6. Coding the cmdWorkspace_Click event.**

```
Private Sub cmdWorkspaces_Click()
    '
    ' show workspaces
    '
    On Error GoTo LocalErr
    '
```

```
        Dim objWS As Workspace
        Dim objItem As Object
        Dim strMsg As String
        '
        strMsg = ""
        For Each objWS In DBEngine.Workspaces
            For Each objItem In objWS.Properties
                strMsg = strMsg & objItem.Name
                strMsg = strMsg & " = "
                strMsg = strMsg & objItem.Value
                strMsg = strMsg & " {"
                strMsg = strMsg & ShowType(objItem.Type) & "}"
                strMsg = strMsg & vbCrLf
            Next
            '
            MsgBox strMsg, vbInformation, "Workspaces"
            '
        Next
        '
        Exit Sub
        '
LocalErr:
        strMsg = strMsg & "<err>"
        Resume Next
        '
End Sub
```

The code in Listing 9.6 should look familiar to you. It is almost identical to the code used to enumerate the DBEngine properties. The only change that has been made is that you now have two For ... Each loops in the routine. The outer loop walks through all defined workspaces in the Workspace collection. The inner loop walks through all the properties of the selected Workspace object.

Save and run the program. When you click on the Workspace button, the program lists all the properties of the object. Your screen should look like Figure 9.5.

Figure 9.5.

Enumerating the Workspace object properties.

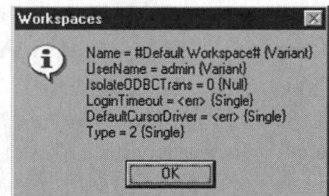

Creating a New Workspace Object

You can create new Workspace objects using the CreateWorkspace method of the DBEngine. Even though Visual Basic 5 creates and uses a default Workspace object when you first begin database operations, you should create an explicit, named Workspace from within Visual

Basic. When you create a unique Workspace object, you isolate all your database operations into a single session. You can then group a set of database transactions into a single session to improve database integrity and security.

Let's add a new command button to the project that will create a new Workspace object. Set the button's Name property to cmdNewWorkSpace and set its Caption property to &New WS. Add the code in Listing 9.7 into the cmdNewWorkSpace_Click code window.

TYPE   **Listing 9.7. Coding the** cmdNewWorkSpace_Click **event.**

```
Private Sub cmdNewWorkSpace_Click()
    '
    ' create a new workspace
    '
    Dim ws As Workspace
    Dim strWSName As String
    Dim strWSUser As String
    Dim strWSPassword As String
    '
    ' init vars
    strWSName = "ws" & App.EXEName
    strWSUser = "admin"
    strWSPassword = ""
    '
    ' create it
    Set ws = DBEngine.CreateWorkspace(strWSName, strWSUser, strWSPassword)
    '
    ' append to collection
    DBEngine.Workspaces.Append ws
    '
    ' show them all
    cmdWorkspaces_Click
    '
End Sub
```

The code in Listing 9.7 establishes local variables and then initializes them to the correct values. Notice that you can use any unique name you like for the Workspace object, but you must use valid User and Password parameters. These values must already exist in the system security file or as the default values if Microsoft Access security is not active. Because you do not use Microsoft Access security here, this example used the default admin user name and empty password.

You used the CreateWorkspace method to create a valid Workspace object. You can now use this object throughout your program. As an option, you can add the new object to the Workspaces collection, by using the Append method. After adding the new object, you can force Visual Basic to display the Workspaces collection to see your results.

9

WARNING

It is not a good idea to append your workspace definitions to the Workspaces collection in a production environment. In rare cases, someone could "listen in" on a network connection that uses workspaces and hack one or more of the valid names, users, and passwords for secured tables. This can be done by locating and walking through the Workspaces collection. To prevent troubles, it is a good idea to never append workspaces to the Workspaces collection.

9

Save and run the project. After you click the New WS button, you see two workspaces displayed on the form. Check your screen against the one in Figure 9.6.

Figure 9.6.

The results of adding a new Workspace object.

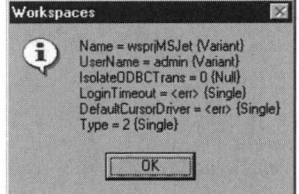

Using the Workspace Object Methods

The Workspace object methods fall into several related groups. Table 9.2 shows the Workspace methods in their respective groups.

Table 9.2. Workspace methods.

Group	Method
Transactions	BeginTrans, CommitTrans, Rollback
Security	CreateUser, CreateGroup
Microsoft Jet	CreateDatabase, OpenDatabase, Close
ODBCDirect	OpenConnection, Close

You learn more about the Transaction group on Day 17, "Multiuser Considerations," and the Security group is covered on Day 21. The ODBCDirect methods are covered in another section in this chapter. That leaves the Microsoft Jet database methods: CreateDatabase, OpenDatabase, and Close.

Using the Microsoft Jet Database Methods

The two database-related Workspace methods are CreateDatabase and OpenDatabase. You use the CreateDatabase method to create a new database, and you use the OpenDatabase method to open an existing database.

Let's first add a command button to create a new database. Set the button's Name property to cmdCreateDB and its Caption property to CreateDB. Add the code in Listing 9.8 to the cmdCreateDB_Click code window.

TYPE   **Listing 9.8. Coding the cmdCreateDB_Click event.**

```
Private Sub cmdCreateDB_Click()
    '
    ' create a new database
    '
    On Error Resume Next
    '
    Dim dbOne As Database
    Dim dbTwo As Database
    Dim ws As Workspace
    Dim dbTemp As Database
    '
    Dim strDBNameOne As String
    Dim strDBNameTwo As String
    Dim strWSName As String
    Dim strWSUser As String
    Dim strWSPassword As String
    Dim strMsg As String
    '
    ' init vars
    strDBNameOne = App.Path & "\CreateDBOne.mdb"
    strDBNameTwo = App.Path & "\CreateDBTwo.mdb"
    strWSName = App.EXEName
    strWSUser = "admin"
    strWSPassword = ""
    '
    ' erase dbs if they exist
    Kill strDBNameOne
    Kill strDBNameTwo
    '
    ' create workspace
    Set ws = DBEngine.CreateWorkspace(strWSName, strWSUser, strWSPassword)
    '
    ' create new jet db
    Set dbOne = ws.CreateDatabase(strDBNameOne, dbLangGeneral, dbVersion30)
    Set dbTwo = ws.CreateDatabase(strDBNameTwo, dbLangGeneral, dbVersion30)
    '
    ' now show db collection
    For Each dbTemp In ws.Databases
        strMsg = strMsg & "Name: " & dbTemp.Name & vbCrLf
```

9

```
    Next
    '
    MsgBox strMsg, vbInformation, "CreateDB"
    '
    ' now clean up your work
    dbOne.Close
    dbTwo.Close
    ws.Close
    '
    Set dbOne = Nothing
    Set dbTwo = Nothing
    Set ws = Nothing
    '
End Sub
```

The code in Listing 9.8 declares some variables, initializes them, and then goes on to create a workspace for this session. It then creates the new Database object and, finally, shows you all the databases that are a part of the current workspace. Database objects are covered in greater detail in the next section of today's lesson. It is important to note here that you create a Workspace object before you create the database to make sure that the Database object becomes a part of the Workspace object. Now all activity on that database is a part of the Workspace. As you can see from the code, you can open more than one database in the same workspace and group the database operations together.

It is also important to note the clean-up code added at the end of the routine. When you finish using DAO objects, you need to close them and release the memory they occupied by setting the program variables to Nothing. If you do not do this, you risk running out of memory in DAO-intensive applications.

Save and run the project. When you click on the CreateDB button, the program creates the new databases and shows the results on the form. Your screen should look like Figure 9.7.

Figure 9.7.

Creating a new database.

You can also open the same database in two different workspaces. This is handy when you want to provide read/write access in one operation, but only want to provide read-only access in another operation. As an example, add a new command button and set its Name property to cmdOpenDB and its Caption property to &OpenDB. Add the code in Listing 9.9 to the cmdOpenDB_Click code window.

TYPE   **Listing 9.9. Coding the `cmdOpenDB_Click` event.**

```
Private Sub cmdOpenDB_Click()
    '
    ' open the same db in two workspaces
    '
    On Error Resume Next
    '
    Dim wsReadWrite As Workspace
    Dim wsReadOnly As Workspace
    Dim dbReadWrite As Database
    Dim dbReadOnly As Database
    Dim wsTemp As Workspace
    Dim dbTemp As Database

    Dim strWSrwName As String
    Dim strWSroName As String
    Dim strDBName As String
    Dim strWSUser As String
    Dim strWSPassword As String
    Dim strMsg As String

    ' init vars
    strWSrwName = "wsReadWrite"
    strWSroName = "wsReadOnly"
    strWSUser = "admin"
    strWSPassword = ""
    strDBName = App.Path & "\..\..\data\books5.mdb"
    '
    ' create workspaces
    Set wsReadWrite = DBEngine.CreateWorkspace(strWSrwName, strWSUser,
➥strWSPassword)
    Set wsReadOnly = DBEngine.CreateWorkspace(strWSroName, strWSUser,
➥strWSPassword)
    '
    ' add them to the workspaces collection
    DBEngine.Workspaces.Append wsReadWrite
    DBEngine.Workspaces.Append wsReadOnly
    '
    ' open database in both ws
    Set dbReadWrite = wsReadWrite.OpenDatabase(strDBName)
    Set dbReadOnly = wsReadOnly.OpenDatabase(strDBName, , True)
    '
    ' now show ws collection
    For Each wsTemp In DBEngine.Workspaces
        strMsg = strMsg & "Workspace: " & wsTemp.Name & vbCrLf
        For Each dbTemp In wsTemp.Databases
            strMsg = strMsg & vbTab & "Database: " & dbTemp.Name & vbCrLf
        Next
    Next
    '
    MsgBox strMsg, vbInformation, "OpenDB"
    '
    ' cleanup code
    dbReadOnly.Close
    dbReadWrite.Close
```

9

```
    wsReadOnly.Close
    wsReadWrite.Close
    '
    Set dbReadOnly = Nothing
    Set dbReadWrite = Nothing
    Set wsReadOnly = Nothing
    Set wsReadWrite = Nothing
    '
End Sub
```

The code in Listing 9.9 declares and initializes several variables for the two Workspace and Database object pairs, along with some temp objects for the collection enumeration at the end of the routine. Then each workspace is created and appended to the collection, and the single database is opened once under each workspace session. Finally, all the workspaces and all their databases are listed on the screen. Note that you do not have to use different user names and passwords for the two Workspace objects.

Save and run the project. When you click the OpenDB button, the program opens the database under two different workspaces and shows the results. Notice that the #Default Workspace# appears in the list. It always exists in the Workspaces collection. Check your screen against Figure 9.8.

Figure 9.8.

The results of the OpenDatabase *method in two workspaces.*

Creating and Opening Non-Microsoft Jet Databases

You can only create Microsoft Jet-format databases using the CreateDatabase method. The other ISAM-type databases (dBASE, FoxPro, Paradox, and Btreive) all use a single directory or folder as the database object. To create non-Microsoft Jet databases, you have to create a new directory or folder on the disk drive. You can then use the OpenDatabase method to open the non-Microsoft Jet database. When it is opened, you can add tables and indexes using the existing Visual Basic data objects and methods. You'll learn about opening non-Microsoft Jet databases in the next section.

The Database Data Object

The Database data object has 5 collections, 8 properties, and 16 methods. The Database object contains all the tables, queries, and relations defined for the database. It is also part of the Databases collection of the Workspace object. The Database object is created whenever you open a database with the OpenDatabase method. Database objects continue to exist in memory until you use the Close method to remove them.

WARNING

> Do not confuse the Database *object* with the database *file*. The Database object is a Visual Basic program construct used to access the physical database file. Throughout this section, you will hear about the Database object.

The Collections of the Database Object

The Database object has five collections:

☐ TableDefs is the collection of Table objects that contain the detailed definition of each data table in the database. This is the default collection.

☐ QueryDefs is the collection of SQL queries stored in the database.

☐ Relations is the collection of database integrity relationship definitions stored in the database.

☐ Recordsets is the collection of active Recordsets opened from this database. Recordsets include any Tables, Dynasets, or Snapshots currently open. Recordsets are temporary objects and are not stored with the database file.

☐ Containers is the collection of all TableDefs, QueryDefs, and Relations stored in the physical database file. You can use the Containers collection to enumerate all the persistent (stored) objects in the database.

The data-access objects are described in later sections of this chapter. This section focuses on the properties and methods associated with the Database data-access object.

The Properties of the Database Object

The Database object has eight properties. To illustrate these properties, add another command button to the CH1001.VBP project. Set its Name property to cmdDBProperties and its Caption property to DB Properties. Enter the code in Listing 9.10 into the cmdDBProperties_Click code window.

Listing 9.10. Coding the `cmdDBProperties_Click` **event.**

```
Private Sub cmdDBProperties_Click()
    '
    ' show all database properties
    '
    On Error GoTo LocalErr
    '
    Dim ws As Workspace
    Dim db As Database
    Dim objItem As Property
    '
    Dim strDBName As String
    Dim strMsg As String
    '
    ' use db created earlier
    strDBName = App.Path & "\CreateDBOne.mdb"
    '
    ' open db in default ws
    Set ws = DBEngine.Workspaces(0)
    Set db = ws.OpenDatabase(strDBName)
    '
    ' enumerate all the properties of the db
    strMsg = ""
    For Each objItem In db.Properties
        strMsg = strMsg & objItem.Name
        strMsg = strMsg & " = "
        strMsg = strMsg & objItem.Value
        strMsg = strMsg & " {"
        strMsg = strMsg & ShowType(objItem.Type) & "}"
        strMsg = strMsg & vbCrLf
    Next
    '
    MsgBox strMsg, vbInformation, "DBProperties"
    strMsg = ""
    Exit Sub
    '
LocalErr:
    strMsg = strMsg & "<err>"
    Resume Next
    '
End Sub
```

In Listing 9.10, you opened an existing Microsoft Jet database in the default workspace (but did not explicitly declare a session). Then you enumerated the properties of the Database object. Save and run the project. Click the DBProperties button and compare your screen to the one in Figure 9.9.

Figure 9.9.

The results of enumerating Data-base object properties.

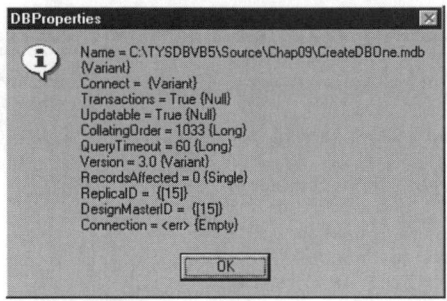

Table 9.3 lists the Database object properties and their meanings.

Table 9.3. Database object properties.

Property	Type/Value	Meaning/Use
Name	String	The name of the physical database file or the name of the ODBC data source.
Connect	String	If the data source is not a Microsoft Jet database, this property contains additional information needed to connect to the data using Microsoft Jet.
Transactions	True/False	If set to `True`, this data source supports the use of the `BeginTrans`, `CommitTrans`, and `Rollback` methods.
Updatable	True/False	If set to `True`, Visual Basic can provide updates to this data source. If set to `False`, this is a read-only data source.
Collating Order	Numeric	This value controls the order in which Microsoft Jet sorts or indexes the records. It is set by the `locale` parameter of the `CreateDatabase` method.
Query Time Out	Numeric (seconds)	This is the amount of time Microsoft Jet waits before reporting an error while waiting for the results of a query.
Version	String	Indicates the Microsoft Jet version used to create the database.
Records Affected	Numeric	Shows the number of records affected by the last database operation on this file.

9

Property	Type/Value	Meaning/Use
ReplicaID	Numeric	This is the unique ID number of this copy of the replicated database. This is set when you initiate replication services (see Day 20, "Database Replication").
ReplicaMaster	Numeric	This is the unique ID value that identifies the Replica Master for this database (see Day 20).
Connection	Object	This is a reference to the ODBCDirect object that can be used to access this database. See the section later in this chapter on ODBCDirect data-access objects.

Let's modify the routine to open a non-Microsoft Jet database in order to compare the differences in the property values between Microsoft Jet and non-Microsoft Jet databases. Change the code to match the following example and run the program again to review the results:

```
'
' use db created earlier
'strDBName = App.Path & "\CreateDBOne.mdb"
strDBName = App.Path
'
' open db in default ws
Set ws = DBEngine.Workspaces(0)
'Set db = ws.OpenDatabase(strDBName)
Set db = ws.OpenDatabase(strDBName, False, False, "Text;")
'
```

You can see from this code snippet that the database name has been set to just the application path and that the OpenDatabase method has been altered to open the directory folder as if it were a Text database. Make the changes to your program, save it, and run it. When you click the DBProperties button this time, you see different property values.

TIP

This last coding example points out a very important fact about the Microsoft Jet database engine. While the Microsoft Jet engine treats the Microsoft Access database as a single file with many tables inside that file, the Microsoft Jet engine treats all other ISAM-type databases quite differently. To Microsoft Jet, the directory folder is the database and the ISAM files are the data tables. This is why it is a good idea to keep all ISAM-type data files in the same directory folder.

The Methods of the Database Object

The Database object has 11 methods, but we won't cover all of them here. Table 9.4 shows the Database object methods grouped in a logical fashion.

Table 9.4. The Database object methods.

Group	Methods
Replication	MakeReplica, PopulatePartial, Synchronize
Security	NewPassword
Child Objects	CreateQueryDef, CreateTableDef, CreateRelation
Database Objects	OpenRecordset, Execute, CreateProperty, Close

You'll learn about the Security methods in Day 20 and the NewPassword method is covered in Day 21. The Child Object methods are covered later in this chapter. That leaves the OpenRecordset, Execute, CreateProperty, and Close methods for review here.

The OpenRecordset Method of the Database Object

You use the OpenRecordset method to access data in existing tables in the database. You can use OpenRecordset to create Dynaset, Snapshot, or Table data objects.

The format of the OpenRecordset method is as follows:

```
Set Variable = Database.OPENRECORDSET(Source, Type, options)
```

In this syntax, Database is the name of the database that will be used to create the Recordset. Type indicates whether the Recordset created is a Table (dbOpenTable), a Dynaset (dbOpenDynaset), or a Snapshot (dbOpenSnapshot). A Table type is created if you don't specify a type. You can also add options for security and record viewing. See Visual Basic online help for a complete description of these options.

Add a new command button to the project. Set its Name property to cmdOpenRS and its Caption property to. Add the code in Listing 9.11 in the cmdOpenRS_Click code window.

Listing 9.11. Coding the cmdRecordset_Click event.

TYPE

```
Private Sub cmdOpenRS_Click()

' open record sets

```

```
        On Error Resume Next
        '
        Dim ws As Workspace
        Dim db As Database
        Dim rsTable As Recordset
        Dim rsDynaset As Recordset
        Dim rsSnapshot As Recordset
        Dim rsTemp As Recordset
        '
        Dim strDBName As String
        Dim strRSTable As String
        Dim strRSDynaset As String
        Dim strRSSnapshot As String
        Dim strMsg As String
        '
        ' init vars
        strDBName = App.Path & "\..\..\data\books5.mdb"
        strRSTable = "Buyers"
        strRSDynaset = "Publishers"
        strRSSnapshot = "Authors"
        '
        ' create ws and open db
        Set ws = DBEngine.Workspaces(0)
        Set db = ws.OpenDatabase(strDBName)
        '
        ' create rs objects
        Set rsTable = db.OpenRecordset(strRSTable, dbOpenTable)
        Set rsDynaset = db.OpenRecordset(strRSDynaset, dbOpenDynaset)
        Set rsSnapshot = db.OpenRecordset(strRSSnapshot, dbOpenSnapshot)
        '
        ' enumerate recordsets in collection
        strMsg = ""
        For Each rsTemp In db.Recordsets
            strMsg = strMsg & rsTemp.Name & vbCrLf
        Next
        '
        MsgBox strMsg, vbInformation, "OpenRS"
        '
End Sub
```

The code in Listing 9.11 creates three Recordsets, one of each type, and then displays the list of open Recordsets on the form. Save and run the form. Compare your results with those in Figure 9.10.

Figure 9.10.
The results of the `OpenRecordset` *method.*

NOTE

> The Recordset created with this method is a very extensive object itself. You'll learn more about the Recordset object's properties and methods later in this chapter.

Using the Execute Method

You can use the Execute method on a database to perform SQL action queries. The Execute method updates the RecordsAffected property of the Database object with the total number of records found or updated by the SQL statement.

NOTE

> An action query is an SQL statement that performs an action on a database (add, edit, or delete records; create or remove data tables; and so on). Action SQL queries are covered in detail on Day 13, "Creating Databases with SQL."

Add a new command button to your project. Set its Name property to cmdExecute and its Caption property to Execute. Add the code in Listing 9.12 to the cmdExecute_Click event.

TYPE   **Listing 9.12. Coding the cmdExecute_Click event.**

```
Private Sub cmdExecute_Click()
    '
    ' execute an SQL statement
    '
    Dim ws As Workspace
    Dim db As Database
    '
    Dim strDBName As String
    Dim strSQL As String
    Dim lngRecords As Long
    '
    ' init vars
    strDBName = App.Path & "\..\..\data\books5.mdb"
    strSQL = "DELETE FROM NewAuthors WHERE AUID<10"
    lngRecords = 0
    '
    ' open db in default ws
    Set ws = DBEngine.Workspaces(0)
    Set db = ws.OpenDatabase(strDBName)
    '
    ' perform SQL & get results
    db.Execute strSQL, dbFailOnError
```

```
lngRecords = db.RecordsAffected
'
' show results
MsgBox CStr(lngRecords), vbInformation, "Deleted Records"
'
' clean up
db.Close
ws.Close
Set db = Nothing
Set ws = Nothing
'
End Sub
```

The code in Listing 9.12 opens a database and performs an SQL action query that deletes records from a table. The routine displays the RecordsAffected property to show you how many records were deleted, and then it closes the database.

Save and run the project. Click Execute and compare your on-screen results with the screen in Figure 9.11.

Figure 9.11.

The results of the Execute *method.*

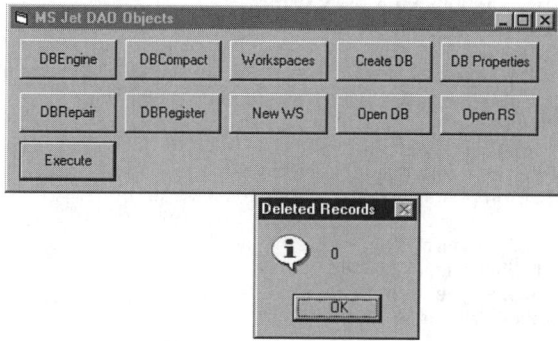

Using the CreateProperty **Method**

Visual Basic lets you create user-defined properties (UDPs) for most data-access objects. These UDPs get stored with the database and can be read and updated by your Visual Basic program. In this example, you use the CreateProperty method to add a UDP to a database.

WARNING

The capability to create and store UDPs is only available when you use the Microsoft Jet version 3.0 or later database format. If you are not using Microsoft Jet 3.0 or later, you can't complete the example in this exercise.

Add a command button to the project. Set its Name property to cmdMakeUDP and its Caption property to MakeUDP. Add the code in Listing 9.13 to the cmdMakeUDP_Click window.

Type **Listing 9.13. Coding the cmdMakeUDP_Click event.**

```
Private Sub cmdMakeUDP_Click()
'
    ' add user-defined properties
    '
    On Error Resume Next
    '
    Dim ws As Workspace
    Dim db As Database
    Dim pr As Property
    Dim prTemp As Property
    '
    Dim strDBName As String
    Dim strUDPName As String
    Dim intUDPType As Integer
    Dim varUDPValue As Variant
    Dim strMsg As String
    '
    ' init vars
    strDBName = App.Path & "\CreateDBOne.mdb"
    '
    ' open ws and db
    Set ws = DBEngine.Workspaces(0)
    Set db = ws.OpenDatabase(strDBName)
    '
    ' add first UDP
    strUDPName = "DBAdmin"
    intUDPType = dbText
    varUDPValue = "D.B. Guru"
    '
    db.Properties.Delete strUDPName
    Set pr = db.CreateProperty(strUDPName, intUDPType, varUDPValue)
    db.Properties.Append pr
    '
    ' add second UDP
    strUDPName = "Programmer"
    intUDPType = dbText
    varUDPValue = "V.B. Coder"
    '
    db.Properties.Delete strUDPName
    Set pr = db.CreateProperty(strUDPName)
    pr.Type = intUDPType
    pr.Value = varUDPValue
    db.Properties.Append pr
    '
    ' now show results
```

9

```
    For Each prTemp In db.Properties
        strMsg = strMsg & prTemp.Name
        strMsg = strMsg & " = "
        strMsg = strMsg & prTemp.Value
        strMsg = strMsg & " {"
        strMsg = strMsg & ShowType(prTemp.Type) & "}"
        strMsg = strMsg & vbCrLf
    Next
    '
    MsgBox strMsg, vbInformation, "MakeUDP"
    '
    ' cleanup
    db.Close
    ws.Close
    Set db = Nothing
    Set ws = Nothing
    '
End Sub
```

The routine in Listing 9.13 adds two user-defined properties to the database. Notice that you attempt to delete the properties first. That way you can run this example several times without getting an error. Notice that you also used two different code structures to create the properties. Either one is correct.

Save and run the project. When you click the MakeUDP button, you should see a screen similar to Figure 9.12.

Figure 9.12.

The results of the CreateProperty *method.*

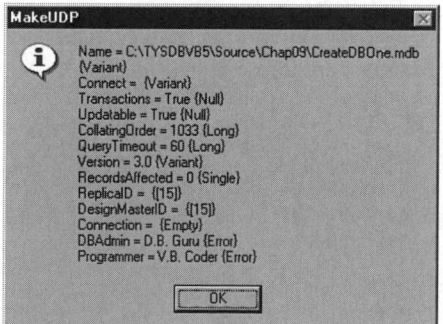

The TableDef Data Object

The TableDef data object contains all the information needed to define a Base table object in the Database. You can access Base table objects using the OpenRecordset method. You use TableDef objects to create and maintain Base tables. TableDef objects have 3 collections, 5 methods, and 10 properties.

The TableDef Collections

The TableDef object has three collections:

☐ Fields is the collection that contains all the information about the database fields defined for the TableDef object. This is the default object.

☐ Indexes is the collection that contains all the information about the database indexes defined for the TableDef object.

☐ Properties is the collection that contains all the information about the current TableDef object.

Details of the Field and Index objects are covered later in this chapter.

The `CreateTableDef` Method and the TableDef Properties

The TableDef properties are set when the table is created. The values of the properties differ depending on whether the TableDef object is a native Microsoft Jet object or an attached object. Listing 9.14 shows the properties of a native Microsoft Jet TableDef object.

Add another button to the project. Set its Name property to cmdTableDef and its Caption property to TableDef. Add the code in Listing 9.14 to the `cmdTableDef_Click` event.

TYPE   **Listing 9.14. Adding the TableDef button.**

```
Private Sub cmdTableDef_Click()
    '
    ' show tabledef properties
    '
    On Error GoTo LocalErr
    '
    Dim ws As Workspace
    Dim db As Database
    Dim td As TableDef
    Dim pr As Property

    Dim strDBName As String
    Dim strTDName As String
    Dim strMsg As String
    '
    ' init vars
    strDBName = App.Path & "\..\..\data\books5.mdb"
    strTDName = "NewTable"
    '
    ' open ws and db
    Set ws = DBEngine.Workspaces(0)
    Set db = ws.OpenDatabase(strDBName)
    '
```

```
          ' now enumerate the empty table defs
          strMsg = ""
          For Each td In db.TableDefs
              For Each pr In td.Properties
                  strMsg = strMsg & pr.Name
                  strMsg = strMsg & " = "
                  strMsg = strMsg & pr.Value
                  strMsg = strMsg & " {"
                  strMsg = strMsg & ShowType(pr.Type) & "}"
                  strMsg = strMsg & vbCrLf
              Next
              '
              MsgBox strMsg, vbInformation, "TableDefs"
              strMsg = ""
              '
          Next
          '
          db.Close
          ws.Close
          Set pr = Nothing
          Set td = Nothing
          Set db = Nothing
          Set ws = Nothing
          '
          Exit Sub
          '
      LocalErr:
          strMsg = strMsg & "<err>"
          Resume Next
          '
      End Sub
```

The code in Listing 9.14 opens a database and then "walks through" all the table definitions in the database, listing the properties of each table. Save and run the project. Click the TableDef button and compare your screen with the one in Figure 9.13.

Figure 9.13.

Viewing the TableDef properties.

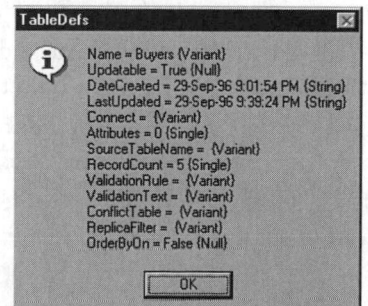

NOTE

You also see several internal data tables in this listing. The tables that start with "MSYS" are used by Microsoft Jet to keep track of indexes, relationships, table definitions, and so on. Do not attempt to read, delete, or modify these tables. Doing so can permanently damage your database.

The actual properties you see on your screen my be different. There are many properties of the TableDef object. Most of them are easy to understand. You can search the Visual Basic online documentation for detailed listings on each of the properties.

NOTE

You may see one or more properties in your TableDefs that are not documented in the Visual Basic online documents. This is because the Microsoft Jet DAO language allows programmers to invent and store their own custom properties. You may be looking at properties invented by some other application (Microsoft Access, MS Project, custom applications, and so on).

The TableDef Methods

Along with the CreateTable method of the database, there are five methods that you can apply to the TableDef object:

- [ ] OpenRecordset enables you to open a Table, Dynaset, or Snapshot Recordset from the TableDef object.
- [ ] RefreshLink updates and refreshes any attached table links for the TableDef object.
- [ ] CreateProperty enables you to create and store a user-defined property. See the UDP example under the Database object elsewhere in this chapter.
- [ ] CreateIndex enables you to add an index to the TableDef object. This method is covered in "The Index Data Object" section later in this chapter.
- [ ] CreateField enables you to add a new field to an existing TableDef object. You learn more about this method in "The Field Data Object" section.

Creating a New Table in the Database

The code in Listing 9.15 enables you to create a very simple database and table. Add another command button to the form. Set its Name property to cmdCreateTable and its Caption property to &CreateTable. Add the code in Listing 9.15 to the cmdCreateTable_Click event.

> **TYPE** **Listing 9.15. Coding the** `cmdCreateTable_Click` **event.**

```
Private Sub cmdCreateTable_Click()
    '
    ' create a new table in a database
    '
    On Error Resume Next
    '
    Dim ws As Workspace
    Dim db As Database
    Dim td As TableDef
    Dim fl As Field
    Dim pr As Property
    '
    Dim strDBName As String
    Dim strTDName As String
    Dim strFLName As String
    Dim intFLType As Integer
    Dim strMsg As String
    '
    ' init values
    strDBName = App.Path & "\NewDB.mdb"
    strTDName = "NewTable"
    strFLName = "NewField"
    intFLType = dbText
    '
    ' erase db if it's there
    Kill strDBName
    '
    ' open ws and create db
    Set ws = DBEngine.Workspaces(0)
    Set db = ws.CreateDatabase(strDBName, dbLangGeneral, dbVersion30)
    '
    ' create a new table
    Set td = db.CreateTableDef(strTDName)
    '
    ' create a new field in table
    Set fl = td.CreateField(strFLName, intFLType)
    '
    ' add new objects to collections
    td.Fields.Append fl
    db.TableDefs.Append td
    '
    ' now show new table properties
    On Error GoTo LocalErr
    strMsg = ""
    For Each pr In td.Properties
        strMsg = strMsg & pr.Name
        strMsg = strMsg & " = "
        strMsg = strMsg & pr.Value
        strMsg = strMsg & " {"
        strMsg = strMsg & ShowType(pr.Type) & "}"
        strMsg = strMsg & vbCrLf
    Next
    '
```

continues

Listing 9.15. continued

```
            MsgBox strMsg, vbInformation, "CreateTable"
            '
            ' clean up
            db.Close
            ws.Close
            Set pr = Nothing
            Set td = Nothing
            Set db = Nothing
            Set ws = Nothing
            '
            Exit Sub
            '
LocalErr:
            strMsg = strMsg & "<err>"
            Resume Next
            '
End Sub
```

The code in Listing 9.15 creates a new database (erasing any old one first), creates a new table object, creates a single field object for the table, and then appends the new objects to their respective collections. Finally, the properties of the new table are displayed. Save and run the project. Check your results against Figure 9.14.

Figure 9.14.

The results of adding a new table.

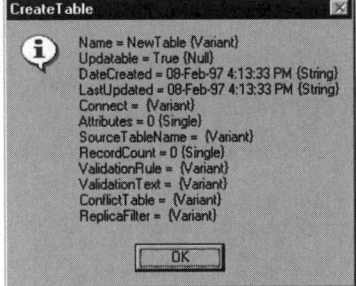

```
CreateTable                                    ⊠
   ⓘ    Name = NewTable (Variant)
         Updatable = True (Null)
         DateCreated = 08-Feb-97 4:13:33 PM (String)
         LastUpdated = 08-Feb-97 4:13:33 PM (String)
         Connect = (Variant)
         Attributes = 0 (Single)
         SourceTableName = (Variant)
         RecordCount = 0 (Single)
         ValidationRule = (Variant)
         ValidationText = (Variant)
         ConflictTable = (Variant)
         ReplicaFilter = (Variant)

                    ┌─────────┐
                    │   OK    │
                    └─────────┘
```

Modifying and Deleting Existing Tables

You can add new fields or delete existing fields by using the Append or Delete methods on the TableDef object. Add a command button with the Name property cmdModifyTable and a Caption property of Modify Table. Add the code in Listing 9.16 to the cmdModifyTable_Click event.

TYPE   **Listing 9.16. Coding the `cmdModifyTable_Click` event.**

```
Private Sub cmdModifyTable_Click()
'
    ' modify an existing table
    '
    On Error Resume Next
    '
    Dim ws As Workspace
    Dim db As Database
    Dim td As TableDef
    Dim fl As Field
    '
    Dim strDBName As String
    Dim strTDName As String
    Dim strFLName As String
    Dim intFLType As Integer
    Dim strMsg As String
    '
    ' init vars
    strDBName = App.Path & "\NewDB.mdb"
    strTDName = "NewTable"
    strFLName = "FollowDate"
    intFLType = dbDate
    '
    ' first create table with other subroutine
    cmdCreateTable_Click
    '
    ' now open ws & db & td
    Set ws = DBEngine.Workspaces(0)
    Set db = OpenDatabase(strDBName)
    Set td = db.TableDefs(strTDName)
    '
    ' add a new field
    Set fl = td.CreateField(strFLName, intFLType)
    td.Fields.Append fl
    '
    ' make list of fields
    strMsg = "Appended Field:"
    For Each fl In td.Fields
        strMsg = strMsg & vbTab & fl.Name & vbCrLf
    Next
    '
    ' now delete the new field
    td.Fields.Delete strFLName
    '
    ' make list again
    strMsg = strMsg & "Deleted Field:"
    For Each fl In td.Fields
        strMsg = strMsg & vbTab & fl.Name & vbCrLf
    Next
    '
```

9

continues

Listing 9.16. continued

```
' show list
MsgBox strMsg, vbInformation, "Deleted Field"
'
' clean up
db.Close
ws.Close
Set fl = Nothing
Set td = Nothing
Set db = Nothing
Set ws = Nothing
'
End Sub
```

In Listing 9.16, you call the previous code section to create the table again. Then you add a new field using the Append method, and delete that field using the Delete method. Save and run the project, and check your final results against Figure 9.15.

Figure 9.15.

The results of adding and deleting fields.

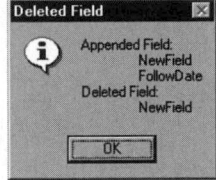

Attaching External Data

You can attach an existing external, non-Microsoft Jet database table to an existing Microsoft Jet-format database. Attaching tables in this way gives you access to the external data using the standard Visual Basic data-access object interface. It also enables you to mix Microsoft Jet and non-Microsoft Jet data in the same database, which is great for handling queries that combine data from both sources.

> **NOTE** You can create and store queries on the attached external data, too. Queries are covered later in this chapter.

You cannot open a table-type Recordset on an attached table. You must use the Dynaset or Snapshot objects for accessing attached tables. Even though you must use Dynaset data objects, attached tables respond faster than external data links.

Let's illustrate attachments by adding another command button to the form. Set its Name property to cmdAttachTable and its Caption property to Attach Table. Add the code in Listing 9.17 to the cmdAttachTable_Click event.

TYPE **Listing 9.17. Coding the** `cmdAttachTable_Click` **event.**

```
Private Sub cmdAttachTable_Click()
    '
    ' attach a non-jet table to database
    '
    Dim ws As Workspace
    Dim db As Database
    Dim td As TableDef

    Dim strDBName As String
    Dim strATName As String
    Dim strATDBType As String
    Dim strATDBName As String
    Dim strATSrcName As String
    Dim strMsg As String
    '
    ' init vars
    strDBName = App.Path & "\NewDB.mdb"
    strATName = "FoxProAttachment"
    strATDBName = App.Path
    strATDBType = "FoxPro 2.5;"
    strATSrcName = "Customer.dbf"
    '
    ' call routine to create table
    cmdCreateTable_Click
    '
    ' now open ws & db
    Set ws = DBEngine.Workspaces(0)
    Set db = OpenDatabase(strDBName)
    '
    ' add a new tabldef
    Set td = db.CreateTableDef(strATName)
    '
    ' define the new def as an attachment
    td.Connect = strATDBType & "DATABASE=" & strATDBName
    td.SourceTableName = strATSrcName
    '
    ' append attachment to collection
    db.TableDefs.Append td
    '
    ' show list of tables
    strMsg = ""
    For Each td In db.TableDefs
        strMsg = strMsg & td.Name & vbCrLf
    Next
```

continues

Listing 9.17. continued

```
        MsgBox strMsg, vbInformation, "AttachTable"
        '
        db.Close
        ws.Close
        Set td = Nothing
        Set db = Nothing
        Set ws = Nothing
        '
End Sub
```

The code in Listing 9.17 calls the routine that creates your test database and then opens the created database and creates a new table definition. This time, instead of creating field definitions to append to the new table definition, you create an attachment to another external database. Attachments always have two parts: the Connect string and the SourceTableName.

The Connect string contains all information needed to connect to the external database. For desktop (ISAM-type) databases, you need to supply the driver name (dBASE III, Paradox 3.*x*, and so on) and the device/path where the data file is located. For back-end database servers, you might need to supply additional parameters.

The SourceTableName contains the name of the data table you want to attach to the Microsoft Jet database. For desktop databases, this is the database filename in the device location (NAMES.DBF, CUSTOMERS.DBF, and so on). For back-end database servers, this is the data table name that already exists in the server database.

Save and run the project. When you click the Attach Table button, you see a few message dialogs flash by. The final dialog lists all the tables in the database (see Figure 9.16).

Figure 9.16.

Viewing the attached tables dialog.

Notice that the FoxProAttachment table now appears. You can now manipulate this table like any native Microsoft Jet data table object.

NOTE
> You also see several internal data tables in this listing. The tables that start with "MSYS" are used by Microsoft Jet to keep track of indexes, relationships, table definitions, and so on. Do not attempt to read, delete, or modify these tables. Doing so can permanently damage your database.

The Field Data Object

The Field object contains all the information about the data table field. In the previous section on TableDef objects, you created and deleted fields. You can also access the Field object to get information on field properties. The Field object has only one collection—the Properties collection. There are 17 properties and 4 methods.

The Field Properties

There are 17 Field properties. You can use these properties to determine the size and type of a field, and whether it is a native Microsoft Jet field object or an attached field from an external database. In version 3.0 Microsoft Jet formats, you can set the default value for the field, and define and enforce field-level validation rules.

Listing 9.18 shows all the properties for selected fields. Add another button to the form. Set its Name property to cmdFields and its Caption property to &Field. Add the code in Listing 9.18 to the `cmdFields_Click` event window.

TYPE **Listing 9.18. Coding the `cmdFields_Click` event.**

```
Private Sub cmdFields_Click()
    '
    ' show all the field properties of a table field
    '
    On Error GoTo LocalErr
    '
    Dim ws As Workspace
    Dim db As Database
    Dim td As TableDef
    Dim fl As Field
    Dim pr As Property
    '
    Dim strDBName As String
    Dim strTDName As String
```

continues

Listing 9.18. continued

```
Dim strFLName As String
Dim strMsg As String
'
' init vars
strDBName = App.Path & "\NewDB.mdb"
strTDName = "NewTable"
strFLName = "NewField"
'
' build new database & table
cmdCreateTable_Click
'
' now open ws and db and td
Set ws = DBEngine.Workspaces(0)
Set db = ws.OpenDatabase(strDBName)
'
' open table and get a field
Set td = db.TableDefs(strTDName)
Set fl = td.Fields(strFLName)
'
' show properties of the field
strMsg = ""
For Each pr In fl.Properties
    strMsg = strMsg & pr.Name
    strMsg = strMsg & " = "
    strMsg = strMsg & pr.Value
    strMsg = strMsg & " {"
    strMsg = strMsg & ShowType(pr.Type) & "}"
    strMsg = strMsg & vbCrLf
Next
'
MsgBox strMsg, vbInformation, "Fields"
'
' cleanup
db.Close
ws.Close
Set pr = Nothing
Set fl = Nothing
Set td = Nothing
Set db = Nothing
Set ws = Nothing
'
Exit Sub
'
LocalErr:
    strMsg = strMsg & "<err>"
    Resume Next
'
End Sub
```

The code in Listing 9.18 creates the database and then opens a single table to access one of the fields. The rest of the code loops through the collection to list the properties for the selected field. The results are displayed in the message box. Check your screen against the one in Figure 9.17.

Figure 9.17.
The Field properties in the Debug window.

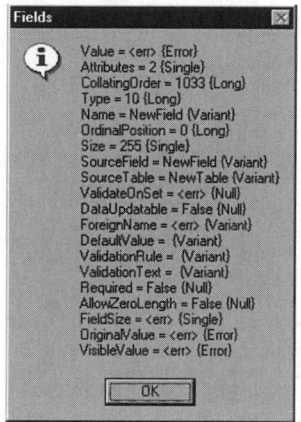

```
Fields                                    ✕
  ⓘ   Value = <err> {Error}
      Attributes = 2 {Single}
      CollatingOrder = 1033 {Long}
      Type = 10 {Long}
      Name = NewField {Variant}
      OrdinalPosition = 0 {Long}
      Size = 255 {Single}
      SourceField = NewField {Variant}
      SourceTable = NewTable {Variant}
      ValidateOnSet = <err> {Null}
      DataUpdatable = False {Null}
      ForeignName = <err> {Variant}
      DefaultValue = {Variant}
      ValidationRule = {Variant}
      ValidationText = {Variant}
      Required = False {Null}
      AllowZeroLength = False {Null}
      FieldSize = <err> {Single}
      OriginalValue = <err> {Error}
      VisibleValue = <err> {Error}

              [ OK ]
```

The list of field properties is quite extensive. You are encouraged to check out the Visual Basic documentation for details on some of the less obvious properties. Also remember that you may be seeing properties added by other DAO applications and that there may be no documentation for these custom properties.

The Index Data Object

The Index object is used to contain information on defined indexes for the associated table. Indexes can only be built for native Microsoft Jet data tables (no attached tables allowed). You can use indexes for two purposes: to enforce data integrity rules and to speed access for single-record lookups.

Indexes are always associated with an existing data table. You must create a native Microsoft Jet data table before you can create an index. Listing 9.19 shows how to create an index through Visual Basic code and view its properties.

Add a command button to the form with a Name property of cmdIndex and a Caption property of &Index. Add the code in Listing 9.19 to the cmdIndex_Click event.

TYPE Listing 9.19. Coding the `cmdIndex_Click` event.

```
Private Sub cmdIndex_Click()
    '
    ' create a new index and display its properties
    '
    Dim ws As Workspace
    Dim db As Database
    Dim td As TableDef
    Dim ix As Index
    Dim fl As Field
    Dim pr As Property
    '
    Dim strDBName As String
    Dim strTDName As String
    Dim strFLName As String
    Dim strIXName As String
    Dim strMsg As String
    '
    ' init vars
    strDBName = App.Path & "\NewDB.mdb"
    strTDName = "NewTable"
    strFLName = "NewField"
    strIXName = "PKNewTable"
    '
    ' create db and table
    cmdCreateTable_Click
    '
    ' open ws, db and table
    Set ws = DBEngine.Workspaces(0)
    Set db = ws.OpenDatabase(strDBName)
    Set td = db.TableDefs(strTDName)
    '
    ' now create an index
    Set ix = td.CreateIndex(strIXName)
    Set fl = ix.CreateField(strFLName)
    ix.Required = True
    ix.Primary = True
    '
    ' add field to index's fields collection
    ix.Fields.Append fl
    '
    ' add index to table's index collection
    td.Indexes.Append ix
    '
    ' now show index properties
    strMsg = ""
    For Each pr In ix.Properties
        strMsg = strMsg & pr.Name
        strMsg = strMsg & " = "
        strMsg = strMsg & pr.Value
        strMsg = strMsg & " {"
        strMsg = strMsg & ShowType(pr.Type)
        strMsg = strMsg & "}"
        strMsg = strMsg & vbCrLf
```

9

```
        Next
        '
        MsgBox strMsg, vbInformation, "Index"
        '
        ' clean up
        db.Close
        ws.Close
        Set pr = Nothing
        Set fl = Nothing
        Set ix = Nothing
        Set td = Nothing
        Set db = Nothing
        Set ws = Nothing
        '
        Exit Sub
        '
LocalErr:
        strMsg = strMsg & "<err>"
        Resume Next
        '
End Sub
```

The code in Listing 9.19 seems pretty familiar, right? After creating a database and adding a table (handled by cmdCreateTable), you build and add the index. Notice that you first name the index, and then create a Field object for the target index. By adding the Field object and setting some other properties, you have completed the index definition. Finally, you append the index to the collection of indexes for the specific table.

TIP

Although you append indexes to a specific table object, the index name is global for the entire database. You cannot create an Index object called Index1 for Table1 and then create another Index1 for Table2. You must have unique index names.

Save and run the project. Click the Index button and check your results against those in Figure 9.18.

Figure 9.18.

The results of adding an index.

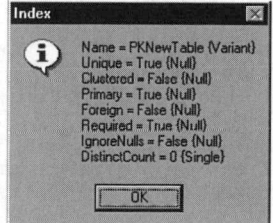

The QueryDef Data Object

The QueryDef object contains information about a stored SQL query. SQL queries can be used as record sources for the Visual Basic data control or as the first parameter in the Recordset object. QueryDef objects run faster than inline SQL queries, because Visual Basic must go through a processing step before executing an SQL query. Stored queries (QueryDef objects) are stored in their processed format. Using QueryDef objects means there is one less processing step to go through before you see your data.

The example in Listing 9.20 creates a simple SELECT SQL query and stores it for later use. After creating the query, you apply it as a record source when creating a Recordset object. Finally, you enumerate the QueryDef properties. Add another button with its Name property set to cmdQuery and its Caption property set to &Query. Add the code in Listing 9.20 to the cmdQuery_Click code window.

TYPE   **Listing 9.20. Coding the `cmdQuery_Click` event.**

```
Private Sub cmdQueryDef_Click()
    '
    ' create a stored query
    '
    On Error Resume Next
    '
    Dim ws As Workspace
    Dim db As Database
    Dim qd As QueryDef
    Dim pr As Property
    '
    Dim strDBName As String
    Dim strQDName As String
    Dim strQDSQL As String
    Dim strMsg As String
    '
    ' init vars
    strDBName = App.Path & "\NewDB.mdb"
    strQDName = "qryNewQuery"
    strQDSQL = "SELECT * FROM NewTable WHERE NewField<>NULL"
    '
    ' create db & table
    cmdCreateTable_Click
    '
    ' open ws and db
    Set ws = DBEngine.Workspaces(0)
    Set db = ws.OpenDatabase(strDBName)
    '
    ' create a new query
    Set qd = db.CreateQueryDef(strQDName)
    qd.SQL = strQDSQL
    '
```

9

```
    ' show properties of the querydef
    strMsg = ""
    For Each pr In qd.Properties
        strMsg = strMsg & pr.Name
        strMsg = strMsg & " = "
        strMsg = strMsg & pr.Value
        strMsg = strMsg & " {"
        strMsg = strMsg & ShowType(pr.Type)
        strMsg = strMsg & "}" & vbCrLf
    Next
    '
    MsgBox strMsg, vbInformation, "QueryDef"
    '
    db.Close
    ws.Close
    Set pr = Nothing
    Set qd = Nothing
    Set db = Nothing
    Set ws = Nothing
    '
    Exit Sub
    '
LocalErr:
    strMsg = strMsg & "<err>"
    Resume Next
    '
End Sub
```

Save and run the project. Check your final screen against the one in Figure 9.19.

Figure 9.19.

The results of creating a QueryDef object.

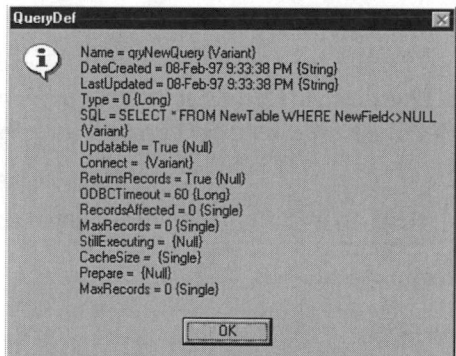

The code in Listing 9.20 exposes one very important aspect of creating QueryDef objects that you might not have noticed. There is no Append method to add the QueryDef to the QueryDefs collection. It is added automatically. As soon as you define the QueryDef with a name property, you have added it to the collection.

TIP

You can also create a QueryDef that *is not* added to the QueryDefs collection. Simply execute the `CreateQueryDef` method with an empty name:

```
set qd = db.CreateQueryDef("")
```

You can then fill the SQL property of the query and execute it to get the resulting dataset. When you close the query, it is destroyed instead of being saved to the QueryDefs collection. This is especially handy when you want to execute dynamic SQL statements, but do not want to create and delete QueryDefs at runtime.

Getting Results from QueryDefs

There are two basic methods for working with QueryDefs—`Execute` and `OpenRecordset`. The `Execute` method is used to perform SQL action queries. Action queries are SQL statements that perform some action on the data table. Examples of action queries are SQL statements that

☐ Add, modify, or remove table records

☐ Add indexes or relationship rules

☐ Add, modify, or remove tables from the database

The other method used when working with QueryDefs is the `OpenRecordset` method. This method is used to retrieve data from the tables into a programming object for manipulation.

Add another button to the form. Set its Name property to cmdRunningQDs and its Caption to Running QDs. Now enter the code from Listing 9.21 into the `cmdRunningQDs_Click` event

TYPE   **Listing 9.21. Coding the `cmdRunningQDs_Click` event.**

```
Private Sub cmdRunningQDs_Click()
    '
    ' running stored queries
    '
    On Error GoTo LocalErr
    '
    Dim ws As Workspace
    Dim db As Database
    Dim qd As QueryDef
    Dim rs As Recordset
    Dim pr As Property

    Dim strDBName As String
    Dim strQDName As String
```

9

```vb
Dim strQDSQLInsert As String
Dim strQDSQLSelect As String
Dim strMsg As String
'
' init vars
strDBName = App.Path & "\NewDB.mdb"
strQDName = "qryNewQuery"
strQDSQLInsert = "INSERT INTO NewTable VALUES('Mike')"
strQDSQLSelect = "SELECT * FROM NewTable"
'
'
' create db & table
cmdCreateTable_Click
'
' open ws & db
Set ws = DBEngine.Workspaces(0)
Set db = ws.OpenDatabase(strDBName)
'
' create temp query and execute
Set qd = db.CreateQueryDef("")
qd.SQL = strQDSQLInsert
qd.Execute
'
' view query properties
strMsg = ""
For Each pr In qd.Properties
    strMsg = strMsg & pr.Name
    strMsg = strMsg & " = "
    strMsg = strMsg & pr.Value
    strMsg = strMsg & " {"
    strMsg = strMsg & ShowType(pr.Type)
    strMsg = strMsg & "}" & vbCrLf
Next
MsgBox strMsg, vbInformation, "TempQueryDef"
'
' create stored query and get results
Set qd = db.CreateQueryDef(strQDName)
qd.SQL = strQDSQLSelect
Set rs = qd.OpenRecordset(dbOpenDynaset)
'
' view query properties
strMsg = ""
For Each pr In qd.Properties
    strMsg = strMsg & pr.Name
    strMsg = strMsg & " = "
    strMsg = strMsg & pr.Value
    strMsg = strMsg & " {"
    strMsg = strMsg & ShowType(pr.Type)
    strMsg = strMsg & "}" & vbCrLf
Next
MsgBox strMsg, vbInformation, "SavedQueryDef"
'
rs.Close
db.Close
ws.Close
```

continues

Listing 9.21. continued

```
        Set pr = Nothing
        Set rs = Nothing
        Set qd = Nothing
        Set db = Nothing
        Set ws = Nothing
        '
        Exit Sub
        '
LocalErr:
        strMsg = strMsg & "<err>"
        Resume Next
        '
End Sub
```

Notice that this code creates and executes two QueryDefs. The first query is an action query—it uses the Execute method. Note also that this first query was never assigned a value for the Name property. It is treated as a temporary query by Microsoft Jet, and it is not appended to the QueryDefs collection.

The second QueryDef selects records from the data table. Because this is not an action query, the OpenRecordset method is used to perform this query. Also, because this query was given a value for the Name property, it is appended automatically to the QueryDefs collection and saved with the database.

Now save and run this code. You see the now familiar CreateTable dialog followed by two more dialogs. The first is the property list for the temporary query. Note that the Name property has been filled by Microsoft Jet with #Temporary QueryDef# and that the RecordsAffected property has been set to 1 (see Figure 9.20).

Figure 9.20.

Viewing the property list for a temporary QueryDef.

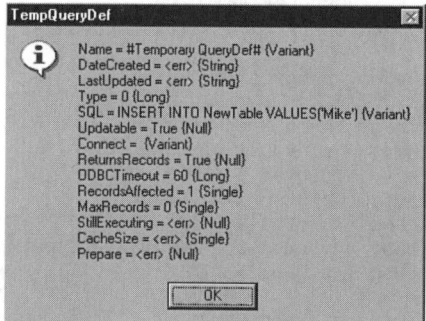

```
TempQueryDef
     Name = #Temporary QueryDef# {Variant}
     DateCreated = <err> {String}
     LastUpdated = <err> {String}
     Type = 0 {Long}
     SQL = INSERT INTO NewTable VALUES('Mike') {Variant}
     Updatable = True {Null}
     Connect = {Variant}
     ReturnsRecords = True {Null}
     ODBCTimeout = 60 {Long}
     RecordsAffected = 1 {Single}
     MaxRecords = 0 {Single}
     StillExecuting = <err> {Null}
     CacheSize = <err> {Single}
     Prepare = <err> {Null}

              OK
```

The next dialog is the property list for the saved QueryDef. This query pulls data from the table into a programming object. Note that the DateCreated and LastUpdated properties are set to valid values (see Figure 9.21).

Figure 9.21.

Viewing the property list for a saved QueryDef.

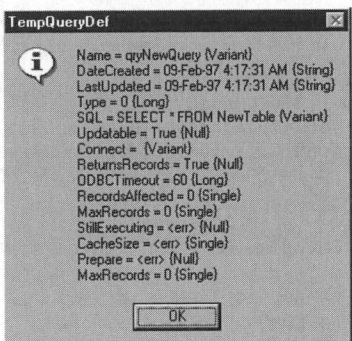

The ODBCDirect Connection Data Object

The Connection object is new to Visual Basic 5.0. This data object is part of the ODBCDirect data access model. This model allows programmers to access ODBC data sources without first defining a Microsoft Jet data object. The ability to open a direct connection to ODBC instead of first opening a Microsoft Jet session provides added flexibility to your programs.

The process of creating and using a Connection object begins at the workspace level. When you create a new workspace, you must explicitly mark it as an ODBCDirect workspace. You can then perform an `OpenConnection` method to open a new connection to an ODBC data source. Once the connection has been established, you can use the `OpenRecordset`, `Execute`, `CreateQueryDef`, and `Close` methods with which you are already familiar.

Add a new button to the form and set its Name property to cmdConnection and its Caption to Connection. Now enter the code from Listing 9.22 into the `cmdConnection_Click` event.

TYPE **Listing 9.22. Coding the `cmdConnection_Click` event.**

```
Private Sub cmdConnection_Click()
    '
    ' show use of ODBCDirect Connection object
    '
    Dim ws As Workspace
    Dim co As Connection
    '
    Dim strWSName As String
    Dim strCOName As String
    Dim strDSN As String
    Dim strDBQ As String
    Dim strCOConnect As String
    Dim strMsg As String
    '
    ' init vars
```

continues

Listing 9.22. continued

```
        strWSName = "wsODBCDirect"
        strCOName = "TDPConnection"
        strDSN = "DSN=MS Access 7.0 Database;"
        strDBQ = "DBQ=C:\TYSDBVB5\Source\Data\Books5.mdb"
        strCOConnect = "ODBC;" & strDSN & strDBQ
        '
        ' create ws for ODBCDirect
        Set ws = DBEngine.CreateWorkspace(strWSName, "admin", "", dbUseODBC)
        '
        ' open a connection
        Set co = ws.OpenConnection(strCOName, dbDriverNoPrompt, False, strCOConnect)
        '
        ' show properties of connection object
        ' connection objects *do not* have a properties collection!
        strMsg = strMsg & "Name = " & co.Name & vbCrLf
        strMsg = strMsg & "Connect = " & co.Connect & vbCrLf
        strMsg = strMsg & "Database = " & co.Database.Name & vbCrLf
        strMsg = strMsg & "QueryTimeOut = " & co.QueryTimeout & vbCrLf
        strMsg = strMsg & "RecordsAffected = " & co.RecordsAffected & vbCrLf
        strMsg = strMsg & "StillExecuting = " & co.StillExecuting & vbCrLf
        strMsg = strMsg & "Transactions = " & co.Transactions & vbCrLf
        strMsg = strMsg & "Updatable = " & co.Updatable & vbCrLf
        '
        MsgBox strMsg, vbInformation, "Connection"
        '
        ' clean up
        co.Close
        ws.Close
        Set co = Nothing
        Set ws = Nothing
        '
End Sub
```

In the code in Listing 9.22, you first create a workspace object with the dbUseODBC parameter added. This creates the ODBCDirect-type workspace. Next, the code performs the Open Connection method on the workspace using the Connect string built-in program variables. This Connect string uses the default Microsoft Access driver that ships with Microsoft Office 95 or later. Notice that you are actually pointing to the BOOKS5.MDB database used throughout this book. Another key point to notice is that you are now using Visual Basic DAO to open an Access database. This is not possible if you are using the standard Microsoft Jet ODBC connection.

TIP

You can now use ODBCDirect to open any ISAM-type database formats, including dBASE, FoxPro, Paradox, and so on, along with Microsoft Access and the back-end RDBMS formats such as SQL Server and Oracle.

Finally, after successfully opening the connection to the database, the Connection object properties are displayed. Unfortunately, the Connection object does not support the use of the Properties collection. This makes coding the property display a bit more labor-intensive than coding the other DAO objects.

Save and run the project. When you press the Connection button, you see the Connection property list appear on your screen (see Figure 9.22).

Figure 9.22.

Viewing the Connection object property list.

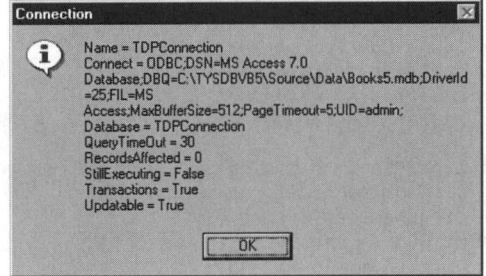

```
Connection                                          X
  (i)    Name = TDPConnection
         Connect = ODBC;DSN=MS Access 7.0
         Database;DBQ=C:\TYSDBVB5\Source\Data\Books5.mdb;DriverId
         =25;FIL=MS
         Access;MaxBufferSize=512;PageTimeout=5;UID=admin;
         Database = TDPConnection
         QueryTimeOut = 30
         RecordsAffected = 0
         StillExecuting = False
         Transactions = True
         Updatable = True

                        OK
```

The Recordset Data Object

By far, the most commonly used objects in Visual Basic programming are the objects that contain datasets. In the Microsoft Jet object model, this object is the Recordset object. Recordset objects can be created from the Database object, the Connection Object, the QueryDef object, and even from another Recordset object. This list of parent objects speaks to the importance of the Recordset as the primary data object in the Microsoft Jet DAO.

The property and method list of the Recordset also reflects its versatility and importance. We have mentioned many of the Recordset's methods in previous chapters. You'll also use the Recordset methods in the next chapter, "Creating Database Programs with Visual Basic Code." The property list of the Recordset object is also quite extensive. Even more important, the exact methods and properties available for the Recordset depend on whether the Recordset was created within an ODBCDirect workspace or a Microsoft Jet workspace.

Rather than take up space in the book to list these methods and properties, look up the "Recordset Object, Recordset Collection Summary" topic in the Visual Basic 5 help files. This help topic lists every method and property with extensive notes regarding the differences between ODBCDirect and Microsoft Jet. You can also use this help topic as a starting point for exploring the details of each method and property.

However, to illustrate the differences and similarities between ODBCDirect Recordsets and Microsoft Jet Recordsets, add a new button to the form. Set its Name property to cmdRecordsets and its caption to Recordsets. Now add the code from Listing 9.23 to the `cmdRecordsets_Click` event.

TYPE **Listing 9.23. Coding the `cmdRecordsets_Click` event.**

```
Private Sub cmdRecordsets_Click()
    '
    ' demonstrate ODBCDirect and MS Jet Recordsets
    '
    On Error GoTo LocalErr
    '
    Dim wsDirect As Workspace
    Dim wsJet As Workspace
    Dim db As Database
    Dim co As Connection
    Dim pr As Property
    Dim rsDirect As Recordset
    Dim rsJet As Recordset
    '
    Dim strWSDName As String
    Dim strWSJName As String
    Dim strDBName As String
    Dim strCOName As String
    Dim strRSDName As String
    Dim strRSJName As String
    Dim strConnect As String
    Dim strMsg As String
    '
    ' init vars
    strWSDName = "wsDirect"
    strWSJName = "wsJet"
    strCOName = "coDirect"
    strConnect = "ODBC;DSN=MS Access 7.0 Database;DBQ=C:\
➥TYSDBVB5\Source\Data\books5.mdb"
    strDBName = App.Path & "\..\..\Source\Data\books5.mdb"
    strRSDName = "SELECT * FROM Buyers"
    strRSJName = "SELECT * FROM Publishers"
    '
    ' establish ODBCDirect connection
    Set wsDirect = DBEngine.CreateWorkspace(strWSDName, "admin", "", dbUseODBC)
    Set co = wsDirect.OpenConnection(strCOName, dbDriverNoPrompt, False,
➥strConnect)
    Set rsDirect = co.OpenRecordset(strRSDName, dbOpenForwardOnly)
    '
    ' establish MS Jet connection
    Set wsJet = DBEngine.CreateWorkspace(strWSJName, "admin", "")
    Set db = wsJet.OpenDatabase(strDBName)
    Set rsJet = db.OpenRecordset(strRSJName, dbOpenDynaset)
    '
    ' now show results
    strMsg = ""
    For Each pr In rsDirect.Properties
        strMsg = strMsg & pr.Name
        strMsg = strMsg & " = "
        strMsg = strMsg & pr.Value
        strMsg = strMsg & " {"
        strMsg = strMsg & ShowType(pr.Type)
        strMsg = strMsg & "}"
        strMsg = strMsg & vbCrLf
```

9

```
    Next
    MsgBox strMsg, vbInformation, "rsDirect"
    '
    strMsg = ""
    For Each pr In rsJet.Properties
        strMsg = strMsg & pr.Name
        strMsg = strMsg & " = "
        strMsg = strMsg & pr.Value
        strMsg = strMsg & " {"
        strMsg = strMsg & ShowType(pr.Type)
        strMsg = strMsg & "}"
        strMsg = strMsg & vbCrLf
        MsgBox strMsg
    Next
    MsgBox strMsg, vbInformation, "rsJet"
    '
    ' cleanup
    rsDirect.Close
    rsJet.Close
    db.Close
    co.Close
    wsDirect.Close
    wsJet.Close
    '
    Set pr = Nothing
    Set rsDirect = Nothing
    Set rsJet = Nothing
    Set db = Nothing
    Set co = Nothing
    Set wsDirect = Nothing
    Set wsJet = Nothing
    '
    Exit Sub
    '
LocalErr:
    strMsg = strMsg & "<err>"
    Resume Next
    '
End Sub
```

When you save and run this routine, you see a long list of Recordset properties for each of
the objects. Note that the lists are different. Even when the property names are the same, some
of the values are different (see Figure 9.23).

The Relation Data Object

The last data-access object covered today is the Relation data object. This object contains
information about established relationships between two tables. Relationships help enforce
database referential integrity. Establishing a relationship involves selecting the two tables you
want to relate, identifying the field you can use to link the tables together, and defining the
type of relationship you want to establish.

Figure 9.23.

Viewing Recordset property lists.

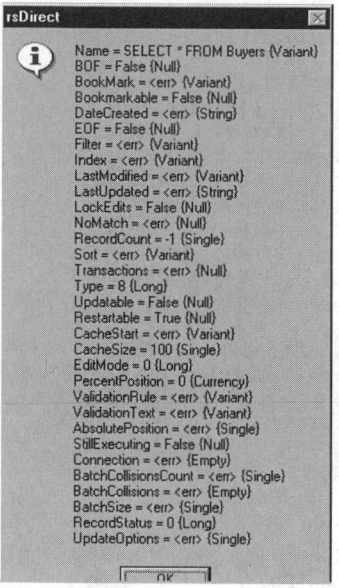

The details of defining relationships are covered next week in the chapters on advanced SQL (Days 15 and 16). For now, remember that you can use the Relation object to create and maintain database relationships within Visual Basic code.

The final coding example for today is to create a new database, add two tables, define fields and indexes for those two tables, and then define a relationship object for the table pair. This example calls on most of the concepts you have learned today. Add one more button to the project. Set its Name property to cmdRelation and its Caption property to Re&lation. Add the code in Listing 9.24 to the cmdRelation_Click event window.

TYPE   **Listing 9.24. Coding the `cmdRelation_Click` event.**

```
Private Sub cmdRelations_Click()
'
'   demonstrate relationship objects
'
On Error Resume Next
'
Dim ws As Workspace
Dim db As Database
```

```
Dim td As TableDef
Dim fl As Field
Dim ix As Index
Dim rl As Relation
Dim pr As Property
'
Dim strDBName As String
Dim strTDLookUp As String
Dim strTDMaster As String
Dim strIXLookUp As String
Dim strIXMaster As String
Dim strRLName As String
Dim strMsg As String
'
' init vars
strDBName = App.Path & "\RelDB.mdb"
strTDLookUp = "ValidUnits"
strTDMaster = "MasterTable"
strIXLookUp = "PKUnits"
strIXMaster = "PKMaster"
strRLName = "relUnitMaster"
'
' erase old db if it's there
Kill strDBName
'
' open ws and create db
Set ws = DBEngine.Workspaces(0)
Set db = ws.CreateDatabase(strDBName, dbLangGeneral, dbVersion30)
'
' now create the lookup list table & fields
Set td = db.CreateTableDef(strTDLookUp)
Set fl = td.CreateField("UnitID", dbText, 10)
td.Fields.Append fl
Set fl = td.CreateField("Description", dbText, 50)
td.Fields.Append fl
'
' now add table to database
db.TableDefs.Append td
'
' index the new table
Set ix = td.CreateIndex(strIXLookUp)
ix.Primary = True
ix.Required = True
Set fl = ix.CreateField("UnitID")
ix.Fields.Append fl
td.Indexes.Append ix
'
' now create master record table
Set td = db.CreateTableDef(strTDMaster)
Set fl = td.CreateField("MasterID", dbText, 20)
td.Fields.Append fl
Set fl = td.CreateField("MasterUnitID", dbText, 10)
td.Fields.Append fl
'
' add index to the master table
```

continues

Listing 9.24. continued

```
Set ix = td.CreateIndex(strIXMaster)
ix.Primary = True
ix.Required = True
Set fl = ix.CreateField("MasterID")
ix.Fields.Append fl
td.Indexes.Append ix
'
' now add defined table
db.TableDefs.Append td
'
' *now* do the relationship!
Set rl = db.CreateRelation(strRLName)
rl.Table = strTDLookUp ' table for lookups
rl.ForeignTable = strTDMaster ' table to verify
Set fl = rl.CreateField("UnitID")
fl.ForeignName = "MasterUnitID"
rl.Fields.Append fl
rl.Attributes = dbRelationUpdateCascade
db.Relations.Append rl
'
' now show relation object
strMsg = "Relation Properties:" & vbCrLf
For Each pr In rl.Properties
    strMsg = vbTab & strMsg & pr.Name
    strMsg = strMsg & " = "
    strMsg = strMsg & pr.Value
    strMsg = strMsg & " {"
    strMsg = strMsg & ShowType(pr.Type)
    strMsg = strMsg & "}"
    strMsg = strMsg & vbCrLf
Next
'
strMsg = strMsg & "Relation Fields:" & vbCrLf
For Each fl In rl.Fields
    strMsg = vbTab & strMsg & fl.Name & vbCrLf
    strMsg = vbTab & strMsg & fl.ForeignName
Next
MsgBox strMsg, vbInformation, "Relation"
'
' cleanup
db.Close
ws.Close
'
Set pr = Nothing
Set fl = Nothing
Set ix = Nothing
Set td = Nothing
Set db = Nothing
Set ws = Nothing
'
```

```
    Exit Sub
    '
LocalErr:
    strMsg = strMsg & "<err>"
    Resume Next
    '

End Sub
```

The code in Listing 9.24 performs the basic tasks. Create a database and build two tables with two fields each. Construct primary key indexes for both tables. Then create the relationship object.

Save and run the project. When you click the Relation command button, the program creates all the data objects, and then displays the resulting Relation object on the form. Compare your results to the screen in Figure 9.24.

Figure 9.24.

Viewing the results of a Relation object.

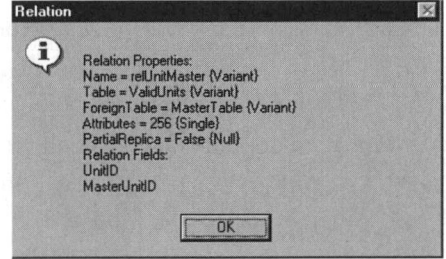

Notice that you added an attribute to make this relationship enforce cascading updates, which means that any time a value is changed in the lookup table, all the corresponding values in the foreign table are updated automatically too. You can also set delete cascades. If the value is deleted from the lookup table, all corresponding records in the foreign table are deleted.

Summary

In today's lesson, you learned the features and functions of Visual Basic Microsoft Jet data access objects and ODBCDirect access objects. These objects are used within Visual Basic code to create and maintain workspaces, databases, tables, fields, indexes, queries, and relations. You learned the properties, methods, and collections of each object. You also learned how to use Visual Basic code to inspect the values in the properties, and how to use the methods to perform basic database operations.

Quiz

1. What does the *Jet* in the Microsoft Jet Database Engine stand for?
2. Describe the difference between a property and a method.
3. What is the top-level data-access object (DAO)?
4. What command would you issue to repair a database? Is this a method or a property?
5. What is the syntax of the CompactDatabase method?
6. What happens if you don't declare a Workspace when you open a database?
7. What data object types can be created with the OpenRecordset method?
8. What is the difference between the Execute and the ExecuteSQL methods?
9. Which TableDef method can be used to create a table in an existing database? What syntax does this method follow?
10. Which data-access object would you use to determine the data type of a table column?
11. Can you use the Index data object to build an index for a FoxPro 2.5 database?
12. What information does the QueryDef object store?

Exercise

Assume that you are a systems consultant to a large multinational corporation. You have been assigned the task of building a program in Visual Basic that creates a database to handle customer information. In this database, you need to track CustomerID, Name, Address (two lines), City, State/Province, Zip, Phone, and Customer Type.

Start a new project and add a single command button to a form that executes the code to build this database. Include the following in your code:

- [ ] A section that deletes the database if it already exists
- [ ] A table for customer information (called Customers) and a table for customer types (called CustomerTypes)
- [ ] Primary keys for both tables
- [ ] A relationship between the two tables on the Customer Type field
- [ ] A message that signifies that the procedure is complete

When you have completed the entry of this code, display the database in Visdata. Add information to both tables. Take note of how the referential integrity is enforced by deleting records from the CustomerTypes table that are used in the Customers table.

Day 10

Creating Database Programs with Visual Basic Code

Today you'll learn how to create complete database entry forms using Visual Basic code instead of the data control. You'll learn how to open a database, establish a Recordset, and prepare a data entry form to allow records to be added, edited, and deleted. You'll also learn how to create a generic record locate routine to use with any data entry form, as well as how to create a set of command buttons to handle all data entry functions. You'll learn about the Visual Basic methods you can use to locate single records and about the Seek method for table objects and the Find and Move methods that you can apply to all Recordsets.

All the routines you create today are generic and portable. You write these routines in an OLE Server library module that you can use in your future database projects. For the lesson today, you'll add these library routines to a new form for the `CompanyMaster` database project you started last week. When you finish today's exercises, you'll be able to build a fully functional data entry form with less than 30 lines of Visual Basic code.

Why Use Code Instead of the Data Control?

Before jumping into the code routines, you should know the difference between writing data entry programs with the Visual Basic data control and writing them without the Visual Basic data control. There are advantages and disadvantages to each method.

The advantage of using the data control is that you can quickly put together solid data entry forms without writing much Visual Basic code. This method works well for small, one-time projects that need to be completed quickly. The disadvantage of using the data control is that once the project is completed, it is not always easy to modify the data entry form or adapt the finished form for another data entry project. Also, forms built using the data control are not always easy to debug or maintain because most of the action goes on in the data control itself. If you think your project needs to be modified or maintained by other programmers, the data control might not be your best choice.

The advantage of using complete Visual Basic code to produce data entry forms is that you have total control over all aspects of the process. You decide when to open the database and Recordset, and you control the record read and write operations, too. This capability can be a real advantage in multiuser settings where increased traffic can cause locking conflicts in programs that use the data control. Another advantage of using Visual Basic code for your data entry forms is that you can create generic code that you can reuse in all your database projects. When you have a fully debugged set of data entry routines, you can quickly create new forms without much additional coding. Because the forms rely on generic routines, they are also easy to modify and maintain in the future.

The primary drawback for using Visual Basic code to create data entry forms is that you have to handle all processes yourself; you can assume nothing. For example, locating and updating a single record in a data table requires that you account for all of the following processes:

- ☐ Opening the database
- ☐ Opening the Recordset
- ☐ Locating the requested record
- ☐ Loading the input controls from the Recordset
- ☐ Handling all user actions during the data entry process
- ☐ Writing the updated controls back to the Recordset

Add the possibility of user errors and database errors, and you have a good bit of responsibility! And you haven't even seen what you need to do to add a new record to the table or delete an existing one. You also need a way for the user to browse the data. Remember that dropping the data control means your form does not automatically display the VCR-style navigation arrows.

Despite this added responsibility, writing your data entry forms with Visual Basic code gives you much greater control over the process and can result in a form that is easy for both programmers and users to deal with. Even though you have to do a good bit of coding to create new data management routines, you can place most of this new code in an OLE Server DLL that can be reused in future projects with a minimum amount of coding.

Searching for a Record

Before you create the generic data entry routines, you need to examine an important topic, record searching. Up until now, we have only touched on this issue. You can use one of several methods to search for a record in a Recordset; some are faster than others. Using the most effective method in your Visual Basic programs can make your programs seem fast and solid. Using an ineffective search method can make your program seem slow.

The Visual Basic data-access object interface is a *set-oriented* interface. It is designed and tuned to quickly return a set of multiple records that meet your search criteria. However, a major part of data entry processing involves *key-oriented* searches. These are searches for a single, specific record that needs to be updated. Visual Basic offers the following three different approaches to handling key-oriented searches:

☐ The Move methods: You can use these methods to browse records one by one (commonly called "walking the dataset"). The Move methods allow you to use Visual Basic code to move from one record to the next in the dataset.

☐ The Seek method: You can use this method to perform an indexed search of the dataset to find the first record that meets your criteria. This search method is the fastest one provided by Visual Basic, and it can only be applied to Recordsets that are opened tables. Dynasets and Snapshots cannot use the Seek method.

☐ The Find methods: You can use these methods to locate a single record in the dataset that meets a set of criteria you establish. This criteria is similar to the SQL WHERE clause you learned about in Day 8, "Selecting Data with SQL." The Find methods perform a sequential search of the dataset to locate the first record that meets your criteria.

10

Using Move **to Navigate Recordsets**

The Move methods offer the most basic form of record searching. There are four methods you can apply to the Recordset object:

☐ MoveFirst: This method moves the record pointer to the first record in the dataset. This method is the same as clicking the double-headed arrow on the left side of the data control.

☐ MovePrevious: This method moves the record pointer to the record just before the current record. This method is the same as clicking the single-headed arrow on the left side of the data control.

☐ MoveNext: This method moves the record pointer to the record just after the current record. This method is the same as clicking the single-headed arrow on the right side of the data control.

☐ MoveLast: This method moves the record pointer directly to the last record in the dataset. This method is the same as clicking the double-headed arrow on the right side of the data control.

To practice using these methods, start a new Visual Basic project. Save the form as FRMMOVE.FRM and the project as PRJMOVE.VBP. Table 10.1 contains a list of controls to add to the form. Refer to Figure 10.1 as a guide as you lay out the form.

Figure 10.1.

Laying out the frmMove form.

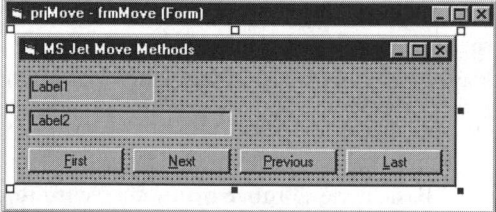

Table 10.1. Controls for project PRJMOVE.VBP.

Control	Property	Setting
VB.Form	Name	frmMove
	Caption	"MS Jet Move Methods"
	ClientHeight	1470
	ClientLeft	60
	ClientTop	345
	ClientWidth	5400

10

Control	Property	Setting
VB.CommandButton	Name	cmdMoveLast
	Caption	"&Last"
	Height	300
	Left	4080
	Top	1080
	Width	1200
VB.CommandButton	Name	cmdMovePrevious
	Caption	"&Previous"
	Height	300
	Left	2760
	Top	1080
	Width	1200
VB.CommandButton	Name	cmdMoveNext
	Caption	"&Next"
	Height	300
	Left	1440
	Top	1080
	Width	1200
VB.CommandButton	Name	cmdMoveFirst
	Caption	"&First"
	Height	300
	Left	120
	Top	1080
	Width	1200
VB.Label	Name	Label2
	BorderStyle	1 'Fixed Single
	Height	315
	Left	120
	Top	600
	Width	2535

continues

Table 10.1. continued

Control	Property	Setting
VB.Label	Name	Label1
	BorderStyle	1 'Fixed Single
	Height	315
	Left	120
	Top	180
	Width	1575

After laying out the form, you need to add the code. Enter Listing 10.1 in the general declarations section of the form. This code declares all the form-level variables you use in the project.

TYPE **Listing 10.1. Coding the form-level variables.**

```
Option Explicit
'
' form-level vars
'
Dim strDBName As String
Dim strRSName As String
Dim ws As Workspace
Dim db As Database
Dim rs As Recordset
```

Listing 10.2 shows the code that opens the database and then opens a Dynaset for your use. Add this code to the Form_Load event.

TYPE **Listing 10.2. Opening the database and a Dynaset.**

```
Private Sub Form_Load()
    '
    ' open db and rs objects
    '
    strDBName = App.Path & "\..\..\data\books5.mdb"
    strRSName = "Authors"

    Set ws = DBEngine.CreateWorkspace("dbTemp", "admin", "")
    Set db = ws.OpenDatabase(strDBName)
    Set rs = db.OpenRecordset(strRSName, dbOpenTable)
    '
End Sub
```

10

This routine initializes the database and Recordset name variables and then creates the related data objects. Performing this step is similar to setting the `DatabaseName`, `RecordSource`, and `RecordsetType` properties of the data control.

You need to create a `Sub` procedure to handle the process of reading the current record and loading the data into the form controls. Create a `Private Sub` procedure called `ReadRow` and then add the following code to the routine:

```
Public Sub ReadRow()
    '
    ' fill controls with current value
    '
    Label1.Caption = rs.Fields(0)
    Label2.Caption = rs.Fields(1)
    '
End Sub
```

This routine copies the first column in the current row of the Recordset to the first form control and then copies the second column of the Recordset to the second form control.

You need to create code for each of the four command buttons on the form. Each button needs to perform two tasks:

☐ Reposition the pointer as requested
☐ Read the data from the new current row

The four code pieces in Listing 10.3 do these tasks. Enter the code in that corresponds to the command button into the `Click` event of that command button. For example, enter `rs.MoveFirst` and `ReadRow` into the `Click` event of the `cmdMoveFirst` command button. Then enter `rs.MoveLast` and `ReadRow` into the `cmdMoveLast` command button, and so on.

TYPE **Listing 10.3. Coding the `cmdMove` events.**

```
Private Sub cmdMoveFirst_Click()
    '
    rs.MoveFirst
    ReadRow
    '
End Sub

Private Sub cmdMoveLast_Click()
    '
    rs.MoveLast
    ReadRow
    '
End Sub

Private Sub cmdMoveNext_Click()
    '
```

continues

Listing 10.3. continued

```
        rs.MoveNext
        ReadRow
        '
End Sub

Private Sub cmdMovePrevious_Click()
        '
        rs.MovePrevious
        ReadRow
        '
End Sub
```

You need to add two more routines to finish up the project. The following code forces the first record onto the screen at startup. Add this code to the Form_Activate event:

```
Private Sub Form_Activate()
        '
        cmdMoveFirst_Click
        '
End Sub
```

The last bit of code performs a safe close of the database at the end of the program. Add this code to the Form_Unload event:

```
Private Sub Form_Unload(Cancel As Integer)
        '
        rs.Close
        db.Close
        Set rs = Nothing
        Set db = Nothing
        '
End Sub
```

Save the form as FRMMOVE.FRM and save the project as PRJMOVE.VBP. When you run the project, you can click the buttons in order to walk the dataset. This project operates the same as the data control arrow buttons.

NOTE

> If you click the First button and then immediately click the Previous button, you get a runtime error. This error is caused by attempting to read past the beginning of the dataset. Later today, you'll create a routine that prevents this error from occurring in your programs.

The project you created in this section is a good example of how you can provide users with a way to browse the dataset on a form. In the next section, you see how to give your users the ability to search for a particular record in the dataset.

Using Seek on Table Recordsets

The fastest way to locate a specific record is to use the Seek method on a table object. The Seek method performs an indexed search for the first occurrence of the record that matches the index criteria. This search uses the type of index used by ISAM-type databases. Indexed searches are easy to perform and are very fast.

Modify the PRJMOVE.VBP project to illustrate index searching by adding another button to the form. Set the button's Name property to cmdSeek and its Caption property to &Seek. Next, add Listing 10.4 to the cmdSeek_Click event.

TYPE | **Listing 10.4. Coding the cmdSeek_Click event.**

```
Private Sub cmdSeek_Click()
    '
    ' use the seek method to locate a record
    '
    Dim strSeek As String
    '
    strSeek = InputBox("Enter an Author ID Seek Value:", "Table Seek", "10")
    strSeek = Trim(strSeek)
    '
    If strSeek <> "" Then
        rs.Seek "=", strSeek
        If rs.NoMatch = True Then
            MsgBox "Unable to locate [" & strSeek & "]", vbExclamation, "Table
Seek Failed"
        Else
            ReadRow
            MsgBox "Found [" & strSeek & "]", vbInformation, "Table Seek Suc-
ceeded"
        End If
    End If
    '
End Sub
```

Listing 10.4 does three things. First, it prompts the user to enter a value for which to search. Second, the code confirms that the user entered a value and then performs the Seek operation. After performing the Seek operation, the code uses the NoMatch method to get the results of the Seek operation (this is the third operation performed in this routine). The results of the search are then posted in a message box. If the search was successful, the new record is loaded into the form controls.

To make this routine work, you have to make a few changes to code in the Form_Load event. Change vbOpenDynaset to vbOpenTable, and then add the following line to the end of the routine, just after the OpenRecordset line:

```
rs.Index = "PrimaryKey" ' set index property
```

Now save and run the project. This time, click the Seek button. When the dialog box appears, accept the default value of 10 and click OK. You should see a message telling you that the search was successful (see Figure 10.2).

Figure 10.2.

The results of the Seek *method on a table object.*

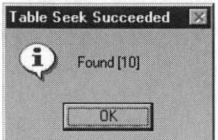

 **TIP**

> You can use other comparison values besides = with the Seek method. You can use <, <=, =, >=, or > as a comparison value.

Although Seek is the fastest search method, you can apply it only to Recordsets opened as table objects. If you want to locate a specific record in a Dynaset or Snapshot, use one of the Find methods.

Using Find on Non-Table Recordsets

Because Dynaset and Snapshot objects do not use indexes, you cannot use the Seek method to search for specific records within them. The Find method is used to locate specific records in non-table objects (Dynasets and Snapshots). The Find method is a sequential search; it starts at the beginning of the dataset and looks at each record until it finds one that matches the search criteria. Although this method is not as fast as Seek, it is still faster than using the Move methods to handle this operation within your own Visual Basic code.

The syntax for the Find methods is almost identical to the SQL WHERE clause (covered in Day 8). The search string consists of a field (or set of fields) followed by a comparison operator (=,<>, and so on) and a search value (for example, MyRS.FindFirst "Au_ID=13").

There are actually four Find methods: FindFirst, FindPrevious, FindNext, and FindLast. The FindFirst method starts its search from the beginning of the file. The FindLast method starts its search from the end of the file and works its way to the beginning. You can use the FindPrevious and FindNext methods to continue a search that can return more than one record. For example, if you are looking for all the records that have their ZipCode column set to 99999, you could use the FindFirst method to locate the first record and then use the FindNext method to continue the search forward until you reach the end of the dataset. Similarly, you can use the FindLast and FindPrevious methods to perform continued searches starting at the end of the dataset. Although the FindNext and FindPrevious methods are available, it is usually better to create a new Recordset using the Find criteria if you expect to locate more than one record that meets the criteria.

Modify the PRJMOVE.VBP project to illustrate the Find method by adding another button to the project. Set the button's Name property to cmdFind and its Caption property to F&ind. Next, add the code in Listing 10.5 to the cmdFind_Click event.

TYPE | **Listing 10.5. Coding the cmdFind_Click event.**

```
Private Sub cmdFind_Click()
    '
    ' use the find method for non-table searches
    '
    Dim strFind As String
    '
    strFind = InputBox("Enter an Author ID to Find:", "Non-table Find", "13")
    strFind = Trim(strFind)
    '
    If strFind <> "" Then
        strFind = "AUID=" & strFind
        rs.FindFirst strFind
        '
        If rs.NoMatch = True Then
            MsgBox "Unable to locate [" & strFind & "]", vbExclamation, "Non-
➥Table Find Failed"
        Else
            ReadRow
            MsgBox "Found [" & strFind & "]", vbInformation, "Non-table Find
➥Succeeded"
        End If
    End If
    '
End Sub
```

Listing 10.5 is almost identical to the code used in the cmdSeek_Click event (refer to Listing 10.4). Notice that you have to build the criteria string to include the name of the field you are searching. Because the Find method can be applied to any field (or fields) in the table, you must supply the field in the search criteria.

Before saving the project, comment out the line in the Form_Load event that sets the index. Also, change dbOpenTable to dbOpenSnapshot. Now save and run the project. When you click the Find button, enter 13 in the input box. You should see a message telling you that the Find operation was successful (see Figure 10.3).

Figure 10.3.

The results of the non-table Find method.

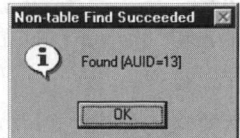

Notice that if you click the Seek button, you eventually get an error message. You cannot apply a Seek method to a non-table object. Also, you cannot apply a Find method to a table object. Later, you'll learn how to write a single locate routine that is smart enough to figure out which search method to use for your Recordset object.

Creating Your Own Bound Controls

Up to this point, you have been creating your Visual Basic database programs by using the data control as the heart of the system. After learning about the Microsoft JET data engine and covering some basics on searching techniques, you are now ready to create an OLE Server library that allows you to build solid data entry forms without using the data control. The rest of this day is devoted to constructing this OLE Server library.

 **NOTE**

> A finished version of the RecObject OLE Server library is contained in the RECOBJECT.CLS class file on the CD that comes with this book.

There is a series of operations that must be handled for any data entry system. First, let's outline these operations, and then you can use that outline as a guide in constructing your library functions. The following is a list of common operations used in almost all data entry forms:

- [ ] RSOpen: This routine opens a database and selects a set of records for processing.
- [ ] RSInit: This routine initializes the data entry form and prepares the on-form controls for reading and writing data records.
- [ ] RSLocate: This routine provides a front end for performing Seek and Find operations on the dataset.
- [ ] RSRead: This routine reads the selected record and loads the on-form controls with the contents of the data fields.
- [ ] RSEnable: This routine handles the enabling and disabling of the input controls to manage user updates to the data form.
- [ ] RSWrite: This routine copies the values from the data entry form back to the dataset for storage.
- [ ] RSDelete: This routine gives the user the power to delete the current record from the dataset.

In addition to the record-handling routines, you also build a set of routines to design and manage a command button toolbar. This toolbar provides access to basic data entry functions such as add, edit, delete, and locate, as well as the four browse actions: first, next, previous, and last moves. These three additional routines handle the actions that involve the command buttons:

☐ BBInit: This routine creates the button set on your form. You can place the button set on the top, bottom, left, or right side of the form.

☐ BBEnable: This short routine enables you to temporarily disable selected buttons on the bar to make sure the user does not mistakenly invoke a search action in the middle of an update action.

☐ BBProcess: This routine is the heart of the data entry form. It links the button set with the previously mentioned record functions to provide a complete, customized data entry form for your applications.

You design these routines to work with any dataset you select, as well as any form layout you choose, using any input controls (not just the Visual Basic data-bound controls). Also, you construct the routines as a set of methods within the standalone OLE Server. That way, you can add the record-handling routines to all your future programming projects.

Finally, the OLE Server library has a handful of properties that you can use to control the behavior of the record-processing routines. The following is a list of the properties you need with the OLE Server:

☐ WSName: This property is the local workspace name.

☐ DBName: This property is the database name.

☐ RSName: This property is the Recordset name or SQL statement.

☐ RSType: This property is the value to indicate a table, Dynaset, or Snapshot object.

☐ Index: This property is the index name to use for table objects.

☐ IndexFlag: This property is a True/False toggle. When this property is True, use the Seek method.

☐ BBAlign: This property is the alignment value that controls the appearance of the control buttons on the form.

☐ Focus: This property is the field that gets first focus when you are adding or editing a record.

In the following sections, you go through the process of building the code library. After the library is built, you build a simple form to add to the CompanyMaster project. This form uses all the library functions covered in this section.

Preparing the Data Entry Form

The routines we have designed make a few assumptions about how your data entry forms are constructed. These assumptions are very general and result in a solid, if not flashy, data entry form. After completing these routines, you might want to modify the library functions to add additional features and options that suit your particular data entry needs.

For each data entry form you design using these routines, you need to stay within the following guidelines:

☐ Each data entry form corresponds to a single dataset. Following this guideline is easy when you are dealing with table-type datasets. You can design a single form for each table. If you need to perform data entry on a set of columns that are the result of a multiple-table SQL JOIN operation, you can use the dataset produced by the JOIN as the basis for the data entry form.

☐ Each data entry form contains a single command button named cmdBtn. You must set its Index property to 0 to indicate that it is part of a control array. All the routines you build expect this command button.

☐ Every column in the dataset row that requires data entry is represented by a single textbox control on the form. The control and the field are related by placing the column name in the Tag property of the input control. This procedure enables you to bind your input controls to your dataset.

After incorporating these guidelines, you can lay out your forms in any manner you like.

Begin this project by building the library of record-handling functions. Start a new Visual Basic 5.0 ActiveX DLL project. Set the class name to recObject by filling the Name property of the class module.

TIP

Be sure to set the Option Explicit option to On for this project. This option forces you to declare all variables before they are used in your program. Using the Option Explicit setting helps reduce the number of program bugs you create as you enter these routines.

Before you begin the heavy coding, complete the declaration section of the library routine. Enter Listing 10.6 at the top of the module.

TYPE   **Listing 10.6. Coding the global variables.**

```
Option Explicit
'
' local enumerations

' recordset types
Enum rsType
```

```
        rsTableType = dbOpenTable
        rsSnapShotType = dbOpenSnapshot
        rsDynasetType = dbOpenDynaset
End Enum
'
' button alignments
Enum bbAlign
    bbTop = 0
    bbBottom = 1
    bbLeft = 2
    bbRight = 3
End Enum


'
' private property storage
Private strWSName As String ' local workspace name
Private strDBName As String ' local database name
Private strRSName As String ' local recordset name/SQL
Private strIndex As String ' local index name
Private blnIndex As Boolean ' use index flag
Private intBBAlign As Integer ' button aligment
Private strFocus As String ' field to get first focus
'
Private ws As workspace
Private db As Database
Private rs As Recordset
Private intRSType As rsType
```

The first two enumerated values in Listing 10.6 are used throughout the routines to indicate the types of datasets and the location of the button bar set on the form. The rest of the values represent local storage for public properties of your OLE Server class. After you have entered the code in Listing 10.6, save the module as RECOBJECT.CLS.

Coding the Property Handling Routines

Now that you've created the local storage for the properties, you can use the Tools | Add Procedure menu option to create Public property procedures, too. Listing 10.7 shows the code for all the property-handling routines in the library. Use the Property names as a guide in creating the properties with the Tools | Add Procedure menu and then enter a associated code into each of the Property Let and Get methods.

TYPE   **Listing 10.7. Coding the property-handling routines.**

```
Public Property Get DBName() As Variant
    DBName = strDBName
End Property
```

continues

Listing 10.7. continued

```
Public Property Let DBName(ByVal vNewValue As Variant)
    strDBName = vNewValue
End Property

Public Property Get RSName() As Variant
    RSName = strRSName
End Property

Public Property Let RSName(ByVal vNewValue As Variant)
    strRSName = vNewValue
End Property

Public Property Get dbObject() As Variant
    dbObject = db
End Property

Public Property Let dbObject(ByVal vNewValue As Variant)
    ' na
End Property

Public Property Get wsObject() As Variant
    wsObject = ws
End Property

Public Property Let wsObject(ByVal vNewValue As Variant)
    ' na
End Property

Public Property Get rsObject() As Variant
    rsObject = rs
End Property

Public Property Let rsObject(ByVal vNewValue As Variant)
    ' na
End Property

Public Property Get WSName() As Variant
    WSName = strWSName
End Property

Public Property Let WSName(ByVal vNewValue As Variant)
    strWSName = vNewValue
End Property

Public Property Get rsType() As rsType
    rsType = intRSType
End Property

Public Property Let rsType(ByVal vNewValue As rsType)
    intRSType = vNewValue
End Property

Public Property Get Index() As Variant
    Index = strIndex
End Property
```

10

```
Public Property Let Index(ByVal vNewValue As Variant)
    strIndex = vNewValue
End Property

Public Property Get IndexFlag() As Boolean
    IndexFlag = blnIndex
End Property

Public Property Let IndexFlag(ByVal vNewValue As Boolean)
    blnIndex = vNewValue
End Property

Public Property Get BtnBarAlign() As bbAlign
    BtnBarAlign = intBBAlign
End Property

Public Property Let BtnBarAlign(ByVal vNewValue As bbAlign)
    intBBAlign = vNewValue
End Property

Public Property Get RSFocus() As Variant
    RSFocus = strFocus
End Property

Public Property Let RSFocus(ByVal vNewValue As Variant)
    strFocus = vNewValue
End Property
```

Next you need to add the code for the `Class_Initialize` and the `Class_Terminate` events. See Listing 10.8 for the code for these two events.

Listing 10.8. Coding the `Class_Initialize` and `Class_Terminate` events.

TYPE

```
Private Sub Class_Initialize()
    '
    ' set inital values
    '
    intRSType = rsDynasetType
    strWSName = "wsTemp"
    strDBName = ""
    strRSName = ""
    '
    intBBAlign = bbTop
    '
End Sub

Private Sub Class_Terminate()
    '
    ' close out class
```

continues

Listing 10.8. continued

```
    '
    On Error Resume Next
    '
    rs.Close
    db.Close
    ws.Close
    Set rs = Nothing
    Set db = Nothing
    Set ws = Nothing
    '
End Sub
```

Now that you have dealt with the properties, you're ready to start coding the main record-handling routines. The next several sections contain the code for all the record-handling routines.

The RSOpen Routine

The RSOpen routine handles the opening of an existing database and the creation of a Recordset to hold the selected records. Enter Listing 10.9 into the class module. Be sure to include the Function declaration line. Visual Basic supplies the End Function line automatically.

> **TIP**
>
> You should save your work after entering each coding section to ensure that you do not lose much work if your computer suffers an unexpected crash.

TYPE **Listing 10.9. Coding the RSOpen function.**

```
Public Function RSOpen(frmTemp As Object)
    '
    ' create ws, db, and rs objects
    '
    On Error GoTo LocalErr
    '
    Dim lngResult As Long
    '
    Set ws = dbengine.createworkspace(WSName, "admin", "")
    Set db = ws.OpenDatabase(strDBName)
    Set rs = db.OpenRecordset(strRSName, intRSType)
    '
```

```
        lngResult = RSInit(frmTemp)
        If lngResult = 0 Then
            lngResult = RSRead(frmTemp)
        End If
        '
        RSOpen = lngResult
        Exit Function
        '
LocalErr:
        RSOpen = Err.Number
        '
End Function
```

This routine accepts the user's form as a parameter, uses the property values to create a complete database and Recordset connection, and then initializes the data entry form and fills it with the first record in the dataset.

Another new twist here is that almost all the routines in this library are declared as Functions instead of Subs. These functions return an integer value that indicates whether any errors occurred during the operation. This value gives you a very easy way to check for errors from within Visual Basic code. Note that any error number returned by the Visual Basic code is sent back to the user's program for handling. This is a simple way to pass internal errors out of the class module into the caller's routine.

TIP

You should comment out the On Error lines of your program while you are first entering the Visual Basic code. When the error trap is on, even simple typing errors set it off. During the construction phase, you want the Visual Basic interpreter to halt and give you a full error message. When you are sure you have eliminated all the programming bugs, you can activate the error handlers by removing the comment mark from the On Error program lines.

The RSInit **Routine**

The RSInit routine clears out any stray values that might exist in the form controls that you are binding to your data table. Remember that you can bind a form control to a dataset column by placing the name of the column in the Tag property of the field. This routine checks that property and, if it contains information, initializes the control to prepare it for receiving dataset values. Enter the code in Listing 10.10 as a new function.

TYPE   **Listing 10.10. Coding the RSInit function.**

```
Public Function RSInit(frmTemp As Object)
    '
    ' clear all input controls on the form
    '
    On Error GoTo LocalErr
    '
    Dim ctlTemp As Control
    Dim strTag As String
    '
    For Each ctlTemp In frmTemp.Controls
        strTag = UCase(Trim(ctlTemp.Tag))
        If strTag <> "" Then
            ctlTemp = ""
        End If
    Next
    '
    RSInit = 0
    Exit Function
    '
LocalErr:
    RSInit = Err.Number
    '
End Function
```

This routine contains a simple loop that checks all the controls on the form to see whether they are bound to a dataset column. If they are, the control is initialized.

The RSLocate Routine

The RSLocate routine prompts the user to enter a value to use as a search criteria on the Recordset. The routine is smart enough to use the Seek method for table objects and the Find method for non-table objects. Add the routine in Listing 10.11 to your module.

TYPE   **Listing 10.11. Coding the RSLocate routine.**

```
Public Function RSLocate(FieldName As String)
    '
    ' search the designated field
    '
    On Error GoTo LocalErr
    '
    Dim strSearch As String
    '
    If blnIndex = True Then
        rs.Index = strIndex
```

10

```
    End If
    '
    strSearch = InputBox("Enter Search Value:", "Searching " & FieldName)
    strSearch = Trim(strSearch)
    '
    If strSearch = "" Then
        RSLocate = False
        Exit Function
    End If
    '
    If rs.Fields(FieldName).Type = dbText Then
        strSearch = "'" & strSearch & "'"
    End If
    '
    If blnIndex = True Then
        rs.Seek "=", strSearch
    Else
        rs.FindFirst FieldName & "=" & strSearch
    End If
    '
    If rs.NoMatch = True Then
        RSLocate = False
    Else
        RSLocate = True
    End If
    '
    Exit Function
    '
LocalErr:
    RSLocate = Err.Number
    '
End Function
```

Notice that if you set the IndexFlag property to True in this routine, the routine uses the Seek method instead of a sequential Find method. Also note the check for a text-type search field. If the target field to search has a dbText data type, the search values are enclosed in single quotes.

The RSRead **Routine**

Now you get one of the important routines! The RSRead routine takes values from the current record of the dataset and loads them into controls on the form. This is done by checking all the controls on the form for a nonblank Tag property. If a control has a value in the Tag property, the routine assumes that the value is a column name for the dataset. The value in this column is then copied from the dataset into the form control. Add this new routine (shown in Listing 10.12) to your library. Note that this routine is built as a Private Function. You do not want external programs to be able to invoke this function directly.

TYPE   **Listing 10.12. Coding the RSRead function.**

```
Private Function RSRead(frmTemp As Object)
    '
    ' move data from recordset to form
    '
    On Error GoTo LocalErr
    '
    Dim ctlTemp As Control
    Dim strTag As String
    Dim strFldName As String
    '
    For Each ctlTemp In frmTemp.Controls
        strTag = UCase(Trim(ctlTemp.Tag))
        If strTag <> "" Then
            If IsNull(rs.Fields(strTag)) = False Then
                ctlTemp = rs.Fields(strTag)
            End If
        End If
    Next
    '
    RSRead = 0
    Exit Function
    '
LocalErr:
    RSRead = Err.Number
    '
End Function
```

This routine and the next routine (RSWrite) are the heart of the record-handling functions.
When you understand how these routines work, you can build your own customized routines
for handling dataset read and write operations.

The RSWrite Routine

The routine in Listing 10.13 performs the opposite function of RSRead (see Listing 10.12).
Again, it's a simple loop through all the controls on the form. If a control is bound to a data
column, the value in the control is copied to the dataset column for storage.

NOTE   Before you can write to a dataset, you need to invoke the Edit or
AddNew methods. After the write operation, you must invoke the Update
method to save the changes. You handle these operations in the button
set routines later in today's lesson.

TYPE **Listing 10.13. Coding the** `RSWrite` **function.**

```
Private Function RSRead(frmTemp As Object)
    '
    ' move data from recordset to form
    '
    On Error GoTo LocalErr
    '
    Dim ctlTemp As Control
    Dim strTag As String
    Dim strFldName As String
    '
    For Each ctlTemp In frmTemp.Controls
        strTag = UCase(Trim(ctlTemp.Tag))
        If strTag <> "" Then
            If IsNull(rs.Fields(strTag)) = False Then
                ctlTemp = rs.Fields(strTag)
            End If
        End If
    Next
    '
    RSRead = 0
    Exit Function
    '
LocalErr:
    RSRead = Err.Number
    '
End Function

Private Function RSWrite(frmTemp As Object)
    '
    ' move values in controls to data set
    '
    On Error GoTo LocalErr
    '
    Dim ctlTemp As Control
    Dim strTag As String
    Dim lngAttrib As Long
    '
    For Each ctlTemp In frmTemp.Controls
        strTag = UCase(Trim(ctlTemp.Tag))
        If strTag <> "" Then
            lngAttrib = rs.Fields(strTag).Attributes
            If (lngAttrib And dbAutoIncrField) = 0 Then
                If rs.Fields(strTag).DataUpdatable = True Then
                    rs.Fields(strTag) = ctlTemp
                End If
            End If
        End If
    Next
    '
    RSWrite = 0
    Exit Function
    '
End Function
```

An added feature in this routine deserves mention. Because Visual Basic does not allow you to write to COUNTER data type fields, this routine checks the Attributes property of each bound column before attempting an update. If the field is a COUNTER data type, the routine does not attempt to write data to the column. Note again that the RSWrite routine is built as a Private Function. This function can be executed only by other methods within your OLE Server class.

The RSEnable Routine

To simplify the management of data entry routines, your form allows users to update form controls only after they select the Edit or Add buttons on a form. The RSEnable routine gives you an easy way to turn on or off the Enabled property of all the bound controls on your form. You call this routine often from your button set routines. Add Listing 10.14 to the library.

TYPE   **Listing 10.14. Coding the RSEnable function.**

```
Public Function RSEnable(frmTemp As Object, Toggle As Boolean)
    '
    ' toggle the controls on/off
    '
    Dim ctlTemp As Control
    Dim strTag As String
    '
    For Each ctlTemp In frmTemp.Controls
        strTag = UCase(Trim(ctlTemp.Tag))
        If strTag <> "" Then
            ctlTemp.Enabled = Toggle
        End If
        If UCase(Trim(ctlTemp.Tag)) = UCase(Trim(strFocus)) Then
            If Toggle = True Then
                ctlTemp.SetFocus
            End If
        End If
    Next
    '
    RSEnable = 0
    Exit Function
    '
LocalErr:
    RSEnable = Err.Number
    '
End Function
```

Notice that the RSEnable routine checks the Focus property to see which input field should get the initial focus on the form.

10

The `RSDelete` Routine

The `RSDelete` routine performs a delete operation on the selected data record. But before committing the deed, the user is given a chance to reverse the process. Add Listing 10.15 to the library.

TYPE **Listing 10.15. Coding the `RSDelete` function.**

```
Private Function RSDelete()
    '
    ' delete current record
    '
    Dim lngResult As Long
    '
    lngResult = MsgBox("Delete current record?", vbYesNo + vbQuestion, rs.Name)
    If lngResult = vbYes Then
        rs.Delete
    End If
    '
    RSDelete = 0
    Exit Function
    '
LocalErr:
    RSDelete = Err.Number
    '
End Function
```

Other Record Routines

You need three more routines to complete the record-handling portion of the library. `RSClose` handles the final closing of the record-handling routines; `RSBack` and `RSNext` provide a safe way to process Visual Basic `MovePrevious` and `MoveNext` operations without encountering end-of-file errors from Visual Basic. Add these three routines, which are provided in Listing 10.16, to the library.

TYPE **Listing 10.16. Coding the `RSClose`, `RSBack`, and `RSNext` routines.**

```
Public Sub RSClose()
    '
    ' close down object
    '
    Class_Terminate
    '
End Sub
```

continues

Listing 10.16. continued

```
Private Function RSBack()
    '
    ' move back one record
    '
    If rs.BOF = True Then
        rs.MoveFirst
    Else
        rs.MovePrevious
        If rs.BOF Then
            rs.MoveFirst
        End If
    End If
    '
    RSBack = 0
    Exit Function
    '
LocalErr:
    RSBack = Err.Number
    '
End Function


Private Function RSNext()
    '
    ' move to next record
    '
    If rs.EOF = True Then
        rs.MoveLast
    Else
        rs.MoveNext
        If rs.EOF Then
            rs.MoveLast
        End If
    End If
    '
    RSNext = 0
    Exit Function
    '
LocalErr:
    RSNext = Err.Number
    '
End Function
```

You have just completed the record-handling portion of the library. There are only three routines left to build. These three routines provide the button set that users see when they perform data entry operations on your form.

10

Creating Your Own Button Bar Routines

The next three routines handle all the operations needed to add a complete set of command buttons to your data entry form. You can use this set for any data entry form that provides the basic add, edit, delete, find, and browse operations needed for most data entry routines.

WARNING

> To make these routines work with your programs, you must add a single command button to your form called cmdBtn. Its Index property must be set to 0 to indicate that it is part of a control array. The details of constructing a working form are covered in the "Creating a Data Entry Form with the Library Routines" section of this lesson.

10

The BBInit Routine

The BBInit routine builds the details of the command button array and places that array on your data entry form. You must first place a single command button on the target form with its Name property set to cmdBtn and its Index property set to 0. This routine creates seven more command buttons, sets their captions and sizes, and places the button set on the top, bottom, left, or right side of the form. You control this feature by setting the BtnBarAlign property you defined earlier. Add this routine (in Listing 10.17) to the OLE Server library module that contains the record-handling routines.

TYPE **Listing 10.17. Coding the BBInit routine.**

```
Public Function BBInit(frmTemp As Object)
    '
    ' initialize a button bar on the form
    '
    Dim intBtnWidth As Integer
    Dim intBtnTop As Integer
    Dim intBtnleft As Integer
    Dim intBtnHeight As Integer
    Dim intLoop As Integer
    Dim varCap As Variant
    '
    varCap = Array("&Add", "&Edit", "&Del", "&Find", "&Top", "&Next",
➥"&Back", "&Last")
    '
```

continues

Listing 10.17. continued

```
' compute btn locations
intBtnWidth = 660
intBtnHeight = 300
'
Select Case intBBAlign
    Case bbTop
        intBtnTop = 60
        intBtnWidth = (frmTemp.ScaleWidth - 60) / 8
        If intBtnWidth < 660 Then intBtnWidth = 660
        intBtnHeight = 300
    Case bbBottom
        intBtnTop = frmTemp.ScaleHeight - 360
        intBtnWidth = (frmTemp.ScaleHeight - 60) / 8
        If intBtnWidth < 660 Then intBtnWidth = 660
        intBtnHeight = 300
    Case bbLeft
        intBtnWidth = 660
        intBtnleft = 60
        intBtnHeight = (frmTemp.ScaleHeight - 60) / 8
        If intBtnHeight < 300 Then intBtnHeight = 300
    Case bbRight
        intBtnWidth = 660
        intBtnleft = frmTemp.ScaleWidth - 720
        intBtnHeight = (frmTemp.ScaleHeight - 60) / 8
        If intBtnHeight < 300 Then intBtnHeight = 300
End Select
'
' now place buttons on the form
For intLoop = 0 To 7
    If intBBAlign = bbTop Or intBBAlign = bbBottom Then
        intBtnleft = intLoop * intBtnWidth
    Else
        intBtnTop = (intLoop * intBtnHeight) + 60
    End If
    '
    On Error Resume Next
    With frmTemp
        If intLoop <> 0 Then
            Load .cmdbtn(intLoop)
        End If
        .cmdbtn(intLoop).Width = intBtnWidth
        .cmdbtn(intLoop).Left = intBtnleft
        .cmdbtn(intLoop).Top = intBtnTop
        .cmdbtn(intLoop).Height = intBtnHeight
        .cmdbtn(intLoop).Caption = varCap(intLoop)
        .cmdbtn(intLoop).Visible = True
    End With
Next
'
BBInit = 0
Exit Function
'
```

```
LocalErr:
    BBInit = Err.Number
    '
End Function
```

Listing 10.17 uses the data form's dimensions to calculate the location and size of the command buttons in the button set. You create a working example of this form in the section "Creating a Data Entry Form with the Library Routines."

The BBEnable Routine

The BBEnable routine is a short routine that allows you to toggle the Enabled property of the command buttons in the button set. This routine is used to turn on or off selected buttons during edit or add operations. Add the routine in Listing 10.18 to the library.

TYPE | **Listing 10.18. Coding the BBEnable routine.**

```
Public Function BBEnable(frmTemp As Object, strList As String)
    '
    ' enable buttons
    '
    On Error GoTo LocalErr
    '
    Dim intLoop As Integer
    '
    strList = Trim(strList)
    '
    For intLoop = 1 To Len(strList)
        If Mid(strList, intLoop, 1) = "1" Then
            frmTemp.cmdbtn(intLoop - 1).Enabled = True
        Else
            frmTemp.cmdbtn(intLoop - 1).Enabled = False
        End If
    Next
    '
    BBEnable = 0
    Exit Function
    '
LocalErr:
    BBEnable = Err.Number
    '
End Function
```

The routine works by accepting a series of eight 1s and 0s. Each position in the eight-byte string represents one of the button bar buttons. If the value is set to 1, the button is enabled. If the value is set to 0, the button is disabled.

The BBProcess Routine

The BBProcess routine handles all the button actions initiated by the user and makes many calls to the other routines in the library. This routine is the high-level method of the class module; it is also the most involved routine in this library. It might look intimidating at first glance. But, after you inspect the first several lines, you see a pattern developing. More than half of the routine is devoted to handling the browse buttons (First, Back, Next, and Last). The rest is used to handle the add, edit, find, and delete operations. Enter Listing 10.19 into the library.

TYPE   **Listing 10.19. Coding the BBProcess routine.**

```
Public Function BBProcess(frmTemp As Object, intBtn As Integer, strSearch As
➥String)
    '
    ' handle all button clicks
    '
    On Error GoTo LocalErr

    Dim lngResult As Long
    '
    Select Case intBtn
        Case 0 ' add/save/cancel
            Select Case frmTemp.cmdbtn(intBtn).Caption
                Case "&Save" ' save new
                    lngResult = RSWrite(frmTemp)
                    If lngResult = 0 Then
                        rs.Update
                    End If
                    If lngResult = 0 Then
                        lngResult = RSInit(frmTemp)
                    End If
                    If lngResult = 0 Then
                        lngResult = RSRead(frmTemp)
                    End If
                    If lngResult = 0 Then
                        lngResult = RSEnable(frmTemp, False)
                    End If
                    If lngResult = 0 Then
                        frmTemp.cmdbtn(0).Caption = "&Add"
                        frmTemp.cmdbtn(1).Caption = "&Edit"
                    End If
                Case "&Add" ' add new
                    rs.AddNew
                    lngResult = RSInit(frmTemp)
                    If lngResult = 0 Then
                        lngResult = RSEnable(frmTemp, True)
                    End If
                    If lngResult = 0 Then
                        frmTemp.cmdbtn(0).Caption = "&Save"
                        frmTemp.cmdbtn(1).Caption = "&Cancel"
```

10

```
                BBEnable frmTemp, "11000000"
            End If
    Case "&Cancel" ' cancel edit
        rs.CancelUpdate
        frmTemp.cmdbtn(0).Caption = "&Add"
        frmTemp.cmdbtn(1).Caption = "&Edit"
        BBEnable frmTemp, "11111111"
        '
        lngResult = RSInit(frmTemp)
        If lngResult = 0 Then
            lngResult = RSRead(frmTemp)
        End If
        If lngResult = 0 Then
            lngResult = RSEnable(frmTemp, False)
        End If
End Select
Case 1 ' edit/save/cancel
    Select Case frmTemp.cmdbtn(1).Caption
        Case "&Save" ' save edit
            rs.Edit
            lngResult = RSWrite(frmTemp)
            If lngResult = 0 Then
                rs.Update
            End If
            If lngResult = 0 Then
                lngResult = RSEnable(frmTemp, False)
            End If
            If lngResult = 0 Then
                frmTemp.cmdbtn(0).Caption = "&Add"
                frmTemp.cmdbtn(1).Caption = "&Edit"
                BBEnable frmTemp, "11111111"
            End If
        Case "&Edit" ' edit existing
            lngResult = RSEnable(frmTemp, True)
            If lngResult = 0 Then
                frmTemp.cmdbtn(0).Caption = "&Cancel"
                frmTemp.cmdbtn(1).Caption = "&Save"
                BBEnable frmTemp, "11000000"
            End If
        Case "&Cancel" ' cancel new
            rs.CancelUpdate
            frmTemp.cmdbtn(0).Caption = "&Add"
            frmTemp.cmdbtn(1).Caption = "&Edit"
            BBEnable frmTemp, "11111111"
            '
            lngResult = RSInit(frmTemp)
            If lngResult = 0 Then
                lngResult = RSRead(frmTemp)
            End If
            If lngResult = 0 Then
                lngResult = RSEnable(frmTemp, False)
            End If
    End Select
    '
```

10

continues

Listing 10.19. continued

```
                    If lngResult = 0 Then
                        lngResult = RSInit(frmTemp)
                    End If
                    If lngResult = 0 Then
                        lngResult = RSRead(frmTemp)
                    End If
                Case 2 ' delete rec
                    lngResult = RSDelete()
                    If lngResult = 0 Then
                        lngResult = RSEnable(frmTemp, False)
                    End If
                    If lngResult = 0 Then
                        lngResult = RSNext()
                    End If
                    If lngResult = 0 Then
                        lngResult = RSInit(frmTemp)
                    End If
                    If lngResult = 0 Then
                        lngResult = RSRead(frmTemp)
                    End If
                    BBEnable frmTemp, "11111111"
                Case 3 ' find
                    lngResult = RSLocate(strSearch)
                    If lngResult = True Then
                        lngResult = RSInit(frmTemp)
                    End If
                    If lngResult = 0 Then
                        lngResult = RSRead(frmTemp)
                    End If
                    BBEnable frmTemp, "11111111"
                Case 4 ' move to top
                    rs.MoveFirst
                    lngResult = RSInit(frmTemp)
                    If lngResult = 0 Then
                        lngResult = RSRead(frmTemp)
                    End If
                    BBEnable frmTemp, "11111111"
                Case 5 ' move next
                    lngResult = RSNext()
                    If lngResult = 0 Then
                        lngResult = RSInit(frmTemp)
                    End If
                    If lngResult = 0 Then
                        lngResult = RSRead(frmTemp)
                    End If
                    BBEnable frmTemp, "11111111"
                Case 6 ' move previous
                    rs.MovePrevious
                    lngResult = RSBack()
                    If lngResult = 0 Then
                        lngResult = RSInit(frmTemp)
                    End If
                    If lngResult = 0 Then
                        lngResult = RSRead(frmTemp)
```

10

```
                End If
                BBEnable frmTemp, "11111111"
            Case 7 ' move last
                rs.MoveLast
                lngResult = RSInit(frmTemp)
                If lngResult = 0 Then
                    lngResult = RSRead(frmTemp)
                End If
                BBEnable frmTemp, "11111111"
        End Select
        '
        BBProcess = 0
        Exit Function
        '
LocalErr:
        BBProcess = Err.Number
        '
End Function
```

NOTE   The routine in Listing 10.19 is the last library function you'll be
adding. Be sure to save the updated library file to disk before exiting
Visual Basic.

Several aspects of Listing 10.19 need review. First, because you are using a command button
array, all operations are dependent on which button was pushed. The outer Select Case
structure handles the action. The comment lines show what each button is labeled. However,
the captions (and functions) of the first two buttons (Add and Edit) can change during the
course of the data entry process. Therefore, these two options have an additional Select Case
to check the caption status of the selected button.

There are a great number of If..End If blocks in the code. These blocks are present because
you are constantly checking the results of previous actions. They clutter up the code a bit,
but they provide solid error-checking capability and program flow control.

Each main section of the outer Select Case performs all the operations needed to complete
a user action. For example, the very first set of operations in the routine is the completion of
the save operation for an Add command. If you ignore the constant checks of the nResult
variable, you see that the essence of this section of the code is as follows:

☐ Write the record to the dataset (RSWrite)

☐ Commit the changes (rs.Update)

☐ Initialize the form controls (RSInit)

☐ Read the current record into the form (RSRead)

☐ Disable data entry in the fields (RSEnable False)

☐ Reset the command button labels and enable all the buttons

The save operation is the most complicated process. The locate, delete, and browse operations are much easier to accomplish and require less coding. The key to remember here is that you are providing all the user-level processes of the data control in this set of Visual Basic code. Although it seems to be a large code piece, you can use it in all your Visual Basic projects once you have it on file.

Compile the OLE Server library so you can use it later. Select File | Make prjRecObject.DLL from the main Visual Basic menu and compile the DLL. In future projects, all you need to do is add a reference to this new object, and you'll be ready to create complete data entry forms with very little coding.

Creating a Data Entry Form with the Library Routines

Now that you have a solid library set for creating data entry forms, you can build a new form for the CompanyMaster project. To do this, you add a new form to the CompanyMaster project. This form is a simple validation list that you can use to validate input for other portions of the project.

If you haven't done it yet, start Visual Basic and load the MASTER.VBP project. This project is a copy of the project you built last week. The first thing you must do is add a reference to the prjRecObject.DLL in the CompanyMaster project. Select Project | References from the main menu and then locate and select prjRecObject.DLL (see Figure 10.4).

Figure 10.4.

Locating and selecting the prjRecObject *OLE Server DLL.*

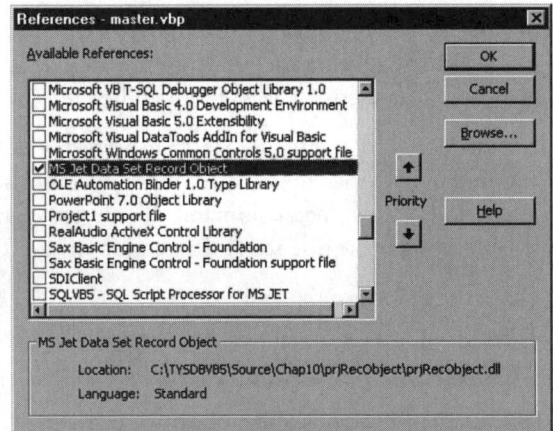

10

NOTE

The CD that ships with the book has a completed version of the library. The CompanyMaster that ships with the CD may also have a reference to the old prjRecObject.DLL instead of a pointer reference to your newer version. If you receive errors loading the CompanyMaster project, ignore them and load the new prjRecObject.DLL as planned.

Modifying the Master Form

Before you add the new form, you need to add a short menu to the CompanyMaster main form. You use this menu to call the new form. Open the frmMaster form and add the menu items listed in Table 10.2. You can also refer to Figure 10.5 as a guide for building the menu.

Figure 10.5.

Adding items to the menu.

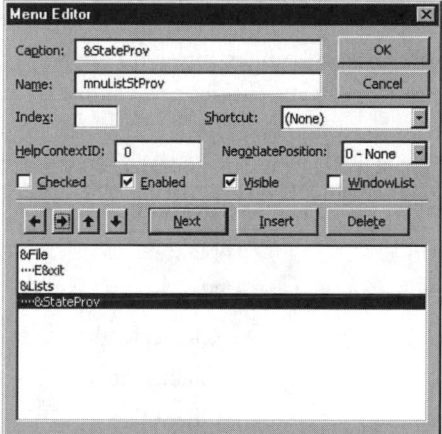

Table 10.2. Menu items for the frmMaster form.

Caption	Menu
&File	mnuFile
E&xit	mnuFileExit
&Lists	mnuList
&State/Prov	mnuListStProv

After building the menu, enter the following code for the Exit menu item:

```
Private Sub mnuFileExit_Click()
    cmdExit_Click    ' do the exit!
End Sub
```

This code calls the existing routine that handles the program exit.

Now you need to add the line of code that calls the new form you are going to create. Enter the following code for the State/Prov menu item:

```
Private Sub mnuListStProv_Click()
    frmStProv.Show 1
End Sub
```

This code calls the new form and forces it to display as a modal form. Because it is modal, users cannot change the focus within their project until they safely exit this form.

Building the State/Province List Form

Now that the housekeeping is done, you can build the new form. Use Table 10.3 and Figure 10.6 as guides as you lay out the new validation form.

Table 10.3. Controls for the State/Province list form.

Control	Property	Setting
VB.Form	Name	frmStProv
	Caption	"State/Province Validation Table"
	ClientHeight	2220
	ClientLeft	60
	ClientTop	345
	ClientWidth	5895
	StartUpPosition	3 'Windows Default
VB.CommandButton	Name	cmdBtn
	Index	0
VB.TextBox	Name	Text2
	Height	255
	Left	1440
	Top	540
	Width	2775

Control	Property	Setting
VB.TextBox	Name	Text1
	Height	255
	Left	1440
	Top	240
	Width	915
VB.Label	Name	Label2
	Caption	"Complete Name"
	Height	300
	Left	120
	Top	600
	Width	1200
VB.Label	Name	Label1
	Caption	"St/Prov Code"
	Height	300
	Left	120
	Top	240
	Width	1200

Figure 10.6.

Laying out the State/ Province form.

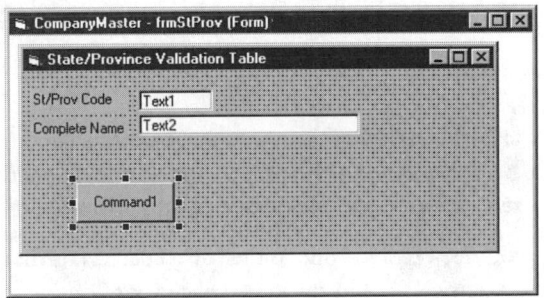

Next, add the code fragments that make this data entry form work. You only have a few items to add because you're using the prjRecObject library you built earlier in this lesson. Add Listing 10.20 to the declaration section of the form.

TYPE   **Listing 10.20. Coding the form-level variables.**

```
Option Explicit
'
Dim objRec As Object
Dim lngResult As Long
```

Create a Sub procedure to handle opening the database and creating the Recordset. Add the new routine in Listing 10.21 to the form.

TYPE   **Listing 10.21. Coding the StartProc routine.**

```
Public Sub StartProc()
    '
    ' handle initial startup of form
    '
    Set objRec = New recObject
    '
    objRec.DBName = App.Path & "\..\..\data\master.mdb"
    objRec.RSName = "StateProvList"
    objRec.rsType = rsDynasetType
    objRec.RSFocus = "StateProv"
    '
    objRec.RSOpen Me
    objRec.RSEnable Me, False
    '
    objRec.BtnBarAlign = bbBottom
    objRec.BBInit Me
    objRec.BBEnable Me, "11111111"
    '
End Sub
```

Listing 10.21 initializes the top-level record object and then sets several properties of the new object before executing the RSOpen and RSEnable methods. Then the routine goes on to initialize and enable the button bar for the form.

Next, you need to add code to the Form_Load event that starts this whole process. Enter the code in Listing 10.22 in the Form_Load event window of the form.

TYPE   **Listing 10.22. Coding the Form_Load routine.**

```
Private Sub Form_Load()
    '
    ' set field tags for data binding
    Text1.Tag = "StateProv"
    Text2.Tag = "Description"
    '
```

```
    ' call routine to start recObject library
    StartProc
    '
End Sub
```

In Listing 10.22, you set the Tag properties of the two textboxes that are used for data entry, and then you call StartProc to start up the local copy of recObject.

Now you need to add the routine that makes the buttons call all of the library routines. Add the following code to the cmdBtn_Click event of the form:

```
Private Sub cmdBtn_Click(Index As Integer)
    '
    ' handle all button selections
    '
    objRec.BBProcess Me, Index, "StateProv"
    '
End Sub
```

This code is called every time you click any of the eight buttons on the data entry form. The BBProcess routine determines which button was pressed and performs the appropriate actions. Note that you are sending the BBProcess method three parameters: the data entry form, the index value that tells you which button was pressed, and the Search field to use if the user has pressed the Find button.

You need to add a few more lines of code to this form before you are done. First, add code that enables the buttons to automatically resize each time the form is resized. Add the following code to the Form_Resize event:

```
Private Sub Form_Resize()
    '
    objRec.BBInit Me
    '
End Sub
```

Finally, add the following code to the Form_Unload event to ensure a safe close of the database when the program ends:

```
Private Sub Form_Unload(Cancel As Integer)
    '
    objRec.RSClose
    '
End Sub
```

Save the new form as FRMSTPROV.FRM, and run the project. When the main form comes up, select Lists | StateProv from the menu to start the new form. Your form should look like the one shown in Figure 10.7.

Notice that the button set appears on the bottom of the form. This placement was handled automatically by the library routines. Resize the form to see how the button bar automatically adjusts to the new form shape. Finally, click the Add button to add a new record to the State/Province table. You see the input controls become enabled and most of the button bar becomes disabled (see Figure 10.8).

Figure 10.7.

Running the new State/Province Validation form.

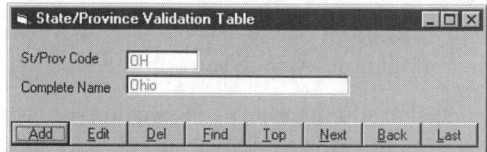

Figure 10.8.

Adding a new record to the State/Province table.

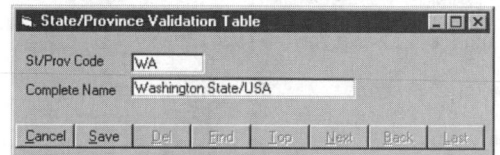

You can enter values in both fields and then click the Save button or the Cancel button to undo the add operation. Click Cancel for now. Test out the form by clicking the Browse and Find buttons. Add a record, edit it, and then delete it. You now have a fully functional data entry form, and you added less than 30 lines of Visual Basic code to the master form!

Summary

Today you learned how to write data entry forms using Visual Basic code. These topics were covered: record search routines, the creation of a procedure library to handle all data entry processes, and the creation of a working data entry form for the CompanyMaster project.

You learned how to perform single-record searches using the three search methods:

☐ The Move methods for browsing the dataset

☐ The Seek method for indexed table objects

☐ The Find methods for non-table objects (Dynasets and Snapshots)

You created an OLE Server library to handle adding, editing, deleting, reading, writing, and locating records in datasets. These routines were written as a generic DLL that you can insert into all Visual Basic programs you write in the future.

You used the new library to add a new form to the CompanyMaster database project. This new form reads a dataset and enables the user to update and browse the table. This new data entry form was built using less than 30 lines of Visual Basic code.

Quiz

To review the material you learned in this chapter, respond to the following questions and check your answers against the ones provided in Appendix C.

1. What are the advantages and disadvantages of using the data control rather than code to manage Visual Basic database applications?
2. What is the main advantage of using code to produce data entry forms?
3. Which approach to searching for a data record—the Move, Find, or Seek method—most resembles the SQL WHERE clause?
4. On what kind of Recordsets can the Seek method be used to search for records?
5. What are the four Move methods that you can apply to the Recordset object?
6. Which of the Find methods starts its search from the beginning of the Recordset? Which of the Find methods starts its search from the end of the Recordset?
7. Which item do you use to remember a specific location in a dataset?
8. What is the fastest search method to locate a record in a dataset?
9. How do you create a control array in Visual Basic?
10. What method(s) do you need to invoke prior to using the Update method to write to a dataset?

Exercise

Assume that you complete the CompanyMaster application and add the State/Province form as discussed in this lesson. After distributing this application to your users, you quickly discover that they are having trouble obtaining zip codes for the companies they enter. You decide to help them by adding a form to this application that lists zip codes and their city equivalents.

Use code to modify the CompanyMaster application so that users can select an item from the List menu (call this item ZipCity) that displays zip codes (field name of Zip) and city (field name of City). Use Visdata to add a data table (ZipCity) to MASTER.MDB.

10

Day 11

Displaying Your Data with Graphs

Today you learn how to add graph displays of your data to your database programs. By creating a simple graphing OLE Server that uses the graph control that ships with Visual Basic Professional Edition, you can easily create visual displays of your database.

You also learn how to use SQL SELECT statements for creating datasets to use as the basis for your graphs. These SQL statements can be built into your code or stored as QueryDef objects in your database.

You also learn how to save the generated graphs to disk as bitmap files, how to share your graphs with other programs by placing them on the Windows Clipboard, and how to send the completed graphs to the printer.

Finally, when you complete this chapter you'll have a graphing OLE Server that you can use in all your future Visual Basic projects. As an example, you add a set of default graphs to the CompanyMaster project you started last week.

The OCX control used for this chapter is GRAPH32.OCX. This control
ships with the professional version of Visual Basic 5, but is not installed
during the normal installation process. If you have already installed
Visual Basic 4, you have the GRAPH32.OCX control installed on your
machine. However, if your machine only has Visual Basic 5 installed,
you need to load the GRAPH32.OCX control from the Tools\Controls
folder on the CD. Also, if you experience errors loading the control on
your form, you need to re-register the GRAPH32.OCX control using the
vbctrl.reg file that is found in the same folder. Just double-click the
file to re-register your GRAPH32.OCX control.

The Advantages of Graphing Your Data

Although generating data graphs is not, strictly speaking, a database function, almost all good
database programs provide graphing capabilities. Visual representations of data are much
easier to understand than tables or lists. Providing graphs in your database programs also gives
users the chance to look at data in more than one way. Often, users discover important
information in their data simply by looking at it from another angle.

Providing graphs also gives your programs an added polish that users appreciate. Quite often,
users want more than a simple data entry program with a few list reports. Many times, users
take data created with a Visual Basic program and export it to another Windows application
in order to develop graphs and charts. Using the techniques you learn today, you can provide
your users with all the graphing tools they need to develop graphs and charts without using
other programs!

Loading and Using the Graph Control

The graph control has a multitude of properties that you can manipulate in order to
customize the graph display. Only the most commonly used options are covered here. (You
can review the Visual Basic documentation for detailed information on all the properties of
the graph control.) In this lesson, you learn how to use graph control properties to manipulate
the way graphs appear on your forms by:

☐ Setting the graph type

☐ Adding graph data using the NumPoints, NumSets, AutoInc, GraphData, and
QuickData properties

☐ Adding titles and legends

You also learn how to use the DrawMode property to send the completed graph to a printer, save it as a file, or copy it to the Windows Clipboard.

Loading the Graph Control into the Visual Basic Toolbox

NOTE

Visual Basic 5 does not install the GRAPH32.OCX control by default. If you cannot locate the GRAPH32.OCX control in your version of Visual Basic 5, you need to copy it from the Tools\Controls folder of the Visual Basic 5 installation CD. You may also need to register the control using the vbctrls.reg file found in that same folder.

Before you can begin to use the graph control tool, you have to make sure it is loaded into the Visual Basic toolbox. To do this, load Visual Basic and select Project | Components from the Visual Basic main menu. In the list of available controls, locate Pinnacle-BPS Graph Control (see Figure 11.1). Click the checkbox to add the control to your toolbox and then click the OK button to exit the form.

Figure 11.1.

Adding the graph control to your toolbox.

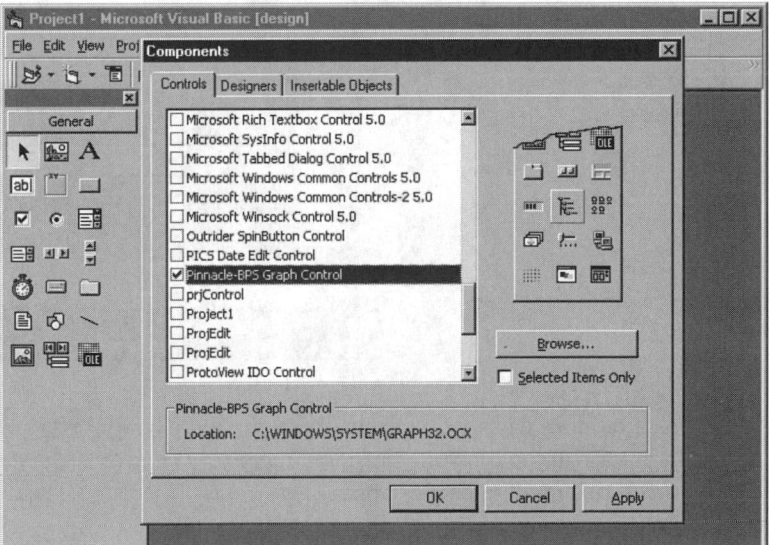

Adding the Graph Control to Your Form

It's very easy to create a good-looking graph using the graph tool. All you need to do is add the control to your form and fill it with data; the graph control does the rest. Let's create a simple graph to illustrate this point.

NOTE

If you have not already loaded Visual Basic and added the graph control to the current project, review the preceding section and perform the required steps.

Add the graph control to a blank form by double-clicking the graph control icon in the toolbox. You see that the graph control automatically displays a two-dimensional bar graph with some data. Stretch the control so that your form looks like the one shown in Figure 11.2.

Figure 11.2.

Adding the graph control to your form.

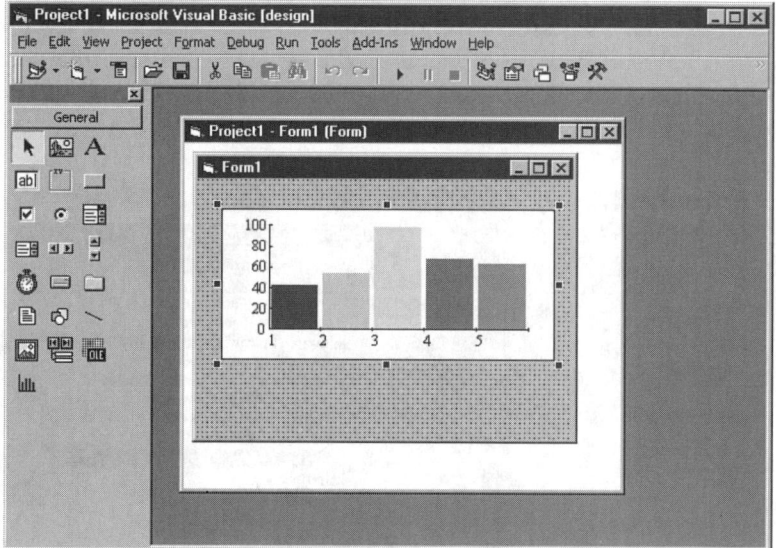

This is random data that the control automatically generates to help you get an idea of how the graph will look in your finished program. When you add your real data to the graph control, this random data disappears.

Setting the Graph Type

You determine the type of graph Visual Basic displays by setting the GraphType property. You can do this using the properties window during design time or through Visual Basic code at runtime. Because you already have the graph up on your form, move to the Properties window and locate the GraphType property. Set the property to display a three-dimensional pie chart by clicking the property in the window and then pulling down the list box. Find and select the 3D Pie option. Your screen should look like the one shown in Figure 11.3.

Figure 11.3.

Changing the GraphType property at design time.

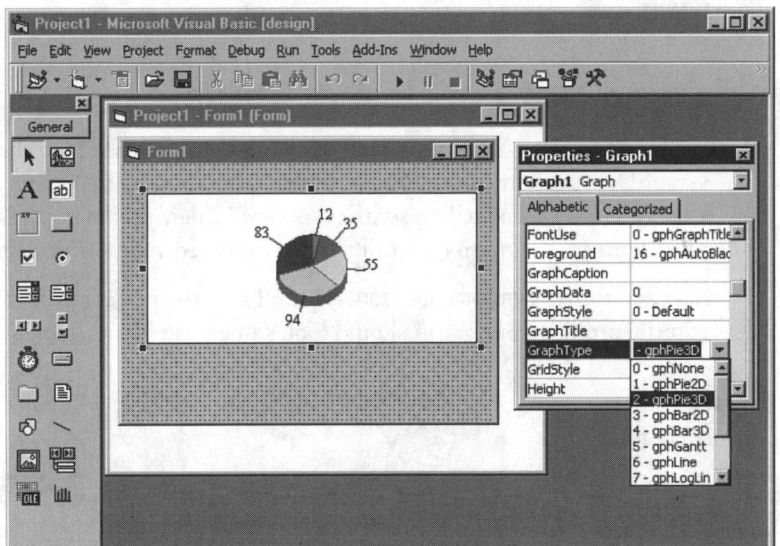

The graph control can display 11 different types of graphs including bar charts, pie charts, line and area graphs, Log/Lin graphs, Gantt charts, scatter graphs, polar graphs, and high/low/close graphs. The three most commonly used formats are covered in this lesson: bar, pie, and line graphs.

How the Graph Control Organizes Your Data

Before you can display data, you have to load it into the graph control. But, before you load it, you need to know how the graph control expects to see the data. The graph control requires that all the data be organized in sets and points. The graph control needs to know how many points of data are in each set you want to graph. Usually, you have a single set of data with multiple points. For example, if you want to graph company sales figures for the last 12 months, you would have a single dataset (company sales figures) with 12 points (one for each month). If you want to create a graph that compares the actual monthly sales figures with the budgeted figures for the last 12 months, you would have two sets of data (actual and budget figures), each with 12 points (one for each month).

You can use the NumSets and NumPoints properties to inform the graph control how the data is to be organized. Create a graph like the one just described. In design mode, use the Property box to set the NumPoints property to 12 and the NumSets property to 1. You have just told the graph control that it should prepare for one set of data containing 12 individual points.

Adding Data in Design Mode

Now add 12 data items at design time so that you can see how the graph looks. Locate the GraphData property in the Property box. It should be set to 0. Now type 1 and press the Enter key. You have just added one of the expected 12 data points for the set. Continue to add data by entering 2, 3, and so on until you have entered values up to 12.

Save the form as FRMGRAPHDESIGN.FRM, and save the project as GRAPHDESIGN.VBP. When you run the project, your graph should look something like the one shown in Figure 11.4.

Figure 11.4.

Adding data in design mode.

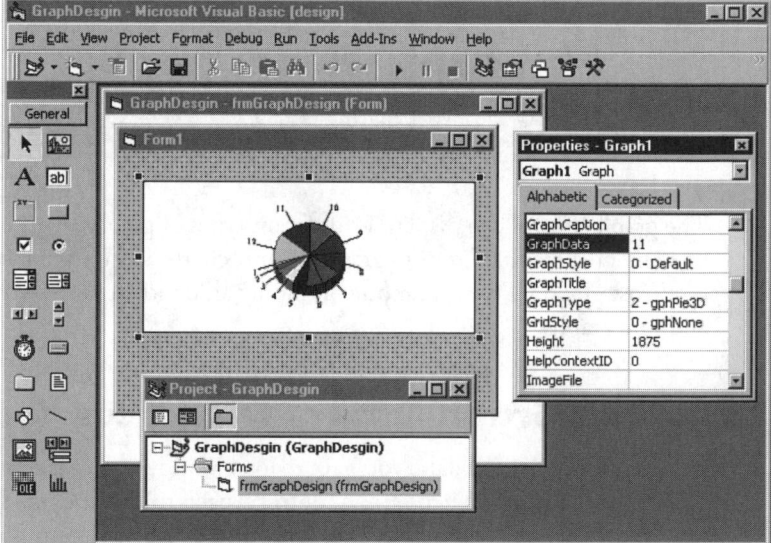

Adding Data at Runtime

You can perform the same task at runtime using Visual Basic code. Add a command button to this form, setting its Name property to cmdSales and its Caption property to Sales. Then add the code in Listing 11.1 in the cmdSales_Click event:

TYPE **Listing 11.1. Adding code to the `cmdSales_Click` event.**

```
Private Sub cmdSales_Click()
    '
    ' add data using VB code
    '
    Dim intLoop As Integer
    '
    Graph1.DataReset = gphAllData    ' clear out all properties
    Graph1.GraphType = gphBar3D      ' use 3d bar chart
    '
    Graph1.NumSets = 1  ' only one set of data
    Graph1.NumPoints = 12 ' one for each month
    '
    ' now add the data
    '
    For intLoop = 1 To 12
        Graph1.ThisPoint = intLoop   ' point to fill
        Graph1.GraphData = intLoop   ' data to load
    Next
    '
    Graph1.DrawMode = gphDraw ' show results
    '
End Sub
```

In Listing 11.1, you do a few things. First, you clear out any data that might already be stored in the graph control. Next, you set the GraphType property to show a three-dimensional bar graph. Also, you set the NumSets and NumPoints properties to 1 and 12, respectively, and then add the data points. Notice that the graph control must be told which set you want filled (using the ThisSet property). Next, you go through a loop—first, setting the ThisPoint property and then adding the data item. Finally, you set the DrawMode property to gphDraw to force Visual Basic to redraw the graph with the new data.

Save and run the project. When you click the Sales button, your form looks similar to the one shown in Figure 11.5.

Although this method works well, there is a faster method. By setting the AutoInc property of the graph control to 1, the graph control automatically increments the NumPoints property. This can simplify and speed up your code. Add a new button to the form, setting its Name property to cmdAutoSales and its Caption property to &AutoSales. Then add the code in Listing 11.2 in the cmdAutoSales_Click event.

Figure 11.5.

Creating a graph using Visual Basic code.

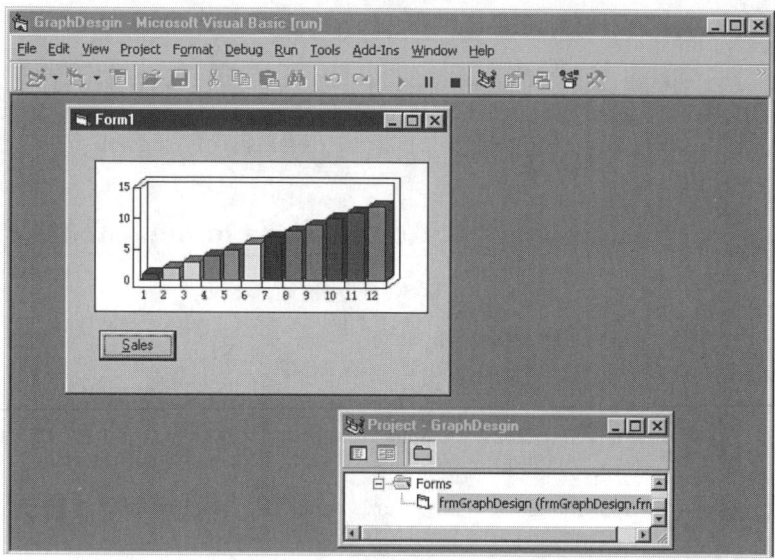

WARNING

If you are using Visual Basic 5's new "code-complete" option, notice that the editor suggests the properties "gphOff" or "gphOn" as valid values for the AutoInc property. In our version of Visual Basic 5, these values returned an error. Be sure to enter a value of 1 for the AutoInc property of the GRAPH32.OCX control.

TYPE **Listing 11.2. Adding code to the CmdAutoSales_Click event.**

```
Private Sub cmdAutoSales_Click()
    '
    ' add data using VB code
    '
    Dim intLoop As Integer
    '
    Graph1.DataReset = gphAllData    ' clear out all properties
    Graph1.GraphType = gphBar3D      ' use 3d bar chart
    '
    Graph1.NumSets = 1  ' only one set of data
    Graph1.NumPoints = 12 ' one for each month
    '
    ' now add the data
    '
```

```
      Graph1.AutoInc = 1   ' turn on auto incrementing
      For intLoop = 1 To 12
          Graph1.GraphData = intLoop  ' data to load
      Next
      '
      Graph1.DrawMode = gphDraw ' show results
      '
End Sub
```

Save and run the project. When you press the AutoSales button, you see the same graph that was generated with the Sales button. Notice that, in this example, you left out the lines of code that set the ThisSet and ThisPoint properties. These values were handled by the graph control using the AutoInc property. This might not seem like a code savings, but it really is. Single-set data is relatively easy to graph. Multiple sets get pretty confusing. It's much easier to use the AutoInc property because it automatically updates the ThisSet property, too. Not only is this approach a bit easier, it is also faster. The fewer lines of code you need to execute within the For...Next loop, the faster your program runs.

There is yet another way to add data to a graph control: by using the QuickData property.

Adding Data Using the QuickData Property

You can use the QuickData property to add graph data in a single command at runtime. The QuickData property accepts a single character string that contains all the datasets and points. Each dataset must be separated by a carriage return/line feed pair. Each data point must be separated by a tab character. This is known as *tab-delimited data*. When you use the QuickData property to load graph data, you do not have to set any of the properties that deal with points or sets. You also do not have to force your Visual Basic code to process any For...Next loops.

Add another command button to the form, setting its Name property to cmdQuickSales and its Caption property to &QuickSales. Then add the code in Listing 11.3 in the cmdQuickSales_Click event window.

NOTE If you're using "code-complete," you notice that the QuickData property is missing from the list of valid selections in the pop-up window. Don't let Visual Basic 5 fool you! The QuickData property is a valid property for the GRAPH32.OCX control. It's just missing from the list.

TYPE **Listing 11.3. Adding code to the `cmdQuickSales_Click` event.**

```
Private Sub cmdQuickData_Click()
    '
    ' show quickdata method for building graphs
    '
    Dim strData As String
    '
    ' create three sets of data, each with four points
    '
    strData = "1" & vbTab & "2" & vbTab & "3" & vbTab & "4" & vbCrLf
    strData = strData & "5" & vbTab & "4" & vbTab & "3" & vbTab & "2" & vbCrLf
    strData = strData & "6" & vbTab & "8" & vbTab & "10" & vbTab & "4" & vbCrLf
    '
    Graph1.GraphType = gphLine
    Graph1.DataReset = gphAllData
    Graph1.QuickData = strData
    '
    Graph1.DrawMode = gphDraw
    '
End Sub
```

Notice that you created a list of data that contained three sets of four points each. When you use the QuickData property, the graph control is able to determine the total number of sets and the number of points in each set without using the NumSets and NumPoints properties. Save and run this project. Your screen should look like the one shown in Figure 11.6.

Figure 11.6.

Adding graph data using the QuickData property.

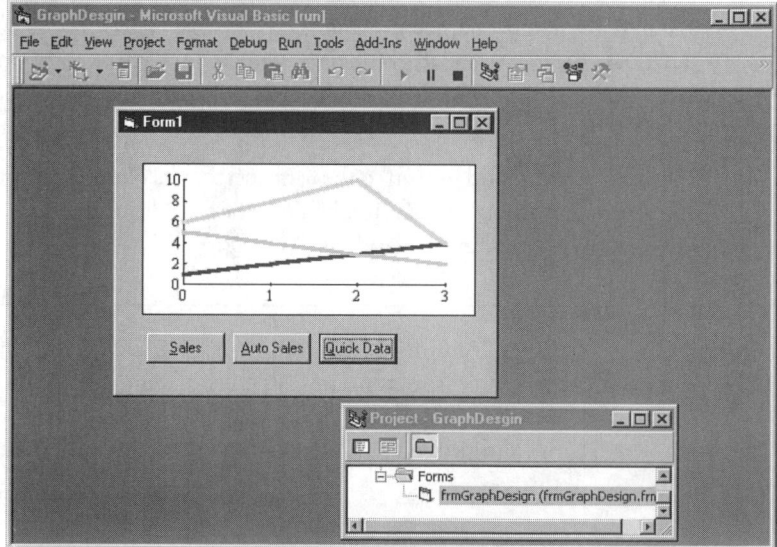

The real advantage of using the QuickData property is that it can accept data from most spreadsheets through Windows cut and paste operations. By placing tab-delimited data on the Windows Clipboard, you can use that data as the input for the QuickData property.

 **NOTE**

> Because you are working with data tables, you won't use the QuickData property to transfer datasets to the graph control. You can refer to the Visual Basic documentation for more information on using the Windows Clipboard and QuickData.

One of the handier uses of the QuickData property is the ability to read a tab-delimited text file and produce a quick graph of the data. You can use Microsoft Notepad, WordPad, or any other text editor to put tab-delimited values into a disk file and then read that file from your Visual Basic program. You can even program Microsoft Word to read data from a Word table and produce a tabbed list of numbers for input into the graph control.

To demonstrate this ability, add a new button to the form. Set its Name property to cmdLoadData and its Caption property to &Load Data. Now add the code from Listing 11.4 to the Click event of the cmdLoadData button.

TYPE **Listing 11.4. Reading a disk file and filling a graph.**

```
Private Sub cmdAutoSales_Click()
    '
    ' add data using VB code
    '
    Dim intLoop As Integer
    '
    Graph1.DataReset = gphAllData    ' clear out all properties
    Graph1.GraphType = gphBar3D      ' use 3d bar chart

    Graph1.NumSets = 1  ' only one set of data
    Graph1.NumPoints = 12 ' one for each month
    '
    ' now add the data
    '
    Graph1.AutoInc = 1  ' turn on auto incrementing
    For intLoop = 1 To 12
        Graph1.GraphData = intLoop  ' data to load
    Next
    '
    Graph1.DrawMode = gphDraw ' show results
    '
End Sub
```

continues

Listing 11.4. continued

```
Private Sub cmdLoadData_Click()
    '
    ' load tabbed data from a file
    '
    Dim strRdLine As String
    Dim strData As String
    Dim strFileName As String
    Dim intFileHandle As Integer
    '
    ' load tab-delimited text file
    strFileName = App.Path & "\..\..\data\graphs\tabdata.txt"
    intFileHandle = FreeFile
    '
    Open strFileName For Input As intFileHandle
        Do While Not EOF(intFileHandle)
            Line Input #1, strRdLine
            strData = strData & strRdLine & vbCrLf
        Loop
    Close #intFileHandle
    '
    ' setup and display graph
    Graph1.GraphType = gphLine
    Graph1.DataReset = gphAllData
    Graph1.QuickData = strData
    '
    Graph1.DrawMode = gphDraw
    '
End Sub
```

When you save and run the project, press the Load Data button. Your screen should look something like the one in Figure 11.7.

Notice that the only difference between the code in Listing 11.3 and Listing 11.4 is that the strData variable is loaded from the disk file in Listing 11.4.

Adding Titles, Labels, and Legends

In addition to loading data and setting the graph type, you can also set graph titles, labels for the data points, and legends for the graph.

Now add another button to the project to illustrate these features of the graph control. Set the button's Name property to cmdTitles and its Caption property to &Titles. Add Listing 11.5 to the cmdTitles_Click event window.

Figure 11.7.

Loading data from a disk file.

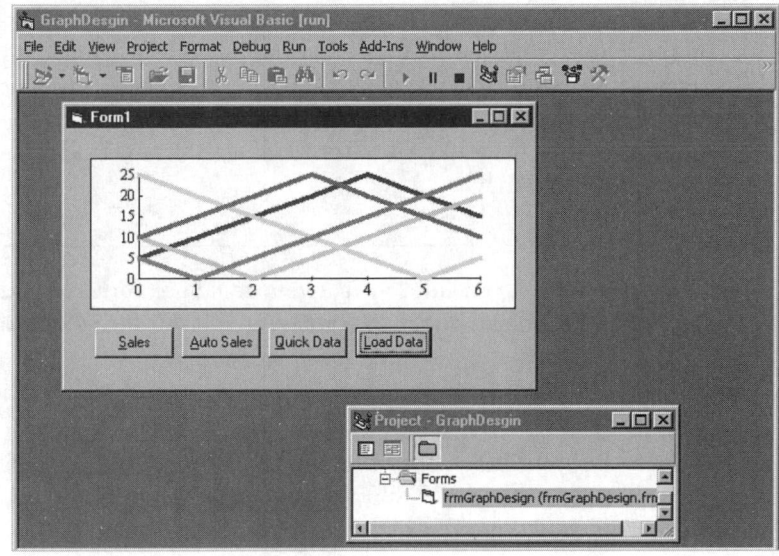

TYPE **Listing 11.5. Adding code to the** `cmdTitles_Click` **event.**

```
Private Sub cmdTitles_Click()
    '
    ' add titles to existing graph
    '
    Dim intLoop As Integer

    ' add the titles
    Graph1.GraphTitle = "Graph Title"
    Graph1.BottomTitle = "Bottom Title"
    Graph1.LeftTitle = "Left Title"
    '
    ' add legends
    Graph1.AutoInc = 1
    For intLoop = 1 To 12
        Graph1.LegendText = "L" & CStr(intLoop)
    Next
    '
    ' add labels
    Graph1.AutoInc = 1
    For intLoop = 1 To 12
        Graph1.LabelText = "X" & CStr(intLoop)
    Next
    '
    Graph1.DrawMode = gphDraw
    '
End Sub
```

In Listing 11.5, you inhialize the three titles and then add legends and labels for the data points. Notice that you used the AutoInc property when adding the legends and labels. Notice, too, that you did not add legends and labels within the same For...Next loop. If you use the AutoInc property, you can only update one element type at a time. When you have more than one element array to update (data, legends, and labels), you must use separate loops for each element array.

NOTE
It is very unlikely that you would use both a legend and data point labels in the same graph. You did this here to illustrate the unique behavior of the AutoInc property.

Save and run the project. You can apply the text features of the graph control to any graph. After clicking a button to produce a graph, click the Titles button to add the text to the graph. Your screen should look like the one shown in Figure 11.8.

Figure 11.8.

Adding titles, labels, and legends to a graph.

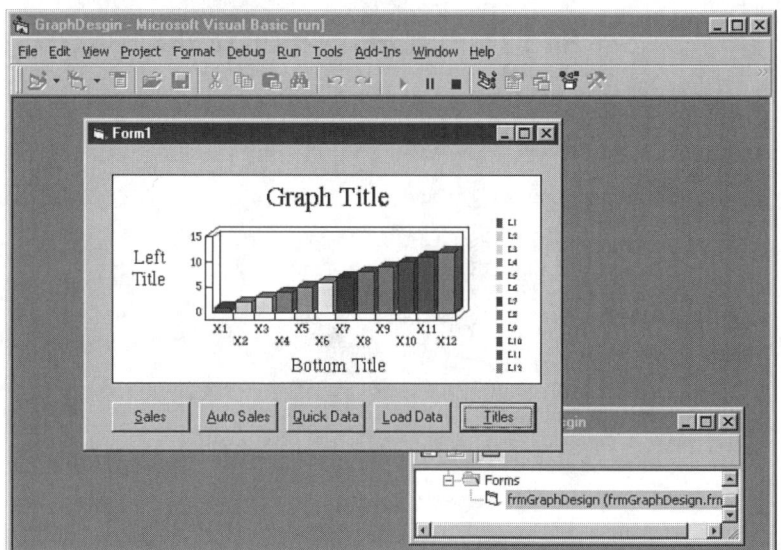

 **TIP**

> If your graph does not show the legends on the right, you may need to enlarge your graph display image. The graph control determines the exact placement and sizing of all titles, legends, and labels.

Display Options

You can also send the completed graph to a file, to the Windows Clipboard, or to your printer. All those options are covered in the next section. For now, you add a button that writes the completed graph to a disk file as a bitmap image.

Add one more command button to the form. Set its Name property to cmdWrite and its Caption property to &Write. Add Listing 11.6 to the cmdWrite_Click event window.

TYPE **Listing 11.6. Adding code to the cmdWrite_Click event.**

```
Private Sub cmdWrite_Click()
    '
    Graph1.ImageFile = App.Path + "\GraphDesign.BMP" ' set file name
    Graph1.DrawMode = gphBlit    ' set for bitmap mode
    Graph1.DrawMode = gphWrite   ' force to file
    Graph1.DrawMode = gphDraw    ' redraw control
    '
End Sub
```

In Listing 11.6, you first set the name of the file to be created. Then you set the drawing mode to bitmap. You then force the creation of the graph file, and, finally, redraw the graph on-screen.

Save and run the project. You see the screen flicker during the redrawing. If you check your disk drive, you find the data file you created. You can load this file using Microsoft Paint or any other program that can read bitmap images. Figure 11.9 shows both the Visual Basic 5 form and Microsoft Paint running at the same time.

Figure 11.9.
*Displaying the graph
in both Visual Basic
and Microsoft Paint.*

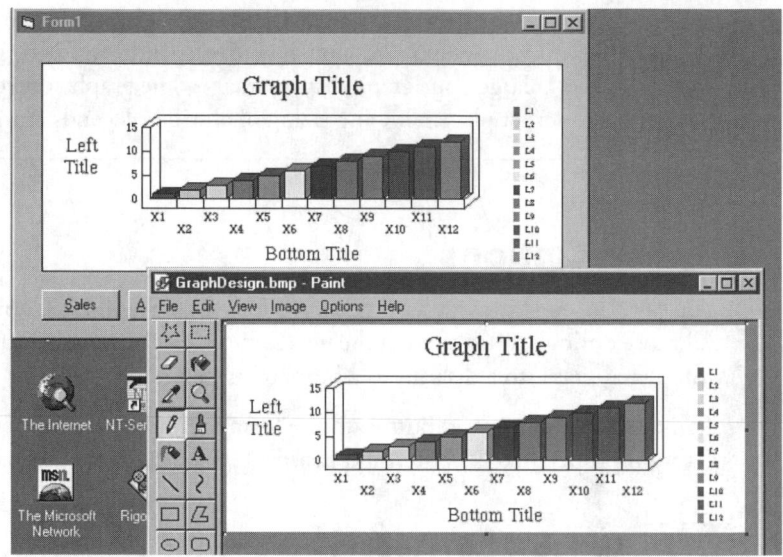

Creating Your Data Graph OLE Server

Now that you have learned the basic techniques of using the graph control, you are ready to build your database graph OLE Server. This OLE Server consists of a single form that contains a graph control and a menu of graphing options. It also has methods that load the form, set the graphing values using your dataset, and display the results. You can pass any valid Visual Basic Recordset object to the data graph OLE Server and display any single-set, multipoint dataset without any further modification of the code.

Building the Data Graph Form

First, start a new ActiveX DLL Visual Basic project. Set the name of the project to prjDataGraph and the name of the default class module to DataGraph. Add a form to the project and set its Name property to frmGraph. You also need to make sure you load the Pinnacle-BPS graph control (GRAPH32.OCX) and the Microsoft common dialog control to the project.

NOTE

Make sure the Pinnacle-BPS graph control is in your Visual Basic toolbox. If not, refer back to the "Loading the Graph Control into the Visual Basic Toolbox" section for instructions on how to add it to your project's toolbox.

Add the graph control to your form. Also add the CommonDialog control to the form. You use this control to add file and print capabilities to the graphing library. You also need to add a menu to the form. Refer to Figure 11.10 and Tables 11.1 and 11.2 as guides for laying out this form.

Figure 11.10.

Laying out the graph library form.

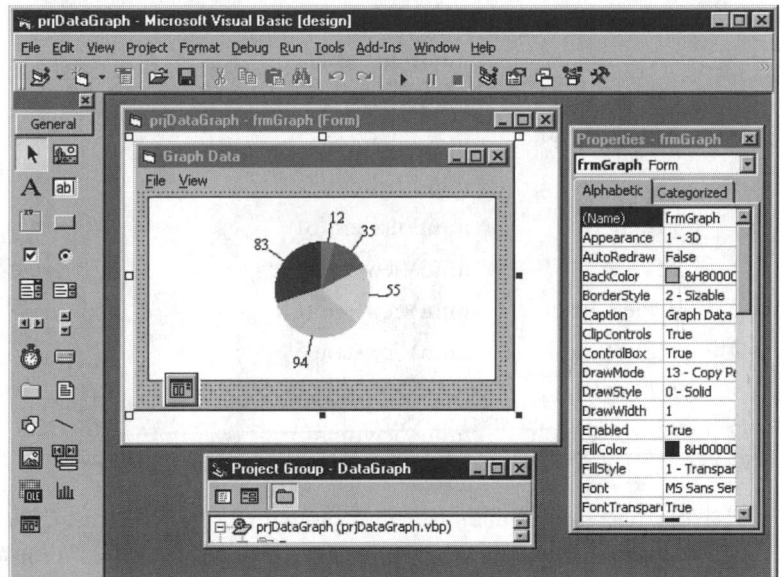

Table 11.1. The control table for the graph library form.

Control	Property	Setting
Form	Name	frmGraph
	Caption	Graph Data
	Height	3375
	Left	2145
	Top	1710
	Width	5280
Graph	Name	Graph1
	Height	2415
	Left	120
	Top	120
	Width	4935
	BorderStyle	1–Fixed Single
CommonDialog	Name	CommonDialog1

Table 11.2. The menu table for the graph library form.

Caption	Menu
&File	mnuFile
&Save	mnuFileItem(0)
&Copy	mnuFileItem(1)
-	mnuFileItem(2)
&Print	mnuFileItem(3)
Print Set&Up	mnuFileItem(4)
-	mnuFileItem(5)
E&xit	mnuFileItem(6)
&View	mnuView
&Pie Chart	mnuViewItem(0)
&Bar Graph	mnuViewItem(1)
&Line Chart	mnuViewItem(2)
&Area Graph	mnuViewItem(3)

Note that you are building menu arrays with the form. Menu arrays, like other control arrays, can speed the processing of your program and simplify the coding and maintenance of your forms.

You need to add some code to this form. But first, save it (FRMGRAPH.FRM) and save the project (PRJDATAGRAPH.VBP). Then add the code in Listing 11.7 to the Form_Load event of the project. This sets the default size of the form to fill 75% of the screen.

TYPE **Listing 11.7. Coding the Form_Load event.**

```
Private Sub Form_Load()
    '
    ' set initial form size
    '
    If Me.WindowState = vbNormal Then
        Me.Width = Screen.Width * 0.75
        Me.Height = Screen.Height * 0.75
    End If
    '
End Sub
```

11

Now, add the code from Listing 11.8 to the Form_Resize event. This code allows users to resize the graph by resizing the form.

TYPE **Listing 11.8. Adding code to the Form_Resize event.**

```
Private Sub Form_Resize()
    '
    ' make graph fill the form
    '
    Graph1.Left = 1
    Graph1.Top = 1
    Graph1.Width = Me.ScaleWidth
    Graph1.Height = Me.ScaleHeight
    '
End Sub
```

The code in Listing 11.9 goes in the mnuFileItem_Click event. This code is executed each time the user selects one of the File menu items. The Index value returns the item number selected by the user. You code the CopyGraph and SaveGraph methods in just a moment.

TYPE **Listing 11.9. Coding the mnuFileItem_Click event.**

11

```
Private Sub mnuFileItem_Click(Index As Integer)
    '
    ' handle file menu selections
    '
    Select Case Index
        Case 0 ' save
            GraphSave
        Case 1 ' copy
            GraphCopy
        Case 2 ' separator
            ' no action
        Case 3 ' print
            Me.PrintForm
        Case 4 ' printer setup
            CommonDialog1.ShowPrinter
        Case 5 ' separator
            ' no action
        Case 6 ' exit
            Unload Me
    End Select
    '
End Sub
```

Now add the code in Listing 11.10 to the `mnuViewItem_Click` event. This allows users to select the type of graph they view.

TYPE **Listing 11.10. Coding the `mnuViewItem_Click` event.**

```
Private Sub mnuViewItem_Click(Index As Integer)
    '
    ' handle view selections
    '
    Dim intGraphType As Integer
    '
    Select Case Index
        Case 0 ' pie chart
            intGraphType = gphPie3D
        Case 1 ' bar graph
            intGraphType = gphBar3D
        Case 2 ' line chart
            intGraphType = gphLine
        Case 3 ' area graph
            intGraphType = gphArea
    End Select
    '
    Graph1.GraphType = intGraphType
    Graph1.DrawMode = gphDraw
    '
End Sub
```

Now you're ready to code the `GraphCopy` method. The code in Listing 11.11 is all you need to copy the graph image to the Windows Clipboard. You can then paste this image of the graph from the Clipboard to any other Windows program that allows image cut and paste operations (Microsoft Write, for example).

TYPE **Listing 11.11. This code copies the graph to the Windows Clipboard.**

```
Public Sub GraphCopy()
    '
    ' copy graph to clipboard
    '
    Graph1.DrawMode = gphBlit
    Graph1.DrawMode = gphCopy
    Graph1.DrawMode = gphDraw
    '
    MsgBox "Graph has been copied to the clipboard", _
        vbInformation, _
        "Copy Graph"
    '
End Sub
```

11

Next, add the GraphSave method code from Listing 11.12 to the project. This code prompts the user for a filename and saves the current graph under that filename.

TYPE | **Listing 11.12. Coding the GraphSave method.**

```
Public Sub GraphSave()
    '
    ' save graph to disk file
    '
    Dim strFileName As String
    '
    CommonDialog1.DefaultExt = ".bmp"
    CommonDialog1.DialogTitle = "Save Graph"
    CommonDialog1.Filter = "Bitmap Files ¦ *.bmp"
    CommonDialog1.ShowSave
    strFileName = CommonDialog1.filename
    '
    If Trim(strFileName) <> "" Then
        Graph1.DrawMode = gphBlit
        Graph1.ImageFile = strFileName
        Graph1.DrawMode = gphWrite
        Graph1.DrawMode = gphDraw
    End If
    '
End Sub
```

That's all the code you need for the form. Save this form now. Next, you create the routine that calls this form.

Building the DataGraph Class Object

In order to display the form you just created, you need to create a class object that allows users to set some properties and executes a ShowGraph method. The basic properties of the DataGraph object are

☐ GraphType: The initial graph type for the display.

☐ DatabaseName: The official name of the database that contains the records to graph.

☐ SQLSelect: The SQL SELECT statement that creates the Recordset to display.

☐ GraphField: The name of the column in the Recordset that contains the values you load into the GraphData property of the graph control.

☐ GraphTitle: The title of the graph.

This is a simple graph tool that is capable of displaying a single-set, multipoint dataset in the most commonly used graph types. Modifications can be made to this routine to add additional labeling, legends, and text. You could also add options in order to graph more than one set of data per graph. For now, just keep the project simple. When you complete this project, you can add your own modifications.

First, you need to add some local storage variables to the class. These contain the passed properties along with a couple of local variables needed for Private methods. Add the code from Listing 11.13 to the class.

TYPE **Listing 11.13. Setting up local storage for the class object.**

```
Option Explicit

'
' enumerated graph types
'
Enum dgType
    dgPie3d = gphPie3D
    dgBar3d = gphBar3D
    dgLine = gphLine
    dgArea = gphArea
End Enum
'
' local property storage
'
Private intGraphType As Integer
Private strDBName As String
Private strSQLSelect As String
Private strFieldPoint As String
Private strTitle As String
'
' for internal use only
Private ws As Workspace
Private db As Database
Private rs As Recordset
Private lngNumPoints As Long
Private lngLoop As Long
'
```

Notice the use of the Enum..End Enum construct in the declarations section. This is a special type of constant declaration that combines a user-defined type (dgType) with a set of predefined values (dgPie3D, dgBar3D, dgLine, dgArea). When you use this class object in your programs, you can see the enumerated types in the code-complete windows that appear as you enter the source code.

Now you need to declare Public properties of the class. These properties allow users to manipulate the local storage variables of the class. Note that all five properties are included in Listing 11.14. You need to add each property individually using the Tools | Add Procedure | Property options from the main menu.

Listing 11.14. Coding the Public properties of the DataGraph.

TYPE

```
Public Property Get GraphType() As Integer
    GraphType = intGraphType
End Property

Public Property Let GraphType(ByVal vNewValue As Integer)
    If IsNumeric(vNewValue) Then
        intGraphType = Int(vNewValue)
    End If
    '
    If intGraphType < 1 Or intGraphType > 11 Then
        Err.Raise 380 ' invalid property
        intGraphType = 0
    End If
    '
End Property

Public Property Get DatabaseName() As String
    DatabaseName = strDBName
End Property

Public Property Let DatabaseName(ByVal vNewValue As String)
    strDBName = vNewValue
End Property

Public Property Get SQLSelect() As String
    SQLSelect = strSQLSelect
End Property

Public Property Let SQLSelect(ByVal vNewValue As String)
    strSQLSelect = vNewValue
End Property

Public Property Get GraphField() As String
    GraphField = strFieldPoint
End Property

Public Property Let GraphField(ByVal vNewValue As String)
    strFieldPoint = vNewValue
End Property

Public Property Get GraphTitle() As String
    GraphTitle = strTitle
End Property

Public Property Let GraphTitle(ByVal vNewValue As String)
    strTitle = vNewValue
End Property
```

Notice some error-checking code in the GraphType property Let method. This checks for a valid graph type and reports an error if a valid value is not found.

Now add the code from Listing 11.15 to the Class_Initialize event. This sets the default values for the properties.

TYPE **Listing 11.15. Coding the Class_Initialize event.**

```
Private Sub Class_Initialize()
    '
    ' set startup values
    '
    strDBName = ""
    strSQLSelect = ""
    strFieldPoint = ""
    strTitle = "Data Graph"
    intGraphType = gphBar3D
    '
End Sub
```

Now you're ready to code the ShowGraph method. This one method collects all the property values, creates a dataset, and builds a graph based on the data. Create a Public Sub called ShowGraph in the class and add the code from Listing 11.16.

TYPE **Listing 11.16. Coding the ShowGraph method.**

```
Public Sub ShowGraph()
    '
    ' display graph
    '
    On Error GoTo LocalErr
    '
    Screen.MousePointer = vbHourglass
    OpenDB
    InitGraph
    LoadGraphData
    Screen.MousePointer = vbNormal
    '
    frmGraph.Graph1.DrawMode = gphDraw
    frmGraph.Show vbModal
    '
    Exit Sub
    '
LocalErr:
    Err.Raise vbObjectError + 4, App.EXEName, "Error displaying graph"
    '
End Sub
```

11

This method calls three other Private methods. Create the `Private Sub OpenDB` and add the code from Listing 11.17.

TYPE **Listing 11.17. Coding the OpenDB method.**

```
Private Sub OpenDB()
    '
    ' open database/recordset
    '
    On Error GoTo LocalErr
    '
    Set ws = dbengine.Workspaces(0)
    Set db = ws.OpenDatabase(strDBName)
    Set rs = db.OpenRecordset(strSQLSelect, dbOpenSnapshot)
    '
    Exit Sub
    '
LocalErr:
    Err.Raise vbObjectError + 1, App.EXEName, "Error creating data set"
    '
End Sub
```

Next, add the `Private Sub InitGraph` and enter the code from Listing 11.18. This code loads the frmGraph form and sets the initial values of the display.

TYPE **Listing 11.18. Coding the InitGraph method.**

```
Private Sub InitGraph()
    '
    ' initialize the graph form
    '
    On Error GoTo LocalErr
    '
    rs.MoveLast
    lngNumPoints = rs.RecordCount
    '
    Load frmGraph
    frmGraph.Graph1.GraphType = intGraphType
    frmGraph.Graph1.GraphTitle = strTitle
    frmGraph.Graph1.NumSets = 1
    frmGraph.Graph1.NumPoints = lngNumPoints
    frmGraph.Graph1.AutoInc = 1
    '
    Exit Sub
    '
LocalErr:
    Err.Raise vbObjectError + 2, App.EXEName, "Error intializing graph form"
    '
End Sub
```

11

Finally, add the `Private Sub LoadGraphData` to the class. This is the code that moves the data from the Recordset into the graph control (see Listing 11.19).

TYPE **Listing 11.19. Coding the `LoadGraphData` method.**

```
Private Sub LoadGraphData()
    '
    ' fill graph with data
    '
    On Error GoTo LocalErr
    '
    rs.MoveFirst
    For lngLoop = 1 To lngNumPoints
        frmGraph.Graph1.GraphData = rs.Fields(strFieldPoint)
        rs.MoveNext
    Next
    '
    Exit Sub
    '
LocalErr:
    Err.Raise vbObjectError + 3, App.EXEName, "Error loading graph data"
    '
End Sub
```

That's all there is to it. You now have a reusable data graphing OLE Server. All you need to do now is save the project and compile the DLL. You can do this by selecting File | Make prjDataGraph.DLL from the main menu. In the next section, you test this library with a simple example.

Testing the Graph OLE Server

You need to build a short program to test your new library. Suppose you have just been told that the marketing department needs a tool to display the year-to-date book sales by sales representative. The data already exists in a database, but there is no easy way to turn that data into a visual display that upper-level management can access on a regular basis. You have been asked to quickly put together a graphing front-end for the sales data.

In order to complete the job, you need to initialize a copy of the DataGraph object; set the DatabaseName and SQLSelect properties; set the GraphType, GraphField, and GraphTitle properties; and then execute the ShowGraph method. From there, users can select various graph styles and, if they wish, save the graph to disk, send it to the printer, or copy it to the Clipboard to paste in other documents.

Because you already have the completed graph library, you can complete your assignment with as few as 10 lines of Visual Basic code.

First, if you don't have it running right now, start Visual Basic and create a new Standard EXE project. If you still have Visual Basic up from the last section of this chapter, select File | Add Project… to add a new Standard EXE project. Make this new project the Default startup project, too.

Now, select Project | References and locate and select the prjDataGraph library. This links your new project with the OLE Server DLL that you built earlier in this chapter.

Add a single button to a blank form. Set its Name property to cmdRepSales and its Caption property to &RepSales. Add the code from Listing 11.20 to support the button.

TYPE   **Listing 11.20. Adding code to the `cmdRepSales_Click` event.**

```
Private Sub cmdRepSales_Click()
    '
    ' test graph libaray
    '
    Dim objDG As Object
    '
    Set objDG = New DataGraph
    '
    objDG.DatabaseName = App.Path & "\..\..\data\books5.mdb"
    objDG.sqlselect = "SELECT SalesRep, SUM(Units) AS UnitsSold FROM BookSales
GROUP BY SalesRep"
    objDG.graphfield = "UnitsSold"
    objDG.graphTitle = "Units Sold by Sales Rep"
    '
    objDG.showgraph
    '
End Sub
```

This code example sets a few properties and then calls the ShowGraph method. That's all there is to it! Save this form as FRMTEST.FRM and the project as PRJTEST.VBP. Now run the project. After you click the single command button, you see the graph displayed on-screen. Your screen should look something like the one shown in Figure 11.11.

You have just completed your first database graphing project using the new OLE Server! Before you end your work on this OLE Server, let's add a few new properties to the class object. These give you (and our users) greater control over the graph display.

11

Figure 11.11.

A graph of book sales data by sales rep.

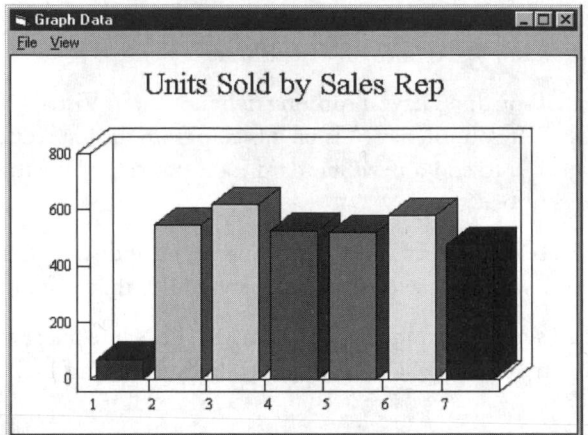

Adding More Properties to the DataGraph Object

Now that the basic DataGraph object is working, let's add some of the bells and whistles that make this a versatile programming tool. Let's add four new properties to the class:

- ☐ LegendField: This is the Recordset column to use for setting the legends of the graph.
- ☐ LabelField: This is the Recordset column to use for setting the labels of the graph.
- ☐ LeftTitle: This is the string to display as the title on the left side of the graph.
- ☐ BottomTitle: This is the string to display as the title at the bottom of the graph.

In order to add these new features, all you need to do is add the property definitions to the DataGraph object and then add code to the ShowGraph method to incorporate these new properties into the displayed graph.

The code in Listing 11.21 shows the changes you need to make to the general declaration section of the DataGraph class. The four new variables are added at the end of the section.

Listing 11.21. Adding local storage variables for the new properties.

TYPE

```
Option Explicit

'
' enumerated graph types
'
Enum dgType
    dgPie3d = gphPie3D
    dgBar3d = gphBar3D
```

11

```
    dgLine = gphLine
    dgArea = gphArea
End Enum
'
' local property storage
'
Private intGraphType As Integer
Private strDBName As String
Private strSQLSelect As String
Private strFieldPoint As String
Private strTitle As String
'
' for internal use only
Private ws As Workspace
Private db As Database
Private rs As Recordset
Private lngNumPoints As Long
Private lngLoop As Long
'
' added properties
Private strLegendField As String
Private strLabelField As String
Private strLeftTitle As String
Private strBottomTitle As String
'
```

The next step is to use the Tools | Add Procedure | Property options from the main menu to add the four new property declarations to the class. Listing 11.22 shows the code for each of these new properties.

TYPE **Listing 11.22. Code for the new properties.**

```
Public Property Get LegendField() As Variant
    LegendField = strLegendField
End Property

Public Property Let LegendField(ByVal vNewValue As Variant)
    strLegendField = vNewValue
End Property

Public Property Get LabelField() As Variant
    LabelField = strLabelField
End Property

Public Property Let LabelField(ByVal vNewValue As Variant)
    strLabelField = vNewValue
End Property

Public Property Get LeftTitle() As Variant
    LeftTitle = strLeftTitle
End Property
```

continues

Listing 11.22. continued

```
Public Property Let LeftTitle(ByVal vNewValue As Variant)
    strLeftTitle = vNewValue
End Property

Public Property Get BottomTitle() As Variant
    BottomTitle = strBottomTitle
End Property

Public Property Let BottomTitle(ByVal vNewValue As Variant)
    strBottomTitle = vNewValue
End Property
```

Because just about any string value could be valid for these properties, no error checking is done at the time the properties are set. In a production application, you might want to add error-checking to protect users.

After adding the new properties, you need to update the `Class_Initialize` event to set the new properties at the start of the object. Listing 11.23 shows the code you need to add to the `Class_Initialize` event.

TYPE **Listing 11.23. Updating the `Class_Initialize` event.**

```
Private Sub Class_Initialize()
    '
    ' set startup values
    '
    strDBName = ""
    strSQLSelect = ""
    strFieldPoint = ""
    strTitle = "Data Graph"
    intGraphType = dgBar3D
    '
    ' initialize added properties
    '
    strLegendField = ""
    strLabelField = ""
    strBottomTitle = ""
    strLeftTitle = ""
    '
End Sub
```

Now you need to build routines to add the legends and labels to the graph. Create a `Private Sub` method called `AddLegends` and enter the code from Listing 11.24.

TYPE **Listing 11.24. Coding the AddLegends method.**

```
Private Sub AddLegends()
    '
    ' add legends to the existing graph
    '
    If Trim(strLegendField) = "" Then Exit Sub
    '
    frmGraph.Graph1.AutoInc = 1
    '
    rs.MoveFirst
    For lngLoop = 1 To lngNumPoints
        frmGraph.Graph1.LegendText = rs.Fields(strLegendField)
        rs.MoveNext
    Next
    '
End Sub
```

Notice the first line of code in Listing 11.24. The line checks to see whether the strLegendField variable contains any printable data. If not, the Exit Sub is executed. No reason to set the legends if no LegendField has been set!

Now add the Private Sub called AddLabels to your class. The code in Listing 11.25 should be added to this new method.

TYPE **Listing 11.25. Coding the AddLabels method.**

```
Private Sub AddLabels()
    '
    ' add labels to the existing graph
    '
    If Trim(strLabelField) = "" Then Exit Sub
    '
    frmGraph.Graph1.AutoInc = 1
    '
    rs.MoveFirst
    For lngLoop = 1 To lngNumPoints
        frmGraph.Graph1.LabelText = rs.Fields(strLabelField)
        rs.MoveNext
    Next
    '
End Sub
```

Next, you need to add the Private Sub called AddTitles to the class. This sets the left and bottom title properties of the graph. Listing 11.26 contains the code needed for this method. Note that the variables strLeftTitle and strBottomTitle are checked for valid data before the graph properties are actually set.

Listing 11.26. Adding the left and bottom titles to the graph.

TYPE

```
Private Sub AddTitles()
    '
    ' add left and bottom titles
    '
    If Trim(strLeftTitle) <> "" Then
        frmGraph.Graph1.LeftTitle = strLeftTitle
    End If
    '
    If Trim(strBottomTitle) <> "" Then
        frmGraph.Graph1.BottomTitle = strBottomTitle
    End If
    '
End Sub
```

Finally, it's time to modify the ShowGraph method to incorporate the new methods into your graph display. Listing 11.27 shows the updated ShowGraph method.

Listing 11.27. The updated ShowGraph method uses the new properties.

TYPE

```
Public Sub ShowGraph()
    '
    ' display graph
    '
    On Error GoTo LocalErr
    '
    Screen.MousePointer = vbHourglass
    OpenDB
    InitGraph
    LoadGraphData
    '
    ' added property handling
    AddLegends
    AddLabels
    AddTitles
    '
    Screen.MousePointer = vbNormal
    '
    frmGraph.Graph1.DrawMode = gphDraw
    frmGraph.Show vbModal
    '
    Exit Sub
    '
LocalErr:
    Err.Raise vbObjectError + 4, App.EXEName, "Error displaying graph"
    '
End Sub
```

11

Now all you need to do is modify the cmdSalesRep_Click event of the frmTest form to test out these new properties. Switch to the prjTest project and add the code from Listing 11.28 to the cmdSalesRep_Click event.

TYPE **Listing 11.28. Updating the cmdSalesRep_Click event.**

```
Private Sub cmdRepSales_Click()
    '
    ' test graph libaray
    '
    Dim objDG As Object
    '
    Set objDG = New DataGraph
    '
    objDG.DatabaseName = App.Path & "\..\..\data\books5.mdb"
    objDG.sqlselect = "SELECT SalesRep, SUM(Units) AS UnitsSold FROM BookSales
GROUP BY SalesRep"
    objDG.graphfield = "UnitsSold"
    objDG.graphTitle = "Units Sold by Sales Rep"
    '
    ' added properties
    objDG.labelfield = "SalesRep"
    objDG.lefttitle = "Units Sold"
    objDG.bottomtitle = "Sales Reps"
    objDG.legendfield = "SalesRep"
    '
    objDG.showgraph
    '
End Sub
```

Save and run the PRJTEST.VBP project. When you click the SalesRep button, your screen should look like the one shown in Figure 11.12.

Figure 11.12.

Viewing the updated graph object display.

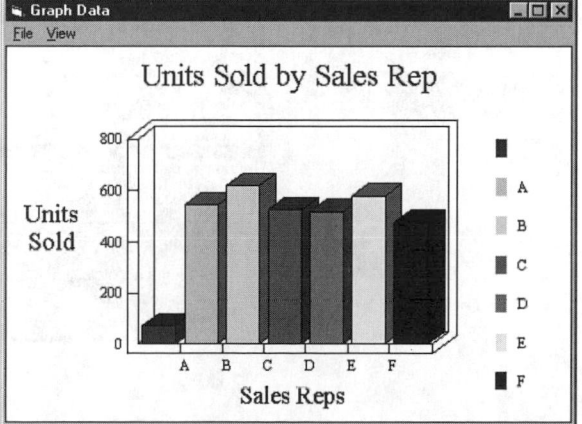

As soon as you confirm that the modifications to the DataGraph object work without errors, recompile the ActiveX DLL. You can use this OLE Server DLL in all your future VBA projects. As an example, you can now add some graphs to the CompanyMaster project you started last week.

Adding Graphs to the CompanyMaster Project

For the last project of the day, you add three graphs to the CompanyMaster project:

☐ A pie graph showing the actual year-to-date sales totals by region

☐ A line graph showing the year-to-date sales totals by month

☐ A bar graph showing the sales by customer

First you have to add a new menu item to the CompanyMaster form that calls the graphs. Then you need to construct SQL statements that select the desired data and feed it to the graph object.

Adding the Graph Menu Option

Adding the graph menu items is pretty easy. First, load the MASTER.VBP project from the CHAP11\COMASTER directory. Add the graph object to the project by selecting Project | References and locating and adding the Databound Graph object library (see Figure 11.13).

Figure 11.13.

Adding the Databound Graph object library.

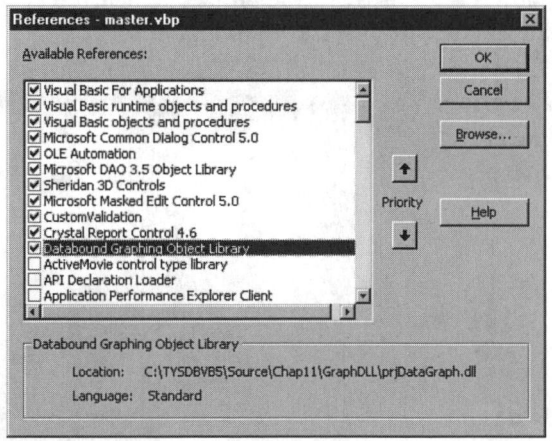

Use Table 11.3 as a guide for adding the following menu items to the CompanyMaster menu.

Table 11.3. Added menu items for the CompanyMaster main menu.

Caption	Menu
&Graphs	mnuGraphs
Sales by &Region	mnuGraphsItem(0)
Sales by &Month	mnuGraphsItem(1)
Sales by &Customer	mnuGraphsItem(2)

Now you need to add code to the form to make the calls to the DataGraph object. For your first graph, you want to create a pie chart showing the total year's sales by region. The fields you have to work with in the SalesData table are CompanyName, Year, Month, Amount, and Region. The database contains records for each month for each customer, along with budget values for the year. These budget records are stored with a CompanyName of Budget.

To get the total customer sales by region, you use the following SQL SELECT statement:

```
SELECT Region, SUM(Amount) AS SalesTotal
   FROM SalesData
   WHERE CompanyName<>'Budget'
   GROUP BY Region
```

This is the SQL statement you use to generate the Snapshot object that is passed to the graph library. Place Listing 11.29 in the mnuGraphsItem Click event.

Listing 11.29. Adding the code to the mnuGraphsItem_Click event.

TYPE

```
Private Sub mnuGraphsItem_Click(Index As Integer)
    '
    ' handle graph menu requests
    '
    Dim objDG As New DataGraph
    Dim strSQL As String
    '
    Select Case Index
        Case 0 ' sales by region
            '
            strSQL = "SELECT Region, SUM(Amount) AS SalesTotal FROM "
            strSQL = strSQL & "SalesData WHERE CompanyName<>'Budget' GROUP BY
            ➥Region"
            '
```

continues

Listing 11.29. continued

```
                objDG.DatabaseName = Data1.DatabaseName
                objDG.SQLSelect = strSQL
                objDG.GraphType = dgPie3d
                objDG.GraphField = "SalesTotal"
                objDG.GraphTitle = "Sales by Region"
                objDG.LegendField = "Region"
                '
        Case 1 ' sales by month
        Case 2 ' sales by customer
    End Select
        '
        objDG.ShowGraph
        '
    End Sub
```

Notice that you used the SQL statement you defined earlier as the SQLSelect property of the
DataGraph object. The rest of the code should be familiar by now: You set several properties
that are required for the graph object library and then you called the ShowGraph method.

 **NOTE**

> It is important to keep in mind that you did not have to load the
> GRAPH32.OCX file into your project. Because this is part of the ActiveX
> DLL, you do not need to identify it in the Visual Basic project that
> uses the DLL. The OCX, and its supporting files, must be present on
> your machine, but you do not have to add it to your project.

Now, save and run the project. When you select Graph | Sales by Region from the main menu,
you should see a graph like the one shown in Figure 11.14.

Figure 11.14.

*Displaying the Sales
by Region pie graph.*

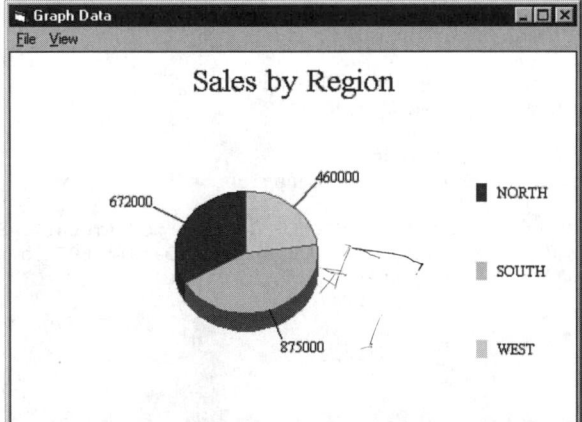

You can resize the form and the graph resizes too. You can also use the menu on the graph to print, save, or copy the graph to the Clipboard.

Now add the Sales by Month graph to the project. This time, you want a line graph that shows the total sales by month. First, you need to construct the SQL statement. It should look like the following:

```
SELECT Month, SUM(Amount) AS SalesTotal
   FROM SalesData
   WHERE CompanyName<>'Budget'
   GROUP BY Month;
```

Now open the `mnuGraphsItem_Click` event and add the code in Listing 11.30.

Listing 11.30. Adding the code for the
TYPE `mnuGraphsMonthSales_Click` **event.**

```
Private Sub mnuGraphsItem_Click(Index As Integer)
    '
    ' handle graph menu requests
    '
    Dim objDG As New DataGraph
    Dim strSQL As String
    '
    Select Case Index
        Case 0 ' sales by region
            '
            strSQL = "SELECT Region, SUM(Amount) AS SalesTotal FROM "
            strSQL = strSQL & "SalesData WHERE CompanyName<>'Budget' GROUP BY
            ➥Region"
            '
            objDG.DatabaseName = Data1.DatabaseName
            objDG.SQLSelect = strSQL
            objDG.GraphType = dgPie3d
            objDG.GraphField = "SalesTotal"
            objDG.GraphTitle = "Sales by Region"
            objDG.LegendField = "Region"
            '
        Case 1 ' sales by month
            '
            strSQL = "SELECT Month, SUM(Amount) AS SalesTotal FROM "
            strSQL = strSQL & "SalesData WHERE CompanyName<>'Budget' GROUP BY
            ➥Month"
            '
            objDG.DatabaseName = Data1.DatabaseName
            objDG.SQLSelect = strSQL
            objDG.GraphType = dgLine
            objDG.GraphField = "SalesTotal"
            objDG.LabelField = "Month"
            objDG.GraphTitle = "Sales by Month"
            objDG.LeftTitle = "($)"
```

continues

11

Listing 11.30. continued

```
                objDG.BottomTitle = "Months"
            '
        Case 2 ' sales by customer
End Select
    '
    objDG.ShowGraph
    '
End Sub
```

The only real difference here is the new SQL statement and the settings for the titles, labels, and legends. Save and run this code. Check your resultant graph with the one shown in Figure 11.15.

Figure 11.15.

Displaying the Sales by Month line graph.

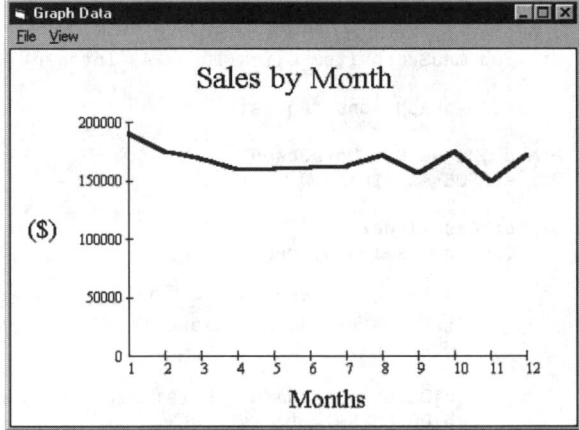

Finally, add the Sales by Company bar graph to the CompanyMaster project. Here is the SQL statement you need to produce a dataset that contains the year-to-date sales figures by company:

```
SELECT CompanyName, SUM(Amount) AS SalesTotal
    FROM SalesData
    WHERE CompanyName<>'Budget'
    GROUP BY CompanyName;
```

Now modify the mnuGraphsItem_Click event to match the code in Listing 11.31.

TYPE **Listing 11.31. Modifying the `mnuGraphsItem_click` event.**

```
Private Sub mnuGraphsItem_Click(Index As Integer)
    '
    ' handle graph menu requests
```

```
'
Dim objDG As New DataGraph
Dim strSQL As String
'
Select Case Index
    Case 0 ' sales by region
        '
        strSQL = "SELECT Region, SUM(Amount) AS SalesTotal FROM "
        strSQL = strSQL & "SalesData WHERE CompanyName<>'Budget' GROUP BY
        ➥Region"
        '
        objDG.DatabaseName = Data1.DatabaseName
        objDG.SQLSelect = strSQL
        objDG.GraphType = dgPie3d
        objDG.GraphField = "SalesTotal"
        objDG.GraphTitle = "Sales by Region"
        objDG.LegendField = "Region"

    Case 1 ' sales by month
        '
        strSQL = "SELECT Month, SUM(Amount) AS SalesTotal FROM "
        strSQL = strSQL & "SalesData WHERE CompanyName<>'Budget' GROUP BY
        ➥Month"
        '
        objDG.DatabaseName = Data1.DatabaseName
        objDG.SQLSelect = strSQL
        objDG.GraphType = dgLine
        objDG.GraphField = "SalesTotal"
        objDG.LabelField = "Month"
        objDG.GraphTitle = "Sales by Month"
        objDG.LeftTitle = "($)"
        objDG.BottomTitle = "Months"
        '
    Case 2 ' sales by customer
        '
        strSQL = "SELECT CompanyName, SUM(Amount) AS SalesTotal FROM "
        strSQL = strSQL & "SalesData WHERE CompanyName<>'Budget' GROUP BY
        ➥CompanyName"
        '
        objDG.DatabaseName = Data1.DatabaseName
        objDG.SQLSelect = strSQL
        objDG.GraphType = dgBar3d
        objDG.GraphField = "SalesTotal"
        objDG.LegendField = "CompanyName"
        objDG.LabelField = "SalesTotal"
        objDG.GraphTitle = "Sales by Company"
        objDG.LeftTitle = "($)"
        objDG.BottomTitle = "Companies"
        '
End Select
'
objDG.ShowGraph
'
End Sub
```

11

Again, the only real difference is in the SQL statement and the titles, labels, and legends. Save and run the project. Your Sales by Company graph should look like the one in Figure 11.16.

Figure 11.16.

Displaying the Sales by Company bar graph.

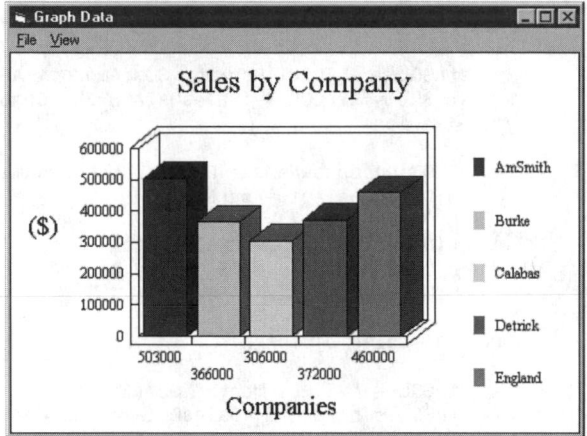

Summary

Today you learned how to use the graph control that ships with Visual Basic in order to create visual displays of your data tables. You learned how to add the control to your project and how to load the graph control with data points, titles, legends, and labels.

Also, you built a graph ActiveX DLL Object Library that you can use to display virtually any dataset in a variety of graph formats. This library lets you save the graph to disk, send the graph to the printer, or copy the graph to the Windows Clipboard for placement in other Windows programs by way of the Paste Special operation.

While building the graph library, you learned how to declare and use enumerated constants to improve the readability of your Visual Basic code.

Finally, you used the new graph library to add three graphs to the CompanyMaster project.

Quiz

1. List the advantages of including graphics in your Visual Basic database applications.
2. Describe the purpose of the NumSets and NumPoints properties of the graph control.
3. When you are using the predefined constants for graph types, is the following code correct?

```
Graph1.GraphType = graphBar3d
```

4. What character separates data points in a series when the QuickData property is used? What character(s) separate a set of points?

5. Is the following code correct?

```
Graph1.GraphTitle = "Sales for October"
```

6. What do the following DrawModes constants do?

```
gphBlit
gphCopy
gphDraw
```

7. What is an enumerated type declaration and why is it useful?

8. Write code to get a count of records in a dataset used for graphing.

Exercises

Assume that you are an analyst for your regional airport. The Manager of Operations wants information on passenger activity throughout the year. He is an extremely busy individual who does not understand database applications. In order to help him perform his job better, you have decided to create some graphs for him to review.

Perform the following steps in completing this project:

1. Build a database using Visdata or Data Manager. Name this database 12ABCEX.MDB.

2. Build a table in this database and name it Activity. Include three fields: Airline (TEXT 10), Month (INTEGER), and Passengers (INTEGER).

3. Insert the following records into your table:

Airline	Month	Passengers
ABC	1	2562
ABC	2	4859
ABC	3	4235
ABC	4	4897
ABC	5	5623
ABC	6	4565
ABC	7	5466
ABC	8	2155
ABC	10	5454
ABC	11	5488
ABC	12	5456
ABC	9	5468
LMN	1	1956

continues

Airline	Month	Passengers
LMN	2	2135
LMN	3	5221
LMN	4	2153
LMN	5	2154
LMN	6	5125
LMN	7	2135
LMN	8	5465
LMN	9	5555
LMN	10	2536
LMN	11	2153
LMN	12	2168
XYZ	1	10251
XYZ	2	12123
XYZ	3	10258
XYZ	4	12000
XYZ	5	21564
XYZ	6	21321
XYZ	7	14564
XYZ	8	12365
XYZ	9	21356
XYZ	10	21357
XYZ	11	21321
XYZ	12	12365

4. Start a new Visual Basic project that uses the LIBGRAPH.BAS module you created today. Build a form and add three command buttons: cmdPie, cmdLine, and cmdBar.

5. Display the following graphs when each button is pressed:

cmdPie: Displays a 3D pie chart that shows comparative activity for the first month.

cmdLine: Displays a line graph that shows total passenger activity by month. Include Passengers as the title on the vertical axis and Month as the title for the horizontal axis.

cmdBar: Displays a 3D bar graph for the activity of ABC Airlines for the entire year.

6. Examine the charts you built. Notice how much easier it is to ascertain trends from these graphs than it is from the data entry table in Exercise 3.

Day 12

Data-Bound List Boxes, Grids, and Subforms

Today you'll learn about the use of data-bound lists, combo boxes, and grids in your Visual Basic 5 database applications. Before Visual Basic, incorporating list boxes, combo boxes, and grids into an application was an arduous task that required a great deal of coding and program maintenance. Now, Visual Basic 5 ships with the tools you need to add lists, combo boxes, and data grids to your project with very little coding.

You'll learn how to add features to your data entry forms that provide pick lists that support and enforce the database relationships already defined in your data tables. You'll also learn the difference between data lists and combo boxes, and you'll learn where it's appropriate to use them.

We will also show you how to easily add a data grid to your form to show more than one record at a time in a table form. This grid can be used for display only, or for data entry, too. We'll show you how to decide which is the best method for your project.

After you learn how to use the data-bound list, combo box, and grid, you'll use them to create a new custom control that provides an easy "find" dialog for all your data entry forms. You also learn how to build a data entry Subform that combines all three controls on a single form.

The Data-Bound List and Combo Boxes

The data-bound list and combo controls are used in conjunction with the data control to allow you to display multiple rows of data in the same control. This provides you with a pick list of values displayed in a list or combo box. You can use these types of controls on your data entry forms to speed data entry, provide tighter data entry validation and control, and give users suggested correct values for the data entry field.

Setting up data-bound lists and combo boxes is a bit trickier than setting up standard data-bound controls. But once you get the hang of it, you'll want to use data-bound lists and combo boxes in every data entry screen you can.

Using the Data-Bound List Box

Although the data-bound list control looks like the standard list control, there are several differences between the two. The data-bound list control has properties that provide the data-binding aspects that are not found in the standard list control (for example, the data-bound list control is self-populating, while the standard list control is not). The first two of these properties are the RowSource and ListField properties of the data-bound list control.

☐ RowSource: The name of the Recordset object that is providing the data set used to fill the data-bound list box.

☐ ListField: The name of the column in the RowSource data set that is used to fill the list box. This is the display field for the list.

These two properties are used to bind the list control to a data control. Once these two properties are set, Visual Basic 5 automatically populates the list control for you when you open the data entry form.

Let's start a new project and illustrate the data-bound list control. Once you start the new project, you must make sure you have added the data-bound list controls to your project. Select the Project | Components... item from the Visual Basic 5 main menu. Locate and select the Microsoft Data Bound List Controls 5.0 item. Your screen should look like the one in Figure 12.1.

Figure 12.1.

Adding the data-bound list controls to your project.

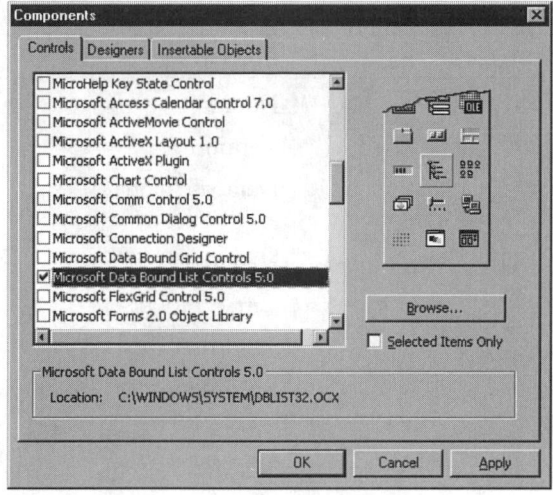

Now you need to add the data-bound list control, a standard data control, and two labels and text boxes. Use Table 12.1 and Figure 12.2 as guides as you build your first data-bound list project. Be sure to save your work periodically. Save the form as LSTCNTRL.FRM and the project as LSTCNTRL.VBP.

TIP

If you lay out the controls in the order in which they are listed in the table, you can use the down arrows of most of the property fields to get a selection list for the field names, and so on. This saves you some typing.

12

Table 12.1. The controls for the CH1301.VBP project.

Controls	Properties	Settings
Form	Name	LSTCNTRL
	Caption	Data-Bound List Controls
	Height	2670
	Left	1215
	Top	1170
	Width	4995

continues

Table 12.1. continued

Controls	Properties	Settings
DataControl	Name	Data1
	Caption	Data1
	DatabaseName	`C:\TYSDBVB5\SOURCE\` `DATA\LSTCNTRL.MDB`
	Height	300
	Left	120
	RecordsetType	2 – Snapshot
	RecordSource	ValidNames
	Top	1860
	Width	1875
DBList	Name	DBList1
	Height	1620
	Left	120
	RowSource	Data1
	ListField	NameText
	Top	120
	Width	1875
Label	Name	Label1
	Alignment	1 – Right justify
	BorderStyle	1 – Fixed Single
	Caption	List Field:
	Height	300
	Left	2160
	Top	120
	Width	1200
Label	Name	Label2
	Alignment	1 – Right Justify
	BorderStyle	1 – Fixed Single
	Caption	Text:
	Height	300
	Left	2160

12

Controls	Properties	Settings
	Top	540
	Width	1200
Textbox	Name	Text1
	Height	300
	Left	3540
	Top	120
	Width	1200
Textbox	Name	Text2
	Height	300
	Left	3540
	Top	540
	Width	1200
Command Button	Name	cmdGetList
	Caption	&Get List
	Height	300
	Left	2160
	Top	1860
	Width	1200

Figure 12.2.
*Laying out the
LSTCNTRL form.*

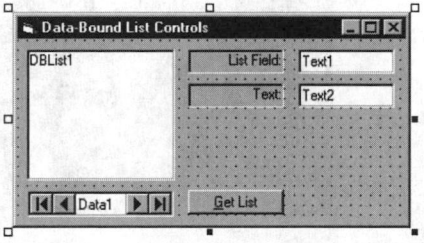

Notice that in the preceding table, a single data control has been added to open the database and create a Snapshot object of the ValidNames table. It's always a good idea to use Snapshot objects as the RowSource for data-bound lists and combo boxes. Snapshot objects are static views of the data set and, even though they take up more workstation memory than Dynaset objects, they run faster. Notice also that we set the ListField property of the data-bound list to NameText. This fills the control with the values stored in the NameText column of the data set.

Now you need to add two lines of code to the project. Open the `cmdGetList_Click` event and enter the following lines of code:

```
Private Sub cmdGetList_Click()
    Text1 = DBList1.ListField
    Text2 = DBList1.TEXT
End Sub
```

These two lines of code update the text box controls each time you press the GetList button on the form. That way you are able to see the current values of the ListField and Text properties of the data-bound list control.

Save the form as LSTCNTRL.FRM and the project as LSTCNTRL.VBP. Now run the project. When the form first comes up, you see the list box already filled with all the values in the NameText column of the data set (that is, the ListField used for the DBList). Select one of the items in the list box by clicking on it. Now press the GetList button. You'll see the two text controls updated with the ListField and Text values of the list control. Your screen should look like the one in Figure 12.3.

Figure 12.3.

Running the LSTCNTRL.VBP project.

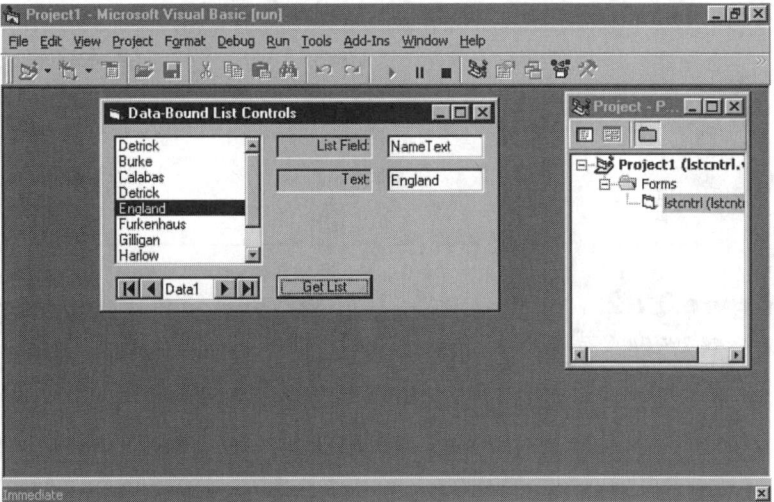

The data-bound list control has two more properties that you need to know. These are the properties that you can use to create an output value based on the item selected from the list. The two properties are

☐ BoundColumn: The name of the column in the RowSource data set that is used to provide the output of the list selection. This can be the same column designated in the ListField property, or it can be any other column in the RowSource data set.

☐ BoundText: The value of the column designated by the BoundColumn property. This is the actual output of the list selection.

12

Usually, data-bound lists present the user with a familiar set of names. The user can pick from these names, and then the program uses the selection to locate a more computer-like ID or code represented by the familiar name selected by the user. The table created for this example contains just such information.

Set the BoundColumn property of the data-bound list control to point to the NameID column of the ValidNames data set. To do this, select the data-bound list control, and then press F4 to bring up the property window. Now locate the BoundColumn property and set it to NameID.

Add two more labels and text boxes to display the new properties. Do this by selecting the existing two labels and the two text controls all as a set. Then select Edit | Copy. This places the four selected controls on the Clipboard. Now select Edit | Paste from the Visual Basic 5 main menu. This places copies of the controls on your new form. Answer Yes to the prompts that ask if you want to create a control array. Set the caption properties of the two new labels to Bound Column: and Bound Text:. Use Figure 12.4 as a guide in laying out the new controls.

Figure 12.4.

Adding new controls to the CH1301.VBP *project.*

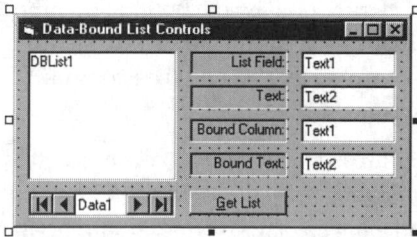

Finally, modify the code in the cmdGetList_Click event to match the following code. This shows you the results of the new BoundColumn and BoundText properties:

```
Private Sub cmdGetList_Click()
    Text1(0) = DBList1.ListField
    Text2(0) = DBList1.TEXT
    Text1(1) = DBList1.BoundColumn
    Text2(1) = DBList1.BoundText
End Sub
```

Notice that you added the array references to the code to account for the new control arrays. Now save and run the project. When you select an item from the list and click the GetList button, you'll see the BoundColumn and BoundText properties displayed in the appropriate textboxes, as shown in Figure 12.5.

Figure 12.5.

Displaying the new BoundColumn and BoundText properties.

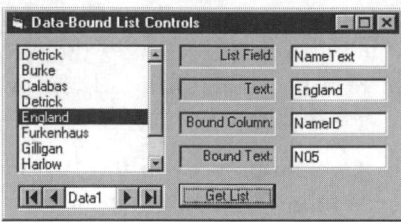

NOTE

You can also activate the Get List event by entering cmdGetList_Click in the Dbl_Click event of DBList. The user can get the same results by selecting the command button, or by double-clicking the item in the list. This type of call provides a quick way of adding functionality to your code. You don't need to enter or maintain the code in both events.

The data that is produced by the BoundText property can be used to update another column in a separate table. The easiest way to do this is to add a second data control and link the data-bound list control to that second data control. You can do this by setting the following two properties of the data-bound list control.

- [ ] DataSource: The data set that is updated by the output of the data-bound list control. This is the data control used to open the destination Recordset.
- [ ] DataField: The name of the column in the Recordset referred to by the DataSource property.

Now let's add a second data control to the form and a bound input control that is updated by the data-bound list. First, add a data control. Set its DatabaseName property to C:\TYSDBVB5\SOURCE\DATA\LSTCNTRL.MDB and its RecordSource property to Destination. Also, set the EOFAction property of the Data2 data control to AddNew. Now add a text control to the project. Set its DataSource property to Data2 and its DataField property to NameID. Use Figure 12.6 as a layout guide.

Before you save and run the project, set the DataSource and DataField properties of the data-bound list control. Set these to Data2 and NameID, respectively. This tells the list control to automatically update the Destination.NameID field. Now, each time a user selects an item in the list and then saves the data set of the *second* control, the designated field of the second data set is automatically updated with the value in the BoundColumn property of the data-bound list.

12

Figure 12.6.

Adding a second data control and text control.

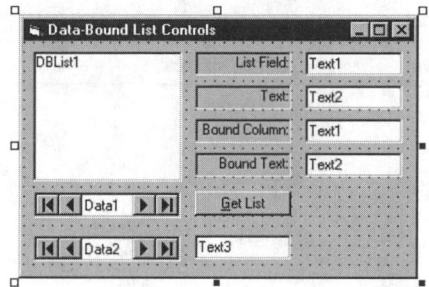

Save and run the project. This time, select the first item in the list by clicking on it. Now click on the GetList button to bring up the list properties in the text boxes. Force the second data control to save its contents by repositioning the record pointer by clicking the left-most arrow to force the second data set to the first record in the set. You should now see that the second data set, Destination, has been updated by the value in the BoundColumn property of the data-bound list. Your screen should look like the one in Figure 12.6.

Do this a few times to add records to the Destination table. Also notice that each time you move the record pointer of the Destination table, the data-bound control reads the value in the bound column and moves the list pointer to highlight the related NameText field. You now have a fully functional data-bound list box!

Using the Data-Bound Combo Box

The data-bound combo box works very much the same as the data-bound list control. The only difference is the way the data is displayed. The data-bound combo control can be used as a basic data entry text box with added validation. Allowing experienced users to type values they know are correct can speed up the data entry process. Also, new users are able to scan the list of valid entries until they learn them. The data-bound combo is an excellent data entry control.

Let's build a new project that shows how you can use the data-bound combo box to create friendly data entry forms. Start a new Visual Basic 5 project. Use Table 12.2 and Figure 12.7 as guides as you build your new form. Save your form as COMBO.FRM and the project as COMBO.VBP.

12

Table 12.2. The controls for the `CH1302.VBP` **project.**

Controls	Properties	Settings
Form	Name	frmCombo
	Caption	Data Bound ComboBox
	Height	2500
	Left	2750
	Top	2500
	Width	3000
DataControl	Name	dtaDestination
	Caption	Destination
	DatabaseName	`C:\TYSDBVB5\SOURCE\DATA\` `LSTCNTRL.MDB`
	EOFAction	2 – AddNew
	Height	300
	Left	120
	RecordsetType	1 – Dynaset
	RecordSource	Destination
	Top	960
	Width	2535
DataControl	Name	dtaValidStates
	Caption	Valid States
	DatabaseName	`C:\TYSDBVB5\SOURCE\DATA\` `LSTCNTRL.MDB`
	Height	300
	Left	120
	RecordsetType	2 – Snapshot
	RecordSource	"ValidStates"
	Top	1320
	Visible	False
	Width	2535
DataControl	Name	dtaValidNames
	Caption	Valid Names

Controls	Properties	Settings
	DatabaseName	C:\TYSDBVB5\SOURCE\DATA\ LSTCNTRL.MDB
	Height	300
	Left	120
	RecordsetType	2 – Snapshot
	RecordSource	ValidNames
	Top	1680
	Visible	False
	Width	2535
DBCombo	Name	DBCombo1
	DataSource	dtaDestination
	DataField	StateCode
	Height	315
	Left	120
	RowSource	dtaValidStates
	ListField	StateName
	BoundColumn	StateCode
	Top	120
	Width	1200
DBCombo	Name	DBCombo2
	DataSource	dtaDestination
	DataField	NameID
	Height	315
	Left	120
	Top	540
	Width	1200
	RowSource	dtaValidNames
	ListField	NameText
	BoundColumn	NameID
Label	Name	Label1
	BorderStyle	1 – Fixed Single

continues

Table 12.2. continued

Controls	Properties	Settings
	DataSource	dtaDestination
	DataField	StateCode
	Height	300
	Left	1440
	Top	120
	Width	1200
Label	Name	Label2
	BorderStyle	1 – Fixed Single
	DataSource	dtaDestination
	DataField	NameID
	Height	300
	Left	1440
	Top	540
	Width	1200

Figure 12.7.

*Laying out the
COMBO.VBP
project.*

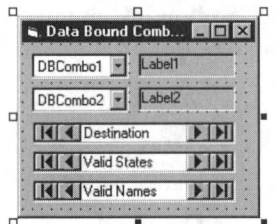

You need to add two lines of code to the project before it's complete. The following lines force
Visual Basic 5 to update the form controls as soon as the user makes a selection in the combo
box:

```
Private Sub DBCombo1_Click(Area As Integer)
    Label1 = DBCombo1.BoundText
End Sub

Private Sub DBCombo2_Click(Area As Integer)
    Label2 = DBCombo2.BoundText
End Sub
```

Save the form as COMBO.FRM and the project as COMBO.VBP. Now run the project and check your
screen against the one in Figure 12.8.

Figure 12.8.

Running the
COMBO.VBP *project.*

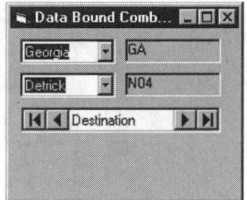

You can make selections in either of the two combo boxes and see that the label controls are updated automatically. Also, you can move through the dataset using the data control arrow buttons and watch the two combo boxes automatically update as each record changes.

Deciding When to Use the List Box or Combo Box

The choice between list and combo controls depends on the type of data-entry screen you have and the amount of real estate available to your data entry form. Typically, you should use lists where you want to show users more than one possible entry. This encourages them to scroll through the list and locate the desired record. The data-bound list control doesn't allow users to enter their own values in the list. Therefore, you should not use the data-bound list control if you want to allow users to add new values to the list.

The data-bound combo box is a good control to use when you are short on form space. You can provide the functionality of a list box without using as much space. Also, combo boxes have the added benefit of allowing users to type in their selected values. This is very useful for users who are performing heads-down data entry. They type the exact values right at the keyboard without using the mouse or checking a list. Also, novices can use the same form to learn about valid list values without slowing down the more experienced users.

The Data-Bound Grid

The data-bound grid control in Visual Basic 5 adds power and flexibility to your database programs. You can easily provide grid access to any available database. You can provide simple display-only access for use with summary data and on-screen reports. You can also provide editing capabilities to your data grid, including modify only, add rights, or delete rights.

Creating Your First Data-Bound Grid Form

It's really quite easy to create a data-bound grid form. First, start a new Visual Basic 5 project. Next, make sure you add the data-bound grid tool to your list of custom controls. To do this, select Project | Components... from the Visual Basic 5 main menu. Locate and select the Microsoft Data Bound Grid Control. Your screen should resemble Figure 12.9.

12

Figure 12.9.

Adding the Data-bound Grid Control to your project.

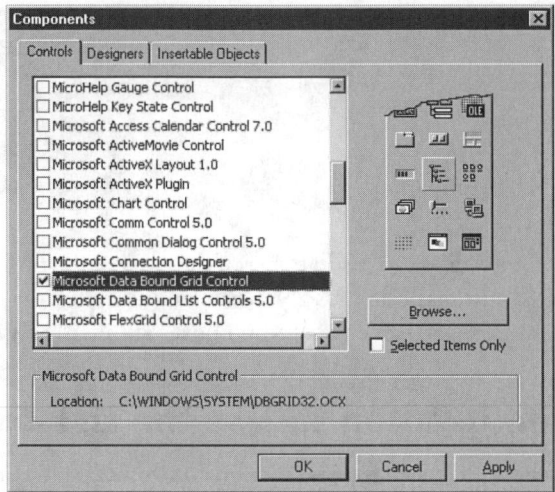

Now drop a standard data control on the form. Place it at the bottom of the form. Set the DatabaseName property to C:\TYSDBVB5\SOURCE\DATA\DBGRID.MDB and the RecordSource property to HeaderTable. Now place the data-bound grid tool on the form and set its DataSource property to Data1. That's all there is to it. Now save the form as DBGRID.FRM and the project as DBGRID.VBP and run the project. Your screen should look like the one in Figure 12.10.

Figure 12.10.

Running the first data-bound grid project.

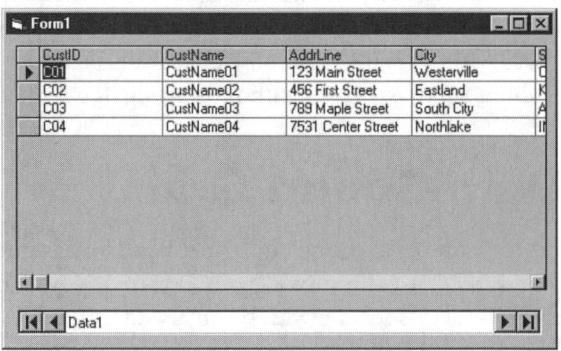

You can move through the grid by clicking the left margin of the grid control. You can also move through the grid by clicking the navigation arrows of the data control. If you select a cell in the grid, you can edit that cell. As soon as you leave the row, that cell is updated by Visual Basic 5. Right now, you cannot add or delete records from the grid. You'll add those features in the next example.

Adding and Deleting Records with the Data-Bound Grid

It's very easy to include add and delete capabilities with the data grid. Bring up the same project you just completed. Select the data grid control and press F4 to bring up the Properties window. Locate the AllowAddNew property and the AllowDelete property and set them to True. You now have add and delete power within the grid.

Before you run this project, make two other changes. Set the Visible property of the data control to False. Because you can navigate through the grid using scroll bars and the mouse, you don't need the data control arrow buttons. Second, set the Align property of the grid control to 1 – vbAlignTop. This forces the grid to hug the top and sides of the form whenever it is resized.

Now save and run the project. Notice that you can resize the columns. Figure 12.11 shows the resized form with several columns adjusted.

Figure 12.11.

Resizing the form and columns of a data grid control.

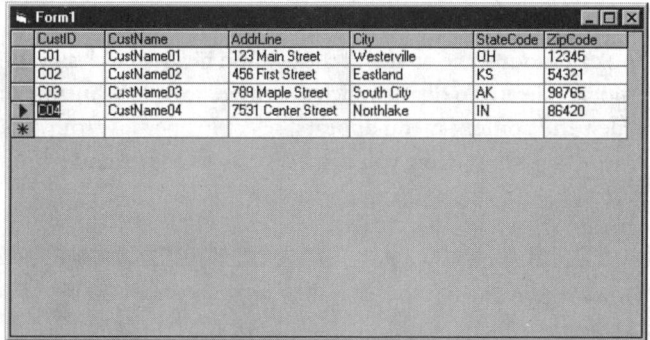

To add a record to the data grid, all you need to do is place the cursor at the first field in the empty row at the bottom of the grid and start typing. Use Figure 12.12 as a guide. Visual Basic 5 creates a new line for you and allows you to enter data. Take note how the record pointer turns into a pencil as you type. When you leave the line, Visual Basic 5 saves the record to the dataset.

Figure 12.12.
Adding a record to the data grid.

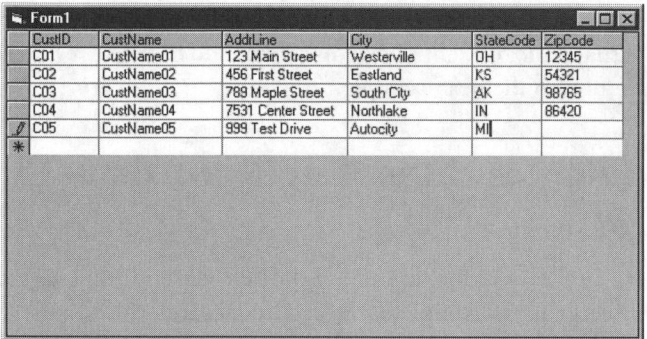

Setting Other Design-Time Properties of the Data Grid

A problem with resizing the form at runtime is that the moment you close the form, all the column settings are lost. You can prevent this problem by resizing the form at design time. Select the data grid control and press the alternate mouse button. This brings up the context menu. Select Retrieve Fields. This loads the column names of the data set into the grid control. Next, select Edit from the context menu. Now you can resize the columns of the control. The dimensions of these columns are stored in the control and used each time the form is loaded.

You can modify the names of the column headers at design time by using the built-in tabbed property sheet. To do this, click the alternate mouse button while the grid control is selected. When the context menu appears, select Properties from this menu. You should now see a series of tabs that allow you to set several grid-level and column-level properties. (See Figure 12.13.)

Figure 12.13.
Using the data grid tabbed properties page.

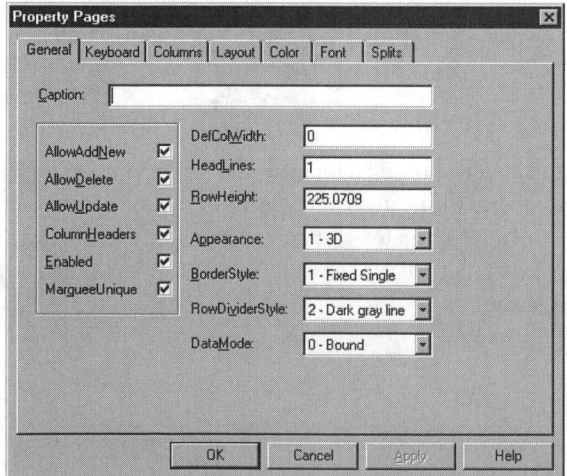

Trapping Events for the Data Grid Control

The data grid control has several unique events that you can use to monitor user actions in your grid. The following events can be used to check the contents of your data table before you allow the user to continue:

- ☐ BeforeInsert: This event occurs before a new row is inserted into the grid. Use this event to confirm that the user wants to add a new record.

- ☐ AfterInsert: This event occurs right after a new row has been inserted into the grid. Use this event to perform clean-up chores after a new record has been added.

- ☐ BeforeUpdate: This event occurs before the data grid writes the changes to the data control. Use this event to perform data validation at the record level.

- ☐ AfterUpdate: This event occurs after the changed data has been written to the data control. Use this event to perform miscellaneous chores after the grid has been updated.

- ☐ BeforeDelete: This event occurs before the selected record(s) are deleted from the grid. Use this event to perform confirmation chores before deleting data.

- ☐ AfterDelete: This event occurs after the user has already deleted the data from the grid. Use this event to perform related chores once the grid has been updated.

You can use the events listed here to perform field and record-level validation and force user confirmation on critical events, such as adding a new record or deleting an existing record. Let's add some code to the DBGRID.VBP project to illustrate the use of these events.

The Add Record Events

First, add code that monitors the adding of new records to the grid. Select the grid control and open the DBGrid1_BeforeInsert event. Add the code in Listing 12.1.

Listing 12.1. Code to monitor addition of new records to a data-bound grid.

TYPE

```
Private Sub DBGrid1_BeforeInsert(Cancel As Integer)
    '
    ' make user confirm add operation
    '
    Dim nResult As Integer
    '
    nResult = MsgBox("Do you want to add a new record?", _
    _vbInformation + vbYesNo, "DBGrid.BeforeInsert")
    If nResult = vbNo Then
        Cancel = True    ' cancel add
    End If
End Sub
```

12

In Listing 12.1, you present a message to the user to confirm the intention to add a new record to the set. If the answer is No, the add operation is canceled.

Now let's add code that tells the user the add operation has been completed. Add the following code in the DBGrid1_AfterInsert event window:

```
Private Sub DBGrid1_AfterInsert()
    '
    ' tell user what you just did!
    '
    MsgBox "New record written to data set!", vbInformation,
    _ "DBGrid.AfterInsert"
End Sub
```

Now save and run the project. Go to the last row in the grid. Begin entering a new record. As soon as you press the first key, the confirmation message appears. (See Figure 12.14.)

Figure 12.14.

Attempting to add a record to the grid.

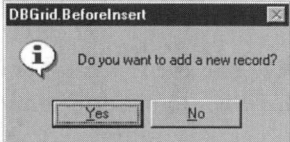

After you fill in all the columns and attempt to move to another record in the grid, you'll see the message telling you that the new record was added to the data set.

The Update Record Events

Now add some code that monitors attempts to update existing records. Add Listing 12.2 to the DBGrid1.BeforeUpdate event.

TYPE   **Listing 12.2. Code to monitor for attempted data updates.**

```
Private Sub DBGrid1_BeforeUpdate(Cancel As Integer)
    '
    ' make user confirm update operation
    '
    Dim nResult As Integer
    '
    nResult = MsgBox("Write any changes to data set?",
    _ vbInformation + vbYesNo, "DBGrid.BeforeUpdate")
    If nResult = vbNo Then
        Cancel = True   ' ignore changes
        DBGrid1.ReBind  ' reset all values
    End If
End Sub
```

12

This code looks similar to the code used to monitor the add record events. The only thing different here is that you force the ReBind method to refresh the data grid after the canceled attempt to update the record.

Now add the code to confirm the update of the record. Add the following code to the DBGrid1.AfterUpdate event:

```
Private Sub DBGrid1_AfterUpdate()
'
    ' tell 'em!
'
    MsgBox "The record has been updated.", vbInformation, "DBGrid.AfterUpdate"
End Sub
```

Now save and run the project. When you press a key in any column of an existing record, you'll see a message asking you to confirm the update. When you move off the record, you'll see a message telling you the record has been updated.

The Delete Record Events

Now add some events to track any attempts to delete existing records. Place the code in Listing 12.3 in the DBGrid1.BeforeDelete event.

TYPE **Listing 12.3. Code to track for record deletes.**

```
Private Sub DBGrid1_BeforeDelete(Cancel As Integer)
'
    ' force user to confirm delete operation
'
    Dim nResult As Integer
'
    nResult = MsgBox("Delete the current record?", _
    vbInformation + vbYesNo, "DBGrid.BeforeDelete")
    If nResult = vbNo Then
        Cancel = True    ' cancel delete op
    End If
End Sub
```

Again, no real news here. Simply ask the user to confirm the delete operation. If the answer is No, the operation is canceled. Now add the code to report the results of the delete. Put this code in the DBGrid1.AfterDelete event:

```
Private Sub DBGrid1_AfterDelete()
'
    ' tell user the news!
'
    MsgBox "Record has been deleted", vbInformation, "DBGrid.AfterDelete"
End Sub
```

12

Now save and run the project. Select an entire record by clicking the left margin of the grid. This highlights all the columns in the row. To delete the record, press the Delete key or Ctrl+X. When the message pops up asking you to confirm the delete, answer No to cancel. (See Figure 12.15.)

Figure 12.15.

Attempting to delete a record from the grid.

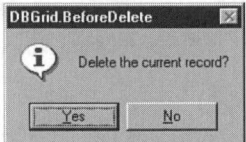

Column-Level Events

Several column-level events are available for the data grid. The following are only two of them:

☐ BeforeColUpdate: This event occurs before the column is updated with any changes made by the user. Use this event to perform data validation before the update occurs.

☐ AfterColUpdate: This event occurs after the column has been updated with user changes. Use this event to perform other duties after the value of the column has been updated.

NOTE

> Refer to the Visual Basic 5 documentation for a list of all the events associated with the DBGrid control.

These events work just like the BeforeUpdate and AfterUpdate events seen earlier. However, instead of occurring whenever the record value is updated, the BeforeColUpdate and AfterColUpdate events occur whenever a column value is changed. This gives you the ability to perform field-level validation within the data grid.

Add some code in the BeforeColUpdate event to force the user to confirm the update of a column. Open the DBGrid.BeforeColUpdate event and enter the code in Listing 12.4.

Listing 12.4. Code to request confirmation on column updates.

```
Private Sub DBGrid1_BeforeColUpdate(ByVal ColIndex As Integer,
_ OldValue As Variant, Cancel As Integer)
'
    ' ask user for confirmation
'
```

```
        Dim nResult As Integer
        '
        nResult = MsgBox("Write changes to Column", vbInformation + vbYesNo,
        _ "DBGrid.BeforeColUpdate")
        If nResult = vbNo Then
            Cancel = False        ' cancel change & get old value
        End If
End Sub
```

Now add the code that tells the user the column has been updated as requested. Place the following code in the DBGrid1.AfterColUpdate event:

```
Private Sub DBGrid1_AfterColUpdate(ByVal ColIndex As Integer)
    '
    ' tell user
    '
    MsgBox "Column has been updated", vbInformation, "DBGrid.AfterColUpdate"
End Sub
```

Save and run the project. Now, each time you attempt to alter a column, you are asked to confirm the column update. (See Figure 12.16.)

Figure 12.16.

Updating a grid column.

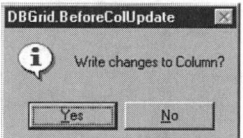

You can also see a message when you leave the column telling you that the data has been changed.

Creating the dbFind Custom Control

A very common use of the data-bound list controls is the creation of a dialog box that lists all the primary keys in a table. This dialog lets users select an item from the list and then displays the complete data record that is associated with the primary key. In this section, you'll learn how to build a custom control that does just that. Once this control is completed, you'll be able to place it on any Visual Basic form and add an instant "Find" dialog to all your Visual Basic forms.

This custom control project has two main parts. The first is the find button. This is the object that users place on their forms. By pressing the button, users see a dialog box containing a list of all the records in the table. The dialog box itself is the second part of the custom control. This dialog contains a data-bound list box, a data control, and two command buttons.

12

TIP

A good custom control also has a property page interface for setting control properties at design time. Because this is not a required feature, it has been left out of our custom control design so that you can concentrate on building the data-bound aspects of the control.

After you build and compile the find dialog custom control, you build a small data entry form that tests the new control.

The dbFind Control Button

The first step in the process is to start a new Visual Basic 5.0 ActiveX Control project. Name the project dbFindCtl and name the UserControl dbFind. Now add a single command button to the UserControl. Set its Height and Width properties to 315 and specify ... as its caption property. Set the font properties to Arial, 8pt Bold. Refer to Figure 12.17 as a guide.

Figure 12.17.

Setting up the dbFind button.

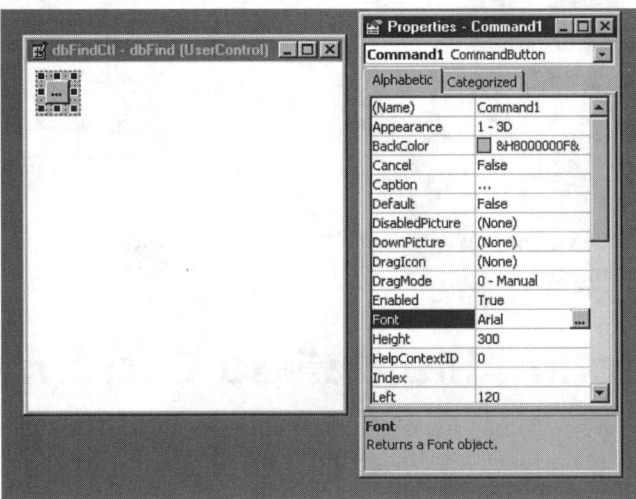

Once you have set these properties, save the control as DBFIND.CTL and the project as DBFINDCTL.VBP.

This custom control has six custom properties and two declared events. Open the code window for the dbFind control and add the code from Listing 12.5 to the general declarations section of the project.

Listing 12.5. Coding the General Declarations section of the dbFind control.

```
Option Explicit
'
' local storage
Private strListField As String
Private strBoundColumn As String
Private strDBName As String
Private strRSName As String
Private strConnect As String
Private strBoundColumn as String
'
' event messages
Public Event Selected(SelectValue As Variant)
Public Event Cancel()
```

After declaring the local storage variables, you're ready to build the actual properties associated with the storage space. Add the DatabaseName property to your project by selecting Tools | Add Procedure... from the main menu and entering DatabaseName as the procedure name and selecting the Property and Public option buttons (see Figure 12.18).

Figure 12.18.
Adding the Databasename property.

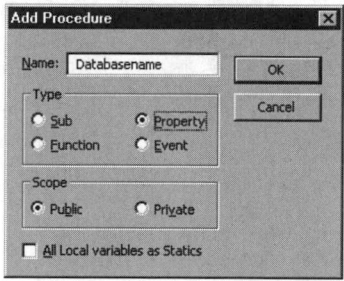

After the Visual Basic editor creates the `Property Let` and `Property Get` functions, edit them to match the code in Listing 12.6.

Listing 12.6. Editing the DatabaseName property functions.

```
Public Property Get DatabaseName() As String
'
    DatabaseName = frmFind.Data1.DatabaseName
'
End Property
```

continues

Listing 12.6. continued

```
Public Property Let DatabaseName(ByVal vNewValue As String)
    '
    strDBName = vNewValue
    frmFind.Data1.DatabaseName = strDBName
    '
End Property
```

> **Note**
>
> All the property routines you'll code here refer to the frmFind form. This form will be built in the next section of the chapter. If you attempt to run this project before building the frmFind form, you'll receive errors.

Next, add the Connect property to the project and enter the code from Listing 12.7.

Type **Listing 12.7. Coding the Connect property procedures.**

```
Public Property Get Connect() As String
    '
    Connect = frmFind.Data1.Connect
    '
End Property

Public Property Let Connect(ByVal vNewValue As String)
    '
    strConnect = vNewValue
    frmFind.Data1.Connect = strConnect
    '
End Property
```

Now add the RecordSource property and enter the code from Listing 12.8.

Type **Listing 12.8. Adding the RecordSource property.**

```
Public Property Get RecordSource() As String
    '
    RecordSource = frmFind.Data1.RecordSource
    '
End Property
```

```
Public Property Let RecordSource(ByVal vNewValue As String)
    '
    strRSName = vNewValue
    frmFind.Data1.RecordSource = strRSName
    '
End Property
```

Next, build the ListField property and add the code from Listing 12.9.

TYPE **Listing 12.9. Building the ListField property.**

```
Public Property Get ListField() As String
    '
    ListField = frmFind.DBList1.ListField
    '
End Property

Public Property Let ListField(ByVal vNewValue As String)
    '
    strListField = vNewValue
    frmFind.DBList1.ListField = strListField
    '
End Property
```

Next, create the BoundColumn property and enter the code from Listing 12.10.

TYPE **Listing 12.10. Adding the BoundColumn property.**

```
Public Property Get BoundColumn() As String
    '
    BoundColumn = frmFind.DBList1.BoundColumn
    '
End Property

Public Property Let BoundColumn(ByVal vNewValue As String)
    '
    strBoundColumn = vNewValue
    frmFind.DBList1.BoundColumn = strBoundColumn
    '
End Property
```

12

Finally, add the BoundText property and enter the code from Listing 12.11.

TYPE | **Listing 12.11. Adding the BoundText property.**

```
Public Property Get BoundText() As Variant
    '
    BoundText = frmFind.DBList1.BoundText
    '
End Property

Public Property Let BoundText(ByVal vNewValue As Variant)
    '
    frmFind.DBList1.BoundText = vNewValue
    '
End Property
```

Now save the control (DBFIND.CTL) and the project (DBFINDCTL.VBP) before continuing.

The next set of routines handles some basics of custom control management. These routines exist in almost all custom controls. First, you need to add a routine to save the design-time state of the custom properties. This ensures that the values you set at design time are available to the runtime version of the control. Add the code in Listing 12.12 to the UserControl_WriteProperties event.

TYPE | **Listing 12.12. Coding the WriteProperties event of the User control.**

```
Private Sub UserControl_WriteProperties(PropBag As PropertyBag)
    '
    ' save design-time vars
    '
    With PropBag
        .WriteProperty "Connect", strConnect, ""
        .WriteProperty "DatabaseName", strDBName, ""
        .WriteProperty "RecordSource", strRSName, ""
        .WriteProperty "ListField", strListField, ""
        .WriteProperty "BoundColumn", strBoundColumn, ""
    End With
    '
End Sub
```

Next, you need to add the routine that reads the saved values. This event occurs when the runtime version of the control first begins. Add the code from Listing 12.13 to the UserControl_ReadProperties event.

TYPE **Listing 12.13. Coding the** `UserControl_ReadProperties` **event.**

```
Private Sub UserControl_ReadProperties(PropBag As PropertyBag)
    '
    ' get design-time vars
    '
    With PropBag
        strDBName = .ReadProperty("DatabaseName", "")
        strConnect = .ReadProperty("Connect", "")
        strRSName = .ReadProperty("RecordSource", "")
        strListField = .ReadProperty("ListField", "")
        strBoundColumn = .ReadProperty("BoundColumn", "")
    End With
    '
End Sub
```

The Initialize and Resize events can be used to set and adjust the size of the control. Enter the code from Listing 12.14 into the Initialize and Resize events of the User control.

TYPE **Listing 12.14. Coding the Initialize and Resize events of the User control.**

```
Private Sub UserControl_Initialize()
    '
    ' set default size
    '
    UserControl.Height = 315
    UserControl.Width = 315
    '
End Sub

Private Sub UserControl_ReadProperties(PropBag As PropertyBag)
    '
    ' get design-time vars
    '
    With PropBag
        strDBName = .ReadProperty("DatabaseName", "")
        strConnect = .ReadProperty("Connect", "")
        strRSName = .ReadProperty("RecordSource", "")
        strListField = .ReadProperty("ListField", "")
        strBoundColumn = .ReadProperty("BoundColumn", "")
    End With
    '
End Sub
```

12

continues

Listing 12.14. continued

```
Private Sub UserControl_Resize()
    '
    ' fill out control space with button
    '
    With Command1
        .Left = 1
        .Top = 1
        .Width = UserControl.Width
        .Height = UserControl.Height
    End With
    '
End Sub
```

Now you need to add just a few more routines to complete this portion of the control. First, you need to create a new private subroutine called LoadProperties. This routine moves all the property values onto the frmFind form that displays the selection dialog box. Enter the code from Listing 12.15 into your project.

TYPE   **Listing 12.15 Coding the LoadProperties subroutine.**

```
Private Sub LoadProperties()
    '
    ' move properties into dialog
    '
    frmFind.Data1.Connect = strConnect
    frmFind.Data1.DatabaseName = strDBName
    frmFind.Data1.RecordSource = strRSName
    frmFind.DBList1.ListField = strListField
    frmFind.DBList1.BoundColumn = strBoundColumn
    frmFind.Data1.Refresh
    frmFind.DBList1.Refresh
    '
End Sub
```

NOTE   The LoadProperties routine is declared private so that users of the ActiveX control cannot see and use this routine. The LoadProperties routine is for internal use and should not be called from outside the control's own code space.

Now you need to add code behind the command button that makes it all work. Enter the code from Listing 12.16 in the Command1_Click event of the control.

TYPE **Listing 12.16. Coding the Command1_Click event of the control.**

```
Private Sub Command1_Click()
    '
    ' user pressed the button!
    '
    Dim varTemp As Variant
    '
    LoadProperties
    frmFind.Show vbModal
    If frmFind.CloseFlag = True Then
        varTemp = frmFind.SelectedValue
        Unload frmFind
        RaiseEvent Selected(varTemp)
    Else
        Unload frmFind
        RaiseEvent Cancel
    End If
    '
End Sub
```

Notice that this last bit of code fires off the Selected and Cancel events, depending on the value stored in the frmFind.CloseFlag variable. You'll code the frmFind form in the next section.

Finally, to round out the control, add the following two subroutines to the project (see Listing 12.17). These create two public methods that can be called from within the user's program.

TYPE **Listing 12.17. Adding the ReturnSelected and ReturnCancel methods.**

```
Public Sub ReturnSelected()
    '
    RaiseEvent Selected(frmFind.DBList1.BoundText)
    '
End Sub

Public Sub ReturnCancel()
    '
    RaiseEvent Cancel
    '
End Sub
```

That is all the coding you need to do for the first part of the custom control. Be sure to save the control and the project before continuing to the next section.

12

The dbFind Dialog Box

Now you're ready to build the dialog box that displays the selection list to the user. Add a new form to the custom control project and set its name to frmFind; its BorderStyle to 3; its ControlBox property to False; and its StartUpPosition to 2. Then add a data-bound list control and a single command button to the form. Copy the command button. Select the command button and then select Edit | Copy and Edit | Paste from the menu. Be sure to answer Yes when asked if you want to create a control array. Finally, add a data control to the form and set its visible property to False. Also, set the DBList1 control's DataSource property to Data1. Your form should look something like the one in Figure 12.19.

Figure 12.19.

Laying out the frmFind form.

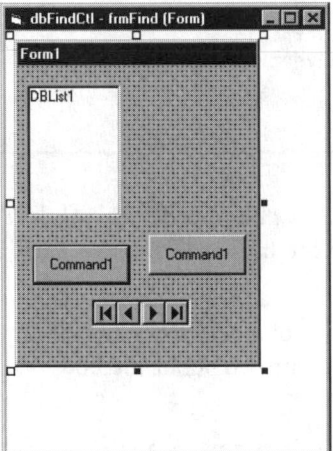

Don't worry about placing the controls on the form, you'll do that at runtime using Visual Basic code. Now save the form (FRMFIND.FRM) and the project (DBFINDCTL.VBP) before going to the next step.

Now it's time to code the frmFind form. First, add the following lines to the general declaration section of the form:

```
Option Explicit
'
Private blnCloseFlag As Boolean
Private varSelectValue As Variant
```

This code declares local storage for two form-level custom properties. Now add the CloseFlag Property (select Tools | Add Procedure) and enter the code from Listing 12.18.

TYPE **Listing 12.18. Adding the CloseFlag property.**

```
Public Property Get CloseFlag() As Variant

    CloseFlag = blnCloseFlag

End Property

Public Property Let CloseFlag(ByVal vNewValue As Variant)

    blnCloseFlag = vNewValue

End Property
```

Next, add the SelectedValue property and enter the code from Listing 12.19.

TYPE **Listing 12.19. Adding the SelectedValue property.**

```
Public Property Get SelectedValue() As Variant

    SelectedValue = varSelectValue

End Property

Public Property Let SelectedValue(ByVal vNewValue As Variant)

    varSelectValue = vNewValue

End Property
```

These properties are used to pass information from the completed form back to the control button you built earlier in the project. Save the form and project before continuing.

Now add the code from Listing 12.20 to the Form_Load event. This code refreshes the dialog at startup.

TYPE **Listing 12.20. Coding the Form_Load event.**

```
Private Sub Form_Load()

    Me.Caption = "Select a Record"
    Data1.Refresh
    DBList1.Refresh

End Sub
```

12

Now enter the code from Listing 21.21 into the `Form_Resize` event. This is the code that sizes and places the list and command buttons on the dialog box.

TYPE **Listing 12.21. Coding the `Form_Resize` event.**

```
Private Sub Form_Resize()
    '
    With DBList1
        .Left = 1
        .Top = 1
        .Width = Me.ScaleWidth
        .Height = Me.ScaleHeight - (300 + 90 + 90)
    End With
    '
    With Command1(0)
        .Left = 120
        .Top = Me.ScaleHeight - (390)
        .Height = 300
        .Width = Me.ScaleWidth * 0.45
        .Caption = "OK"
        .Default = True
    End With
    '
    With Command1(1)
        .Left = Me.ScaleWidth * 0.5
        .Top = Command1(0).Top
        .Height = Command1(0).Height
        .Width = Command1(0).Width
        .Caption = "Cancel"
        .Cancel = True
    End With
    '
End Sub
```

Now it's time to write the code for the `Command1_Click` event. This is the code that executes when the user presses a command button. Add the code from Listing 12.22 to your form.

TYPE **Listing 12.22. Coding the `Command1_Click` event.**

```
Private Sub Command1_Click(Index As Integer)
    '
    ' handle user button selection
    '
    Select Case Index
        Case 0 ' OK
            CloseFlag = True
            varSelectValue = frmFind.DBList1.BoundText
        Case 1 ' cancel
            CloseFlag = False
    End Select
```

```
'
    If Trim(varSelectValue) = "" Then
        CloseFlag = False
    End If
'
    Me.Hide
'
End Sub
```

Note that the CloseFlag is set along with the SelectedValue property. These property values are used by the control button you created earlier.

Finally, you need to add a bit of code to make the dialog box more user friendly. The code in Listing 12.23 executes when the user clicks or double-clicks the list. Add this to your project.

TYPE **Listing 12.23. Coding the `Click` and `DblClick` events of the DBList control.**

```
Private Sub DBList1_Click()
'
    SelectedValue = DBList1.BoundText
'
End Sub

Private Sub DBList1_DblClick()
'
    Command1_Click 0
'
End Sub
```

That's all the coding you need to complete the custom control. Now save the control and project. In the next section, you'll test the control in a sample data entry form.

Before you go to the next section, you should compile the dbFind.ocx control. This forces Visual Basic to review all the code and report any coding errors you may have in your project.

Testing the dbFind Custom Control

Now add a new Standard EXE project to the group (select File | Add Project... from the main menu). Use Table 12.3 and Figure 12.20 as guides when building the test form.

12

Figure 12.20.

Laying out the test form.

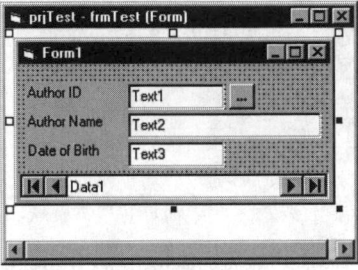

Table 12.3. Test Form layout.

Control	Property	Setting
VB.Form	Name	FrmTest
	Caption	"Form1"
	ClientHeight	1680
	ClientLeft	60
	ClientTop	345
	ClientWidth	3885
	StartUpPosition	2 'CenterScreen
dbFindCtl.dbFind	Name	dbFind1
	Height	315
	Left	2640
	Top	240
	Width	315
VB.Data	Name	Data1
	Align	2 'Align Bottom
	DatabaseName	C:\TYSDBVB5\Source\Data\BOOKS5.MDB
	RecordSource	"Authors"
	Top	1335
	Width	3885
VB.TextBox	Name	Text3
	DataSource	"Data1"
	Height	315
	Left	1380
	Top	960
	Width	1200

12

Control	Property	Setting
VB.TextBox	Name	Text2
	DataSource	"Data1"
	Height	315
	Left	1380
	Top	600
	Width	2400
VB.TextBox	Name	Text1
	DataSource	"Data1"
	Height	315
	Left	1380
	Top	240
	Width	1200
VB.Label	Name	Label3
	Caption	"Date of Birth"
	Height	315
	Left	120
	Top	960
	Width	1215
VB.Label	Name	Label2
	Caption	"Author Name"
	Height	315
	Left	120
	Top	600
	Width	1215
VB.Label	Name	Label1
	Caption	"Author ID"
	Height	315
	Left	120
	Top	240
	Width	1215

12

Note the use of the new dbFind control on the form. You need to add very little code to this project. Listing 12.24 shows the code for the Form_Load event. Add this to your project.

TYPE **Listing 12.24. Coding the Form_Load event.**

```
Private Sub Form_Load()
    '
    ' set database control values
    Data1.DatabaseName = "c:\tysdbvb5\source\data\books5.mdb"
    Data1.RecordSource = "Authors"
    '
    ' set field binding
    Text1.DataField = "AUID"
    Text2.DataField = "Name"
    Text3.DataField = "DOB"
    '
    ' set up dbfind control
    dbFind1.DatabaseName = Data1.DatabaseName
    dbFind1.RecordSource = "SELECT * FROM Authors ORDER BY Name"
    dbFind1.BoundColumn = "AUID"
    dbFind1.ListField = "Name"
    dbFind1.Refresh
    '
    ' some other nice stuff
    Me.Caption = Data1.RecordSource
    '
End Sub
```

The code in Listing 12.24 sets up the data control properties, binds the text boxes to the Data1 control, and then sets up the dbFind1 control properties. You'll notice that the RecordSource for the dbFind1 control is the same data table used for the Data1 control. The only difference is that the dbFind1 control data set is sorted by Name. This means that when the user presses the Find button, the dbFind dialog displays the records in Name order.

NOTE
Most of the code in Listing 12.24 repeats property settings that can be performed at design time. They are set here in order to show you how the Data1 and dbFind1 properties are closely related.

The only other code you need in this form is a list of code in the dbFind1_Selected event that repositions the data pointer to display the record selected by the user. Add the following code to the dbfind1_Selected event:

```
Private Sub dbFind1_Selected(SelectValue As Variant)
    '
    ' re-position record based on return value
    '
    Data1.Recordset.FindFirst Text1.DataField & "=" & SelectValue
    '
End Sub
```

Now save the form (FRMTEST.FRM) and project (PRJTEST.VBP), then run the test form. When you press the Find button, you should see a dialog box that lists all the records in the table, in Name order (see Figure 12.21).

Figure 12.21.

Running the test form.

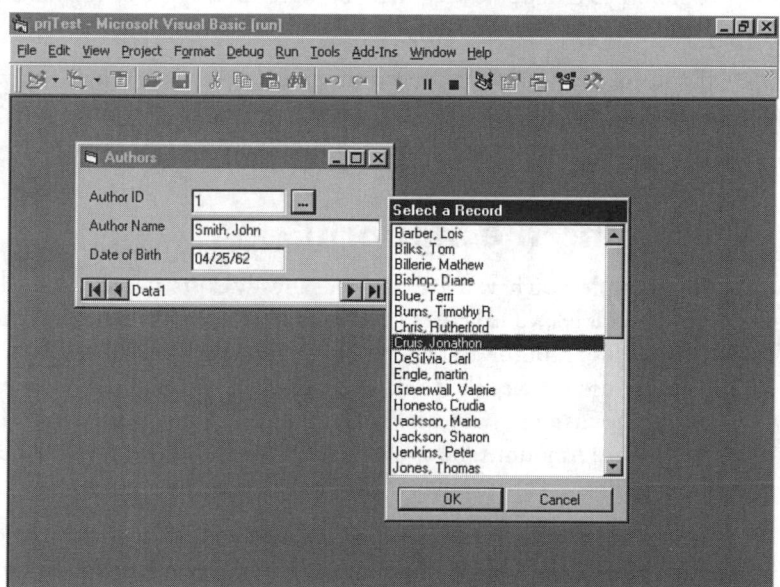

When you select a name from the list (highlight a name and press OK or double-click the name), you'll see that the main form returns to focus and the data pointer is moved to display the selected record. You now have a custom control that offers instant "find" features by adding just a few lines of code to your projects.

Using the Data Grid to Create a Subform

In this last section of the chapter, you'll use the data grid to create one of the most common forms of data entry screens, the Subform. Subforms are data entry forms that actually contain two forms within the same screen. Usually, Subforms are used to combine standard form layout data entry screens with view-only or view and edit lists. For example, if you want to create a form that shows customer information (name, address, and so on) at the top of the form and a list of invoices outstanding for that customer at the bottom of the form, you have a Subform type entry screen.

Typically, Subforms are used to display data tables linked through relationship definitions. In the case just mentioned, the customer information is probably in a single master table, and the invoice data is probably in a related list table that is linked through the customer ID or some other unique field. When you have these types of relationships, Subforms make an excellent way to present data.

If you spend much time programming databases, you'll meet up with the need for a good Subform strategy. Let's go through the process of designing and coding a Subform using Visual Basic 5 data-bound controls, especially the data grid.

Designing the Subform

For example, you have a database that already exists, CH1203.MDB, which contains two tables. The first table is called Header. It contains all the information needed to fill out a header on an invoice or monthly statement, such as CustID, CustName, Address, City, State, and Zip. There is also a table called SalesData. This table contains a list of each invoice currently on file for the customer, and it includes the CustID, Invoice Number, Invoice Description, and the Invoice Amount. The two tables are linked through the CustID field that exists in both tables. There is a one-to-many (Header-to-SalesData) relationship defined for the two tables.

You need to design a form that allows users to browse through the master table (Header), displaying all the address information for review and update. At the same time, you need to provide the user with a view of the invoice data on the same screen. As the customer records are changed, the list of invoices must also be changed. You need a Subform.

Laying Out and Coding the Subform with Visual Basic 5

Start a new project in Visual Basic 5. Lay out the Header table information at the top of the form and the SalesTable information in a grid at the bottom of the form. You need two data controls (one for the Header table and one for the SalesTable), one grid for the sales data, and several label and input controls for the Header data. Use Table 12.4 and Figure 12.22 as guides as you lay out the Subform.

The controls table and Figure 12.22 contain almost all the information you need to design and code the Visual Basic 5 Subform. Notice that all the textbox and label controls have the same name. These are part of a control array. Lay out the first label/textbox pair. Then use the alternate mouse button to copy and repeatedly paste these two buttons until you have all the fields you need for your form.

TIP

Not only is it easier to build forms using data controls because you save a lot of typing, but it also saves workstation resources. To Visual Basic 5, each control is a resource that must be allotted memory for tracking. Control arrays are counted as a single resource, no matter how many members you have in the array.

Figure 12.22.

Laying out the Header/SubForm example.

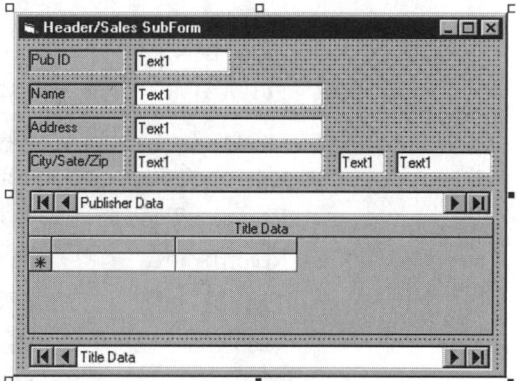

Table 12.4. The Controls for the Subform Project.

Controls	Properties	Settings
Form	Name	frmSubForm
	Caption	Header/Sales SubForm
	Height	4545
	Left	1395
	Top	1335
	Width	6180
Data Control	Name	Data1
	Caption	Publisher Data

continues

Table 12.4. continued

Controls	Properties	Settings
	DatabaseName	`C:\TYSDBVB5\SOURCE\DATA\BOOKS5.MDB`
	EOfAction	2 – AddNew
	Height	300
	Left	120
	RecordsetType	1 – Dynaset
	RecordSource	Publishers
	Top	1800
	Width	5835
Data Control	Name	Data2
	Caption	Titles Data
	DatabaseName	`C:\TYSDBVB5\SOURCE\DATA\BOOKS5.MDB`
	EOFAction	2 – AddNew
	Height	300
	Left	120
	RecordsetType	1 – Dynaset
	RecordSource	Titles
	Top	3780
	Visible	0 – False
	Width	5835
Text Box	Name	Text1
	DataSource	Data1
	DataField	PubID
	Height	300
	Left	1440
	Top	120
	Width	1200
Text Box	Name	Text1
	DataSource	Data1
	DataField	Name
	Height	300

Controls	Properties	Settings
	Left	1440
	Top	540
	Width	2400
Text Box	Name	Text1
	DataSource	Data1
	DataField	Address
	Height	300
	Left	1440
	Top	960
	Width	2400
Text Box	Name	Text1
	DataSource	Data1
	DataField	City
	Height	300
	Left	1440
	Top	1380
	Width	2400
Text Box	Name	Text1
	DataSource	Data1
	DataField	StateProv
	Height	300
	Left	4020
	Top	1380
	Width	600
Text Box	Name	Text1
	DataSource	Data1
	DataField	Zip
	Height	300
	Left	4740
	Top	1380
	Width	1200

continues

12

Table 12.4. continued

Controls	Properties	Settings
Label	Name	Label1
	BorderStyle	1 – Fixed Single
	Caption	PubID
	Height	300
	Left	120
	Top	120
	Width	1200
Label	Name	Label1
	BorderStyle	1 – Fixed Single
	Caption	Name
	Height	300
	Left	120
	Top	540
	Width	1200
Label	Name	Label1
	BorderStyle	1 – Fixed Single
	Caption	Address
	Height	300
	Left	120
	Top	960
	Width	1200
Label	Name	Label1
	Borderstyle	1 – Fixed Single
	Caption	City/State/Zip
	Height	300
	Left	120
	Top	1380
	Width	1200
MSDBGrid	Name	DBGrid1
	Height	1455

Controls	Properties	Settings
	Left	120
	Top	2222
	Width	5835

It would be nice to say that you could build a Subform without using any Visual Basic 5 code, but that's not quite true. You need just over 10 lines of code to get your data grid at the bottom of the form linked to the master table at the top of the form. Place the code in Listing 12.25 in the Data1_Reposition event of the Publishers table data control.

TYPE

Listing 12.25. Code to update the Subform with the Reposition event.

```
Private Sub Data1_Reposition()
    '
    Dim strSQL As String
    Dim strKey As String
    '
    ' create select to load grid
    If Text1(0).Text = "" Then
        strKey = "0"
    Else
        strKey = Trim(Text1(0).Text)
    End If
    '
    strSQL = "SELECT ISBN,Title,YearPub FROM Titles WHERE PubID=" & strKey
    Data2.RecordSource = strSQL  ' load grid-bound data control
    Data2.Refresh    ' refresh data control
    DBGrid1.ReBind   ' refresh grid
    '
End Sub
```

The preceding code is used to create a new SQL SELECT statement using the PubID value of the Publishers table. This SQL statement is used to generate a new data set for the Data2 data control. This is the control that supplies the data grid. Once the new record source has been created, invoke the Refresh method to update the data control and the ReBind method to update the data grid. That's it; there are only eleven lines of Visual Basic code, including the comments. Now save the form as SUBFORM.FRM and the project as SUBFORM.VBP, and run the program. When the form loads, you see the first record in the Header table displayed at the top of the form, and a list of all the outstanding invoices for that customer in the grid at the bottom of the form (see Figure 12.23).

12

Figure 12.23.

*Running the Header/
Subform example.*

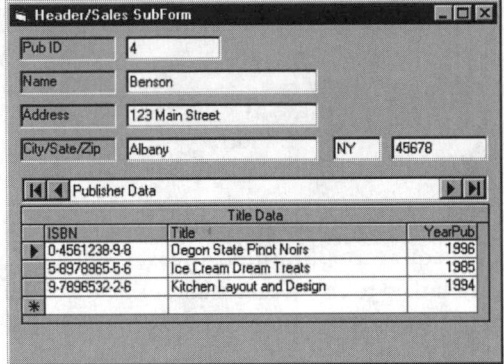

As you browse through the Publishers table, you'll see the data grid is updated, too. You can add records to the data grid or to the Publisher master. If this were a production project, you would add event-trapping features like the ones mentioned in the previous section in order to maintain data integrity. You can also add the dbFind button to the header section of the form.

Summary

Today, you learned how to load and use three of the new data-bound controls that are shipped with Visual Basic 5.

- ☐ The data-bound list box
- ☐ The data-bound combo box
- ☐ The data-bound grid

You learned how to link these new controls to Recordsets using the Visual Basic 5 data controls and how to use these links to update related tables.

You also learned several of the important Visual Basic 5 events associated with the data grid. These events let you create user-friendly data entry routines using just a data control and the data grid.

You also built a new dbFind custom control that uses the DBList control to build a data-bound list of all records in a table. This new control can be used to provide primary key (or some other unique value) selection dialogs to all your Visual Basic data entry forms.

Finally, you drew upon your knowledge of data grids, SQL, and form layout to design and implement a data entry Subform. This form showed a master table at the top and a related list table at the bottom of the form in a data-bound grid.

Quiz

1. What are some of the advantages of using a data-bound list or combo box?

2. What property of the data-bound list box do you set to identify the name of the Recordset object that provides the data to fill the list box?

3. What function does the BoundColumn property of the data-bound list box serve?

4. What data-bound list/combo box properties do you set to identify the destination data set and field to be updated.

5. What properties of the data-bound grid control must be set to allow additions and removal of records?

6. What event of the data-bound grid control would you modify to prompt the user to confirm deletion of a record?

7. Why would you use the column-level events of the data-bound grid control?

8. When would you use the data-bound combo box instead of the data-bound list box?

9. What data-bound grid control method do you use to refresh the grid?

10. In what scenarios would you employ a Subform using a data grid?

Exercises

Assume that you have been assigned the responsibility of maintaining the BIBLIO.MDB database application that ships with Visual Basic 5. Your organization has determined that the information contained in this database will be of value to Help Desk personnel. The Help Desk Manager has come to you and requested a Visual Basic 5 application for Help Desk use.

Build a data form that contains a data-bound list box that displays the Name field from the Publishers table. Once selection is made in this list box, text boxes should display PubID, CompanyName, Address, City, State, Zip, Telephone, and Fax of the publisher selected.

In addition, a listing of all publications of the selected publisher should appear in a data-bound grid Subform. For each entry, display the Title, Year Published, and ISBN from the Titles table.

Hint: You will need to use three data controls for this form.

12

Day 13

Creating Databases with SQL

The earlier chapter on SQL (Day 8, "Selecting Data with SQL") focused on SQL's Data Manipulation Language (DML) keywords. Today's work focuses on SQL's Data Definition Language (DDL) keywords.

On Day 8, you learned how easy it is to select and order data using the SQL SELECT_FROM clause. You also learned that using SQL statements to perform data selection means that your Visual Basic programs work with almost any back-end database server you might encounter in the future.

In today's lesson, you'll learn that you can use SQL statements to create your databases, too. Using SQL keywords to create your data tables, to set relationships, and to create indexes gives your programs an added level of portability. The SQL words you learn today work not only on Microsoft Access-formatted databases, but also on any database format that is SQL compliant. The skills you learn today can be applied to almost every database engine on the market.

By the time you are through with today's lesson, you will be able to use SQL keywords to perform the following tasks:

☐ Create and delete data tables with the CREATE TABLE and DROP TABLE keywords.

☐ Add and delete fields in an existing data table using the ADD COLUMN and DROP COLUMN keywords.

☐ Create and delete indexes using the CREATE INDEX and DROP INDEX keywords.

☐ Define table relationships including foreign keys using the PRIMARY KEY and FOREIGN KEY_REFERENCES keywords.

Throughout today's lesson, you'll use a program called SQL-VB. This is a Visual Basic program that processes SQL scripts. All the commands you learn today are in the form of SQL scripts. You can use the SQL-VB5 program without knowing much about how it was built. However, if you are curious about how SQL-VB5 works, you can refer to Appendix A, "The SQL-VB Project." This appendix walks you through a step-by-step construction of SQL-VB. It also contains information on how to use SQL-VB5 with this book and with other projects you create in the future.

Using the SQL-VB5 Interpreter

Before you begin today's lesson in advanced SQL commands, you'll take a quick tour of the SQL-VB5 program. You'll learn how to use SQL-VB5 to create, edit, and run SQL scripts. The SQL-VB5 Interpreter is a program that reads and executes SQL command scripts. You'll use this program throughout the lesson today. You might also find this program useful in the future for creating and managing SQL databases.

Loading and Running the SQL-VB5 Interpreter

To load the SQL-VB5 Interpreter, locate the TYSDBVB5\SOURCE\SQLVB5 directory that was created from the installation CD (for installation information, refer to the last page of this book). In the Windows Explorer or in File Manager, double-click on the SQLVB5.EXE file (this is a 32-bit application) to start the program. After the program loads, you should see a screen that looks similar to the one in Figure 13.1.

The opening screen is actually a multidocument interface. You can load and run one or more scripts from this interface. To test the system, load and run a simple test script. Using SQL-VB5, select File | Run, and at the Load SQLVB File dialog, locate and select SQLVB01.SQV (see Figure 13.2).

13

Figure 13.1.

The opening screen for the SQL-VB5 *Interpreter.*

Figure 13.2.

Loading the SQLVB01.SQV *SQL script.*

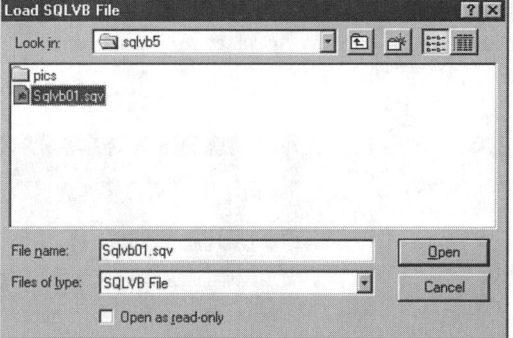

When you select the script, SQL-VB5 begins to read and process the SQL commands in the file. This test script opens the BOOKS5.MDB database and then creates six result sets and displays them on the screen. When the script is completed, you see a dialog box announcing the completion of the script along with several result sets displayed on the screen, as shown in Figure 13.3.

13

Figure 13.3.

The completed
SQLVB01.SQV *script.*

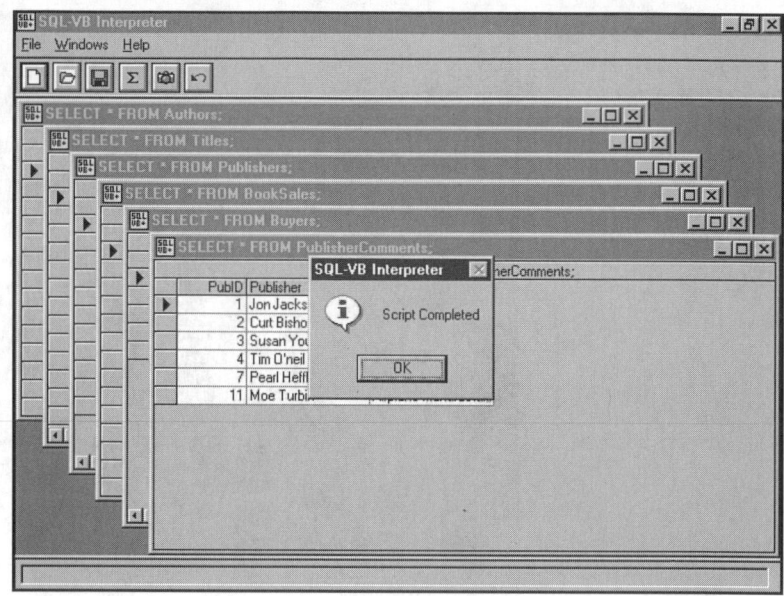

SQL-VB5 creates all result set forms in a cascade starting at the top left of the screen. You can change this to a tiled view by selecting Windows | Tile Horizontal from the main menu (see Figure 13.4).

Figure 13.4.

Tiling the open forms.

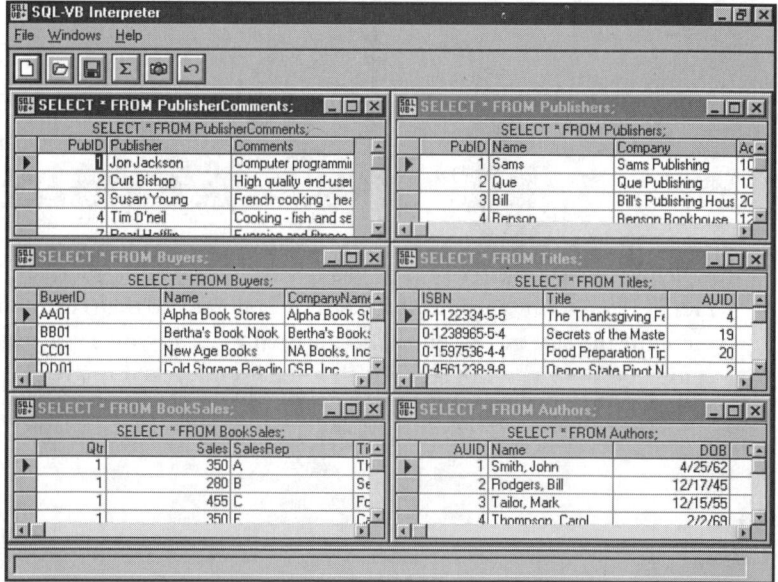

You can also use your mouse pointer to resize, minimize, or maximize any form. You can even resize individual columns and rows within a form. Figure 13.5 shows several of the ways you can alter the view of forms.

Figure 13.5.

Altering the form views within SQL-VB5.

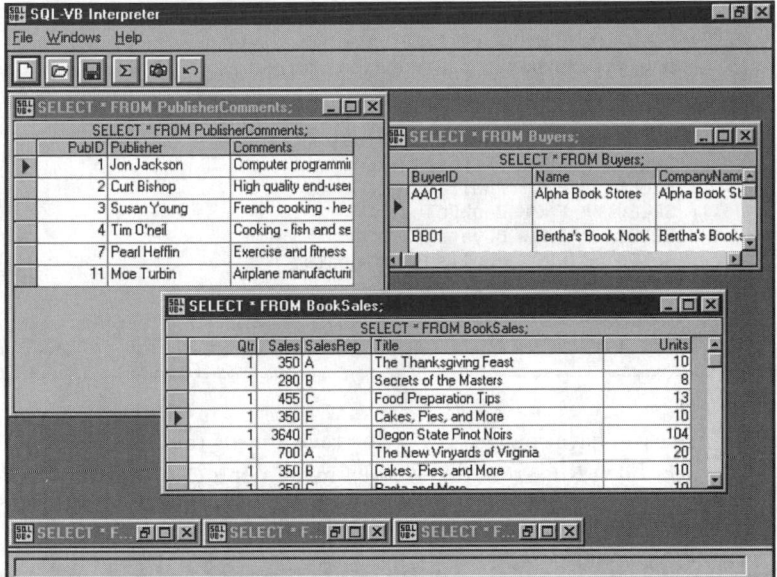

Creating and Editing SQL-VB5 Scripts

You can also use SQL-VB5 to create and edit SQL command scripts. For example, edit the SQLVB01.SQV script you tested earlier. First, load the script for editing by selecting File | Edit from the main menu. Locate and select the SQLVB01.SQV script. When you select the script, SQL-VB5 launches the Notepad editor and loads the selected SQL script.

Let's change the SQL script so that the first result set includes only authors whose AUID is less than 7. To do this, add the text WHERE AUID<7; to the first SELECT statement. Be sure to place the semicolon (;) at the end of the line. SQL-VB5 needs this character to indicate the end of an SQL statement. Also, let's comment out the rest of the view sets for now. You only want to see one result set in this test. To do this, add two slashes (//) to the start of all the other lines that contain SELECT statements. Be sure to place a space after the // comment sign. Your script should now resemble Listing 13.1.

13

TYPE   **Listing 13.1. Modifying a SQL-VB5 script.**

```
//
// test sql command file for sqlvb interpreter
//

// open the database
dbOpen \tysdbvb5\source\data\books5.mdb;

// open some tables to view
SELECT * FROM Authors WHERE AUID<7;
// SELECT * FROM Titles;
// SELECT * FROM Publishers;
// SELECT * FROM BookSales;
// SELECT * FROM Buyers;
// SELECT * FROM PublisherComments;


//
// eof
//
```

After you have changed the script, save it using the File | Save command of Notepad. Now select File | Run from the SQL-VB5 main menu to run the updated SQLVB01.SQV command script. Your results should look similar to those in Figure 13.6.

Figure 13.6.

The results of the edited SQLVB01.SQV *script.*

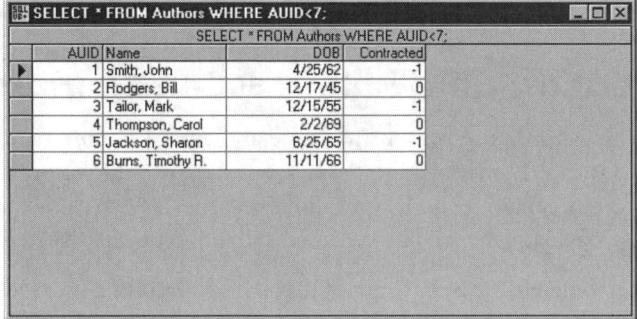

You can create new SQL-VB5 scripts by selecting File | New from the menu and entering any valid SQL statement into the editor. After you've created your script, save it with an .SQV file extension. Then use the File | Run menu option to execute your script.

You need to know a few SQL-VB5 command syntax rules before you can create your own SQL-VB5 scripts. This is covered in the next section.

SQL-VB5 **Command Syntax**

The command syntax for SQL-VB5 is very similar to standard ANSI SQL syntax. In fact, any valid SQL command is a valid SQL-VB5 command. However, there are a few additional commands in SQL-VB5 that you should know about.

Three special command words work in SQL-VB5, but they are not SQL commands. These special commands are used to create, open, and close Microsoft Jet databases. SQL-VB5 also has a comment command. The comment command indicates to SQL-VB5 that the information on this line is for comment only and should not be executed. Finally, each command line must end with a semicolon (;). The semicolon tells SQL-VB5 where the command line ends. The special command words, their meanings, and examples are included in Table 13.1.

Table 13.1. Special SQL-VB5 commands.

SQL-VB5 Command	Example	Description
//	// this is a comment	Any line that begins with // is treated as a comment line and is not processed by the SQL-VB5 Interpreter. Comments cannot be placed at the end of SQL command lines, but must occupy their own line. Don't use the single quotation mark for comments as in Visual Basic because that character is a valid SQL character. Also, you must leave at least one space after the // for SQL-VB5 to recognize it as a comment marker.
dbOpen	dbOpen C:\DATA.MDB;	The dbOpen command opens a Microsoft Jet database. SQL-VB5 can only open and process Microsoft Jet-format databases. A dbOpen command must be executed before any SQL statements are processed.
dbMake	dbMake C:\NEWDATA.MDB;	The dbMake command creates a new, empty Microsoft Jet database on the drive path indicated in the command. When a database is created using the dbMake command, you do not have to issue a dbOpen command.

continues

13

Table 13.1. continued

SQL-VB5 Command	Example	Description
dbClose	dbClose;	The dbClose command closes the Microsoft Jet database that was opened using the dbOpen or dbMake command.
;	SELECT * FROM Table1;	The semicolon is used to indicate the end of a command. Commands can stretch over several lines of text but each command must always end with a semicolon (;).

You now have enough information about SQL-VB5 to use it in the rest of the lesson today. As you go through the examples, you learn more about SQL-VB5 and how you can create your own SQL scripts. If you want to know more about how SQL-VB5 works, see Appendix A.

Why Use SQL to Create and Manage Data Tables?

Before you jump into the details of SQL keywords, let's talk about the advantages of using SQL statements to create and manage your data tables.

Although Visual Basic offers several powerful commands for performing the same functions within a Visual Basic program, you might find that using SQL keywords to perform database management gives you an advantage. By using SQL statements to create and maintain your database structures, you can easily create useful documentation on how your databases are structured. Are you trying to debug a problem at a client site and can't remember how the tables are laid out? If you used a set of SQL statements to create the tables, you can refer to that script when you are solving your client's problems.

It is also easy to generate, test, or sample data tables using SQL statements. If you are working on a database design and are still experimenting with table layouts and relationships, you can quickly put together an SQL DDL script, run it through SQL-VB5, and review the results. If, after experimenting, you find you need a new field in a table, you can alter your existing script and rerun it. Or you can write a short script that makes only the changes you need, preserving any data you have loaded into the existing tables.

You can even use SQL statements to load test data into your new tables. After you have created the tables, you can add SQL statements to your script that load test data into the columns.

This test data can exercise defined relationships, check for data table integrity, and so on. Using an SQL script to load data is an excellent way to perform repeated tests on changing data tables. As you make changes to your table structures, you can use the same data each time until you know you have the results you are looking for.

Also, you can use the same SQL statements to create data tables within other database systems, including Microsoft's SQL Server, Oracle, and others. After you create the test files using Microsoft Access Jet databases, you can then regenerate the tables for other database engines using the same SQL statements. This increases the portability of your application and eases the migration of your data from one database platform to another.

Table Management SQL Keywords

The type of SQL keywords you learn today are the table management keywords. These keywords enable you to create new data tables, alter the structure of existing data tables, and remove existing data tables from the database.

Designing New Tables with CREATE TABLE

The CREATE TABLE keyword allows you to create new tables in an existing database. In its most basic form, the CREATE TABLE statement consists of three parts: the CREATE TABLE clause; a TableName; and a list of column names, column types, and column sizes for each column in the new table. The following example shows a simple CREATE TABLE SQL statement.

```
CREATE TABLE NewTable (Field1 TEXT(30), Field2 INTEGER);
```

This SQL statement creates a data table called NewTable that has two columns. The column named Field1 is a TEXT column 30 bytes long. The column named Field2 is an INTEGER column. Notice that no size was designated for the INTEGER column. Microsoft Access Jet SQL statements only accept size values for TEXT columns. All other columns are set to a predefined length. See Table 2.1 in Day 2, "Creating Databases," for a list of the default field lengths for Microsoft Access Jet data fields.

13

NOTE   If you omit the size definition for the TEXT field, Microsoft Access Jet uses the default value of 255 bytes. Because this can result in rather large tables with empty space, it's a good habit to declare a size for all TEXT fields.

Test this SQL statement by creating the SQL script in Listing 13.2 and running it using the SQL-VB5 application. Start the application and select File | New... to create a new script called SQLVB02.SQV. Enter the following script commands into Notepad.

TYPE **Listing 13.2. Creating the SQLVB02.SQV script.**

```
//
// SQLVB02.SQV - Testing SQL Table Management Keywords
//
// create a new database for our tests
dbMake sqlvb02.mdb;
// create a simple table
CREATE TABLE NewTable (Field1 TEXT(30), Field2 INTEGER);
// show the empty table
SELECT * FROM NewTable;
// eof (end of file)
```

This script creates a new database, creates a new table in the database, and displays the empty table in a result set. Use SQL-VB5 to run the script by selecting File | Run... and locating and loading the SQLVB02.SQV script file. Your results should appear as shown in Figure 13.7. Please note that this screen is followed by several error screens which are a result of executing an SQL statement against an empty table. Simply press OK and move past each message.

Figure 13.7.

Results of the CREATE TABLE *statement.*

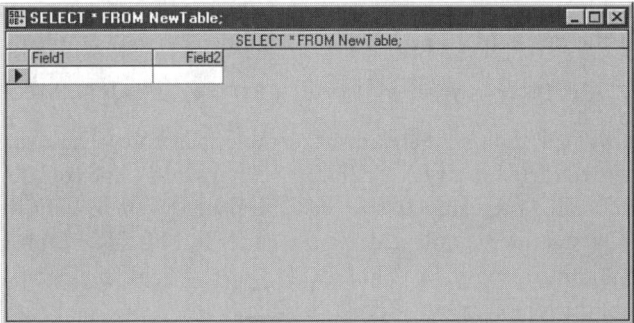

You can also use the PRIMARY KEY command when you CREATE a data table. This can be done by following the name of the primary key field with a CONSTRAINT clause. Use SQL-VB5 to edit the SQLVB02.SQV script so that it sets the Field1 column as a primary key. See Listing 13.3 for an example.

TYPE **Listing 13.3. Adding the** PRIMARY KEY CONSTRAINT.

```
//
// testing SQL Table Management Keywords
//
// create a new database for our tests
dbMake sqlvb02.mdb;
// create a simple table
CREATE TABLE NewTable
    (Field1 TEXT(30) CONSTRAINT PKNewTable PRIMARY KEY,
     Field2 INTEGER);
// show the empty table
SELECT * FROM NewTable;
// eof
```

Notice that the CREATE TABLE SQL statement is spread out over more than one line of text. SQL statements can stretch over several lines, as long as each complete SQL statement ends with a semicolon. The continued lines need not be indented, but doing so makes it easier to read the SQL scripts.

You look at the CONSTRAINT clause in depth a bit later. For now, remember that you can create both primary and foreign keys in a CREATE TABLE statement.

Modifying Tables with ALTER TABLE_ADD COLUMN and DROP COLUMN

There are two forms of the ALTER TABLE statement: the ADD COLUMN form and the DROP COLUMN form. The ADD COLUMN form enables you to add new columns to an existing table without losing any data in the existing columns. Edit the SQLVB02.SQV script using SQL-VB5 so that it matches the script in Listing 13.4.

TYPE **Listing 13.4. Using the** ADD COLUMN **clause.**

13

```
//
// testing SQL Table Management Keywords
//
// create a new database for our tests
dbMake sqlvb02.mdb;
// create a simple table
CREATE TABLE NewTable
    (Field1 TEXT(30) CONSTRAINT PKNewTable PRIMARY KEY,
     Field2 INTEGER);
// add a two new columns
ALTER TABLE NewTable ADD COLUMN Field3 DATE;
ALTER TABLE NewTable ADD COLUMN Field4 CURRENCY;
// show the empty table
SELECT * FROM NewTable;
// eof
```

Notice that you had to add two ALTER TABLE statements to add two columns to the same table. The ALTER TABLE statement can only deal with one column at a time. Run the SQLVB02.SQV script and inspect the results. Your screen should look similar to the one in Figure 13.8.

Figure 13.8.

Results of using ALTER TABLE_ADD COLUMN *keywords.*

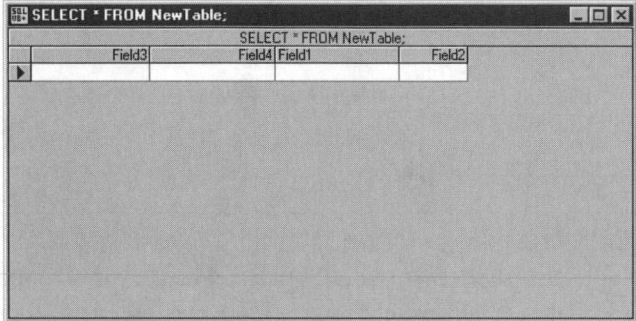

> **NOTE**
>
> Note that the ADD COLUMN clause always adds columns starting at the left-most column in the table. You can always control the order of the columns in a display using the SELECT_FROM clause (see Day 8). If you want to control the physical order of the fields, you must add the fields in a CREATE TABLE statement.

You can also use the ALTER TABLE statement to remove columns from an existing table without losing data in the unaffected columns. This is accomplished using the DROP COLUMN clause. Edit SQLVB02.SQV to match the example in Listing 13.5.

TYPE **Listing 13.5. Using the DROP COLUMN clause.**

```
//
// testing SQL Table Management Keywords
//
// create a new database for our tests
dbMake sqlvb02.mdb;
// create a simple table
CREATE TABLE NewTable
    (Field1 TEXT(30) CONSTRAINT PKNewTable PRIMARY KEY,
     Field2 INTEGER);
// add two new columns
ALTER TABLE NewTable ADD COLUMN Field3 DATE;
ALTER TABLE NewTable ADD COLUMN Field4 CURRENCY;
// drop one of the new columns
ALTER TABLE newTable DROP COLUMN Field3;
// show the empty table
SELECT * FROM NewTable;
// eof
```

13

Run the `SQLVB02.SQV` script and check your results against the screen shown in Figure 13.9.

Figure 13.9.
Results of the ALTER
TABLE_DROP COLUMN
keywords.

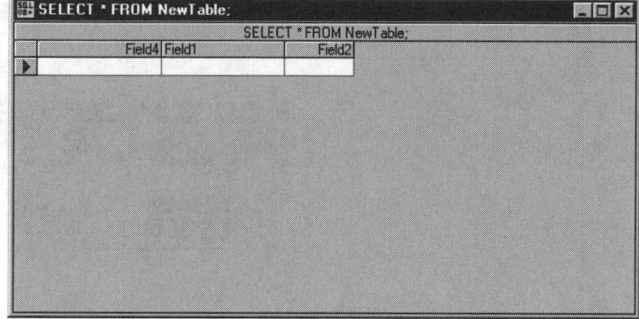

NOTE

You can also use the ALTER TABLE statement to ADD or DROP CONSTRAINTs. We cover CONSTRAINTs in depth later in this chapter.

Deleting Tables with DROP TABLE

You can use the DROP TABLE statement to remove a table from the database. This is often used to remove temporary tables, or it can be used as part of a process that copies data from one table to another or from one database to another. Edit and save `SQLVB02.SQV` to match the code example in Listing 13.6.

TYPE **Listing 13.6. Using the DROP TABLE clause.**

```
//
// testing SQL Table Management Keywords
//
// create a new database for our tests
dbMake sqlvb02.mdb;
// create a simple table
CREATE TABLE NewTable
    (Field1 TEXT(30) CONSTRAINT PKNewTable PRIMARY KEY,
     Field2 INTEGER);
// add two new columns
ALTER TABLE NewTable ADD COLUMN Field3 DATE;
ALTER TABLE NewTable ADD COLUMN Field4 CURRENCY;
// drop one of the new columns
ALTER TABLE NewTable DROP COLUMN Field3;
// remove the table from the database
DROP TABLE NewTable;
// show the empty table
SELECT * FROM NewTable;
// eof
```

13

Save and run the updated SQLVB02.SQV. You should see an SQL error message telling you that it could not find the table NewTable. This happened because the script executed the DROP TABLE statement just before the SELECT_FROM statement. The error message appears in Figure 13.10.

Figure 13.10.
Results of the DROP
TABLE *statement.*

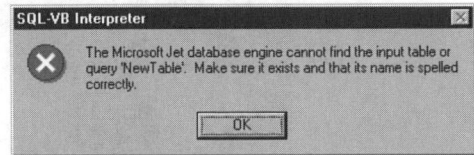

Relationship SQL Keywords

You can create and delete indexes or constraints on a data table using the SQL keywords CREATE INDEX and DROP INDEX, and the CONSTRAINT clause of CREATE TABLE and ALTER TABLE statements. SQL constraints are just indexes with another name. However, CONSTRAINT clauses are usually used with CREATE TABLE statements to establish relationships between one or more tables in the same database. INDEX statements are usually used to add or delete search indexes to existing tables.

Managing Indexes with CREATE INDEX and DROP INDEX

The CREATE INDEX statement is used to create a search index on an existing table. The most basic form of the CREATE INDEX statement is shown in the following line:

```
CREATE INDEX NewIndex ON NewTable (Field1);
```

Several variations on the CREATE INDEX statement allow you to add data integrity to the data table. Table 13.2 shows a list of the various CREATE INDEX options and how they are used.

Table 13.2. The CREATE INDEX options.

CREATE INDEX Statement	Meaning and Use
CREATE INDEX NewIndex ON NewTable(Field1) WITH PRIMARY	Creates a primary key index. A primary key index ensures that each row of the table has a unique value in the index field. No nulls are allowed in the index field.
CREATE UNIQUE INDEX NewIndex ON NewTable(Field1)	Creates a unique index on the designated field. In this example, no two columns could have the same value, but null values would be allowed.

CREATE INDEX Statement	Meaning and Use

`CREATE INDEX NewIndex ON`
`NewTable (Field1)`
`WITH DISALLOW NULL`
	Creates an index that is not unique, but does not allow null columns.

`CREATE INDEX NewIndex ON`
`NewTable (Field1) WITH`
`IGNORE NULL`
	Creates a non-unique index that allows null records in the index column.

Use SQL-VB5 to create a new SQL script that contains the code from Listing 13.7. After you enter the code, save the script as SQLVB03.SQV.

TYPE **Listing 13.7. Testing the relationship SQL keywords.**

```
//
// sqlvb03.sqv - Test Relationship SQL keywords
//
// create a database
dbMake sqlvb03.mdb;
// create a test table to work with
CREATE TABLE NewTable1
    (EmployeeID    TEXT(10),
     LastName      TEXT(30),
     FirstName     TEXT(30),
     LoginName     TEXT(15),
     JobTitle      TEXT(20),
     Department    TEXT(10));
// create primary key
CREATE INDEX PKEmployeeID
   ON NewTable1(EmployeeID) WITH PRIMARY;
// create unique key column
CREATE UNIQUE INDEX UKLoginName
   ON NewTable1(LoginName) WITH IGNORE NULL;
// create non-null column
CREATE INDEX IKJobTitle
   ON NewTable1(JobTitle) WITH DISALLOW NULL;
// create multi-column sort key
CREATE INDEX SKDeptSort
   ON NewTable1(Department,LastName,FirstName);
// show empty table
SELECT * FROM NewTable1;
// eof
```

The preceding SQL script shows several examples of the CREATE INDEX statement. You can use SQL-VB5 to run this script. Your screen should look similar to the one in Figure 13.11.

13

Figure 13.11.
Results of
`SQLVB03.SQV` *script.*

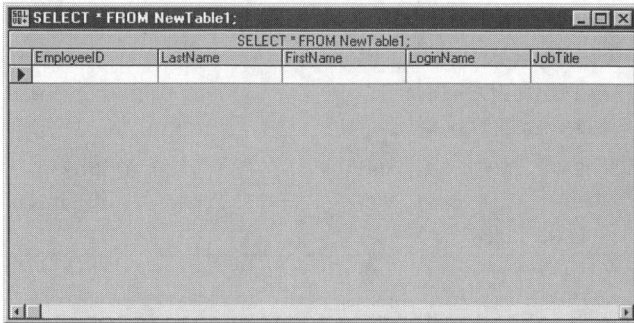

The code example in Listing 13.7 introduced a naming convention for indexes. This convention is widely used by SQL programmers. All primary key indexes should start with the letters PK (PKEmployeeID). All keys created for sorting purposes should begin with the letters SK (SKDeptSort). All index keys that require unique values should begin with UK (UKLoginName). All keys that define foreign key relationships should start with FK. (You learn more about foreign keys in the next section.) Finally, any other index keys should start with IK (IKJobTitle) to identify them as index keys.

Using the ASC and DESC Keywords in the INDEX Statement

You can control the index order by adding ASC (ascending) or DESC (descending) keywords to the CREATE INDEX SQL statement. For example, to create an index on the LastName column, but listing from Zilckowicz to Anderson, you use the following CREATE INDEX statement:

```
CREATE INDEX SKLastName ON NewTable1(LastName DESC);
```

Notice that the DESC goes inside the parentheses. If you want to control the index order on a multiple column index, you can use the following CREATE INDEX statement:

```
CREATE INDEX SKDeptSort ON NewTable1(Department ASC, LastName DESC);
```

If you omit an order word from the CREATE INDEX clause, SQL uses the default ASC order.

Using Indexes to Speed Data Access

In Listing 13.7, the index SKDeptSort is a special index key. This is a *sort key index*. Sort key indexes can be used to speed data access while performing single-record lookups (using the Visual Basic Find method), or for speeding report processing by ordering the data before running a list report. Sort key indexes are not used to enforce data integrity rules or perform data entry validation.

13

Although sort key indexes are very common in non-relational databases, they are not often used in relational databases. All the related indexes in a database must be updated by the database engine each time a data table is updated. If you have created several sort key indexes, you might begin to see a performance degradation when dealing with large data files or when dealing with remote (ODBC-connected) databases. For this reason, we do not recommend extensive use of sort key indexes in your database.

Using Indexes to Add Database Integrity

You have just about all the possible indexes created in the SQLVB03.SQV example. Many of the indexes serve as database integrity enforcers. In fact, only one of the indexes is meant to be used as a tool for ordering the data (SKDeptSort). All the other indexes in SQLVB03.SQV add database integrity features to the table. This is an important point. In SQL databases, you have much more opportunity to build database editing and field-level enforcement into your database structures than you do with non-relational desktop databases. When you use the database enforcement options of SQL databases, you can greatly decrease the amount of Visual Basic code you need to write to support data entry routines. Also, by storing the database integrity enforcement in the database itself, all other programs that access and update the database have to conform to the same rules. The rules are no longer stored in your program; they're stored in the database itself!

PRIMARY KEY Enforcement

The PRIMARY KEY index (PKEmployeeID) is familiar to you by now. By defining the index as the primary key, no record is allowed to contain a NULL value in the column EmployeeID, and every record must contain a unique value in the EmployeeID column.

IGNORE NULL UNIQUE Enforcement

The index key UKLoginName allows records in the table that have this field blank (IGNORE NULL). However, if a user enters data into this column, the database checks the other records in the table to make sure that the new entry is unique (UNIQUE keyword). This shows an excellent method for enforcing uniqueness on columns that are not required to have input. For example, if you have an input form that allows users to enter their social security number, but does not require that they do so, you can ensure that the value for the field is unique by using the IGNORE NULL and UNIQUE keywords in the INDEX definition.

DISALLOW NULL Enforcement

The index key IKJobTitle is another example of using the SQL database engine to enforce data integrity rules. By defining the IKJobTitle index as DISALLOW NULL, you have set a data rule that defines this field as a required field. No record can be saved to the data table unless it has a valid value in the JobTitle column. Notice that you have not required that the value be unique. That would require every person in the database to have a unique job title. Instead, you allow duplicate job titles in this column. In real life, you would probably want to check the value entered here against a list of valid job titles. That involves creating a foreign key relationship using the CONSTRAINT keyword. Read the next section for more on CONSTRAINTs.

Managing Relationships with CONSTRAINTs

CONSTRAINTs are really the same as indexes from the standpoint of SQL statements. The CONSTRAINT keyword is used to create indexes that add data integrity to your database. You must use the CONSTRAINT keyword with the CREATE TABLE or ALTER TABLE SQL statement. There is no such thing in Microsoft Access Jet SQL as CREATE CONSTRAINT.

There are three forms of the CONSTRAINT clause:

- [ ] PRIMARY KEY
- [ ] UNIQUE
- [ ] FOREIGN KEY

Microsoft Access SQL syntax does not allow you to use the IGNORE NULL or DISALLOW NULL keywords within the CONSTRAINT clause. If you want to create data integrity indexes that include the IGNORE NULL or DISALLOW NULL keywords, you have to use the CREATE INDEX keyword to define your index.

Using the PRIMARY KEY CONSTRAINT

The most commonly used CONSTRAINT clause is the PRIMARY KEY CONSTRAINT. This is used to define the column (or set of columns) that contains the primary key for the table. The SQL-VB5 script in Listing 13.8 creates a new database and a single table that contains two fields, one of which is the primary key column for the table. The other field is a MEMO field. MEMO fields can contain any type of free-form text and cannot be used in any CONSTRAINT or INDEX definition.

TYPE   **Listing 13.8. Testing the PRIMARY KEY CONSTRAINT.**

```
//
// sqlvb04.sqv - Test CONSTRAINT SQL keyword
//
// create a database
dbMake sqlvb04.mdb;
// create jobs title table
CREATE TABLE JobsTable
    (JobTitle TEXT (20) CONSTRAINT PKJobTitle PRIMARY KEY,
     JobDesc  MEMO
```

13

```
    );
// show the table
SELECT * FROM JobsTable;
// eof
```

Enter this code into the SQL-Visual Basic editor, save the script as SQLVB04.SQV and execute it. You see a simple table that shows two fields. See Figure 13.12 for an example.

Figure 13.12.

Defining the
PRIMARY KEY
CONSTRAINT.

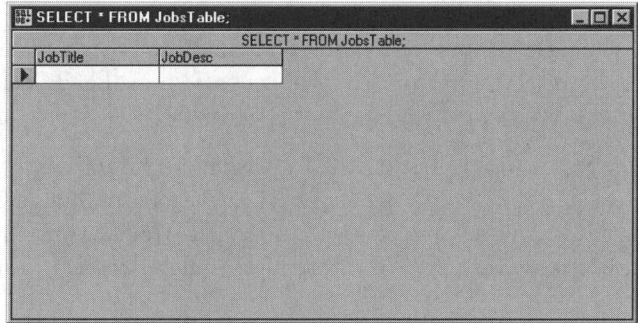

The SQL script in Listing 13.9 performs the same task, except it uses the CREATE INDEX keyword to define the primary key index.

TYPE   **Listing 13.9. Using CREATE INDEX to define the PRIMARY KEY.**

```
//
// create index using CREATE INDEX keywords
//
// create database
dbMake sqlvb04.mdb;
// create table
CREATE TABLE JobsTable
    (JobTitle TEXT(20),
     JobDesc MEMO
    );
// create index
CREATE INDEX PKJobTitle ON JobsTable(JobTitle) WITH PRIMARY;
// eof
```

13

Although the code examples in Listing 13.8 and Listing 13.9 both perform the same task, the first code example (Listing 13.8) is the preferred method for creating primary key indexes. Listing 13.8 documents the creation of the index at the time the table is created. This is easier to understand and easier to maintain over time. It is possible to create primary key indexes using the CREATE INDEX statement, but this can lead to problems. If you attempt to use the CREATE INDEX_PRIMARY KEY statement on a table that already has a primary key index defined, you get a database error. It is best to avoid this error by limiting the creation of primary key indexes to CREATE TABLE statements.

Using the UNIQUE KEY CONSTRAINT

Another common use of the CONSTRAINT clause is in the creation of UNIQUE indexes. By default, the index key created using the UNIQUE CONSTRAINT clause allows null entries in the identified columns. However, when data is entered into the column, that data must be unique or the database engine returns an error message. This is the same as using the IGNORE NULL keyword in the CREATE INDEX statement. You should also note that you cannot use the DISALLOW NULL keywords when creating a UNIQUE CONSTRAINT clause. By default, all keys created using the UNIQUE CONSTRAINT are IGNORE NULL index keys.

The SQL script in Listing 13.10 shows a new column in the JobsTable data table that was created in the last SQL-VB5 script. The new column, BudgetCode, is defined as an optional data column that must contain unique data. Update your version of the SQLVB04.SQV script, save it, and execute it. Your result set should resemble the one shown in Figure 13.13.

TYPE   **Listing 13.10. Adding a UNIQUE CONSTRAINT.**

```
//
// sqlvb04.sqv - Test CONSTRAINT SQL keyword
//
// create a database
dbMake sqlvb04.mdb;
// create jobs title table
CREATE TABLE JobsTable
   (JobTitle TEXT (20) CONSTRAINT PKJobTitle PRIMARY KEY,
    BudgetCode TEXT(10) CONSTRAINT UKJobCode UNIQUE,
    JobDesc  MEMO
    );
// show table
SELECT * FROM JobsTable;
// eof
```

Figure 13.13.

Defining a UNIQUE CONSTRAINT *index.*

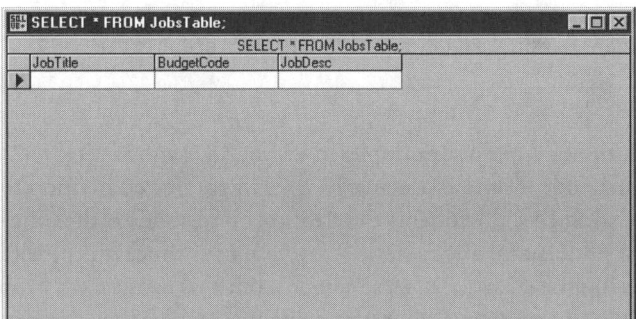

You can use the UNIQUE CONSTRAINT clause in a multicolumn index. This is especially handy if you have a data table containing more than one field that must be evaluated when deciding uniqueness. For example, what if the preceding data table, in addition to BudgetCode, had BudgetPrefix and BudgetSuffix, too? You can make sure that the combination of the three fields is always unique by building a multicolumn CONSTRAINT clause. Use the code example in Listing 13.11 as a guide. Update your SQLVB04.SQV script to match the example in Listing 13.11 and execute it to make sure you have written the syntax correctly.

TYPE **Listing 13.11. Defining a multicolumn UNIQUE CONSTRAINT.**

```
//
// sqlvb04.sqv - Test CONSTRAINT SQL keyword
//
// create a database
dbMake sqlvb04.mdb;
// create jobs title table
CREATE TABLE JobsTable
   (JobTitle TEXT (20) CONSTRAINT PKJobTitle PRIMARY KEY,
    BudgetPrefix TEXT(5),
    BudgetCode   TEXT(10),
    BudgetSuffix TEXT(5),
    JobDesc MEMO,
    CONSTRAINT UKBudget UNIQUE (BudgetPrefix,BudgetCode,BudgetSuffix)
   );
// show table
SELECT * FROM JobsTable;
// eof
```

Once the script has executed, your screen should look similar to the one in Figure 13.14.

Figure 13.14.

The results of a multicolumn CONSTRAINT *clause.*

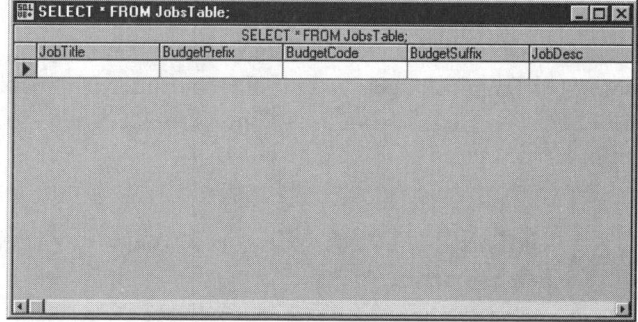

You should also be aware of an important difference between the single-column and multicolumn CONSTRAINT clause formats. Notice that when you are defining a *single-column* CONSTRAINT, you place the CONSTRAINT clause directly after the column definition *without* a comma between the column type and the CONSTRAINT keyword. In the *multicolumn*

CONSTRAINT clause, you separate the CONSTRAINT clause *with* a comma and enclose the column names within parentheses. Mixing these two formats can lead to frustration when you are trying to debug an SQL script!

> **TIP**
>
> Think of it this way. In the case of a single-column CONSTRAINT, these are additional qualifiers of the column; the constraint belongs *within* the column definition. A multicolumn CONSTRAINT, however, is a standalone definition that is not an extension of any one column definition. For this reason, multicolumn constraints are treated as if they are on an equal level with a column definition. They stand alone in the column list.

Using the FOREIGN KEY_REFERENCES Relationship

The most powerful of the CONSTRAINT formats is the FOREIGN KEY_REFERENCES format. This format is used to establish relationships between tables. Commonly, a FOREIGN KEY relationship is established between a small table containing a list of valid column entries (usually called a *validation table*) and another table. The second table usually has a column defined with the same name as the primary key column in the validation table. By establishing a foreign key relationship between the two files, you can enforce a database rule that says the only valid entries in a given table are those values that already exist in the primary key column of the validation table. Once again, you are using the database engine to store data integrity rules. This reduces your volume of Visual Basic code and increases database integrity.

Let's use the script from Listing 13.11 (SQLVB04.SQV) to create a foreign key relationship. You already have a table defined—JobsTable. This is an excellent example of a validation table. It has few fields and has a single column defined as the primary key. Now let's add another table—the EmpsTable. This table holds basic information about employees, including their respective job titles. Listing 13.12 shows modifications to SQLVB04.SQV that include the definition of the EmpsTable data table.

TYPE **Listing 13.12. Adding a PRIMARY KEY CONSTRAINT to the EmpsTable.**

```
//
// sqlvb04.sqv - Test CONSTRAINT SQL keyword
//
// create a database
dbMake sqlvb04.mdb;
// create jobs title table
CREATE TABLE JobsTable
    (JobTitle TEXT (20) CONSTRAINT PKJobTitle PRIMARY KEY,
```

13

```
      BudgetPrefix TEXT(5),
      BudgetCode   TEXT(10),
      BudgetSuffix TEXT(5),
      JobDesc MEMO,
      CONSTRAINT UKBudget UNIQUE (BudgetPrefix,BudgetCode,BudgetSuffix)
      );
// create a test table to work with
CREATE TABLE EmpsTable
   (EmployeeID    TEXT(10) CONSTRAINT PKEmployeeID PRIMARY KEY,
    LastName      TEXT(30),
    FirstName     TEXT(30),
    LoginName     TEXT(15),
    JobTitle      TEXT(20),
    Department    TEXT(10)
    );
// show empty table
SELECT * FROM JobsTable;
SELECT * FROM EmpsTable;
// eof
```

The SQL-VB5 script in Listing 13.12 defines the EmpsTable with only one CONSTRAINT—that of the PRIMARY KEY index. Now let's define a relationship between the EmpsTable.JobTitle column and the JobsTable.JobTitle column. You do this by using the FOREIGN KEY CONSTRAINT syntax. The modified SQLVB04.SQV is shown in Listing 13.13.

TYPE | **Listing 13.13. Adding the FOREIGN KEY_REFERENCES CONSTRAINT.**

```
//
// sqlvb04.sqv - Test CONSTRAINT SQL keyword
//
// create a database
dbMake sqlvb04.mdb;
// create jobs title table
CREATE TABLE JobsTable
   (JobTitle TEXT (20) CONSTRAINT PKJobTitle PRIMARY KEY,
    BudgetPrefix TEXT(5),
    BudgetCode   TEXT(10),
    BudgetSuffix TEXT(5),
    JobDesc MEMO,
    CONSTRAINT UKBudget UNIQUE (BudgetPrefix,BudgetCode,BudgetSuffix)
    );
// create a test table to work with
CREATE TABLE EmpsTable
   (EmployeeID    TEXT(10) CONSTRAINT PKEmployeeID PRIMARY KEY,
    LastName      TEXT(30),
    FirstName     TEXT(30),
    LoginName     TEXT(15),
    JobTitle      TEXT(20) CONSTRAINT FKJobTitle REFERENCES JobsTable(JobTitle),
    Department    TEXT(10)
    );
// show empty table
SELECT * FROM JobsTable;
SELECT * FROM EmpsTable;
// eof
```

13

Notice that the exact SQL syntax for single-column foreign key indexes is

```
CONSTRAINT IndexName REFERENCES Tablename(ColumnName)
```

As long as the column name you are referencing defines the PRIMARY KEY of the referenced table, you can omit the (ColumnName) portion of the CONSTRAINT clause. However, it is good programming practice to include the column name for clarity.

Use the SQL-VB5 editor window to load SQLVB04.SQV. Modify the script to match the code in Listing 13.13, save it, and run the script. Your screen should resemble Figure 13.15.

Figure 13.15.

A foreign key constraint cascades the related tables on-screen.

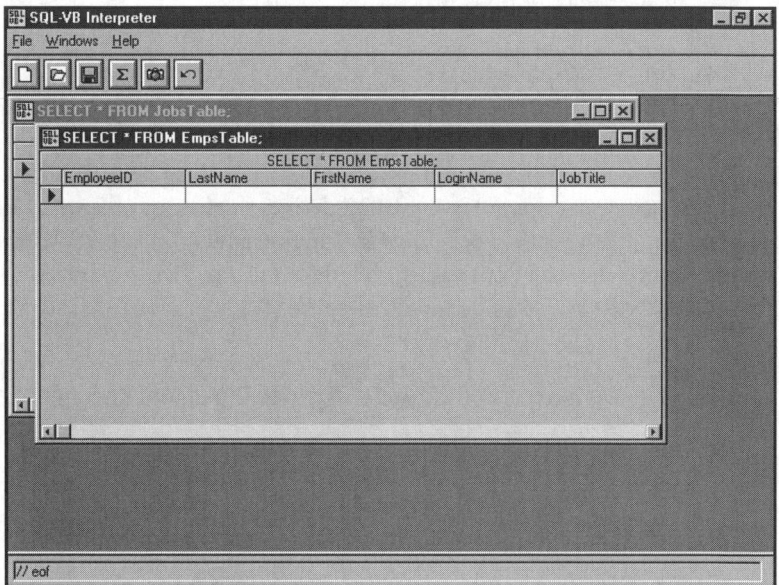

What you have defined here is a rule that tells the Microsoft Jet database engine that, any time a user enters data into the EmpsTable.JobTitle column, the engine should refer to the JobsTable.JobTitle column to make sure that the value entered in EmpsTable.JobTitle can be found in one of the rows of JobsTable.JobTitle. If not, return an error message to the user and do not save the record to the data table. All that is done without writing any input validation code at all!

You can set up foreign key relations between any two columns in any two tables. They need not have the same column name, but they must have the same data type. For example, you can add a table to the SQLVB04.MDB database that holds information about job titles and pay grades. However, in this table the column that holds the job title is called JobName. Enter the script in Listing 13.14, save it, and execute it. See Figure 13.16 for a guide.

13

**Listing 13.14. Creating a foreign key relationship on
unmatched field names.**

TYPE

```
//
// sqlvb04.sqv - Test CONSTRAINT SQL keyword
//
// create a database
dbMake sqlvb04.mdb;
// create jobs title table
CREATE TABLE JobsTable
    (JobTitle TEXT (20) CONSTRAINT PKJobTitle PRIMARY KEY,
     BudgetPrefix TEXT(5),
     BudgetCode   TEXT(10),
     BudgetSuffix TEXT(5),
     JobDesc MEMO,
     CONSTRAINT UKBudget UNIQUE (BudgetPrefix,BudgetCode,BudgetSuffix)
    );
// create job pay grade table
CREATE TABLE PayGrades
    (GradeID   TEXT(5)  CONSTRAINT PKGradeID PRIMARY KEY,
     JobName   TEXT(20) CONSTRAINT FKJobName REFERENCES JobsTable(JobTitle),
     PayMin    CURRENCY,
     PayMax    CURRENCY
    );

// create a test table to work with
CREATE TABLE EmpsTable
   (EmployeeID  TEXT(10) CONSTRAINT PKEmployeeID PRIMARY KEY,
    LastName    TEXT(30),
    FirstName   TEXT(30),
    LoginName   TEXT(15),
    JobTitle    TEXT(20) CONSTRAINT FKJobTitle REFERENCES JobsTable(JobTitle),
    Department  TEXT(10)
    );
// show empty table
SELECT * FROM JobsTable;
SELECT * FROM PayGrades;
SELECT * FROM EmpsTable;
// eof
```

13

Notice that the column PayGrades.JobName does not have the same name as its referenced column (JobsTable.JobTitle). You can still define a foreign key relationship for these columns. This relationship operates exactly the same as the one defined for EmpsTable.JobTitle and JobsTable.JobTitle.

It is also important to point out the order in which you must create tables when you are establishing foreign key constraints. You must always create the *referenced* table before you refer to it in a CONSTRAINT clause. Failure to adhere to this rule results in a database error when you run your SQL-VB5 script. SQL must see that the table exists before a foreign key reference to it can be established.

Figure 13.16.

Results of a foreign key constraint on unmatched column names.

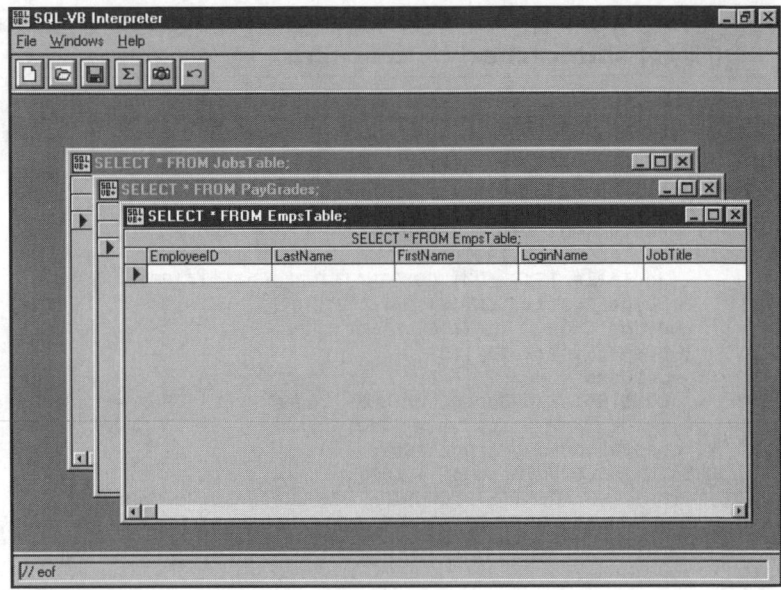

It is also possible to create a multicolumn foreign key constraint. When you create multicolumn foreign key constraints, you must reference the same number of columns on each side of the relationship. For example, if you have a primary key index called PKBudgetCode that contains three columns, any foreign key constraint you define in another table that references PKBudgetCode must also contain three columns.

The example in Listing 13.15 shows an added foreign key constraint in the JobsTable. This constraint sets up a relationship between the Budget columns in the BudgetTrack table and JobsTable. Make the changes to the SQLVB04.SQV script and execute it to check for errors. See Figure 13.17 to compare your results.

TYPE

Listing 13.15. Creating a multicolumn foreign key constraint.

```
// create a database
dbMake sqlvb04.mdb;
// create budget tracking file
CREATE TABLE BudgetTrack
    (BudgetPrefix TEXT(5),
     BudgetCode   TEXT(10),
     BudgetSuffix TEXT(5),
     CONSTRAINT PKBudgetCode PRIMARY KEY (BudgetPrefix,BudgetCode,BudgetSuffix),
     AnnBudgetAmt CURRENCY,
     YTDActualAmt CURRENCY
     );
// create jobs title table
CREATE TABLE JobsTable
```

13

```
     (JobTitle TEXT (20) CONSTRAINT PKJobTitle PRIMARY KEY,
      BudgetPrefix TEXT(5),
      BudgetCode   TEXT(10),
      BudgetSuffix TEXT(5),
      JobDesc MEMO,
      CONSTRAINT FKBudget
         FOREIGN KEY (BudgetPrefix,BudgetCode,BudgetSuffix)
         REFERENCES  BudgetTrack
     );
// create job pay grade table
CREATE TABLE PayGrades
   (GradeID  TEXT(5)   CONSTRAINT PKGradeID PRIMARY KEY,
    JobName   TEXT(20) CONSTRAINT FKJobName REFERENCES JobsTable(JobTitle),
    PayMin    CURRENCY,
    PayMax    CURRENCY
    );
// create a test table to work with
CREATE TABLE EmpsTable
   (EmployeeID  TEXT(10) CONSTRAINT PKEmployeeID PRIMARY KEY,
    LastName    TEXT(30),
    FirstName   TEXT(30),
    LoginName   TEXT(15),
    JobTitle    TEXT(20) CONSTRAINT FKJobTitle REFERENCES JobsTable(JobTitle),
    Department  TEXT(10)
    );
// show empty table
SELECT * FROM JobsTable;
SELECT * FROM EmpsTable;
SELECT * FROM PayGrades;
SELECT * FROM BudgetTrack;
// eof
```

Figure 13.17.

The results of adding a multicolumn foreign key constraint.

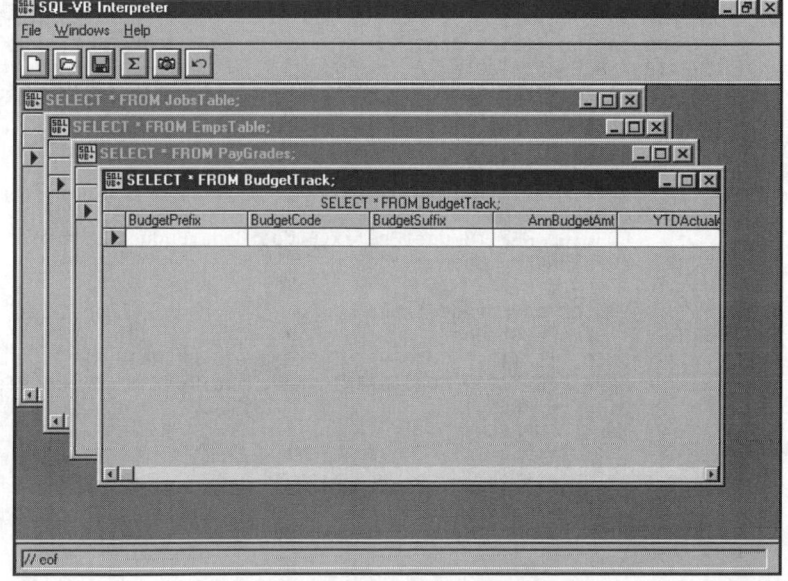

13

Notice that the syntax for adding multicolumn foreign key constraints differs from that used when creating single-column foreign key relationships. When creating multicolumn foreign key relationships, you have to actually use the keywords FOREIGN KEY. Also, you list the columns in parentheses in the same order in which they are listed in the referenced key for the referenced table.

Using ALTER TABLE to ADD and DROP Constraints

You can also use the ALTER TABLE statement to add constraints or drop constraints from existing data tables. The code example in Listing 13.16 adds a new constraint to an existing table, and then removes it. You should be careful adding or dropping constraints outside of the CREATE TABLE statement. Although SQL allows you to do this, it can often lead to data integrity errors if data already exists within the target table. We recommend that you only establish CONSTRAINTs at the time you create the table using the CREATE TABLE statement.

TYPE   **Listing 13.16. Using ALTER TABLE to ADD and DROP constraints.**

```
// create a database
dbMake sqlvb04.mdb;
// create budget tracking file
CREATE TABLE BudgetTrack
    (BudgetPrefix TEXT(5),
     BudgetCode   TEXT(10),
     BudgetSuffix TEXT(5),
     CONSTRAINT PKBudgetCode PRIMARY KEY (BudgetPrefix,BudgetCode,BudgetSuffix),
     AnnBudgetAmt CURRENCY,
     YTDActualAmt CURRENCY
    );
// create jobs title table
CREATE TABLE JobsTable
    (JobTitle TEXT (20) CONSTRAINT PKJobTitle PRIMARY KEY,
     BudgetPrefix TEXT(5),
     BudgetCode    TEXT(10),
     BudgetSuffix TEXT(5),
     JobDesc MEMO,
     CONSTRAINT FKBudget
        FOREIGN KEY (BudgetPrefix,BudgetCode,BudgetSuffix)
        REFERENCES  BudgetTrack
    );
// create job pay grade table
CREATE TABLE PayGrades
    (GradeID TEXT(5)  CONSTRAINT PKGradeID PRIMARY KEY,
     JobName  TEXT(20) CONSTRAINT FKJobName REFERENCES JobsTable(JobTitle),
     PayMin   CURRENCY,
     PayMax   CURRENCY
    );
// create a test table to work with
CREATE TABLE EmpsTable
```

13

```
  (EmployeeID  TEXT(10) CONSTRAINT PKEmployeeID PRIMARY KEY,
   LastName     TEXT(30),
   FirstName    TEXT(30),
   LoginName    TEXT(15),
   JobTitle     TEXT(20) CONSTRAINT FKJobTitle REFERENCES JobsTable(JobTitle),
   Department   TEXT(10)
   );
// use alter table to add and drop a constraint
ALTER TABLE EmpsTable ADD CONSTRAINT FKMoreJobs
   FOREIGN KEY (JobTitle) REFERENCES JobsTable(JobTitle);
ALTER TABLE EmpsTable DROP CONSTRAINT FKMoreJobs;

// show empty table
SELECT * FROM JobsTable;
SELECT * FROM EmpsTable;
SELECT * FROM PayGrades;
SELECT * FROM BudgetTrack;
// eof
```

In today's lesson, you saw SQL keywords that create and alter tables and establish table indexes and relationship constraints. Now you are ready for tomorrow's lesson, in which you learn the SQL keywords that you can use to add data to the tables you have created. You'll also see keywords that you can use to copy tables, including the data.

Summary

In today's lesson you learned how to create, alter, and delete database table structures using DDL (Data Definition Language) SQL keywords. You also learned that using DDL statements to build tables, create indexes, and establish relationships is an excellent way to automatically document table layouts. You learned how to maintain database structures using the following DDL keywords:

- [ ] CREATE TABLE enables you to create entirely new tables in your existing database.

- [ ] DROP TABLE enables you to completely remove a table, including any data that is already in the table.

- [ ] ALTER TABLE enables you to ADD a new column or DROP an existing column from the table without losing existing data in the other columns.

- [ ] CREATE INDEX and DROP INDEX enable you to create indexes that can enforce data integrity or speed data access.

- [ ] The CONSTRAINT clause can be added to the CREATE TABLE or ALTER TABLE statement to define relationships between tables using the FOREIGN KEY clause.

13

Quiz

1. What are the benefits of using SQL to create and manage data tables?

2. What is the format of the CREATE TABLE statement?

3. What is the default size of a Microsoft Jet TEXT field?

4. What SQL statement do you use to add a column to a table? What is its format?

5. What SQL statement do you use to remove a table from a database? What is the format of this statement?

6. What SQL statement creates an index to a data table?

7. What are the three forms of the CONSTRAINT clause?

Exercise

You have been assigned the responsibility of building a database of customers for your company. After careful review of the business processes and interviews with other users, you have determined that the following data must be maintained for the Customer database:

Table	Name	Field Type
CustomerType	CustomerType	TEXT(6)
	Description	TEXT(30)
Customers	CustomerID	TEXT(10)
	Name	TEXT(30)
	CustomerType	TEXT(6)
	Address	TEXT(30)
	City	TEXT(30)
	State	TEXT(30)
	Zip	TEXT(10)
	Phone	TEXT(14)
	FAX	TEXT(14)

Use SQL-VB5 to build this structure. Include a primary key for each table and an index on Zip in the Customers table. Include any foreign key relationships that you think would increase database integrity. Name your database CH13EX.MDB. (You can use any path that you like for the .MDB file).

Day 14

Error Handling in Visual Basic 5

Today's lesson covers a very important aspect of programming—handling runtime errors. Although you should always work to make sure your program can anticipate any problems that might occur while a user is running your software, you can't account for every possibility. That's why every good program should have a solid error-handling system.

Today you learn just what an error handler is and why error handlers are so important. You also learn about some of the inner workings of Visual Basic and how they affect error handling.

You learn about the difference between local error-handling methods and global error-handling methods. You also learn the advantages and disadvantages of each method. You see the various types of errors your program is likely to encounter and get some guidelines on how to handle each type of error.

You also learn about the Err object and the Error collection and how to use these objects to improve the accuracy of error reporting within your application. You also learn how to use the `Raise` method of the Err object to flag errors from within custom controls or OLE Server objects.

You also learn how to create error logs to keep track of errors that occur in your program. You learn how to create a trace log to analyze your programs. And you learn how you can write your programs to turn these features on or off without having to rewrite program code.

Finally, you build an OLE Server DLL that contains an improved error handler, an error logging facility, and a module trace routine. You can use this new OLE Server in all your future VBA-compliant programming projects.

Error Handling in General

Error handling is an essential part of any program. No program is complete unless it has good error handling. It is important to write your programs in a way that reduces the chance that errors occur, but you won't be able to think of everything. Errors do happen! Well-designed programs don't necessarily have fewer errors; they just handle them better.

Writing error handlers is not difficult. In fact, you can add consistent error handling to your program by adding only a few lines of code to each module. The difficult part of writing good error handlers is knowing what to expect and how to handle the unexpected. You learn how to do both in today's lesson.

Adding error handling to your program makes your program seem much more polished and friendly to your users. Nothing is more annoying—or frightening—to a user than seeing the screen freeze up, hearing a startling beep, or watching the program (and any file the user had been working on) suddenly disappear from the screen. This only needs to happen a few times before the user vows never to use your program again.

Polite error messages, recovery routines that allow users to fix their own mistakes or correct hardware problems, and opportunities for the user to save any open files before the program halts because of errors are all essential parts of a good error-handling strategy.

Error Handling in Visual Basic

Writing error handlers in Visual Basic is a bit trickier than in most PC languages. There are several reasons for this. First, Visual Basic follows an *event-driven* language model, rather than a *procedure-driven* model like most PC languages. Second, Visual Basic uses a call stack method that isolates local variables. This means that when you exit the routine, you can lose track of the values of internal variables, which can make resuming execution after error handling difficult. Third, in Visual Basic all errors are local. If an error occurs, it's best to handle it within the routine in which the error occurred, which means you have to write a short error handler for each routine in your Visual Basic program.

NOTE

Technically, Visual Basic does allow the use of a global error handler. However, after Visual Basic travels up the procedure stack to locate the error handler, it can't travel back down the stack to resume execution after the error has been corrected. (This is typical of most object-oriented languages.) For this reason, we highly recommend using local error handlers in your Visual Basic programs.

The Built-In Visual Basic Error Objects

Visual Basic 5 has two built-in objects that can be used to track and report errors at runtime. The Err object is a built-in object that exists in all Visual Basic programs. This object contains several properties and two methods. Each time an error occurs in the program, the Err object properties are filled with information you can use within your program.

The second built-in object that helps in tracking errors is the Error object, and its associated Errors collection. These are available to any Visual Basic 5 program that has loaded one of the Microsoft data access object libraries. The Error object is a child object of the DBEngine. You can use the Error object to get additional details on the nature of the database errors that occur in a program.

WARNING

The Error object is only available if you have loaded a Microsoft data-access object library. If you attempt to access the Error object from a Visual Basic program that does not have a Microsoft data access object library loaded, you receive an error.

The advantage of the Error object over the Err object is that the Error object contains more information about the database-related errors than the Err object. In some cases, back-end database servers return several error messages to your Visual Basic application. The Err object only reports the last error received from the back-end server. However, the Errors collection can report all of the errors received. For this reason, it is always a good idea to use the Error object when you are working with Visual Basic database applications.

14

Working with the Err Object

Visual Basic 5 has a built-in object called the Err object. This object holds all the information about the most recent error that occurred within the running application space.

WARNING

> There is a bit of confusion regarding the Err keyword in Visual Basic. Visual Basic 5 still supports the outdated Err and Error functions, but we do not advise you to use them in your programs. In some rare cases, the values reported by the Err and Error functions are not the same as those reported by the Err object. Throughout this book, when we mention "Err" we are referring to the Err object, not the Err function.

The Err object has several important properties. Table 14.1 shows these properties and explains their use.

Table 14.1. The properties of the Err object.

Property	Type	Value
Number	Long	The actual internal error number returned by Visual Basic.
Source	String	Name of the current Visual Basic file in which the error occurred. This could be an EXE, DLL, or OCX file.
Description	String	A string corresponding to the internal error number returned in the Number property, if this string exists. If the string doesn't exist, Description contains "Application-defined or object-defined error."
HelpFile	String	The fully qualified drive, path, and filename of the Help file. This help file can be called to support the reported errors.
HelpContext	Long	The Help file context (topic) ID in the help file indicated by the HelpFile property.
LastDLLError	Long	The error code for the last call to a dynamic-link library (DLL). This is available only on 32-bit Microsoft platforms.

When an error occurs in your Visual Basic program, the Err object properties are populated with the details of the error. You can inspect these values during your program execution and, if possible, use Visual Basic code to correct the error and continue the program.

For example, once an error occurs, you can inspect the properties of the object using the following code:

```
Msgbox "<" & CStr(Err.Number) & "> " & Err.Description & "[" & Err.Source & "]"
```

Once the error occurs and the Err object properties are updated, the Err object values do not change until another error is reported or the error-handling system is re-initialized.

NOTE The error handling system is re-initialized each time a procedure exit or end occurs, or when the special error-handling keywords Resume or On Error are executed. You learn more about these keywords later in this chapter.

If the error that was reported has an associated help file and help context ID, these properties are also filled in. You can use the HelpFile and HelpContext properties of the Err object to display an online help topic to explain the error condition to the user.

TIP Although help file composition and the construction of context-sensitive help is beyond the scope of a database book, Appendix B at the back of this book shows you how to create help files and how to link them to your Visual Basic programs.

If your application has called a dynamic-link library (DLL), you may be able to use the LastDLLError property of the Err object to get additional information about an error that occurred in a DLL. This property is only available on the 32-bit platform and may not be supported by the DLL you are calling.

Working with the Error Object and the Errors Collection

In addition to the built-in Err object, Visual Basic 5 also has a built-in Error object for database errors. This object is a child object of the DBEngine object. For this reason, you can only access the Error object if you have loaded a Microsoft data access object library (select Project | References from the main menu).

14

The primary advantage of the Error object is that it can report additional error information not included in the standard Err object mentioned earlier in this chapter. Many times, your database application needs to depend on external processes such as ODBC data connections or OLE Server modules. When an error occurs in these external processes, they may report more than one error code back to your Visual Basic application.

The Err object is only able to remember the *most recent* error reported. However, the Error object (and its associated Errors collection) can remember *all* of the errors reported by external processes. That is why it is a good idea to use the Error object for reporting errors in all your Visual Basic database programs.

The properties of the Microsoft data access Error object are almost identical to the properties of the Visual Basic Err object (see the discussion earlier in this chapter). The only difference is that the Error object does not have the optional LastDLLError property. Therefore, the calling convention for the Error object is basically the same as that for the Err object:

```
Msgbox "<" & CStr(Error.Number) & "> " & Error.Description & "[" & Error.Source
➥& "]"
```

While the Error and Err objects are quite similar, there is one major difference worth noting. While the Err object stands alone, the Microsoft data access Error object belongs to the Errors collection. This is very important when dealing with back-end database servers, especially when your Visual Basic program is connected to databases through the Open Database Connectivity (ODBC) interface. When an error occurs during an ODBC transaction, the Err object always returns the same error message, ODBC failed. However, the Errors collection often contains more than one error message, which can tell you a great deal more about the nature of the problem. You can retrieve all the error information by enumerating all the Error objects in the Errors collection. The code in Listing 14.1 shows how that can be done.

TYPE **Listing 14.1. Enumerating the Errors collection.**

```
Dim objTempErr as Object
Dim strMsg as String

For Each objTempErr In Errors
    StrMsg = "<" & CStr(objTempErr.Number) & "> "
    StrMsg = strMsg & objTempErr.Description
    StrMsg = strMsg & " in [" & objTempErr.Source & "]" & vbCrLf
Next

Msgbox strMsg
```

The code in Listing 14.1 creates a single line of text (strMsg) that contains all the error messages reported by the back-end database server. You learn more about using both the Err and Error objects in the next section of the chapter.

14

Creating Your Own Error Handlers

Before getting into the details of using the Err and Error objects in your Visual Basic programs, let's take a look at a basic error handler in Visual Basic. Error handlers in Visual Basic have three main parts:

☐ The On Error Goto statement

☐ The error handler code

☐ The exit statement

The On Error Goto statement appears at the beginning of the Sub or Function. This is the line that tells Visual Basic what to do when an error occurs, as in the following example:

```
On Error Goto LocalErrHandler
```

In the preceding code line, every time an error occurs in this Sub or Function, the program immediately jumps to the LocalErrHandler label in the routine and executes the error handler code. The error handler code can be as simple or as complex as needed to handle the error. A very simple error handler would just report the error number and error message, like this:

```
LocalErrHandler:
    MsgBox CStr(Err.Number) & " - " & Err.Description
```

In the preceding code example, as soon as the error occurs, Visual Basic reports the error number (Err.Number) and the error message (Err.Description) in a message box.

The third, and final, part of a Visual Basic error handler is the exit statement. This is the line that tells Visual Basic where to go after the error handler is done with its work. There are four different ways to exit an error handler routine:

☐ Use the Resume keyword to return to the location in the program that caused the error in order to re-execute the same instruction.

☐ Use the Resume Next keywords to resume execution at the Visual Basic code line immediately following the line that caused the error.

☐ Use the Resume label keywords to resume execution at a specified location within the routine that caused the error. This location could be anywhere within the routine—before or after the line that caused the error.

☐ Use the Exit Sub or Exit Function keywords to immediately exit the routine in which the error occurred.

Which exit method you use depends on the type of error that occurred and the error handling strategy you employ throughout your program. Error types and error handling strategies are covered later in this chapter.

Now that you have the basics of error handling, you can write some error-handling routines.

14

Creating a Simple Error Handler

To start, let's write a simple error-handling routine to illustrate how Visual Basic behaves when errors occur. Start up a new Standard EXE project in Visual Basic 5. Add a single command button to the default form. Set its Name property to cmdSimpleErr and its Caption Property to Simple. Now add the code in Listing 14.2 to support the command button.

TYPE   **Listing 14.2. Writing a simple error handler.**

```
Private Sub cmdSimpleErr_Click()
    '
    ' a simple error handler
    '
    On Error GoTo LocalErr  ' turn on error handling
    '
    Dim intValue As Integer ' declare integer
    Dim strMsg As String    ' declare string
    intValue = 10000000     ' create overflow error
    GoTo LocalExit          ' exit if no error
    '
    ' local error handler
LocalErr:
    strMsg = CStr(Err.Number) & " - " & Err.Description ' make message
    MsgBox strMsg, vbCritical, "cmdSimpleErr_Click"  ' show message
    Resume Next  ' continue on
    '
    ' routine exit
LocalExit:
    '
End Sub
```

Save the form as BASICERR.FRM, and save the project as BASICERR.VBP. Then execute the program and click the command button. You see the error message displayed on the screen (see Figure 14.1).

The example in Listing 14.2 exhibits all the parts of a good error handler. The first line in the routine tells Visual Basic what to do in case of an error. Notice that the name for the error-handling code is given as LocalErr. (Every local error handler written in this book is called LocalErr.) Next, the routine declares an integer variable and then purposely loads that variable with an illegal value. This causes the error routine to kick in.

The error routine is very simple. It is a message that contains the error number and the associated text message. The routine then displays that message along with the warning symbol and the name of the routine that is reporting the error.

Figure 14.1.
Displaying the results of a simple error handler.

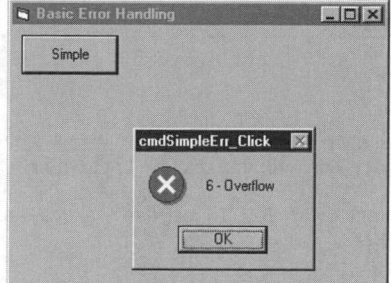

The next line tells Visual Basic what to do after the error is handled. In this case, Visual Basic resumes execution with the line of program code that immediately follows the line that caused the error (Resume at the Next line).

When Visual Basic resumes execution, the routine hits the line that tells Visual Basic to go to the exit routine (Goto LocalExit). Notice again the naming convention for the exit routine. All exit jump labels in this book are called LocalExit.

Handling Cascading Errors

What happens if you get an error *within* your error routine? Although it isn't fun to think about, it can happen. When an error occurs inside the error-handling routine, Visual Basic looks for the next declared error routine. This would be an error routine started in the previous calling routine using the On Error Goto label statement. If no error routine is available, Visual Basic halts the program with a fatal error.

As an example, let's add a new button to the BASICERR project and create a cascading error condition. Set the button's Name property to cmdCascadeErr and its Caption property to Cascade. First, create a new Sub procedure called CreateErr. Then enter the code from Listing 14.3.

TYPE   **Listing 14.3. Coding the CreateErr routine.**

```
Public Sub CreateErr()
    '
    ' create an internal error
    '
    On Error GoTo LocalErr
    '
    Dim strMsg As String
    Dim intValue As Integer
    '
    intValue = 900000 ' create an error
```

continues

Listing 14.3. continued

```
    GoTo LocalExit ' all done
    '
LocalErr:
    strMsg = CStr(Err.Number) & " - " & Err.Description
    MsgBox strMsg, vbCritical, "CreateErr"
    '
    Open "junk.txt" For Input As 1 ' create another error
    Resume Next
    '
LocalExit:
    '
End Sub
```

Notice that this routine is quite similar to the code from Listing 14.2. The biggest difference is in the lines of code in the error-handling portion of the subroutine. Notice that Visual Basic attempts to open a text file for input. Since this file does not currently exist, this action causes an error.

Now add the code from Listing 14.4 to the cmdCascadeErr_Click event. This is the code that calls the CreateErr routine.

TYPE **Listing 14.4. Coding the cmdCascadeErr routine.**

```
Private Sub cmdCascadeErr_Click()
    '
    ' create an error cascade
    '
    On Error GoTo LocalErr

    Dim strMsg As String
    '
    CreateErr ' call another routine
    GoTo LocalExit ' all done
    '
LocalErr:
    strMsg = CStr(Err.Number) & " - " & Err.Description
    MsgBox strMsg, vbCritical, "cmdCascadeErr"
    Resume Next
    '
LocalExit:
    '
End Sub
```

Save the program and run it to see the results. When you first click the command button, you see the error message that announces the overflow error. Notice that the title of the message box indicates that the error is being reported by the CreateErr routine (see Figure 14.2).

Figure 14.2.

Reporting the error from CreateErr.

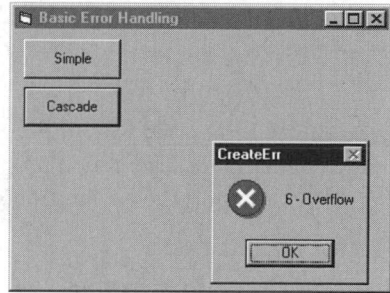

When you click the OK button in the message box, you see another error message. This one reports an `Error 53-File not found` message, which occurred when `CreateErr` tried to open the nonexistent file (see Figure 14.3).

Figure 14.3.

Reporting the File not found *error.*

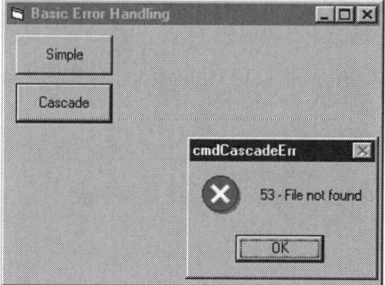

Here's the important point. Notice that the second error message box tells you that the error is being reported from the `cmdCascadeErr` routine—even though the error occurred in the `CreateErr` routine! The error that occurred in the `CreateErr` error-handling routine could not be handled locally, and Visual Basic searched upward in the call stack to find the next available error handler to invoke. This action by Visual Basic can be a blessing and a curse. It's good to know that Visual Basic uses the next available error-handling routine when things like this happen, but it's also likely to cause confusion for you and your users if you are not careful. For all you can tell in this example, an error occurred in `cmdCascadeErr`. You must keep this in mind when you are debugging Visual Basic error reports.

Using Resume to Exit the Error Handler

The simplest way to exit an error handler is to use the `Resume` method. When you exit an error handler with the `Resume` keyword, Visual Basic returns to the line of code that caused the error and attempts to run that line again. The `Resume` keyword is useful when you encounter an error that the user can easily correct, such as attempting to read a disk drive when the user

14

forgot to insert a diskette or close the drive door. You can use the Resume keyword whenever you are confident that the situation that caused the error has been remedied, and you want to retry the action that caused the error.

Let's modify the BASICERR project by adding a new button to the project. Set its Name property to cmdResumeErr and its Caption property to Resume. Now add the Visual Basic code in Listing 14.5 to support the new button's Click event.

TYPE   **Listing 14.5. Using the Resume keyword.**

```
Private Sub cmdResumeErr_Click()
    '
    ' show resume keyword
    '
    On Error GoTo LocalErr
    '
    Dim intValue As Integer
    Dim strMsg As String
    '
    intValue = InputBox("Enter an integer:")
    GoTo LocalExit
    '
LocalErr:
    strMsg = CStr(Err.Number) & " - " & Err.Description
    MsgBox strMsg, vbCritical, "cmdResumeErr"
    Resume ' try it again
    '
LocalExit:
    '
End Sub
```

Save and run the project. When you press the Resume button, you are prompted to enter an integer value. If you press the Cancel button or the OK button without entering data (or if you enter a value that is greater than 32,767), you invoke the error handler and receive an error message from Visual Basic (see Figure 14.4).

Figure 14.4.

Reporting an error message from the input box.

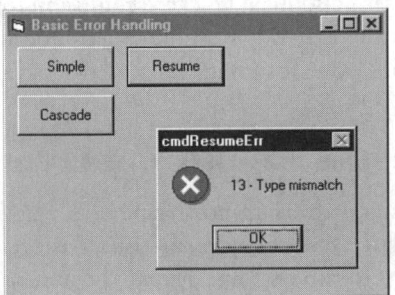

When you click the OK button, Visual Basic redisplays the input prompt and waits for your reply. If you enter another invalid value, you see the error message, and then you see the prompt again. This is the Resume exit method in action. You can't get beyond this screen until you enter a valid value.

This can be very frustrating for users. What if they don't know what value to enter here? Are they stuck in this terrible error handler forever? Whenever you use the Resume keyword, you should give your users an option to ignore the error and move on or cancel the action completely. Those options are covered next.

Using Resume Next to Exit the Error Handler

Using the Resume Next method to exit an error handler allows your user to get past a problem spot in the program as if no error has occurred. This is useful when you use code within the error handler to fix the problem, or when you think the program can go on even though an error has been reported.

Deciding whether to continue the program even though an error has been reported is sometimes a tough call. It is usually not a good idea to assume that your program will work fine even though an error is reported. This is especially true if the error that occurs is one related to physical devices (missing diskette, lost communications connection, and so on) or file errors (missing, corrupted, or locked data files, and so on). The Resume Next keywords are usually used in error-handling routines that fix any reported error before continuing.

To illustrate the use of Resume Next, add a new command button to the project. Set its Name property to cmdResumeNext and its Caption property to Next. Now enter the code in Listing 14.6 behind the button's Click event.

TYPE   **Listing 14.6. Using the Resume Next keywords.**

```
Private Sub cmdResumeNextErr_Click()
    '
    ' show use of resume next
    '
    On Error GoTo LocalErr
    '
    Dim intValue As Integer
    Dim strMsg As String
    Dim lngReturn As Long
    '
    intValue = InputBox("Enter a valid Integer")
    MsgBox "intValue has been set to " + CStr(intValue)
    GoTo LocalExit
    '
```

14

continues

Listing 14.6. continued

```
LocalErr:
    If Err.Number = 6 Then ' was it an overflow error?
        strMsg = "You have entered an invalid integer value." & vbCrLf
        strMsg = strMsg & "The program will now set the value to 0 for you." &
➥vbCrLf
        strMsg = strMsg & "Select YES to set the value to 0 and continue." &
➥vbCrLf
        strMsg = strMsg & "Select NO to return to enter a new value."
        '
        lngReturn = MsgBox(strMsg, vbCritical + vbYesNo, "cmdResumeNextErr")
        If lngReturn = vbYes Then
            intValue = 0
            Resume Next
        Else
            Resume
        End If
    Else ' must have been some other error(!)
        strMsg = CStr(Err.Number) & " - " & Err.Description
        MsgBox strMsg, vbCritical, "cmdResumeNext"
        Resume
    End If
    '
LocalExit:
    '
End Sub
```

In Listing 14.6, you added a section of code to the error handler that tests for the anticipated overflow error. You explain the options to the user and then give the user a choice of how to proceed. This is a good general model for error handling that involves user interaction. Tell the user the problem, explain the options, and let the user decide how to go forward.

Notice, also, that this routine includes a general error trap for those cases when the error is not caused by an integer overflow. Even when you think you have covered all the possible error conditions, you should always include a general error trap.

Save and run this project. When you press the Next command button and enter an invalid value (that is, any number greater than 32,767), you see the error message that explains your options (see Figure 14.5).

Using `Resume label` to Exit an Error Handler

There are times when you need your program to return to another spot within the routine in order to fix an error that occurs. For example, if you ask the user to enter two numbers that you use to perform a division operation, and it results in a divide-by-zero error, you want to ask the user to enter both numbers again. You might not be able to just use the `Resume` statement after you handle the error.

14

Figure 14.5.

*An error message that
asks for user input.*

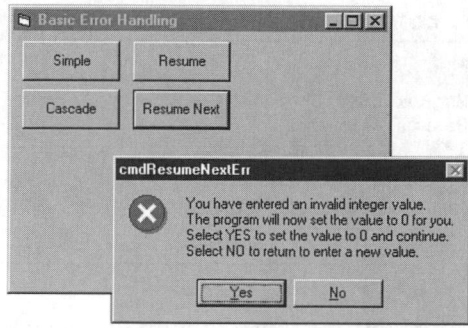

When you need to force the program to return to a specific point in the routine, you can use the Resume label exit method. The Resume label method enables you to return to any place within the current procedure. You can't use Resume label to jump to another Sub or Function within the project.

Now let's modify the BASICERR project to include an example of Resume label. Add a new command button to the project. Set its Name property to cmdResumeLabelErr and its Caption property to Resume Label. Now, place the code in Listing 14.7 behind the Click event.

TYPE **Listing 14.7. Using the Resume label keywords.**

```
Private Sub cmdResumeLabelErr_Click()
    '
    ' show resume label version
    '
    On Error GoTo LocalErr
    '
    Dim intX As Integer
    Dim intY As Integer
    Dim intZ As Integer
    '
cmdLabelInput:
    intX = InputBox("Enter a Divisor:", "Input Box #1")
    intY = InputBox("Enter a Dividend:", "Input Box #2")
    intZ = intX / intY
    MsgBox "The Quotient is: " + Str(intZ), vbInformation, "Results"
    GoTo LocalExit
    '
LocalErr:
    If Err = 11 Then      ' divide by zero error
        MsgBox CStr(Err.Number) & " - " & Err.Description, vbCritical,
➥"cmdResumeLabelErr"
        Resume cmdLabelInput ' back for more
```

14

continues

Listing 14.7. continued

```
        Else
            MsgBox CStr(Err) & " -" & Error$, vbCritical, "cmdLabel"
            Resume Next
        End If
        '
LocalExit:
        '
End Sub
```

Save and run the project. Enter 13 at the first input box and 0 at the second input box. This causes a divide-by-zero error, and the error handler takes over from there. You see the error message shown in Figure 14.6 and then return to the line that starts the input process.

Figure 14.6.

Displaying the
Divide by Zero
error message.

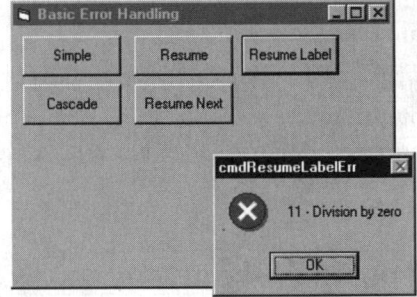

Using the Exit or End Method to Exit an Error Handler

There are times when an error occurs and there is no good way to return to the program. A good example of this type of error can occur when the program attempts to open files on a network file server and the user has forgotten to log onto the server. In this case, you need to either exit the routine and return to the calling procedure, or exit the program completely. Exiting to a calling routine can work if you have written your program to anticipate these critical errors. Usually it's difficult to do that. Most of the time, critical errors of this type mean you should end the program and let the user fix the problem before restarting the program.

14

Let's add one more button to the BASICERR project. Set its Caption property to End and its Name property to cmdEndErr. Enter the code in Listing 14.8 to support the cmdEnd_Click event.

TYPE **Listing 14.8. Using the End keyword.**

```
Private Sub cmdEndErr_Click()
    '
    ' use End to exit handler
    '
    On Error GoTo LocalErr
    '
    Dim strMsg As String
    Open "junk.txt" For Input As 1
    GoTo cmdEndExit
    '
LocalErr:
    If Err.Number = 53 Then
        strMsg = "Unable to open JUNK.TXT" & vbCrLf
        strMsg = strMsg & "Exit the program and check your INI file" & vbCrLf
        strMsg = strMsg & "to make sure the JUNKFILE setting is correct."
        MsgBox strMsg, vbCritical, "cmdEnd"
        Unload Me
    Else
        MsgBox Str(Err) + " - " + Error$, vbCritical, "cmdEnd"
        Resume Next
    End If
    '
LocalExit:
    '
End Sub
```

In Listing 14.8, you add a check in the error handler for the anticipated File not found error. You give the user some helpful information and then tell him you are closing down the program. It's always a good idea to tell the user when you are about to exit the program. Notice that you did not use the Visual Basic End keyword; you used Unload Me. Remember that End stops all program execution immediately. Using Unload Me causes Visual Basic to execute any code placed in the Unload event of the form. This event should contain any file-closing routine needed to safely exit the program.

Save and run the project. When you click the End button, you see a message box explaining the problem and suggesting a solution (see Figure 14.7). When you click the OK button, Visual Basic ends the program.

14

Figure 14.7.

*Showing the error
message before exiting
the program.*

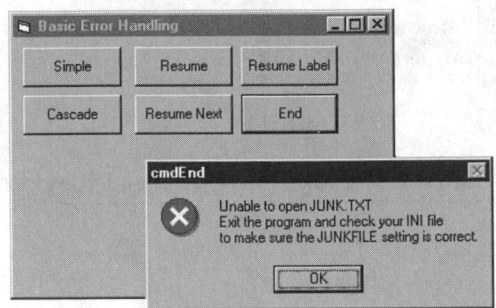

Using the `Err.Raise` Method to Create Your Own Error Conditions

Many times it is not practical, or desirable, to display an error message when an error occurs. Other times, you may want to use the error-handling capabilities of Visual Basic 5 to your advantage by creating your own error codes and messages. You can do this using the `Raise` method of the Err object. Using the `Raise` method allows you to alert users (or other calling applications) that an error has occurred, but gives both you and the user additional flexibility on how the error is handled.

The `Raise` method takes up to five parameters:

☐ `ErrorNumber`: This is a unique number identifying the error that just occurred.

☐ `ErrorSource`: This is the code module that generated the error.

☐ `ErrorDescription`: This is the text message associated with the error.

☐ `HelpFile`: This is the help file that contains support information on the error.

☐ `HelpcontextID`: This is the ID number of the help topic associated with this error.

When you raise your own errors, you are required to report an error number. This number can be any unique value. If you use a number already defined as a Visual Basic error, you automatically get the `ErrorDescription` and any associated `HelpFile` and `HelpContextID` information as well. If you generate your own unique number, you can fill in the other parameters yourself. It is recommended that you use the vbObjectError constant as a base number for your own error codes. This guarantees that your error number does not conflict with any Visual Basic errors.

Here is a typical call to use the `Err.Raise` method:

```
'
LocalErr:
    ' trouble with file stuff!
```

14

```
    Err.Raise vbObjectError + 1, "errHandler.LogError", "Can't write log file ["
 ➥& errLogFileName & "]"
        '
End Sub
```

It is especially important to use this method for marking errors when you are coding ActiveX DLL servers. Since servers may run at a remote location on the network, you cannot be sure that users ever see any error dialog you display. Also, remember that, even if the DLL is running on the local PC, error dialog boxes are application-modal. No other processing occurs until the dialog box is dismissed. You learn to use the `Err.Raise` method when you create your errHandler object library later in this chapter.

So far, you have seen how to build a simple error handler and the different ways to exit error handlers. Now you need to learn about the different types of errors that you may encounter in your Visual Basic programs and how to plan for them in advance.

Types of Errors

In order to make writing error handlers easier and more efficient, you can group errors into typical types. These error types can usually be handled in a similar manner. When you get an idea of the types of errors you may encounter, you can begin to write error handlers that take care of more than one error. You can write handlers that take care of error types.

There are four types of Visual Basic errors:

☐ General file errors: These are errors you encounter when you are attempting to open, read, or write simple files. This type of error does not include errors related to internal database operations (read/write table records).

☐ Physical media errors: These are errors caused by problems with physical devices— errors such as unresponsive communications ports or printers and low-level disk errors (`Unable To Read Sector`, and so on).

☐ Program code errors: These are errors that appear in your programs due to problems with your code. Errors include `Divide by zero`, `Invalid Property`, and other errors that can only be corrected by changing the Visual Basic code in your programs.

☐ Database errors: These are errors that occur during database operations, usually during data read/write or data object create/delete operations.

Each of these types of errors needs to be handled differently within your Visual Basic programs. You learn general rules for handling these errors in the following sections.

14

General File Errors

General file errors occur because of invalid data file information such as a bad filename, data path, or device name. Usually the user can fix these errors, and the program can continue from the point of failure. The basic approach to handling general file errors is to create an error handler that reports the problem to the user and asks for additional information to complete or retry the operation.

In Listing 14.9, the error handler is called when the program attempts to open a control file called CONTROL.TXT. The error handler then prompts the user for the proper file location and continues processing. Start a new Standard EXE project (ERRTYPES.VBP) and add a command button to the form. Set its Caption property to Control and its Name property to cmdControl. Also, add a CommonDialog control to the project. Enter the code in Listing 14.9 into the cmdControl_Click event.

TYPE   Listing 14.9. Adding code to the cmdControl_Click event.

```
Private Sub cmdControl_Click()
    '
    ' show general file errors
    '
    On Error GoTo LocalErr
    '
    Dim strFile As String
    Dim strMsg As String
    Dim lngReturn As Long
    '
    strFile = "\control.txt"
    '
    Open strFile For Input As 1
    MsgBox "Control File Opened"
    GoTo LocalExit
    '
LocalErr:
    If Err.Number = 53 Then ' file not found?
        strMsg = "Unable to Open CONTROL.TXT" & vbCrLf
        strMsg = strMsg & "Select OK to locate CONTROL.TXT" & vbCrLf
        strMsg = strMsg & "Select CANCEL to exit program."
        '
        lngReturn = MsgBox(strMsg, vbCritical + vbOKCancel, "cmdControl")
        '
        If lngReturn = vbOK Then
            CommonDialog1.filename = strFile
            CommonDialog1.DefaultExt = ".txt"
            CommonDialog1.ShowOpen
            Resume
        Else
            Unload Me
        End If
    Else
```

14

```
        MsgBox CStr(Err.Number) & " - " + Err.Description
        Resume Next
    End If
    '
LocalExit:
    '
End Sub
```

Save the form as FRMERRTYPES.FRM and the project as PRJERRTYPES.VBP. Now run this project. When you click on the Control button, the program tries to open the CONTROL.TXT file. If it can't be found, you see the error message (see Figure 14.8).

Figure 14.8.

Displaying the File not Found *error.*

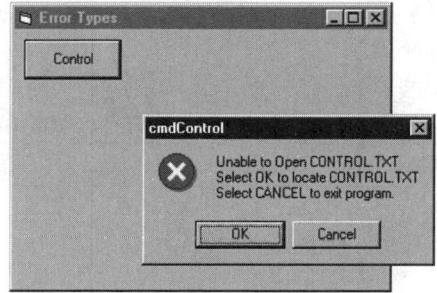

If the user selects OK, the program calls the CommonDialog control and prompts the user to locate the CONTROL.TXT file. It can be found in the \TYSDBVB5\SOURCE\CHAP14 directory (see Figure 14.9).

Figure 14.9.

Attempting to locate the CONTROL.TXT *file.*

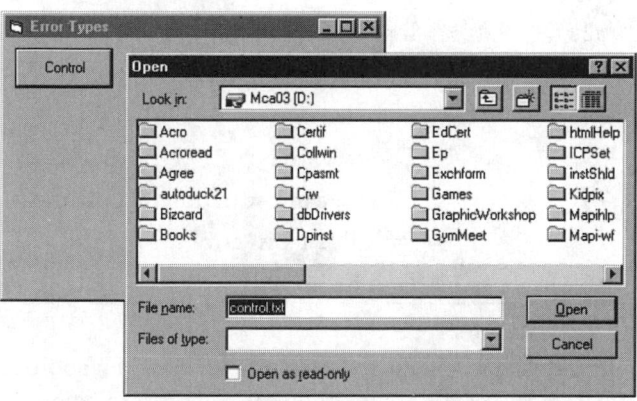

14

TIP

Notice the use of the `CommonDialog` control to open the file. Whenever you need to prompt users for file-related action (open, create, save), you should use the `CommonDialog` control. This is a familiar dialog for your users, and it handles all of the dirty work of scrolling, searching, and so on.

Table 14.2 lists errors that are similar to the `File not found` error illustrated in Listing 14.9. Errors of this type usually involve giving the user a chance to re-enter the filename or reset some value. Most of the time, you can write an error trap that anticipates these errors, prompts the user to supply the corrected information, and then retries the operation that caused the error.

Table 14.2. Common general file errors.

Error Code	Error Message
52	Bad filename or number
53	File not found
54	Bad file mode
55	File already open
58	File already exists
59	Bad record length
61	Disk full
62	Input past end of file
63	Bad record number
64	Bad filename
67	Too many files
74	Can't rename with different drive
75	Path/File access error
76	Path not found

In cases when it is not practical to prompt a user for additional information (such as during initial startup of the program), it is usually best to report the error in a message box. Then give the user some ideas about how to fix the problem before you exit the program safely.

14

Physical Media Errors

Another group of common errors is caused by problems with physical media. Unresponsive printers, disk drives that do not contain diskettes, and downed communications ports are the most common examples of physical media errors. These errors might, or might not, be easily fixed by your user. Usually, you can report the error, wait for the user to fix the problem, and then continue with the process. For example, if the printer is jammed with paper, all you need to do is report the error to the user, and then wait for the OK to continue.

Let's add another button to the PRJERRTYPES.VBP project to display an example of physical media error handling. Add a new command button to the project. Set its Caption property to &Media and its Name property to cmdMedia. Enter the code in Listing 14.10 into the cmdMedia_Click event.

TYPE **Listing 14.10. Trapping media errors.**

```
Private Sub cmdMedia_Click()
    '
    ' show handling of media errors
    '
    On Error GoTo LocalErr
    Dim strMsg As String
    Dim lngReturn As Long
    '
    ' open a file on the a drive
    ' an error will occur if there
    ' is no diskette in the drive
    '
    Open "a:\junk.txt" For Input As 1
    Close #1
    GoTo LocalExit
    '
LocalErr:
    If Err.Number = 71 Then
        strMsg = "The disk drive is not ready." & vbCrLf
        strMsg = strMsg + "Please make sure there is a diskette" & vbCrLf
        strMsg = strMsg + "in the drive and the drive door is closed."
        '
        lngReturn = MsgBox(strMsg, vbCritical + vbRetryCancel, "cmdMedia")
        '
        If lngReturn = vbRetry Then
            Resume
        Else
            Resume Next
        End If
    Else
        MsgBox Str(Err.Number) & " - " & Err.Description
        Resume Next
```

continues

Listing 14.10. continued

```
    End If
    '
LocalExit:
    '
End Sub
```

In Listing 14.10, you attempt to open a file on a disk drive that has no disk (or has an open drive door). The error handler prompts the user to correct the problem and allows the user to try the operation again. If all goes well the second time, the program continues. The user also has an option to cancel the operation.

Save and run the project. When you click on the Media button, you should get results that look like those in Figure 14.10.

Figure 14.10.

The results of a physical media error.

Program Code Errors

Another common type of error is the program code error. These errors occur as part of the Visual Basic code. Errors of this type cannot be fixed by users and are usually due to unanticipated conditions within the code itself. Error messages such as Variable Not Found, Invalid Object, and so on, create a mystery for most of your users. The best way to handle errors of this type is to tell the user to report the message to the programmer and close the program safely.

Database Errors with the Data Control

A very common type of error that occurs in database applications is the data-related error. These errors include those that deal with data type or field size problems, table access restrictions including read-only access, locked tables due to other users, and so on. Database errors fall into two groups. Those caused by attempting to read or write invalid data to or from tables, including data integrity errors, make up the most common group. The second group includes those errors caused by locked tables, restricted access, or multiuser conflicts.

NOTE

Errors concerning table locks, restricted access, and multiuser issues are covered in depth in the last week of the book. In this chapter, you focus on the more common group of errors.

In most cases, all you need to do is trap for the error, report it to the user, and allow the user to return to the data entry screen to fix the problem. If you use the Visual Basic data control in your data forms, you can take advantage of the automatic database error reporting built into the data control. As an example, let's put together a simple data entry form to illustrate some of the common data entry-oriented database errors.

Start a new Visual Basic Standard EXE project to illustrate common database errors. Add a data control, two bound input controls, and two label controls. Use Table 14.3 as a reference for adding the controls to the form. Refer to Figure 14.11 as a guide for placing the controls.

Figure 14.11.

Laying out the DataErr form.

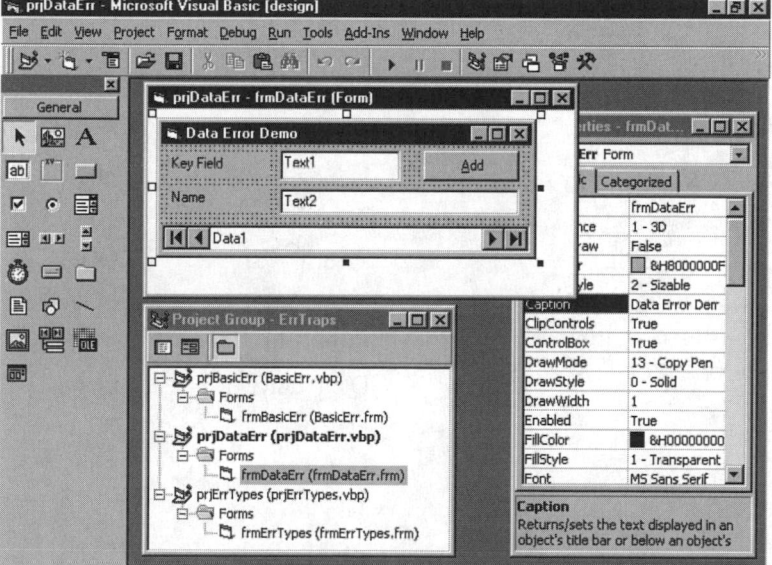

14

Table 14.3. Controls for the frmDataErr form.

Control	Property	Setting
VB.Form	Name	frmDataErr
	Caption	"Data Error Demo"
	ClientHeight	1335
	ClientLeft	60
	ClientTop	345
	ClientWidth	4665
	StartUpPosition	3 'Windows Default
VB.CommandButton	Name	cmdAdd
	Caption	"&Add"
	Height	375
	Left	3300
	Top	60
	Width	1215
VB.TextBox	Name	txtName
	DataField	"Name"
	DataSource	"Data1"
	Height	315
	Left	1500
	Top	540
	Width	3015
VB.TextBox	Name	txtKeyField
	DataField	"KeyField"
	DataSource	"Data1"
	Height	375
	Left	1500
	Top	60
	Width	1515
VB.Data	Name	Data1
	Align	2 'Align Bottom
	Caption	"Data1"
	Connect	"Access"

14

Control	Property	Setting
	DatabaseName	`C:\TYSDBVB5\SOURCE\DATA\ERRORS\ERRORDB.MDB`
	Height	360
	RecordSource	"Table1"
	Top	975
	Width	4665
VB.Label	Name	lblName
	Caption	"Name"
	Height	255
	Left	120
	Top	540
	Width	1215
VB.Label	Name	lblKeyField
	Caption	"Key Field"
	Height	255
	Left	120
	Top	120
	Width	1215

The only code you need to add to this form is a single line to support the Add button. Place the following code behind the `cmdAdd_Click` event.

```
Private Sub cmdAdd_Click()
   Data1.Recordset.AddNew
End Sub
```

Now save the new form as `DATAERR.FRM` and the project as `DATAERR.VBP`. When you run the project, you can test the built-in error trapping for Microsoft data controls by adding a new, duplicate record to the table. Press the Add button, then enter `KF109` in the KeyField input box and press one of the arrows on the data control to force it to save the record. You should see a database error message that looks like the one in Figure 14.12.

Are you surprised? You didn't add an error trap to the data entry form, but you still got a complete database error message! The Visual Basic data control is kind enough to provide complete database error reporting even if you have no error handlers in your Visual Basic program. Along with the automatic errors, the data control also has the `Error` event. Each time a data-related error occurs, this event occurs. You can add code in the `Data1_Error` event to automatically fix errors, display better error messages, and so on.

14

Figure 14.12.

A sample Microsoft data control error message.

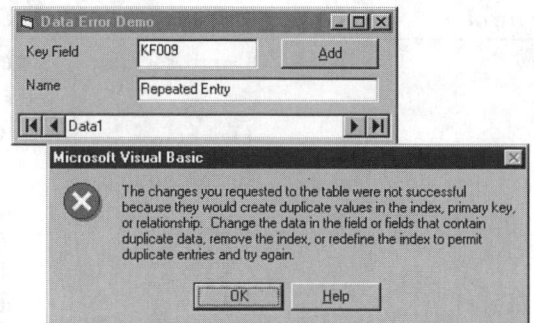

Let's modify the program a bit to show you how you can use the Data1_Error event. First, add a CommonDialog control to your form. Then edit the DatabaseName property of the data control to read C:\ERRORDB.MDB. Next, add the code from Listing 14.11 to the Data1_Error event.

TYPE **Listing 14.11. Coding the Data1_Error event.**

```
Private Sub Data1_Error(DataErr As Integer, Response As Integer)
    '
    ' add error-trapping for data errors
    '
    Dim strFileName As String
    '
    Select Case DataErr
        Case 3044 ' database not found
            MsgBox "Unable to locate data file", vbExclamation, "Database
➥Missing"
            '
            CommonDialog1.DialogTitle = "Locate ERRORDB.MDB"
            CommonDialog1.filename = "ERRORDB.MDB"
            CommonDialog1.Filter = "*.mdb"
            CommonDialog1.ShowOpen
            Data1.DatabaseName = CommonDialog1.filename
            '
            Response = vbCancel ' cancel auto-message
    End Select
    '
End Sub
```

Notice that the code in Listing 14.11 checks to see whether the error code is 3044. This is the error number that corresponds to the "database missing" message. If the 3044 code is reported, the user sees a short message and then the file open dialog, ready to locate and load the database. Finally, notice the line that sets the Response parameter to vbCancel. This step tells Visual Basic *not* to display the default message.

14

 **TIP** Usually, it is not a good idea to attempt to override this facility with your own database errors. As long as you use the Visual Basic data control, you do not need to add database error-trapping routines to your data entry forms. The only time you need to add error-related code is when you want to perform special actions in the `Error` event of the data control.

You need to add one more bit of code to complete this error trap. Add the following line of code to the `Form_Activate` event.

```
Private Sub Form_Activate()
    Data1.Refresh
End Sub
```

This code makes sure the data entry fields on the form are updated with the most recent data from the database.

Now save and run the project. You first see a message telling you that the database is missing (Figure 14.13).

Figure 14.13.

Custom error message in the `Data1_Error` *event.*

Next, the open file dialog waits for you to locate and load the requested database (Figure 14.14).

Figure 14.14.

Locating the requested database.

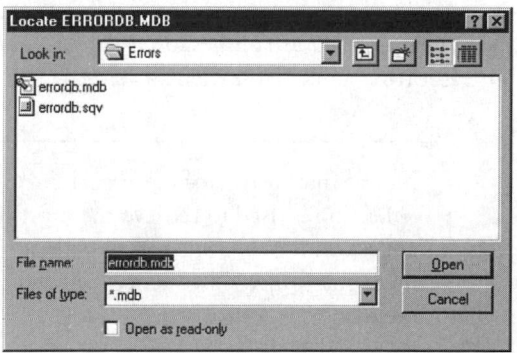

Finally, once you load the database, the data entry screen comes up ready for your input.

Database Errors with Microsoft Data Access Objects

If you use Microsoft data access objects instead of the Visual Basic data control, you need to add error-handling routines to your project. For example, if you want to create a Dynaset using Visual Basic code, you need to trap for any error that might occur along the way.

Add the code in Listing 14.12 to the Form_Load event of frmData. This code opens the database and creates a Dynaset to stuff into the data control that already exists on the form.

TYPE **Listing 14.12. Adding code to the Form_Load event.**

```
Private Sub Form_Load()
    '
    ' create recordset using DAO
    '
    On Error GoTo LocalErr
    '
    Dim ws As Workspace
    Dim db As Database
    Dim rs As Recordset
    Dim strSQL As String
    '
    strSQL = "SELECT * FROM Table2"
    Set ws = DBEngine.Workspaces(0)
    Set db = ws.OpenDatabase(App.Path & "\..\..\Data\Errors\ErrorDB.mdb")
    Set rs = db.OpenRecordset(strSQL, dbOpenDynaset)
    Exit Sub
    '
LocalErr:
    MsgBox "<" & CStr(Errors(0).Number) & "> " & Errors(0).Description,
➥vbCritical, "Form_Load Error"
    Unload Me
    '
End Sub
```

The code in Listing 14.12 establishes some variables and then opens the database and creates a new Dynaset from a data table called Table2.

NOTE Notice that instead of the Visual Basic Err object, the DAO Errors collection is used to retrieve the most recent database error. The Errors collection is only available if you loaded the Microsoft DAO library using the Project | References option from the main Visual Basic 5 menu.

14

Because there is no Table2 in ERRORDB.MDB, you see a database error when the program runs. The error message is displayed, and then the form is unloaded completely (see Figure 14.15).

Figure 14.15.

Displaying an error message from the `Form_Load` *event.*

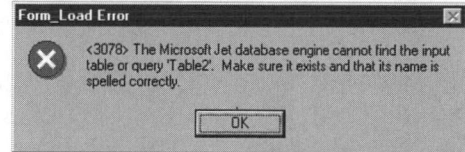

It is a good idea to open any data tables or files that you need for a data entry form during the `Form_Load` event. That way, if there are problems, you can catch them before data entry begins.

Creating Your Error Handler OLE Server

In the previous sections, you created several error handlers, each tuned to handle a special set of problems. Although this approach works for small projects, it can be tedious and burdensome if you have to put together a large application. Also, after you've written an error handler that works well for one type of error, you can use that error handler in every other program that might have the same error. Why write it more than once?

Even though Visual Basic requires error traps to be set for each `Sub` or `Function`, you can still create a generic approach to error handling that takes advantage of code you have already written. In this section, you write a set of routines that you can install in all your Visual Basic programs—the error-handling OLE Server. This OLE Server offers some generic error-handling capabilities along with the ability to log these errors to a disk file and to keep track of the procedure call stack. These last two services can be very valuable when you encounter a vexing bug in your program and need to get additional information on the exact subroutines and functions that were executed before the error occurred.

To build the new error handling OLE Server, you need to start a new Visual Basic ActiveX DLL project. Name the default Class module errHandler and set the project Name to prjErrHandler. You also need to add a BAS module and a form to the project. The form acts as the new customized error dialog box. The BAS module holds a new user-defined type and some API definitions for use with the customized error dialog box.

Building the errHandler Class

Building the errHandler class involves several steps. First, add some code to the general declaration section of the Class object (see Listing 14.13).

14

TYPE
Listing 14.13. Adding code to the Declaration section of the errHandler class.

```
Option Explicit

'
' error types
Enum errType
    erritem = 0
    errcoll = 1
End Enum

'
' return/option values
Enum errReturn
    errExit = 0
    errresume = 1
    errNext = 2
    errselect = 3
End Enum

'
' handler storage
Private errDefRtn As errReturn
Private errDefType As errType
'
```

The first two items in the declaration section define enumerated types. These are a special type of user-defined type that are a mix between a standard user-defined type and a Public constant. Enumerated types make it easy to write well-documented code. Along with the enumerated types, you see two Private variables declared for local use.

Next, you need to add some declaration code to the BAS module in your DLL project. This code defines a special custom data type that you can use to control the display of your custom error dialog box. The errHandler DLL allows you to access any possible help topics associated with the error messages, too. For this reason, the BAS module contains the WinHelp API declaration. This is used on the custom dialog box. Open the BAS module, set its Name property to modErrHandler and enter the code in Listing 14.14 into the general declaration section of the module.

TYPE
Listing 14.14. Adding code to the general declaration section of the modErrHandler BAS module.

```
Option Explicit

'
' define dialog data type
Public Type errDialog
```

14

```
        Message As String
        Buttons As Variant
        Title As String
        HelpFile As String
        HelpID As Long
        Return As Long
End Type
'
Public udtErrDialog As errDialog

'
' declare winHelp API
Declare Function WinHelp Lib "user32" Alias "WinHelpA" (ByVal hwnd As Long, _
    ByVal lpHelpFile As String, _
    ByVal wCommand As Long, _
    ByVal dwData As Long) As Long
'
Public Const HELP_CONTEXT = &H1
Public Const HELP_QUIT = &H2
```

That's all that you need to add to the modErrHandler. Next, you need to add code to the Initialize event of the errHandler Class module. Add the code from Listing 14.15 to the Class_Initialize event.

TYPE | **Listing 14.15. Adding code to the `Class_Initialize` event of the errHandler class.**

```
Private Sub Class_Initialize()
    '
    ' set starting values
    errDefRtn = errExit
    errDefType = errItem
    '
    udtErrDialog.Buttons = ""
    udtErrDialog.HelpFile = ""
    udtErrDialog.HelpID = -1
    udtErrDialog.Message = ""
    udtErrDialog.Return = -1
    udtErrDialog.Title = ""
    '
End Sub
```

This errHandler class has two Public properties—the DefaultAction and DefaultType properties. These defaults were set in the Initialize event and can be overridden by setting the properties at runtime. Create the DefaultAction property (using the Tools | Add Procedure menu option) and add the code from Listing 14.16 into the Property Let and Property Get routines.

14

Listing 14.16. Defining the `Property Let` **and** `Property Get`
TYPE   routines for the DefaultAction property.

```
Public Property Get DefaultAction() As errReturn
    '
    ' return default
    '
    DefaultAction = errDefRtn
    '
End Property

Public Property Let DefaultAction(ByVal vNewValue As errReturn)
    '
    ' verify parm and store
    '
    If vNewValue >= errExit Or vNewValue <= errselect Then
        errDefRtn = vNewValue
    End If
    '
End Property
```

Note that the data type for the property is errReturn. This is one of the enumerated types
defined in the declaration section of the class module. Next, create the `Property Let` and
`Property Get` routines for the DefaultType property, and enter the code from Listing 14.17
into the project.

Listing 14.17. Coding the `Property Let` **and** `Property Get`
TYPE   routines for the DefaultType property.

```
Public Property Get DefaultType() As errType
    '
    DefaultType = errDefType
    '
End Property

Public Property Let DefaultType(ByVal vNewValue As errType)
    '
    If vNewValue >= errcoll Or vNewValue <= erritem Then
        errDefType = vNewValue
    End If
    '
End Property
```

Finally, you're ready to write the main error handler method. This method can be called from
any VBA-compliant program. You pass the Visual Basic Err object (or database Errors
collection) along with a few optional parameters that can control the behavior of the message
dialog box. After the method has been completed, a value is returned. This value can be used
to control program flow and error recovery.

14

Create a new function method in your class module called errHandler and enter the code
from Listing 14.18.

TYPE **Listing 14.18. Coding the errHandler function.**

```
Public Function errHandler(objErrColl As Variant, Optional intType As errType, _
➥Optional errOption As errReturn, Optional errRefName As String) As errReturn

    ' ----------------------------------------------------------------------
    ' produce msg and prompt for response
    '
    ' inputs:
    '   objErrColl  - DAO collection -OR- VBA Err object
    '   intType     - errType enum that describes objErrColl (coll or item)
    '   errOption   - errReturn enum sets dialog behavior (exit, resume, next,
    '   ➥select)
    '   errRefName  - string to reference caller
    '
    ' returns:
    '   errExit     - end program
    '   errResume   - try again
    '   errNext     - skip to next line
    ' ----------------------------------------------------------------------
    '
    Dim strMsg As String
    Dim strTitle As String
    Dim rtnValue As errReturn
    '
    ' retrieve action option
    If IsMissing(errOption) Then
        errOption = errDefRtn
    End If
    '
    ' retrieve reference name
    If IsMissing(errRefName) Then
        errRefName = ""
    Else
        errRefName = " from " & errRefName
    End If
    '
    ' build full message
    strMsg = errMsg(objErrColl, intType)
    '
    ' write it out, if allowed
    If errLogFlag = True Then
        LogError strMsg
    End If
    '
    ' evaluate things
    Select Case errOption
        Case errExit
            udtErrDialog.Title = "Exiting Program"
            udtErrDialog.Message = strMsg
```

continues

14

Listing 14.18. continued

```
                udtErrDialog.Buttons = Array("&Exit")
                frmErrDialog.Show vbModal
                rtnValue = errExit
            '
        Case errresume, errNext
            udtErrDialog.Title = "Error Message" & errRefName
            udtErrDialog.Message = strMsg
            udtErrDialog.Buttons = Array("&OK")
            frmErrDialog.Show vbModal
            rtnValue = errOption
        '
        Case Else
            udtErrDialog.Title = "Error Message" & errRefName
            udtErrDialog.Message = strMsg
            udtErrDialog.Buttons = Array("&Cancel", "&Retry", "&Ignore")
            frmErrDialog.Show vbModal
            rtnValue = udtErrDialog.Return
    End Select
    '
    ' give it back
    errHandler = rtnValue
    '
End Function
```

The code in Listing 14.18 calls a support function (errMsg) and a dialog box (frmErrDialog).
You need to code these two remaining objects before you can test your error handler. Create
a new function (errMsg) in the class module and enter the code from Listing 14.19 into the
project.

TYPE   **Listing 14.19. Adding the errMsg support function.**

```
Public Function errMsg(objErrColl As Variant, intType As errType) As String
    '
    ' build and return complete error msg
    '
    Dim strMsg As String
    Dim objItem As Error
    '
    strMsg = ""
    '
    If intType = errcoll Then
        For Each objItem In objErrColl
            strMsg = strMsg & "<" & CStr(objItem.Number) & "> "
            strMsg = strMsg & objItem.Description
            strMsg = strMsg & " (in " & objItem.Source & ")." & vbCrLf
        Next
    Else ' intType= errItem
        strMsg = "<" & objErrColl.Number & "> "
        strMsg = strMsg & objErrColl.Description
```

14

```
        strMsg = strMsg & " (in " & objErrColl.Source & ")"
        '
        udtErrDialog.HelpFile = objErrColl.HelpFile
        udtErrDialog.HelpID = objErrColl.HelpContext
    End If
    '
    errMsg = strMsg
    '
End Function
```

The main job of the errMsg routine is to build a complete error message for display to the user. In order to do this, errMsg needs to know if the object that was passed was a single VBA Err object or the DAO Errors collection. That is why the errType parameter is included in the call. Also note that the errMsg method has been declared as a Public method. You can call this method from your Visual Basic 5 programs, too. That way, even if you don't want to perform all of the error-handing operations, you can use errMsg to get an improved error message for your use.

Coding the frmErrDialog Form

The last main piece of the errHandler class is a custom dialog box to display the error message and get input from the user. Often, you want to do more than just display the message and let the user press "OK." You may ask them to retry the same process, or ask if they want to ignore the error and continue. This dialog box not only displays the message and gives you an opportunity to get a response from the user, it also allows you to provide an optional "Help" button to give the user greater support in discovering how to resolve the error.

 **NOTE**

> Creating Help files for your Visual Basic project is covered in Appendix B of this book.

With the prjErrHandler project still open, add a form to the project. Use Table 14.4 and Figure 14.16 as guides in laying out the form.

Table 14.4. Control table for the frmErrDialog form.

Control	Property	Setting
VB.Form	Name	frmErrDialog
	BorderStyle	3 'Fixed Dialog
	Caption	"Error Report"

14

continues

Table 14.4. continued

Control	Property	Setting
	ClientHeight	1755
	ClientLeft	45
	ClientTop	330
	ClientWidth	5460
	ControlBox	0 'False
	MaxButton	0 'False
	MinButton	0 'False
	ShowInTaskbar	0 'False
	StartUpPosition	2 'CenterScreen
VB.TextBox	Name	txtErrMsg
	BackColor	&H80000000&
	Height	1035
	Left	900
	Locked	-1 'True
	MultiLine	-1 'True
	ScrollBars	2 'Vertical
	Top	120
	Width	4395
VB.CommandButton	Name	cmdBtn
	Caption	"&Help"
	Height	315
	Index	3
	Left	4080
	Top	1320
	Visible	0 'False
	Width	1215
VB.CommandButton	Name	cmdBtn
	Caption	"&Ignore"
	Height	315

Control	Property	Setting
	Index	2
	Left	2760
	Top	1320
	Visible	0 'False
	Width	1215
VB.CommandButton	Name	cmdBtn
	Caption	"&Retry"
	Height	315
	Index	1
	Left	1440
	Top	1320
	Visible	0 'False
	Width	1215
VB.CommandButton	Name	cmdBtn
	Caption	"&OK"
	Height	315
	Index	0
	Left	120
	Top	1320
	Visible	0 'False
	Width	1215
VB.Image	Name	Image1
	Height	600
	Left	120
	Picture	C:\TYSDBVB5\SOURCE\CHAP14\ ERRHANDLER\INTL_NO.BMP
	Stretch	-1 'True
	Top	120
	Width	600

14

Be sure you build the command buttons as a control array and that you set their Visible property to False. You write code to arrange and enable these buttons as needed at runtime.

Figure 14.16.

*Laying out the
frmErrDialog form.*

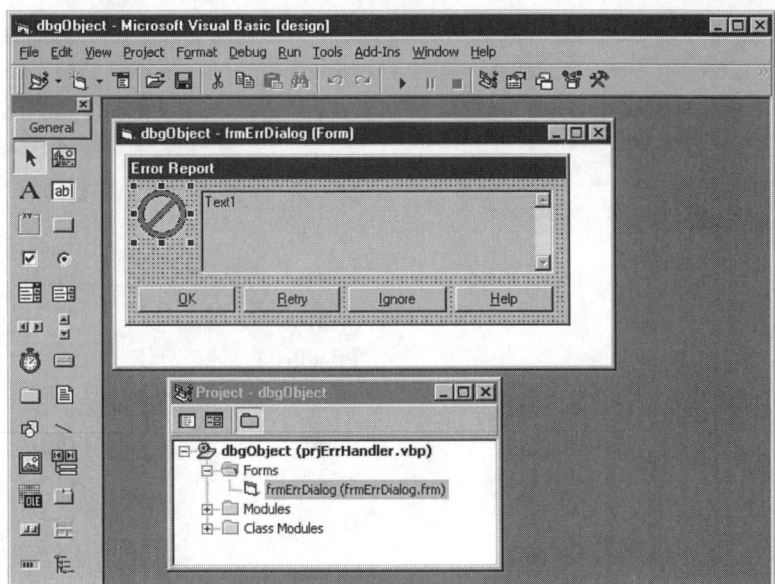

Only two events need to be coded for this form. The Form_Load event handles most of the
dirty work. Listing 14.20 shows the code that you should add to the Form_Load event.

**Listing 14.20. Coding the Form_Load event of the frmErrDialog
form.**

TYPE

```
Private Sub Form_Load()
    '
    Dim intBtns As Integer
    Dim intLoop As Integer
    '
    txtErrMsg = udtErrDialog.Message
    Me.Caption = udtErrDialog.Title
    '
    intBtns = UBound(udtErrDialog.Buttons)
    For intLoop = 0 To intBtns
        cmdBtn(intLoop).Caption = udtErrDialog.Buttons(intLoop)
        cmdBtn(intLoop).Visible = True
        cmdBtn(intLoop).Top = Me.ScaleHeight - 420
        cmdBtn(intLoop).Left = 120 + (1300 * intLoop)
    Next
    '
    ' check for help file
    If udtErrDialog.HelpFile <> "" Then
        cmdBtn(3).Visible = True
        cmdBtn(3).Top = Me.ScaleHeight - 420
        cmdBtn(3).Left = 120 + (1300 * 3)
    End If
    '
End Sub
```

14

The code in Listing 14.20 first sets the dialog caption and message box. Then, based on the properties of the udtErrDialog type, the buttons are arranged on the form. The only other code that needs to be added to this form is the code that goes behind the command button array. Place the code from Listing 14.21 in the cmdBtn_Click event of the form.

TYPE | **Listing 14.21. Coding the cmdBtn_Click event.**

```
Private Sub cmdBtn_Click(Index As Integer)
    '
    ' return user selection
    '
    Dim lngReturn As Long
    '
    Select Case Index
        Case 0
            udtErrDialog.Return = errExit
            lngReturn = WinHelp(Me.hwnd, udtErrDialog.HelpFile, HELP_QUIT, &H0)
            Unload Me
        Case 1
            udtErrDialog.Return = errresume
            lngReturn = WinHelp(Me.hwnd, udtErrDialog.HelpFile, HELP_QUIT, &H0)
            Unload Me
        Case 2
            udtErrDialog.Return = errNext
            lngReturn = WinHelp(Me.hwnd, udtErrDialog.HelpFile, HELP_QUIT, &H0)
            Unload Me
        Case 3
            lngReturn = WinHelp(Me.hwnd, udtErrDialog.HelpFile, HELP_CONTEXT,
udtErrDialog.HelpID)
    End Select
    '
End Sub
```

The code in Listing 14.21 allows the user to select the command button appropriate for the moment. If the user presses the Help button, the properties from the udtErrDialog type are used to fill in the parameters of the WinHelp API call.

That's all the code you need to create your errHandler ActiveX DLL. Save the project and then compile it (File | Make prjErrHandler.dll). If it compiles without error, you're all set for a quick test!

Testing the ErrHandler Object Library

Start a new Visual Basic 5 Standard EXE project. Set the form name to frmTest and the project name to prjTest. Add a data control and a command button to the form. Refer to Figure 14.17 while laying out the form.

14

Figure 14.17.

Laying out the frmTest form.

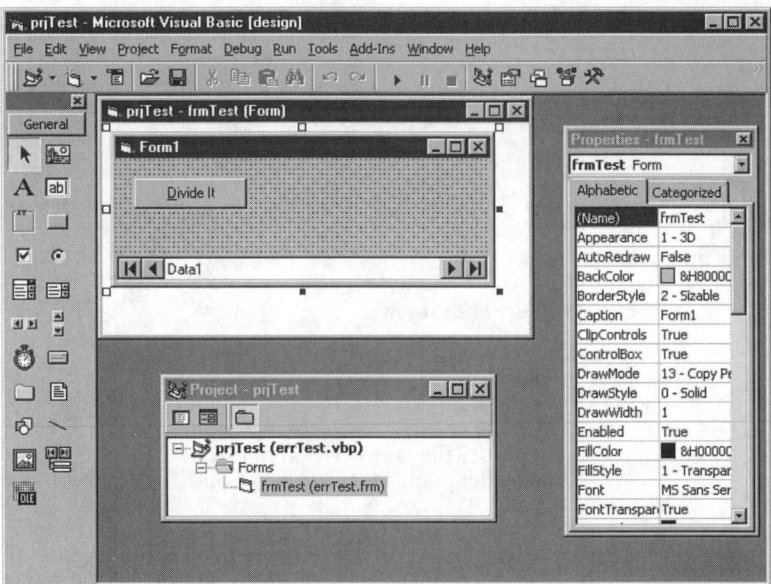

Next you need to add a reference to the error handler object library to your project. Select Project | References and locate and add the prjErrHandler DLL (see Figure 14.18).

Figure 14.18.

Adding the error handler object library to the project.

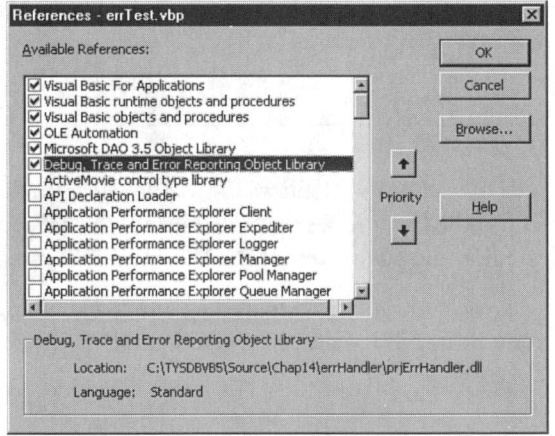

Now you can add a bit of code to the form to set up the error handler, and then cause an error to be handled. First, add the following line to the general declaration section of the form. This declares the object that contains the error handler.

```
Option Explicit
'
Public objErr As Object
```

Next, add the code from Listing 14.22 to the Form_Load event of the project.

TYPE **Listing 14.22. Coding the Form_Load event.**

```
Private Sub Form_Load()
    '
    Data1.DatabaseName = "junk"
    Set objErr = New errHandler
    '
End Sub
```

This code creates the new error handler object and then sets up the data control with a bogus database name. Now add the code from Listing 14.23 to the Data1_Error event. This code intercepts the database error and displays the new custom dialog box.

TYPE **Listing 14.23. Trapping the data control error.**

```
Private Sub Data1_Error(DataErr As Integer, Response As Integer)
    '
    Dim rtn As Long

    Response = 0
    rtn = objErr.errHandler(Errors, errcoll)
    '
End Sub
```

Now save the form (FRMTEST.FRM) and the project (PRJTEST.VBP) and run the code. You should see your new object library error dialog telling you about the database error (see Figure 14.19).

Now add some code behind the Command1_Click event to create a divide-by-zero error. The code in Listing 14.24 does just that.

14

Figure 14.19.

*The new error object
library in action.*

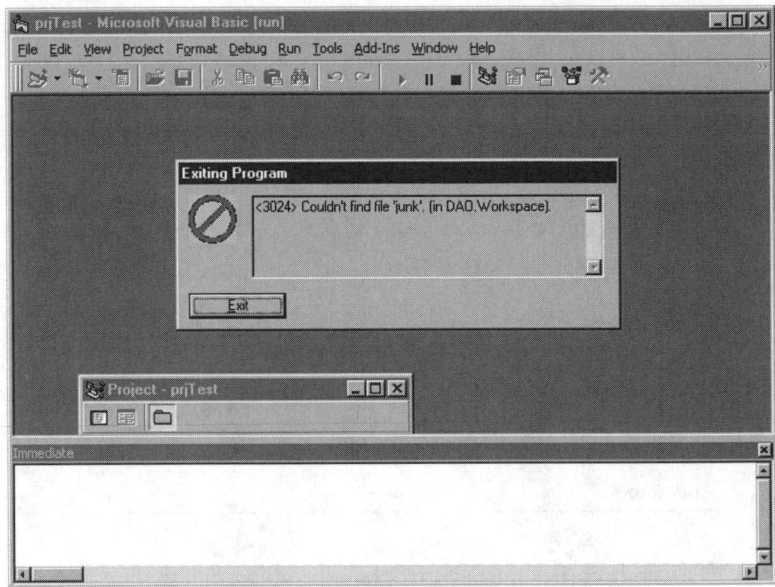

TYPE   **Listing 14.24. Creating a divide-by-zero error in code.**

```
Private Sub Command1_Click()
    '
    On Error GoTo Localerr
    Dim rtn as Long
    '
    Print 6 / 0
    '
    Exit Sub
    '
Localerr:
    rtn = objErr.errHandler(Err, erritem, errresume, "prjTest.
➥Form1.Command1_Click")
    Resume Next
    '
End Sub
```

When you save and run this code, press the command button to see the new error report. You
should see that the Help button is active. Press the Help button to display Visual Basic 5 help
for dealing with the divide-by-zero error (see Figure 14.20).

NOTE

Check out Appendix B for information on how you can create your
own help files for your Visual Basic 5 projects.

14

Figure 14.20.

Viewing help on the divide-by-zero error.

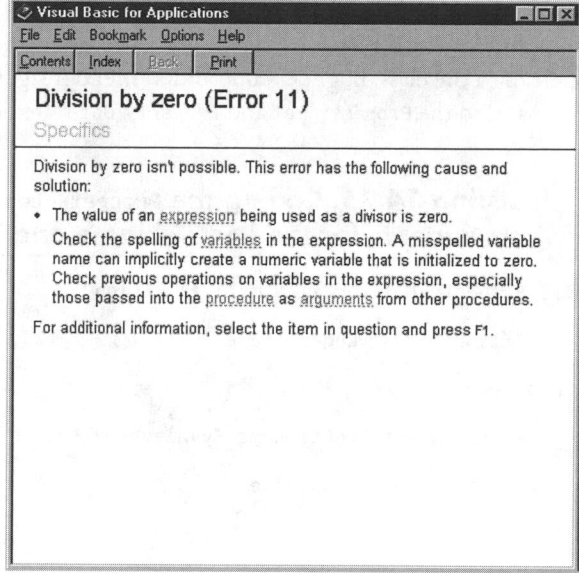

Now let's add an option that creates an error report file whenever the error handler is activated.

Adding Error Logs to the Error Handler

When errors occur, users often do not remember details that appear in the error messages. It's much more useful to create an error log on disk whenever errors occur. This enables programmers or system administrators to review the logs and see the error messages without having to be right next to the user when the error occurs.

To build error-logging features into the existing errhandler class, you need to declare two new properties (LogFileName and WriteLogFlag), create a LogError method to write the errors to a disk file, add some code to the general declarations area, the Class_Initialize and Class_Terminate events, and add a few lines to the errHandler method to call the LogError method.

First, restart the errhandler DLL project and add the code below to the general declaration section of the class module.

```
'
' logging storage
Private errLogFileName As String
Private errLogFlag As Boolean
```

14

These two lines of code appear at the end of the section. They declare local storage space for the new properties. Now use the Tools | Add Procedure menu option to add two new Public properties to the class: LogFileName and WriteLogFlag. Listing 14.25 shows the code you need to add to the `Property Let` and `Property Get` statements for these two new properties.

TYPE

Listing 14.25. Coding the `Property Let` and `Property Get` statements for the LogFileName and WriteLogFlag properties.

```
Public Property Get LogFileName() As String
    '
    LogFileName = errLogFileName
    '
End Property

Public Property Let LogFileName(ByVal vNewValue As String)
    '
    errLogFileName = vNewValue
    '
End Property

Public Property Get WriteLogFlag() As Boolean
    '
    WriteLogFlag = errLogFlag
    '
End Property

Public Property Let WriteLogFlag(ByVal vNewValue As Boolean)
    '
    errLogFlag = vNewValue
    '
End Property
```

The LogFileName property is used to hold the name of the disk file that holds the log records. The LogFlag property controls the status of the error logging. If the LogFlag property is set to `True`, log records are created. Now add the following code to the end of the `Class_Initialize` event. This sets the default values for the two new properties.

```
errLogFileName = App.EXEName & ".err"
errLogFlag = False
'
```

Now create a new `Private Sub` method called `LogError` and enter the code from Listing 14.26 into the routine. This is the code that actually creates the log entries.

TYPE **Listing 14.26. Coding the `LogError` method.**

```
Private Sub LogError(strErrMsg As String)
    '
    ' write error to disk file
    On Error GoTo LocalErr
    '
    Dim intChFile As Integer
    '
    intChFile = FreeFile
    Open errLogFileName For Append As intChFile
        Print #intChFile, Format(Now, "general date")
        Print #intChFile, strErrMsg
        Print #intChFile, ""
    Close intChFile
    '
    Exit Sub
    '
LocalErr:
    ' trouble with file stuff!
    Err.Raise vbObjectError + 1, "errHandler.LogError", "Can't write log file ["
& errLogFileName & "]"
    '
End Sub
```

Notice that you added an error handler in this routine. Because you are about to perform disk operations, you need to be ready for errors here, too! Notice also that the internal error is not displayed in a message box. Instead the `Raise` method of the Err object is used to generate a unique error number and description. This is sent back to the calling application for handling.

 **TIP**

> The Visual Basic `FreeFile()` function is used to return a number that represents the first available file channel that Visual Basic uses to open the data file. Using `FreeFile()` guarantees that you do not select a file channel that Visual Basic is already using for another file.

Now all you need to do is add a call to the `LogError` method from within the Public `errHandler` method. Listing 14.27 shows the code you need to add in the routine. Make sure you add these lines of code right after the call to the `errMsg` function and just before the start of the `Select Case` statement.

14

TYPE **Listing 14.27. Updating the errHandler method.**

```
' build full message
    strMsg = errMsg(objErrColl, intType)
    '
    ' write it out, if allowed          <<< new code
    If errLogFlag = True Then           <<< new code
        LogError strMsg                 <<< new code
    End If                                      <<< new code
    '
    ' evaluate things
    Select Case errOption
```

That's the end of the code to add logging to the error handler. Save the project and compile the ActiveX DLL. Once the DLL has been successfully compiled, close this project and open the test project you built earlier.

Open the Form_Load event of the frmTest form and add two lines to set the LogFileName and WriteLogFlag properties of the errHandler object. Listing 14.28 shows how to modify the code.

TYPE **Listing 14.28. Modifying the Form_Load event to include error logging.**

```
Private Sub Form_Load()
    '
    Data1.DatabaseName = "junk"
    Set objErr = New errHandler
    '
    objErr.WriteLogFlag = True
    objErr.LogFileName = App.Path & "\" & App.EXEName & ".log"
    '
End Sub
```

Now, when you run the project, each error is logged to a file with the same name as the application in the same folder as the application. In the preceding example, a file called errTest.log was created in the C:\TYSDBVB5\SOURCE\CHAP14\ folder. Listing 14.29 shows the contents of this error log file.

TYPE **Listing 14.29. Contents of the errTest.log file.**

```
05-Feb-97 5:27:01 AM
<3024> Couldn't find file 'junk'. (in DAO.Workspace).

05-Feb-97 5:27:08 AM
<11> Division by zero (in prjTest)
```

You can easily modify the layout and the contents of the log reports. You need only change a few lines of code in the LogError method.

Adding a Module Trace to the Error Handler

The final touch to add to your error handler library is the option to keep track of and print a module trace. A module trace keeps track of all the modules that have been called and the order in which they were invoked. This can be very valuable when you're debugging programs. Often, a routine works just fine when it is called from one module, but it reports errors if called from another module. When errors occur, it's handy to have a module trace to look through to help find the source of your problems.

We implement our module trace routines as a new objclass object in the prjErrHandler project. Reload the ActiveX DLL project and add a new class module to the project. Set its Name property to TraceObject and keep its Instancing property set to the default, 5 - MultiUse.

You need two new properties for this object (TraceFileName and TraceFlag) and a handful of new Public methods:

- [ ] Push adds a sub or function name to the call list.
- [ ] Pop removes a sub or function name from the call list.
- [ ] List returns an array of all the names on the call list.
- [ ] Dump writes the complete call list to a disk file.
- [ ] Show displays the complete call list in a message box.
- [ ] Clear resets the call list.

First, add the code in Listing 14.30 to the general declarations area of the class module.

TYPE   **Listing 14.30. Declaring the TraceObject variables.**

```
Option Explicit
'
' local property storage
Private trcFileName As String
Private trcFlag As Boolean
'
' internal variables
Private trcStack() As String
Private trcPointer As Long
```

14

Next, create the two new Public properties, TraceFile and TraceFlag, and enter the code from Listing 14.31 into the `Property Let` and `Property Get` statements for these two new properties.

Listing 14.31. Coding the `Property Let` and `Property Get` statements for the TraceFile and TraceLog properties.

TYPE

```
Public Property Get TraceFileName() As String
    '
    TraceFileName = trcFileName
    '
End Property

Public Property Let TraceFileName(ByVal vNewValue As String)
    '
    trcFileName = vNewValue
    '
End Property

Public Property Get TraceFlag() As Boolean
    '
    TraceFlag = trcFlag
    '
End Property

Public Property Let TraceFlag(ByVal vNewValue As Boolean)
    '
    trcFlag = vNewValue
    '
End Property
```

Now add the code from Listing 14.32 to the `Class_Initialize` event. This code sets the default values for the two Public properties.

TYPE   **Listing 14.32. Coding the `Class_Initialize` event.**

```
Private Sub Class_Initialize()
    '
    ' startup stuff
    trcFileName = App.EXEName & ".trc"
    trcFlag = False
    '
End Sub
```

14

Now it's time to code the various methods you need to manage call tracing in Visual Basic 5. First, create the Public Sub methods Push and Pop. These two routines handle the details of keeping track of each function or sub as it is executed. Listing 14.33 shows the code for these two Public methods.

TYPE **Listing 14.33. Coding the Push and Pop methods of the TraceObject.**

```
Public Sub Push(ProcName As String)
    '
    ' push a proc onto the stack
    trcPointer = trcPointer + 1
    ReDim Preserve trcStack(trcPointer)
    trcStack(trcPointer) = ProcName
    '
End Sub

Public Sub Pop()
    '
    ' pop a proc off the stack
    If trcPointer <> 0 Then
        trcPointer = trcPointer - 1
        ReDim Preserve trcStack(trcPointer)
    End If
    '
End Sub
```

Now create another Public Sub method (Clear) and a Public Function method (List). Add the code from Listing 14.34 to the class.

TYPE **Listing 14.34. Coding the List and Clear methods of the TraceObject.**

```
Public Function List() As Variant
    '
    ' return an array of the trace log
    List = trcStack
    '
End Function

Public Sub Clear()
    '
    ' clear off the stack
    trcPointer = 0
    ReDim Preserve trcStack(0)
    '
End Sub
```

14

TIP Notice the use of the Variant data type to return an array of items. This is a very efficient way to pass array data among Visual Basic methods.

Now create a new `Public Sub` called `Dump`. This writes the trace list to a disk file. Fill in the method with the code from Listing 14.35.

TYPE **Listing 14.35. Coding the `Dump` method of the TraceObject.**

```
Public Sub Dump()
    '
    ' write trace log to file
    Dim intFile As Integer
    Dim intLoop As Integer
    '
    intFile = FreeFile
    Open trcFileName For Append As intFile
        Print #intFile, "***TRACE STACK DUMP***"
        Print #intFile, "***DATE: " & Format(Now(), "general date")
        Print #intFile, ""
        '
        For intLoop = trcPointer To 1 Step -1
            Print #intFile, vbTab & Format(intLoop, "000") & ": " &
➥trcStack(intLoop)
        Next
        '
        Print #intFile, ""
        Print #intFile, "***EOF"
    Close #intFile
    '
    Exit Sub
    '
LocalErr:
    Err.Raise vbObjectError + 3, "Trace.Dump", "Can't write trace file [" &
➥trcFileName & "]"

End Sub
```

Finally, create the `Public Sub` method called `Show` and enter the code from Listing 14.36.

TYPE **Listing 14.36. Coding the `Show` method of the TraceObject.**

```
Public Sub Show()
    '
    ' show trace log in dialog
    '
    Dim intLoop As Integer
    Dim strMsg As String
```

```
        '
        strMsg = ""
        For intLoop = trcPointer To 1 Step -1
            strMsg = strMsg & Format(intLoop, "000")
            strMsg = strMsg & ": "
            strMsg = strMsg & Trim(trcStack(intLoop))
            strMsg = strMsg & vbCrLf
        Next
        '
        MsgBox strMsg, vbInformation, "Trace Stack"
        '
End Sub
```

Notice that the code in Listing 14.36 prints the call array in *reverse* order. This is the conventional way to print trace lists. The top-most entry shows the most recently executed routine, and the bottom-most entry shows the first routine in this trace.

After adding this last code, save and compile the ActiveX DLL and then load your errTest project. After you load the frmTest form, add the following code to the general declarations area of the form.

```
Public objTrace As Object
```

Next, update the Form_Load event as shown in Listing 14.37. This adds the use of the trace module to the project.

TYPE **Listing 14.37. Updating the Form_Load event to include module tracing.**

```
Private Sub Form_Load()
    '
    Data1.DatabaseName = "junk"
    '
    Set objErr = New errHandler
    Set objTrace = New TraceObject
    '
    objTrace.Push "Form_Load"
    '
    objErr.WriteLogFlag = True
    objErr.LogFileName = App.Path & "\" & App.EXEName & ".log"
    '
    objTrace.Pop
    '
End Sub
```

Note the use of objTrace.Push to add the name of the method onto the trace stack. This should happen as early as possible in the method code. Note, also the objTrace.Pop line at the very end of the method. This removes the name of the method from the stack just as the method is complete.

14

Let's also add trace coding to the Command1_click event. Update your form's command1_Click event to match the one in Listing 14.38.

TYPE **Listing 14.38. Updating the Command1_click event to use module tracing.**

```
Private Sub Command1_Click()
    '
    On Error GoTo Localerr
    Dim varList As Variant
    Dim rtn As Long
    '
    objTrace.Push "Command1_Click"
    '
    Print 6 / 0
    '
    Exit Sub
    '
Localerr:
    '
    rtn = objErr.errHandler(Err, erritem, errresume,
"prjTest.Form1.Command1_Click")
    '
    objTrace.Show
    objTrace.Pop
    Resume Next
    '
End Sub
```

Save this code and run the project. When you press the command button, you get a trace report on the screen (see Figure 14.21).

Figure 14.21.

Viewing the trace message.

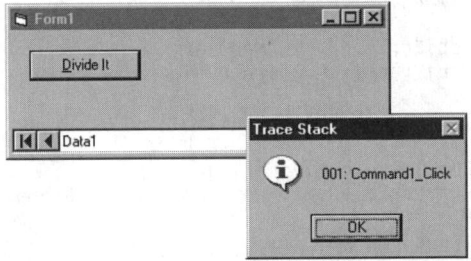

Notice that, in order to add module tracing to a project, you only need to add a .Push line at the start of the routine and a .Pop line at the end of the routine. This is all you need to do in order to update the procedure stack for the program. But, for this to be really valuable, you have to do this for each routine that you want to track.

14

In a real application environment, you wouldn't want to show the procedure stack each time an error is reported. The best place for a stack dump is at exit time due to a fatal error. You should probably use the TraceFile option to write the stack to disk rather than displaying it to the user.

Other Error Handler Options

Now that you have the basics of error handling under your belt, you can continue to add features to the generic error handler. As you add these features, your programs take on a more professional look and feel. Also, using options such as error report logs and procedure stack logs makes it easier to debug and maintain your applications.

Additional features that you can add to your error handler include:

☐ Add the name of the user or workstation address to the reports.

☐ If you have created an error trap for common errors, such as Error 53—File not found, add that recovery code to your generic handler. Now you can count on consistent handling of common errors without adding code to every project.

Summary

Today's lesson covered all the basics of creating your own error-handling routines for Visual Basic applications. You learned that an error handler has three basic parts:

☐ The `On Error Goto` statement

☐ The body of the error handler code

☐ The error handler exit

You learned that an error handler has four possible exits:

☐ `Resume`: Re-executes the code that caused the error.

☐ `Resume Next`: Continues processing at the line immediately following the code line that caused the error.

☐ `Resume label`: Continues processing at the location identified by the label.

☐ `EXIT` or `END`: `EXIT` ends processing for the current routine, and `END` exits the program completely.

You learned how to use the `Err.Raise` method to flag errors without resorting to modal dialog boxes.

14

You learned about the major types of errors that you are likely to encounter in your program:

☐ General file errors: These include errors such as `File not found` and `Invalid path`. Errors of this type can usually be fixed by the user and then the operation retried. Use `Resume` as an exit for these types of errors.

☐ Database errors: These include errors related to data entry mistakes, integrity violations, and multiuser-related errors, such as locked records. Errors of this type are best handled by allowing the user to correct the data and attempt the operation again. If you use the Visual Basic data control, you do not have to write error handlers—the data control handles them for you. For operations that do not use the data control, you need to write your own error-handling routines.

☐ Physical media errors: These errors relate to device problems, such as unresponsive printers, downed communications ports, and so on. Sometimes users can fix the problems and continue (such as refilling the paper tray of the printer). Other times, users cannot fix the problem without first exiting the program. It is a good idea to give users the option of exiting the program safely when errors of these types are reported.

☐ Program code errors: These errors occur because of problems within the Visual Basic code itself. Examples of program code errors include `Object variable not set` and `For loop not initialized`. Usually the user cannot do anything to fix errors of this type. It is best to encourage the user to report the error to the system administrator and exit the program safely.

You also learned that you can declare a global error handler or a local error handler. The advantage of the global error handler is that it allows you to create a single module that handles all expected errors. The disadvantage is that, due to the way Visual Basic keeps track of running routines, you are not able to resume processing at the point the error occurs once you arrive at the global error handler. The advantage of the local error handler is that you are always able to use `Resume`, `Resume Next`, or `Resume label` to continue processing at the point the error occurs. The disadvantage of the local error handler is that you need to add error-handling code to every routine in your program.

Finally, you learned how to create an error handler object library that combines local error trapping with global error messages and responses. The error handler object library also contains modules to keep track of the procedures currently running at the time of the error, a process for printing procedure stack dumps to the screen and to a file, and a process that creates an error log on file for later review.

14

Quiz

1. What are the three main parts of error handlers in Visual Basic?
2. What are the four ways to exit an error handler routine?
3. When would you use `Resume` to exit an error handler?
4. When would you use `Resume Next` to exit an error handler?
5. When would you use `Resume label` to exit an error handler?
6. When would you use the `EXIT` or `END` command to exit an error handler?
7. List the four types of Visual Basic errors.
8. Should you use error trapping for the Visual Basic data control?
9. In what Visual Basic event should you open data tables or files in which the user enters data?
10. What are the advantages and disadvantages of global error handlers?
11. What is the `Err.Raise` method and why is it useful?

Exercises

1. Create a new project and add code to a command button that opens the file `C:\ABC.TXT`. Include an error handler that notifies the user that the file cannot be opened, and then terminates the program.

2. Modify the project started in Exercise 1 by adding a new command button. Attach code to this button that attempts to load a file named `C:\ABC.TXT`. Notify the user that this file cannot be opened, and give the user the option and the dialog box to search for the file. Exit the program when a selection has been made or if the user chooses not to proceed.

   Run this program and elect to find the file. Cancel out of any common dialogs that appear. After this, create the file using Notepad and run the process again. Finally, move the file to a location other than the C drive and run the program. Use the common dialog to search for and select the file.

14

Week

2

8

9

10

11

12

13

14

In Review

Week 2 concentrated on topics that are of value to developers in the standalone and workgroup environments. A wide variety of topics were covered in Week 2, including

- [ ] How to use Visdata to build and manage databases
- [ ] How to use the Structured Query Language (SQL) to extract data from existing databases
- [ ] What the Microsoft Jet engine is, and how you can use Visual Basic code to create and maintain data-access objects
- [ ] How to create data entry forms with Visual Basic code

☐ How to use the Microsoft graph control to create graphs and charts of your data

☐ How to use data-bound list boxes, data-bound combo boxes, and data-bound grids to create advanced data entry forms

☐ How to make applications more solid with error trapping

Here is a more detailed look at the topics covered in each lesson:

Day 8: Selecting Data with SQL

You learned in Day 8 how to create basic SQL statements that select data from existing tables. You learned that the most fundamental form of the SQL statement is the SELECT_FROM clause. This clause is used to select one or more columns from a table and display the results of in a *result set*, or *view*.

You also learned about the optional clauses that you can add to the SELECT_FROM clause:

☐ The WHERE clause: Used to limit the rows in the result set using logical comparisons (for example, WHERE Table.Name = "SMITH") and to link two tables in a single, nonupdatable, view (for example, WHERE Table1.Name = Table2.Name).

☐ The ORDER BY clause: Used to control the order in which the result set is displayed (for example, ORDER BY Name ASC).

☐ The GROUP BY clause: Used to create a subtotal result set based on a break column (for example, GROUP BY Name).

☐ The HAVING clause: Used only with the GROUP BY clause, the HAVING clause acts as a WHERE clause for the GROUP BY subtotal clause (for example, GROUP BY Name HAVING SUM(SalesTotal)>1000).

☐ The INNER JOIN clause: Used to join two tables together into a single, updatable result set. The INNER JOIN returns rows that have a corresponding match in both tables.

☐ The LEFT JOIN and RIGHT JOIN: Used to join two tables into a single, updatable result set. The LEFT JOIN includes all records from the first (left-hand) table and all rows from the second table that have a corresponding match. The RIGHT JOIN works in reverse.

☐ The UNION clause: Used to combine two or more complete SQL queries into a single result set (for example, SELECT * FROM Table1 UNION SELECT * FROM Table2).

☐ The TRANSFORM_PIVOT clause: Used to create a cross-tab query as a result set (for example, TRANSFORM SUM(MonthlySales) FROM SalesTable GROUP BY Product PIVOT Month).

You also learned about additional SQL keywords that you can use to control the contents of the result set:

- [ ] `BETWEEN_AND`
- [ ] `DISTINCT` and `DISTINCTROW`
- [ ] `AS`
- [ ] `TOP n` and `TOP n PERCENT`
- [ ] `AVG`, `COUNT`, `MAX`, `MIN`, and `SUM`

Day 9: Visual Basic and the Microsoft Jet Engine

In Day 9's lesson, you learned the features and functions of Visual Basic Microsoft Jet data-access objects and ODBCDirect access objects. These objects are used within Visual Basic code to create and maintain workspaces, databases, tables, fields, indexes, queries, and relations. You learned the properties, methods, and collections of each object. You also learned how to use Visual Basic code to inspect the values in the properties, and how to use the methods to perform basic database operations.

Day 10: Creating Database Programs with Visual Basic Code

On Day 10, you learned how to write data entry forms using Visual Basic code. These topics were covered: record search routines, the creation of a procedure library to handle all data entry processes, and creating a working data entry form for the CompanyMaster project.

You learned how to perform single-record searches using the three search methods:

- [ ] `Move` for browsing the dataset
- [ ] `Seek` for indexed table objects
- [ ] `Find` for non-table objects (Dynasets and Snapshots)

You created an OLE Server library to handle adding, editing, deleting, reading, writing, and locating records in datasets. These routines were written as a generic DLL that can be inserted into all Visual Basic programs you write in the future.

You used the new library to add a new form to the CompanyMaster database project. This new form reads a dataset and allows the user to update and browse the table. This new data entry form was built using fewer than 30 lines of Visual Basic code.

Day 11: Displaying Your Data with Graphs

On Day 11, you learned how to use the graph control that ships with Visual Basic 5 to create visual displays of your data tables. You learned how to add the control to your project and how to load the graph control with data points, titles, legends, and labels.

Also, you built a graph ActiveX DLL object library that you can use to display virtually any dataset in a variety of graph formats. This library lets you save the graph to disk, send the graph to the printer, or copy the graph to the Windows Clipboard for placement in other Windows programs through the Paste Special operation.

While building the graph library, you learned how to declare and use enumerated constants to improve the readability of your Visual Basic code.

Finally, you used the new graph library to add three graphs to the CompanyMaster project.

Day 12: Data-Bound List Boxes, Grids, and Subforms

On Day 12, you learned how to load and use three of the data-bound controls that are shipped with Visual Basic 5:

☐ The data-bound list box
☐ The data-bound combo box
☐ The data-bound grid

You learned how to link these new controls to Recordsets using the Visual Basic 5 data controls and how to use these links to update related tables.

You also learned several of the important Visual Basic 5 events associated with the data grid. These events let you create user-friendly data entry routines using just a data control and the data grid.

Finally, you drew upon your knowledge of data grids, SQL, and form layout to design and implement a data entry subform. This form showed a master table at the top, and a related list table at the bottom of the form in a data-bound grid.

Day 13: Creating Databases with SQL

On Day 13, you learned how to create, alter, and delete database table structures using DDL (Data Definition Language) SQL keywords. You also learned that using DDL statements to build tables, create indexes, and establish relationships is an excellent way to automatically document table layouts. You learned how to maintain database structures using the following DDL keywords:

☐ CREATE TABLE enables you to create entirely new tables in your existing database.

☐ DROP TABLE enables you to completely remove a table, including any data that is already in the table.

☐ ALTER TABLE enables you to ADD a new column or DROP an existing column from the table without losing existing data in the other columns.

☐ CREATE INDEX and DROP INDEX enable you to create indexes that can enforce data integrity or speed data access.

☐ The CONSTRAINT clause can be added to the CREATE TABLE or ALTER TABLE statement to define relationships between tables using the FOREIGN KEY clause.

Day 14: Error Handling in Visual Basic 5

The final lesson of the second week covered all the basics of creating your own error-handling routines for Visual Basic applications. You learned that an error handler has three basic parts:

☐ The On Error Goto statement
☐ The body of the error handler code
☐ The error handler exit

You learned that an error handler has four possible exits:

☐ Resume: Re-executes the code that caused the error.

☐ Resume Next: Continues processing at the line immediately following the line that caused the error.

☐ Resume label: Continues processing at the location identified by the label.

☐ EXIT or END: EXIT ends processing for the current routine and END exits the program completely.

You learned how to use the Err.Raise method to flag errors without resorting to modal dialog boxes.

You learned about the major types of errors that you are likely to encounter in your program:

☐ General file errors: These include errors such as File not Found and Invalid Path. Errors of this type can usually be fixed by the user and then the original procedure re-attempted. Use Resume as an exit for these types of errors.

☐ Database errors: These include errors related to data entry mistakes, integrity violations, and multiuser-related errors, such as locked records. Errors of this type are best handled by allowing the user to correct the data and attempt the operation again. If you use the Visual Basic data control, you do not have to write error handlers—the data control handles them for you. For operations that do not use the data control, you need to write your own error-handling routines.

☐ Physical media errors: These errors relate to device problems, such as unresponsive printers, downed communications ports, and so on. Sometimes users can fix the problems and continue (for example, refilling the paper tray of the printer). Other times, users cannot fix the problem without first exiting the program. It is a good idea to give users the option of exiting the program safely when errors of these types are reported.

☐ Program code errors: These errors occur because of problems within the Visual Basic code itself. Examples of program code errors include Object variable not Set and For loop not initialized. Usually the user cannot do anything to fix errors of this type. It is best to encourage the user to report the error to the system administrator and then exit the program safely.

You also learned that you can declare a global error handler or a local error handler. The advantage of the global error handler is that it allows you to create a single module that handles all expected errors. The disadvantage is that, because of the way Visual Basic keeps track of running routines, you are not able to resume processing at the point the error occurs once you arrive at the global error handler. The advantage of the local error handler is that you are always able to use Resume, Resume Next, or Resume label to continue processing at the point the error occurs. The disadvantage of the local error handler is that you need to add error-handling code to every routine in your program.

Finally, you learned how to create an error handler object library that combines local error trapping with global error messages and responses. The error handler object library also contains modules to keep track of the procedures currently running at the time of the error, a process for printing procedure stack dumps to the screen and to a file, and a process that creates an error log on file for later review.

WEEK 3

15

16

17

18

19

20

21

At a Glance

Week 1 focused on developing skills necessary to build Visual Basic database applications in the desktop environment. Week 2 focused on the skills needed in the workgroup environment. This week focuses on skills needed for developing enterprise-level Visual Basic applications.

The following topics are covered:

☐ Using Advanced SQL statements to add, edit, and delete data from database tables.

☐ Using database normalization techniques to improve the organization, integrity, and performance of your databases.

☐ Issues to consider when developing multiuser applications, including Jet locking schemes, the use of cascading updates and deletes for referential integrity, and how transaction management can improve both the speed of your programs and the quality of your data.

☐ Using the Remote Data Control and Remote Data Objects to attach to external relational database management systems.

☐ How to use the ODBC (Open Database Connectivity) API set to build ODBC-enabled applications that run on both 16-bit and 32-bit platforms.

☐ Using database replication to distribute and maintain data across an entire organization.

☐ How to add application-level security features to your program, including user login/logout, programmable access rights for critical operations, and the use of audit trails to track database updates and all secured user activity.

When you complete this week, you will have several reusable ActiveX objects that you can place into any Visual Basic application.

Here's a review of the upcoming lessons:

Day 15: You continue your study of SQL, using Data Manipulation Language to insert records into tables, append records to tables, and update records that currently exist in data tables. You also learn how to use Make Table queries to build tables with data from other tables. Finally, you learn how to create Delete Table queries that remove multiple records from a data table.

Day 16: This lesson focuses on using data normalization to increase database integrity and processing speed. The five rules of data normalization are covered, with logical examples that build upon your knowledge of SQL.

Day 17: This lesson centers on multiuser considerations. You learn the nuances of cascading updates and cascading deletes. You spend time on transaction management using the BeginTrans, CommitTrans, and Rollback methods. By the time you finish, you have a good understanding of database-level, table-level, and page-level locking schemes.

Day 18: In Day 18's lesson, you use two alternate methods to access external database information using Visual Basic 5. You are introduced to the Remote Data Control and to Remote Data Objects. You learn to use the properties, events, and methods of these tools to attach to RDBMS data sources. You also learn some of the basics of remote data access in general.

Day 19: This day's topic is Open Database Connectivity (ODBC) through the ODBC API. You learn how to create data forms that use low-level API calls to access existing databases. This chapter presents topics that are essential to the development of client-server Visual Basic applications that can run on both 16-bit and 32-bit operating systems. You see how to build Visual Basic applications that bypass the Microsoft Jet database engine and link directly to the data source through the ODBC interface. You also learn how to build reusable code that creates data-entry screens for applications that connect to ODBC data sources.

Day 20: Database replication is the focus of Day 20. You learn how to use database replication to distribute data changes across a replica set. You learn to use data-access objects to create Design Masters and replicas. You also use data-access objects to synchronize data changes. Finally, you use data-access objects to keep objects from replicating.

Day 21: The main focus of Day 20 is securing your Visual Basic database applications. All quality applications have security to protect the precious data they control. Database security, encryption, and the securing of processes are covered. You look at applying audit trails to track critical activities in your application. Throughout the day, you build security modules that you can insert into any Visual Basic project you create.

Day 15

Updating Databases with SQL

In today's lesson, you learn about the SQL Data Manipulation Language (DML) keywords you can use to update and modify data in existing tables. Although most of the time you use Visual Basic data entry forms and Visual Basic program code to perform data table updates, there are often times when it is more desirable to use SQL statements to update your data tables.

When you complete the examples in this chapter, you will be able to:

- ☐ Alter the contents of existing tables using the UPDATE statement.
- ☐ Add new rows to existing tables with the INSERT INTO statement.
- ☐ Append rows from one table to another using the INSERT INTO_FROM clause.
- ☐ Copy one or more rows from an existing table to a new table using the SELECT_INTO keywords.
- ☐ Remove selected rows from a table using the DELETE_FROM clause.

NOTE

Throughout this chapter, you use the SQL-VB5 program to create and run SQL scripts. The lesson on Day 13, "Creating Databases with SQL," contains a short tutorial on where to locate the SQL-VB5 program and how to use it. If you have not worked through the lesson on Day 13 yet, now is a good time to review at least the first half of that chapter.

Data Manipulation SQL Keywords

The Data Manipulation Language (DML) SQL keywords are used to add new data to existing tables, edit existing table data, append data from one table to another, copy data from one table to an entirely new table, and delete data rows from existing tables.

Most of the time, your Visual Basic programs use data-entry screens to perform these tasks. However, sometimes the DML keywords come in handy. In some back-end database systems, these SQL keywords are the only way you can add, edit, or delete data from tables. At other times, these SQL keywords give you the power to produce updates to large tables with very few lines of code and in a relatively short amount of time.

Also, many times you might need to select a small subset of data from your tables for a report or a graphic display. Instead of creating Dynaset views of existing tables, you might want to create a frozen Snapshot of the data to use for this purpose. What you need to do is copy some records from an existing table into a new table for use in reporting and displays. SQL DML keywords can help create these select tables quickly without extensive Visual Basic code.

Another example of using SQL DML keywords is when you want to append a set of records from one table to another. Instead of writing Visual Basic code routines that read a record from one table and then write it to another, you can use SQL DML keywords to perform the table update—many times with just one line of SQL code.

Finally, SQL DML keywords allow you to quickly delete entire tables or subsets of data in a single SQL statement. This reduces the amount of Visual Basic code you need to write and also greatly speeds the processing in most cases.

Adding Rows with the INSERT Statement

The INSERT statement is used to insert values into data tables. You can use the INSERT statement to populate data tables automatically—without the need for data-entry screens. Also, you can perform this automatic data entry using very little Visual Basic code.

15

Why Use INSERT **Statements?**

Even though you most often perform data entry using Visual Basic–coded data-entry screens tied to Visual Basic data controls, there are times when using the INSERT statement can prove more efficient. An excellent example of using INSERT statements is the installation of a new database system. Often, several data tables need to be populated with default values before people can start using a system. You can use the INSERT statement to perform the initial data load.

Another use for the INSERT statement is in converting data from one database to another. Often, you can use INSERT statements to load existing data in one format into your newly designed relational database.

Finally, you can use INSERT statements to quickly add data to tables that would be too tedious to enter using data-entry screens.

Using the INSERT INTO **Statement**

The basic form of the INSERT statement is

```
INSERT INTO TableName(field1, field2) VALUES (value1, value2);
```

NOTE | INSERT and INSERT INTO statements are often used interchangeably. For the most part, this book uses the latter term.

The INSERT SQL statement has three parts. The *TableName* identifies the table that you want to update. The (*field1, field2*) part of the statement identifies the columns into which you add data. The (*value1, value2*) part of the statement identifies the exact values you add to the fields you identified. You can name as few or as many fields as you like in the field portion of the statement. However, you must supply a list of values that has the same number of values and the same data type as those identified in the field portion of the statement. Also, you must list the values in the same order as the fields. The first value is placed in the first field, the second value in the second field, and so on.

Let's use SQL-VB5 to create a working example of the INSERT statement. Open a new .SQV script called SQLVB05.SQV using the File | New command from the main menu. Enter the script shown in Listing 15.1, save it, and execute it using the File | Run menu option. Refer to Figure 15.1 to compare your results.

`TYPE` **Listing 15.1. Testing the INSERT INTO keyword.**

```
//
// sqlvb05.sqv - Testing the INSERT INTO keyword
//
// create a new database
dbMake sqlvb05.mdb;
// create a new table
CREATE TABLE JobTitles
   (JobID TEXT(5) CONSTRAINT PKJobTitle PRIMARY KEY,
    JobName TEXT(20),
    JobDesc MEMO
    );
// insert some data
INSERT INTO JobTitles(JobID, JobName, JobDesc) VALUES
   ('J001',
    'President',
    'Presides over the company'
    );
INSERT INTO JobTitles(JobID, JobName, JobDesc) VALUES
   ('J002',
    'Vice President',
    'Does what the President tells him to do'
    );
// display results
SELECT * FROM JobTitles;
// eof
```

Figure 15.1.

The results of the
INSERT INTO
statement.

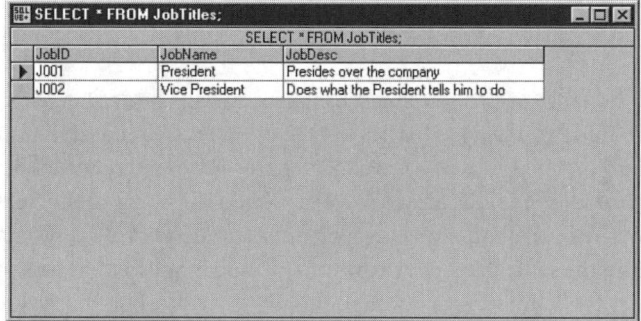

Notice that you must use a separate INSERT INTO statement for each row you want to add to the table. If you wanted to add 10 more job descriptions to the JobTitles table, you would need to add 10 more INSERT INTO statements to the script.

Also, because you defined the JobsTitles.JobID column as the primary key, you are required to fill that field with unique, non-null data each time you execute the INSERT INTO statement. If you provide a null value or leave the JobsTitles.JobID field out of the INSERT INTO statement, you get a database error message.

15

If you use a COUNTER data type field in your table, you can't include that in the field list of the INSERT INTO statement. Visual Basic and the SQL engine fill the COUNTER field with an appropriate value. Also, you do not have to add data to every column in the row. If there are fields in the data table that are not required and that can be left null, you can simply omit them from the INSERT INTO statement. The code example in Listing 15.2 illustrates these last two points. Use SQL-VB5 to edit the SQLVB05.SQV script to match the one in Listing 15.2. Save and execute the script. Check your results against those in Figure 15.2.

TYPE

Listing 15.2. Handling COUNTER and blank fields in INSERT statements.

```
//
// sqlvb05.sqv - Testing the INSERT INTO keyword
//
// create a new database
dbMake sqlvb05.mdb;
// create a new table
CREATE TABLE JobTitles
   (JobCounter COUNTER,
    JobID TEXT(5) CONSTRAINT PKJobTitle PRIMARY KEY,
    JobName TEXT(20),
    JobPay CURRENCY,
    JobDesc MEMO
    );
// insert some data
INSERT INTO JobTitles (JobID, JobName, JobDesc, JobPay) VALUES
   ('J001',
    'President',
    'Presides over the company',
    '50000'
    );
INSERT INTO JobTitles (JobID, JobName, JobDesc, JobPay) VALUES
   ('J002',
    'Vice President',
    'Does what the President tells him to do',
    '40000'
    );
INSERT INTO JobTitles (JobID, JobPay, JobName) VALUES
   ('J003',
    '35000',
    'Chief Engineer'
    );
// display results
SELECT * FROM JobTitles;
// eof
```

Notice that the JobTitles.JobCounter column was automatically populated by Visual Basic. Also, you can see that the JobTitles.JobDesc column was left blank for the third record in the table.

Figure 15.2.

The results of using INSERT INTO *with* COUNTER *and optional fields.*

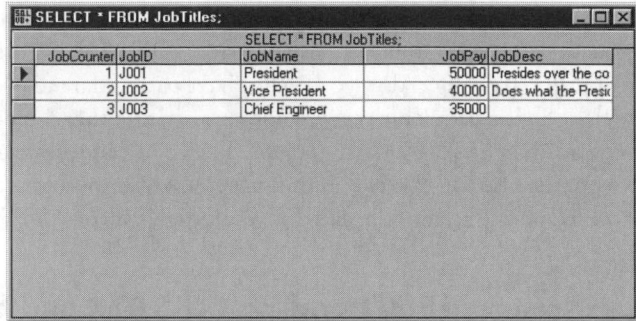

Two other interesting things about the INSERT INTO statement are illustrated in the code example in Listing 15.2. Notice that the values for the JobTitles.JobPay column were surrounded by quotation marks even though the data type is CURRENCY. When you use the INSERT INTO statement, all values must be surrounded by quotation marks. SQL and Visual Basic handle any type conversions needed to insert the values into the identified fields.

The second interesting thing to note in Listing 15.2 is the order in which columns are listed in the INSERT INTO statements. If you look at each of the statements, you see that the JobTitles.JobPay column appears in different places within the field list. When you use the INSERT INTO statement, you can list the columns in any order. You only need to make sure that you list the values to be inserted in the same order in which you list the columns.

You have learned how to use the INSERT INTO statement to add individual rows to a table. This is commonly called a *single-record* insert. In the next section, you learn about a more powerful version of the INSERT INTO statement, commonly called an *append query*.

Creating Append Queries with INSERT INTO_FROM

The INSERT INTO_FROM version of the INSERT statement allows you to insert multiple records from one table into another table. This multirecord version of INSERT INTO is called an *append query* because it enables you to append rows from one table to the end of another table. As long as the two tables you are working with have fields with the same name, you can use the INSERT INTO_FROM statement.

The basic format of the INSERT INTO_FROM statement is

```
INSERT INTO TargetTable SELECT field1, field2 FROM SourceTable;
```

There are three important parts of the INSERT INTO_FROM statement. The first part is the *TargetTable*. This is the table that is updated by the statement. The second part is SELECT fields. This is a list of the fields that are updated in the *TargetTable*. These are also the fields that are supplied by the third part of the statement—the *SourceTable*. As you can see, the

INSERT INTO_FROM statement is really just a SELECT_FROM query with an INSERT INTO *TargetTable* in front of it.

Now, let's update the SQLVB05.SQV to provide an example of the INSERT INTO_FROM statement. First, use SQL-VB5 to load and edit the SQLVB05.SQV script. Make changes to the script so that it matches Listing 15.3. Save the script and run it. Check your results against those shown in Figure 15.3.

TYPE   Listing 15.3. Using the INSERT INTO_FROM statement.

```
//
// sqlvb05.sqv - Testing the INSERT INTO keyword
//
// create a new database
dbMake sqlvb05.mdb;
// create a new table
CREATE TABLE JobTitles
    (JobCounter COUNTER,
     JobID TEXT(5) CONSTRAINT PKJobTitle PRIMARY KEY,
     JobName TEXT(20),
     JobPay CURRENCY,
     JobDesc MEMO
     );
// insert some data
INSERT INTO JobTitles (JobID, JobName, JobDesc, JobPay) VALUES
    ('J001',
     'President',
     'Presides over the company',
     '50000'
     );
INSERT INTO JobTitles (JobID, JobName, JobDesc, JobPay) VALUES
    ('J002',
     'Vice President',
     'Does what the President tells him to do',
     '40000'
     );
INSERT INTO JobTitles (JobID, JobPay, JobName) VALUES
    ('J003',
     '35000',
     'Chief Engineer'
     );
// create a second table to hold some of the info from JobTitles
CREATE TABLE JobReport
    (JobID TEXT(5) CONSTRAINT PKJobReport PRIMARY KEY,
     JobName TEXT(20),
     JobDesc MEMO,
     DeptID TEXT(5)
     );
// now append records from JobTitles into JobReport
INSERT INTO JobReport
    SELECT JobID, JobName, JobDesc FROM JobTitles;
```

continues

Listing 15.3 continued.

```
// display results
SELECT * FROM JobTitles;
SELECT * FROM JobReport;
// eof
```

Figure 15.3.

The results of the
INSERT INTO_FROM
statement.

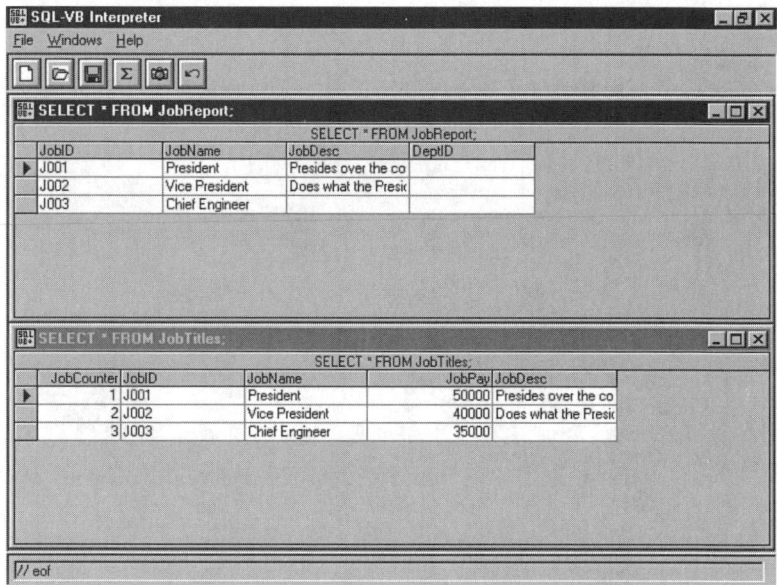

 **NOTE**

> You might have noticed in Listing 15.3 that you created two indexes, each on an identical column name, but you gave the two indexes different names. SQL does not allow you to use the same name on different indexes, even if they refer to different tables. Indexes appear as independent data objects in a Microsoft Access database. Each object must have a unique name.

Notice that the INSERT INTO_FROM statement lists only those fields that are present in both tables. You need to list the columns by name in this example because the JobReport table does not contain all the fields that the JobTitles table contains. If both tables were an exact match, you could use the asterisk wildcard (*) character in the SELECT clause. For example, if JobTitles and JobReport shared all the same column names, you could use the following SQL statement to append data from one to the other:

```
INSERT INTO JobReport SELECT * FROM JobTitles;
```

15

You can also use the INSERT INTO statement to append rows to tables in another database. You accomplish this by adding an IN clause to the first part of the statement. For example, you can add rows from the JobTitles table in SQLVB05.MDB to a similar table in another database called SQLVB05B.MDB. The syntax for the IN clause of an INSERT INTO_FROM statement is

```
IN "DatabaseFileName" "DatabaseFormat"
```

DatabaseFileName is the complete database filename including the drive identifier and the path name of the destination (or external) database. *DatabaseFormat* is the name of the database format of the destination database, such as FoxPro, dBASE, Paradox, and so on. For example, if you want to update TableOne in the external database called EXTERNAL.MDB on drive C in the directory called DB, you would use the following IN clause for the SELECT INTO statement:

```
SELECT INTO TableOne IN "c:\db\external.mdb" "access"
```

Listing 15.4 shows how this is done using a real set of database files. Use SQL-VB5 to load and edit SQLVB05.SQV to match the modifications outlined in Listing 15.4. Save the script and execute it. Your results should look similar to those in Figure 15.4.

TYPE **Listing 15.4. Adding the IN clause.**

```
//
// sqlvb05.sqv - Testing the INSERT INTO keyword
//
// create sqlvgb05b database
dbMake sqlvb05b.mdb;
// make a table
CREATE TABLE OtherTitles
   (JobCounter COUNTER,
    JobID TEXT(5) CONSTRAINT PKJobTitle PRIMARY KEY,
    JobName TEXT(20),
    JobPay CURRENCY,
    JobDesc MEMO
    );
// insert some rows
INSERT INTO OtherTitles (JobID, JobName, JobDesc, JobPay) VALUES
   ('J004',
    'Line Foreman',
    'Supervises production line',
    '30000'
    );
INSERT INTO OtherTitles (JobID, JobName, JobDesc, JobPay) VALUES
   ('J005',
    'Line Worker',
    'Does what the Line Foreman tells him to do',
    '25000'
    );
// show results
```

continues

Listing 15.4. continued

```
SELECT * FROM OtherTitles;
// now close this database
dbClose;
// **********************************************************
// create a new database
dbMake sqlvb05.mdb;
// create a new table
CREATE TABLE JobTitles
   (JobCounter COUNTER,
    JobID TEXT(5) CONSTRAINT PKJobTitle PRIMARY KEY,
    JobName TEXT(20),
    JobPay CURRENCY,
    JobDesc MEMO
    );
// insert some data
INSERT INTO JobTitles (JobID, JobName, JobDesc, JobPay) VALUES
   ('J001',
    'President',
    'Presides over the company',
    '50000'
    );
INSERT INTO JobTitles (JobID, JobName, JobDesc, JobPay) VALUES
   ('J002',
    'Vice President',
    'Does what the President tells him to do',
    '40000'
    );
INSERT INTO JobTitles (JobID, JobPay, JobName) VALUES
   ('J003',
    '35000',
    'Chief Engineer'
    );
// create a second table to hold some of the info from JobTitles
CREATE TABLE JobReport
   (JobID TEXT(5) CONSTRAINT PKJobReport PRIMARY KEY,
    JobName TEXT(20),
    JobDesc MEMO
    );
// now append records from JobTitles into JobReport
INSERT INTO JobReport
   SELECT JobID, JobName, JobDesc FROM JobTitles;

// display results
SELECT * FROM JobTitles;
SELECT * FROM JobReport;
// now append data from one database to another
INSERT INTO OtherTitles IN "sqlvb05b.mdb" "Access"
   SELECT JobID, JobName, JobDesc, JobPay FROM JobTitles;
// close this db
dbClose;
// open other db
dbOpen sqlvb05b.mdb
// show updated table
SELECT * FROM OtherTitles;
// eof
```

Figure 15.4.

The results of the
`INSERT INTO_FROM`
statement with the `IN`
clause.

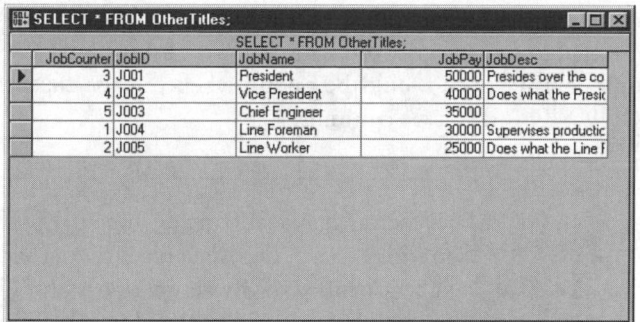

The script in Listing 15.4 first creates a database with a single table (OtherTitles) that has two records in the table. Then the script displays the table for a moment before the database is closed. Notice that the records in the table have OtherTitles.JobCounter values of 1 and 2. Then the script creates the JobTitles table in another database and populates that table with three records. Other tables are populated (this was done in previous examples), and eventually the JobTitles table is displayed. The three records have JobTitles.JobCounter values of 1, 2, and 3. Finally, the `INSERT INTO_FROM_IN` statement is executed to update the external data table. Then the external table is opened so that you can view the results.

Now look at the OtherTitles.JobCounter values. What has happened? When you append COUNTER data fields to another table, the new records are renumbered. This ensures unique counter values in the table. If you want to retain the old numbers, you can include the COUNTER field in your `INSERT INTO` list. To illustrate this, add the JobCounter column name to the field list in the `INSERT INTO` statement that updated the external table (see Figure 15.5). Now execute the script again to see the results.

Figure 15.5.

*The results
of the* `INSERT
INTO_FROM_IN`
*with an updated
counter column.*

JobCounter	JobID	JobName	JobPay	JobDesc
▶ 1	J001	President	50000	Presides over the co
2	J002	Vice President	40000	Does what the Presi
3	J003	Chief Engineer	35000	
1	J004	Line Foreman	30000	Supervises productic
2	J005	Line Worker	25000	Does what the Line F

As you can see in Figure 15.5, you now have duplicate COUNTER values in your table. This can lead to data integrity problems if you are using the COUNTER data type as a guaranteed unique value. You should be careful when you use INSERT INTO statements that contain COUNTER data type columns.

WARNING

> The Microsoft Visual Basic documentation for the behavior of INSERT INTO with COUNTER data types states that duplicate counter values are not appended to the destination table. This is not correct. The only time duplicates are not included in the destination tables is when the COUNTER data type column is defined as the primary key.

We should point out here that if you attempt to append records to a table that has a duplicate primary key value, the new record is not appended to the table—and you do not receive an error message! If you edit the SQLVB05.SQV script to renumber the OtherTitles.JobID values to J001 and J002, you see a different set of results when you run the script. Figure 15.6 shows what you get when you attempt to update duplicate primary key rows.

Figure 15.6.

The results of attempting to append duplicate primary key rows.

JobCounter	JobID	JobName	JobPay	JobDesc
1	J001	Line Foreman	30000	Supervises productic
2	J002	Line Worker	25000	Does what the Line F
3	J003	Chief Engineer	35000	

SELECT * FROM OtherTitles;

The fact that SQL does not append records with a duplicate key can be used as an advantage. You can easily merge two tables that contain overlapping data and get a single result set that does not contain duplicates. Anyone who has worked with mailing lists can find a use for this feature of the INSERT INTO statement.

Now that you know how to insert rows into tables, it's time to learn how you can update existing rows using the UPDATE_SET statement.

15

Creating UPDATE Queries with the UPDATE_SET Statement

The UPDATE_SET statement enables you to update a large amount of data in one or more tables very quickly with very little coding. You use the UPDATE_SET statement to modify data already on file in a data table. The advantage of the UPDATE_SET statement is that you can use a single statement to modify multiple rows in the table.

For example, assume that you have a table of 500 employees. You are told by the Human Resources department that all employees are to be given a 17.5 percent increase in their pay starting immediately (wouldn't it be nice?). You could write a Visual Basic program that opens the table, reads each record, computes the new salary, stores the updated record, and then goes back to read the next record. Your code would look something like the pseudocode sample in Listing 15.5.

NOTE

Listing 15.5 is not a real Visual Basic program; it is just a set of statements that read like program code. Such pseudocode is often used by programmers to plan out programs without having to deal with the details of a particular programming language. Another benefit of using pseudocode to plan programs is that people do not need to know a particular programming language to be able to understand the example.

TYPE **Listing 15.5. Sample code for record-oriented updates.**

```
OPEN EmpDatabase
OPEN EmpTable
DO UNTIL END-OF-FILE (EmpTable)
   READ EmpTable RECORD
   EmpTable.EmpSalary = EmpTable.EmpSalary * 1.175
   WRITE EmpTable RECORD
END DO
CLOSE EmpTable
CLOSE EmpDatabase
```

This is a relatively simple process, but—depending on the size of the data table and the speed of your workstation or the database server—this kind of table update could take quite a bit of time. You can use the SQL UPDATE statement to perform the same task.

```
OPEN database
UPDATE EmpTable SET EmpSalary = EmpSalary * 1.175
CLOSE database
```

The preceding example shows how you can accomplish the same task with less coding. Even better, this code runs much faster than the walk-through loop shown in Listing 15.5, and this single line of code works for any number of records in the set. Furthermore, if this statement is sent to a back-end database server connected by ODBC and not processed by the local workstation, you could see an even greater increase in processing speed for your program.

Let's start a new program that illustrates the UPDATE_SET statement. Use SQL-VB5 to create a new script file called SQLVB06.SQV and enter the commands in Listing 15.6. After you save the script, execute it and check your results against those in Figure 15.7.

TYPE   **Listing 15.6. Using the UPDATE_SET statement.**

```
//
// sqlvb06.sqv - testing the UPDATE ... SET statement
//
// create a database
dbMake sqlvb06.mdb;
// create a table
CREATE TABLE EmpTable
    (EmpID TEXT(5) CONSTRAINT PKEmpTable PRIMARY KEY,
     EmpName TEXT(30),
     EmpSalary CURRENCY
     );
// insert some data
INSERT INTO EmpTable VALUES
    ('E001',
     'Anderson, Shannon',
     '35000'
     );
INSERT INTO EmpTable VALUES
    ('E002',
     'Billings, Jesse',
     '30000'
     );
INSERT INTO EmpTable VALUES
    ('E003',
     'Caldwell, Dana',
     '25000'
     );
// show first result set
SELECT * FROM EmpTable AS FirstPass;
// now perform update
UPDATE empTable SET EmpSalary = EmpSalary * 1.175;
// show new results
SELECT * FROM EmpTable AS SecondPass;
// eof
```

Figure 15.7.

The results of using the UPDATE_SET *statement.*

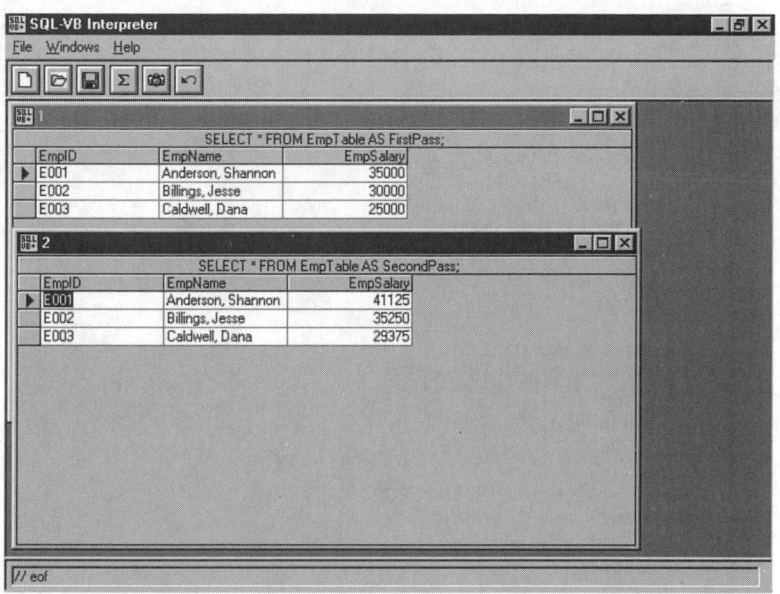

15

NOTE

Notice that you did not include the column names in the INSERT INTO statements in this example. As long as you are supplying *all* the column values for a table, in the same order that they appear in the physical layout, you can omit the column names from the statement.

As you can see in Figure 15.7, all the records in the table are updated by the UPDATE_SET statement. The SET statement works for both numeric and character fields. It can contain any number of column updates, too. For example, if you have a table that has three fields that need to be updated, you can use the following SQL statement:

```
UPDATE MyTable SET
    CustType="RETAIL",
    CustDiscount=10,
    CustDate=#01/15/96#;
```

You can also add a WHERE clause to the UPDATE statement to limit the rows that are affected by the SET portion of the statement. What if you want to give anyone whose salary is over $30,000 a 10 percent raise and anyone whose salary is $30,000 or under a 15 percent raise? You could accomplish this with two UPDATE_SET statements that each contain a WHERE clause. Use the code in Listing 15.7 as a guide to modifying the SQLVB06.SQV script. Save your changes and run the script. Check your results against Figure 15.8.

TYPE   **Listing 15.7. Adding the WHERE clause to the UPDATE statement.**

```
//
// sqlvb06.sqv - testing the UPDATE ... SET statement
//
// create a database
dbMake sqlvb06.mdb;
// create a table
CREATE TABLE EmpTable
   (EmpID TEXT(5) CONSTRAINT PKEmpTable PRIMARY KEY,
    EmpName TEXT(30),
    EmpSalary CURRENCY
    );
// insert some data
INSERT INTO EmpTable VALUES
   ('E001',
    'Anderson, Shannon',
    '35000'
    );
INSERT INTO EmpTable VALUES
   ('E002',
    'Billings, Jesse',
    '30000'
    );
INSERT INTO EmpTable VALUES
   ('E003',
    'Caldwell, Dana',
    '25000'
    );
// show first result set
SELECT * FROM EmpTable AS FirstPass;
// now perform updates
UPDATE EmpTable SET EmpSalary = EmpSalary * 1.10
   WHERE EmpSalary > 30000;
UPDATE empTable SET EmpSalary = EmpSalary * 1.15
   WHERE EmpSalary <= 30000;
// show new results
SELECT * FROM EmpTable AS SecondPass;
// eof
```

In Listing 15.7, you use the WHERE clause to isolate the records you want to modify with the UPDATE_SET statement. The WHERE clause can be as simple or as complicated as needed to meet the criteria. In other words, any WHERE clause that is valid within the SELECT_FROM statement can be used as part of the UPDATE_SET statement.

15

Figure 15.8.

The results of the
UPDATE *query with a*
WHERE *clause.*

15

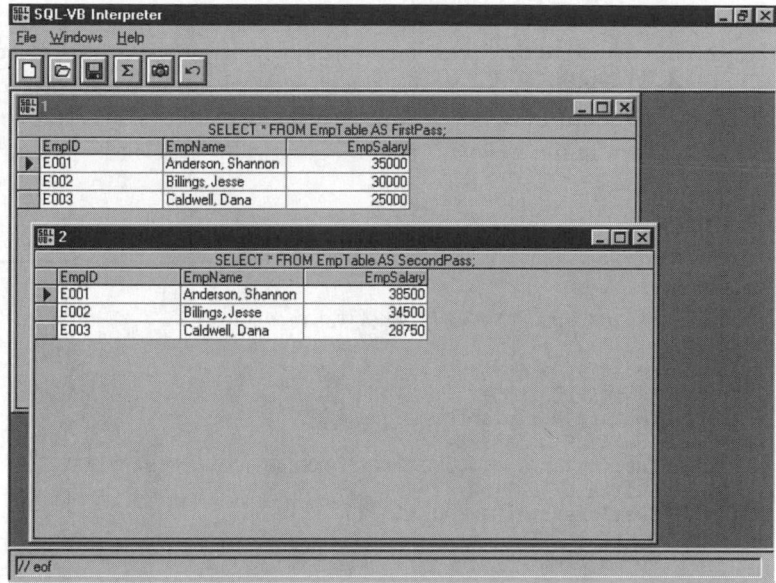

Creating Make Table Queries Using the
SELECT_INTO_FROM **Statement**

The SELECT_INTO_FROM statement allows you to create entirely new tables, complete with data from existing tables. This is called a *Make Table query* because it enables you to make a new table. The difference between Make Table queries and the CREATE TABLE statement is that you use the Make Table query to copy both the table structure and the data within the table from an already existing table. Because the Make Table query is really just a form of a SELECT statement, you can use all the clauses valid for a SELECT statement when copying data tables, including WHERE, ORDER BY, GROUP BY, and HAVING.

Make Table queries are excellent for making backup copies of your data tables. You can also create static read-only tables for reporting and reviewing purposes. For example, you can create a Make Table query that summarizes sales for the period and save the results in a data table that can be accessed for reports and on-screen displays. Now you can provide summary data to your users without giving them access to the underlying transaction tables. This can improve overall processing speed and help provide data security, too.

The basic form of the Make Table query is

```
SELECT field1, field2 INTO DestinationTable FROM SourceTable;
```

In the preceding example, the *field1*, *field2* list contains the list of fields in the *SourceTable* that is copied to the *DestinationTable*. If you want to copy all the columns from the source to the destination, you can use the asterisk wildcard (*) character for the field list. Enter the SQL-VB5 script in Listing 15.8 as SQLVB07.SQV. Save and execute the script, and check your on-screen results against those in Figure 15.9.

TYPE   **Listing 15.8. Testing Make Table queries.**

```
//
// sqlvb07.sqv - Testing Make Table Queries
//
// create a database
dbMake sqlvb07.mdb;
// create a base table
CREATE TABLE BaseTable
   (CustID TEXT(10) CONSTRAINT PKBaseTable PRIMARY KEY,
    CustName TEXT(30),
    CustBalance CURRENCY,
    CustType TEXT(10),
    Notes MEMO
   );
// add some data
INSERT INTO BaseTable VALUES
   ('CUST01',
    'Willingham & Associates',
    '300.65',
    'RETAIL',
    'This is a comment'
   );
INSERT INTO BaseTable VALUES
   ('CUST02',
    'Parker & Parker',
    '1000.29',
    'WHOLESALE',
    'This is another comment'
   );
INSERT INTO BaseTable VALUES
   ('CUST03',
    'Anchor, Smith, & Hocking',
    '575.25',
    'RETAIL',
    'This is the last comment'
   );
// now make a new table from the old one
SELECT * INTO CopyTable FROM BaseTable;
// show results
SELECT * FROM BaseTable;
SELECT * FROM CopyTable;
// eof
```

15

Figure 15.9.

The results of a simple Make Table query.

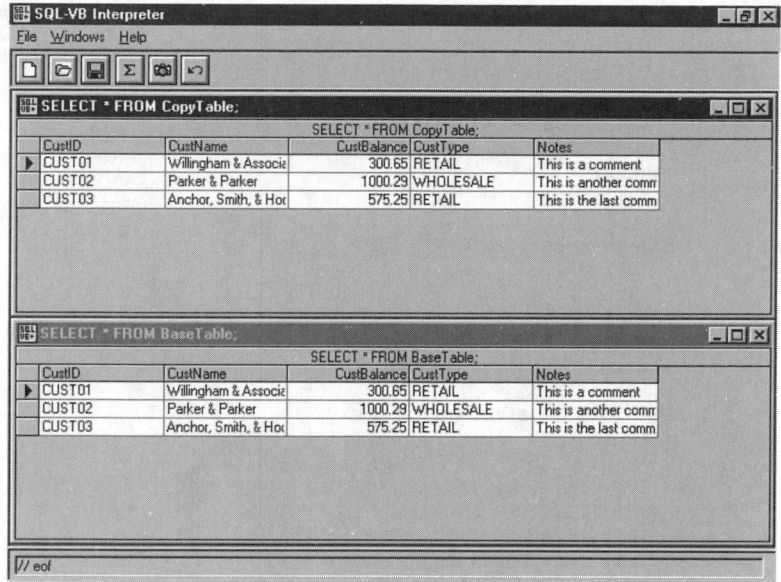

In Listing 15.8, you created a database with one table, populated the table with some test data, and then executed a Make Table query that copied the table structure and contents to a new table in the same database.

You can use the WHERE clause to limit the rows copied to the new table. Modify SQLVB07.SQV to contain the new SELECT_INTO statement and its corresponding SELECT_FROM, as shown in Listing 15.9. Save the script and execute it. Your results should look similar to those shown in Figure 15.10.

Listing 15.9. Using the WHERE clause to limit Make Table queries.

TYPE

```
//
// sqlvb07.sqv - Testing Make Table Queries
//
// create a database
dbMake sqlvb07.mdb;
// create a base table
CREATE TABLE BaseTable
    (CustID TEXT(10) CONSTRAINT PKBaseTable PRIMARY KEY,
     CustName TEXT(30),
     CustBalance CURRENCY,
     CustType TEXT(10),
     Notes MEMO
    );
// add some data
```

continues

Listing 15.9. continued

```
INSERT INTO BaseTable VALUES
   ('CUST01',
    'Willingham & Associates',
    '300.65',
    'RETAIL',
    'This is a comment'
   );
INSERT INTO BaseTable VALUES
   ('CUST02',
    'Parker & Parker',
    '1000.29',
    'WHOLESALE',
    'This is another comment'
   );
INSERT INTO BaseTable VALUES
   ('CUST03',
    'Anchor, Smith, & Hocking',
    '575.25',
    'RETAIL',
    'This is the last comment'
   );
// now make a new table from the old one
SELECT * INTO CopyTable FROM BaseTable;
// select just some of the records
SELECT * INTO RetailTable FROM BaseTable
   WHERE CustType='RETAIL';
// show results
SELECT * FROM BaseTable;
SELECT * FROM CopyTable;
SELECT * FROM RetailTable;
// eof
```

As you can see from Figure 15.10, only the rows with WHERE CustType = 'RETAIL' are copied to the new table.

You can also use the GROUP BY and HAVING clauses to limit and summarize data before copying to a new table. Let's modify the SQLVB07.SQV script to produce only one record for each customer type, with each new row containing the customer type and total balance for that type. Let's also order the records in descending order by customer balance. Let's rename the CustBalance field to Balance. The modifications to SQLVB07.SQV are shown in Listing 15.10. Make your changes, save and run the script, and compare your results to Figure 15.11.

15

Figure 15.10.

Using the WHERE clause to limit Make Table queries.

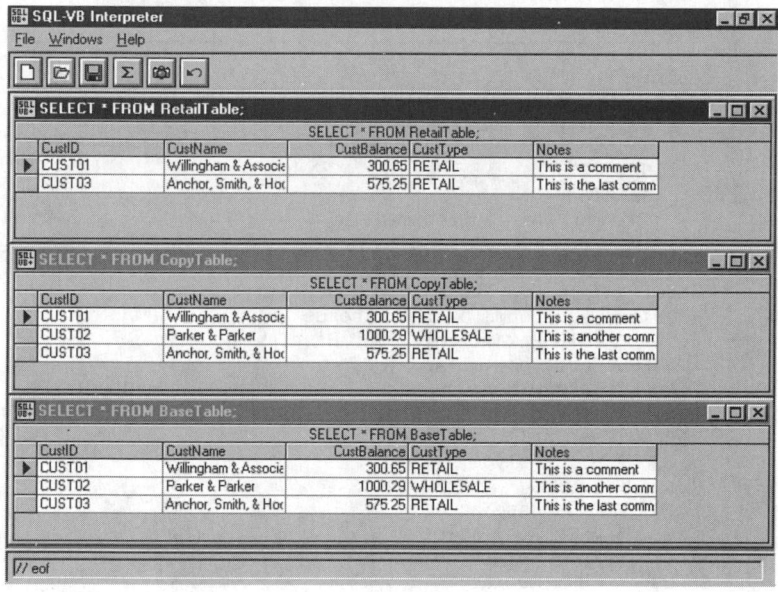

TYPE   **Listing 15.10. Using GROUP BY and HAVING to summarize data.**

```
//
// sqlvb07.sqv - Testing Make Table Queries
//
// create a database
dbMake sqlvb07.mdb;
// create a base table
CREATE TABLE BaseTable
    (CustID TEXT(10) CONSTRAINT PKBaseTable PRIMARY KEY,
     CustName TEXT(30),
     CustBalance CURRENCY,
     CustType TEXT(10),
     Notes MEMO
    );
// add some data
INSERT INTO BaseTable VALUES
    ('CUST01',
     'Willingham & Associates',
     '300.65',
     'RETAIL',
     'This is a comment'
    );
INSERT INTO BaseTable VALUES
    ('CUST02',
     'Parker & Parker',
     '1000.29',
     'WHOLESALE',
     'This is another comment'
```

continues

Listing 15.10. continued

```
   );
INSERT INTO BaseTable VALUES
   ('CUST03',
   'Anchor, Smith, & Hocking',
   '575.25',
   'RETAIL',
   'This is the last comment'
   );
// now make a new table from the old one
SELECT * INTO CopyTable FROM BaseTable;
// select just some of the records
SELECT * INTO RetailTable FROM BaseTable
   WHERE CustType='RETAIL';
// create a new summary table with fancy stuff added
SELECT CustType, SUM(CustBalance) AS Balance INTO SummaryTable
   FROM BaseTable
   GROUP BY CustType;
// show results
SELECT * FROM BaseTable;
SELECT * FROM CopyTable;
SELECT * FROM RetailTable;
SELECT * FROM SummaryTable;
// eof
```

Figure 15.11.

Using GROUP BY *and* HAVING *to summarize data.*

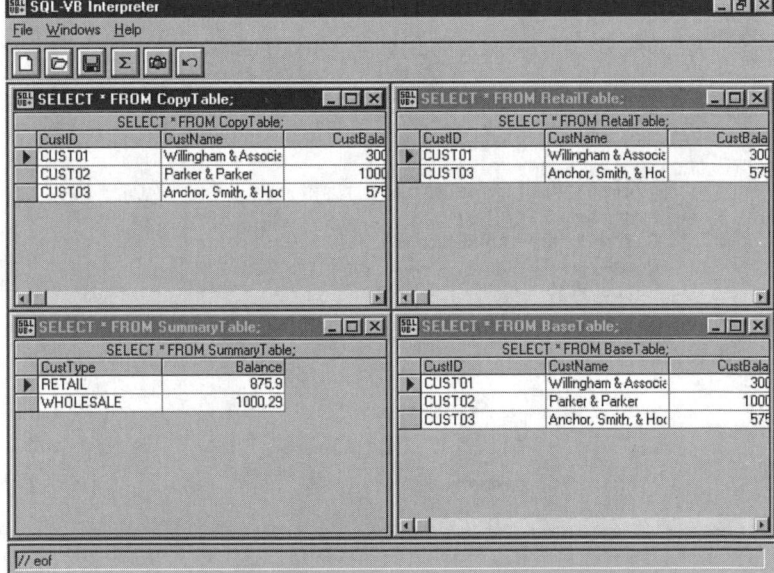

15

In all the examples so far, you have used the SELECT_INTO statement to copy existing tables to another table within the database. You can also use SELECT_INTO to copy an existing table to another database by adding the IN clause. You can use this feature to copy entire data tables from one database to another, or to copy portions of a database or data tables to another database for archiving or reporting purposes.

For example, if you want to copy the entire BaseTable you designed in the previous examples from SQLVB07.MDB to SQLVB07B.MDB, you could use the following SELECT_INTO statement:

```
SELECT * INTO CopyTable IN sqlvb07b.mdb FROM BaseTable;
```

You can use all the WHERE, ORDER BY, GROUP BY, HAVING, and AS clauses you desire when copying tables from one database to another.

WARNING

When you copy tables using the SELECT_INTO statement, none of the indexes or constraints are copied to the new table. This is an important point. If you use SELECT_INTO to create tables that you want to use for data entry, you need to reconstruct the indexes and constraints using CREATE INDEX to add indexes and ALTER TABLE to add constraints.

Creating Delete Table Queries Using DELETE_FROM

The final SQL statement you learn today is the DELETE_FROM statement, commonly called the *Delete Table query*. Delete Table queries are used to remove one or more records from a data table. The delete query can also be applied to a valid view created using the JOIN keyword. Although it is not always efficient to use the DELETE statement to remove a single record from a table, it can be very effective to use the DELETE statement to remove several records from a table. In fact, when you need to remove more than one record from a table or view, the DELETE statement outperforms repeated uses of the Delete method in Visual Basic code.

In its most basic form, the DELETE statement looks like this:

```
DELETE FROM TableName;
```

In the preceding example, TableName represents the name of the base table from which you are deleting records. In this case, all records in the table are removed using a single command. If you want to remove only some of the records, you could add an SQL WHERE clause to limit the scope of the DELETE action.

```
DELETE FROM TableName WHERE Field = value;
```

This example removes only the records that meet the criteria established in the WHERE clause.

Now let's create some real DELETE statements using SQL-VB. Start a new script file called SQLVB08.SQV, and enter the script commands in Listing 15.11. Save the script and execute it. Check your results against those shown in Figure 15.12.

TYPE **Listing 15.11. Using the DELETE statement.**

```
//
// sqlvb08.sqv - Testing DELETE statements
//
// create a new database
dbMake sqlvb08.mdb;
// create a table to work with
CREATE TABLE Table1
   (RecID TEXT(10),
    LastName TEXT(30),
    FirstName TEXT(30),
    RecType TEXT(5),
    Amount CURRENCY,
    LastPaid DATE
   );
// add some records to work with
INSERT INTO Table1 VALUES
    ('R01',
     'Simmons',
     'Chris',
     'LOCAL',
     '3000',
     '12/15/95'
    );
INSERT INTO Table1 VALUES
    ('R02',
     'Walters',
     'Curtis',
     'INTL',
     '5000',
     '11/30/95'
    );
INSERT INTO Table1 VALUES
    ('R03',
     'Austin',
     'Moro',
     'INTL',
     '4500',
     '01/15/96'
    );
// show loaded table
SELECT * FROM Table1 AS FirstPass;
// now delete LOCAL records
DELETE FROM Table1
    WHERE RecType = 'LOCAL';
// show results
SELECT * FROM Table1 AS SecondPass;
// eof
```

15

Figure 15.12.

The results of a simple DELETE *statement.*

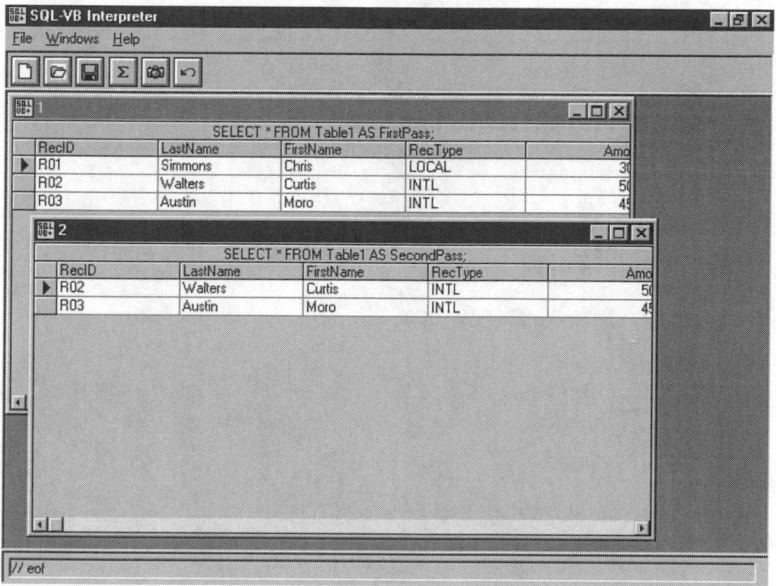

The SQLVB08.SQV script in Listing 15.11 creates a database with one table in it, populates that table with test data, and then shows the loaded table. Next, a DELETE statement is executed to remove all records that have a Table1.RecType that contains LOCAL. When this is done, the results are shown on-screen.

You can create any type of WHERE clause you need to establish the proper criteria. For example, what if you want to remove all international (INTL) records where the last payment is after 12/31/95? Edit your copy of SQLVB08.SQV. Then save and run it to check your results against Figure 15.13. Our version of the solution appears in Listing 15.12.

TYPE **Listing 15.12. Using a complex WHERE clause with a DELETE statement.**

```
//
// sqlvb08.sqv - Testing DELETE statements
//
// create a new database
dbMake sqlvb08.mdb;
// create a table to work with
CREATE TABLE Table1
    (RecID TEXT(10),
    LastName TEXT(30),
    FirstName TEXT(30),
    RecType TEXT(5),
    Amount CURRENCY,
    LastPaid DATE
```

continues

Listing 15.12. continued

```
    );
// add some records to work with
INSERT INTO Table1 VALUES
    ('R01',
     'Simmons',
     'Chris',
     'LOCAL',
     '3000',
     #12/15/95#
    );
INSERT INTO Table1 VALUES
    ('R02',
     'Walters',
     'Curtis',
     'INTL',
     '5000',
     #11/30/95#
    );
INSERT INTO Table1 VALUES
    ('R03',
     'Austin',
     'Moro',
     'INTL',
     '4500',
     #01/15/96#
    );
// show loaded table
SELECT * FROM Table1 AS FirstPass;
// now delete LOCAL records
DELETE FROM Table1
    WHERE RecType = 'INTL' AND LastPaid > #12/31/95#;
// show results
SELECT * FROM Table1 AS SecondPass;
// eof
```

As you can see from the code in Listing 15.12, you only need to change the WHERE clause (adding the date criteria) in order to make the DELETE statement function as planned.

NOTE

You might have noticed that you enclose date information with the pound symbol (#). This ensures that Microsoft Jet handles the data as DATE type values. Using the pound symbol works across language settings within the Windows operating system. This means that if you ship your program to Europe, where many countries use the date format DD/MM/YY (instead of the U.S. standard MM/DD/YY), Windows converts the date information to display and compute properly for the regional settings on the local PC.

15

Figure 15.13.

The results of the
DELETE *statement*
with a complex WHERE
clause.

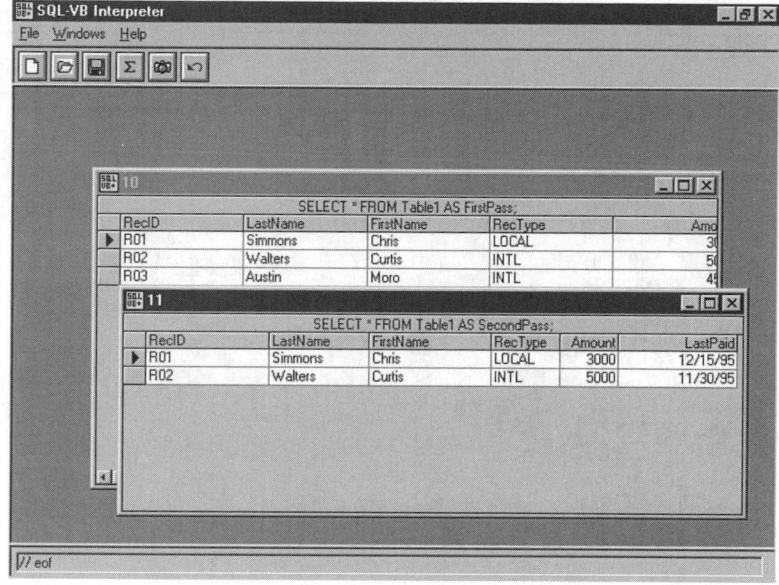

You can also use the DELETE statement to delete records in more than one table at a time. These multitable deletes can only be performed on tables that have a one-to-one relationship. The example in Listing 15.13 shows modifications to SQLVB08.SQV to illustrate the use of the JOIN clauses to create a multitable DELETE statement. Use SQL-VB5 to edit your copy of SQLVB08.SQV to match the one in Listing 15.13. Save and execute the script and refer to Figure 15.14 for comparison.

TYPE **Listing 15.13. Using JOIN to perform a multitable DELETE.**

```
//
// sqlvb08.sqv - Testing DELETE statements
//
// create a new database
dbMake sqlvb08.mdb;
// create a table to work with
CREATE TABLE Table1
   (RecID TEXT(10),
    LastName TEXT(30),
    FirstName TEXT(30),
    RecType TEXT(5),
    Amount CURRENCY,
    LastPaid DATE
   );
// add some records to work with
INSERT INTO Table1 VALUES
   ('R01',
```

continues

Listing 15.13. continued

```
        'Simmons',
        'Chris',
        'LOCAL',
        '3000',
        #12/15/95#
        );
INSERT INTO Table1 VALUES
    ('R02',
     'Walters',
     'Curtis',
     'INTL',
     '5000',
     #11/30/95#
     );
INSERT INTO Table1 VALUES
    ('R03',
     'Austin',
     'Moro',
     'INTL',
     '4500',
     #01/15/96#
     );
// create a second table for JOIN purposes
CREATE TABLE Table2
    (RecID TEXT(10),
     BizPhone TEXT(20),
     EMailAddr TEXT(30)
     );
// load some data
INSERT INTO Table2 VALUES
    ('R01',
     '(111)222-3333',
     'chris@link.net'
     );
INSERT INTO Table2 VALUES
    ('R03',
     '(777)888-9999',
     'moro@band.edu'
     );
INSERT INTO Table2 VALUES
    ('R04',
     '(222)444-6666',
     'person@mystery.uk'
     );
// show loaded table
SELECT * FROM Table1 AS FirstPass1;
SELECT * FROM Table2 AS FirstPass2;
// now delete records
DELETE Table1.*, Table2.* FROM
    Table1 INNER JOIN Table2 ON Table1.RecID = Table2.RecID;
// show results
SELECT * FROM Table1 AS SecondPass1;
SELECT * FROM Table2 AS SecondPass2;
// eof
```

15

Figure 15.14.

Results of a multitable DELETE.

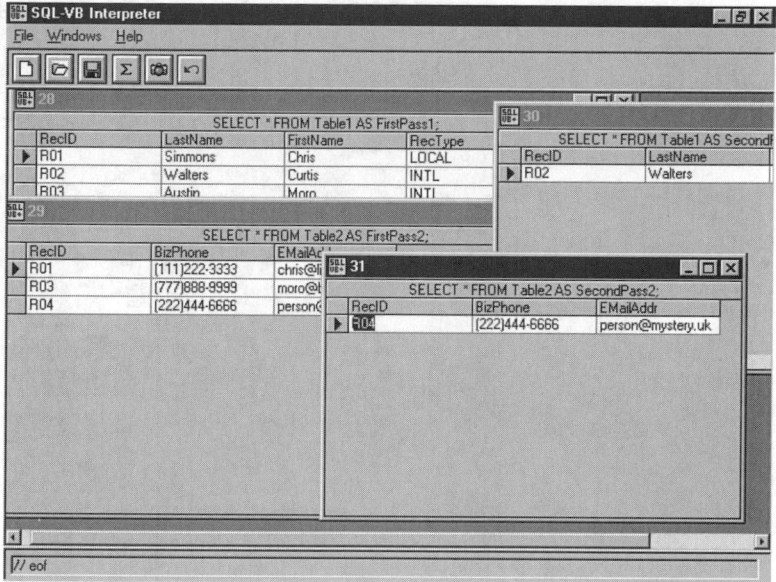

The results of this DELETE query might surprise you. Because there is no WHERE clause in the DELETE statement that could limit the scope of the SQL command, you might think that the statement deletes all records in both tables. In fact, this statement only deletes the records that have a matching RecID in both tables. The reason for this is that you used an INNER JOIN. INNER JOIN clauses operate only on records that appear in both tables. You now have an excellent way to remove records from multiple tables with one DELETE statement! It must be pointed out, however, that this technique only works with tables that have a one-to-one relationship defined. In the case of one-to-many relationships, only the first occurrence of the match on the many side is removed.

Here is a puzzle for you. What happens if you only list Table1 in the first part of that last DELETE statement?

```
DELETE Table1.* FROM
Table1 INNER JOIN Table2 ON Table1.RecID = Table2.RecID;
```

What records (if any) are deleted from Table1? Edit SQLVB08.SQV, save it, and execute it to find out. Check your results against Figure 15.15.

As you can see from Figure 15.15, a DELETE query that contains an INNER JOIN only removes records from Table1 that have a match in Table2. And the records in Table2 are left intact! This is a good example of using JOIN clauses to limit the scope of a DELETE statement. This technique is very useful when you want to eliminate duplicates in related or identical tables. Note also that this INNER JOIN works just fine without the use of defined constraints or index keys.

Figure 15.15.

The results of a one-sided DELETE *using an* INNER JOIN.

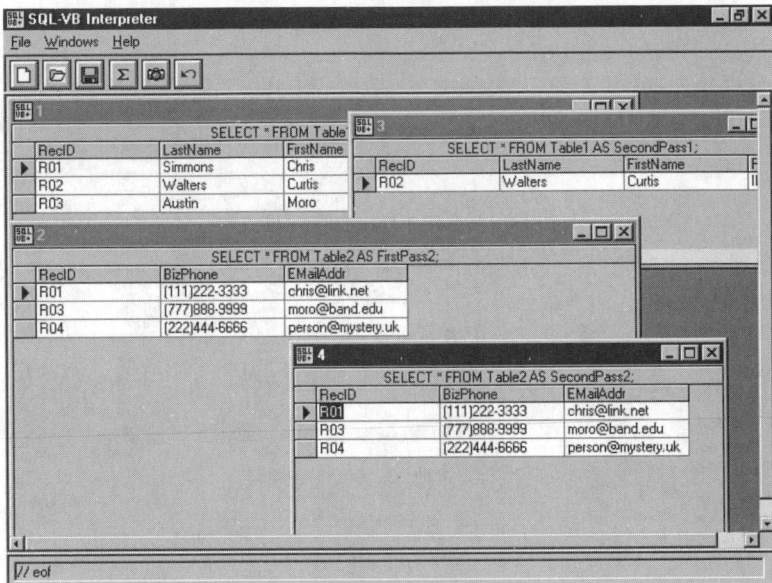

Summary

You have learned how to add, delete, and edit data within tables using the DML (Data Manipulation Language) SQL keywords. You've learned that, by using DML statements, you can quickly create test data for tables and load default values into startup tables. You also learned that DML statements—such as Append queries, Make Table queries, and Delete queries—can outperform equivalent Visual Basic code versions of the same operations.

You learned how to manage data within the tables using the following DML keywords:

☐ The INSERT INTO statement can be used to add new rows to the table using the VALUES clause.

☐ You can create an Append query by using the INSERT INTO_FROM syntax to copy data from one table to another. You can also copy data from one database to another using the IN clause of an INSERT INTO_FROM statement.

☐ You can create new tables by copying the structure and some of the data using the SELECT_INTO statement. This statement can incorporate WHERE, ORDER BY, GROUP BY, and HAVING clauses to limit the scope of the data used to populate the new table you create.

☐ You can use the DELETE FROM clause to remove one or more records from an existing table. You can even create customized views of the database using the JOIN clause and remove only records that are the result of a JOIN statement.

Quiz

1. What SQL statement do you use to insert a single data record into a table? What is the basic form of this statement?

2. What SQL statement do you issue to insert multiple data records into a table? What is its format?

3. What SQL statement do you use to modify data that is already in a data table? What is the form of this statement?

4. What SQL statement is used to create new tables that include data from other tables? What is the format of this statement?

5. What SQL statement do you use to delete one or more records from a data table? What is the basic format of this statement?

Exercises

1. Modify the SQL-VB5 script you created in Exercise 1 of Day 13 to add the following records.

Data for the CustomerType Table

Customer Type	Description
INDV	Individual
BUS	Business—Non-Corporate
CORP	Corporate Entity

Data for the Customers Table

Field	Customer #1	Customer #2	Customer #3
CustomerID	SMITHJ	JONEST	JACKSONT
Name	John Smith	Jones Taxi	Thomas Jackson
CustomerType	INDV	BUS	INDV
Address	160 Main Street	421 Shoe St.	123 Walnut St.
City	Dublin	Milford	Oxford
State	Ohio	Rhode Island	Maine
Zip	45621	03215	05896
Phone	614-555-8975	555-555-5555	444-444-4444
Fax	614-555-5580	555-555-5555	444-444-4444

2. Create a third table that includes data from the CustomerID, City, and State fields of the Customers table. Call your table Localities.

3. Write an SQL statement that would delete the SMITHJ record from the Customers table. What SQL statement would you issue to delete the entire Customers table?

Day 16

Database Normalization

Now that you understand the Data Definition Language (DDL) portion of SQL, it's time to apply that new knowledge to a lesson on database theory. Today you learn about the concept of data normalization. You develop a working definition of data normalization and learn about the advantages of normalizing your databases. You also explore each of the five rules of data normalization, including reasons for applying these rules. When you have completed today's lesson, you will be able to identify ways to use data normalization to improve database integrity and performance.

Throughout today's lesson, you normalize a real database using the data definition SQL statements you learned about on Day 13 ("Creating Databases with SQL") and Day 15 ("Updating Databases with SQL"), and by using Visual Basic's Visdata application that you learned about in the first week (see Day 7, "Using the Visdata Program").

The topic of data normalization could easily take up an entire book—and there are several excellent books on it. This lesson approaches data normalization from a practical standpoint rather than a theoretical standpoint. Here you focus on two particular questions: What are the rules? How can these rules help me improve my Visual Basic database applications? To start, let's develop a working definition of data normalization and talk about why it can improve your Visual Basic applications.

What Is Data Normalization?

Data normalization is a process of refining database structures to improve the speed at which data can be accessed and to increase database integrity. This is not easy. Very often, optimizing a table for speed is not the same as optimizing for integrity. Putting a database together involves discovering the data elements you need and then creating a set of tables to hold those elements. The tables and fields you define make up the structure of the database. The structure you decide upon affects the performance of your database programs. Some database layouts can improve access speed. For example, placing all related information in a single table allows your programs to locate all needed data by looking in one place. On the other hand, you can lay out your database in a way that improves data integrity. For example, placing all the invoice line item data in one table and the invoice address information in another table prevents users from deleting complete addresses when they remove invoice line items from the database. Well-normalized databases strike a balance between speed and integrity.

High-speed tables have few index constraints and can have several, sometimes repetitive, fields in a single record. The few constraints make updates, insertions, and deletions faster. The repetitive fields make it easier to load large amounts of data in a single SQL statement instead of finding additional, related data in subsidiary tables linked through those slower index constraints.

Databases built for maximum integrity have many small data tables. Each of these tables can have several indexes—mostly foreign keys referencing other tables in the database. If a table is built with high integrity in mind, it is difficult to add invalid data to the database without firing off database error messages. Of course, all that integrity checking eats precious ticks off the microchip clock.

Good data normalization results in data tables that make sense in a fundamental way. Well-normalized tables are easy to understand when you look at them. It is easy to see what kind of data they store and what types of updates need to be performed. Usually, it is rather easy to create data entry routines and simple reports directly from well-normalized tables. In fact, the rule of thumb is this: If it's hard to work with a data table, it probably needs more normalization work.

For the rest of this lesson, you use the Visdata application to build data tables. If you have not already looked at the lesson on Day 7, turn there first for information on how to use Visdata to maintain relational databases.

A Typical Database Before Normalization

To illustrate the process of normalization, let's start with an existing database table. The database NORMDAT1.MDB can be found in the TYSDBVB5\SOURCE\DATA directory of the CD that shipped with this book. Load this into the Visdata application and open the Table1 data table in design mode. Your screen should look something like the one in Figure 16.1.

Figure 16.1.

Displaying Table1 before normalization.

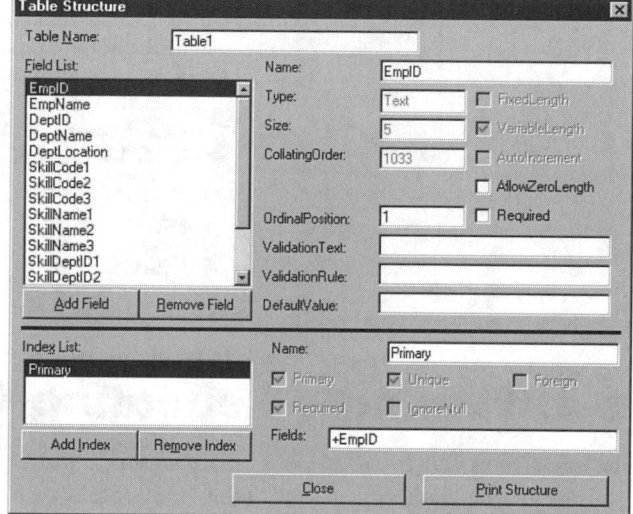

This data table holds information about employees of a small company. The table contains fields for the employee ID and employee name, and the ID, name, and location of the department to which this employee is currently assigned. It also includes fields for tracking the employee's job skills, including the skill code, the name, the department in which the skill was learned, and the ability level that the employee has attained for the designated skill. Up to three different skills can be maintained for each employee.

This table is rather typical of those you find in existing record-oriented databases. It is designed to quickly give users all the available information on a single employee. It is also a fairly simple task to build a data entry form for this data table. The single form can hold the employee and department fields at the top of the form and the three skill field sets toward the bottom of the form. Figure 16.2 shows a simple data form for this table generated by Visdata.

Access to the information in the table is fast and the creation of a data entry screen is easy. So this is a well-normalized table, right? Wrong. Three of the five rules of normalization that you learn in the rest of this lesson are broken, and the other two are in jeopardy! Some of the problems are obvious, some are not. Let's go through each of the five rules of normalization and see how applying these rules can improve the data table.

Figure 16.2.

The data entry form for Table1.

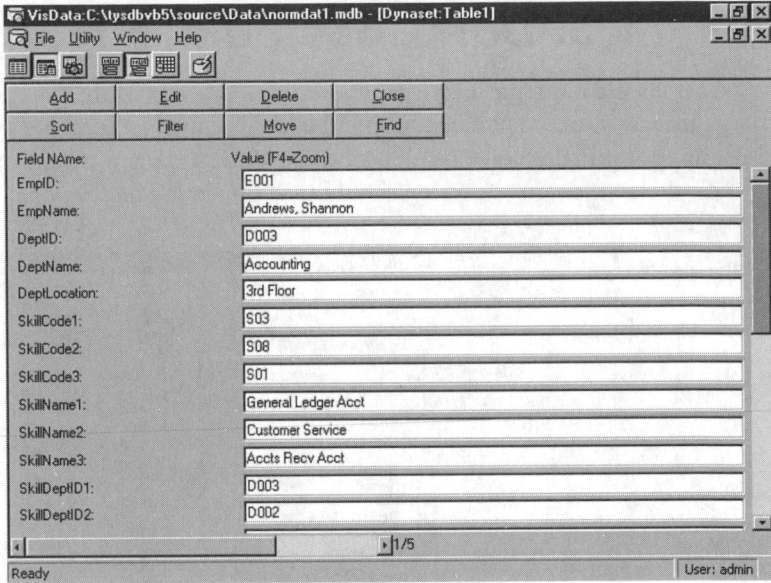

Rule 1: Eliminate Repeating Groups

The first area in which Table1 needs some work is in the repeating skill fields. Why include columns in the data table called SkillCode1, SkillCode2, SkillCode3, or SkillName1, SkillName2, SkillName3, and so forth? You want to be able to store more than one set of skills for an employee, right? But what if you want to store data on more than three skills acquired by a single employee? What if most of the employees only have one or two skills, and very few have three skills? Why waste the blank space for the third skill? Even more vexing, how easy will it be to locate all employees in the data table that have a particular skill?

NOTE

> The first rule of data normalization states that you should make a separate table for each set of related columns and give each table a primary key. Databases that adhere to this first rule of normalization are said to be in the *First Normal Form.*

The first rule of data normalization is to eliminate repeating groups of data in a data table. Repeating groups of data, such as the skill fields (SkillCodeX, SkillNameX, SkillDeptIDX, and SkillLevelX), usually indicates the need for an additional table. Creating the related table greatly improves readability and allows you to keep as few or as many skill sets for each employee as you need without wasting storage space.

The fields that relate to employee skills need to be separated from the others in the table. You don't need to put all 12 skill fields in the new table, though. You only need one of each of the unique data fields. The new database now has not one, but two data tables. One, called Skills, contains only the skill fields. The other table, called Employees, contains the rest of the fields. Table 16.1 shows how the two new tables look.

Table 16.1. Eliminating repeating data.

Skills Table	Employees Table
EmpID	EmpID
SkillCode	EmpName
SkillName	DeptID
SkillDeptID	DeptName
SkillLevel	DeptLocation

Notice that the first field in both tables is the EmpID field. This field is used to relate the two tables. Each record in the Skill table contains the employee ID and all pertinent data on a single job skill (code, name, department learned, and ability level). If a single employee has several skills, there is a single record in the Skill table for each job skill acquired by an employee. For example, if a single employee has acquired five skills, there are five records with the same employee ID in the Skills table.

Each record in the Skills table must contain a valid value in the EmpID field or it should be rejected. In other words, each time a record is added to the Skills table, the value in the EmpID field should be checked against values in the EmpID field of the Employees table. If no match is found, the Skills record must be corrected before it is written to the database. You remember from the discussion of SQL Data Definition Language statements on Day 13 that this is a FOREIGN KEY CONSTRAINT. The field EmpID in the Skills table is a foreign key that references the field EmpID in the Employees table. Also, the EmpID field in the Employees table should be a primary field to make sure that each record in the Employee table has a unique EmpID value.

Now that you know the fields and index constraints you need, you can use SQL DDL to create two new tables. If you have not already done so, start the Visdata application and open the NORMDAT1.MDB database. Now you create two new tables that bring the database into compliance with the first rule of data normalization.

First, create the table that holds all the basic employee data. This table has all the fields that were in the Table1 table, minus the skill fields. Using the information in Table 16.1 as a guide, enter an SQL DDL statement in the SQL window of Visdata that creates the Employees data table. Your SQL statement should resemble Listing 16.1.

TYPE **Listing 16.1. Creating the Employees table.**

```
CREATE TABLE Employees
   (EmpID TEXT(5),
    EmpName TEXT(30),
    DeptID TEXT(5),
    DeptName TEXT(20),
    DeptLocation TEXT(20),
    CONSTRAINT PKEmpID PRIMARY KEY (EmpID));
```

The EmpID field has been designated as a primary key field. This guarantees that no two records in the Employees data table can have the same EmpID value. You can use the EmpID field in the next table you create (the Skills table) as the reference field that links the two tables. Because you are using the EmpID field as a link, it must be a unique value in the Employees table in order to maintain database integrity. What you are doing here is setting up a one-to-many relationship between the Employees table (the one-side) and the Skills table (the many-side). Any time you establish a one-to-many relationship, you must make sure that the reference field (in this case, the EmpID field) is unique on the one-side of the relationship.

Now that you have built the Employees table, you can create the table that holds all the skills data. Use the information in Table 16.1 to write an SQL DDL statement that creates a table called Skills. Make sure the new table has the field EmpID and that the EmpID field is built with the correct index constraint to enforce one-to-many database integrity. Your SQL statement should look like the one in Listing 16.2.

TYPE **Listing 16.2. Creating the Skills table.**

```
CREATE TABLE Skills
   (EmpID TEXT(5),
    SkillCode TEXT(5),
    SkillName TEXT(20),
    SkillDeptID TEXT(5),
    SkillLevel INTEGER,
    CONSTRAINT PKSkills PRIMARY KEY (SkillCode,EmpID),
    CONSTRAINT FKEmpID FOREIGN KEY (EmpID) REFERENCES Employees(EmpID));
```

You can see in Listing 16.2 that you have used the FOREIGN KEY_REFERENCES syntax to establish and maintain the table relationship. As you remember from the SQL lessons on Day 13 and Day 15, the FOREIGN KEY_REFERENCES syntax makes sure that any entry in the Skills.EmpID field can be found in the related Employees.EmpID field. If users enter a value in the Skills.EmpID field that cannot be found in any Employees.EmpID field, Visual Basic automatically issues a database error message. This message is generated by Visual Basic, not by your program.

16

That is how you build tables that adhere to the first rule of data normalization. To see how these tables look when they have live data in them, use Visdata to load the TYSDBVB5\SOURCE\DATA\NORMDAT2.MDB database. This database contains the Employees and Skills tables with data already loaded into them. Figure 16.3 shows how Visdata displays the two new tables that have live data.

Figure 16.3.

The new Employees and Skills tables from NORMDAT2.MDB.

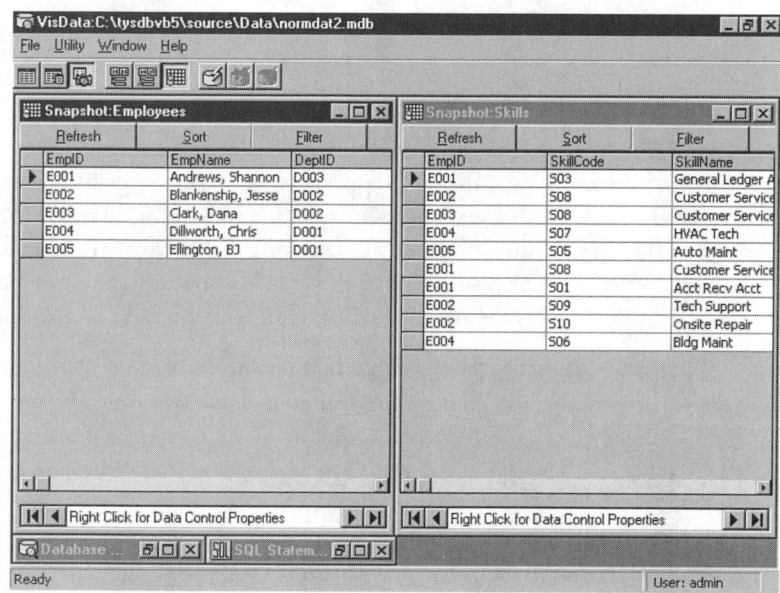

16

NOTE

Before continuing with today's lesson, load the NORMDAT2.MDB database into Visdata.

Rule 2: Eliminate Redundant Data

Another aspect of the Skills table also needs attention. Although moving the repeating skills fields into a separate table improves the database, you still have work to do. The Skills table contains *redundant data.* That is, data is stored in several places in the database. Redundant data in your database can lead to serious database integrity problems. It's best to eliminate as many occurrences of redundant data as possible.

NOTE  The second rule of data normalization states that if a column depends only on part of a multivalued key, you remove it to a separate table. In other words, if you need to fill in two fields in order to truly identify the record (JobID and JobName), but only one of those fields is needed to perform a lookup in the table, you need a new table. Databases that conform to this rule are said to be in the *Second Normal Form*.

For example, the Skills table includes a field called SkillCode. This field contains a code that identifies the specific skill (or skills) each employee has acquired. If two employees have gained the same skill, that skill appears twice in the Skills file. The same table also includes a field called SkillName. This field contains a meaningful name for the skill represented by the value in the SkillCode field. This name is much more readable and informative than the SkillCode value. In essence, these two fields contain the same data, represented slightly differently. This is the dreaded redundant data you have to eliminate!

Before you jump into fixing things, first review the details regarding redundant data and how it can adversely affect the integrity of your database.

Update Integrity Problems

When you keep copies of data elements in several rows in the same table or in several different tables (such as job names to go with job ID codes), you have a lot of work ahead of you when you want to modify the copied data. If you fail to update one or more of these copies, you can ruin the integrity of your database. Redundant data can lead to what are known as *update integrity* problems.

Imagine that you have built a huge database of employee skills using the tables you built in the preceding section. All is going great when, suddenly, the Human Resources Department informs you that it has designed a new set of names for the existing skill codes. You now have to go through the entire database and update all the records in the Skills table, searching out the old skill name and updating the SkillName field with the new skill name. Because this is an update for the entire data table, you have to shut down the database until the job is complete in order to make sure no one is editing records while you're performing this update. Also, you probably have to change some Visual Basic code that you built to verify the data entry. All in all, it's a nasty job. If that isn't enough, how about a little power outage in the middle of your update run? Now you have some records with the old names, and some with the new names. Things are really messed up!

Delete Integrity Problems

Although the update integrity problem is annoying, you can suffer through most of those problems. In fact, almost all database programmers have had to face similar problems before. The more troublesome integrity problem resulting from redundant data comes not during updates, but during deletes. Let's assume you have properly handled the mass update required by the Human Resources Department. Then you discover that there is only one employee in the entire database that has the SkillCode S099 (Advanced Customer Service course). No other employee has attained this high level of training. Now, that employee is leaving the organization. When you delete the employee record from the file, you delete the only reference to the Advanced Customer Service course! There is no longer any record of the Advanced Customer Service course in your entire database, which is a real problem.

The Normalization Solution

The way to reduce these kinds of data integrity problems is to pull out the redundant data and place it in a separate table. You need a single table, called SkillMaster, that contains only the SkillCode and the SkillName data fields. This table is linked to the Skills table through the SkillCode field. Now, when the Human Resources department changes the skill names, you only need to update a single record—the one in the SkillMaster table. Because the Skills table is linked to the SkillMaster table, when you delete the employee with the certification for SkillCode S099, you don't delete the last reference to the skill. It's still in the SkillMaster table.

TIP
Another plus to this type of table separation is in speeding data entry. With only one field to enter, and especially a brief code, data entry operators can more quickly fill in fields on the table's form.

Also, you now have a single table that lists all the unique skills that can be acquired by your employees. You can produce a Skills list for employees and managers to review. If you add fields that group the skills by department, you can even produce a report that shows all the skills by department. This would be very difficult if you were stuck with the file structure you developed in the preceding section.

So let's redefine the Skills table and the SkillMaster table to conform to the second rule of data normalization. Table 16.2 shows the fields you need for the two tables.

Table 16.2. The field list for the Skills and SkillMaster tables.

EmpSkills	SkillMaster
EmpID	SkillCode
SkillCode	SkillName
SkillDeptID	
SkillLevel	

You can see that you have renamed the Skills table to EmpSkills to better reflect its contents. You have also moved the SkillName field out of the EmpSkills table and created SkillMaster, a small table that contains a list of all the valid skills and their descriptive names. Now you have the added bonus of being able to add a FOREIGN KEY constraint to the EmpSkills table. This improves database integrity without adding any additional programming code!

Listing 16.3 shows the two SQL DDL statements that create the EmpSkills and the SkillMaster data tables. Note the use of FOREIGN KEY constraints in the EmpSkills table.

TYPE **Listing 16.3. Creating the SkillMaster and EmpSkills tables.**

```
CREATE TABLE SkillMaster
    (SkillCode TEXT(5),
     SkillName TEXT(20),
     CONSTRAINT PKSkillMaster PRIMARY KEY (SkillCode))
CREATE TABLE EmpSkills
    (EmpID TEXT(5),
     SkillCode TEXT(5),
     SkillDeptID TEXT(5),
     SkillLevel INTEGER,
     CONSTRAINT PKSkills PRIMARY KEY (SkillCode,EmpID),
     CONSTRAINT FKEmpID2 FOREIGN KEY (EmpID)
        REFERENCES Employees(EmpID),
     CONSTRAINT FKSkillCode FOREIGN KEY (SkillCode)
        REFERENCES SkillMaster(SkillCode));
```

Use Visdata to add these two new tables to the NORMDAT2.MDB database. The database TYSDBVB5\SOURCE\DATA\NORMDAT3.MDB contains a complete database with the data tables Employees, EmpSkills, and SkillMaster fully populated with data. This is demonstrated in Figure 16.4.

You now have a database that conforms to the first two rules of data normalization. You have eliminated repeating data and redundant data. You have one more type of data to eliminate from your tables. You handle that in the following section.

Figure 16.4.

The new Employees, EmpSkills, and SkillMaster tables.

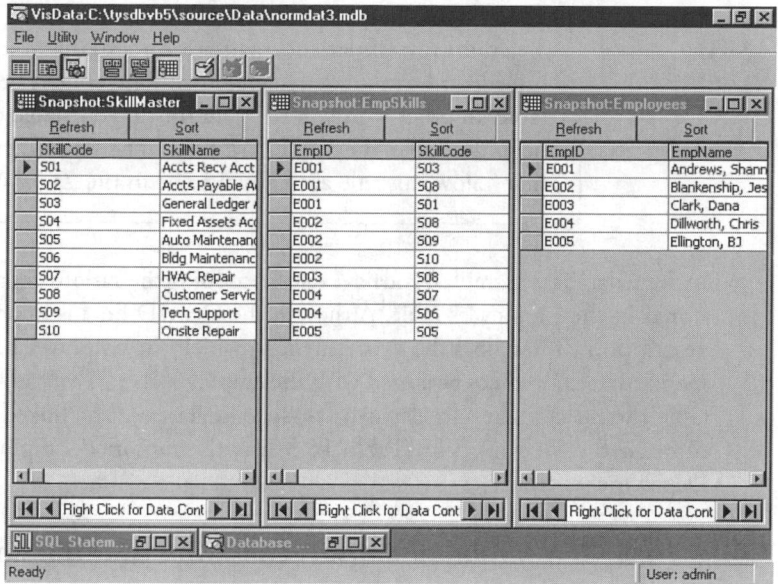

NOTE

Before continuing with the lesson, load the NORMDAT3.MDB database into Visdata.

Rule 3: Eliminate Columns Not Dependent on the Primary Key

By now, you're probably getting the idea. You are looking for hints in the table structure that lead you into traps further down the road. Will this table be easy to update? What happens if you delete records from this table? Is it easy to get a comprehensive list of all the unique records in this table? Asking questions like these can uncover problems that are not so apparent when you first build a table.

When you are building a data table, you should also be concerned about whether a field describes additional information about the key field. In other words, is the field you are about to add to this table truly related to the key field? If not, the field in question should not be added to the table. It probably needs to be in its own table. This process of removing fields that do not describe the key field is how you make your data tables conform to the third rule of data normalization—eliminate columns not dependent on keys.

NOTE

> The third rule of data normalization states that if a column does not fully describe the index key, that column should be moved to a separate table. In other words, if the columns in your table don't really need to be in this table, they probably need to be somewhere else. Databases that follow this rule are known to be in the *Third Normal Form.*

In these database examples, you have data describing the various departments in the company stored in the Employees table. Although the DeptID field is important to the Employees description (it describes the department to which the employee belongs), the *department-specific* data should not be stored with the employee data. Yes, you need another table. This table should contain only department-specific data and be linked to the Employees table through the DeptID field. Table 16.3 lists the modified Employees table and the new Departments table.

Table 16.3. The modified Employees table and the new Departments table.

Employees	Departments
EmpID	DeptID
EmpName	DeptName
DeptID	DeptLocation

Notice that the Employees table is much simpler now that you have eliminated all unrelated fields. Use Visdata to construct SQL DDL statements that create the new Departments table and then modify the Employees table and the EmpSkills table to increase database integrity (yes, more foreign keys!). First, use the SQL DDL in Listing 16.4 to create the Departments table. Check your work against Figure 16.5.

TYPE   **Listing 16.4. Creating the Departments table.**

```
CREATE TABLE Departments
  (DeptID TEXT(5),
   DeptName TEXT(20),
   DeptLocation TEXT(20),
   CONSTRAINT PKDeptID PRIMARY KEY (DeptID))
```

Now alter the Employees table. You need to do two things:

☐ Remove the DeptName column from the table.

☐ Add a FOREIGN KEY constraint to enforce referential integrity on the Employees.DeptID field.

Listing 16.5 contains the SQL DDL statements to create the modified Employees table.

TYPE   **Listing 16.5. Creating the new Employees table.**

```
CREATE TABLE Employees
   (EmpID TEXT(5),
    EmpName TEXT(30),
    DeptID TEXT(5),
    CONSTRAINT PKEmpID PRIMARY KEY (EmpID),
    CONSTRAINT FKEmpDept FOREIGN KEY (DeptID)
      REFERENCES Departments(DeptID))
```

Now you need to modify the EmpSkills table to add the referential integrity check on the EmpSkills.SkillDeptID field. The new SQL DDL should look like Listing 16.6.

TYPE   **Listing 16.6. Creating the new EmpSkills table.**

```
CREATE TABLE EmpSkills2
   (EmpID TEXT(5),
    SkillCode TEXT(5),
    SkillDeptID TEXT(5),
    SkillLevel INTEGER,
    CONSTRAINT PKEmpSkill2 PRIMARY KEY (SkillCode,EmpID),
    CONSTRAINT FKSkillMast FOREIGNKEY (SkillCode)
      REFERENCES SkillMaster(SkillCode),
    CONSTRAINT FKSkillDept FOREIGN KEY (SkillDeptID)
      REFERENCES Departments(DeptID));
```

The database NORMDAT4.MDB contains a complete set of tables that conform to the third rule of data normalization. Use Visdata to load NORMDAT4.MDB and review the data tables. Attempt to add some data that does not follow the integrity rules. Try deleting records. This shows you how Visual Basic issues database error messages when you try to save a record that breaks the referential integrity rules.

The first three rules of data normalization involve the elimination of repeating, redundant, or unrelated data fields. The last two rules involve isolating multiple relationships to improve overall database integrity. The first three rules are usually all that you need to produce well-designed databases. However, there are times when additional normalization can improve the quality of your database design. In the next two sections, you learn rules 4 and 5 of data normalization.

Figure 16.5.

The Departments table added to NORMDAT4.MDB.

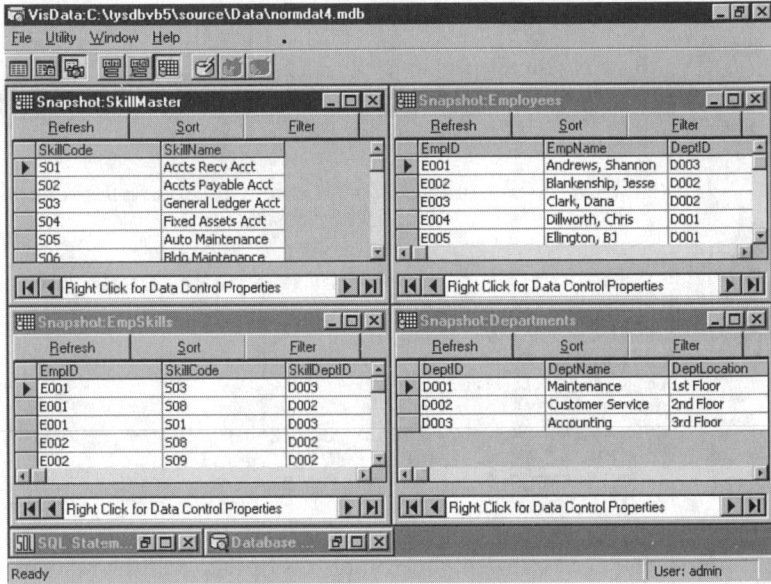

Do Not Store Calculated Data in Your Tables

It is important to note here that one of the results of the third rule of data normalization is that you should not store calculated fields in a data table. Calculated fields are fields that contain derived data such as year-to-date totals, a line in the invoice table that contains the totals of several other rows in the invoice table, and so forth. Calculated fields do not describe the primary key. Calculated fields are *derived data*. It is a bad practice to store derived data in live data tables.

Derived data can easily fall out of sync with the individual rows that make up the total data. What happens if the individual rows that add up to the total are altered or deleted? How do you make sure the row that holds the total is updated each time any line item row is changed? Storing derived data might seem to be faster, but it is not easier. And dealing with derived data opens your database to possible update and delete integrity problems each time a user touches either the prime data rows or the total data rows. Calculated data should not be stored. It should always be computed using the prime data at the time it is needed.

NOTE  | Before continuing with this lesson, load the NORMDAT4.MDB database into Visdata.

16

Rule 4: Isolate Independent Multiple Relationships

The fourth rule of data normalization concerns the handling of independent multiple relationships. This rule is applied whenever you have more than one one-to-many relationship on the same data table. The relationship between the Employees table and the EmpSkills table is a one-to-many relationship. There can be many EmpSkills records related to one Employee record. Let's add an additional attribute of employees to create a database that has more than a single one-to-many relationship.

Assume that the Human Resources Department has decided it needs more than just the skill names and skill levels attained for each employee. Human Resources also wants to add the level of education attained by the employee for that skill. For example, if the employee has an accounting skill and has an associate's degree in bookkeeping, Human Resources wants to store the degree information, too. If an employee has been certified as an electrician and works in the Maintenance Department, the Human Resources group wants to know that.

The first thing you might want to do is add a new column to the EmpSkills table—maybe a field called Degree, maybe even a field for YearCompleted. This makes sense because each skill might have an associated education component. It makes sense, but it is not a good idea. What about the employee who is currently working in the Customer Service Department but has an accounting degree? Just because the employee has a degree does not mean that employee has the skills to perform a particular job or is working in a position directly related to his or her degree. The degree and the job skills are independent of each other. Therefore, even though the skills data and the degree data are related, they should be isolated in separate tables and linked through a foreign key relationship.

 **NOTE**

> The fourth rule of data normalization dictates that no table can contain two or more one-to-many or many-to-many relationships that are not directly related. In other words, if the data element is important (the college degree) but not directly related to other elements in the record (the customer service rep with an accounting degree), you need to move the college degree element to a new table. Databases that follow this rule are in the *Fourth Normal Form*.

Table 16.4 shows a sample Training table that can be used to hold the education information for each employee. Now the Human Resources department can keep track of education achievements independent of acquired job skills. Note that the EmpID directly connects the two relationships. If the Training table has only one entry per employee, the two relationships are a one-to-one relationship between the Employees table and the Training table, and a one-to-many relationship between the Employees table and the EmpSkills table. Of course, if any employee has more than one degree, both relationships become one-to-many.

Table 16.4. The sample training data table.

EmpID

Degree

YearCompleted

InstitutionName

Listing 16.7 is a sample SQL DDL statement that creates the Training data table with the proper relationship constraint. Enter this statement in the SQL window of Visdata while you have the NORMDAT4.MDB database open. Check your results against Figure 16.6.

TYPE **Listing 16.7. Creating the Training table.**

```
CREATE TABLE Training
    (EmpID TEXT(5),
    Degree TEXT(20),
    YearCompleted INTEGER,
    InstitutionName TEXT(30),
    CONSTRAINT PKTraining PRIMARY KEY (EmpID,Degree),
    CONSTRAINT FKEmpTrn FOREIGN KEY (EmpID)
        REFERENCES Employees (EmpID))
```

The database NORMDAT5.MDB contains a complete version of the database normalized up to the fourth rule of data normalization. Use Visdata to open the database and review the table structure.

NOTE Before continuing with the lesson, load the NORMDAT5.MDB database into Visdata.

Figure 16.6.

The Training table shows the degree achievements for the Employees table.

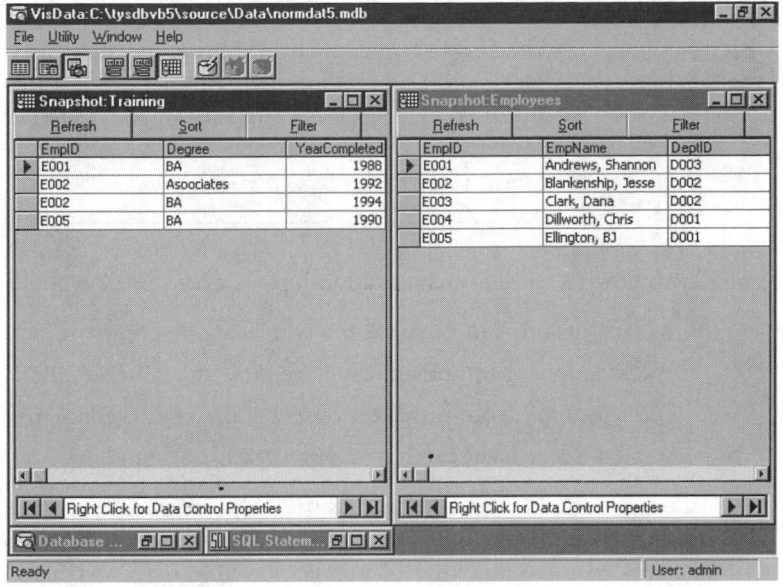

Rule 5: Isolate Related Multiple Relationships

The last remaining rule of data normalization covers the handling of related multiple relationships in a database. Unlike the fourth rule, which deals with independent, one-to-many, multiple relationships, the fifth rule is used to normalize related, many-to-many multiple relationships. Related, many-to-many multiple relationships do not occur frequently in databases. However, when they do come up, these types of data relations can cause a great deal of confusion and hassle when you're normalizing your database. You won't invoke this rule often, but when you do it pays off!

Imagine that the Maintenance Department decides it wants to keep track of all the large equipment used on the shop floor by various departments. It uses this data to keep track of where the equipment is located. The Maintenance Department also wants to keep a list of suppliers for the equipment in cases of repair or replacement. When you were a novice, you might have decided to design a single table that held the department ID, equipment name, and supplier name. But, as I'm sure you have guessed by now, that is not the correct response. What if the Maintenance Department has more than one supplier for the same type of equipment? What if a single supplier provides more than one of the types of equipment used in the plant? What if some departments are restricted in the suppliers they can use to repair or replace their equipment?

NOTE

> The fifth rule of data normalization dictates that you should isolate related multiple relationships within a database. In other words, if several complex relationships exist in your database, separate each of the relationships into its own table. Databases that adhere to this rule are known to be in the *Fifth Normal Form*.

The following list shows the relationships that have been exposed in this example:

☐ Each department can have several pieces of equipment.

☐ Each piece of equipment can have more than one supplier.

☐ Each supplier can provide a variety of pieces of equipment.

☐ Each department can have a restricted list of suppliers.

Although each of the preceding business rules are simple, putting them all together in the database design is tough. It's the last item that really complicates things. There is more than one way to solve this kind of puzzle. The one suggested here is just one of the many possibilities.

First, you need to expose all the tables that you need to contain the data. The preceding list describes two one-to-many relationships (department to equipment, and department to supplier, with restrictions) and one many-to-many relationship (equipment to supplier, supplier to equipment). Each of those relationships can be expressed in simple tables. Two additional tables not mentioned, but certainly needed, are a table of all the equipment in the building (regardless of its location) and a table of all the suppliers (regardless of their department affiliation). Table 16.5 shows sample field layouts for the required tables. The Equipment and Supplier tables are shortened in this example. If you were designing these tables for a real database project, you would add several other fields.

Table 16.5. The Fifth Rule sample data tables.

Equipment	Supplier
EquipID	SupplierID
EquipName	SupplierName
DatePurchased	SupplierAddress

Listing 16.8 contains the SQL DDL statements to create these tables. Figure 16.7 shows the results of executing these statements.

TYPE

Listing 16.8. Creating the Equipment and the Supplier tables.

```
CREATE TABLE Equipment
   (EquipID TEXT (10),
    EquipName TEXT(30),
    DatePurchased DATE,
    CONSTRAINT PKEquipID PRIMARY KEY (EquipID))
CREATE TABLE Supplier
   (SupplierID TEXT (10),
    SupplierName TEXT(30),
    SupplierAddress MEMO,
    CONSTRAINT PKSupplier PRIMARY KEY (SupplierID))
```

Figure 16.7.

Supplier and Equipment tables in

NORMDAT6.MDB.

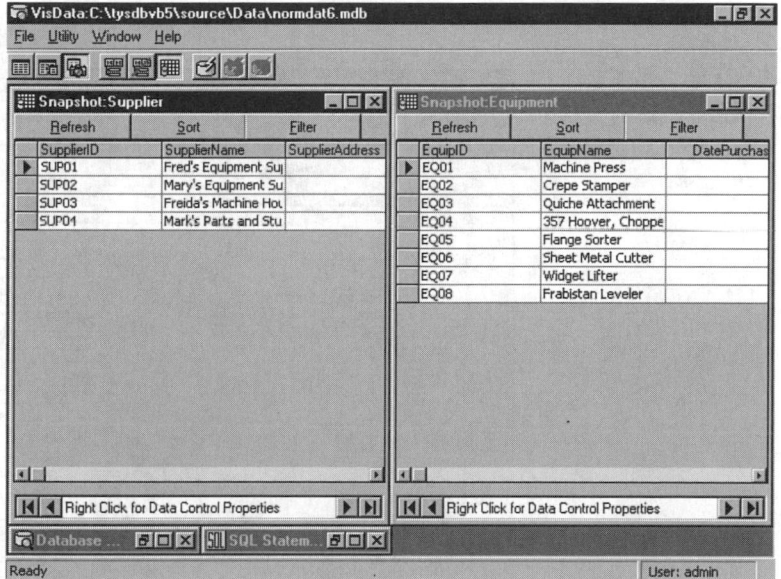

The next two data tables describe the relationships between Supplier and Equipment and between Supplier and Departments. You remember that departments can be restricted to certain suppliers when repairing or replacing equipment. By setting up a table such as the DeptSupplier table described next, you can easily maintain a list of valid suppliers for each department. Similarly, as new suppliers are discovered for equipment, they can be added to the EquipSupplier table. Refer to Table 16.6 for a sample list of fields.

Table 16.6. EquipSupplier and DeptSupplier tables.

EquipSupplier	DeptSupplier
EquipID	DeptID
SupplierID	SupplierID

These two tables are short because they are only needed to enforce expressed simple relationships between existing data tables. Creating small tables such as these is a handy way to reduce complex relationships to more straightforward ones. It is easier to create meaningful CONSTRAINT clauses when the tables are kept simple, too. The SQL DDL statements for these two tables appear in Listing 16.9. The result of executing these statements in Visdata appears in Figure 16.8.

Figure 16.8.

EquipSupplier and DeptSupplier tables.

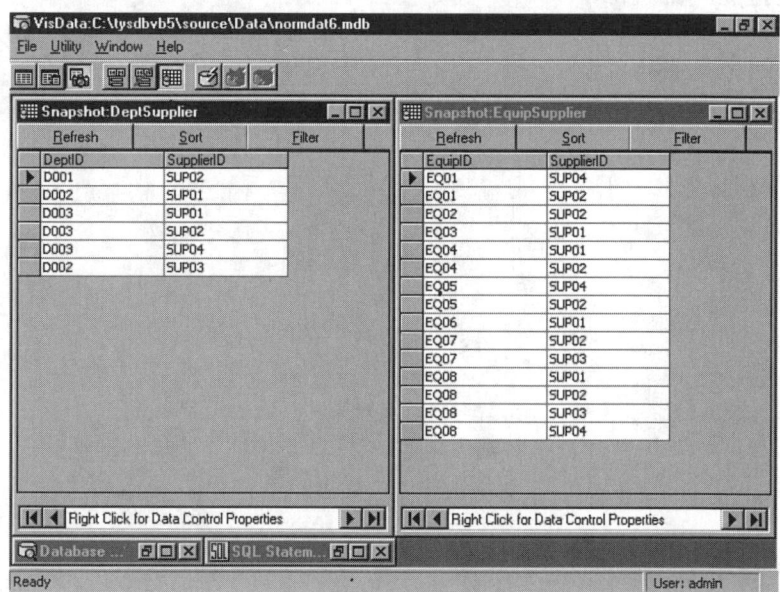

Listing 16.9. Creating the EquipSupplier and DeptSupplier tables.

TYPE

```
CREATE TABLE EquipSupplier
    (EquipID TEXT(10),
     SupplierID TEXT(10),
     CONSTRAINT PKEqSpl PRIMARY KEY (EquipID,SupplierID),
     CONSTRAINT FKEqSplEquip FOREIGN KEY (EquipID)
        REFERENCES Equipment(EquipID),
     CONSTRAINT FKEqSplSupplier FOREIGN KEY (SupplierID)
```

16

```
        REFERENCES Supplier(SupplierID))
CREATE TABLE DeptSupplier
   (DeptID TEXT(5),
    SupplierID TEXT(10),
    CONSTRAINT PKDeptSpl PRIMARY KEY (DeptID,SupplierID),
    CONSTRAINT FKDptSplDept FOREIGN KEY (DeptID)
       REFERENCES Departments(DeptID),
    CONSTRAINT FKDptSplSupplier FOREIGN KEY (SupplierID)
       REFERENCES Supplier(SupplierID))
```

Notice that, in these two tables, the CONSTRAINT definitions are longer than the field definitions. This is common when you begin to use the power database integrity aspects of SQL databases.

Finally, you need a single table that expresses the Equipment-Supplier-Department relationship. This table shows which department has which equipment supplied by which supplier. More importantly, you can build this final table with tight constraints that enforce all these business rules. Both the Department-Supplier relationship and the Equipment-Supplier relationship are validated before the record is saved to the database. This is a powerful data validation tool—all without writing any Visual Basic code! Table 16.7 and the SQL DDL statement in Listing 16.10 show how this table can be constructed. See Figure 16.9 to review the results of executing these statements.

Table 16.7. The Department-Equipment-Supplier data table.

DeptID

EquipID

SupplierID

TYPE **Listing 16.10. Creating the DeptEqpSuplr table.**

```
CREATE TABLE DeptEqpSuplr
   (DeptID TEXT(5),
    EquipID TEXT(10),
    SupplierID TEXT(10),
    CONSTRAINT PFDeptEq PRIMARY KEY (DeptID, EquipID),
    CONSTRAINT FKEqSupl FOREIGN KEY (EquipID,SupplierID)
       REFERENCES EquipSupplier(EquipID,SupplierID),
    CONSTRAINT FKDeptSupl FOREIGN KEY (DeptID,SupplierID)
       REFERENCES DeptSupplier(DeptID,SupplierID))
```

The Microsoft Access database NORMDAT6.MDB contains a set of live data for the tables described in this section. Use Visdata to open the database and review the table structure. Try adding or deleting records in ways that would break integrity rules. Notice that none of the last three tables defined (EquipSupplier, DeptSupplier, and DeptEqpSuplr) allow edits on any existing record. This is because you defined the primary key as having all the fields in a record. Because you cannot edit a primary key value, you must first delete the record, and then add the modified version to the data table.

Figure 16.9.

The EquipSupplier, DeptSupplier, and DeptEqpSuplr tables.

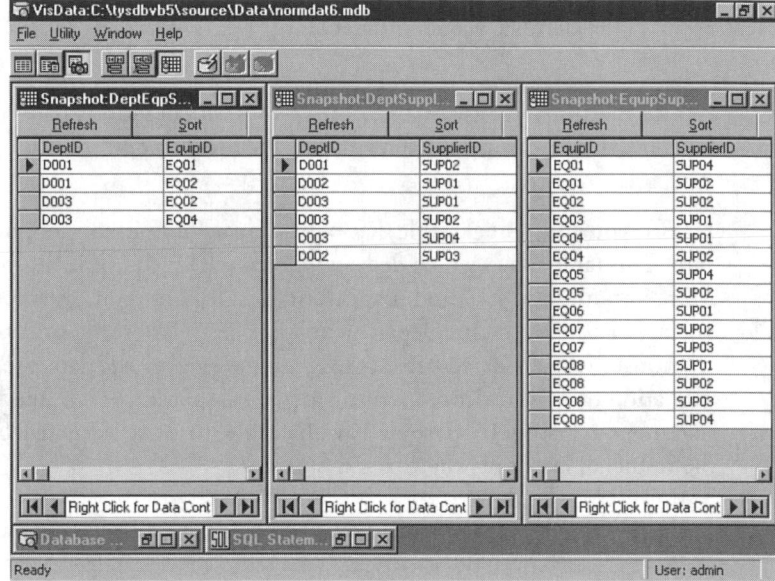

Summary

In today's lesson, you learned how to improve database integrity and access speed using the five rules of data normalization. You learned the following five rules:

☐ **Rule 1: Eliminate Repeating Groups.** If you have a set of fields that have the same name followed by a number (Skill1, Skill2, Skill3, and so forth), remove these repeating groups, create a new table for the repeating data, and relate it to the key field in the first table.

☐ **Rule 2: Eliminate Redundant Data.** Don't store the same data in two different locations. This can lead to update and delete errors. If equivalent data elements are entered in two fields, remove the second data element, create a new master table with the element and its partner as a key field, and then place the key field as a relationship in the locations that formerly held both data elements.

☐ **Rule 3: Eliminate Columns Not Dependent on Keys.** If you have data elements that are not directly related to the primary key of the table, these elements should be removed to their own data table. Only store data elements that are directly related to the primary key of the table. This particularly includes derived data or other calculations.

☐ **Rule 4: Isolate Independent Multiple Relationships.** Use this rule to improve database design when you are dealing with more than one one-to-many relationship in the database. Before you add a new field to a table, ask yourself whether this field is really dependent upon the other fields in the table. If not, create a new table with the independent data.

☐ **Rule 5: Isolate Related Multiple Relationships.** Use this rule to improve database design when you are dealing with more than one many-to-many relationship in the database. If you have database rules that require multiple references to the same field or sets of fields, isolate the fields into smaller tables and construct one or more link tables that contain the required constraints that enforce database integrity.

Quiz

1. Is it a good idea to optimize your database strictly for speed?

2. What is meant by the term *First Normal Form*?

3. Explain how the second rule of data normalization differs from the first rule of normalization.

4. Should you include fields in a data table that are the calculated results of other fields in the same table?

5. When would you invoke the fourth rule of data normalization?

6. When would you invoke the fifth rule of data normalization?

Exercises

1. As a computer consultant, you have landed a contract to build a customer tracking system for your local garage. After several days of interviews with the owner, mechanics, and staff members, you have determined that the following data fields should be included in your database. Many of the customers of this garage have more than one automobile. Therefore, you are requested to leave room for tracking two cars per customer.

   Use these fields: CustomerID, CustomerName, Address, City, State, Zip, Phone, SerialNumber, License, VehicleType1, Make1, Model1, Color1, Odometer1, VehicleType2, Make2, Model2, Color2, Odometer2.

   Optimize this data into tables using the rules of data normalization discussed in today's lesson. Identify all primary and foreign keys.

2. Write the SQL statements that create the tables you designed in Exercise 1.

Day 17

Multiuser Considerations

Today you'll look at some issues related to designing and coding applications that serve multiple users. Multiuser applications pose some unique challenges when it comes to database operations. These challenges are the main topics of this chapter:

☐ *Database locking schemes:* You'll examine the locking system used by the Microsoft Jet database engine, and you'll look at the differences between optimistic and pessimistic locking schemes. You'll learn a scheme for performing multitable locking of data tables in highly relational databases.

☐ *Cascading updates and deletes:* You'll learn how to use these features of the Microsoft Jet database engine to enforce database relations using the Cascading Updates and Deletes options.

☐ *Transaction management:* You'll see the process of transaction management, as well as how to add transaction management to your Visual Basic applications by using the `BeginTrans`, `CommitTrans`, and `Rollback` methods. Transaction management using the SQL pass-through method with back-end databases also is covered.

By the time you complete this chapter, you'll be able to add transaction management to your Visual Basic applications, and you'll understand using cascading updates and deletes to maintain the referential integrity of your database. You also will know how to perform database-level, table-level, and page-level locking schemes in your database applications.

Database Locking Schemes

Whenever more than one person is accessing a single database, some type of process must be used to prevent two users from attempting to update the same record at the same time. This process is a *locking scheme*. In its simplest form, a locking scheme allows only one user at a time to update information in the database.

The Microsoft Jet database engine provides three levels of locking:

☐ *Database locking:* At this level, only one user at a time can access the database. Use this locking level when you need to perform work on multiple, related database objects (such as tables, queries, indexes, and relations) at the same time.

☐ *Table locking:* At this level, only one user at a time can access the locked table. Use this locking level when you need to perform work on multiple records in the same table.

☐ *Page locking:* At this level, only one user can access the page of records in the database table. This is the lowest locking level provided by Microsoft Jet. Page locking is handled automatically by Visual Basic whenever you attempt to edit or update a record in a dataset.

Database Locking

Database-level locking is the most restrictive locking scheme you can use in your Visual Basic application. When you open the database using the Visual Basic data control, you can lock the database by setting the Exclusive property of the data control to True. After you open the database by using Visual Basic code, you can lock the database by setting the second parameter of the OpenDatabase method to True. Here's an example:

```
Set db = DbEngine.OpenDatabase("c:mydb",True)
```

When the database is locked, no other users can open it. Other programs cannot read or write any information until you close the database. You should use database-level locking only when you must perform work that affects multiple data objects (such as tables, indexes, relations, and queries). The Visual Basic CompactDatabase operation, for example, affects all the data objects, so the database must be opened exclusively.

17

If you need to perform an operation to update the customer ID values in several tables and you also need to update several queries to match new search criteria, you should use database-level locking.

Take a look at a Visual Basic project to see how database-level locking works. Load Visual Basic and open a new project. Add a data control to the form. Set its DataBaseName property to C:\TYSDBVB5\SOURCE\DATA\MULTIUSE.MDB and its Exclusive property to True. Save the form as MULTIUS1.FRM and the project as MULTIUS1.VBP. Now create an executable version of the project by choosing File | Make MULTIUS1.EXE from the Visual Basic main menu. Use MULTIUS1.EXE as the name of the executable file.

Now run the executable file. It loads and displays the data control. Run a second instance of the executable file. This is an attempt to run a copy of the same program. Because this second copy attempts to open the same database for exclusive use, you see an error message when the second program starts (see Figure 17.1).

Figure 17.1.

Attempting to open a locked database.

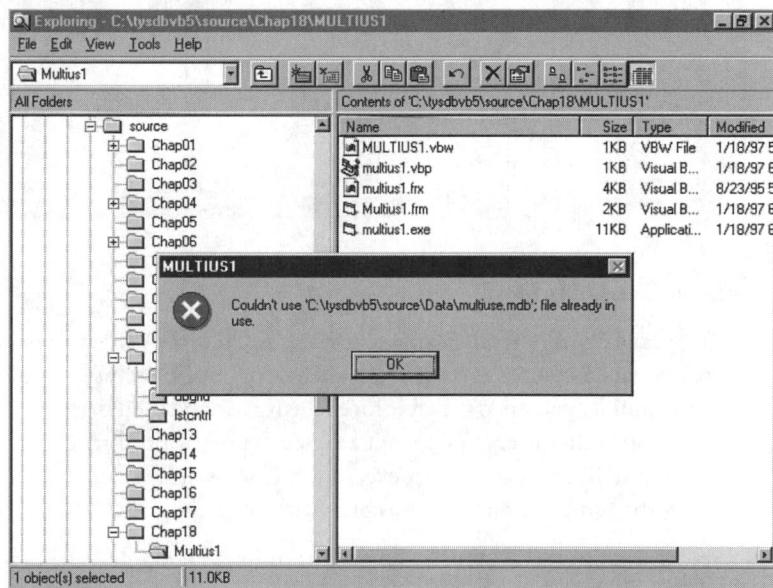

Notice that the second program continues after the error occurs, even though the database is not opened. You can check for the error when you first load the project by adding the following code to the Error event of the data control:

```
Private Sub Data1_Error(DataErr As Integer, Response As Integer)
    If Err <> 0 Then
        MsgBox Error$(Err)+Chr(13)+"Exiting Program", vbCritical, "Data1_Error"
        Unload Me
    End If
End Sub
```

Add this code to the Data1_Error event and then recompile the program. Again, attempt to run two instances of this program. This time, when you attempt to start the second instance, you receive a similar message, after which the program exits safely. (See Figure 17.2.)

Figure 17.2.

Trapping the locked database error.

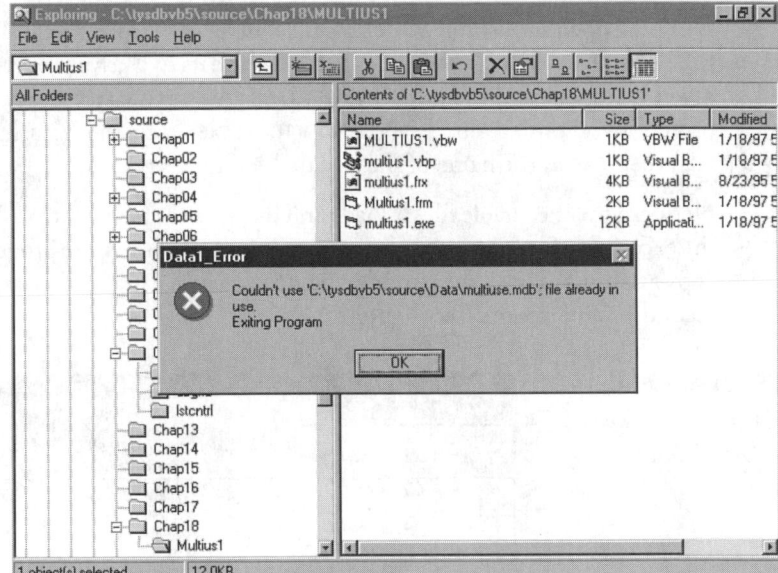

Table Locking

You can use table-level locking to secure a single table while you perform sensitive operations on the table. If you want to increase the sale price of all items in your inventory by five percent, for example, you open the table for exclusive use and then perform the update. After you close the table, other users can open it and see the new price list. Using table-level locking for an operation like this can help prevent users from writing sales orders that contain some records with the old price and some records with the new price.

Now modify the MULTIUS1.VBP project to illustrate table-level locking. Reopen the project and set the Exclusive property of the data control to False. This setting allows other users to open the database while your program is running. Now set the RecordSource property to MasterTable and set the Options property to 3. Setting the Options property to 3 opens the Recordset with the DenyWrite (1) and DenyRead (2) options turned on. This prevents other programs from opening MasterTable while your program is running.

Save and recompile the program. Start a copy of the executable version of the program. It runs without error. Now attempt to start a second copy of the same program. You see an error message telling you that the table could not be locked because it is in use elsewhere—that is, by the first instance of the program (see Figure 17.3).

Figure 17.3.

Attempting to open a locked table.

You can perform the same table-locking operation by using this Visual Basic code:

```
Sub OpenTable()
    On Error GoTo OpenTableErr
    '
    Dim db As Database
    Dim rs As Recordset
    '
    Set db = DBEngine.OpenDatabase("C:\TYSDBVB5\SOURCE\DATA\MULTIUSE.MDB")
    Set rs = db.OpenRecordset("MasterTable", dbOpenTable,
    _dbDenyRead + dbDenyWrite)
    '
    GoTo OpenTableExit
    '
OpenTableErr:
    MsgBox Error$(Err) + Chr(13) + "Exiting Program", vbCritical, "OpenTable"
    GoTo OpenTableExit
    '
OpenTableExit:
    '
End Sub
```

Notice the use of the dbDenyRead and dbDenyWrite constants in the OpenRecordset method. This is the same as setting the Option property of the data control to 3. Also notice that an error trap is added to the module to replace the code in the Error event of the data control.

Page Locking

The lowest level of locking available in Visual Basic is page-level locking. *Page-level locking* is handled automatically by the Microsoft Jet engine and cannot be controlled through Visual Basic code or with data-bound control properties. Each time a user attempts to edit or update a record, the Microsoft Jet performs the necessary page locking to ensure data integrity.

What Is Page Locking?

A data page can contain more than one data record. Currently, the Microsoft Jet data page is always 2KB. Locking a data page locks all records that are stored on the same data page. If you have records that are 512 bytes in size, each time Microsoft Jet performs a page lock, four data records are locked. If you have records that are 50 bytes in size, each Microsoft Jet page lock can affect 40 data records.

The exact number of records that are locked on a page cannot be controlled or accurately predicted. If your data table contains several deleted records that have not been compacted out by using the CompactDatabase method, you have "holes" in your data pages. These holes do not contain valid records. Also, data pages contain records that are physically adjacent to each other—regardless of any index, filter, or sort order that has been applied to create the dataset. Even though records in a dataset are listed one after another, they might not be physically stored in the same manner. Therefore, editing one of the dataset records might not lock the next record in the dataset list.

Pessimistic and Optimistic Locking

Even though page-level locking is performed automatically by Microsoft Jet, you can use the LockEdits property of a record set to control how page-locking is handled by your application. Two page-locking modes are available: pessimistic locking (LockEdits=True) and optimistic locking (LockEdits=False). The default locking mode is pessimistic.

In *pessimistic locking mode*, Microsoft Jet locks the data page whenever the Edit or AddNew method is invoked. The page stays locked until an Update or Cancel method is executed. When a page is locked, no other program or user can read or write any data records on the locked data page until the Update or Cancel method has been invoked. The advantage of using the pessimistic locking mode is that it provides the highest level of data integrity possible at the page level. The disadvantage of using the pessimistic locking mode is that it can lock data pages for a long period of time. This can cause other users of the same database to encounter error messages as they attempt to read or write data in the same table.

In *optimistic locking mode*, Microsoft Jet only locks the data page whenever the Update method is invoked. Users can invoke the Edit or AddNew method and begin editing data without causing Microsoft Jet to execute a page lock. When the user is done making changes and saves the record using the Update method, Microsoft Jet attempts to place a lock on the page. If it is successful, the record is written to the table. If Microsoft Jet discovers that someone else also has edited the same record and already has saved it, the update is canceled and the user is informed with an error message saying that someone already has changed the data.

The advantage of using optimistic locking is that page locks are in place for the shortest time possible. This reduces the number of lock messages users receive as they access data in your database. The disadvantage of using optimistic locking is that it is possible for two users to edit the same record at the same time. This can lead to lock errors at update time rather than at read time.

An Example of Page-Level Locking

In this section, you build a new Visual Basic project to demonstrate page-level locking as well as the differences between pessimistic and optimistic locking. Load Visual Basic and start a new project.

Place a command button on the form. Set its Name property to cmdEdit and its Caption property to &Edit. Add a frame control to the form and set its Caption property to Page Locking. Place two option button controls in the frame control. Set the Caption property of Option1 to Pessimistic and the Caption property of Option2 to Optimistic. Use Figure 17.4 as a layout guide.

Figure 17.4.

Laying out the page-locking project.

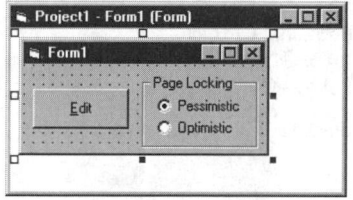

Now you need to add code to this demo. First, place the following variable declarations in the general declarations section of the form:

```
Option Explicit

Dim db As Database
Dim rs As Recordset
Dim cName As String
Dim nMax As Integer
```

Now add the following code to the Form_Load event. This code prompts you for a name for the form header. It then opens the database and data table, and it counts all the records in the table:

```
Private Sub Form_Load()
    ' get instance ID
    cName = InputBox("Enter Job Name:")
    Me.Caption = cName
    '
    ' load db and open set
    Set db = OpenDatabase("C:\TYSDBVB5\SOURCE\DATA\MULTIUSE.MDB")
    Set rs = db.OpenRecordset("mastertable", dbOpenTable, dbSeeChanges)
    '
    ' count total recs in set
    rs.MoveLast
    nMax = rs.RecordCount
    '
End Sub
```

Now add the following two code pieces to the Click events of the option buttons. These routines toggle the LockEdits property of the Recordset between pessimistic locking (LockEdits=True) and optimistic locking (LockEdits=False).

This code snippet turns on pessimistic locking:

```
Private Sub Option1_Click()
    If Option1 = True Then
        rs.LockEdits = True
    Else
        rs.LockEdits = False
    End If
End Sub
```

This code snippet turns on optimistic locking:

```
Private Sub Option2_Click()
    If Option2 = True Then
        rs.LockEdits = False
    Else
        rs.LockEdits = True
    End If
End Sub
```

Finally, add the following code to the cmdEdit_Click event of the form. While in Edit mode, this code prompts you for a record number. It then moves to that record, invokes the Edit method, makes a forced change in a Recordset field, and updates some titles and messages. When the form is in Update mode, this routine attempts to update the Recordset with the changed data and then resets some titles. Here's the code:

```
Private Sub cmdEdit_Click()
    On Error GoTo cmdEditClickErr    ' set trap
    '
    Dim nRec As Integer ' for rec select
    Dim X As Integer     ' for locator
    '
    ' are we trying to edit?
    If cmdEdit.Caption = "&Edit" Then
        ' get rec to edit
        nRec = InputBox("Enter Record # to Edit [1 - " +
```

```
        _Trim(Str(nMax)) + "]:", cName)
        ' locate rec
        If nRec > 0 Then
            rs.MoveFirst
            For X = 1 To nRec
                rs.MoveNext
            Next
            rs.Edit ' start edit mode
            ' change rec
            If Left(rs.Fields(0), 1) = "X" Then
                rs.Fields(0) = Mid(rs.Fields(0), 2, 255)
            Else
                rs.Fields(0) = "X" + rs.Fields(0)
            End If
            ' tell 'em you changed it
            MsgBox "Modified field to: [" + rs.Fields(0) + "]"
            ' prepare for update mode
            cmdEdit.Caption = "&Update"
            Me.Caption = cName + " [Rec: " + Trim(Str(X - 1)) + "]"
        End If
    Else
        rs.Update     ' attempt update
        cmdEdit.Caption = "&Edit"    ' fix caption
        Me.Caption = cName           ' fix header
        dbengine.idle dbfreelocks    ' pause VB
    End If
    '
    GoTo cmdEditClickExit
    '
cmdEditClickErr:
    ' show error message
    MsgBox Trim(Str(Err)) + ": " + Error$, vbCritical, cName + "[cmdEdit]"
    '
cmdEditClickExit:
    '
End Sub
```

Notice that there is a new line in this routine: the DBEngine.Idle method. This method forces Visual Basic to pause for a moment to update any Dynaset or Snapshot objects that are opened by the program. It is a good idea to place this line in your code so that it is executed during some part of the update process. This ensures that your program has the most recent updates to the dataset.

Save the form as MULTIUS2.FRM and the project as MULTIUS2.VBP. Compile the project and save it as MULTIUS2.EXE. Now you're ready to test it. Load two instances of the compiled program. When it starts up, you are prompted for a job name. It does not matter what you enter for the job name, but make sure that you enter different names for each instance. The name you enter is displayed on messages and form headers so that you can tell the two programs apart. Position the two instances apart from each other on the screen. (See Figure 17.5.)

First, you'll test the behavior of pessimistic page locking. Make sure that the Pessimistic radio button in the Page Locking frame is selected in both instances of the program. Now click the Edit button of the first instance of the program; when prompted, enter 1 as the record to edit.

This program now has locked a page of data. Switch to the second instance of the program and click the Edit button. You'll see error 3260, which tells you that the data is unavailable. (See Figure 17.6.)

Figure 17.5.

Running two in-stances of the page-locking project.

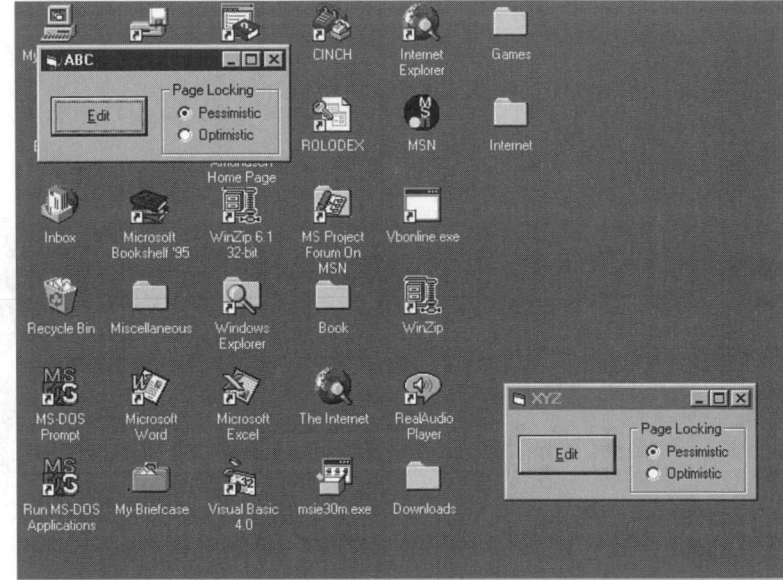

Figure 17.6.

A failed attempt at editing during pessimistic locking.

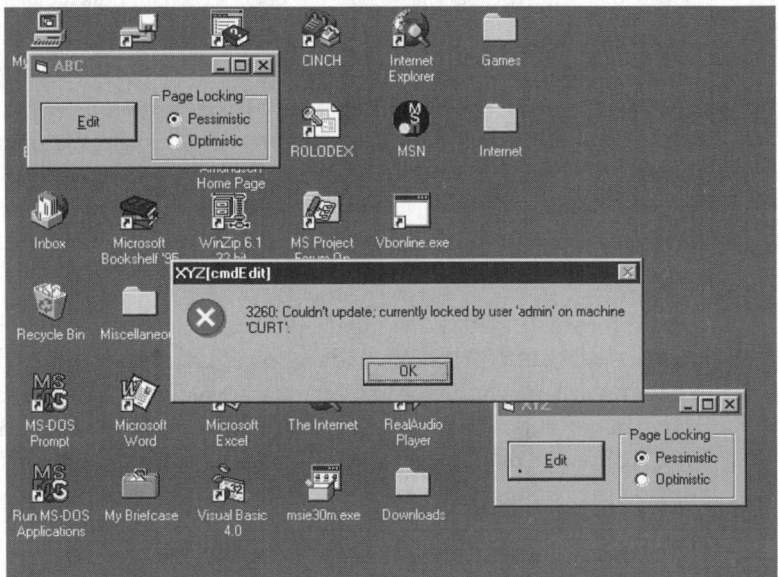

17

Remember that pessimistic locking locks the data page as soon as a user begins an edit operation on a record. This lock prevents anyone else from accessing any records on the data page until the first instance releases the record by using `Update` or `UpdateCancel`. Now click the error message box and then click the Update button to release the record and unlock the data page.

Now you test the behavior of Microsoft Jet during optimistic locking. Select the Optimistic radio button on both forms. In the first form, click Edit and enter 1 when prompted. The first instance now is editing record 1. Move to the second instance and click Edit. This time, you do not see an error message. When prompted, enter 1 as the record to edit. Again, you see no error message as Microsoft Jet allows you to begin editing record 1 of the set. Now both programs are editing record 1 of the set.

Click the Update button of the second instance of the program to save the new data to the dataset. The second instance now has read, edited, and updated the same record opened earlier by the first instance. Now move to the first instance and click the Update button to save the changes made by this instance. You'll see Error 3197, which tells you that data has been changed and that the update has been canceled. (See Figure 17.7.)

17

Figure 17.7.

A failed attempt to update during optimistic locking.

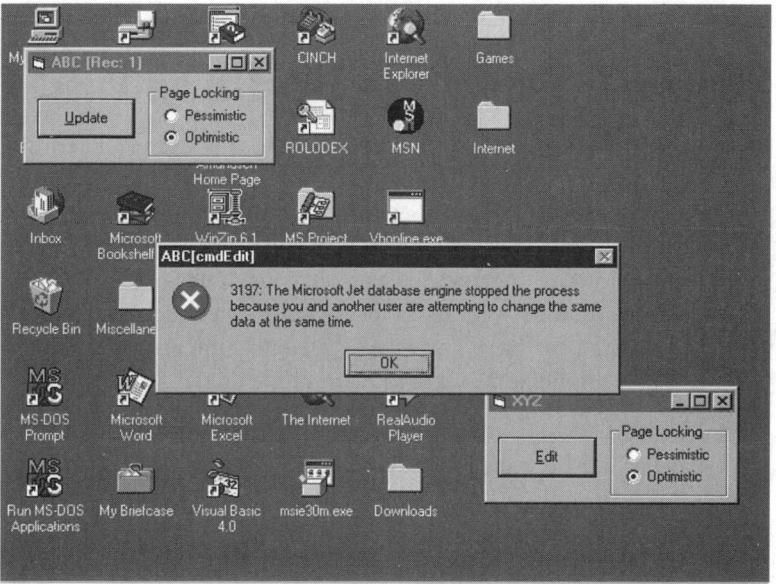

Optimistic locking occurs at the moment the `Update` method is invoked. Under the optimistic scheme, a user can read and edit any record he or she chooses. When the user attempts to write the record back out to disk, the program checks to see whether the original record was updated by any other program since the user's version last read the record. If changes were saved by another program, error 3197 is reported.

When to Use Pessimistic or Optimistic Page Locking

The advantage of using pessimistic locking is that once you begin editing a record, you can save your work because all other users are prevented from accessing that record. The disadvantage of using pessimistic locking is that if you have many people in the database, it is possible that quite a bit of the file is unavailable at any one time.

The advantage of using optimistic locking is that it occurs only during an update and then only when required. Optimistic locks are the shortest in duration. The disadvantage of using optimistic locking is that, even though more than one user can edit a dataset record at one time, only one person can *save* that dataset record. This usually is the first person to complete the edit (not the person who opened the record first or the person who saves it last). This can be very frustrating for users who have filled out a lengthy data entry screen only to discover that they cannot update the data table! Except in rare cases where there is an extreme amount of network traffic, you probably will find that optimistic locking is enough.

NOTE   All ODBC data sources use optimistic locking *only*.

Using Cascading Updates and Deletes

In the lesson on Day 9, "Visual Basic and the Microsoft Jet Engine," you learned how to identify and define cascading updates and delete relationships by using the relation data-access object. At the time, a particular aspect of relation objects was not fully covered: the capability to define cascading updates and deletes in order to enforce referential integrity. By using cascading updates and deletes in your database definition, you can ensure that changes made to columns in one data table are distributed properly to all related columns in all related tables in the database. This type of referential integrity is essential when designing and using database applications accessed by multiple users.

Microsoft Jet can enforce update and delete cascades only for native Microsoft Jet format databases. Microsoft Jet cannot enforce cascades that involve an attached table.

TIP   Cascading options should be added at database design time and can be accomplished by using the Visdata program (see Day 7, "Using the Visdata Program") or by using Visual Basic code (see Day 9).

17

Cascading occurs when users update or delete columns in one table that are referred to (via the relation object) by other columns in other tables. When this update or delete occurs, Microsoft Jet automatically updates or deletes all the records that are part of the defined relation. If you define a relationship between the column Valid.ListID and the column Master.ListID, for example, any time a user updates the value of Valid.ListID, Microsoft Jet scans the MasterTable and updates the values of all Master.ListID columns that match the updated values in the Valid.ListID column. In this way, as users change data in one table, all related tables are kept in sync through the use of cascading updates and deletes.

Building the Cascading Demo Project

The MULTIUSE.MDB database used in the earlier exercise is also used for this exercise. This database has a one-to-many relationship with enforced referential integrity for both cascading updates and cascading deletes. ValidTypes is the base table, and CustType is the base field. MasterTable is the foreign table, and CustType is the foreign field. You might find it helpful to open this database in the Visual Data Manager (Visdata) and explore the structure of these two tables.

TIP

It might seem to you that the terms *base table* and *foreign table* are used incorrectly in the relation definition. It might help you to remember that all relation definitions are based on the values in the ValidTypes table. Also, it might help to remember that any data table related to the ValidTypes table is a foreign table.

Now you build a project that illustrates the process of cascading updates and deletes. Use the information in Table 17.1 and Figure 17.8 to build the MULTIUS3.VBP project.

Table 17.1. The control table for the MULTIUS3.VBP project.

Control	Property	Setting
Form	Name	Ch1703
	Caption	Cascading Demo
	Left	1020
	Height	4275
	Top	1170
	Width	6480
DBGrid	Name	DBGrid1

continues

Table 17.1. continued

Control	Property	Setting
	AllowAddNew	True
	AllowDelete	True
	Height	2715
	Left	120
	Top	120
	Width	3000
DBGrid	Name	DBGrid2
	AllowAddNew	True
	AllowDelete	True
	Height	2715
	Left	3240
	Top	120
	Width	3000
Data Control	Name	Data1
	Caption	Master Table
	DatabaseName	C:\TYSDBVB5\SOURCE\DATA\MULTIUSE.MDB
	Height	300
	Left	120
	RecordsetType	1–Dynaset
	RecordSource	MasterTable
	Top	3000
	Width	3000
Data Control	Name	Data2
	Caption	Valid Types
	DatabaseName	C:\TYSDBVB5\SOURCE\DATA\MULTIUSE.MDB
	Height	300
	Left	3240
	RecordsetType	1–Dynaset
	RecordSource	ValidTypes

17

Control	Property	Setting
	Top	3000
	Width	3000
Command Button	Name	Command1
	Caption	Refresh
	Height	300
	Left	2580
	Top	3480
	Width	1200

Figure 17.8.

Laying out the
MULTIUS3.FRM *form.*

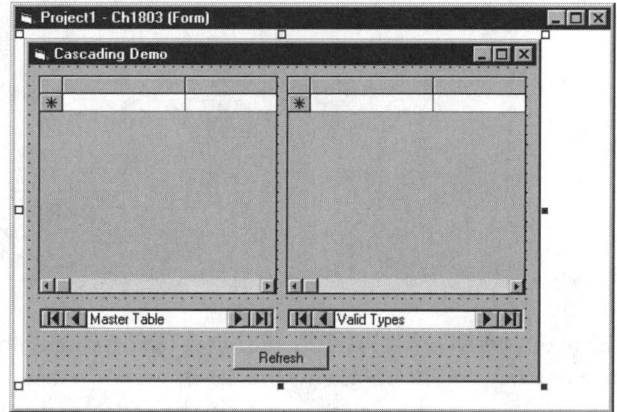

Only two lines of Visual Basic code are needed to complete the form. Add the following lines to the Command1_Click event. These two lines update both data controls and their associated grids:

```
Private Sub Command1_Click()
    Data1.Refresh
    Data2.Refresh
End Sub
```

Save the form as MULTIUS3.FRM and the project as MULTIUS3.VBP, and then run the project. Now you're ready to test the cascading updates and deletes.

Running the Cascading Demo Project

When you run the project, you see the two tables displayed in each grid, side by side. First, test the update cascade by editing one of the records in the Valid Types table. Select the first record and change the CustType column value from T01 to T09. After you finish the edit and move the record pointer to another record in the ValidTypes grid, click the Refresh button to update both datasets. You see that all records in the MasterTable that had a value of T01 in their CustType field now have a value of T09. The update of ValidTypes was cascaded into the MasterTable by Microsoft Jet.

Now add a new record with the CustType value of T99 to the ValidTypes table (set the Description field to any text you want). Add a record to the MasterTable that uses the T99 value in its CustType field. Your screen should look something like the one shown in Figure 17.9.

Figure 17.9.

Adding new records to the MULTIUSE.MDB *database.*

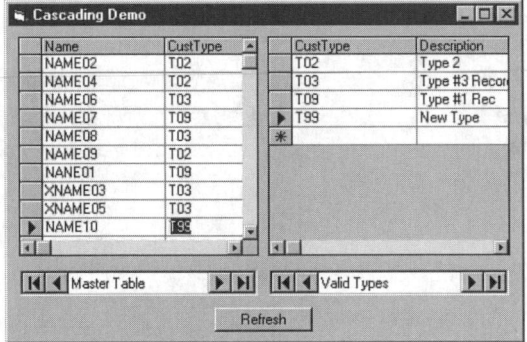

Delete the T99 record from the ValidTypes table by highlighting the entire row and pressing Delete. After you delete the record, click the Refresh button again to update both data controls. What happens to the record in the MasterTable that contains the T99 value in the CustType field? It is deleted from the MasterTable! This shows the power of the cascading delete. When cascading deletes are enforced, any time a user deletes a record from the base table, all related records in the foreign table also are deleted.

When to Use the Cascading Updates and Deletes

The capability to enforce cascading updates and deletes as part of the database definition is a powerful tool. With this power comes some responsibility, too, however. Because database cascades cannot easily be undone, you should think through your database design carefully before you add cascading features to your database. It is not always wise to add both update and delete cascades to all your relationships. At times, you might not want to cascade all update or delete operations.

Whenever you define a relation object in which the base table is a validation table and the foreign table is a master table, it is wise to define an update cascade. This ensures that any changes made to the validation table are cascaded to the related master table. It is not a good idea to define a delete cascade for this type of relation. Rarely do you want to delete all master records whenever you delete a related record from the validation table. If the user attempts to delete a record from the validation table that is used by one or more records in the master table, Microsoft Jet issues an error message telling the user that it is unable to delete the record.

Whenever you define a relation object in which the base table is a master table and the foreign table is a child table (for example, CustomerMaster.CustID is the base table and CustomerComments.CustID is the foreign table), you might want to define both an update and a delete cascade. It is logical to make sure that any changes to the CustomerMaster.CustID field would be updated in the CustomerComments.CustID field. It also might make sense to delete all CustomerComments records whenever the related CustomerMaster record is deleted. This is not always the case, though. If the child table is CustomerInvoice, for example, you might not want to automatically delete all invoices on file. Instead, you might want Microsoft Jet to prevent the deletion of the CustomerMaster record if a related CustomerInvoice record exists.

The key point to remember is that cascades are performed automatically by Microsoft Jet, without any warning message. You cannot create an optional cascade or receive an automatic warning before a cascade begins. If you choose to use cascades in your database, be sure to think through the logic and the relations thoroughly, and be sure to test your relations and cascades before using the database in a production setting.

Transaction Management

Another important tool for maintaining the integrity of your database is the use of transactions to manage database updates and deletes. Visual Basic enables you to enclose all database update operations as a single transaction. *Transactions* involve two steps: First, mark the start of a database transaction with the BeginTrans keyword; second, mark the end of the database transaction with the CommitTrans or RollBack keyword. You can start a set of database operations (add, edit, and delete records) and then, if no error occurs, you can use the CommitTrans keyword to save the updated records to the database. If you encounter an error along the way, though, you can use the RollBack keyword to tell Microsoft Jet to reverse all database operations completed up to the point where the transaction first began.

Suppose that you need to perform a series of database updates to several tables as part of a month-end update routine for an accounting system. This month-end processing includes totaling transactions by customer from the TransTable, writing those totals to existing columns in a CustTotals table, appending the transactions to the HistoryTable, and deleting the transactions from the TransTable. The process requires access to three different tables and involves updating existing records (appending new records to a table and deleting existing records from a table). If your program encounters an error part of the way through this process, it will be difficult to reconstruct the data as it existed before the process began. In other words, it will be difficult unless you used Visual Basic transactions as part of the update routine.

Microsoft Jet Transactions and the Workspace Object

All Microsoft Jet transactions are applied to the current workspace object. (See Day 10, "Creating Database Programs with Visual Basic Code," for a discussion of the Workspace object.) If you do not name a Workspace object, Visual Basic uses the default workspace for your program. Because transactions apply to an entire workspace, it is recommended that you explicitly declare workspaces when you use transactions. This gives you the capability to isolate datasets into different workspaces and better control the creation of transactions.

Here's the exact syntax for starting a transaction:

```
Workspace(0).BeginTrans    ' starts a transaction
...
If Err=0 Then
    Workspaces(0).CommitTrans   ' completes a transaction
Else
    Workspaces(0).Rollback   ' cancels a transaction
End If
```

In this code, the default workspace for the transaction area is used. In an actual program, you should name a workspace explicitly.

Building the Microsoft Jet Transaction Project

You now build a small project that illustrates one possible use for transactions in your Visual Basic applications. You create a database routine that performs the tasks listed in the previous example. You open a transaction table, total the records to a subsidiary table, copy the records to a history file, and then delete the records from the original table.

TIP	To avoid errors when running this project, make sure that you selected the appropriate DAO reference before executing the program. Do this by choosing Project	References from the Visual Basic 5 menu. Then enable the checkbox next to Microsoft DAO 3.5 object library.

Write two main routines: one to declare the workspace and open the database, and one to perform the database transaction. First, add the following code to the general declarations section of a new form in a new project:

```
Option Explicit

Dim db As Database         ' database object
Dim wsUpdate As workspace  ' workspace object
Dim nErrFlag As Integer    ' error flag
```

These are the form-level variables you need to perform the update.

Add the following code, which creates the workspace and opens the database. Create a new Sub called OpenDB and place the following code in the routine:

```
Sub OpenDB()
    On Error GoTo OpenDBErr
    '
    nErrFlag = 0 ' assume all is OK
    '
    Set wsUpdate = DBEngine.CreateWorkspace("wsUpdate", "admin", "")
    Set db = wsUpdate.OpenDatabase("C:\TYSDBVB5\SOURCE\DATA\MULTIUS4.MDB", True)
    '
    GoTo OpenDBExit

OpenDBErr:
    MsgBox Trim(Str(Err)) + " " + Error$(Err), vbCritical, "OpenDB"
    nErrFlag = Err
    '
OpenDBExit:
    '
End Sub
```

This routine creates a new workspace object to encompass the transaction and then opens the database for exclusive use. You don't want anyone else in the system while you perform this major update. An error-trap routine has been added here in case you can't open the database exclusively.

Now you can add the code that performs the actual month-end update. Do this by using the SQL statements you learned in the lessons on Days 13, "Creating Databases with SQL," and 15, "Updating Databases with SQL." Create a new Sub called ProcMonthEnd and then add the following code:

```
Sub ProcMonthEnd()
    On Error goto ProcMonthEndErr
    '
    Dim cSQL As String
    Dim nResult As Integer
    '
    wsUpdate.BeginTrans ' mark start of transaction
    '
    ' append totals to transtotals table
    cSQL = "INSERT INTO TransTotals SELECT TransTable.CustID,
    _SUM(TransTable.Amount) as Amount FROM TransTable
    _GROUP BY TransTable.CustID"
    db.Execute cSQL
    '
    ' append history records
    cSQL = "INSERT INTO TransHistory SELECT * FROM TransTable"
    db.Execute cSQL
    '
    ' delete the transaction records
    cSQL = "DELETE FROM TransTable"
    db.Execute cSQL
    '
```

```
    ' ask user to commit transaction
    '
    nResult = MsgBox("Transaction Completed. Ready to Commit?",
    _vbInformation + vbYesNo, "ProcMonthEnd")
    If nResult = vbYes Then
        wsUpdate.CommitTrans
        MsgBox "Transaction Committed"
    Else
        wsUpdate.Rollback
        MsgBox "Transaction Canceled"
    End If
    '
    nErrFlag = 0
    GoTo ProcMonthEndExit
    '
ProcMonthEndErr:
    MsgBox Trim(Str(Err)) + " " + Error$(Err), vbCritical, "ProcMonthEnd"
    nErrFlag = Err
    '
ProcMonthEndExit:
    '
End Sub
```

This code executes the three SQL statements that perform the updates and deletes needed for the month-end processing. The routine is started with a BeginTrans. When the updates are complete, the user is asked to confirm the transaction. In a production program, you probably wouldn't ask for transaction confirmation; however, this helps you see how the process is working.

Finally, you need to add the code that puts everything together. Add the following code to the Form_Load event:

```
Private Sub Form_Load()
    OpenDB
    If nErrFlag = 0 Then
        ProcMonthEnd
    End If
    '
    If nErrFlag <> 0 Then
        MsgBox "Error Reported", vbCritical, "FormLoad"
    End If
    Unload Me
End Sub
```

This routine calls the OpenDB procedure. Then, if no error is reported, it calls the ProcMonthEnd procedure. If an error has occurred during the process, a message is displayed.

Save the form as MULTIUS4.FRM and the project as MULTIUS4.VBP, and then run the project. All you'll see is a message that tells you the transaction is complete and asks for your approval. (See Figure 17.10.)

Figure 17.10.

Waiting for approval to commit the transaction.

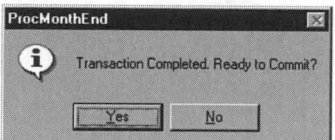

If you choose No in this message box, Microsoft Jet reverses all the previously completed database operations between the Rollback and the BeginTrans statements. You can confirm this by clicking No, using Visdata or Data Manager to load the MULTIUS4.MDB database, and then inspecting the contents of the tables.

 An SQL-Visual Basic script called MULTIUS4.SQV is included on the CD-ROM that accompanies this book. You can use this script with the SQL-VB program (see Days 13 and 15) to create a "clean" MULTIUS4.MDB file. After you run MULTIUS4.VBP once and answer Yes to commit the transaction, you might want to run the MULTIUS4.SQV script to refresh the database.

Advantages and Limitations of Transactions

The primary advantage of using transactions in your Visual Basic programs is that they can greatly increase the integrity of your data. You should use transactions whenever you are performing database operations that span more than one table or even operations that affect many records in a single table. A secondary advantage of using transactions is that they often increase the processing speed of Microsoft Jet.

As useful as transactions are, there are still a few limitations. First, some database formats might not support transactions (for example, Paradox files do not support transactions). You can check for transaction support by checking the Transactions property of the database. If transactions are not supported, Microsoft Jet ignores the transaction statements in your code; you do not receive an error message. Some Dynasets might not support transactions, depending on how they are constructed. Usually, sets that are the result of SQL JOIN and WHERE clauses or result sets that contain data from attached tables do not support transactions.

Transaction operations are kept on the local workstation in a temporary directory (the one pointed to by the TEMP environment variable). If you run out of available space on the TEMP drive, you'll receive error 2004. You can trap for this error. The only solution is to make more disk space available or to reduce the number of database operations between the BeginTrans and the CommitTrans statements.

Microsoft Jet enables you to nest transactions up to five levels deep. If you are using external ODBC databases, however, you cannot nest transactions.

Summary

Today, you learned about the three important challenges that face every database programmer writing multiuser applications:

☐ Using database locking schemes

☐ Using cascading updates and deletes to maintain database integrity

☐ Using database transactions to provide commit/rollback options for major updates to your database

You learned that three levels of locking are available to Visual Basic programs:

☐ *Database level:* You can use the Exclusive property of the data control or the second parameter of the OpenDatabase method to lock the entire database. Use this option when you need to perform work that affects multiple database objects (such as tables, queries, indexes, relations, and so on).

☐ *Table level:* You can set the Options property of the data control to 3 or the third parameter of the OpenRecordset method to dbDenyRead+dbDenyWrite in order to lock the entire table for your use only. Use this option when you need to perform work that affects multiple records in a single table (for example, increasing the sales price on all items in the inventory table).

☐ *Page level:* Microsoft Jet automatically performs page-level locking whenever you use the data control to edit and save a record, or whenever you use Visual Basic code to perform the Edit/AddNew and Update/CancelUpdate methods. You can use the LockEdits property of the Recordset to set the page locking to pessimistic (to perform locking at edit time) or optimistic (to perform locking only at update time).

You learned how to use Visual Basic to enforce referential integrity and automatically perform cascading updates or deletes to related records. You learned that there are times when it is not advisable to establish cascading deletes (for example, do not use cascading deletes when the base table is a validation list and the foreign table is a master).

Finally, you learned how to use database transactions to protect your database during extended, multitable operations. You learned how to use the BeginTrans, CommitTrans, and Rollback methods of the workspace object. Finally, you learned some of the advantages and limitations of transaction processing.

17

Quiz

1. What are the three levels of locking provided by the Microsoft Jet database engine?
2. Which form of locking would you use when compacting a database?
3. Which form of locking would you use if you needed to update price codes in the price table of a database?
4. Which property of a Recordset do you set to control whether your application's data has optimistic or pessimistic page locking?
5. What is the difference between pessimistic and optimistic page locking?
6. Can you use pessimistic locking on an ODBC data source?
7. What happens to data when cascading deletes are used in a relationship?
8. Why would you use transaction management in your applications?
9. What are the limitations of transactions?
10. Do you need to declare a workspace when using transactions?

Exercises

1. Write Visual Basic code that exclusively opens a database (C:\DATA\ABC.MDB) during a Form Load event. Include error trapping.
2. Build on the code you wrote in the previous exercise to exclusively open the table Customers in ABC.MDB.
3. Suppose that you are building a new accounts receivable system for your company. You have saved all tables and data into a single database named C:\DATA\ABC.MDB. You have discovered that all invoices created must be posted to a history file on a daily basis. Because this history file is extremely valuable (it is used for collections, reporting, and so on), you don't want your posting process to destroy any of the data that it currently contains. Therefore, you decide to use transactions in your code.

   Write the Visual Basic code that takes invoice transactions from the temporary holding table, Transactions, and inserts them into a table named History, which keeps the cumulative history information.

   The History table contains four fields: HistoryItem (counter and primary key), CustID (a unique identifier for the customer), InvoiceNo (the number of the invoice issued to the customer), and Amount.

   The Transactions table also has four fields: TransNo (counter and primary key), CustID (a unique identifier for the customer), InvoiceNo (the number of the invoice issued to the customer), and Amount.

Complete this project by starting a new project and dropping a single command button (named Post) onto a form. Clicking this button should trigger the posting process.

Include error trapping in your routines. Also, include messages to notify the user that the transaction posting is complete or that problems have been encountered.

Day 18

Using the Remote Data Control and the Remote Data Objects

Today, you'll learn about two alternative methods for accessing database information using Visual Basic 5: the *Remote Data Control* (RDC) and the *Remote Data Objects* (RDOs). Both these alternative methods are designed for reading and updating data stored in *relational database management systems* (RDBMSs) that are external to Visual Basic and to the Microsoft Jet data engine. Although it is possible to use the standard data control and Microsoft Jet data object collections to access data stored in RDBMS, the RDC and RDOs have properties and methods that make them better suited to manipulating data in remote systems.

> The RDC and RDOs are shipped as part of the Visual Basic 5 Enterprise Edition. If you do not have the Enterprise Edition of Visual Basic 5, you cannot complete the examples in this chapter or run the code that ships on the CD-ROM with this book. You still can get a lot out of this chapter by reading through the text and inspecting the code examples, though.

Along with the details of the RDC and the RDOs, you learn some of the basics of remote data access in general. These basics are hidden from you when you use the data control, or they do not apply unless you are accessing remote data. You'll learn the meaning and use of these elements:

☐ Cursor drivers

☐ Key sets

☐ Lock types

In today's lesson, you'll learn the properties, methods, and events of the RDC and how you can use these to develop data-entry forms using the same data-bound controls you learned about in the first week's lessons. After you learn the details of the RDC programming tool, you'll build a simple data-entry form based on the RDC. In this chapter, you even use an ODBC definition that links your RDC to a Microsoft Jet Access database.

You also learn the details of the RDOs. The RDOs are programming objects similar to the Microsoft Jet *data-access objects* (DAOs) you learned about in Week 2. Like the RDC, the RDO collection has special properties and methods that make it better suited to accessing data from remote storage systems. In this chapter, you'll learn how to use the RDO programming objects listed in Table 18.1.

Table 18.1. RDO programming objects.

Object	Description
rdoColumn	The RDO version of the Microsoft Jet Field object
rdoConnection	The RDO equivalent of the Microsoft Jet Database object
rdoEngine	The top-level data engine used to access remote data
rdoEnvironment	The RDO equivalent of the Microsoft Jet Workspace object
rdoParameters	A special collection of query parameters for the rdoQuery object
rdoQuery	The RDO version of the Microsoft Jet QueryDef object
rdoResultset	The RDO equivalent of the Microsoft Jet Recordset object
rdoTable	The RDO version of the Microsoft Jet Table object

As Table 18.1 shows, most RDOs have a parallel in the Microsoft Jet DAO collections. If you have not read through the chapter covering the Microsoft Jet Database objects (Day 9, "Visual Basic and the Microsoft Jet Engine"), you might want to review that material before you continue with this chapter.

When you complete this chapter, you'll be able to create data-bound entry forms using the RDCs and to build Visual Basic programs that manipulate RDBMS data using the RDOs.

The Basics of Remote Data Access

Before getting into the details of the RDC and RDO programming tools, it is important to review a few basic principles of remote data access. When you use the Microsoft Jet DAOs or the standard data control, you usually do not need to deal with some of the issues covered here. The three concepts covered here are cursor drivers, dataset types, and lock types. Manipulating the parameters of these three properties affects the type of dataset you are working with and the types of operations you can perform on that data. By default, all remote connections to data are non-updatable (read-only) datasets. You can change this behavior by manipulating the three properties covered here.

Cursor Drivers

You use the cursor drivers to define the way in which you can move within a set of data. When you connect to data using the standard data control or the Microsoft Jet DAOs, you can, by default, move forward and backward in the dataset and move to any record in the collection. You can use any of the Move and Find methods (MoveFirst, MoveLast, MoveNext, MovePrevious, FindFirst, FindLast, FindNext, and FindPrevious), for example.

In order to have this movement capability, the database engine must be able to keep track of all the records in the collection and their place in the dataset. This process of keeping track of the location of the data pointer in the dataset is called *cursor management*. You can use two primary locations to keep track of the cursor location: the client workstation or the database server. Under the RDC and RDOs, the local workstation version of cursor management is handled by the ODBC driver. The server-side cursor management is handled by the database server that holds the data.

Under RDC and RDOs, there are two other possible settings for cursor management: Client Batch and None. You can use the Client Batch option with advanced data servers that allow multiple data requests to be sent simultaneously over the same connection. In this case, you can batch up multiple SQL statements in a single string and send them to the server at one time. The server manages the requests and reports results back to you as each SQL statement is completed.

18

You also can choose to use no cursor driver when accessing remote data. This results in the server sending you a single record from the dataset each time you request it. You cannot request previous records from the server and, if you want to start at the top of the collection, you must restart the query. This is the most limited cursor management available for a remote connection.

TIP

> Although using no cursor management severely limits your capability to navigate a large set of data, it is the fastest connection possible. Even more valuable, you can use non-cursor driver sets to execute action queries such as SET UPDATE, INSERT INTO, and SELECT INTO queries. This means that you can perform multirecord updates without having to declare a cursor.

Cursor drivers can have five possible settings when you are working with RDC and RDOs. Table 18.2 shows these values and their meanings.

Table 18.2. Cursor driver options with RDC and RDOs.

Driver Option	Integer Value	Description
rdUseIfNeeded	0	Instructs RDOs/RDC to determine the best cursor driver to use for the requested operation. This is the default setting.
rdUseOdbc	1	Instructs RDC/RDOs to use the client-side ODBC cursor driver to keep track of the data pointer in the dataset.
rdUseServer	2	Instructs RDC/RDO to use the remote RDBMS cursor driver to keep track of the data pointer in the dataset.
rdUseClientBatch	3	Instructs RDC/RDO to use the remote RDBMS to manage multiple cursors in response to batch requests sent from the client workstation. This is available only on advanced RDBMS systems (SQL Server 6.0 and higher).
rdUseNone	4	Instructs RDC/RDO to use no cursor driver. The result is a return on only one row, no matter how may rows are in the result set. This option still can be used to perform action queries, such as SET UPDATE, INSERT INTO, SELECT INTO, and so on.

18

As you can see in Table 18.2, the default option for RDC/RDOs is to allow rdoEngine to select the most appropriate cursor available. When rdUseIfNeeded is in place, RDC/RDOs attempt to use server-side cursors if they are available (rdUseServer or rdUseClientBatch if Batch mode is in force). If the RDBMS does not support server-side cursor management, RDC/RDOs use the client workstation cursor manager (rdUseOdbc). The rdUseNone option is used only if the value is explicitly selected.

Again, the important thing to remember about cursor drivers is that they govern the way you can navigate the dataset. The other important aspect of cursor drivers is that, with RDC/RDOs, you can select the driver you prefer: client-side or server-side. The only caveat to all this is that the data source (RDBMS) must support your cursor request in order for you to be able to select certain server-side options.

Dataset Type

The selection of cursor drivers is just one of the options you must determine when accessing remote data. Another important parameter is the dataset type property of the connection. Several types of datasets can be returned by the remote data source. Table 18.3 outlines these types.

Table 18.3. Dataset type options with RDC/RDOs.

Dataset Option	Integer Value	Description
rdOpenForwardOnly	0	Creates a read-only, scroll-forward-only dataset. All members are copied to the client workstation for use. This is the default option.
rdOpenStatic	1	Creates an updatable dataset that has non-changing membership. New records added to the set may (or may not) appear as part of the set, depending on the cursor driver. All members are copied to the client workstation for use.
rdOpenDynamic	2	Creates an updatable dataset that has changing membership. New records added to the set *will* appear as part of the set. Actual data records are buffered to the client workstation as needed. Record keys are *not* used.
rdOpenKeyset	3	Creates an updatable dataset that has changing membership. New records added to the set *will* appear as part of the set. Actual data records are buffered to the client workstation as needed. Record keys (the key set) are created to point to all members of the set. This enables you to use bookmarks with the dataset.

18

The information in Table 18.3 deserves some additional comment. Remember that the primary work of dataset management from the workstation point of view is gaining access to the actual rows of data stored in the remote system. The most efficient method for gaining access is to receive a set of row pointers from the RDBMS, not to actually receive the complete rows of data. In this way, the RDBMS can allow multiple users to have access to the same set of records without having to deal with major synchronization work if more than one user attempts to update the same row of data.

For this reason, RDC/RDOs support the use of rdOpenKeyset datasets. These are sets of data that contain not just data rows, but also key-set pointers to other rows in the requested dataset. rdOpenKeysets are the remote data-access versions of Microsoft Jet Dynaset-type datasets.

The rdOpenDynamic datasets do not support keys, but they do act as dynamically changing sets of data. These dynamic datasets reflect newly added or deleted records just as rdOpenKeyset datasets, but they do not support the use of bookmarks. This is because the rdOpenDynamic datasets are kept dynamic through the use of recurring refreshes of the data membership from the remote data source. Although this method is accurate, it is hardly efficient. If you have large sets of data, using the rdOpenDynamic option can result in decreased throughput, because all data members are shipped to the client each time the set is refreshed.

It also is important to note that rdOpenStatic datasets are updatable. Even though their membership is kept static (there is no constant refresh from the remote data source), it still is possible to update the records in the set. These datasets act much like an updatable version of the Microsoft Jet Snapshot dataset.

Lock Types

The final concept that deserves special attention when dealing with remote data access is the lock type used to manage dataset updates. With Microsoft Jet data access, you have two options: pessimistic (lock at start of edit) and optimistic (lock at start of update). RDC/RDOs offer a few additional variations to these two basic options. Table 18.4 shows the lock-type options with RDC/RDOs.

Table 18.4. Dataset lock-type options with RDC/RDOs.

Lock-Type Option	Integer Value	Description
rdConcurReadOnly	0	Provides no row-level locking. Forces the dataset to act as a read-only set. You can use this option to perform action queries, though. This is the default option.

Lock-Type Option	Integer Value	Description
rdConcurLock	1	Provides pessimistic locking for the entire row set. The lock occurs as soon as the data is accessed—not when an Edit operation begins.
rdConcurRowver	2	Provides optimistic locking based on internal row ID values (usually, the TimeStamp column).
rdConcurValues	3	Provides optimistic locking based on a column-by-column check of the data in each row.
rdConcurBatch	4	Provides optimistic locking based on the value in the UpdateCriteria property when using Batch Update mode. Not supported by all RDBMSs.

The type of locking mechanism used can have a great effect on the performance of your application and the capability of others to access the shared data. The rdConcurReadOnly option allows anyone else to access the same data your application is using. Your application cannot update the dataset unless you are using action queries, however. The rdConcurLock option provides the greatest degree of locking. As soon as your dataset is created, all buffered rows in the dataset are locked. Because locks occur on pages, this can result in hundreds of record locks while your application browses the dataset.

The rdConcurRowver and rdConcurValues options allow optimistic locking schemes. In the rdConcurRowver option, each record's ID value (usually, the TimeStamp column) is checked at the time the row is updated. If the ID has changed since your application retrieved the data, an error is reported. In the rdConcurValues option, each value in the row's columns is checked against the original value. If the value has changed since your application received the dataset, an error is reported.

The least intrusive form of locking for read/write datasets is the rdConcurRowver or rdConcurValues option. The most secure form of locking for read/write datasets is the rdConcurLock option. An advantage that RDC/RDOs have over Microsoft Jet is that you easily can tune the number of rows in the row set by using the RowsetSize property. If you set this property sufficiently low, you can use the rdConcurLock option without adversely affecting other users who are attempting to access the remote data.

Now that you understand the basics of accessing remote data, you are ready to begin using the RDC and RDO tools to build Visual Basic programs that read and update remote data sources.

18

Building an ODBC Definition

Before you can complete any of the projects in this chapter, you need to build an ODBC connection to the BOOKS5.MDB database that ships on the CD-ROM with this book. After you build this ODBC data source definition, you'll be able to use both RDC and RDO programming tools to access the BOOKS5.MDB database.

WARNING

> You might have both the 32-bit and the 16-bit ODBC Administrator applets in your Control Panel group. Be sure to use the 32-bit ODBC Administrator to define your new data source. The RDC and RDO programming objects recognize only data-source definitions built with the 32-bit ODBC Administrator.

To build an ODBC definition, you need to call up the ODBC Administrator. Follow these steps:

1. Choose Start | Settings | Control Panel from the main Windows 95 (or WinNT4) menu. The Control Panel appears, as shown in Figure 18.1. Double-click the 32-bit ODBC icon to open the ODBC Administrator.

Figure 18.1.

Accessing the 32-bit ODBC Administrator applet from the Control Panel group.

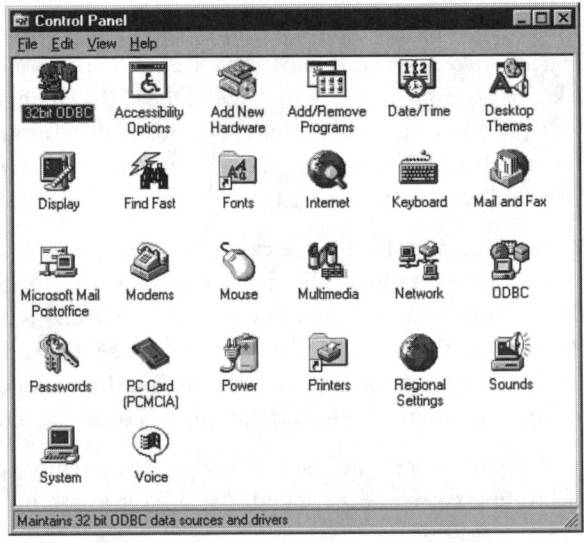

18

NOTE
If you are using WinNT 3.51, double-click the ODBC Administrator applet from the Control Panel group.

2. After the ODBC Data Source Administrator dialog box appears, select the User DSN tab and click Add. The Create New Data Source dialog box appears, as shown in Figure 18.2.

Figure 18.2.

Adding a new definition to the User DSN collection.

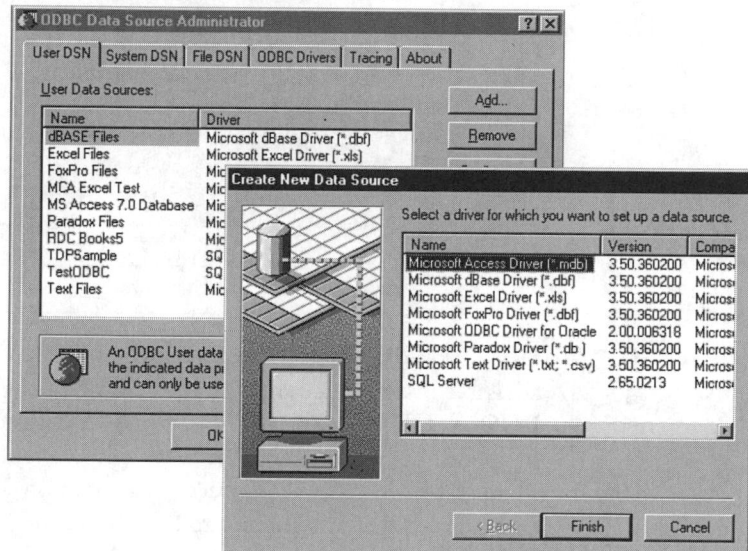

3. Double-click the Microsoft Access 7.0 Database driver. The OBBC Microsoft Access 97 Setup dialog box appears. In the Data Source Name field, enter RDC Books5. In the Description field, enter Remote Data Connection to books5.mdb. In the Database section, specify the path C:\TYSDBVB5\SOURCE\DATA\BOOKS5.MDB by clicking Select and navigating to it in the Select Database dialog box. Figure 18.3 shows what the dialog box should look like at this point.

4. Click OK to save the definition and then exit the ODBC Administrator applet. You now have an ODBC data source definition that you can use with the RDC and the RDOs.

Figure 18.3.

Filling out the Microsoft Access 97 Setup dialog box.

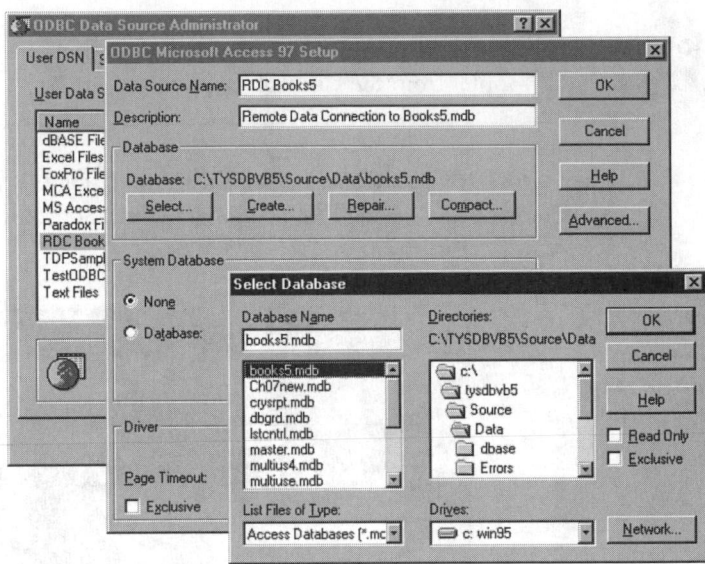

 **NOTE**

Using RDC/RDOs to connect to a Microsoft Jet Access database is not advisable in a production setting. The process of going through RDC/RDOs to ODBC to Microsoft Access is very wasteful and limits the programming options available to the application. Using Microsoft Access tables in this way, however, is a common method of prototyping tables that will later be moved to SQL Server or some other RDBMS. If you have SQL Server or some other RDBMS available to your workstation, you can substitute the DSN built in this section for another one that uses your own remote data.

Programming with the Remote Data Control

Programming with the RDC is very similar to programming with the standard data control that ships with all versions of Visual Basic 5.0. The RDC has unique property names, but these properties are quite similar to the standard data-control properties and they provide almost the same functionality. Also notice that the RDC has methods and events that are close, if not identical, to the methods and events of the standard data control.

18

In the following sections, you learn the properties, methods, and events of the RDC. As you review these items, it might help to refer to the material covered in Day 3, "Visual Basic Database Objects."

The RDC Properties

The RDC has a number of unique properties you can use to establish and manage your connection to the remote data source. Table 18.5 shows these unique properties, their types, default settings, and short descriptions of their meaning and use.

Table 18.5. Unique properties of the RDC.

Property	Type	Default Setting	Description
Connection	rdoConnection	<none>	Contains an object reference to the RDO Connection object created by the RDC. You can use this as you use the Database property of the standard data control.
CursorDriver	Integer	rdUseIfNeeded (0)	Controls the source and behavior of the cursor manager.
DataSourceName	String	<none>	Specifies the name of the ODBC data source you want to access. This is the RDO equivalent of the database name.
EditMode	Integer	rdEditNone (0)	Indicates whether an edit or AddNew operation is in effect. You can use this to determine whether an Update method must be used to complete a pending action.

continues

18

Table 18.5. continued

Property	Type	Default Setting	Description
Environment	rdoEnvironment	<none>	Contains an object reference to the RDO Environment object created by the RDC. You can use this as you use the Workspace object in Microsoft Jet data access.
KeysetSize	Integer	100	Specifies the number of rows in the keyset buffer. Using this value and the MaxRows and RowsetSize properties can affect the way records are buffered and locked.
LockType	Integer	rdConcurReadOnly (0)	Controls how records are locked for update.
LoginTimeOut	Integer	0	Using a value greater than zero indicates the length of time (in seconds) that RDC/RDOs wait before reporting a time-out error when trying to log onto the remote data source. A typical LAN connection time-out value is 15 seconds. RAS/Internet connections may need a longer time-out setting.

18

Property	Type	Default Setting	Description
LogMessages	String	<none>	Setting this value to a valid drive/path/filename enables the creation of a trace file for ODBC conversations. This file can get quite long and should be used only for temporary debugging of questionable connections.
MaxRows	Integer	–1	Controls how many rows are affected by an action. When set to –1 (default) all rows matching the criteria are affected. You can set this value to 1 to ensure that only one record is updated when using an UPDATE query.
Prompt	Integer	rdDriverPrompt (0)	Controls the behavior of the ODBC logon process. Setting this value to rdDriverNoPrompt suppresses the ODBC logon screen. You can use this setting to log onto the data source without asking the user for additional parameters. If the values set in the programmatic logon are invalid, an error is reported.

18

continues

Table 18.5. continued

Property	Type	Default Setting	Description
Resultset	rdoResultset	<none>	Contains an object reference to the rdoResultset object created by the RDC. you can use this as you use the Recordset object of the standard data control.
ResultsetType	Integer	rdOpenStatic (0)	Controls the type of dataset returned by the RDC. The rdOpenStatic option returns an updatable dataset with un-changing member-ship; the rdOpenKeyset opens an updatable dataset with changing mem-bership.
RowsetSize	Integer	100	Controls the number of rows buffered to your application. This is also the num-ber of rows locked when using pessimis-tic locking (rdConcurLock).
SQL	String	<none>	Specifies the SQL statement used to populate the dataset for the RDC. This is the RDC equivalent of the RecordSource property of the stan-dard data control.

18

Property	Type	Default Setting	Description
StillExecuting	Boolean	False	Indicates whether the dataset is still in the process of being created. You can check this periodically on long data connections.
Transactions	Boolean	False	Indicates whether the remote data source supports the use of `BeginTrans`, `CommitTrans`, and `RollbackTrans` methods. You can check this before you attempt to use these methods.

18

The RDC Methods

Several methods are associated with the RDC. Most of these methods have counterparts with the standard data control. Table 18.6 lists the RDC methods.

Table 18.6. The RDC methods.

Method	Function
`BeginTrans,` `CommitTrans,` `RollbackTrans`	Enables programmers to provide transaction management for RDC actions. This improves data integrity on action queries and can speed up processing on single-row updates.
`Cancel`	Cancels any pending `Query`, `Edit`, `AddNew`, or `Delete` operation.
`Refresh`	Repopulates the dataset.
`UpdateControls`	Refreshes the data-bound controls with the contents of the dataset.
`UpdateRows`	Refreshes the dataset with the values in the data-bound controls.

The most important items to note in Table 18.6 are the transaction-management methods and the UpdateRows method. These methods are unique to the RDC and are not available with the standard Microsoft Jet data control.

The RDC Events

The RDC offers a set of unique events that are similar to the events supported by the Microsoft Jet data control: Validate, Reposition, and Error. The RDC has an additional event not supported by the Microsoft Jet data control: the QueryCompleted event. This event is fired after the dataset has returned successfully from the remote data source. This event can be used to alert users of the completion of delayed queries because of slow connections or a large dataset size.

The events, methods, and properties covered in the previous sections are illustrated in the RDC data-entry project in the next section.

Laying Out the RDC Data-Entry Forms

In this section, you create a simple data-entry form using the RDC. This form illustrates the use of most of the properties, methods, and events covered in previous sections of this chapter. If you haven't already done so, start Visual Basic 5.0 and select a new, Standard EXE project.

Before you begin laying out the data-entry form, be sure to load the RDC by choosing Project | Components. The Components dialog box appears, as shown in Figure 18.4.

Figure 18.4.

Loading the RDC.

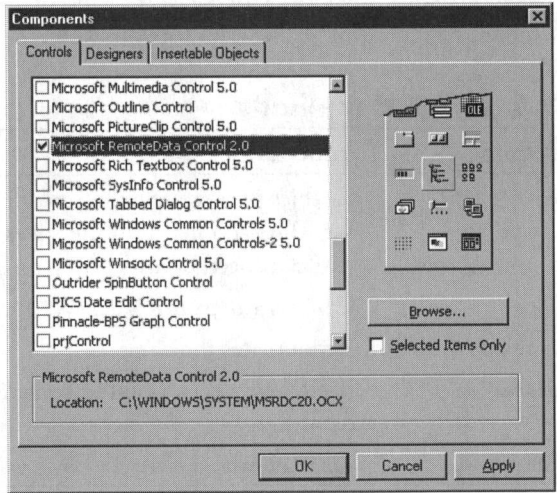

After adding the RDC to the project, create your data-entry form based on Figure 18.5 and Table 18.7.

Table 18.7. Laying out the RDC data-entry form.

Control	Property	Setting
VB.Form	Name	frmDataEntry
	Caption	"Form1"
	ClientHeight	2250
	ClientLeft	60
	ClientTop	345
	ClientWidth	6510
	StartUpPosition	3 'Windows Default
VB.CommandButton	Name	cmdBtn
	Caption	"&Close"
	Height	300
	Index	4
	Left	5160
	Top	1500
	Width	1200
VB.CommandButton	Name	cmdBtn
	Caption	"&Refresh"
	Height	300
	Index	3
	Left	3900
	Top	1500
	Width	1200
VB.CommandButton	Name	cmdBtn
	Caption	"&Update"
	Height	300
	Index	2
	Left	2640
	Top	1500
	Width	1200
VB.CommandButton	Name	cmdBtn
	Caption	"&Delete"

18

continues

Table 18.7. continued

Control	Property	Setting
	Height	300
	Index	1
	Left	1380
	Top	1500
	Width	1200
VB.CommandButton	Name	cmdBtn
	Caption	"&Add"
	Height	300
	Index	0
	Left	120
	Top	1500
	Width	1200
VB.TextBox	Name	txtDOB
	DataSource	"MSRDC1"
	Height	285
	Left	1440
	Text	"Text2"
	Top	960
	Width	1200
VB.TextBox	Name	txtName
	DataSource	"MSRDC1"
	Height	285
	Left	1440
	Text	"Text1"
	Top	540
	Width	2400
MSRDC.MSRDC	Name	MSRDC1
	Align	Bottom
	Height	330
	Left	0
	Top	1920

Control	Property	Setting
	Width	6510
VB.Label	Name	lblDOB
	Caption	"DOB"
	Height	255
	Left	120
	Top	1020
	Width	1200
VB.Label	Name	lblName
	Caption	"Name"
	Height	255
	Left	120
	Top	600
	Width	1200
VB.Label	Name	lblAuthorID
	Caption	"Author ID"
	Height	255
	Left	120
	Top	180
	Width	1200
VB.Label	Name	lblAUID
	BorderStyle	1 'Fixed Single
	Caption	"Label1"
	DataSource	"MSRDC1"
	Height	255
	Left	1440
	Top	180
	Width	1200

In addition to the main data-entry form, you need to build a second form to display status messages while the data-entry form is running. Add a new standard form to your project. Set its Name property to frmMsgs, and place a single textbox on the form. Set the textbox Name property to txtMsgs, and set its Multiline property to True and its Scrollbars property to Both.

Figure 18.5.

*Laying out the RDC
data-entry form.*

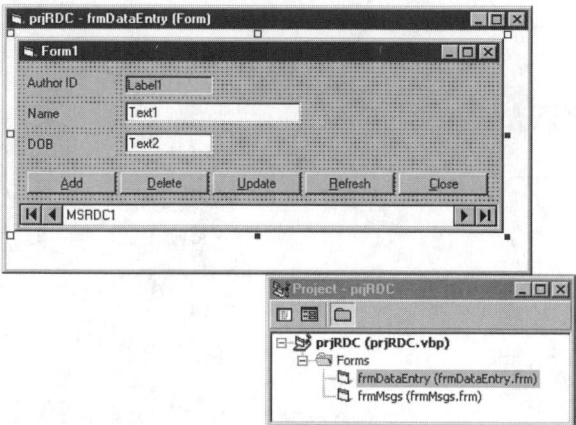

Now save the project as PRJRDC.VBP, the main form as FRMDATAENTRY.FRM, and the support
form as FRMMSGS.FRM. Now you're ready to add Visual Basic code to the forms.

Coding the RDC Data-Entry Forms

First, you need to add code to two events in the frmMsgs form. Listing 18.1 shows the code
for the Form_Load and Form_Resize events. Add this code to your support form.

TYPE **Listing 18.1. Coding the events for the frmMsgs support
form.**

```
Private Sub Form_Load()
    '
    Me.Caption = "MSRDC Event Messages"
    txtMsg.Text = ""
    '
End Sub

Private Sub Form_Resize()
    '
    ' make text box fill the form
    '
    If Me.WindowState <> vbMinimized Then
        txtMsg.Left = 1
        txtMsg.Top = 1
        txtMsg.Width = Me.ScaleWidth
        txtMsg.Height = Me.ScaleHeight
    End If
    '
End Sub
```

18

The code in Listing 18.1 sets up the initial caption and textbox on the form and then forces the textbox to fill the entire frmMsgs form space. This form displays progress messages reported by the main data-entry form. You can save and close this form. This is all the code you need to add to the frmMsgs form.

Now open the main data-entry form (frmDataEntry) and add the code from Listing 18.2 to the Form_Load event of the form.

Listing 18.2. Coding the `Form_Load` event of the frmDataEntry form.

`TYPE`

```
Private Sub Form_Load()
    '
    ' project setup actions
    '
    frmMsgs.Show ' launch message window
    '
    ' set up RDC
    MSRDC1.DataSourceName = "RDC Books5"
    MSRDC1.SQL = "SELECT * FROM Authors"
    MSRDC1.CursorDriver = rdUseClientBatch
    MSRDC1.LockType = rdConcurBatch
    MSRDC1.ResultsetType = rdOpenStatic
    MSRDC1.Refresh
    '
    ' bind inputs to rdc
    lblAUID.DataField = "AUID"
    txtName.DataField = "Name"
    txtDOB.DataField = "DOB"
    '
    ' set form title
    Me.Caption = "Remote Data Control Demo"
    '
End Sub
```

The code in Listing 18.2 sets up the basic parameters to the RDC, uses the Refresh method to fetch the data, and then updates the DataField properties of the bound input controls in order to link them to the dataset returned in the RDC. Note that you are using the rdOpenStatic option to create an updatable, fixed-membership dataset.

Now add the code from Listing 18.3 to the cmdBtn_Click event of the form. This single set of code handles all the command buttons, because the buttons were added as a control array.

TYPE **Listing 18.3. Coding the `cmdBtn_Click` event.**

```
Private Sub cmdBtn_Click(Index As Integer)
    '
    ' handle button selections
    '
    Select Case Index
        Case 0 ' add
            MSRDC1.Resultset.AddNew
        Case 1 ' delete
            MSRDC1.Resultset.Delete
        Case 2 ' update
            MSRDC1.UpdateRow
        Case 3 ' refresh
            MSRDC1.UpdateControls
        Case 4 ' close
            Unload Me
    End Select
    '
End Sub
```

Listing 18.4 shows the code you need to add to the four RDC-related events. Note that all four of these routines use a `PostMsg` subroutine and that the `Validate` event calls a `ShowAction` function. You build these routines in the next step of the project.

TYPE **Listing 18.4. Coding the events of the RDC.**

```
Private Sub MSRDC1_Error(ByVal Number As Long, Description As String, ByVal
➥Scode As Long, ByVal Source As String, ByVal HelpFile As String, ByVal
➥HelpContext As Long, CancelDisplay As Boolean)
    '
    PostMsg "MSRDC1_Error - Number=" & CStr(Number) & ", Description = " &
➥Description & ", Scode = " & CStr(Scode) & ", Source = " & Source & ",
➥HelpFile = " & HelpFile & ", HelpContext = " & CStr(HelpContext) & ",
➥CancelDisplay = " & CStr(CancelDisplay)
    '
End Sub

Private Sub MSRDC1_QueryCompleted()
    '
    PostMsg "MSRDC1_QueryCompleted"
    '
End Sub

Private Sub MSRDC1_Reposition()
    '
    PostMsg "MSRDC1_Reposition"
    '
End Sub

Private Sub MSRDC1_Validate(Action As Integer, Reserved As Integer)
    '
```

18

```
    PostMsg "MSRDC1_Validate - Action=" & ShowAction(Action) & ", Reserved=" &
➥CStr(Reserved)
    '
End Sub
```

After adding the code for all the events, add the code in Listing 18.5 to the form to create the ShowAction function. This function converts the integer value passed from the Validate event into a friendly string name. This is used to display progress messages in the frmMsg form.

TYPE **Listing 18.5. Coding the ShowAction function.**

```
Public Function ShowAction(intAction As Integer) As String
    '
    ' convert numeric action value
    ' into friendly string value
    '
    Dim strMsg As String
    '
    Select Case intAction
        Case rdActionCancel   '0
            strMsg = "Cancel"
        Case rdActionMoveFirst      '1
            strMsg = "MoveFirst"
        Case rdActionMovePrevious    '2
            strMsg = "MovePrevious"
        Case rdActionMoveNext    '3
            strMsg = "MoveNext"
        Case rdActionMoveLast    '4
            strMsg = "MoveLast"
        Case rdActionAddNew   '5
            strMsg = "AddNew"
        Case rdActionUpdate   '6
            strMsg = "Update"
        Case rdActionDelete   '7
            strMsg = "Delete"
        Case rdActionFind  '8
            strMsg = "Find"
        Case rdActionBookmark  '9
            strMsg = "Bookmark"
        Case rdActionClose  '10
            strMsg = "Close"
        Case rdActionUnload  '11
            strMsg = "Unload"
        Case rdActionUpdateAddNew  '12
            strMsg = "UpdateAddNew"
        Case rdActionUpdateModified  '13
            strMsg = "UpdateModified"
        Case rdActionRefresh  '14
            strMsg = "Refresh"
        Case rdActionCancelUpdate  '15
            strMsg = "CancelUpdate"
        Case rdActionBeginTransact  '16
```

18

continues

Listing 18.5. continued

```
            strMsg = "BeginTrans"
        Case rdActionCommitTransact '17
            strMsg = "CommitTrans"
        Case rdActionRollbackTransact '18
            strMsg = "RollbackTrans"
        Case rdActionNewParameters '19
            strMsg = "NewParameters"
        Case rdActionNewSQL '20
            strMsg = "NewSQL"
    End Select
    '
    ShowAction = strMsg
    '
End Function
```

Notice that the Validate event of the RDC has several action values that are not available with the standard Microsoft Jet data control. These additional values come in handy when managing remote data connections.

Now add the PostMsg method to your data-entry form. Listing 18.6 shows the code for this support routine.

TYPE **Listing 18.6. Coding the PostMsg subroutine.**

```
Public Sub PostMsg(strMsg As String)
    '
    ' post a message to a text box
    '
    Static lngCounter As Long
    '
    lngCounter = lngCounter + 1
    frmMsgs.txtMsg = Format(lngCounter, "000") & ":" & strMsg & vbCrLf &
➥frmMsgs.txtMsg
    '
End Sub
```

As mentioned earlier, the sole purpose of this routine is to post messages to the supporting form so that you can see the progress of data requests using the RDC. Now save the form (FRMDATAENTRY.FRM) and the project (PRJRDC.VBP) before running it.

When you run the project, the message form and the data form appear. Note the messages that have been posted to the support form. Modify the first record (change the value of the Name field) and move the record pointer. You see a number of messages appear in the support form indicating the validation of the new data, the updating of the modified data, and the repositioning of the record pointer on the new record (see Figure 18.6).

18

Figure 18.6.

Running the RDC data-entry project.

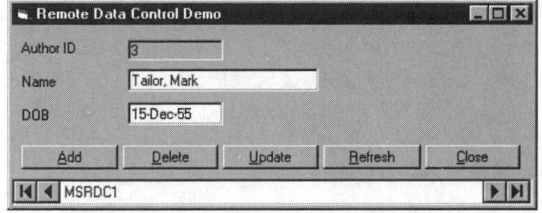

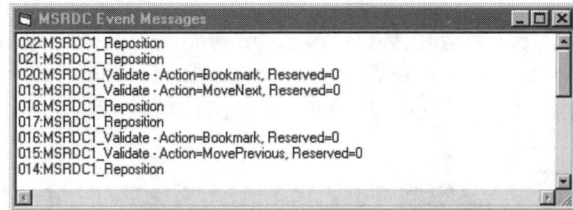

That's all there is to creating data-entry forms using data-bound controls and the RDC. In the next section, you'll learn how to create database applications that use the RDOs instead of a data-bound control set.

Programming with RDOs

Creating database applications that use the RDOs is quite similar to programming with the Microsoft Jet DAOs. Most of the material in this section of the chapter refers to Chapter 9. If you have not already completed that chapter, you might want to review it before you continue with this chapter.

The RDO programming objects are arranged in a hierarchy of collections. The top-level object is the rdoEngine object. This is the programmatic access to the Microsoft remote data engine used by Visual Basic 5 to gain access to all remote data. All requests using the RDO objects are handled by the rdoEngine.

The rdoEngine creates one or more rdoEnvironment objects. These objects are used to manage the details of the various connections to datasets. rdoEnvironment objects can create rdoConnection objects. These are the actual connections to existing data sources at the remote data system. Each rdoConnection can create one or more rdoResultset objects. The rdoResultset object contains the actual rows of data. You also can create and access rdoQuery objects or rdoTable objects from the rdoConnection object. The rdoQuery object also has an rdoParameter object to manage the passing of parameters during the processing of queries.

In the sections that follow, you code examples of each of the RDO objects, inspect their properties, and exercise their methods. To do this, start a new Visual Basic 5 Standard EXE project. Set the project name to prjRDO and the form name to frmRDO. Save the empty form as FRMRDO.FRM and the project as PRJRDO.VBP. In each of the following sections, you add code that illustrates each of the RDO objects.

The rdoEngine Object

The rdoEngine object is the top-level object in the RDO collection. This object has only a handful of parameters and has no collection of its own. You can have only one rdoEngine instance in your Visual Basic programs. Add a new command button to your form. Set its Name property to cmdRDOEngine and its Caption to RDO Engine. Now add the code in Listing 18.7 to the cmdRDOEngine_Click event.

TYPE **Listing 18.7. Coding the cmdRDOEngine_Click event.**

```
Private Sub cmdRDOEngine_Click()
    '
    ' show rdo engine properties
    '
    Dim strMsg As String
    Dim rdoEng As rdoEngine
    Dim aryCursorDriver As Variant
    '
    aryCursorDriver = Array("rdUseIfNeeded", "rdUseOdbc", "rdUseServer",
➥"rdUseClientBatch", "rduseNone")
    '
    Set rdoEng = rdoEngine
    '
    strMsg = strMsg & "rdoDefaultCursorDriver=" &
➥aryCursorDriver(rdoEng.rdoDefaultCursorDriver) & vbCrLf
    strMsg = strMsg & "rdoDefaultErrorThreshold=" &
➥CStr(rdoEng.rdoDefaultErrorThreshold) & vbCrLf
    strMsg = strMsg & "rdoDefaultLoginTimeOut=" &
➥CStr(rdoEng.rdoDefaultLoginTimeout) & vbCrLf
    strMsg = strMsg & "rdoDefaultPassword=" & rdoEng.rdoDefaultPassword & vbCrLf
    strMsg = strMsg & "rdoDefaultUser=" & rdoEng.rdoDefaultUser & vbCrLf
    strMsg = strMsg & "rdoLocaleID=" & CStr(rdoEng.rdoLocaleID) & vbCrLf
    strMsg = strMsg & "rdoVersion=" & CStr(rdoEng.rdoVersion) & vbCrLf
    '
    MsgBox strMsg, vbInformation, "RDOEngine"
    '
    Set rdoEng = Nothing
    '
End Sub
```

Save and run the project. After you click the RDO Engine command button, you should see something like the message in Figure 18.7.

18

Figure 18.7.

Displaying the RDO Engine properties.

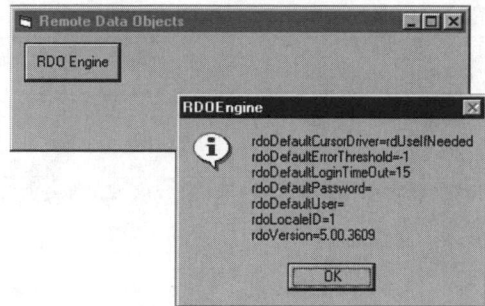

The rdoEnvironment Object

The rdoEnvironment object contains information about the current environment for data connections. The rdoEnvironment object is the RDO equivalent of the Microsoft Jet Workspaces object. rdoEnvironment objects can be used to group rdoConnection objects together for transaction-management purposes as well.

You can create multiple rdoEnvironment objects under the rdoEngine object. All rdoEnvironment objects are contained in the rdoEnvironments collection object.

Add a new button to the form. Set its Name property to cmdRDOEnvironment and its Caption to Environment. Now enter the code from Listing 18.8 to the cmdRDOEnvironment_Click event.

TYPE | **Listing 18.8. Coding the cmdRDOEnvironment_Click event.**

```
Private Sub cmdRDOEnvironment_Click()
    '
    ' show environment collection as properties
    '
    Dim strMsg As String
    Dim rdoEnv As rdoEnvironment
    Dim rdoNewEnv As rdoEnvironment
    Dim aryCursorDriver As Variant
    '
    aryCursorDriver = Array("rdUseIfNeeded", "rdUseOdbc", "rdUseServer",
➥"rdUseClientBatch", "rduseNone")
    '
    Set rdoNewEnv = rdoEngine.rdoCreateEnvironment("rdoTEMP", "admin", "")
    '
    For Each rdoEnv In rdoEngine.rdoEnvironments
        strMsg = strMsg & "rdoCursorDriver=" &
➥aryCursorDriver(rdoEnv.CursorDriver) & vbCrLf
        strMsg = strMsg & "hEnv=" & CStr(rdoEnv.hEnv) & vbCrLf
        strMsg = strMsg & "LoginTimeOut=" & CStr(rdoEnv.LoginTimeout) & vbCrLf
        strMsg = strMsg & "Name=" & rdoEnv.Name & vbCrLf
```

continues

Listing 18.8. continued

```
        'strMsg = strMsg & "Password=" & rdoEnv.Password & vbCrLf
        strMsg = strMsg & "UserName=" & rdoEnv.UserName & vbCrLf
        strMsg = strMsg & vbCrLf
    Next
    '
    MsgBox strMsg, vbInformation, "rdoEnvironment"
    '
    rdoNewEnv.Close
    Set rdoEnv = Nothing
    Set rdoNewEnv = Nothing
    '
End Sub
```

After you save and run the project, click the Environment button to display a dialog box similar to the one in Figure 18.8.

Figure 18.8.

*Displaying the
rdoEnvironment
properties.*

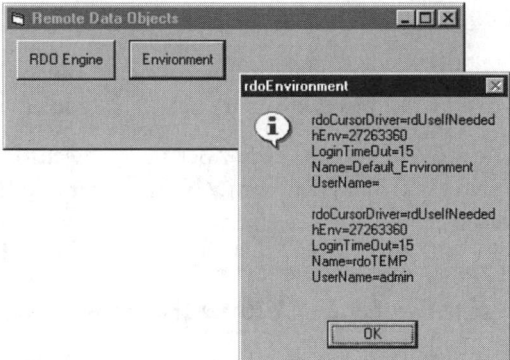

Notice that a default environment always is available to your application. It is advisable, however, to create your own environment before you attempt to establish a connection to remote data sources.

The rdoConnection Object

The rdoConnection object contains the details needed to establish a connection between your application and the remote data source. The rdoConnection object is similar to the Microsoft Jet Database object.

You can create more than one rdoConnection object under the same rdoEnvironment object. All rdoConnection objects are stored in the rdoConnections collection.

Add a new button to the form. Set its Name to cmdRDOConnection and its Caption to Connection. Then add the code in Listing 18.9 to the `cmdRDOConnection_Click` event.

TYPE   **Listing 18.9. Coding the `cmdRDOConnection_Click` event.**

```
Private Sub cmdRDOConnection_Click()
    '
    ' show resultsets
    '
    Dim strMsg As String
    Dim rdoEnv As rdoEnvironment
    Dim rdoCon As rdoConnection
    Dim rdoNewCon As rdoConnection
    Dim aryCursorDriver As Variant

    aryCursorDriver = Array("rdUseIfNeeded", "rdUseOdbc", "rdUseServer",
➥"rdUseClientBatch", "rduseNone")
    '
    Set rdoEnv = rdoEngine.rdoCreateEnvironment("rdoTEMP", "admin", "")
    Set rdoNewCon = rdoEnv.OpenConnection("RDC Books5")
    '
    For Each rdoCon In rdoEnv.rdoConnections
        strMsg = strMsg & "AsyncCheckInterval=" &
➥CStr(rdoCon.AsyncCheckInterval) & vbCrLf
        strMsg = strMsg & "Connect=" & rdoCon.Connect & vbCrLf
        strMsg = strMsg & "CursorDriver=" & aryCursorDriver(rdoCon.CursorDriver)
➥& vbCrLf
        strMsg = strMsg & "hDbc=" & CStr(rdoCon.hDbc) & vbCrLf
        strMsg = strMsg & "LoginTimeOut=" & CStr(rdoCon.LoginTimeout) & vbCrLf
        strMsg = strMsg & "LogMessages=" & rdoCon.LogMessages & vbCrLf
        strMsg = strMsg & "Name=" & rdoCon.Name & vbCrLf
        strMsg = strMsg & "QueryTimeOut=" & CStr(rdoCon.QueryTimeout) & vbCrLf
        strMsg = strMsg & "RowsAffected=" & CStr(rdoCon.RowsAffected) & vbCrLf
        strMsg = strMsg & "StillConnecting=" & CStr(rdoCon.StillConnecting) &
➥vbCrLf
        strMsg = strMsg & "StillExecuting=" & CStr(rdoCon.StillExecuting) &
➥vbCrLf
        strMsg = strMsg & "Transactions=" & CStr(rdoCon.Transactions) & vbCrLf
        strMsg = strMsg & "Updatable=" & CStr(rdoCon.Updatable) & vbCrLf
        strMsg = strMsg & "Version=" & rdoCon.Version & vbCrLf
    Next
    '
    MsgBox strMsg, vbInformation, "rdoConnection"
    '
    rdoNewCon.Close
    rdoEnv.Close
    Set rdoEnv = Nothing
    Set rdoCon = Nothing
    Set rdoNewCon = Nothing
    '
End Sub
```

18

Save and run the project. After you click the Connection button, you'll see a display of all the default properties of an rdoConnection object, as shown in Figure 18.9.

Figure 18.9.

Displaying the rdoConnection properties.

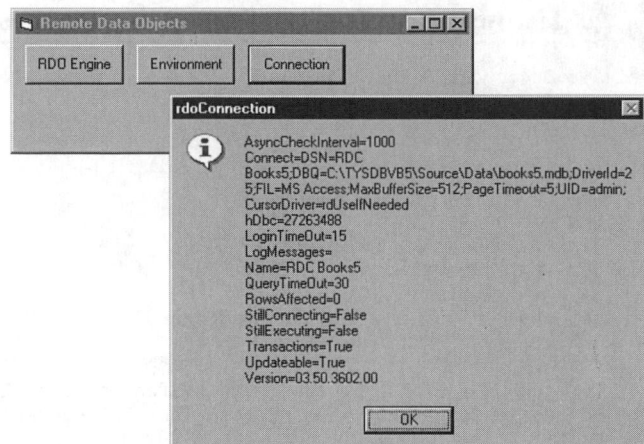

Note that the Version property of the rdoConnection object reports the version number of the ODBC driver used to establish the connection to the remote data source.

The rdoResultset Object

After a connection is established between your program and the remote data, you can use the rdoResultset object to create a collection of records. The rdoResultset object is the RDO equivalent of the Microsoft Jet Recordset object. rdoResultset contains a direct reference to all the rows and columns in the dataset.

You can have multiple rdoResultset objects for each rdoConnection object. All Resultset objects are stored in the Resultsets collection of the rdoConnection object.

Add a new button to the project. Set its Name property to cmdRDOResultset and its Caption to Resultset. Now add the code in Listing 18.10 to the cmdRDOResultset_Click event.

TYPE **Listing 18.10. Coding the cmdRDOResultset_Click event.**

```
Private Sub cmdRDOResultset_Click()
    '
    ' show result set properties
    '
    Dim rdoEnv As rdoEnvironment
    Dim rdoCon As rdoConnection
    Dim rdoRS As rdoResultset
    Dim strMsg As String
    Dim aryEditMode As Variant
    Dim aryLockType As Variant
```

18

```
    Dim aryType As Variant
    '
    aryEditMode = Array("rdEditNone", "rdEditInProgress", "rdEditAdd")
    aryLockType = Array("rdConcurReadOnly", "rdConcurLock", "rdConcurRowVer",
➥"rdConcurValues", "rdConCurBatchEdit")
    aryType = Array("rdOpenForwardOnly", "rdOpenKeyset", "rdOpenDynamic",
➥"rdOpenStatic")
    '
    ' set up env/con/rs
    Set rdoEnv = rdoEngine.rdoCreateEnvironment("rdoTEMP", "admin", "")
    Set rdoCon = rdoEnv.OpenConnection("RDC Books5")
    Set rdoRS = rdoCon.OpenResultset("SELECT * FROM Authors")
    '
    ' show properties of the rdoRS
    strMsg = strMsg & "AbsolutePosition=" & CStr(rdoRS.AbsolutePosition) &
➥vbCrLf
    strMsg = strMsg & "BOF=" & CStr(rdoRS.BOF) & vbCrLf
    strMsg = strMsg & "Bookmark=" & rdoRS.Bookmark & vbCrLf
    strMsg = strMsg & "Bookmarkable=" & CStr(rdoRS.Bookmarkable) & vbCrLf
    strMsg = strMsg & "EditMode=" & aryEditMode(rdoRS.EditMode) & vbCrLf
    strMsg = strMsg & "EOF=" & CStr(rdoRS.EOF) & vbCrLf
    strMsg = strMsg & "hStmt=" & CStr(rdoRS.hStmt) & vbCrLf
    strMsg = strMsg & "LastModified=" & rdoRS.LastModified & vbCrLf
    strMsg = strMsg & "LockEdits=" & CStr(rdoRS.LockEdits) & vbCrLf
    strMsg = strMsg & "LockType=" & aryLockType(rdoRS.LockType) & vbCrLf
    strMsg = strMsg & "Name=" & rdoRS.Name & vbCrLf
    strMsg = strMsg & "PercentPosition=" & CStr(rdoRS.PercentPosition) & vbCrLf
    strMsg = strMsg & "Restartable=" & CStr(rdoRS.Restartable) & vbCrLf
    strMsg = strMsg & "RowCount=" & CStr(rdoRS.RowCount) & vbCrLf
    strMsg = strMsg & "Status=" & CStr(rdoRS.Status) & vbCrLf
    strMsg = strMsg & "StillExecuting=" & CStr(rdoRS.StillExecuting) & vbCrLf
    strMsg = strMsg & "Transactions=" & CStr(rdoRS.Transactions) & vbCrLf
    strMsg = strMsg & "Type=" & aryType(rdoRS.Type) & vbCrLf
    strMsg = strMsg & "Updatable=" & CStr(rdoRS.Updatable) & vbCrLf
    '
    MsgBox strMsg, vbInformation, "rdoResultset"
    '
    rdoRS.Close
    rdoCon.Close
    rdoEnv.Close
    Set rdoRS = Nothing
    Set rdoCon = Nothing
    Set rdoEnv = Nothing
    '
End Sub
```

Note the use of the OpenResultset method of the rdoConnection object to create the rdoResultset. Save and run the project. After you click the Resultset button, you'll see a display similar to the one in Figure 18.10.

Figure 18.10.
Displaying the rdoResultset properties.

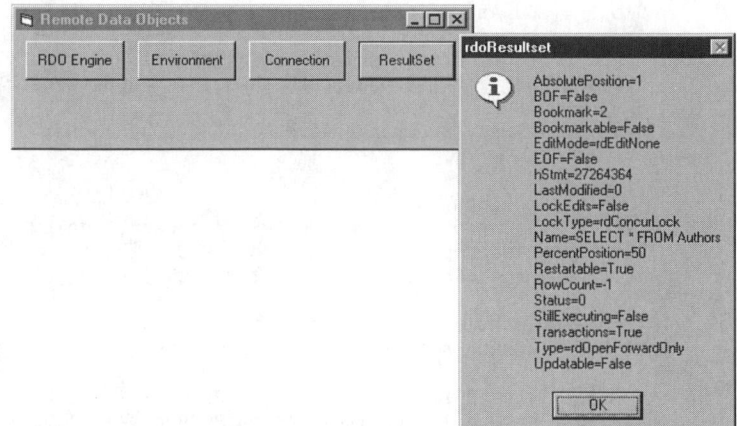

The rdoTable Object

You also can open an rdoTable object from the rdoConnection object. This object contains information about each of the columns in the base table that exist on the remote data source. You can use the rdoTables collection to get a listing of all the base objects available through the rdoConnection. The rdoTables collection returns more than just the defined base tables. You also receive all the stored queries (views) available at the remote data source.

WARNING

> The rdoTable object is included in Visual Basic 5.0 for backward compatibility with previous versions of the RDO Engine. Although the rdoTable object works as expected in this version of Visual Basic, it might not be supported in future versions of Visual Basic.

Add a new button to the project. Set its Name property to cmdRDOTables and its Caption to RDO Tables. Now add the code in Listing 18.11 to the cmdRDOTables_Click event.

TYPE **Listing 18.11. Coding the cmdRDOTables_Click event.**

```
Private Sub cmdRDOTables_Click()
    '
    ' get rdo table collection
    '
    Dim rdoEnv As rdoEnvironment
    Dim rdoCon As rdoConnection
    Dim rdoTbl As rdoTable
    Dim strMsg As String
    '
```

18

```
' set env/con
Set rdoEnv = rdoEngine.rdoCreateEnvironment("rdoTEMP", "admin", "")
Set rdoCon = rdoEnv.OpenConnection("RDC Books5")
'
' update the tables collection
rdoCon.rdoTables.Refresh
'
' show table properties
For Each rdoTbl In rdoCon.rdoTables
    strMsg = strMsg & "Name=" & rdoTbl.Name & vbCrLf
    strMsg = strMsg & "RowCount=" & CStr(rdoTbl.RowCount) & vbCrLf
    strMsg = strMsg & "Type=" & CStr(rdoTbl.Type) & vbCrLf
    strMsg = strMsg & "Updatable=" & CStr(rdoTbl.Updatable)
    strMsg = strMsg & vbCrLf
    '
    MsgBox strMsg, vbInformation, "rdoTable"
    strMsg = ""
Next
'
rdoCon.Close
rdoEnv.Close
Set rdoTbl = Nothing
Set rdoCon = Nothing
Set rdoEnv = Nothing
'
End Sub
```

Notice the use of the Refresh method on the rdoTables collection. This is required if you want to get a list of all the table and view objects available from the data source. The rdoTables collection is not automatically refreshed when you create the rdoConnection object.

Save and run the project. After you click the RDO Tables button, you'll see a list of the tables and views available from the data source. Figure 18.11 shows one of those displays.

Figure 18.11.
Inspecting the rdoTable properties.

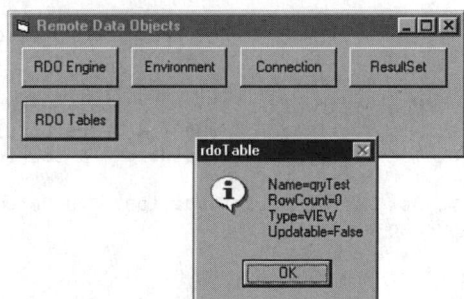

The rdoColumns Object

The rdoColumns object contains detailed information about the contents and properties of each data column in the rdoTable or rdoResultset object. The rdoColumn object corresponds to the Microsoft Jet Field object. Usually, more than one rdoColumn object exists for each rdoTable or rdoResultset object. All rdoColumn objects are stored in the rdoColumns collection.

Add a new button to the project. Set its Name to cmdRDOColumns and its Caption to Columns. Now add the code in Listing 18.12 to the cmdRDOColumns_Click event.

TYPE **Listing 18.12. Coding the** `cmdRDOColumns_Click` **event**

```
Private Sub cmdRDOColumns_Click()
    '
    ' show rdo columns collection
    '
    Dim rdoEnv As rdoEnvironment
    Dim rdoCon As rdoConnection
    Dim rdoTbl As rdoTable
    Dim rdoCol As rdoColumn
    Dim strMsg As String
    '
    ' set up connection
    Set rdoEnv = rdoEngine.rdoCreateEnvironment("rdoTEMP", "admin", "")
    Set rdoCon = rdoEnv.OpenConnection("RDC Books5")
    '
    ' get table info
    rdoCon.rdoTables.Refresh
    Set rdoTbl = rdoCon.rdoTables("Authors")
    '
    ' get column info
    For Each rdoCol In rdoTbl.rdoColumns
        strMsg = strMsg & "AllowZeroLength=" & CStr(rdoCol.AllowZeroLength) &
➥vbCrLf
        strMsg = strMsg & "Attributes=" & Hex(rdoCol.Attributes) & vbCrLf
        strMsg = strMsg & "ChunkRequired=" & CStr(rdoCol.ChunkRequired) & vbCrLf
        strMsg = strMsg & "Name=" & rdoCol.Name & vbCrLf
        strMsg = strMsg & "OrdinalPosition=" & CStr(rdoCol.OrdinalPosition) &
➥vbCrLf
        strMsg = strMsg & "Required=" & CStr(rdoCol.Required) & vbCrLf
        strMsg = strMsg & "Size=" & CStr(rdoCol.Size) & vbCrLf
        strMsg = strMsg & "SourceColumn=" & rdoCol.SourceColumn & vbCrLf
        strMsg = strMsg & "SourceTable=" & rdoCol.SourceTable & vbCrLf
        strMsg = strMsg & "Type=" & CStr(rdoCol.Type) & vbCrLf
        strMsg = strMsg & "Updatable=" & CStr(rdoCol.Updatable) & vbCrLf
        '
        MsgBox strMsg, vbInformation, "rdoColumn"
        strMsg = ""
        '
    Next
    '
    rdoCon.Close
    rdoEnv.Close
    Set rdoCol = Nothing
    Set rdoTbl = Nothing
    Set rdoCon = Nothing
    Set rdoEnv = Nothing
    '
End Sub
```

18

The code in Listing 18.12 displays detailed properties for each column in the Authors table at the data source. Note that the .Value and the .OriginalValue properties have been left out of this example. You also can access these properties in your programs. Also, the value of the .Type property maps to a set of predefined Visual Basic constants. Table 18.8 lists those values.

Table 18.8. Various type values of the rdoColumns.Type property.

Visual Basic Constant	Integer Value	Description
rdTypeCHAR	1	Fixed-length character string. Length set by Size property.
rdTypeNUMERIC	2	Signed, exact numeric value with precision p and scale s (1 p 15; 0 s p).
rdTypeDECIMAL	3	Signed, exact numeric value with precision p and scale s (1 p 15; 0 s p).
rdTypeINTEGER	4	Signed, exact numeric value with precision 10, scale 0 (signed: -231 n 231-1; unsigned: 0 n 232-1).
rdTypeSMALLINT	5	Signed, exact numeric value with precision 5, scale 0 (signed: -32,768 n 32,767; unsigned: 0 n 65,535).
rdTypeFLOAT	6	Signed, approximate numeric value with mantissa precision 15 (zero or absolute value 10-308 to 10308).
rdTypeREAL	7	Signed, approximate numeric value with mantissa precision 7 (zero or absolute value 10-38 to 1038).
rdTypeDOUBLE	8	Signed, approximate numeric value with mantissa precision 15 (zero or absolute value 10-308 to 10308).
rdTypeDATE	9	Date: Data-source dependent.
rdTypeTIME	10	Time: Data-source dependent.
rdTypeTIMESTAMP	11	TimeStamp: Data-source dependent.
rdTypeVARCHAR	12	Variable-length character string. Maximum length: 255.
rdTypeLONGVARCHAR	−1	Variable-length character string. Maximum length determined by data source.

continues

18

Table 18.8. continued

Visual Basic Constant	Integer Value	Description
rdTypeBINARY	–2	Fixed-length binary data. Maximum length: 255.
rdTypeVARBINARY	–3	Variable-length binary data. Maximum length: 255.
rdTypeLONGVARBINARY	–4	Variable-length binary data. Maximum data-source dependent.
rdTypeBIGINT	–5	Signed, exact numeric value with precision 19 (signed) or 20 (unsigned); scale 0 (signed: -263 n 263-1; unsigned: 0 n 264-1).
rdTypeTINYINT	–6	Signed, exact numeric value with precision 3, scale 0; (signed: -128 n 127; unsigned: 0 n 255).
rdTypeBIT	–7	Single binary digit.

The exact data type returned in each column is data-source dependent. Not all data sources support all data types listed here.

Save and run the project. After you click the RDO Columns button, you'll see a series of dialog boxes that show the details of each column in the Authors table. Figure 18.12 shows one of those dialog boxes.

Figure 18.12.

Viewing the rdoColumn properties.

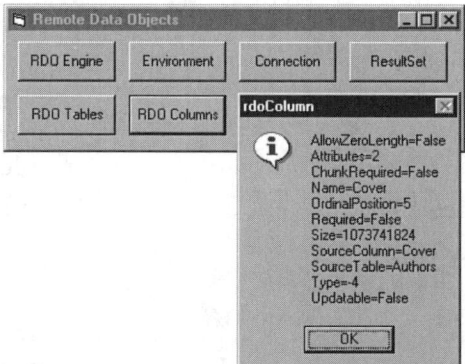

18

The rdoQuery Object

The rdoQuery object provides a method for creating and executing defined queries or views on the remote data source. The rdoQuery object is the RDO version of the Microsoft Jet QueryDef object. You can create more than one rdoQuery object on each rdoConnection object. All rdoQuery objects are accessed through the rdoQueries collection object.

Add a new button to the form. Set its Name to cmdRDOQueries and its Caption to RDO Queries. Add the code in Listing 18.13 to the cmdRDOQueries_Click event.

TYPE **Listing 18.13. Coding for the cmdRDOQueries_Click event.**

```
Private Sub cmdRDOQueries_Click()
    '
    ' example rdo query
    '
    Dim rdoEnv As rdoEnvironment
    Dim rdoCon As rdoConnection
    Dim rdoQry As rdoQuery
    Dim rdoNewQry As rdoQuery
    Dim rdoRS As rdoResultset
    Dim strMsg As String
    Dim strSQL As String
    Dim aryLockType As Variant
    Dim aryType As Variant
    Dim aryCursorDriver As Variant
    '
    aryCursorDriver = Array("rdUseIfNeeded", "rdUseOdbc", "rdUseServer",
➥"rdUseClientBatch", "rduseNone")
    aryLockType = Array("rdConcurReadOnly", "rdConcurLock", "rdConcurRowVer",
➥"rdConcurValues", "rdConCurBatchEdit")
    aryType = Array("rdOpenForwardOnly", "rdOpenKeyset", "rdOpenDynamic",
➥"rdOpenStatic")
    '
    strSQL = "SELECT * FROM Publishers,Titles WHERE
➥Publishers.PubID=Titles.PubId"
    '
    ' set env/con
    Set rdoEnv = rdoEngine.rdoCreateEnvironment("rdoTEMP", "admin", "")
    Set rdoCon = rdoEnv.OpenConnection("RDC Books5")
    '
    ' build a new query & collect data set
    Set rdoNewQry = rdoCon.CreateQuery("rdoQryTest", strSQL)
    Set rdoRS = rdoNewQry.OpenResultset()
    '
    ' show details
    For Each rdoQry In rdoCon.rdoQueries
        strMsg = strMsg & "BindThreshold=" & CStr(rdoQry.BindThreshold) & vbCrLf
        strMsg = strMsg & "CursorType=" & aryCursorDriver(rdoQry.CursorType) &
➥vbCrLf
        strMsg = strMsg & "hStmt=" & CStr(rdoQry.hStmt) & vbCrLf
        strMsg = strMsg & "KeysetSize=" & CStr(rdoQry.KeysetSize) & vbCrLf
```

continues

18

Listing 18.13. continued

```
        strMsg = strMsg & "LockType=" & aryLockType(rdoQry.LockType) & vbCrLf
        strMsg = strMsg & "MaxRows=" & CStr(rdoQry.MaxRows) & vbCrLf
        strMsg = strMsg & "Name=" & rdoQry.Name & vbCrLf
        strMsg = strMsg & "Prepared=" & rdoQry.Prepared & vbCrLf
        strMsg = strMsg & "QueryTimeOut=" & CStr(rdoQry.QueryTimeout) & vbCrLf
        strMsg = strMsg & "RowsAffeced=" & CStr(rdoQry.RowsAffected) & vbCrLf
        strMsg = strMsg & "RowsetSize=" & CStr(rdoQry.RowsetSize) & vbCrLf
        strMsg = strMsg & "SQL=" & rdoQry.SQL & vbCrLf
        strMsg = strMsg & "StillExecuting=" & CStr(rdoQry.StillExecuting) &
➥vbCrLf
        strMsg = strMsg & "Type=" & aryType(rdoQry.Type) & vbCrLf
        '
        MsgBox strMsg, vbInformation, "rdoQuery"
        strMsg = ""
        '
    Next
    '
    rdoNewQry.Close
    rdoCon.Close
    rdoEnv.Close
    Set rdoQry = Nothing
    Set rdoNewQry = Nothing
    Set rdoCon = Nothing
    Set rdoEnv = Nothing
    '
End Sub
```

Notice the use of the OpenResultset method on the rdoQuery object. This is the way to fetch rows from the data source using the rdoQuery object as the base. Save and run the project. After you click the RDO Queries button, you'll see a detailed listing of the properties of the query, as shown in Figure 18.13.

Figure 18.13.

Displaying the rdoQuery properties.

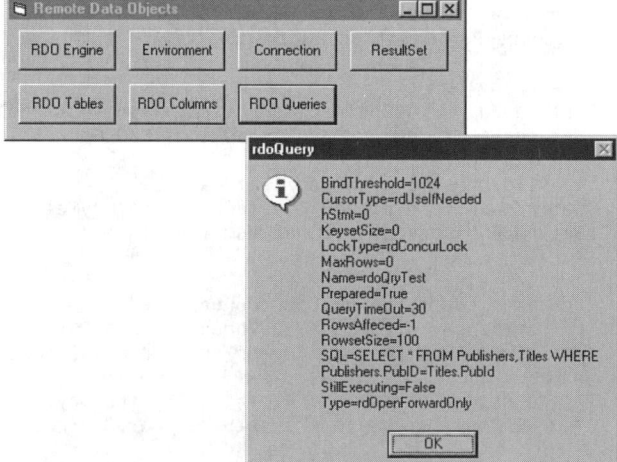

The rdoParameter Object

The rdoParameter object enables you to populate the various predefined runtime parameters of a sorted query so that you can create flexible queries that can be adjusted at runtime by programming code or user input. You can define more than one rdoParameter object for each rdoQuery object. All the parameter objects are accessed via the rdoParameters collection.

Add one last button to the project. Set its Name to cmdRDOParameter and its Caption to Parameters. Then add the code in Listing 18.14 to the cmdRDOParameter_Click event.

TYPE   **Listing 18.14. Coding for the cmdRDOParameter_Click event.**

```
Private Sub cmdRDOParameters_Click()
    '
    ' example of rdo parameters
    '
    Dim rdoEnv As rdoEnvironment
    Dim rdoCon As rdoConnection
    Dim rdoQry As rdoQuery
    Dim rdoRS As rdoResultset
    Dim rdoPrm As rdoParameter
    Dim strMsg As String
    Dim strSQL As String
    '
    strSQL = "SELECT * FROM Authors WHERE Name Like ?"
    '
    ' open env/con
    Set rdoEnv = rdoEngine.rdoCreateEnvironment("rdoTEMP", "admin", "")
    Set rdoCon = rdoEnv.OpenConnection("RDC Books5")
    '
    ' create a parameter query
    Set rdoQry = rdoCon.CreateQuery("rdoQryPrm", strSQL)
    '
    ' load parameter
    rdoQry.rdoParameters(0).Value = "%s%"
    rdoQry.rdoParameters(0).Type = rdTypeCHAR
    '
    ' get result from parameterized query
    Set rdoRS = rdoQry.OpenResultset(rdOpenKeyset)
    rdoRS.MoveLast
    '
    ' show some details
    strMsg = strMsg & "Name=" & rdoRS.Name & vbCrLf
    strMsg = strMsg & "Parameter=" & rdoQry.rdoParameters(0) & vbCrLf
    strMsg = strMsg & "RowCount=" & CStr(rdoRS.RowCount) & vbCrLf
    '
    MsgBox strMsg, vbInformation, "rdoParameters"
    '
    rdoQry.Close
    rdoCon.Close
    rdoEnv.Close
    Set rdoPrm = Nothing
```

18

continues

Listing 18.14. continued

```
        Set rdoQry = Nothing
        Set rdoRS = Nothing
        Set rdoCon = Nothing
        Set rdoEnv = Nothing
    '
    End Sub
```

The code in Listing 18.14 first opens the data connection and then creates a parameterized query (note the ? that represents the parameter portion of the statement). Then the rdoParameter object is populated by using the Value and Type properties. Notice that it is not necessary to surround string parameters in single or double quotation marks. This is handled by the remote data source. Then the OpenResultset method is used to populate the dataset, and the MoveLast method is used to force the cursor to traverse the entire record collection. This ensures an accurate value for the Rowcount property of the rdoResultset. Finally, the results appear in a dialog box, as shown in Figure 18.14.

Figure 18.14.

Viewing the rdoParameters properties.

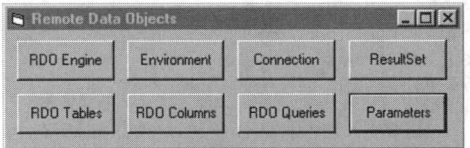

TIP

> The code in Listing 18.14 uses the Type property of the rdoParameter object. This is not a required property when creating rdoParameter objects, but it is highly recommended. If no Type property is set, the remote data source makes a guess at the data type of the parameter. This can lead to unexpected errors. If you have a CHAR column in your table that contains a shoe size (8.5, 9, and so on), for example, and use this column in a parameterized query, it is possible that passing a value of 8 will be misinterpreted by the RDBMS as an integer or long value instead of a CHAR value.

That completes your tour of the RDO programming object collection.

Summary

In today's lesson, you learned about two alternative methods for accessing remote data. You learned that you can use the RDC to create simple data-entry forms with data-bound controls. You also learned to use the RDOs to create Visual Basic 5 programs that can access data from a remote RDBMS.

Along with the details of the RDC and the RDOs, you also learned some of the basics of remote data access in general:

- [ ] Cursor drivers: The tools that manage the location of the Recordset pointer in a dataset. You learned that you can use client-side or server-side cursor drivers with RDC/RDO connections.

- [ ] Dataset types: You learned that a number of dataset types are available to you when you connect to remote data sources, including forward-only/read-only sets, static sets, key sets, and dynamic sets.

- [ ] Lock types: You learned that you can use several lock types when accessing data from your remote data source. You can use ConcurrentLock sets that perform locks as soon as you receive the data rows, or you can use several versions of optimistic locking that only attempt to lock the rows when you update them.

You also learned the details of the following Microsoft RDOs:

- [ ] rdoColumn: The RDO version of the Microsoft Jet Field object
- [ ] rdoConnection: The RDO equivalent of the Microsoft Jet Database object
- [ ] rdoEngine: The top-level data engine used to access remote data
- [ ] rdoEnvironment: The RDO equivalent of the Microsoft Jet Workspace object
- [ ] rdoParameters: A special collection of query parameters for the rdoQuery object
- [ ] rdoResultset: The RDO equivalent of the Microsoft Jet Recordset object
- [ ] rdoQuery: The RDO version of the Microsoft Jet QueryDef object
- [ ] rdoTable: The RDO version of the Microsoft Jet Table object

18

Quiz

1. What is the difference between the standard data control and the Remote Data Control?
2. What is a cursor driver?
3. What are the four dataset types?
4. What are the five lock types?

5. What is the Microsoft Jet equivalent of the rdoResultset object?

6. What is the RDO equivalent of the Microsoft Jet Workspace object?

Exercise

You have been asked to build a quick utility that scans any RDBMS database and provides a list of all the tables and views in that database. This will be used to catalog old RDBMS databases and assist in maintenance chores.

Create a simple data entry form that allows users to select any available ODBC data source and then view all tables and views in the data source in a list box. Hint: Use the `rdo.connection` method with an empty DSN string to get the ODBC dialog to appear.

Day 19

ODBC Data Access via the ODBC API

Today, you learn how to create data-entry forms that use the low-level *Open Database Connectivity* (ODBC) API routines to access existing databases. The ODBC API provides an alternative to using the Microsoft Jet database engine to access data. The ODBC interface usually is faster than the Microsoft Jet engine and uses less workstation memory than Microsoft Jet. The ODBC interface is capable of accessing data in client-server databases, desktop ISAM databases (such as dBASE, FoxPro, and so on), Microsoft Access format databases, and even Excel spreadsheets and text files.

Although data access via ODBC is fast, you can work only with Snapshot-type datasets. All data is accessed by using SQL statements to pass data to and from the ODBC data source. Also, data access via the ODBC API requires more code than using data controls or Visual Basic programming code. For these reasons, the ODBC API is not a good choice for every program. After you get an idea of what it takes to write a Visual Basic program using ODBC for data access, you can decide for yourself when to use the ODBC for data access.

NOTE

> You have a number of ODBC-type connection options with Visual Basic 5. In many cases, it is easier to use RDOs/RDC (for Visual Basic 5 Enterprise users) or the ODBCDirect options of the standard data control. This material is included here for those who want direct access to the ODBC interface via Visual Basic code instead of by using the object and ActiveX interfaces.

In today's lesson, you look at installing the ODBC Administrator on your system and using the Administrator program to define and register an ODBC data source for use with the ODBC API. You also briefly examine the ODBC operational model and the minimum ODBC APIs you need to create your own database programs using the ODBC interface.

You then use your knowledge of the ODBC API to construct an ActiveX DLL library that contains the essential API calls and a series of wrapper routines that you can use with all your Visual Basic programs to create data-entry screens for ODBC data sources. Finally, you build a Visual Basic data-entry form that calls the library routines and shows you how to implement a simple data-entry form by using standard Visual Basic controls.

When you complete this lesson, you will know how to register new data sources by using the ODBC Administrator program. You also will have a code library you can use to build solid Visual Basic applications that bypass the Microsoft Jet engine and use the ODBC API set to read and write databases.

Understanding the ODBC Interface

The ODBC interface is a direct interface between your Visual Basic program and the target database. This interface was developed by Microsoft as a way to provide seamless access to external data formats. The first versions of ODBC were a bit buggy and, in some cases, slow. Although the ODBC interface now is one of the fastest data interfaces available, many programmers still mistakenly think the ODBC interface is too slow for production applications. This is not the case. As you'll see in today's lesson, using the ODBC interface usually is faster than using the Microsoft Jet database engine.

When you use the Microsoft Jet interface to access an ODBC data source, the Microsoft Jet interface does the talking to the ODBC interface, which then talks to the intermediate driver, which talks to the data source your Visual Basic program requested. When you use ODBC API calls, you bypass the Microsoft Jet layer, and your Visual Basic program talks directly to the ODBC interface. Figure 19.1 shows how this process looks on paper.

Figure 19.1.

*ODBC versus
Microsoft Jet
interface.*

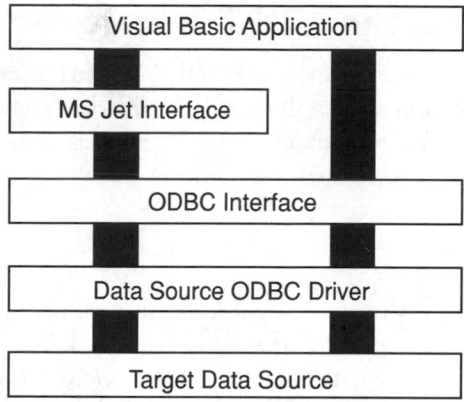

The ODBC interface doesn't really talk to databases. Instead, it links your Visual Basic program to defined data sources. These sources of data can be flat-file databases (such as dBASE and FoxPro), relational databases (such as Microsoft Access and SQL Server), or any file format for which an ODBC interface driver is available. Microsoft provides an ODBC interface driver for Excel spreadsheets and even delimited text files, for example. As long as a driver is available, you can use ODBC to access the data.

Even more important, when you use the ODBC interface to link to a data source, your Visual Basic program is not really talking to the data source directly. Your program talks to the ODBC front-end alone. The ODBC front-end uses removable drivers to translate your requests into a format understood by the target data source. The ODBC drivers exist as a middleman between the ODBC front-end and the target data file. Your Visual Basic programs talk to the ODBC front-end. The ODBC front-end talks to the appropriate driver. The driver talks to the target data file. The advantage of this design is that you easily can replace the translator routines (the drivers) to add improved performance or functionality without having to change your Visual Basic program or the target data source. Also, because the ODBC interface rules are published information, anyone who wants to make data available to users can create a new driver, and that driver then can work with all the installed versions of the ODBC interface that already exist.

Using the ODBC API interface has its limits, however. When you use the basic ODBC API to select and retrieve data, you actually are dealing with Snapshot-type data objects. You collect a set of data, bring it to your machine, make additions or modifications to the dataset, and send those changes back to the data source. Although this method is fast, it can be a bit cumbersome. Also, when you use the ODBC API, you are not able to use any data-bound controls. You are responsible for reading the data, placing it into form controls, and moving the data from the form controls back to the data source when needed. This means that you have more programming to do before you get a data-entry form up and running. Even with these drawbacks, using the ODBC API to access your data can add increased flexibility to your Visual Basic database programs.

Installing the ODBC Interface

The most recent version of the ODBC interface is included in the Visual Basic 5 installation files. If you did not install the ODBC interface when you first installed Visual Basic 5, you need to do it now in order to continue the lesson. If you already have installed the ODBC interface, you can skip this section and move on to the section "Registering an ODBC Data Source."

NOTE

You also might have other software packages that installed the ODBC interface on your system. Look for a program called ODBCAD32.EXE. If you do not find this program, refer to the Visual Basic 5 installation disks or CD-ROM to install the ODBC interface.

The ODBC kit that ships with Visual Basic 5 contains drivers for SQL Server. Drivers also are available for accessing desktop file formats such as dBASE, FoxPro, Microsoft Access, and Excel spreadsheets. The ODBC installation options appear when you first install Visual Basic 5. For a full installation, you need to check not just the SQL Server and Oracle Drivers, but also the ISAM drivers (for Microsoft Jet use) and the Desktop ODBC drivers (for ODBC use).

Now that you have the ODBC Administrator installed, you are ready to define an ODBC data source that you can use with your Visual Basic 5 programs.

Registering an ODBC Data Source

The ODBC interface is based on the idea that defined data sources are available for users and programs to access. Each desktop has its own list of available ODBC data sources. On 16-bit systems, this list of ODBC data sources is kept in the ODBC.INI file in the \WINDOWS\SYSTEM directory. On 32-bit systems, the information is stored in the Registry under the SOFTWARE/ODBC keys.

WARNING

Even though you can call up the ODBC.INI file with a text editor or open the Windows Registry by using REGEDIT.EXE, I do not recommend that you alter these entries using anything other than the ODBC Administrator program. Incorrect data in the ODBC entries in the INI file or in the Registry can cause the ODBC interface to behave unpredictably or to fail completely.

Each of these entries contains basic information about the defined data source, the drive used to access the data, and possibly additional information, depending on the data source and driver used. It is easy to define and register a new ODBC data source; to understand this process, create an ODBC data source that you can use later in this lesson.

First, load the ODBC Administrator program by locating and executing the ODBCAD32.EXE program. You can find it in the Control Panel, as shown in Figure 19.2; just double-click the icon.

Figure 19.2.

Locating the ODBC Administrator program (ODBCAD32.EXE).

When you first start the ODBC Administrator, you see a tabbed dialog box that lists all the data sources currently registered for your workstation, as shown in Figure 19.3.

Figure 19.3.

Viewing the registered ODBC data sources.

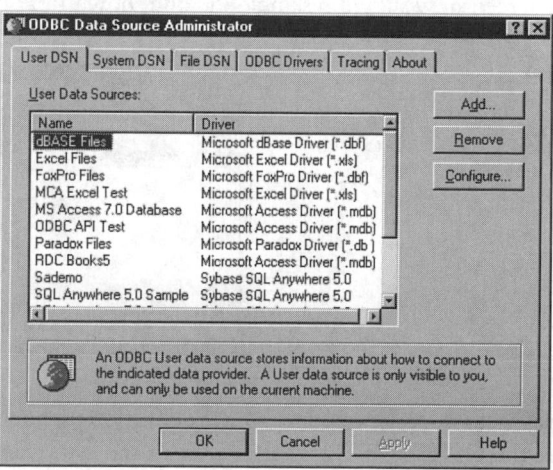

19

To define a new ODBC data source, make sure that the User DSN tab is selected and click Add. The Create New Data Source dialog box appears. Select the Microsoft Access Driver (*.mdb) and click Finish. The ODBC Microsoft Access 97 Setup dialog box for creating a new ODBC data source then appears.

The Data Source Name field contains the string you use when you call the ODBC connection from your Visual Basic 5 program. The Description field just contains a comment to remind you of the contents of the data source. Enter ODBC API Test in the Data Source Name field and Testing the ODBC API Set in the Description field (see Figure 19.4).

Figure 19.4.

Defining a new ODBC data source.

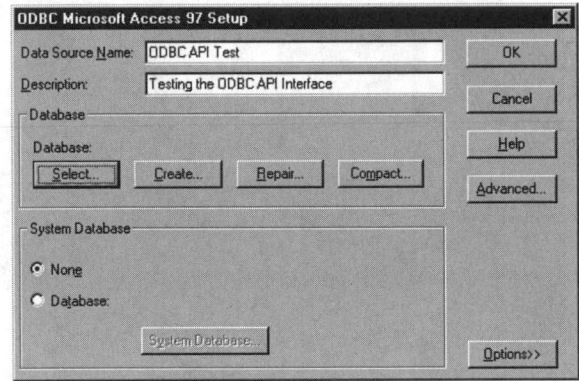

In the Database section, click Select to access the Select Database dialog box shown in Figure 19.5. Locate and select the C:\TYSDBVB5\SOURCE\CHAP19\TEST\SQLODBC.MDB database. This is the database your program connects to each time it calls the ODBC data source TYSODBC. Your screen now should resemble the one shown in Figure 19.5.

Figure 19.5.

Setting the Database property of the ODBC.

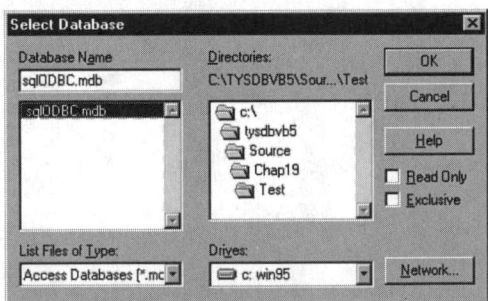

Click OK to store the new data-source definition to the ODBC.INI file. You now should be able to see the ODBC API Test data source in the listbox in the first ODBC dialog box form.

19

Figure 19.6 shows the entries in the My Computer\HKEY_CURRENT_USER\Software\ODBC\ODBC.INI section of the Registry file that were created when you added the ODBC API Test data source. Your entries might vary slightly.

Figure 19.6.

Viewing the Registry entries for the new data source.

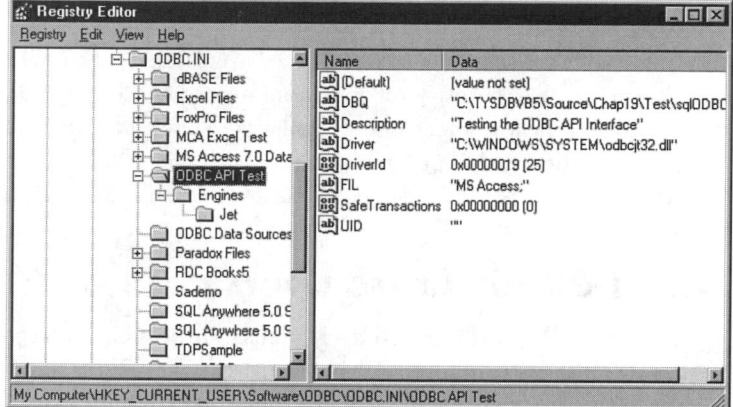

You can register as many data sources as you want. You can add various options to the data-source definition, depending on the target data file with which you are working. With Microsoft Jet databases, for example, you can add the SYSTEM security file to the data source to force users to provide valid user IDs and passwords. You also can adjust time-out values and mark the data source for exclusive use only. Other possible entries for other data file formats exist as well.

TIP

Review the ODBC Administrator online help file for more information on configuring ODBC data sources.

Creating the ODBC API Library Routines

Now that you know how to define ODBC data sources, you are ready to put together a Visual Basic 5 program that uses the ODBC interface to read and write data. To build your ODBC application, you need to declare several Windows API calls. These calls, along with a handful of predefined constants, are the heart of creating an ODBC-capable database program. This chapter doesn't review all the ODBC API calls—only the essential ones you need to get your ODBC application working.

TIP Visual Basic 5 ships with an API viewer that enables you to search for a particular API call and then copy and paste the information from the viewer directly into your Visual Basic 5 application.

After you declare the basic APIs, you need to create a set of Visual Basic routines that use these APIs to perform the low-level operations needed to execute ODBC commands from Visual Basic. After the low-level routines, you write a few mid-level functions that hide most of the grittier features of API programming. Finally, you create a few high-level routines you can use from any Visual Basic data-entry form to start off and maintain your ODBC connections.

An ODBC API Crash Course

Dozens of API calls for the ODBC interface are possible. You can write calls that enable you to inspect the type of ODBC driver you are using, to inspect the various details of the data source (database name, format, and so on), to gather information about the dataset (column names, data types for each field, length of each field, and so on), and to actually connect to the data source and move data to and from the ODBC data source. For this lesson, you focus only on those routines needed to move data back and forth through the ODBC interface.

Before you start coding the API calls and wrapper routines, you need to review the basic sequence of ODBC events required to connect to and share data with a registered ODBC data source. Several preliminary steps are involved before you actually can get any data from an ODBC data source. These steps involve defining an environment space for the ODBC connection, completing the actual connection, and then establishing an area of memory for passing data back and forth. Many of the API calls require or return unique values (called *handles*) to identify the memory spaces reserved for the ODBC interface. Figure 19.7 shows these operations. Most of the preliminary work for establishing an ODBC connection involves creating the handles you use throughout your program.

After the connection is established, you easily can share data with the target data source by using standard SQL statements. You can select a set of rows by using the SELECT_FROM statement. Whenever you request a dataset from the ODBC source, you need to go through several steps to actually pass the rows and columns from the source to your Visual Basic program. First, you execute the SQL statement. Then, to receive the dataset, you must determine the number of columns to receive and use that information to tell ODBC to queue up a row of data and send you each column in the row. You do this until you have received all the rows in the dataset. Figure 19.8 illustrates the process of executing the SELECT statement and collecting the resulting data.

Figure 19.7.

The preliminary steps to establish an ODBC data-source connection.

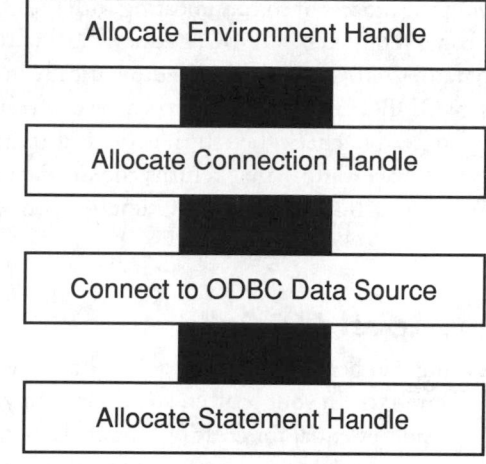

Allocate Environment Handle

Allocate Connection Handle

Connect to ODBC Data Source

Allocate Statement Handle

Figure 19.8.

Collecting results of a SELECT query from an ODBC connection.

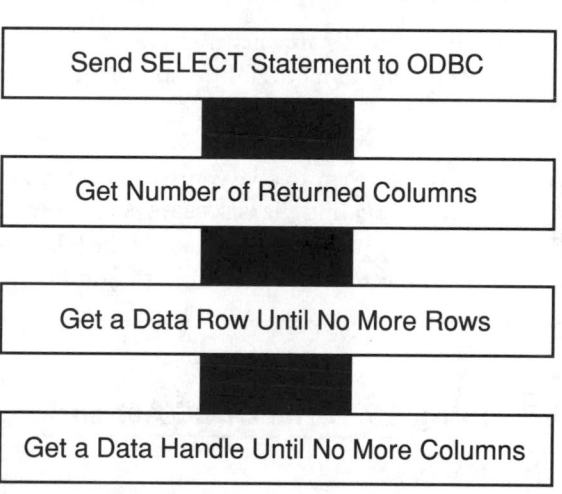

Send SELECT Statement to ODBC

Get Number of Returned Columns

Get a Data Row Until No More Rows

Get a Data Handle Until No More Columns

You can perform single record adds, updates, and deletes by using SQL INSERT, UPDATE, and DELETE statements. You accomplish this simply by sending the SQL statement to the data source. You even can perform data table CREATE and DROP statements for most data sources.

The last set of ODBC routines you need to call from Visual Basic are the ones that safely close down the ODBC interface before your program exits. The shutdown routine is basically the same as the startup routine in reverse. First, you need to release the statement handle; then, close the ODBC connection and release the connection handle. Finally, you release the environment handle.

Throughout the process of communicating with the ODBC interface, you need to check for any error codes returned by ODBC. Because the functions are executing outside your Visual Basic program, ODBC errors do not automatically invoke your Visual Basic error handler. Every major ODBC call returns a success code or an error code. After you execute an ODBC API call, you need to check the return code. If it indicates that an error occurred, you also can call an ODBC routine that returns the detailed error message generated by the data source. When you build your ODBC library, you write a routine to perform this error checking.

The Low-Level API Calls

The first thing you need to do to build your library is to declare the necessary API calls for the ODBC interface. In your project, you declare only a subset of the total ODBC API calls; these are the calls essential for creating a basic data-entry form. You also need a handful of Visual Basic constants that you use throughout the library.

Load Visual Basic 5 and start a new ActiveX project. Add a BAS module to the project and set its Name property to modODBC. Add the API calls in Listing 19.1 to the project.

TIP

If you want to save yourself some typing (and possible typing errors), you can find the MODODBC.BAS file in the C:\TYSDBVB5\SOURCE\ CHAP19\PRJODBC directory on the CD. You can load this file into your project by choosing Project | Add File.

TYPE **Listing 19.1. The ODBC API declarations.**

```
Option Explicit

' ----------------------------------------------------------
' ODBC API Declarations
' ----------------------------------------------------------

'
' basic ODBC Declares
Declare Function SQLAllocEnv Lib "odbc32.dll" (env As Long) As Integer

Declare Function SQLFreeEnv Lib "odbc32.dll" (ByVal env As Long) As Integer

Declare Function SQLAllocConnect Lib "odbc32.dll" (ByVal env As Long, _
  hDbc As Long) As Integer

Declare Function SQLConnect Lib "odbc32.dll" (ByVal hDbc As Long, _
  ByVal Server As String, ByVal serverlen As Integer, _
```

19

```
          ByVal uid As String, ByVal uidlen As Integer, ByVal pwd As String, _
          ByVal pwdlen As Integer) As Integer

     Declare Function SQLFreeConnect Lib "odbc32.dll" (ByVal hDbc As Long) _
          As Integer

     Declare Function SQLDisconnect Lib "odbc32.dll" (ByVal hDbc As Long) _
          As Integer

     Declare Function SQLAllocStmt Lib "odbc32.dll" (ByVal hDbc As Long, _
          hStmt As Long) As Integer

     Declare Function SQLFreeStmt Lib "odbc32.dll" (ByVal hStmt As Long, _
          ByVal EndOption As Integer) As Integer

     Declare Function SQLExecDirect Lib "odbc32.dll" (ByVal hStmt As Long, _
          ByVal sqlString As String, ByVal sqlstrlen As Long) As Integer

     Declare Function SQLNumResultCols Lib "odbc32.dll" (ByVal hStmt As Long, _
          NumCols As Integer) As Integer

     Declare Function SQLFetch Lib "odbc32.dll" (ByVal hStmt As Long) As Integer

     Declare Function SQLGetData Lib "odbc32.dll" (ByVal hStmt As Long, _
          ByVal Col As Integer, ByVal wConvType As Integer, ByVal lpbBuf As String, _
          ByVal dwbuflen As Long, lpcbout As Long) As Integer

     Declare Function sqlError Lib "odbc32.dll" Alias "SQLError" (ByVal env As _
          Long, ByVal hDbc As Long, ByVal hStmt As Long, ByVal SQLState As _
          String, NativeError As Long, ByVal Buffer As String, ByVal Buflen As _
          Integer, OutLen As Integer) As Integer

     Declare Function SQLSetConnectOption Lib "odbc32.dll" (ByVal hDbc&, _
          ByVal fOption%, ByVal vParam&) As Integer

     Declare Function SQLSetStmtOption Lib "odbc32.dll" (ByVal hStmt&, _
          ByVal fOption%, ByVal vParam&) As Integer
```

Listing 19.1 contains the ODBC API calls needed to implement basic connect, data-transfer, and disconnect operations. Now add the constants in Listing 19.2 to the module.

TYPE   **Listing 19.2. The ODBC constant declarations.**

```
'
' misc constants
Public Const sqlChar = 1
Public Const sqlMaxMsgLen = 512
Public Const sqlFetchNext = 1
Public Const sqlFetchFirst = 2
Public Const sqlStillExecuting = 2
Public Const sqlODBCCursors = 110
Public Const sqlConcurrency = 7
Public Const sqlCursorType = 6
```

19

Save the module as MODODBC.BAS, and save the project as PRJODBC.VBP. Now you are ready to build the library functions that use these API calls to perform ODBC operations.

The ODBC Library Routines

The next set of routines are separated into two groups. The first group are routines that deal primarily with the ODBC interface. These routines are just wrappers for the API calls. *Wrappers* are Visual Basic routines that encapsulate the API call. Using wrappers makes it easy to change the underlying API call without having to change your code. If you want to use the 16-bit version of the ODBC, for example, you only need to change the ODBC32.DLL reference in each of the API calls to ODBC.DLL. Because you are using Visual Basic wrappers, you won't have to make any changes to your Visual Basic programs in order to use 16-bit ODBC.

The second set of library routines deals primarily with Visual Basic. These routines take the data from the ODBC and store it in Visual Basic variables and controls for use on your data-entry forms.

First, you need to add a few global variables that you use throughout the library. Select the default class module for the project and set its Name property to objODBC. Now add the declarations in Listing 19.3 to the file.

TYPE   **Listing 19.3. Adding the local variables to LIBODBC.BAS.**

```
Option Explicit
'
'
Private Const BUFFERLEN = 256
'
' sql lock types
Public Enum sqlLockType
    sqlreadonly = 1
    sqllock = 2
    sqlrowver = 3
    sqlValues = 4
End Enum


' sql cursor drivers
Public Enum sqlCursorDriverType
    sqluseifneeded = 0
    sqlUseODBC = 1
    sqlUseDriver = 2
End Enum


' cursor types
Public Enum sqlResultSetType
```

```
        sqlforwardonly = 0
        sqlKeyset = 1
        sqldynamic = 2
        sqlStatic = 3
    End Enum

    '
    ' sqlerror type
    Public Enum sqlErrorType
        sqlSuccess = 0
        sqlSuccessWithInfo = 1
        sqlerr = -1
        sqlNoDataFound = 100
    End Enum

    Public Enum sqlStatement
        sqlClose = 0
        sqlDrop = 1
        sqlUnbind = 2
        sqlResetParams = 3
    End Enum


    ' shared ODBC handle properties:
    Public hEnv As Long
    Public hDbc As Long
    Public hStmt As Long
    Public NumCols As Integer
    '
    ' local storage for properties
    Private strDataSource As String
    Private strUserID As String
    Private strPassword As String
    Private strSQL As String
    Private intRecordCount As Integer
    Private strTable As String
    Private strKey As String
    Private intCursorDriver As Integer
    Private intLockType As Integer
    Private intResultSetType As Integer

    ' internal use
    Dim intRecNum As Integer
```

Most of the items in Listing 19.3 define shared Public variables or enumerated data types for properties of the new class object. You use these values and storage locations both internally within the new class and from your external programs that call this class.

Now define the various properties by using the Visual Basic Property Let and Property Get statements. Listing 19.4 shows the complete listing of all property routines for this class object.

Listing 19.4. Coding the property routines for the `objODBC` class.

```
Public Property Get DataSource() As Variant
    DataSource = strDataSource
End Property

Public Property Let DataSource(ByVal vNewValue As Variant)
    strDataSource = vNewValue
End Property

Public Property Get UserID() As Variant
    UserID = strUserID
End Property

Public Property Let UserID(ByVal vNewValue As Variant)
    strUserID = vNewValue
End Property

Public Property Get Password() As Variant
    Password = strPassword
End Property

Public Property Let Password(ByVal vNewValue As Variant)
    strPassword = vNewValue
End Property

Public Property Get RecordCount() As Variant
    RecordCount = intRecordCount
End Property

Public Property Let RecordCount(ByVal vNewValue As Variant)
    ' na
End Property

Public Property Get SQL() As Variant
    SQL = strSQL
End Property

Public Property Let SQL(ByVal vNewValue As Variant)
    strSQL = vNewValue
End Property

Public Property Get Table() As Variant
    Table = strTable
End Property

Public Property Let Table(ByVal vNewValue As Variant)
    strTable = vNewValue
End Property

Public Property Get Key() As Variant
    Key = strKey
End Property

Public Property Let Key(ByVal vNewValue As Variant)
    strKey = vNewValue
```

```
End Property

Public Property Get CursorDriver() As sqlCursorDriverType
    CursorDriver = intCursorDriver
End Property

Public Property Let CursorDriver(ByVal vNewValue As sqlCursorDriverType)
    intCursorDriver = vNewValue
End Property

Public Property Get LockType() As sqlLockType
    LockType = intLockType
End Property

Public Property Let LockType(ByVal vNewValue As sqlLockType)
    intLockType = vNewValue
End Property

Public Property Get ResultSetType() As sqlResultSetType
    ResultSetType = intResultSetType
End Property

Public Property Let ResultSetType(ByVal vNewValue As sqlResultSetType)
    intResultSetType = vNewValue
End Property
```

After coding all the property handlers, add the code from Listing 19.5 to the `Class_Initialize` event.

TYPE **Listing 19.5. Coding the `Class_Initialize` event.**

```
Private Sub Class_Initialize()
    '
    ' init props
    '
    strDataSource = ""
    strUserID = ""
    strPassword = ""
    strSQL = ""
    intRecordCount = 0
    intCursorDriver = sqlforwardonly
    intLockType = sqlreadonly
    '
End Sub
```

Save the class modules as `objODBC.cls` before continuing to the next section. Now you're ready for the first set of Visual Basic routines.

Mid-Level Routines

The mid-level routines handle the direct calls to the ODBC API and provide simple error checking. The first of the routines allocates an environment handle. This handle is needed before you can attempt to connect to the ODBC interface.

Create a new function called `AllocateEnv` and add the code in Listing 19.6.

TYPE **Listing 19.6. Coding the `AllocateEnv` function.**

```
Private Function AllocateEnv()
    '
    ' Allocates an ODBC environment handle.
    ' Stores result to hEnv property
    '
    Dim intResult As Integer
    '
    intResult = SQLAllocEnv(hEnv)
    '
    If intResult <> sqlSuccess Then
        Err.Raise vbObjectError + 1, App.EXEName, "Cannot allocate environment
handle"
    End If
    '
    AllocateEnv = sqlSuccess
    '
End Function
```

The routine in Listing 19.6 calls the `SQLAllocEnv` API and checks for any errors. The `SQLAllocEnv` API establishes an environment for all ODBC transactions for this session. The `hEnv` variable that is set here holds a unique number that identifies all transactions that pass from your Visual Basic program to the ODBC interface.

Create a new function called `Connect`, as shown in Listing 19.7. This routine handles the details of completing a connection to the ODBC data source.

TYPE **Listing 19.7. Coding the `Connect` function.**

```
Public Function Connect() As Integer
    '
    ' Allocates and establishes connection
    ' to DataSource stored in DataSource
    ' property.
    '
    Dim intResult As Integer
    '
    AllocateEnv
    '
```

19

```
    ' Allocate connection handle:
    intResult = SQLAllocConnect(hEnv, hDbc)
    If intResult <> sqlSuccess Then
        Err.Raise vbObjectError + 3, App.EXEName, "Unable to allocate connection
handle"
        Connect = intResult
        Exit Function
    End If
    '
    ' Set cursor driver
    intResult = SQLSetConnectOption(hDbc, sqlODBCCursors, intCursorDriver)
    If intResult <> sqlSuccess Then
        sqlErrorMsg "Error Setting CursorDriver"
        Exit Function
    End If
    '
    ' Login to data source
    intResult = SQLConnect(hDbc, strDataSource, Len(strDataSource), strUserID,
Len(strUserID), strPassword, Len(strPassword))
    If intResult <> sqlSuccess And intResult <> sqlSuccessWithInfo Then
        sqlErrorMsg "Unable to connect to DataSource [" & strDataSource & "]"
        Connect = intResult
        Exit Function
    End If
    '
    ' Allocate statement handle.
    intResult = SQLAllocStmt(hDbc, hStmt)
    If intResult <> sqlSuccess Then
        sqlErrorMsg "Unable to allocate statement handle"
        Connect = intResult
        Exit Function
    End If
    '
    ' set cursor type (result set)
    intResult = SQLSetStmtOption(hStmt, sqlCursorType, intResultSetType)
    If intResult <> sqlSuccess Then
        sqlErrorMsg "Error Setting ResultsetType"
        Exit Function
    End If
    '
    ' set locktype
    intResult = SQLSetStmtOption(hStmt, sqlConcurrency, intLockType)
    If intResult <> sqlSuccess Then
        sqlErrorMsg "Error Setting LockType"
        Exit Function
    End If
    '
    Connect = sqlSuccess
    '
End Function
```

19

The routine in Listing 19.7 performs several chores. The first operation establishes a data-source connection handle. Then, after setting the connection type by using the selected CursorDriver, the actual attempt to connect to the data source is performed. The DataSource,

UserID, and Password properties are used for this. Next, the ODBC statement handle is established, and the ResultSetType and LockType properties are used to define the details of the connection. The statement handle is used as the unique identifier whenever you want to share data with the ODBC data source.

You also need to disconnect the ODBC link when you exit the program. Create a new function called Disconnect and add the code in Listing 19.8.

TYPE   **Listing 19.8. Coding the Disconnect method.**

```
Public Function Disconnect()
    '
    ' disconnect from the data source
    '
    Dim intResult As Integer
    '
    ' Deallocate statement handle:
    If hStmt <> 0 Then
        intResult = SQLFreeStmt(hStmt, sqlDrop)
        If intResult <> sqlSuccess Then
            Err.Raise vbObjectError + 6, App.EXEName, "Unable to free statement
handle"
            Disconnect = intResult
        End If
    End If
    '
    ' Disconnect
    If hDbc <> 0 Then
        intResult = SQLDisconnect(hDbc)
        If intResult <> sqlSuccess Then
            Err.Raise vbObjectError + 7, App.EXEName, "Unable to disconnect from
data source"
            Disconnect = intResult
        End If
    End If
    '
    ' Deallocate connection handle
    If hDbc <> 0 Then
        intResult = SQLFreeConnect(hDbc)
        If intResult <> sqlSuccess Then
            Err.Raise vbObjectError + 8, App.EXEName, "Unable to deallocate
connection handle"
            Disconnect = intResult
        End If
    End If
    '
    DeallocateEnv
    '
    Disconnect = sqlSuccess
    '
End Function
```

19

You can see that Listing 19.8 performs the same three functions as ODBCConnect, only this time in reverse. First, it releases the statement handle, and then it performs the actual disconnect of the ODBC interface. Finally, the routine releases the connection handle.

Of course, you need a routine to release the environment handle, too. Create the DeallocateEnv function and enter the code in Listing 19.9.

TYPE | **Listing 19.9. Coding the DeallocateEnv function.**

```
Private Function DeallocateEnv()
    '
    ' Frees specified env. handle
    ' clears stored in hEnv property
    '
    Dim intResult As Integer
    '
    If hEnv <> 0 Then
        intResult = SQLFreeEnv(hEnv)
        If intResult <> sqlSuccess Then
            Err.Raise vbObjectError + 2, App.EXEName, "Unable to free environ-
ment handle"
            DeallocateEnv = intResult
            Exit Function
        End If
    End If
    '
    DeallocateEnv = sqlSuccess
    '
End Function
```

Listing 19.9 is a simple routine. It tells the ODBC interface that you are done with the session and returns any resulting codes.

The last mid-level routine you need is an ODBC error routine. This routine gathers any error information sent to your Visual Basic program from the ODBC data source. ODBC data sources are capable of sending more than one line of error information. For this reason, you write the routine as a loop that continues to ask for error messages until there are none to be found.

Create a new Public Sub called sqlErrorMsg and enter the code in Listing 19.10.

TYPE | **Listing 19.10. Coding the sqlErrorMsg subroutine.**

```
Public Sub sqlErrorMsg(strMsg As String)
    '
    ' report detailed SQL Error
    '
    Dim strSQLState As String * 16
```

19

continues

Listing 19.10. continued

```
        Dim strErrorMsg As String * sqlMaxMsgLen
        Dim intErrorMsgLen As Integer
        Dim intOutLen As Integer
        '
        Dim lngErrCode As Long
        Dim strErrCode As String
        Dim intResult As Integer
        Dim intTemp As Integer
        '
        strSQLState = String(16, 0)
        strErrorMsg = String(sqlMaxMsgLen - 1, 0)
        '
        Do
            intResult = sqlError(hEnv, hDbc, hStmt, strSQLState, lngErrCode,
    strErrorMsg, Len(strErrorMsg), intErrorMsgLen)

        If intResult = sqlSuccess Or intResult = sqlSuccessWithInfo Then
            If intErrorMsgLen = 0 Then
                Err.Raise vbObjectError + 9, App.EXEName, "Success or
    SuccessWithInfo Error"
            Else
                If lngErrCode = 0 Then
                    strErrCode = ""
                Else
                    strErrCode = Trim(CStr(lngErrCode)) & " "
                End If
                Err.Raise vbObjectError + 10, App.EXEName, "<" & strMsg & "> " &
    strErrCode & Left(strErrorMsg, intErrorMsgLen)
            End If
        End If
    Loop Until intResult <> sqlSuccess
        '
End Sub
```

The routine in Listing 19.10 checks the state of the error code and returns any messages it can find. There are times when the error code is set by ODBC, but no message is returned. The routine checks for this and creates its own message, if needed.

Save this class module before you continue with the last set of ODBC library routines.

High-Level Routines

The last set of ODBC library routines deals primarily with the duties required to make Visual Basic capable of displaying, reading, and writing data via the ODBC interface. These routines take the datasets returned by ODBC and store them in Visual Basic list and grid controls. These controls then are used as holding areas by your Visual Basic program for filling and updating textboxes on your data-entry form. This method of storing result sets in a Visual Basic control reduces the amount of traffic over the ODBC link and improves the response time of your program.

In the examples here, you access relatively small datasets. If your ODBC interface requires the passing of very large datasets, you need to develop more sophisticated methods for storing and retrieving the resulting datasets. It is always a good idea to limit the size of the result set as much as possible, though, because passing large amounts of data over the ODBC link can adversely affect not just your Visual Basic program, but all programs that are using the same network.

The first high-level routine you build actually creates a dataset for your Visual Basic program. This routine handles the creation of the dataset by using all the properties that already have been set. This method is called right after the Connect method.

Create a new function called Refresh and add the code in Listing 19.11.

TYPE Listing 19.11. Coding the Refresh function.

```
Public Function Refresh()
    '
    ' collect data from result set
    '
    Dim intResult As Integer
    Dim intCols As Integer
    Dim intRows As Integer
    Dim strBuffer As String * BUFFERLEN
    Dim strItem As String
    Dim strData As String
    Dim lngOutLen As Long
    Dim intLoop As Integer


    '
    ' run the query
    intResult = ExecDirect
    If intResult <> sqlSuccess Then
        Refresh = sqlerr
        Exit Function
    End If
    '
    ' get the column count
    intResult = NumResultCols(intCols)
    If intCols = 0 Then
        Refresh = sqlerr
        Exit Function
    Else
        NumCols = intCols
    End If
    '
    ' set up for collection
    frmSQLData.rtbSQlData = ""
```

continues

Listing 19.11. continued

```
            strBuffer = String(BUFFERLEN, 0)
            intRows = 0
            '
            ' get data
            Do
                intResult = FetchRow() ' get a row
                Select Case intResult
                    Case sqlNoDataFound
                        If intRows > 0 Then
                            Exit Do ' we're done
                        Else
                            Refresh = sqlerr
                            Exit Function
                        End If
                    Case sqlSuccess
                        intRows = intRows + 1
                        strItem = ""
                        For intLoop = 1 To intCols
                            intResult = GetColumn(strBuffer, intLoop)
                            SaveColumn strItem, strBuffer
                        Next ' get another column
                        SaveRow strItem
                    Case Else
                        intResult = SQLFreeStmt(hStmt, sqlClose)
                        Refresh = sqlerr
                        Exit Function
                End Select
            Loop ' get another row
            '
            intRecNum = 0 ' clear record pointer
            intRecordCount = intRows
            Refresh = sqlSuccess
            frmSQLData.Refresh
            '
End Function
```

The routine in Listing 19.11 performs a number of important tasks. First, it calls the internal ExecDirect method. This method executes the actual SQL statement. Then, after returning from the ExecDirect call, the routine gets the number of data columns and clears a utility form that holds a rich text control. This rich text control is used as an internal buffer area for the downloaded dataset. You build that form in just a moment. Finally, a Do loop is established to collect each column of data and save it as a new row. When all rows have been collected, the routine exits.

Now add a single form to your project. Set its Name property to frmSQLData. Add a rich text control to the form and set its Name property to rtbSQLData. Now save the form as frmSQLData. It should look similar to the form shown in Figure 19.9 at this point. You refer to this form again later in the project.

Figure 19.9.

*Adding the
frmSQLData utility
form to the project.*

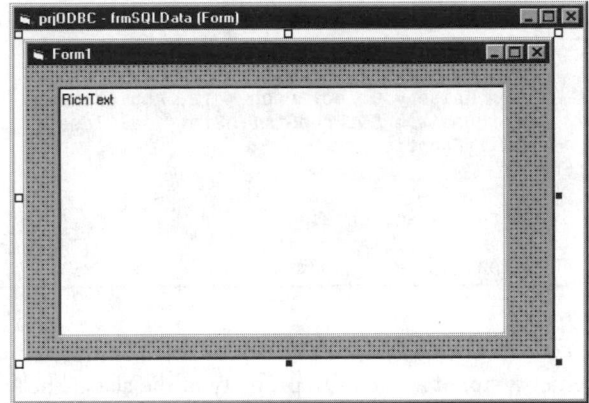

Next, you need to code the ExecDirect method. This is the wrapper method for the
SQLDirectExec API call. Add the code in Listing 19.12 to the class module.

TYPE   **Listing 19.12. Coding the ExecDirect method.**

```
Public Function ExecDirect()
    '
    ' perform an SQL statement
    '
    Dim intResult As Integer
    '
    ' clear any in-process stuff
    If hStmt <> 0 Then
        intResult = SQLFreeStmt(hStmt, sqlClose)
        intResult = SQLFreeStmt(hStmt, sqlUnbind)
        intResult = SQLFreeStmt(hStmt, sqlResetParams)
    End If
    '
    If intResult <> sqlSuccess Then
        ExecDirect = intResult
        Err.Raise vbObjectError + 11, App.EXEName, "Error freeing old statement
handle"
        intResult = SQLFreeStmt(hStmt, sqlClose)
        Exit Function
    End If
    '
    ' Do the query & wait
    intResult = SQLExecDirect(hStmt, SQL, Len(SQL))
    Do While intResult = sqlStillExecuting
        intResult = SQLExecDirect(hStmt, SQL, Len(SQL))
        DoEvents
    Loop
    '
    ' check for errors
    If intResult <> sqlSuccess Then
```

continues

Listing 19.12. continued

```
            ExecDirect = intResult
            Err.Raise vbObjectError + 12, App.EXEName, "Error executing Query"
            intResult = SQLFreeStmt(hStmt, sqlClose)
            Exit Function
    End If
    '
    ExecDirect = sqlSuccess
    '
End Function
```

The code in Listing 19.12 clears any current pending statement and then executes the SQL statements stored in the SQL property of the class. The Refresh method calls a number of other important methods. The first of these is the FetchRow method. This gets a row of data from the ODBC data source. Add the code in Listing 19.13 to your class.

TYPE   **Listing 19.13. Coding the FetchRow method.**

```
Public Function FetchRow()
    '
    ' get a row of data
    '
    Dim intResult As Integer
    '
    intResult = SQLFetch(hStmt)
    If intResult <> sqlSuccess Then
        If intResult <> sqlNoDataFound Then
            Err.Raise vbObjectError + 14, App.EXEName, "Error fetching row"
            FetchRow = intResult
        Else
            FetchRow = intResult
        End If
    Else
        FetchRow = sqlSuccess
    End If
    '
End Function
```

Next, you need to add the GetColumn method. This moves a column of data from the data source to the local memory space. Add the code in Listing 19.14 to the class.

TYPE   **Listing 19.14. Coding the GetColumn method.**

```
Private Function GetColumn(strBuffer As String, intCol As Integer)
    '
    ' get a column from the current row
```

19

```
       '
       Dim intResult As Integer
       Dim lngBufferLen As Long
       '
       intResult = SQLGetData(hStmt, intCol, sqlChar, strBuffer, BUFFERLEN,
   lngBufferLen)
       If intResult <> sqlSuccess Then
           GetColumn = intResult
           Err.Raise vbObjectError + 15, App.EXEName, "Error retrieving column
   data"
           Exit Function
       Else
           If lngBufferLen > 0 Then
               strBuffer = Left(strBuffer, lngBufferLen)
           Else
               strBuffer = ""
           End If
       End If
       '
       GetColumn = sqlSuccess
       '
   End Function
```

Now, add the SaveColumn method in Listing 19.15 to the class.

TYPE   **Listing 19.15. Adding the SaveColumn method to the class.**

```
Private Sub SaveColumn(strRow As String, strColumn As String)
    '
    ' add column to row line
    '
    If Trim(strColumn) <> "" Then
        If Trim(strRow) = "" Then
            strRow = "¦¦" & Trim(strColumn) ' mark first field
        Else
            strRow = strRow & "¦" & (strColumn)
        End If
    Else
        strRow = strRow & "¦"
    End If
    '
End Sub
```

This routine just copies the retrieved column data into a hold variable. The marking values "¦¦" (for a new record) and "¦" (for a new field) are used to retrieve the data from local storage to the caller's data-input form controls later.

Now add the code in Listing 19.16 to the class. This is the SaveRow method. This is the code that copies the complete line of data into the rich textbox control for storage.

19

TYPE   **Listing 19.16. Adding the SaveRow method.**

```
Private Sub SaveRow(strRow As String)
    '
    ' save row to rtb control
    '
    frmSQLData.rtbSQLData.Text = frmSQLData.rtbSQLData.Text & strRow & vbCrLf
    '
End Sub
```

Now that you have loaded the rich textbox control with the data from the data source, you need a routine that moves individual rows from the control to the caller's input controls on the data-entry form. To do this, you need some support routines: the GetSQLRec and GetSQLField methods. Add the code in Listing 19.17 to your class.

TYPE   **Listing 19.17. Coding the GetSQLRec method.**

```
Private Sub GetSQLRec(intLine As Integer, strLine As String, frmTemp As Object)
    '
    ' move a rec from the rtb into array
    '
    Dim intLoop As Integer
    Dim lngPosMark As Long
    Dim lngRecEnd As Long
    Dim intRec As Integer
    Dim strData As String
    '
    strData = frmSQLData.rtbSQLData.Text
    '
    lngPosMark = 1
    For intLoop = 1 To intRecordCount
        lngPosMark = InStr(lngPosMark, strData, "¦¦")
        If lngPosMark <> 0 Then
            intRec = intRec + 1
            If intRec = intLine Then
                Exit For
            End If
            lngPosMark = lngPosMark + 1
        End If
    Next
    '
    If intRec <> 0 Then
        lngRecEnd = InStr(lngPosMark, strData, vbCrLf)
        strLine = Mid(strData, lngPosMark + 2, lngRecEnd - (lngPosMark + 2))
    End If
    '
    ' now get fields
    If strLine <> "" Then
        For intLoop = 1 To NumCols
            frmTemp.sqlfield(intLoop - 1) = GetSQLField((strLine), intLoop)
'frmTemp.sqlfield(intLoop) = GetSQLField(strRecLine, intLoop)
```

```
        Next
    End If

End Sub
```

Note that the code in Listing 19.17 requires a few parameters. The first is the number of the rows requested. The second parameter is the data row returned, and the last is the caller's data form that contains the input controls. Notice that the routine assumes that the controls on the caller's form are called sqlField and are part of a control array. This is a requirement for all forms that call this library.

Next, you need the GetSQLField method. Add this from the code in Listing 19.18.

TYPE **Listing 19.18. Coding the GetSQLField method.**

```
Private Function GetSQLField(strLine As String, intField As Integer)
    '
    ' get a field from the line
    '
    Dim intLoop As Integer
    Dim lngPosMark As Long
    Dim lngPosEnd As Long
    Dim intCol As Integer
    '
    strLine = "¦" & strLine & "¦"
    lngPosMark = 1
    lngPosEnd = 0
    intCol = 0
    '
    For intLoop = 1 To NumCols
        lngPosMark = InStr(lngPosMark, strLine, "¦")
        If lngPosMark <> 0 Then
            intCol = intCol + 1
            If intCol = intField Then
                lngPosEnd = InStr(lngPosMark + 1, strLine, "¦")
                Exit For
            End If
            lngPosMark = lngPosMark + 1
        End If
    Next
    '
    If lngPosEnd <> 0 Then
        GetSQLField = Mid(strLine, lngPosMark + 1, lngPosEnd - (lngPosMark + 1))
    Else
        GetSQLField = ""
    End If
    '
End Function
```

19

The routine in Listing 19.18 asks for the control to read the column number and the character used to delimit the columns in the list control. It takes this information and returns a string that can be used to populate a text control (or any other control) on a data-entry form. You learn how to use this in your data-entry forms in the next section.

Now that you have a method for retrieving a row and each field, you're ready to build the routines that handle moving the record pointer and loading the caller's form. Listing 19.19 shows all the code for the MoveFirst, MoveNext, MovePrevious, and MoveLast methods of the class. Add these methods to your project.

TYPE   **Listing 19.19. Coding the Move methods for the class.**

```
Public Sub MoveFirst(frmTemp As Object)
    '
    ' move items from rtb into form controls
    '
    Dim strRecLine As String
    '
    ' position record pointer
    intRecNum = 1
    '
    GetSQLRec intRecNum, strRecLine, frmTemp
    '
End Sub

Public Sub MoveLast(frmTemp As Object)
    '
    ' move items from rtb into form controls
    '
    Dim strRecLine As String
    '
    ' position record pointer
    intRecNum = intRecordCount
    '
    GetSQLRec intRecNum, strRecLine, frmTemp
    '
End Sub

Public Sub MovePrevious(frmTemp As Object)
    '
    ' move items from rtb into form controls
    '
    Dim strRecLine As String
    '
    ' position record pointer
    If intRecNum > 1 Then
        intRecNum = intRecNum - 1
    Else
        intRecNum = 1
    End If

    GetSQLRec intRecNum, strRecLine, frmTemp
```

```
    '
End Sub

Public Sub MoveNext(frmTemp As Object)

    ' move item from rtb into form controls
    '
    Dim strRecLine As String
    '
    ' position record pointer
    If intRecNum < intRecordCount Then
        intRecNum = intRecNum + 1
    End If
    '
    GetSQLRec intRecNum, strRecLine, frmTemp
    '
End Sub
```

You need only three more library functions before you have a complete ODBC database kit. You need routines that can write an updated existing record, add a new record, and delete an existing record from the dataset. These three routines can be called from your data-entry form and look much like the standard add, edit, and delete operations used with data-bound controls.

First, create the DelRow method and enter the code in Listing 19.20.

TYPE **Listing 19.20. Coding the DelRow method.**

```
Public Sub DelRow(frmTemp As Object)
    '
    ' remove a row from the table
    '
    Dim intResult As Integer
    Dim strSQL As String
    '
    ' make statement
    strSQL = "DELETE * FROM " & strTable & " WHERE "
    strSQL = strSQL & strKey & "='" & frmTemp.sqlfield(0) & "'"
    '
    ' make the call
    intResult = SQLExecDirect(hStmt, strSQL, Len(strSQL))
    If intResult <> sqlSuccess Then
        sqlErrorMsg "Unable to delete row"
        intResult = SQLFreeStmt(hStmt, sqlClose)
    End If
    '
End Sub
```

19

The routine in Listing 19.20 is designed to delete the current record loaded into the text controls on the form, and it requires only a pointer to the form as a parameter. The name of the data table you are updating and name of the key field are pulled from properties already set by the user. For all your ODBC datasets, you are assuming that the first field in the list is the primary key field.

NOTE

Assuming that the primary key field is always the first physical field in the dataset can be a limitation when you're dealing with secondary tables and other non-normalized datasets. For now, however, this assumption handles most of your data-entry needs. As you develop more skill with ODBC routines, you can modify these routines or add others that give you more flexibility in sharing data over ODBC connections.

The routine in Listing 19.20 builds a standard DELETE query using the parameters you supplied to it and then executes the SQL DELETE, returning any error messages that might result.

Now you build the AddRow method. This routine builds a standard APPEND query using the INSERT INTO syntax. Create the new function and add the code in Listing 19.21.

TYPE   **Listing 19.21. Coding the AddRow method.**

```
Public Sub AddRow(frmTemp As Object)
    '
    ' add a new row of data to the table
    '
    Dim intResult As Integer
    Dim strSQL As String
    Dim intLoop As Integer
    '
    strSQL = "INSERT INTO " & strTable & " VALUES("
    '
    For intLoop = 1 To NumCols
        strSQL = strSQL & "'" & frmTemp.sqlfield(intLoop - 1) & "'"
        If intLoop <> NumCols Then
            strSQL = strSQL & ","
        End If
    Next
    strSQL = strSQL & ")"
    '
    ' now make the call
    intResult = SQLExecDirect(hStmt, strSQL, Len(strSQL))
    If intResult <> sqlSuccess Then
        sqlErrorMsg "Unable to add row"
        intResult = SQLFreeStmt(hStmt, sqlClose)
    End If
    '
End Sub
```

19

The last routine in your library performs an update of an existing record. The simplest way to accomplish this is to delete the existing record and replace it with the new updated version. This can be done with two SQL statements: a DELETE query, followed by an INSERT INTO statement. A more sophisticated approach would be to build a series of UPDATE statements that update each field of the row, one at a time. For the example here, you use the DELETE/INSERT method, because it takes less code and is easier to understand.

WARNING

In certain situations, you do not want to perform updates by using the DELETE/INSERT method. If you have defined a delete cascade in a relationship between two tables, performing a DELETE/INSERT on the *one* side of the one-to-many relationship results in the deletion of all the related records on the *many* side of the relationship. In cases where yot might define delete cascades, you should use only the UDPATE method.

Create the UpdateRow method and add the code in Listing 19.22.

TYPE | **Listing 19.22. Coding the UpdateRow method.**

```
Public Sub UpdateRow(frmTemp As Object)
    '
    ' replace an existing row
    '
    Dim intResult As Integer
    Dim strDelSQL As String
    Dim strAddSQL As String
    Dim intLoop As Integer
    '
    strDelSQL = "DELETE * FROM " & strTable & " WHERE "
    strDelSQL = strDelSQL & strKey & "='" & frmTemp.sqlfield(0) & "'"
    '
    strAddSQL = "INSERT INTO " & strTable & " VALUES("
    '
    For intLoop = 1 To NumCols
        strAddSQL = strAddSQL & "'" & frmTemp.sqlfield(intLoop - 1) & "'"
        If intLoop <> NumCols Then
            strAddSQL = strAddSQL & ","
        End If
    Next
    strAddSQL = strAddSQL & ")"
    '
    ' make the calls
    intResult = SQLExecDirect(hStmt, strDelSQL, Len(strDelSQL))
    If intResult <> sqlSuccess Then
        sqlErrorMsg "Unable to delete row"
        intResult = SQLFreeStmt(hStmt, sqlClose)
    End If
```

continues

19

Listing 19.22. continued

```
    '
    intResult = SQLExecDirect(hStmt, strAddSQL, Len(strAddSQL))
    If intResult <> sqlSuccess Then
        sqlErrorMsg "Unable to add row"
        intResult = SQLFreeStmt(hStmt, sqlClose)
    End If
    '
End Sub
```

As you can see, this routine first executes a DELETE query, and then it executes an INSERT statement.

Save the class module. You now have completed the ODBC library routines. The next step is to build a simple data-entry form that uses the ODBC library to open a dataset and pass information to and from the data via the ODBC interface.

Using the ODBC Library to Create a Data-Entry Form

Now that you have your ODBC library, you are ready to build a data-entry form that uses the ODBC interface for database access. For this example, you build a simple data-entry form that has the usual navigation buttons (First, Next, Back, and Last) and the record buttons (Add, Delete, and Update).

You write this form by using the new class library in a way that is almost identical to the way you create a data-entry form using the standard data control. You add controls, set a few properties, and then execute a few methods.

Building the ODBC Test Data-Entry Form

Add a new Standard EXE project to the current project group (the one with the prjODBC project). Use Figure 19.10 and Table 19.1 as a guide for laying out the test form.

Figure 19.10.

Laying out the SQLTest form.

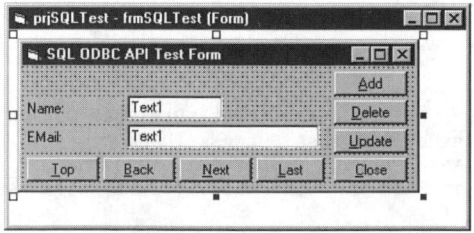

Table 19.1. Controls for the SQLTest form.

Control	Property	Setting
VB.Form	Name	frmSQLTest
	Caption	"SQL ODBC API Test Form"
	ClientHeight	1515
	ClientLeft	60
	ClientTop	345
	ClientWidth	4890
VB.CommandButton	Name	cmdAction
	Caption	"&Close"
	Height	300
	Index	3
	Left	3900
	Top	1140
	Width	900
VB.CommandButton	Name	cmdAction
	Caption	"&Update"
	Height	300
	Index	2
	Left	3900
	Top	780
	Width	900
VB.CommandButton	Name	cmdAction
	Caption	"&Add"
	Height	300
	Index	0
	Left	3900
	Top	60
	Width	900
VB.CommandButton	Name	cmdMove
	Caption	"&Last"
	Height	300
	Index	3

19

continues

Table 19.1. continued

Control	Property	Setting
	Left	2940
	Top	1140
	Width	840
VB.CommandButton	Name	cmdMove
	Caption	"&Next"
	Height	300
	Index	2
	Left	1980
	Top	1140
	Width	900
VB.CommandButton	Name	cmdMove
	Caption	"&Back"
	Height	300
	Index	1
	Left	1020
	Top	1140
	Width	900
VB.CommandButton	Name	cmdMove
	Caption	"&Top"
	Height	300
	Index	0
	Left	60
	Top	1140
	Width	900
VB.TextBox	Name	sqlField
	Height	300
	Index	1
	Left	1320
	Top	720
	Width	2400

Control	Property	Setting
VB.TextBox	Name	sqlField
	Height	300
	Index	0
	Left	1320
	Top	360
	Width	1200
VB.CommandButton	Name	cmdAction
	Caption	"&Delete"
	Height	300
	Index	1
	Left	3900
	Top	420
	Width	900
VB.Label	Name	Label2
	Caption	"EMail:"
	Height	300
	Left	60
	Top	780
	Width	1200
VB.Label	Name	Label1
	Caption	"Name:"
	Height	300
	Left	60
	Top	420
	Width	1200

Save this form as FRMSQLTEST.FRM and the project as PRJSQLTEST.VBP. Now you're ready to add the code to the form.

Coding the ODBC Data-Entry Form

You need to add code in just a few places on the form. First, you need to add two form-level variables, as shown in Listing 19.23. These variables are used throughout the form.

Listing 19.23. Coding the general declaration section of the form.

```
Option Explicit

'
' form-level vars
Dim objSQL As Object
Dim blnAdding As Boolean
```

Next, you need to create a custom routine that sets the new class properties and initializes the data connection. Create a new Public Sub called StartDB and enter the code in Listing 19.24.

TYPE **Listing 19.24. Coding the StartDB routine.**

```
Public Sub StartDB()
    '
    ' handle chores of connecting and getting data
    '

    ' create reference to ODBC object
    Set objSQL = New objODBC
    '
    ' populate properties
    objSQL.DataSource = "ODBC API Test"
    objSQL.UserID = "admin"
    objSQL.Password = ""
    objSQL.SQL = "SELECT * FROM TestTable"
    objSQL.Table = "TestTable"
    objSQL.Key = "Name"
    objSQL.ResultSetType = sqlStatic
    objSQL.CursorDriver = sqlUseODBC
    objSQL.LockType = sqlValues
    '
    ' do real work
    objSQL.Connect ' establish connection
    objSQL.Refresh ' build dataset
    objSQL.MoveFirst Me ' display first row
    '
End Sub
```

Most of the material here should look familiar. After creating a reference to the class and setting several properties, the Connect, Refresh, and MoveFirst methods are executed to fill the form with data.

NOTE

> The values used to initialize the variables are related to the ODBC data source you defined in the "Registering an ODBC Data Source" section of this chapter. If you have not completed the first part of this chapter, you cannot run this program with these variables.

Now add the following lines to the Form_Load event of the form:

```
Private Sub Form_Load()
    '
    ' startup connection
    '
    StartDB
    '
End Sub
```

You need to add the code that handles all the user actions behind the cmdMove command button array. This button array handles the navigation chores (First, Last, Next, and Back). Enter the code in Listing 19.25 into the Click event of the cmdMove button.

Type **Listing 19.25. Coding the `cmdMove_Click` event.**

```
Private Sub cmdMove_Click(Index As Integer)
    '
    ' move record pointer
    '
    Select Case Index
        Case 0 '
            objSQL.MoveFirst Me
        Case 1
            objSQL.MovePrevious Me
        Case 2
            objSQL.MoveNext Me
        Case 3
            objSQL.MoveLast Me
    End Select
    '
End Sub
```

Finally, you need to code the Click event of the cmdAction button. This handles the record-modification chores (Add, Update, Delete, and Refresh). Add the code in Listing 19.26 to the project.

19

TYPE　**Listing 19.26. Coding the cmdAction_Click event.**

```
Private Sub cmdAction_Click(Index As Integer)
    '
    ' handle action selections
    '
    Select Case Index
        Case 0 ' add
            sqlField(0) = ""
            sqlField(1) = ""
            blnAdding = True
        Case 1 ' delete
            If blnAdding = True Then
                blnAdding = False
            End If
            objSQL.DelRow Me
        Case 2 ' udpate
            If blnAdding = True Then
                objSQL.AddRow Me
                blnAdding = False
            Else
                objSQL.UpdateRow Me
            End If
        Case 3 ' close
            objSQL.Disconnect
            Unload Me
    End Select
    '
End Sub
```

NOTE

The code in Listing 19.26 is only the most basic code needed to add, delete, and update a record. If you want to use this form in a production setting, you should add code to confirm deletes and enable users to cancel updates or adds.

Now save the project as PRJTEST.VBP. You now are ready to run the ODBC data-entry form.

Running the ODBC Data-Entry Form

Now that both the library and the form routines are completed, you are ready to run the program. When you first run the program, you see the data-entry form with the first record displayed, as shown in Figure 19.11.

You now can use this screen to walk through the dataset by using the command buttons (First, Last, Next, and Back). You also can add, edit, and delete records in the dataset by using the appropriate buttons.

19

Figure 19.11.
Running the SQLTest project.

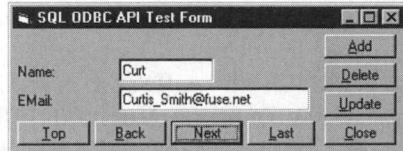

You now have a fully functional data-entry screen for ODBC data sources. You can improve this form by adding other routines that improve the error handling and increase the user friendliness of the form. You even can use this form as a basis for your own ODBC data-entry forms.

Looking at Other ODBC Considerations

Now that you know how to build ODBC data-entry forms, you should keep in mind a few ODBC-related items as you build ODBC-enabled Visual Basic applications:

☐ *ODBC connection usage:* With some RDMBS systems, each connection you make counts as a user connection to the back-end data source. If your client has a 10-user license and your Visual Basic application opens three ODBC datasets, only seven connections are left for the entire network. If you run three versions of the same program at the same time, you are using nine connections. SQL Server is able to use smart caching to eliminate this problem, but some systems do not. It is a good idea to minimize the number of open connections your Visual Basic programs require.

☐ *Install files:* If you are using ODBC to connect to data, you need to include the ODBC setup files with your Visual Basic program setup kit. See the Visual Basic documentation on the Setup Wizard for more information on the required files to include for ODBC-enabled applications.

☐ *.INI and Registry settings:* A number of ODBC-related variables can affect performance. The 16-bit ODBC interface uses ODBC.INI (the list of defined data sources), ODBCINST.INI (the list of installed ODBC drivers available), and ODBCISAM.INI and ODBCDDP.INI (which deal with the ISAM-type interfaces, such as Microsoft Access, Excel, FoxPro, and so on). In 32-bit systems, this information is stored in the system Registry. Although you should not edit these files directly, you should know where these values are stored when you're debugging your ODBC applications.

☐ *Tracing ODBC activity:* You can turn on ODBC trace files from the ODBC Administrator program. This enables you to watch the message activity between your application and the ODBC interface, which can be very informative when you're attempting to locate bugs or performance problems. The Trace log does take up a lot of disk space after a short time, though. You should turn on the trace capability only when you absolutely need it.

☐ *Remote data control alternative:* If your Visual Basic program will be operating only in a 32-bit environment and you have the Enterprise Edition of Visual Basic, you can use the RDC and the RDOs to connect to the ODBC data source. The RDC/RDOs platform is a replacement for the ODBC API you learned today. Although it is easier to deal with the RDC/RDOs platform, you must use the 32-bit version of Visual Basic, and your program must run on a 32-bit operating system. If your program must run on a 16-bit operating system, you still can use the ODBC API and the examples from this chapter.

Summary

Today you learned how to use the ODBC API set to directly link your Visual Basic program to target data sources via the ODBC interface. The ODBC interface generally is faster than Microsoft Jet when it comes to linking to ODBC-defined data sources.

You also looked at installing the ODBC interface on your workstation and using the ODBC Administrator program to install ODBC driver sets and to define data sources for ODBC connections.

You learned how to build a program library that uses a minimum set of ODBC API calls along with several Visual Basic wrapper routines. This library set provides the basic functions necessary to read and write data to and from a defined ODBC data source. You can use these routines to create fully functional data-entry forms for ODBC data sources.

Finally, you used the library routines to build a data-entry form that opens a link to a defined ODBC data source and enables users to read and write data records for the ODBC data source.

Quiz

1. What do the letters *ODBC* stand for?
2. Why is the ODBC API interface faster than the Microsoft Jet interface when connecting to defined ODBC data sources?
3. What are some of the drawbacks to using the ODBC API to link to databases?
4. What program do you use to define an ODBC data source for the workstation?
5. Can you use the ODBC interface to connect to nondatabase files, such as spreadsheets or text files?

6. When you write ODBC-enabled Visual Basic applications, can you use the same set of API declarations for the 16-bit version of Visual Basic 5 that you use for the 32-bit version of Visual Basic 5?

7. What are the four preliminary steps you must complete before you can pass an SQL SELECT statement to the newly opened ODBC data source?

Exercises

Suppose that you have been given the assignment of creating a remote data-entry form for reviewing and updating data in a centrally located data file. The data currently is stored in a Microsoft Access database on the central file server, but it might soon be converted to an SQL Server database in another location.

You cannot always know the actual columns that exist in the data table, because the layout of the table changes based on information entered each month. The form should be flexible enough to determine the columns available and present those columns to the user for data entry. The program also should be flexible enough to allow for minimum disruption of the file even when the database is converted from Microsoft Access to SQL Server database format.

Your first task is to define an ODBC data source at your workstation that has the Microsoft Access data file C:\TYSDBVB\CHAP19\EXER19.MDB as its data source name. You want to access the Transactions table that exists in the EXER19.MDB database. The key field of the Transactions table is called OrderNbr.

Then, modify the TYSODBC.VBP project to open this data source and enable users to review and update data in the spreadsheet.

19

Day 20

Database Replication

In the 1970s, the mainframe computer was the main instrument used in the delivery of data to the enterprise. Databases were centralized, and clients were merely dumb terminals. This paradigm, however, met its partial demise because it was expensive and unfriendly to the user.

In the 1980s, the local area network (LAN) came into being, and data was distributed among groups of users tied into a common network. This reduced development costs for some, but fragmented the data into smaller databases. Organizational data was spread out over multiple locations, which meant much data entry effort was duplicated and groups did not communicate efficiently.

The 1990s has brought the need for organizations to communicate on a much larger scale. Wide area networks (WANs) provide a means for communicating among individuals. The speed and reliability of WANs, however, are not generally fast enough to allow for constant connection to databases located in other cities or countries. It is necessary to have databases located locally that communicate with one another.

The 90s have also brought about the widespread use of laptop PCs. More and more workers are performing their daily chores off-line. These individuals want access to data contained on WANs, but are unable to attach economically from cars, airplanes, hotels, and client offices.

The purpose of this chapter is to show you how to facilitate the environment in which we now work on a daily basis. You learn about creating databases that can be copied to other sites. You then learn how to coordinate the changes made to these databases among users at different sites. You learn about *database replication*.

What Is Database Replication?

When we refer to database replication, we are talking about the act of creating copies of a database and coordinating the changes made to the data among all copies. The original database is referred to as the *Design Master*. Each copy of the database is referred to as a *replica*. The combination of the Design Master and all the replicas of the Design Master is referred to as the *replica set*. The act of creating the components of the replica set, and keeping the data contained in it synchronized, is referred to as *database replication*.

By performing database replication, you permit users to work on the data that is most convenient for them to use. This is important in large organizations with offices in multiple sites, or among organizations with a significant population of remote or mobile users.

The Microsoft Jet engine allows for several ways to perform database replication. This includes the use of the Windows 95 Briefcase and the Microsoft Access Replication Manager, and through programming using Data Access Objects (DAO). The lesson today focuses on the use of DAO to perform replication.

Why Use Database Replication?

There are numerous reasons why you may want to consider using database replication in your Visual Basic 5 database application. If you work in a large organization, you may need to deploy your application over a wide area network environment. This typically requires you to keep the main copy of the database, the Design Master, at the central office, and create replica sets across all the other offices.

You may also need to build an application for use by remote users. An example of this might be a customer contact management system for your sales staff. Each salesperson could have a replica of the Design Master to review and update while visiting clients. All the salespeople could then update all the changes they make to the Design Master. In turn, each salesperson could receive all changes made by all other members of the sales force to the Design Master. This is referred to as *synchronizing* the data.

20

Generally, to back up a database, the data files must be closed to all users. This is sometimes not practical, however, or even possible. Database replication can be used in this situation to make a replica of the original database, without having to close any files or hinder user access to the data contained in the database.

You might also want to use database replication to create a static database for reporting. In many applications, such as financial applications, data changes constantly. Mass confusion reigns if users create reports that differ each time they are generated. By using replication, you can create an unchanging copy of the data to a separate database that users can then use for reporting and analysis.

When Is Database Replication Not a Good Idea?

Though database replication can be an invaluable tool, there are scenarios where it should not be deployed. For example, you may not want to deploy replication when you are delivering data in an intranet environment. Before deploying a typical Visual Basic 5 database application in a large organization (for example, an application with a front-end located on a user workstation and the data on a separate server), you may want to test the performance of a database application that uses a Web browser as the front end. This can greatly reduce the maintenance required for the application and the deployment time to individuals.

You do not want to use replication in applications that are heavily transaction-oriented. For example, an airline would not want to use replication for a reservation system. It makes little sense for users to work with a copy of a database that is unreliable, and therefore unusable, the second after the data is replicated. (Many cynical travelers believe, however, that airlines *do* use two reservation systems—one for passengers and one for baggage.)

You also do not want to use replication in a system where data accuracy is extremely important, such as emergency response systems. In databases used by law enforcement or fire departments, for example, you might not be able to replicate data fast enough to be of value to the user. If, for example, a bank is robbed in Columbus, Ohio, and the criminal is fleeing towards Cincinnati, you may not have the time to perform the replication so that the police force in Cincinnati has a description of the criminals. Additionally, the mode of data transfer used in the synchronization may not be operating due to circumstances beyond your control.

Making a Database Replicable

The focus of this exercise is to turn an existing database into a Design Master. We use the REPLMAST.MDB database that shipped on the CD that came with this text as our original

20

database. Please locate this database in the \\TYSDBVB5\SOURCE\DATA directory now and place it into the directory you want to use for this project.

Before we begin, let's open the REPLMAST.MDB file using the Visual Data Manager (Visdata). This can be done by selecting Add Ins | Visual Data Manager from the Visual Basic 5 menu. When Visdata loads, select File | Open Database | Microsoft Access and locate REPLMAST.MDB. Your screen should resemble Figure 20.1.

Figure 20.1.

The REPLMAST.MDB *database before it becomes a Design Master.*

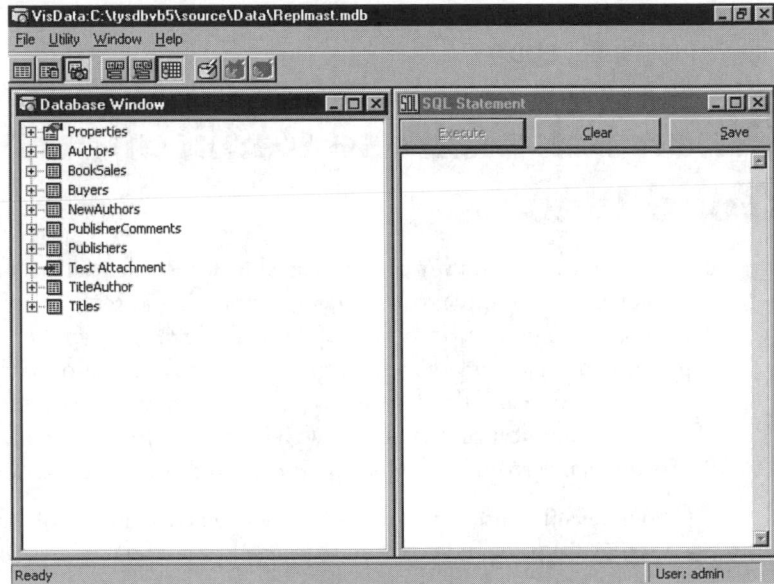

Note that there are nine tables in this database. You may also recognize this as a copy of the BOOKS5.MDB database that we used in previous lessons.

Now select Utility | Preferences | Include System Tables. This displays all of the system tables for this database in the Database window. Your screen should look like Figure 20.2.

Select the Authors table and open the Fields property. Notice that there are five fields defined for this table. Open the same property for the BookSales table. Use Figure 20.3 as a reference.

Finally, open the Properties object in the Database window. Take a look at the properties that currently exist for this database. Your screen should look similar to Figure 20.4.

The purpose of this quick exercise was to show you what tables and fields exist within the database. You now create a Visual Basic project that turns the REPLMAST.MDB database into a Design Master. After that, you return to Visdata and view the changes made to this database as a result of becoming a Design Master.

20

Figure 20.2.

The REPLMAST.MDB *database and system tables.*

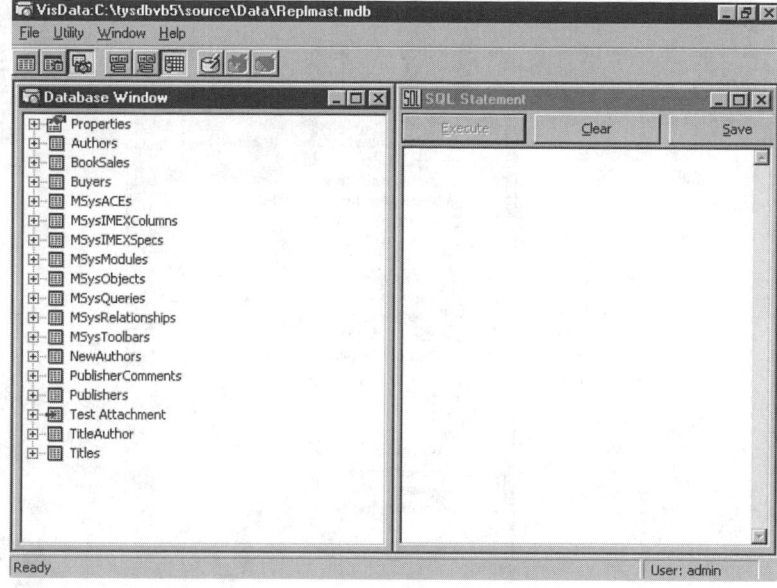

Figure 20.3.

The fields of the Authors and BookSales tables.

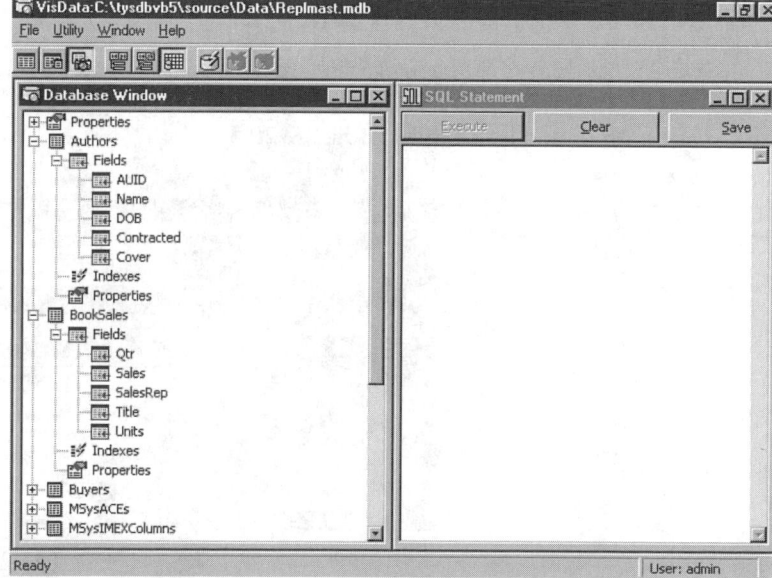

20

Figure 20.4.

Database properties before the Design Master is created.

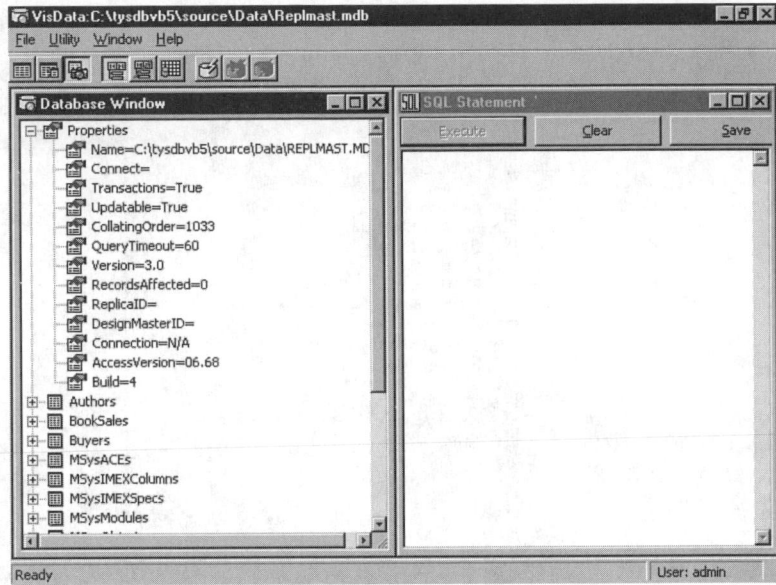

Creating the Design Master

Start Visual Basic 5 and begin a Standard EXE project. Add a command button to a form. Set its name property to cmdCreateMaster and its Caption property to &Create Master. Your form should look similar to Figure 20.5.

Figure 20.5.

The main form of REPLDEMO.VBP.

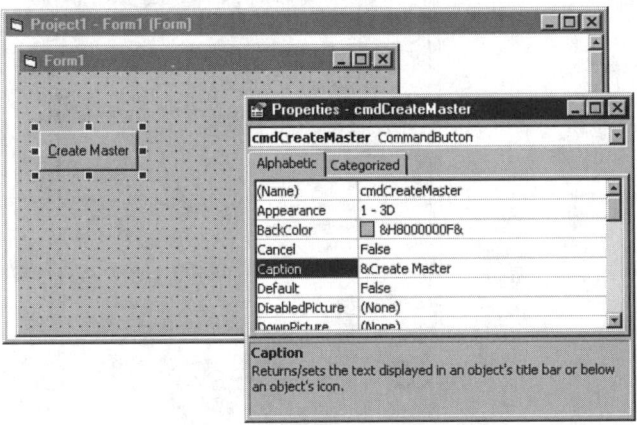

Save the form as REPLDEMO.FRM and the project as REPLDEMO.VBP.

NOTE

Make sure that you have set the Microsoft DAO 3.5 object library before performing the exercises in this chapter. This can be done by selecting Project from the main menu, then choosing Preferences. Find the option for the object library in the dialog that appears and then press OK.

Now, double-click the command button and enter the code from Listing 20.1 in its Click event.

TYPE **Listing 20.1. Visual Basic code for the Create Master command button.**

```
Private Sub cmdCreateMaster_Click()

    Dim dbMaster As Database
    Dim repProperty As Property

    'Open the database in exclusive mode
    Set dbMaster = OpenDatabase("c:\tysdbvb5\source\data\replmast.mdb", True)

    'Create and set the replicable property
    Set repProperty = dbMaster.CreateProperty("Replicable", dbText, "T")
    dbMaster.Properties.Append repProperty
    dbMaster.Properties("Replicable") = "T"

    'Display a message box
    MsgBox "You have created a Design Master!"

End Sub
```

This code opens the REPLMAST.MDB exclusively, creates the Replicable property and appends it to the database, and then sets the Replicable property to T. Please note that you must first create this property because it does not exist in a standard database.

NOTE

Always make a backup copy of your database before converting it into a Design Master. Once the Design Master is created and data changes are made, destroy the copy. Later today you will see that making and using backup copies of the Design Master is dangerous business.

Add a second command button and name it cmdExit, and use E&xit as the caption. Enter the code from Listing 20.2 into the Click event of this project.

20

Listing 20.2. The `cmdExit_Click` event.

```
Private Sub cmdExit_Click()

    Unload Me

End Sub
```

Run the project and click the Create Master button. You should see a message box when the Design Master is created. See Figure 20.6.

Figure 20.6.

Confirmation that the Design Master has been created.

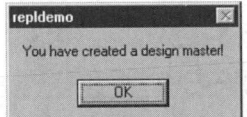

You have created the Design Master. You did not create a new file; rather, you modified the existing file. Don't try to perform this operation on this same file a second time. A file can be made a Design Master only once.

Select the Exit button to close the project.

What Happens to a Database When You Make It Replicable?

The simple routine you wrote and executed in the preceding example made quite a few changes to the REPLMASTER.MDB database. This section explores these changes in detail.

Fields Added to a Replicated Database

Open the Visual Data Manager (Visdata) and load the REPLMAST.MDB database. Open the BookSales table and then expand the fields. Your screen should look like Figure 20.7. Compare Figure 20.7 and Figure 20.3 to find the fields that were added.

The following three fields are added to each table when the Design Master is created:

- ☐ s_Generation
- ☐ s_GUID
- ☐ s_Lineage

Figure 20.7.
*Fields added when
the Design Master
is created.*

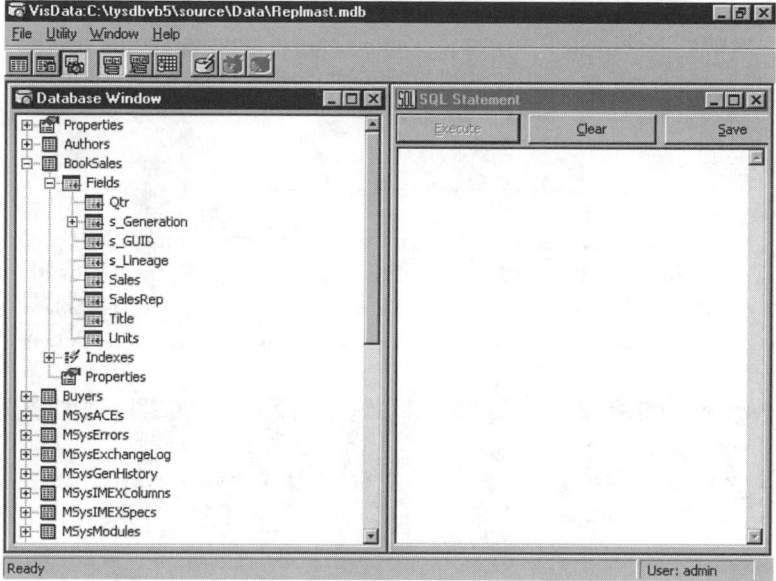

Figure 20.7.
Fields added when the Design Master is created.

The s_Generation field identifies records that have been changed. All records start out with a number 1 in this field. This number changes to 0 when the record is modified in any way. During synchronization between members of the replica set (discussed later in this chapter) only the records with a 0 in this field are transferred. This speeds the synchronization process by requiring the transmission of only the records that were actually changed.

The s_GUID field is a 16-bit GUID field that serves as a unique identifier for each record. This number remains the same for each record across all members of the replica set.

The s_Lineage field contains the name of the last replica member to update a record. This field is not readable by the users of the database.

We discuss these fields as we make changes to the database.

System Tables Added to a Replicated Database

With the REPLMAST.MDB database still open, let's take a look at the system tables that now exist. For comparison, refer back to Figure 20.2 to see a listing of the tables that existed before the creation of the Design Master.

As you can see, many new tables have been added to the REPLMAST.MDB database. The purpose of these tables is to keep track of synchronization activities to ensure that members of the replica set are updated properly. For a complete description of the tables added, look at Visual Basic Books Online and search using the phrase "Replication System Tables." Then choose the "Changes to Your Database" topic.

 **NOTE**

> You cannot change the information contained in most of the system tables that are added when a Design Master is created. The Microsoft Jet engine makes most necessary changes during the synchronization process.

At this point, let's just explore the MSysReplicas table by opening it. This table contains information on each member of the replica set. At this point, there is only one member in this set (see Figure 20.8). In the exercise on creating replicas later in this chapter, this table gains a record for each replica of the Design Master that is created.

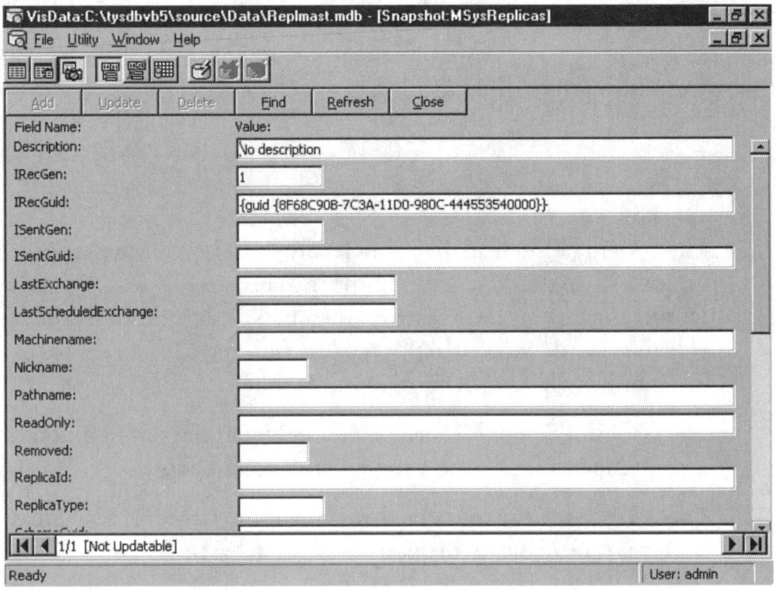

Figure 20.8.

The MSysReplicas table when the Design Master is first created.

VisData:C:\tysdbvb5\source\Data\Replmast.mdb - [Snapshot:MSysReplicas]

```
File   Utility   Window   Help
```

Add	Update	Delete	Find	Refresh	Close

Field Name:	Value:
Description:	No description
IRecGen:	1
IRecGuid:	{guid {8F68C90B-7C3A-11D0-980C-444553540000}}
ISentGen:	
ISentGuid:	
LastExchange:	
LastScheduledExchange:	
Machinename:	
Nickname:	
Pathname:	
ReadOnly:	
Removed:	
ReplicaId:	
ReplicaType:	

1/1 [Not Updatable]

Ready   User: admin

Properties Added to the Replicated Database

The creation of the Design Master added properties to the database. Open the Properties object in the Database window. Your screen should look similar to Figure 20.9.

Notice that a property named Replicable now exists and has a value of T. This means that replicas can now be made of this database.

Also note that a property called ReplicaID was added. As you might expect, this is the unique identifier for this database. Each replica receives its own ReplicaID as it is created.

20

Figure 20.9.

Database Properties after the Design Master is created.

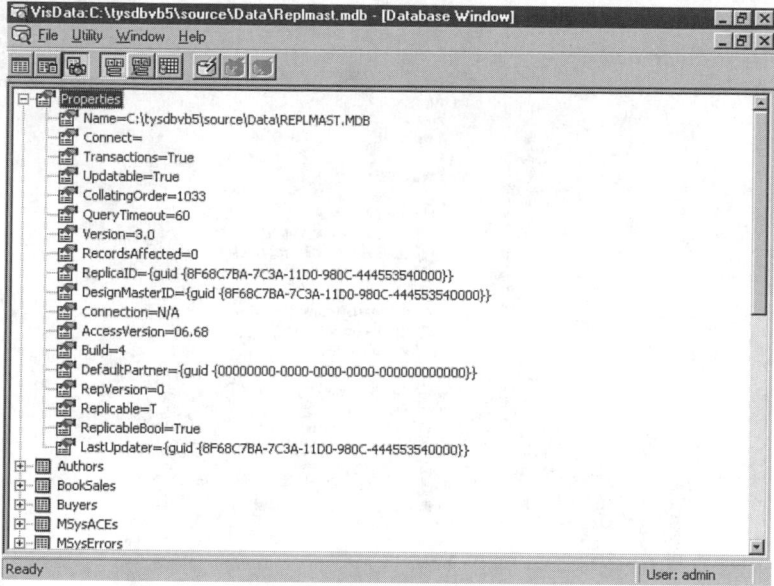

A property called DesignMasterID was also created. This property identifies the Design Master of the replica set. Notice that the DesignMasterID and the ReplicaID for this database are the same.

For Microsoft Jet version 3.5, the ReplicableBool property is new. This property performs the same function as the Replicable property, but uses a Boolean data type where the Replicable property uses a TEXT data type. Note, that the value of the property is set to True.

The final property added to the database was LastUpdated. This field stores the ID of the last member of the replica set to update the database.

Properties Added to a Replicated Table

Open the table properties for any table in the REPLMAST.MDB database. Notice that fields were added to each table during the creation of the Design Master. See Figure 20.10.

The Replicable and ReplicableBool properties serve the same function for the table as for database properties. When these values are set to T, it indicates that the table can be replicated.

20

Figure 20.10.

*Table properties after
the Design Master is
created.*

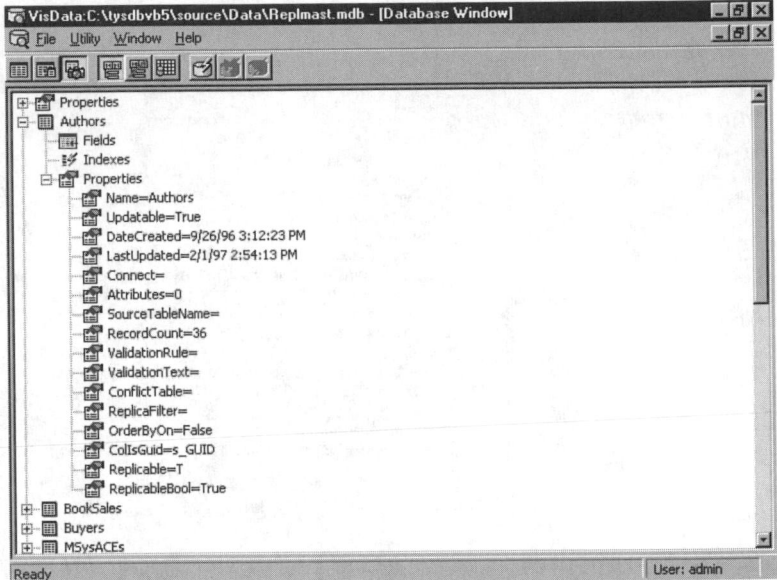

Physical Size Changes Made to a Database When It Becomes Replicable

If you're thinking that the addition of these tables, fields, and properties to the Design Master will increase the size of your database, you're correct. Approximately 28 bytes are added to each record contained to allow for the replication feature. This is not much in itself, but when you consider all the tables in a typical application, and all the records in each table, it can add up to something significant.

Let's perform some mathematical calculations. Say that you have a database with five tables—a main table and four validation tables. Let's say there are 100,000 records in the main table, and 1,000 records in each of the four validation tables. Adding replication functionality adds 2,912,000 bytes ([100,000 + 4,000] × 28) to the total size of each member of your replica set. As you can see, the numbers can add up quickly!

In addition to the increase for each record, replication adds many new tables, each of which takes up hard drive space. The space requirements of these tables vary dramatically depending on the frequency of synchronization, the number of members in the replica set, and the number of conflicts and errors encountered during the synchronization process.

In addition to the physical hard drive space you consume, remember that you are using up fields in each table to track replication information. The Microsoft Jet engine allows for 255 fields in a table, including the replication fields. Although it is extremely rare to have tables with 255 fields, it is possible.

20

NOTE

If you have a table in your database that is approaching 255 fields in size, you should probably be more concerned about database normalization than you are with the number of fields consumed by replication. Please refer to Chapter 16, "Database Normalization," for a complete discussion of database normalization issues.

The Effect of Database Replication on AutoNumber Fields

A typical AutoNumber field is incremented by 1 each time a record is added. When a database is made replicable, these fields become random numbers. Let's look at a quick example.

Open the database AUTONUMB.MDB found in the \\TYSDBVB5\SOURCE\DATA directory on the CD that shipped with this book. Now open the tblSupervisors table as a Dynaset. Your screen should look similar to Figure 20.11.

Figure 20.11.

The AUTONUMB.MDB *file before it becomes replicable.*

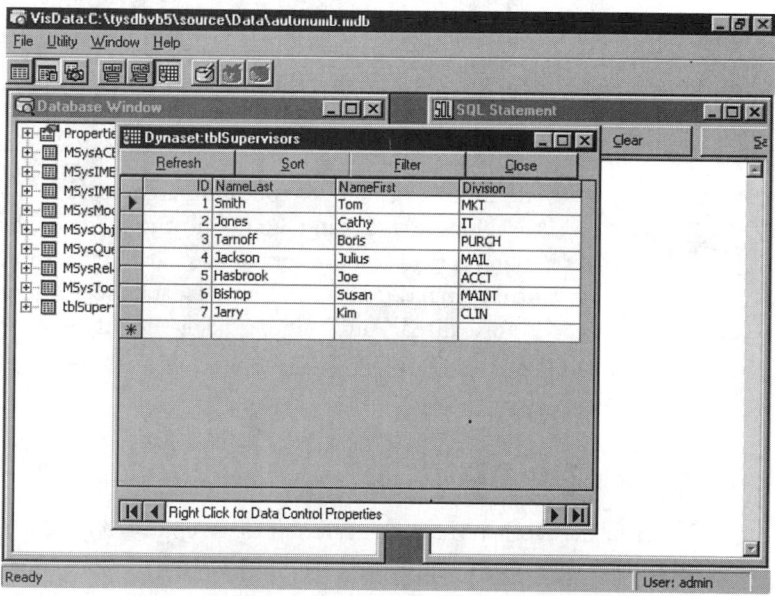

Insert a new record and watch how the ID field increments by 1. Now you can return to the Visual Basic 5 project REPLDEMO.VBP and modify the cmdCreateMaster Click event by substituting AUTONUMB.MDB for REPLMAST.MDB. Run the project and make the AUTONUMB.MDB database replicable.

Now open the database AUTONUMB.MDB in Visdata. Open the tblSupervisors table and notice what happens to the AutoNumber field when you add a new record. A random number has been inserted in the AutoNumber field. (See Figure 20.12.)

Figure 20.12.

The AutoNumber field becomes random after the Design Master is created.

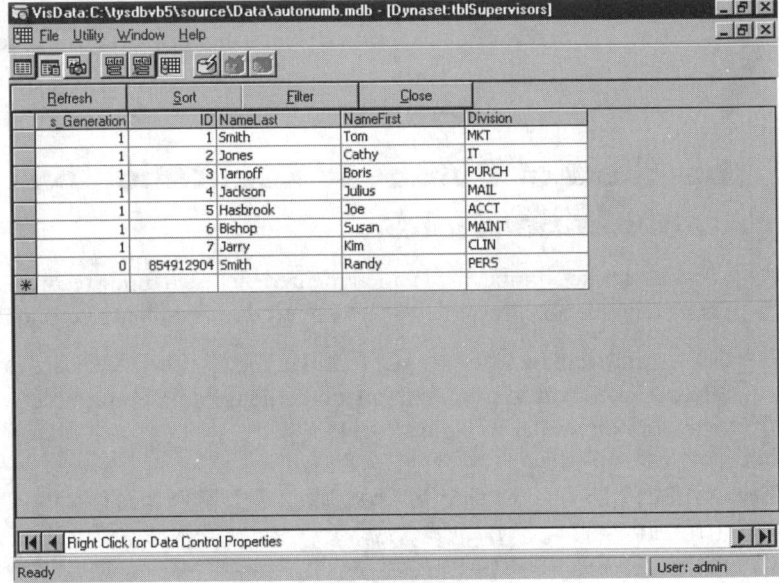

NOTE  The effects of database replication are not the only reason not to use AutoNumber fields in your application. The use of an AutoNumber, or Counter, field as a primary key in a data table should raise a red flag for the developer, indicating that the database is not properly constructed or normalized. AutoNumber fields should be used sparingly, if at all.

Creating Replicas

Copies of the Design Master are referred to as replicas. We now modify the REPLDEMO.VBP project to create a copy of the REPLMAST.MDB file.

If you need to, start Visual Basic 5 and load the REPLDEMO.VBP project. Add another command button to your form and name it cmdMakeReplica; insert the caption &Make Replica.

Next, insert the code from Listing 20.3 into the cmdMakeReplica_Click event.

TYPE **Listing 20.3. The Visual Basic code to make a replica.**

```
Private Sub cmdMakeReplica_Click()
    Dim dbMaster As Database

    'Open the database in exclusive mode
    Set dbMaster = OpenDatabase("c:\tysdbvb5\source\data\replmast.mdb", True)

    dbMaster.MakeReplica "c:\tysdbvb5\source\data\copy.mdb", "Replica of " &
"dbMaster"

    dbMaster.Close

    MsgBox "You have created a copy of your database"

End Sub
```

This code first opens the database REPLMAST.MDB (our Design Master), and then uses the MakeReplica method to create a new member of the replica set named COPY.MDB.

NOTE　　Create the COPY.MDB file only once. Trying to create another replica named COPY.MDB causes the program to fail.

NOTE　　Always make a backup copy of a database before you create a replica. This should be done whether you are creating a copy of the Design Master, or another replica.

Save your project and execute it. Select the Make Replica button to create the new database.

NOTE　　You can't depend on the traditional backup and restore methodology to safeguard a Design Master. Changes occur to the Design Master during the synchronization process. Restoring a backup from a tape drive might insert a database that is out of synch, and that might not be able to perform synchronization with other members of the replica set. It is a far better practice to use replication to create a backup copy that can be made the Design Master in case the original is corrupted.

20

Select Exit when COPY.MDB is created. Open your new replica in Visdata. Explore the properties of the new replica. Notice that you have all of the same tables.

Now open the MSysReplicas table. When we first looked at this table in the Design Master, there was only one entry. Now there are two. Also note that the Description field for the new record is the same description you added in the MakeReplica method you executed earlier. (See Figure 12.13.)

Figure 20.13.

The MSysReplicas table after creation of a replica.

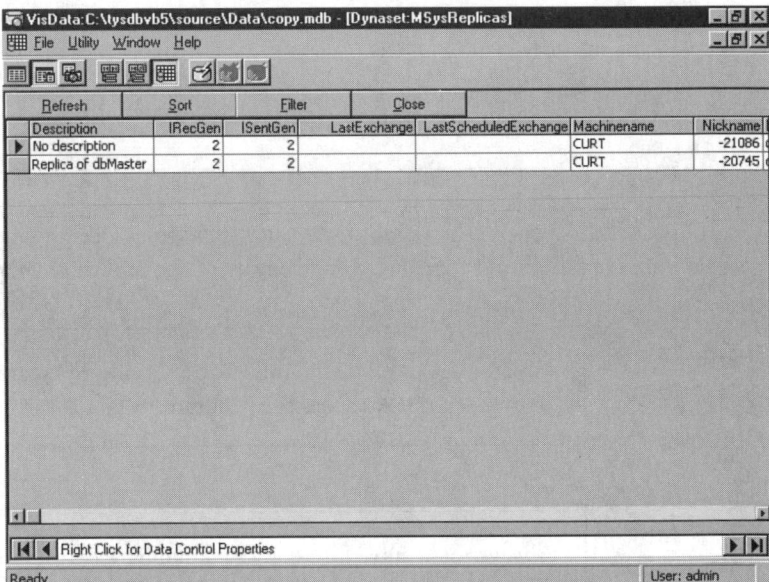

As you can see, it is quite easy to make a replica. A replica can be made out of any member of the replica set. For example, you could now create a third member of the set from either REPLMAST.MDB or COPY.MDB.

Synchronizing Members of a Replica Set

The act of making data in all members of the replica set identical is referred to as *synchronizing* data. In this exercise we make data changes to the Design Master and the replica you created in the previous exercise, and then perform a synchronization to apply the data changes to the other member of the replica set.

Open COPY.MDB in Visdata. Next, open the Authors table. Add a few records to this table (make them up). Take note of how the s_Generation field resets to zero when you add a record. The zero tells the Jet engine that the record is ready to be copied during the next synchronization.

20

Also make a change to any existing record in this table. Notice how the 1 in the s_Generation field also changes to zero. Again, this record is marked to be synchronized. Your screen should look similar to Figure 20.14.

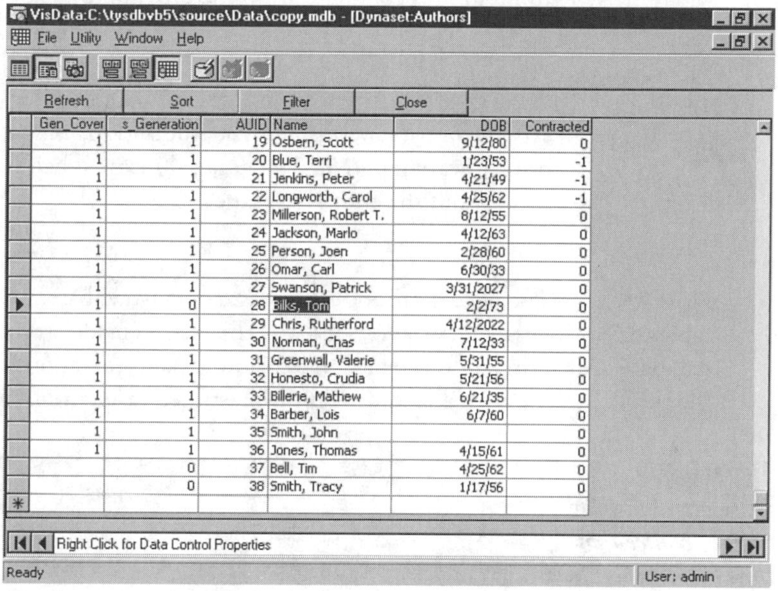

Figure 20.14.

Changes to records cause the s_Generation field to be set to 0.

Open the REPLMAST.MDB database in Visdata, and open the BookSales table. Make a change to the first record. When we perform the synchronization, notice how changes get updated in both members of the replica set.

Now close Visdata and open the REPLDEMO.VBP project in Visual Basic 5. Add one more command button to the form. Name this button cmdSynch, and set its caption to &Synchronize. Enter the code from Listing 20.4 into the cmdSynch_Click event.

TYPE

Listing 20.4. Code to perform a bidirectional synchronization.

```
Private Sub cmdSynch_Click()
    Dim dbMaster As Database

    'Open the database
    Set dbMaster = OpenDatabase("c:\tysdbvb5\source\data\replmast.mdb")

    dbMaster.Synchronize "c:\tysdbvb5\source\data\copy.mdb"

    MsgBox "The synchronization is complete."

End Sub
```

20

This code uses the `Synchronize` method to copy changes from `REPLMAST.MDB` to `COPY.MDB`, and vice versa.

Run the project and click the Synchronize button. You receive a dialog box notifying you when the synchronization is complete. Stop the program by selecting Exit.

NOTE

> It is a good practice to compact your database (repair it first, if necessary) before you perform a synchronization. This ensures that you are not replicating potentially damaged records that might propagate throughout the entire replica set.

Now open Visdata once more and load the `COPY.MDB` database. Look first at the BookSales table and notice that it now reflects the data change you made previously in the `REPLMAST.MDB` database. Open the Authors table. Notice how the s_Generation field has been updated for the new and the changed records. This is illustrated in Figure 20.15.

Figure 20.15.

Data after synchronization. Notice that the s_Generation field has a new value.

Gen_Cover	s_Generation	AUID	Name	DOB	Contracted
1	1	19	Osbern, Scott	9/12/80	0
1	1	20	Blue, Terri	1/23/53	-1
1	1	21	Jenkins, Peter	4/21/49	-1
1	1	22	Longworth, Carol	4/25/62	-1
1	1	23	Millerson, Robert T.	8/12/55	0
1	1	24	Jackson, Marlo	4/12/63	0
1	1	25	Person, Joen	2/28/60	0
1	1	26	Omar, Carl	6/30/33	0
1	4	27	Swanson, Patrick	3/31/80	0
1	4	28	Bilks, Tom	2/2/73	0
1	1	29	Chris, Rutherford	4/12/2022	0
1	1	30	Norman, Chas	7/12/33	0
1	1	31	Greenwall, Valerie	5/31/55	0
1	1	32	Honesto, Crudia	5/21/56	0
1	1	33	Billerie, Mathew	6/21/35	0
1	1	34	Barber, Lois	6/7/60	0
1	1	35	Smith, John		0
1	1	36	Jones, Thomas	4/15/61	0
	4	37	Bell, Tim	4/25/62	0
	4	38	Smith, Tracy	1/17/56	0

The s_Generation field is incremented by 1 each time a record is changed and a synchronization is performed. The replica keeps track of the last record sent to a particular member of the replica set, and only sends records with record numbers that are greater than the last record sent, and of course, all records with an s_Generation value of zero.

Open the REPLMAST.MDB file and its BookSales table. Notice that the s_Generation field was updated on the record that was changed.

The Synchronize Method

In the preceding example, we used the Synchronize method to perform a bidirectional synchronization of data. This two-way synchronization is the default implementation of this method. The Synchronize method can also be used to import information from another database, export changes to another database, and even synchronize with databases over the Internet.

The structure of the Synchronize statement is

```
Database.Synchronize pathname, exchange
```

where pathname is a string value naming the destination of the replication, and exchange is one of dbRepExportChanges, dbRepImportChanges, dbRepImpExpChanges, or dbRepSyncInternet.

Use the dbRepExportChanges to send changes to another database without receiving updates from that database. Use dbRepImportChanges to bring in changes from another replica set member without sending out any changes. If you enter no exchange value, or use dbRepImpExpChanges, data flows both ways during a synchronization. Finally, use dbRepSyncInternet to perform a synchronization over the Internet.

NOTE
You need the Microsoft Office 97 Developer Edition if you want to perform data synchronization over the Internet.

NOTE
Be aware that the .MDB format is used by the Microsoft Jet database engine. The Microsoft Jet engine is used by both Visual Basic and Microsoft Access. It is common practice by Access developers to store data, forms, reports, and queries in the same .MDB file. When you synchronize, changes to forms or reports contained within the database are also synchronized.

20

Resolving Synchronization Conflicts

Data conflicts are quite common among members of a replica set. They can occur when the same record gets changed in different replicas in between synchronizations. This means that two different users might see two different values for the record. How does the Microsoft Jet engine know which value should be used? Better yet, how does it know which value to use and distribute throughout the entire replica set?

The logic that the Microsoft Jet engine uses to resolve synchronization conflicts is simple and consistent. The replica set member that changes the record the greatest number of times wins the conflict. If this number is equal for all the replica members being synchronized, the Microsoft Jet engine selects the record from the table with the lowest ReplicaID.

As you remember, the s_Lineage field stores the number of changes to a record. This is the field that the Microsoft Jet engine examines to determine which replica set member wins the conflict.

Load COPY.MDB into Visdata and open the Authors table. Change the first record by changing the name of the Author in the first record from "Smith, John" to "Smith, Copy." Now open the REPLMAST.MDB database in Visdata, load the Authors table, and change the Name field of the first record to "Smith, Curtis." Now save the record and close the table. Reopen the table and change the DOB (Date of Birth) field to 9/2/64. Save the record and close the table.

You have now changed the first record of the Authors table of COPY.MDB database once, and the same record in the REPLMAST.MDB database twice. In a synchronization, which change do you think prevails?

To find out, close Visdata and load the REPLDEMO.VBP project. Run the project and click the Synchronize button. When you are informed that the synchronization is complete, close the project by pressing Exit.

Return to Visdata and load COPY.MDB. Open the Authors table and notice that the first record is updated based upon the values that were entered into the REPLMAST.MDB database. That is to say, the Microsoft Jet engine knows that this record changed more times in the REPLMAST.MDB files than in COPY.MDB, and therefore chooses that record as the one to use in the synchronization.

But what happened to the change made in the COPY.MDB file? To find out, close the Authors table, and you notice that a new table was added to this database during the synchronization process, the Authors_Conflict table. Open this table and you find a record with the single change. Your screen should look similar to Figure 20.16.

Open the REPLMAST.MDB database in Visdata. Notice in the Database window that the Authors_Conflict table does not exist. The error table created by a synchronization conflict is stored only in the table that lost the conflict. Open the Authors table, and you should see that both changes made to the first record were preserved.

Figure 20.16.

The Authors_Conflict table.

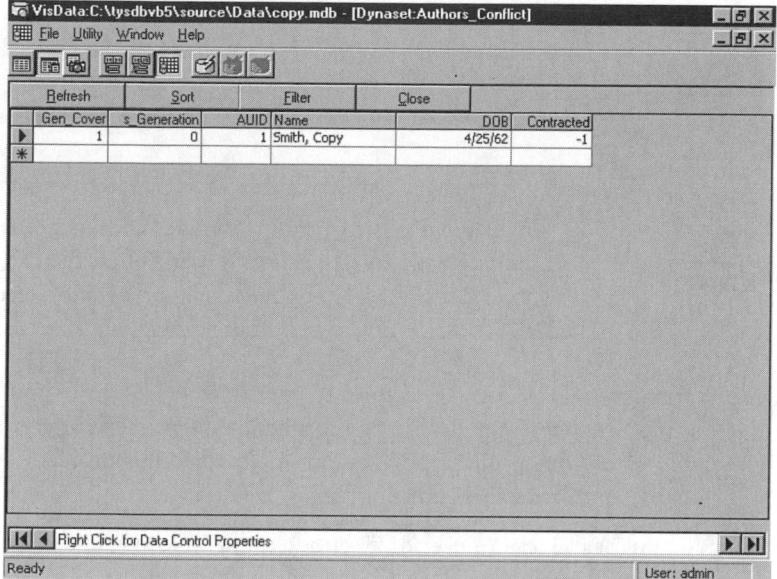

Errors That May Occur During Replication

Along with record conflicts, more serious errors can occur during synchronization. There are several actions that may cause an error during synchronization. For example, you can implement table-level validation rules after replicas have been created. This is not bad in itself, but an error occurs during synchronization if you try to replicate the rule and if a member of the replica set has entered and saved data that violates the rule.

This same type of error may occur if you change the primary key of a table. You could try replicating this change only to find that you receive an error when a replica has two equal values in two separate records in the field you tried to create as the primary key.

In both cases, you are performing serious design changes in mid-stream. You should therefore be careful and limit the design changes you make to members of a replica set.

An error may also occur when one replica set member deletes an entry from a validation table that has been used by another member in updating a master record. You receive an error when you try to import the master record into the replica set that deleted the validation table entry. Each member by itself doesn't violate referential integrity rules, but when combined, they do so in grand style. To avoid this situation, make validation tables read-only to all but the Design Master whenever possible.

20

NOTE   Try to limit users to read-only access to validation tables in a replicated environment.

NOTE   Try to avoid using cascading updates and cascading deletes in your application when replication is used. These features make it easy for you to cause a large number of synchronization errors.

You might also receive a synchronization error when you try to update a record that is locked by another user in a multiuser environment. An entry is written to the MSysErrors system table when you encounter such an error. To avoid this problem, it is best to have all users locked out of a database during synchronization.

You might also receive an error if you add a new table to your database and use the same name that another replica used for a different table. To avoid this, all members of the replica set need to communicate all database changes.

In summary, synchronization errors can occur as a result of design changes, as a result of violation of referential integrity rules on a consolidated basis, or as a result of record locking by users of a replica set member. You can avoid most of these errors by completing development before replication begins, by securing validation tables whenever possible, and by locking the replica members involved in a synchronization.

NOTE   Errors encountered during synchronization are stored in the MSysErrors table. This table is replicated during the synchronization process. Therefore, try to correct all encountered errors before they are passed to other members of the replica set.

Replication Topologies

When you implement database replication in your application, you most likely will make more than one replica of the original Design Master. When you do, you will be faced with the logistical question of how and when to update replica set members.

You need to implement a schema for the order in which data updates get dispersed throughout the replica set. The design of the order in which replica set members get updated

is referred to as the *replication topology*. We cover the various topologies in this section. It is important, however, to note that there is no universal best topology. You need to investigate the needs of your application's users thoroughly before you can decide on which topology to implement.

The most commonly used topology implemented in database replication is the *star topology*. In the star topology, there is one central database, usually the Design Master, with which all members of the replica set perform a synchronization. No replication occurs directly between members of the replica set. As an example, let's assume you created a replica set with one Design Master (DM) and four replicas (A, B, C, D). To begin, A first synchronizes with DM. Next, B synchronizes with DM, then C with DM, and D with DM. A, B, C, and D don't talk to one another directly, but pass all data changes through DM.

The star topology is the simplest topology to implement. It doesn't require a strict synchronization order be maintained. Replica A could synchronize after B, and C could synchronize before B. This is therefore a good topology to use when you are working with a large number of replicas, such as in a sales force automation application. Users can synchronize in this topology without having to worry about when other members of the replica set synchronize.

There are two drawbacks to the star topology, however, of which you should be aware. First of all, the central database with which all replicas synchronize serves as a single point of failure. If this database is down, no one can talk to anyone else. You should therefore be prepared to move one of the replica set members into the central role if necessary. Remember, though, that use of a backup is not recommended as a means of safeguarding a database in a replicated environment.

The other problem with this topology is that it permits some replicas to synchronize infrequently, or not at all. This is actually a very common problem in contact management databases, because some users don't see the need for sharing their entries with other members of the replica set, or just don't get around to performing the synchronization.

NOTE

It is not realistic to believe that humans can stick to a strict replication schedule. Or that they will voluntarily perform a synchronization if it is difficult. If implemented in an end-user application, synchronization must be made extremely easy to use, or it will not be used.

20

A *linear topology* can also be used for synchronization. In this topology, replica A synchronizes with B, then B synchronizes with C, and then C synchronizes with D. To restart the process, D would synchronize with C, and then C with B, and finally B with A.

A *ring topology* is similar to a linear topology, except, the reverse track is not performed. In this scenario, replica A synchronizes with B, B synchronizes with C, and then C synchronizes with D. Replica D then restarts the process by synchronizing with A, and then A synchronizes with B, and so on.

The linear and ring topologies are good in that they do not have a single point of failure. They are bad in that the synchronization can be stopped, or delayed if one member goes down. Also, the transfer to other members of the replica set is slower. In a linear topology, a change to C would have to go first to D, then back to C, and then to B before it is sent to A. This is a total of four synchronizations.

The fourth topology that can be used in a replicated database structure is referred to as the *fully connected topology*. In this scenario, replica A synchronizes directly with B, C, and D; replica B synchronizes directly with A, C, and D; replica C synchronizes directly with A, B, and D; and D synchronizes directly with A, B, and C. This topology requires the greatest amount of work, and should be used in applications that require constant availability of data.

NOTE

> You might want to reconsider the use of database replication in your application if you are using the fully connected topology to guarantee data availability. Web-enabled applications with centralized data may be a better solution.

The topology you ultimately choose for your application depends on the timeline requirement of data. If this is unknown, start with the star topology and make changes as necessary.

Keeping Database Elements from Replicating

There might be some data tables that you do not want to replicate to other members of a replica set. This might be the case with data that is highly sensitive in nature, or data that is of little value to other replicas. For example, you might want to replicate general employee information to remote offices of your organization, but you might not want to distribute payroll information outside of the main office. Or, you might not want to replicate a table of office supply vendors used by your California office to your office in Vermont.

In the following example we create the KeepLocal property for the Authors table of a new database named KEEPLOC.MDB. This file can be found in the \\TYSDBVB5\SOURCE\DATA directory on the CD that shipped with this text. We then convert this database into a Design Master and make a replica named COPYKL.MDB. This replica does not have the Authors table as part of its object collection.

Start this exercise by loading the REPLDEMO.VBP project into Visual Basic 5. Add a command button to the form REPLDEMO.FRM. Set the Name property of this button to cmdKeepLocal, and its Caption to &Keep Local. Now add the code in Listing 20.5 to the cmdKeepLocal_Click event.

Listing 20.5. The Visual Basic 5 code to keep a table object from replicating.

`TYPE`

```
Private Sub cmdKeepLocal_Click()

    Dim dbMaster As Database
    Dim LocalProperty As Property
    Dim KeepTab As Object
    Dim repProperty As Property

    'Open the database in exclusive mode
    Set dbMaster = OpenDatabase("c:\tysdbvb5\source\data\keeploc.mdb", True)

    Set KeepTab = dbMaster.TableDefs("Authors")
    Set LocalProperty = dbMaster.CreateProperty("KeepLocal", dbText, "T")
    KeepTab.Properties.Append LocalProperty
    KeepTab.Properties("Keeplocal") = "T"

    MsgBox "The Authors table is set to not replicate"

    'Create and set the replicable property
    Set repProperty = dbMaster.CreateProperty("Replicable", dbText, "T")
    dbMaster.Properties.Append repProperty
    dbMaster.Properties("Replicable") = "T"

    'Display a message box
    MsgBox "You have created a Design Master out of KEEPLOC.MDB!"

    dbMaster.MakeReplica "c:\tysdbvb5\source\data\copykl.mdb", "Replica of " &
    ➥"dbMaster"

    dbMaster.Close

    MsgBox "You have created a copy of KEEPLOC.MDB"

End Sub
```

20

This code first opens our database, KEEPLOC.MDB, and sets the KeepLocal property of the Authors table to T. Note that the KeepLocal property must be set *before* the Design Master is created. The program then turns KEEPLOC.MDB into a Design Master, and creates a replica named COPYKL.MDB.

Now run the application and select the Keep Local Command button. You are prompted with a Message Box when the KeepLocal property is set to T for the Authors table, when the

KEEPLOC.MDB database is converted into a Design Master, and when the COPYKL.MDB file is created. Finally, select Exit to unload the project.

After the program is completed, open the KEEPLOC.MDB database in Visdata. Expand the Authors table object in the Database Window and then expand the Properties of the Authors table. Notice that the KeepLocal property is set to T. This is illustrated in Figure 20.17. Open the BookSales table. Notice that there isn't a KeepLocal property.

Figure 20.17.

To prevent this table from replicating, the KeepLocal property was created and set to T.

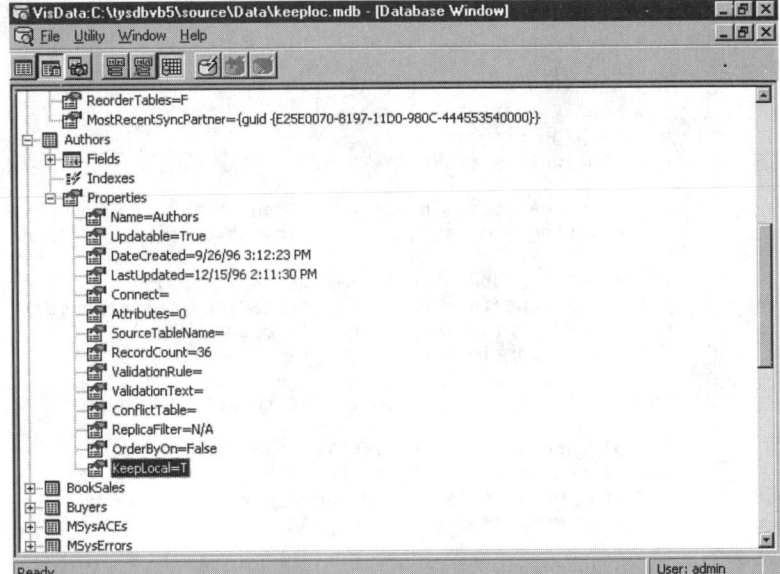

Now open the COPYKL.MDB file in Visdata. Notice that this database does not have an Authors table. You have successfully made a replica of the Design Master and excluded a table!

NOTE

Objects created after a replica is created do not flow to other members of the replica set. You must first set their Replicable property to T to replicate them.

Summary

In database replication terminology, the main, or central, database is referred to as the *Design Master*. A copy of the Design Master is referred to as the *replica*. The combination of the Design Master and all replicas is referred to as the *replica set*. *Database replication* is the process of synchronizing data so that it is the same across all members of the replica set.

Database replication is a good tool to use in the development of systems deployed across a WAN or to remote users. Replication can also be used to make copies of databases that cannot be shut down. Replication is also good for creating reporting databases.

Do not use database replication when a centralized data storage facility can be used, such as a Web-enabled application. Also, don't use replication in heavily transaction-oriented applications, or in applications where up-to-the-minute accuracy is of paramount importance.

Tables, fields, and properties are added to a database when it is made a Design Master. The addition of these items is necessary to track changes to data and to facilitate the synchronization between members of the replica set. These additions, however, consume additional hard drive space.

Creating and changing the Replicable property of a database to T creates a Design Master. Once the Design Master is created, you can use the MakeReplica method to make copies of it. Finally, you use the Synchronize method to replicate data changes to members of the replica set. *Data synchronization* is the act of copying data changes from one member of a replica set to another.

The Synchronize method can be used to import data changes, export data changes, perform "two-way" data changes, and even perform data exchanges over the Internet.

Synchronization errors occur when two members of a replica set try to synchronize records that each has changed. Errors can also occur during the synchronization process when design changes are made to a database but violated by replicas prior to synchronization of the changes. Violation of referential integrity can be encountered by replicas that add records to a database that uses validation records deleted in another replica. Record locking in a multiuser environment can also cause synchronization errors.

There are four topologies for the synchronization of replicas. These are the *star, linear, ring,* and *fully connected* topologies. The star topology is the most common, but like all the other topologies, has certain strengths and weaknesses.

There may be times when you do not want to replicate objects contained in one database to other members of the replica set. If such is the case, use the KeepLocal method before you create the Design Master. This method keeps the object from being copied to other replica set members.

20

Quiz

1. Define database replication.

2. Cite examples of applications that can make good use of database replication.

3. Cite examples of systems in which database replication should not be used.

4. What fields are added to all data tables when a database is turned into a Design Master?

5. What properties are added to the database during the creation of the Design Master to indicate that it can be replicated?

6. How much hard drive space is consumed by a database when it is turned into a Design Master?

7. What happens to an AutoNumber field when a database is turned into a Design Master?

8. What method do you use to create a copy of a Design Master?

9. What is the logic that the Microsoft Jet engine uses to resolve synchronization conflicts?

10. What topologies can be used for database synchronization? Which topology is the most commonly used?

11. What method do you use to keep database objects from replicating to other members of a replica set?

Exercises

Design an implementation strategy for the rollout of a database application that you built to track and deliver your company's employee information. This application needs to be installed at your corporate office in Cincinnati, and then delivered to offices in Chicago, Los Angeles, and New York. Use the following information as you design your strategy:

☐ The database is named EMPLOYEE.MDB and has four tables: EmployeeMaster, EmergencyInfo, Education, and SalaryInfo.

☐ All payroll is performed in the Cincinnati office.

☐ Updates need to be made at each site, and shared with all other sites. The order in which updates are made to the database is not important.

☐ Cincinnati is the largest office. Chicago is the second largest, and is three times the size of the Los Angeles or the New York offices.

Include the following items as part of your implementation plan:

- ☐ Names of the tables to be distributed to each site
- ☐ Backup methodology
- ☐ Synchronization topology
- ☐ Code to keep the payroll information (SalaryInfo) from replicating
- ☐ Code to create the Design Master
- ☐ Code to create the Chicago replica
- ☐ Code to synchronize your Chicago and your Cincinnati databases

20

Day 21

Securing Your Database Applications

In our final lesson, we cover topics related to securing your database and your application. Almost all software that is deployed in a multiuser environment should use some level of security. Security schemes can be used for more than just limiting user access to the database. Security schemes can also limit user access to the applications that use the database. You can also install security features in your Visual Basic database applications to limit the function rights of users within your applications. You can even develop routines that record user activity within your applications—including user login/logout activity—each time a user updates a database record, and even each time a user performs a critical operation such as printing a sensitive report or graph, updating key data, or running restricted routines.

Throughout today's lesson, you build a new OLE Server library. You can use this library to add varying levels of security to all your future Visual Basic database applications.

When you have completed this chapter, you will understand how Microsoft Access database security and encryption works and the advantages and disadvantages of both. You'll also know how to implement an application security scheme, including adding user login and logout history, implementing audit trails that show when database records have been updated, and recording each time users perform critical application operations.

Database Security

The first level of security you can employ in Visual Basic database applications is at the database level. The Microsoft Jet database format enables you to establish user and group security schemes using the Microsoft Access SYSTEM security file. You can also add database encryption to your Microsoft Jet databases to increase the level of security within your database.

Although the Microsoft Access SYSTEM security file and Microsoft Jet data encryption are powerful tools, they have some disadvantages. When adding either of these features, you should understand the limitations and pitfalls of the security features. In the following sections, you learn the most notable of these limitations, as well as some suggestions on how you can avoid unexpected results.

Limitations of the Microsoft Access SYSTEM Security

If you have a copy of Microsoft Access, you can install a database security scheme for your Visual Basic applications. The security scheme requires the presence of a single file (called SYSTEM.MDA or SYSTEM.MDW). This file must be available to your Visual Basic application either in the application path, or pointed to through the application .INI file or system Registry. After the SYSTEM security file is defined, all attempts to open the secured database cause the Microsoft Jet engine to request a user name and password before opening the database.

NOTE

> Some 32-bit systems have a Microsoft Jet security file called SYSTEM.MDW (for example, Access 95). Others continue to use SYSTEM.MDA in both 16- and 32-bit modes (for example, Visual Basic 4). The difference between the SYSTEM.MDW and SYSTEM.MDA files is in name only. Throughout this lesson, you will see SYSTEM, SYSTEM.MDW, and SYSTEM.MDA. They can be used interchangeably.

We won't review the details of creating and updating the SYSTEM security file here (see Day 7, "Using the Visdata Program" for details on defining SYSTEM security). Instead, this section covers the advantages and limitations of using the SYSTEM security scheme employed by Microsoft Access and Microsoft Jet.

Microsoft Access Is Required

Once you have a SYSTEM security file registered on your workstation, you can use Microsoft Access or you can use Visdata to define the system security details. However, only Microsoft Access can create the original SYSTEM file. You cannot use any Visual Basic application to create a SYSTEM file. You can, however, use Visual Basic to modify existing SYSTEM security files.

Multiple SYSTEM Files Are Possible

You can have multiple versions of the SYSTEM security file available on your workstation or network. In this way you can create unique security schemes for each of your Microsoft Jet databases. The disadvantage here is that it is possible to install the wrong SYSTEM security file for an application. This could result in preventing all users from accessing any of the data. Depending on the SYSTEM file installed, it could also result in reducing security to the point of allowing all users access to critical data not normally available to them. If you are using multiple SYSTEM security files, be sure to store these files in the same directory as the application files and include the specific path to the SYSTEM file in all installation procedures.

Removing the SYSTEM File Removes the Security

Because all security features are stored in a single file, removing SYSTEM from the workstation or network effectively eliminates all database security. You can limit this possibility by storing the SYSTEM file on a network in a directory where users do not have delete or rename rights. Setting these rights requires administrator-level access to the network and knowledge of your network's file rights utilities.

Some Applications Might Not Use SYSTEM Files

If you are using the database in an environment where multiple applications can access the database, you might find that some applications do not use the SYSTEM files at all. These applications might be able to open the database without having to go through the security features. For example, you could easily write a Visual Basic application that opens a database without first checking for the existence of the SYSTEM file. By doing this, you can completely ignore any security features built into the SYSTEM security file.

21

Limitations of Microsoft Jet Encryption

You can also use the encryption feature of Microsoft Jet to encode sensitive data. However, you have no control over the type of encryption algorithm used to encode your data. You can only turn encryption on or off using the `dbEncrypt` or `dbDecrypt` option constants with the `CreateDatabase` and `CompactDatabase` methods.

The following list outlines other limitations to consider when using Microsoft Jet encryption.

☐ You cannot encrypt selected tables within a database. When you turn encryption on, it affects all objects in the database. If you have only a few tables that are sensitive, you should consider moving those tables into a separate database for encryption.

☐ If you are deploying your database in an environment where multiple applications access your data, it is possible that these applications might not be able to read the encrypted data.

☐ If you want to take advantage of the replication features of Microsoft Jet, you cannot use encrypted databases.

Application Security

Application security is quite different from database security. Application security focuses on securing not only data but also processes. For example, you can use application security to limit users' ability to use selected data entry forms, produce certain graphs or reports, or run critical procedures (such as month-end closing or mass price updates).

Any good application security scheme has two main features. The first is a process that forces users to log into your application using stored passwords. This provides an additional level of security to your Visual Basic database application. As you see later in this chapter, forcing users to log into and out of your application also gives you the opportunity to create audit logs of all user activity. These audit logs can help you locate and fix problems reported by users and give you an additional tool for keeping track of just who is using your application.

The second process that is valuable in building an application security system is an access rights scheme. You can use an access rights scheme to limit the functions that particular users can perform within your application. For example, if you want to allow only certain users to perform critical tasks, you can establish an access right for that task and check each user's rights before he or she is allowed to attempt that operation. You can establish access rights for virtually any program operation, including data form entry, report generation, even special processes such as price updates, file exports, and so on.

NOTE

> Because application security works only within the selected application, it cannot affect users who are accessing the database from other applications. Therefore, you should not rely on application-level security as the only security scheme for your critical data. Still, application security can provide powerful security controls to your Visual Basic database applications.

In order to provide user login and logout and access rights checking, in this lesson you build a set of routines in a new OLE Server library called usrObject. This library contains all the properties and methods needed to install and maintain application-level security for all your Visual Basic database applications.

Developing a User Login/Logout System

The first routines you need to build as part of your application security OLE library enable application administrators to create and maintain a list of valid application users. This involves creating a simple data entry form that contains add, edit, and delete operations for a Users table. Next, you need routines to process user logins and logouts. The login routine prompts potential users for their user ID and password, and checks the values entered against the data table on file. As usual, you construct these routines in a way that makes it easy for you to use them in any future Visual Basic database applications.

Building the User Maintenance Form

Load Visual Basic 5 and start a new ActiveX DLL project. The first thing you do is create a form to manage the list of valid application users. This form enables you to add, edit, and delete users from a table called secUsers. This is the same table used to verify user logins at the start of all your secured applications. Use Table 21.1 and Figure 21.1 to build the first page of the User Maintenance tabbed dialog.

Before building this form, however, you need to add two reference entries and two custom controls to your project. Refer to the following list to make sure you load all the additional files needed for this project.

- ☐ Microsoft Data Bound Grid control
- ☐ Microsoft Tabbed Dialog control 5.0
- ☐ TYSDBVB5, the data entry library (prjRecObject.dll)
- ☐ Microsoft DAO 3.5 object library

21

 **NOTE** This project uses several control arrays. You can save yourself additional typing by building the first member of the control array, setting all the control properties, and then copying the additional members. You still have to retype some property settings, but it is considerably less tedious than if you had to set them all manually.

Figure 21.1.

*Laying out the User
Maintenance form.*

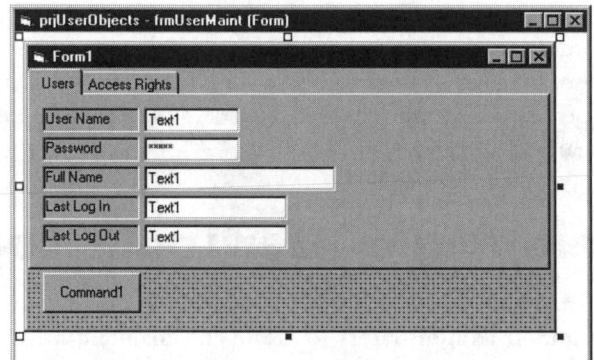

Table 21.1. Controls for the User Maintenance form.

Control	Property	Setting
VB.Form	Name	frmUserMaint
	Caption	"Form1"
	ClientHeight	3195
	ClientLeft	60
	ClientTop	345
	ClientWidth	6510
	StartUpPosition	2 'CenterScreen
VB.CommandButton	Name	cmdBtn
	Caption	"Command1"
	Height	495
	Index	0
	Left	180
	TabIndex	0
	Top	2520
	Width	1215

Control	Property	Setting
TabDlg.SSTab	Name	SSTab1
	Height	2475
	Left	0
	TabIndex	6
	Top	0
	Width	6495
	Style	1
	Tabs	2
	TabsPerRow	2
	TabCaption(0)	"Users"
	TabCaption(1)	"Access Rights"
VB.TextBox	Name	txtField
	Height	300
	Index	0
	Left	1440
	TabIndex	1
	Text	"Text1"
	Top	480
	Width	1200
VB.TextBox	Name	txtField
	Height	300
	Index	4
	Left	1440
	TabIndex	5
	Text	"Text1"
	Top	1920
	Width	1800
VB.TextBox	Name	txtField
	Height	300
	Index	3
	Left	1440
	TabIndex	4

continues

Table 21.1. continued

Control	Property	Setting
	Text	"Text1"
	Top	1560
	Width	1800
VB.TextBox	Name	txtField
	Height	300
	Index	2
	Left	1440
	TabIndex	3
	Text	"Text1"
	Top	1200
	Width	2400
VB.TextBox	Name	txtField
	Height	300
	Index	1
	Left	1440
	PasswordChar	"*"
	TabIndex	2
	Text	"Text1"
	Top	840
	Width	1200
VB.Label	Name	Label5
	BorderStyle	1 'Fixed Single
	Caption	"Last Log Out"
	Height	300
	Left	180
	TabIndex	11
	Top	1920
	Width	1200
VB.Label	Name	Label4
	BorderStyle	1 'Fixed Single
	Caption	"Last Log In"

21

Control	Property	Setting
	Height	300
	Left	180
	TabIndex	10
	Top	1560
	Width	1200
VB.Label	Name	Label3
	BorderStyle	1 'Fixed Single
	Caption	"Full Name"
	Height	300
	Left	180
	TabIndex	9
	Top	1200
	Width	1200
VB.Label	Name	Label2
	BorderStyle	1 'Fixed Single
	Caption	"Password"
	Height	300
	Left	180
	TabIndex	8
	Top	840
	Width	1200
VB.Label	Name	Label1
	BorderStyle	1 'Fixed Single
	Caption	"User Name"
	Height	300
	Left	180
	TabIndex	7
	Top	480
	Width	1200

21

Save the form as FRMUSERMAINT.FRM and the project as PRJUSROBJET.VBP after you add all the controls and position them on the form. Now you need to add some Visual Basic code to make the form work.

Place the following initialization code in the Declaration section of the User Maintenance form.

```
Option Explicit
'
' user maint and login vars
Dim objRec As Object
Dim lgnResult As Long
Public strDBName As String
'
```

Next, place the code in Listing 21.1 in the Form_Load event of the form.

TYPE **Listing 21.1. Setting up the User Maintenance form.**

```
Private Sub Form_Load()
    '
    Me.Caption = "User Maintenance"
    Bin8dInputs
    StartProc
    '
End Sub
```

Listing 21.1 calls two routines that perform the initialization operations. Now add a new subroutine to the form called BindInputs and enter the code from Listing 21.2.

TYPE **Listing 21.2. Adding the BindInputs method.**

```
Public Sub BindInputs()
    '
    ' bind inputs to database
    '
    txtField(0).Tag = "UserID"
    txtField(1).Tag = "Password"
    txtField(2).Tag = "UserName"
    txtField(3).Tag = "LastLogIn"
    txtField(4).Tag = "LastLogOut"
    '
End Sub
```

Now add the code from Listing 21.3 to the new StartProc subroutine.

21

TYPE **Listing 21.3. Coding the** `StartProc` **routine.**

```
Public Sub StartProc()
    '
    ' start database
    '
    Set objRec = New recObject
    '
    objRec.DBName = strDBName
    objRec.RSName = "SELECT * FROM secUsers ORDER BY UserID"
    objRec.rsType = rsDynasetType
    objRec.RSFocus = "UserID"
    '
    objRec.RSOpen Me
    objRec.RSEnable Me, False
    '
    objRec.BtnBarAlign = bbBottom
    objRec.BBInit Me
    objRec.BBEnable Me, "11111111"
    '
End Sub
```

The code in Listing 21.3 initializes the record object, sets several properties, and then it's ready for you to begin.

Add the code in Listing 21.4 to the `cmdBtn_Click` event. This code calls the `BBProcess` method of the record object library to handle all data entry functions.

TYPE **Listing 21.4. Coding the** `cmdBtn_Click` **event.**

```
Private Sub cmdBtn_Click(Index As Integer)
    '
    objRec.BBProcess Me, Index, "UserID"
    '
    ' add default date/time for new recs
    If Index = 0 And cmdBtn(0).Caption = "&Save" Then
        txtField(3) = Now()
        txtField(4) = Now()
    End If
    '
End Sub
```

Next, add the code in Listing 21.5 to your project. This is the code that resizes the controls when the user resizes the form.

21

TYPE   **Listing 21.5. Resizing the controls at runtime.**

```
Private Sub Form_Resize()
    '
    If Me.WindowState <> vbMinimized Then
        With SSTab1
            .Left = 1
            .Top = 1
            .Width = Me.ScaleWidth
            .Height = Me.ScaleHeight - 540
        End With
    End If
    '
    objRec.BBInit Me
    '
End Sub
```

You also need to add some code (shown in Listing 21.6) to the Text1_KeyPress event. This code prevents users from editing the Last Log In or Last Log Out fields on the form.

TYPE   **Listing 21.6. Disabling entry in the Text1_KeyPress event.**

```
Private Sub txtField_KeyPress(Index As Integer, KeyAscii As Integer)
    '
    ' trap keystrokes
    '
    Select Case Index
        Case 0 ' userid
            KeyAscii = Asc(UCase(Chr(KeyAscii)))
        Case 1 ' password
        Case 2 ' username
        Case 3 ' last log in
            KeyAscii = 0
        Case 4 ' last log out
            KeyAscii = 0
    End Select
    '
End Sub
```

Now save the project. Before you can run this project, you need to add some code to the class module, too. First, set its name to usrObject and save the project just to be safe. Next, add some declarations to the top of the module, based on Listing 21.7.

TYPE   **Listing 21.7. User-related declarations for the usrObject class.**

```
Option Explicit
'
' user login/out vars
```

```
Private wsUsers As Workspace
Private dbUsers As Database
Private rsUsers As Recordset
Private blnUsersLoaded As Boolean
Private strDBName As String
Private intMaxTries As Integer
Private strUserIDProp As String
Private strTitle As String
'
Enum urUserAction
    urLogIn = 0
    urLogOut = 1
End Enum
```

You use these variables to handle user logins and logouts, too.

Now add the Property Let and Property Get routines to the class module (see Listing 21.8)

TYPE **Listing 21.8. Opening the dataset with the `usrInit` function.**

```
Public Property Get DBName() As Variant
    DBName = strDBName
End Property

Public Property Let DBName(ByVal vNewValue As Variant)
    strDBName = vNewValue
End Property

Public Property Get UserID() As Variant
    UserID = strUserIDProp
End Property

Public Property Let UserID(ByVal vNewValue As Variant)
    ' na
End Property

Public Property Get LoginTitle() As Variant
    LoginTitle = strTitle
End Property

Public Property Let LoginTitle(ByVal vNewValue As Variant)
    strTitle = vNewValue
End Property

Public Property Get MaxTries() As Variant
    MaxTries = intMaxTries
End Property

Public Property Let MaxTries(ByVal vNewValue As Variant)
    intMaxTries = vNewValue
End Property
```

21

This code just declares Public properties for the class. You need to add the `Class_Initialize` routine, too. Enter the code from Listing 21.9.

TYPE **Listing 21.9. Coding the `Class_Initialize` event.**

```
Private Sub Class_Initialize()
    '
    ' initial settings
    '
    strDBName = App.Path & "\security.mdb"
    intMaxTries = 3
    strTitle = "User Maintenance Library"
    strUserIDProp = ""
    blnRightsLoaded = False
    '
End Sub
```

This routine passes the local version of the database name property to the form and then calls the form. Note the use of the `Err.Raise` method in the error handler. This simply passes the error back to the calling program with some additional information that you can use to diagnose the problem.

Finally, to test this library you need to start a second project (Visual Basic 5 Standard EXE) in the same group (select File | New Project from the main menu). This second project is used to instantiate a new `recObject` and call it from within your program. This is all handled through a single BAS module, not a form. All you need to do is remove the default form from your EXE project, and add the module to your form. Add the code from Listing 21.10 to your new module file.

TYPE **Listing 21.10. Building a second project to test the usrObject library.**

```
Option Explicit
'
' project-level vars
'
Public objUser As Object

Public Sub Main()
    '
    ' main entry for form-less project
    '
    Set objUser = New usrObject
    objUser.DBName = App.Path & "\..\..\data\security\security.mdb"
    '
    objUser.UsersForm
    '
    End
    '
End Sub
```

21

TIP

There are several advantages to using a Main() routine as the startup for your application. You can handle numerous initialization processes before you load a form, and you can even design your application to use different forms from the same Main() routine. Programs that start with a Main() routine are usually easier to maintain and modify than programs that start with a startup form.

Now save the new module as modUsrTest.bas and the project as prjUsrTest.vbp, and run the project. Your screen should look similar to the one in Figure 21.2.

Figure 21.2.

Running the User Maintenance form.

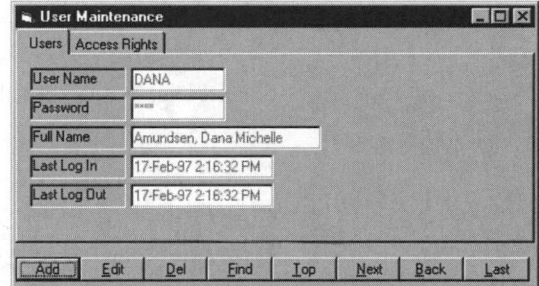

You can now add, edit, and delete user records. A few records have already been added for you. Make sure this includes a record for USERA. If one does not exist, add it. If it is already on file, edit the record and set the Password field to USERA. Notice that the Password field does not display its contents. This is because you set the PasswordChar property of the textbox to show only an asterisk (*) for every character in the field. The actual characters are stored in the database table.

Building the User LogIn and LogOut Routines

Now that you have a method for managing the list of valid users, it's time to create the routines that enable users to log into and out of your applications. First you need to create a user login form. Then you need to add a routine to verify the user login and a routine to log the user out when the application is terminated.

First, build the user login form. Add a new form to the existing PRJUSROBJECT.VBP project, using Table 21.2 and Figure 21.3 as guides in building the form.

21

Figure 21.3.

*Laying out the User
Login form.*

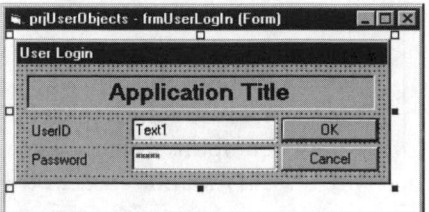

Table 21.2. Controls for the User Login form.

Control	Property	Setting
VB.Form	Name	frmUserLogIn
	BorderStyle	3 'Fixed Dialog
	Caption	"User Login"
	ClientHeight	1440
	ClientLeft	45
	ClientTop	330
	ClientWidth	4605
	StartUpPosition	2 'CenterScreen
VB.CommandButton	Name	cmdCancel
	Cancel	-1 'True
	Caption	"Cancel"
	Height	300
	Left	3300
	Top	1020
	Width	1200
VB.CommandButton	Name	cmdOK
	Caption	"OK"
	Default	-1 'True
	Height	300
	Left	3300
	Top	660
	Width	1200
VB.TextBox	Name	txtPassword
	Height	300
	Left	1440

21

Control	Property	Setting
	PasswordChar	"*"
	Text	"Text1"
	Top	1020
	Width	1800
VB.TextBox	Name	txtUserID
	Height	300
	Left	1440
	Text	"Text1"
	Top	660
	Width	1800
VB.Label	Name	lblPassword
	Caption	"Password"
	Height	300
	Left	180
	Top	1080
	Width	1200
VB.Label	Name	lblUserID
	Caption	"UserID"
	Height	300
	Left	180
	Top	720
	Width	1200
VB.Label	Name	lblAppTitle
	Alignment	2 'Center
	BorderStyle	1 'Fixed Single
	Caption	"Application Title"
	Font	Name="MS Sans Serif"
		Size=13.5
	Height	435
	Left	120
	Top	120
	Width	4335

21

You need to add only a few lines of code to this form. First, add the code shown in Listing 21.11 to the declaration area of the form.

TYPE **Listing 21.11. Coding the declaration section of the form.**

```
Option Explicit
'
' public vars
Public blnOK As Boolean
Public strTitle As String
```

Next, add the code in Listing 21.12 to the Form_Activate event to initialize form values at startup.

TYPE **Listing 21.12. Initializing form values.**

```
Private Sub Form_Activate()
    '
    ' form setup
    '
    lblAppTitle = strTitle
    txtUserID = ""
    txtPassword = ""
    txtUserID.SetFocus
    '
End Sub
```

You need to add a few lines to support the command buttons. First, add the code in Listing 21.13 for the OK button.

TYPE **Listing 21.13. Code for the OK button.**

```
Private Sub cmdOK_Click()
    '
    blnOK = True
    Me.Hide
    '
End Sub
```

This code sets a global variable and hides the login form. Now add the code from Listing 21.14 to support the Cancel button.

TYPE **Listing 21.14. Code for the Cancel button.**

```
Private Sub cmdCancel_Click()
    '
    blnOK = False
    Me.Hide
    '
End Sub
```

That's it for the User Login form. Save this form as FRMUSERLOGIN.FRM.

Now you need to add more code to the PRJUSROBJECT class library file. You need three routines. The first routine to add is the UserLogin method. This method calls the login form and then calls other routines to verify the login and update the user's record in the secUsers table.

Create a new Public function called UserLogin and add the code from Listing 21.15.

TYPE **Listing 21.15. Adding the LoginUser function to the DLL library.**

```
Public Function UserLogin() As Boolean
    '
    ' handle user login attempts
    '
    On Error GoTo LocalErr
    '
    Static intTries As Integer
    Dim blnValidUser As Boolean
    Dim intAnswer As Integer
    '
UserLoginAttempt:
    '
    frmUserLogIn.strTitle = strTitle
    frmUserLogIn.Show vbModal
    '
    ' did user cancel login?
    If frmUserLogIn.blnOK = False Then
        UserLogin = False
        GoTo UserLoginExit
    End If
    '
    ' verify login
    If frmUserLogIn.blnOK = True Then
        intTries = intTries + 1
        blnValidUser = CheckUser(frmUserLogIn.txtUserID,
frmUserLogIn.txtPassword)
        If blnValidUser = True Then
            strUserIDProp = frmUserLogIn.txtUserID ' save to properties
            modUsrObject.strUserIDSaved = strUserIDProp
            LogUser urLogIn ' update table
```

continues

21

Listing 21.15. continued

```
                UserLogin = True ' set flag
                GoTo UserLoginExit ' exit
        End If
    End If
    '
    ' did user max attempts?
    If intTries = intMaxTries Then
        MsgBox "Login failed - access denied", vbCritical, "User Login"
        UserLogin = False
        GoTo UserLoginExit
    End If
    '
    ' go try again
    intAnswer = MsgBox("Invalid Login", vbRetryCancel + vbInformation, "User
Login")
    If intAnswer = vbRetry Then
        GoTo UserLoginAttempt
    Else
        UserLogin = False
        GoTo UserLoginExit
    End If
    '
UserLoginExit:
    Unload frmUserLogIn
    '
    Exit Function
    '
LocalErr:
    Err.Raise Err.Number, App.EXEName & ".usrObject", Err.Description
    '
End Function
```

The module in Listing 21.15 first sets some variables and then calls the login form and waits for the user to press OK or Cancel on the form. The default settings allow the user three login attempts. If the user presses the OK button on the form, the routine calls the CheckUser function to check for a valid user. If the user is valid, the routine stores the user's ID, updates the user's record in the secUsers table, and then exits. If the user cannot pass the security check after three tries, the login is terminated.

Now let's code the CheckUser routine. This is the module that looks up the user ID and password to see if they match in the data table. Create a new Private function called CheckUser and enter the code in Listing 21.16.

TYPE   **Listing 21.16. Coding the `CheckUser` routine.**

```
Private Function CheckUser(strUserID As String, strPassword As String) As
Boolean
    '
    ' check login parms against table
    '
    Dim strFind As String
    '
    strFind = "UserID = '" & strUserID & "' AND Password='" & strPassword & "'"
    '
    If blnUsersLoaded = False Then
        LoadUsers
    End If
    '
    rsUsers.FindFirst strFind
    If rsUsers.NoMatch = True Then
        CheckUser = False
    Else
        CheckUser = True
    End If
    '
End Function
```

This routine first checks to see if the dataset containing the users is already loaded. If not, the `LoadUsers` method is called. Then, the method searches the dataset for the User ID and password in a single record. If all is okay, the routine updates the LastLogIn field of the dataset and exits. If the search comes up empty, the routine reports a value of FALSE upon exit.

Now add the Private subroutine `LoadUsers` from Listing 21.17.

TYPE   **Listing 21.17. Coding the `LoadUsers` method.**

```
Private Sub LoadUsers()
    '
    ' load users data set
    '
    Dim strSQL As String
    '
    strSQL = "SELECT * FROM secUsers ORDER BY UserID"
    '
    Set wsUsers = DBEngine.CreateWorkspace("usrLogin", "admin", "")
    Set dbUsers = wsUsers.OpenDatabase(strDBName)
    Set rsUsers = dbUsers.OpenRecordset(strSQL, dbOpenDynaset)
    '
    blnUsersLoaded = True
    '
End Sub
```

21

This routine simply initializes the data connection between the class object and the database that holds the security tables.

You need only one more routine—the `LogUser` routine. This procedure just needs to locate the requested user record and update the LastLogIn or LastLogOut fields—depending on the parameter passed. Create a new function called `usrLogOut` and add the code from Listing 21.18.

TYPE **Listing 21.18. Adding the `LogUser` routine.**

```
Public Sub LogUser(urAction As urUserAction)
    '
    ' make entry in the user table
    '
    On Error GoTo LocalErr
    '
    Dim strAction As String
    '
    If urAction = urLogIn Then
        strAction = "In"
    Else
        strAction = "Out"
    End If
    '
    If blnUsersLoaded = False Then
        LoadUsers
    End If
    '
    With rsUsers
        .FindFirst "UserID='" & strUserIDProp & "'"
        If .NoMatch = False Then
            .Edit
            .Fields("LastLog" & strAction) = Now()
            .Update
        End If
    End With
    '
    Exit Sub
    '
LocalErr:
    Err.Raise Err.Number, App.EXEName & ".usrObject", Err.Description
    '
End Sub
```

There is a line in the `UserLogin` method that saves a copy of the UserID to a Public property of a BAS module. This is needed so that you can share the user ID with other class objects in this DLL (you build another one a bit later today). Add a BAS module to the DLL project. Set its Name to modUsrObject and save it as `modUsrObject.bas`. Now add the code from Listing 21.19 to this new module.

21

TYPE **Listing 21.19. Coding the properties for the `modUsrObject.bas` module.**

```
Option Explicit
'
Private strLocalUserID As String

Public Property Get strUserIDSaved() As Variant
    strUserIDSaved = strLocalUserID
End Property

Public Property Let strUserIDSaved(ByVal vNewValue As Variant)
    strLocalUserID = vNewValue
End Property
```

That's all the coding you need to do in the DLL project for now. Before continuing, save this project (`PRJUSEROBJEC.VBP`) and all its components.

Now you need to modify the Main procedure in the test project you created earlier to call the new User Login form. Modify the Main routine to match the lines of code in Listing 21.20.

TYPE **Listing 21.20. Modifying the `Main` routine to add the new User Login form.**

```
Public Sub Main()
    '
    ' main entry for form-less project
    '
    Set objUser = New usrObject
    objUser.DBName = App.Path & "\..\..\data\security\security.mdb"
    '
    ' now try to start up
    If objUser.UserLogin = True Then
        objUser.UsersForm
        objUser.LogUser urLogOut
    Else
        MsgBox "You do not have rights to this application", vbExclamation,
"Login Failed"
    End If
    '
    End
    '
End Sub
```

Now, instead of just calling the UsersForm routine right away, you first make the user login with a valid ID and password. If the user successfully logs in, the program runs the UsersForm routine. When the user returns from the User Maintenance form, the LogUser method is called with the urLogOut parameter. This updates the LastLogOut field of the secUsers table.

Save and run this project. Your screen should look similar to the one in Figure 21.4.

21

Figure 21.4.
Running the User
Login form.

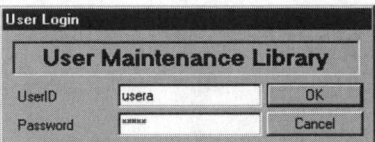

When you see the login form, enter USERA as the User ID and USERA as the password (remember, you added this in the previous example). Next, you see the User Maintenance form. When you exit this form, the routine automatically updates your logout time stamp.

You now have a complete and portable user login and logout system for your Visual Basic applications. Now let's add an additional application security feature—user access rights.

Developing a User Access Rights System

You can add an increased level of application security to your Visual Basic programs by establishing a user access rights scheme. An access rights scheme enables you to define a set of secured operations within your program and then define access rights for each of the operations on a user-by-user basis. For example, you might want to restrict the ability to print certain reports to specifically qualified users. You might also want to limit the number of users who can access data entry forms. You might even want to allow some users to modify data, but not create new records or delete existing records. Any of these arrangements can be handled by defining and implementing a user access rights security scheme.

Defining the User Access Rights Scheme

Before you can code the new features, you need to consider how the scheme will be implemented in your Visual Basic applications. This exercise uses a typical rights scheme that uses a sliding scale—the lowest level on the scale has no rights at all; the highest level has all possible rights. Table 21.3 shows the proposed set of access rights.

Table 21.3. The scale of access rights levels.

Rights Level	Access Rights
Level 0	No rights
Level 1	Read-only rights
Level 2	Read and modify rights
Level 3	Read, modify, and add rights
Level 4	Read, modify, add, and delete rights
Level 5	All, plus extended rights

In Table 21.3, each level adds additional privileges. The final level (Level 5) includes all previously defined rights plus special extended rights. You can use this level to define any special powers, depending on the object or system (supervisor control, for example).

Set up a data table that contains three columns—User ID, Object, and Level. The User ID should match the one in the AppUser table you already defined. The Level column contains values 0 through 5, and the Object column contains the name of a secured program object. This object could be a report, a data entry form, or even a menu item or command button.

There is a single record in the dataset for each secured program object. This default set is used to establish the base security profile for the system. If an object is in the default set, it is a secured object, and any users who attempt access to the program object must have their own access record defined for the requested object. If no object is present for a particular user, the user cannot access the program object.

You need to add just a bit of new code to the prjUsrObject class library in order to implement an access rights scheme. First, you need a routine that verifies the user access information when requested. You need a few support routines along the way, too (you get to those later). But first, you need to modify the User Maintenance form to include data entry for access rights.

Building the User Access Rights Maintenance Form

The first order of business is to create the data entry form needed to create and edit user access rights. This form is the second page of the tabbed dialog you built to manage the User table. Use Table 21.4 and Figure 21.5 as guides in laying out the Access Rights tab of the User Maintenance form.

Figure 21.5.

Laying out the Access Rights tab.

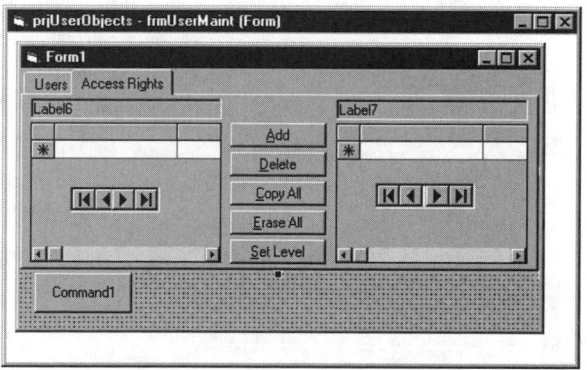

21

NOTE

This form contains a control button array. Be sure to add the first button (cmdAccess), set its properties, and then copy and paste the button onto the form.

Table 21.4. Controls for the access rights maintenance form.

Controls	Properties	Settings
VB.Data	Name	dtaUserID
	Caption	"Data1"
	Connect	"Access"
	DatabaseName	""
	DefaultCursorType=	'DefaultCursor
	DefaultType	2 'UseODBC
	Exclusive	0 'False
	Height	345
	Left	-70560
	Options	0
	ReadOnly	0 'False
	RecordsetType	1 'Dynaset
	RecordSource	""
	Top	1380
	Visible	0 'False
	Width	1275
VB.Data	Name	dtaDefault
	Caption	"Data1"
	Connect	"Access"
	DatabaseName	""
	DefaultCursorType=	'DefaultCursor
	DefaultType	2 'UseODBC
	Exclusive	0 'False
	Height	345
	Left	-74400
	Options	0

21

Controls	Properties	Settings
	ReadOnly	0 'False
	RecordsetType	1 'Dynaset
	RecordSource	""
	Top	1440
	Visible	0 'False
	Width	1155
VB.CommandButton	Name	cmdAccess
	Caption	"&Set Level"
	Height	300
	Index	4
	Left	-72360
	TabIndex	20
	Top	2100
	Width	1200
VB.CommandButton	Name	cmdAccess
	Caption	"&Erase All"
	Height	300
	Index	3
	Left	-72360
	TabIndex	19
	Top	1740
	Width	1200
VB.CommandButton	Name	cmdAccess
	Caption	"&Copy All"
	Height	300
	Index	2
	Left	-72360
	TabIndex	18
	Top	1380
	Width	1200
VB.CommandButton	Name	cmdAccess
	Caption	"&Delete"

21

continues

Table 21.4. continued

Controls	Properties	Settings
	Height	300
	Index	1
	Left	-72360
	TabIndex	17
	Top	1020
	Width	1200
VB.CommandButton	Name	cmdAccess
	Caption	"&Add"
	Height	300
	Index	0
	Left	-72360
	TabIndex	16
	Top	660
	Width	1200
MSDBGrid.DBGrid	Name	dbgDefault
	Height	1725
	Left	-74880
	TabIndex	12
	Top	660
	Width	2400
MSDBGrid.DBGrid	Name	dbgUserID
	Height	1725
	Left	-71040
	TabIndex	13
	Top	660
	Width	2400
VB.Label	Name	lblUserName
	BorderStyle	1 'Fixed Single

Controls	Properties	Settings
	Caption	"Label7"
	Height	255
	Left	-71040
	TabIndex	15
	Top	360
	Width	2400
VB.Label	Name	lbluserID
	BorderStyle	1 'Fixed Single
	Caption	"Label6"
	Height	255
	Left	-74880
	TabIndex	14
	Top	360
	Width	2400

After you add the data-bound grid objects to the form, you need to set some of their properties using the pop-up menu. Select the dbgDefault grid and click the alternate mouse button. Then select Retrieve Fields to load the fields. Now click the alternate button again and select Properties and click the Columns tab. Make the User ID column invisible. Perform the same steps for the dbgUserID data grid. Save the project before you add the code.

The first step in coding the User Access Rights page is to add three form-level variables to the User Maintenance Form.

```
Option Explicit
'
' user maint and login vars
Dim objRec As Object
Dim lgnResult As Long
Public strDBName As String
'
'***new >>> access rights vars
Dim strSQLDefault As String
Dim strSQLUserID As String
Public intRights As Integer
```

Next, add the code in Listing 21.21 to the SSTab1_Click event. This code fills out the rights form for the selected user.

21

Listing 21.21. Selecting the Access Rights form.

```
Private Sub SSTab1_Click(PreviousTab As Integer)
    '
    ' handle tab changes
    '
    Select Case PreviousTab
        Case 0 ' leaving users
            lblUserID = txtField(0)
            lblUserName = txtField(2)
            accLoadLists
        Case 1 ' leaving access
    End Select
    '
End Sub
```

Then add code for the new accLoadLists method. This is the code that actually loads the grid boxes with live data (see Listing 21.22).

Listing 21.22. Coding the accLoadLists method.

```
Public Sub accLoadLists()
    '
    ' load form dbgrids
    '
    strSQLDefault = "SELECT Object,[Level],UserID FROM secAccess WHERE
UserID='DEFAULT' ORDER BY Object"
    strSQLUserID = "SELECT Object,[Level],UserID FROM secAccess WHERE UserID =
'" & lblUserID & "' ORDER BY Object"
    '
    dtaDefault.DatabaseName = strDBName
    dtaDefault.RecordSource = strSQLDefault
    dbgDefault.Caption = "Secure Objects"
    dtaDefault.Refresh
    dbgDefault.ReBind
    dbgDefault.Columns(0).Width = 1440
    dbgDefault.Columns(1).Width = 600
    '
    dtaUserID.DatabaseName = strDBName
    dtaUserID.RecordSource = strSQLUserID
    dbgUserID.Caption = "User Access"
    dtaUserID.Refresh
    dbgUserID.ReBind
    dbgUserID.Columns(0).Width = 1440
    dbgUserID.Columns(1).Width = 600
    '
End Sub
```

Next, add the code from Listing 21.23 behind the cmdAccess button array. This control array handles all the routines that add and delete rights objects and set the access level for the rights objects.

Listing 21.23. Setting up access levels and command buttons.

`TYPE`

```
Private Sub cmdAccess_Click(Index As Integer)
    '
    ' handle user selections
    '
    Select Case Index
        Case 0 ' add object
            accAddObject
        Case 1 ' delete object
            If dtaUserID.Recordset.RecordCount > 0 Then
                accDelObject
            Else
                MsgBox "No objects to Delete", vbExclamation, "Delete Object"
            End If
        Case 2 ' copy all
            accCopyAll
        Case 3 ' erase all
            If dtaUserID.Recordset.RecordCount > 0 Then
                accDelAll
            Else
                MsgBox "No objects to Delete", vbExclamation, "Erase All"
            End If
        Case 4 ' set level
            If dtaUserID.Recordset.RecordCount > 0 Then
                accSetLevel
            Else
                MsgBox "No objects on File", vbInformation, "Set Level"
            End If
    End Select
    '
End Sub
```

This module calls a set of routines. Each of them handles the real dirty work. You also add some error checking here to make the program a bit more friendly.

To start off, you enter the code that adds an object from the Default Set to the current User's Set. Create a new subroutine called accAddObject and place the code in Listing 21.24 in the routine.

`TYPE`   **Listing 21.24. Creating the accAddObject routine.**

```
Public Sub accAddObject()
    '
    ' add an object to the UserID set
    '
    On Error GoTo LocalErr
    '
    Dim strObject As String
```

21

continues

Listing 21.24. continued

```
        '
        ' is this the default user account?
        If lblUserID = "DEFAULT" Then
            strObject = InputBox("Enter new secure object:", "Create new Object")
            strObject = UCase(Trim(strObject))
        Else
            strObject = dtaDefault.Recordset!object
        End If
        '
        ' try to add it to the collection
        If strObject <> "" Then
            With dtaUserID.Recordset
                .FindFirst "UserID='" & lblUserID & "' AND object='" & strObject &
    "'"
                If .NoMatch = True Then
                    .AddNew
                    .UserID = lblUserID
                    !object = strObject
                    ![Level] = 0
                    .Update
                Else
                    MsgBox "Object Already on File", vbExclamation, "Add Object"
                End If
            End With
        End If
        '
        accLoadLists
        '
        Exit Sub
        '
LocalErr:
        MsgBox Err.Description, vbExclamation, Err.Number
        '
End Sub
```

This routine gets some variables from the form and then checks to see whether you are trying
to add an object to the Default user. If so, you are prompted for the new object name, and
if a valid one is entered, that object is added to the Default list. If you are attempting to add
a new object to a real user, the routine checks to make sure the object does not already exist
for that user before adding it to your list.

The next routine to add (shown in Listing 21.25) deletes an object from the User List. Create
a new subroutine called accDelObject and add the code in Listing 21.25.

TYPE **Listing 21.25. Deleting an object with accDelObject.**

```
Public Sub accDelObject()
    '
    ' delete an object from the User list
    '
    Dim strObject As String
```

```
    Dim intAnswer As Integer
    '
    strObject = dtaUserID.Recordset!object
    intAnswer = MsgBox("Delete [" & strObject & "] from User Access?",
vbQuestion + vbYesNo, "Delete Object")
    If intAnswer = vbYes Then
        dtaUserID.Recordset.Delete
        accLoadLists
    End If
    '
End Sub
```

The routine first asks for confirmation before deleting the object from the list.

Now you tackle a tougher one. The subroutine called accDelAll removes all the existing rights objects for the current user. Add the code in Listing 21.26.

Listing 21.26. Deleting all existing rights objects with accDelAll.

TYPE

```
Public Sub accDelAll()
    '
    ' delete all objects from user list
    '
    Dim strUserID As String
    Dim intAnswer As Integer
    Dim strSQL As String
    Dim ws As Workspace
    Dim db As Database
    '
    ' init vars
    strUserID = lblUserID
    strSQL = "DELETE FROM secAccess WHERE UserID='" & strUserID & "'"
    '
    ' confirm delete
    intAnswer = MsgBox("Delete ALL objects for UserID [" & strUserID & "]?",
vbQuestion + vbYesNo, "Erase All")
    If intAnswer = vbYes Then
        Set ws = DBEngine.CreateWorkspace("usrDelAll", "admin", "")
        Set db = ws.OpenDatabase(strDBName)
        '
        On Error Resume Next
        ws.BeginTrans
        db.Execute strSQL
        If Err.Number = 0 Then
            ws.CommitTrans
        Else
            ws.Rollback
            MsgBox "Unable to complete transaction", vbExclamation, "Erase All"
        End If
        '
```

21

continues

Listing 21.26. continued

```
        db.Close
        ws.Close
        Set db = Nothing
        Set ws = Nothing
    End If
    '
    accLoadLists
    '
End Sub
```

Notice that you use an SQL statement to perform this task. Because you are using the `Execute` method, you need to open another copy of the database. Also, because the single SQL statement might be deleting multiple records in the same table, you encapsulate the delete process in a `BeginTrans_CommitTrans` loop.

Now for the hardest one of the bunch, the `accCopyAll` routine. Because some records might already be on file, you first must delete any existing items. The routine in Listing 21.27 contains several SQL statements and, of course, they are covered by Visual Basic transactions, too.

TYPE   **Listing 21.27. The `accCopyAll` routine.**

```
Public Sub accCopyAll()
    '
    ' copy all objects from default to user
    '
    Dim strUserID As String
    Dim strSQLDelete As String
    Dim strSQLTemp As String
    Dim strSQLUpdate As String
    Dim strSQLDrop As String
    Dim strSQLInsert As String
    Dim intAnswer As Integer
    Dim ws As Workspace
    Dim db As Database
    '
    ' init vars
    strUserID = lblUserID
    strSQLDelete = "DELETE FROM secAccess WHERE UserID='" & strUserID & "'"
    strSQLTemp = "SELECT * INTO secTemp FROM secAccess WHERE UserID='DEFAULT'"
    strSQLUpdate = "UPDATE secTemp SET UserID='" & strUserID & "'"
    strSQLInsert = "INSERT INTO secAccess SELECT * FROM secTemp"
    strSQLDrop = "DROP Table secTemp"
    '
    ' now do it
    intAnswer = MsgBox("Replace all current objects for UserID [" & strUserID &
"]?", vbQuestion + vbYesNo, "CopyAll")
    If intAnswer = vbYes Then
        '
        Set ws = DBEngine.CreateWorkspace("wsCopyAll", "admin", "")
        Set db = ws.OpenDatabase(strDBName)
        '
```

```
        On Error Resume Next
        ws.BeginTrans
        db.Execute strSQLDelete
        db.Execute strSQLTemp
        db.Execute strSQLUpdate
        db.Execute strSQLInsert
        db.Execute strSQLDrop
        '
        If Err.Number = 0 Then
            ws.CommitTrans
        Else
            ws.Rollback
            MsgBox "Unable to complete transaction", vbExclamation, "Copy All"
        End If
        '
        db.Close
        ws.Close
        Set db = Nothing
        Set ws = Nothing
        '
        accLoadLists
    End If
    '
End Sub
```

The last routine you need to add is the one for the Set Level button. This routine calls another small form that you build next. The second form is where you set the access level for the selected rights object. Create a new subroutine called accSetLevel and add the code in Listing 21.28.

TYPE   **Listing 21.28. The accSetLevel routine.**

```
Public Sub accSetLevel()
    '
    ' set user access level
    '
    Dim strRightsName As String
    '
    strRightsName = lblUserID & " ["
    strRightsName = strRightsName & dtaUserID.Recordset.Fields("Object") & "]"
    intRights = dtaUserID.Recordset![Level]

    frmRights.fraRights = strRightsName
    frmRights.Caption = "User Access Rights"
    '
    frmRights.Show vbModal
    '
    ' update object rights
    With dtaUserID.Recordset
        .Edit
        .Fields("[Level]") = intRights
        .Update
```

21

continues

Listing 21.28. continued

```
    End With
    '
    accLoadLists
    '
End Sub
```

This routine loads some controls on the new form and then shows the form for input. When the form is closed, this routine transfers some of the information back into the data control and refreshes the on-screen lists.

Now you need to build the last data form. Add a new form to the DLL project. Use Table 21.5 and Figure 21.6 as guides in laying out the Rights List.

Figure 21.6.

Laying out the access level form.

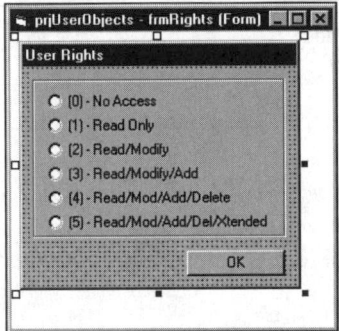

Table 21.5. Controls for the Rights List form.

Control	Property	Setting
VB.Form	Name	frmRights
	BorderStyle	3 'Fixed Dialog
	Caption	"User Rights"
	ClientHeight	2715
	ClientLeft	45
	ClientTop	330
	ClientWidth	3390
	ControlBox	0 'False
	LinkTopic	"Form1"
	MaxButton	0 'False
	MinButton	0 'False
	ScaleHeight	2715

Control	Property	Setting
	ScaleWidth	3390
	ShowInTaskbar	0 'False
	StartUpPosition	2 'CenterScreen
VB.CommandButton	Name	cmdOK
	Caption	"OK"
	Height	315
	Left	2040
	TabIndex	1
	Top	2280
	Width	1200
VB.Frame	Name	fraRights
	Height	2055
	Left	120
	TabIndex	0
	Top	60
	Width	3135
VB.OptionButton	Name	optRights
	Caption	"(5)–Read/Mod/Add/Del/Xtended"
	Height	255
	Index	5
	Left	180
	TabIndex	7
	Top	1740
	Width	2775
VB.OptionButton	Name	optRights
	Caption	"(4)–Read/Mod/Add/Delete"
	Height	255
	Index	4
	Left	180
	TabIndex	6
	Top	1440
	Width	2775

21

continues

Table 21.5. continued

Control	Property	Setting
VB.OptionButton	Name	optRights
	Caption	"(3)–Read/Modify/Add"
	Height	255
	Index	3
	Left	180
	TabIndex	5
	Top	1140
	Width	2775
VB.OptionButton	Name	optRights
	Caption	"(2)–Read/Modify"
	Height	255
	Index	2
	Left	180
	TabIndex	4
	Top	840
	Width	2775
VB.OptionButton	Name	optRights
	Caption	"(1)–Read Only"
	Height	255
	Index	1
	Left	180
	TabIndex	3
	Top	540
	Width	2775
VB.OptionButton	Name	optRights
	Caption	"(0)–No Access"
	Height	255
	Index	0
	Left	180
	TabIndex	2
	Top	240
	Width	2775

21

There is very little code to add to this form. All the code you need for this form is found in Listing 21.29. Add this code to the frmRights form.

TYPE **Listing 21.29. Coding the frmRights form.**

```
Option Explicit

Private Sub cmdOK_Click()
    Unload Me
End Sub

Private Sub Form_Load()
    '
    ' set rights button
    '
    optRights(frmUserMaint.intRights) = True
    '
End Sub

Private Sub optRights_Click(Index As Integer)
    '
    ' set rights level
    '
    frmUserMaint.intRights = Index
    '
End Sub
```

Now save this form as FRMRIGHTS.FRM. In the next section, you walk through a session of setting user rights and adding new secured objects to the database.

Running the Access Rights Maintenance Forms

After building the Access Rights forms, you are ready to test the project again. When you start the program, you are prompted to enter a password. As before, enter USERA for both the User ID and the Password. This brings up the User Maintenance form. First, add a new user, TEMPUSER. Be sure to include a password and a name. After saving the new user record, select the User Access tab to add user access rights. Your form should look similar to the one in Figure 21.7.

You can see a set of default access objects on the left of Figure 21.7, and you can see that the new user does not have any defined security levels for the objects in the box on the right. First, add one of the default objects to the user's list by clicking a row selector in the Secure Objects list (the Default List) and clicking the Add button. You see that the selected object has been copied to the User Access list with the default access rights setting (see Figure 21.8).

21

Figure 21.7.

Editing the access rights for a user.

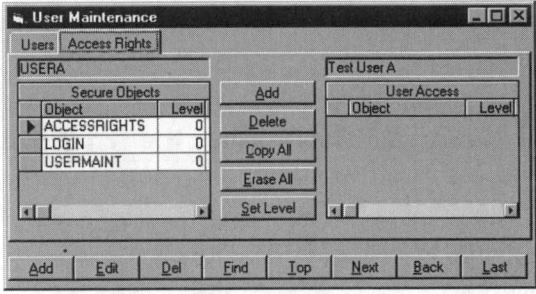

Figure 21.8.

Adding an object to the User Access list.

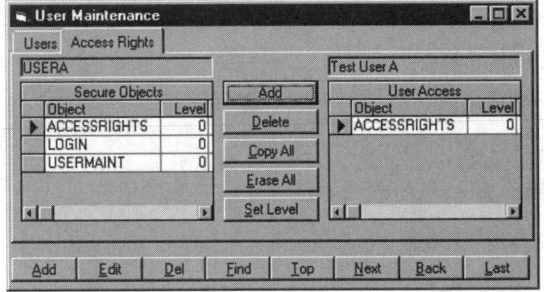

You can change the access level for the new object by pressing the Set Level button. This brings up a window that shows all the possible access levels (see Figure 21.9).

Figure 21.9.

Changing the Access Level for an object.

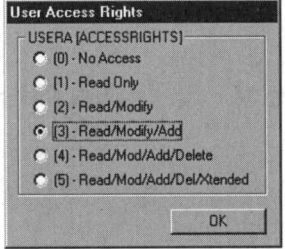

Select the Read/Modify/Add radio button and click the OK button. When you return to the previous form, you see that the access level for that user has been updated.

You can practice adding, deleting, and modifying secured objects for any user you add to the database. You can define new secured objects by opening the Default user profile and selecting Access | Set User Access from the main menu. Any entirely new objects must first be added to the Default user.

WARNING

Although it is possible to delete all the objects from the Default user profile, it is not recommended. Doing so makes it impossible to add or edit existing access rights of other new users.

Implementing Access Rights Security in Your Application

Now that you have the tools to create and manage user access rights, you need to build a routine to check those user rights and then add rights-checking to a working Visual Basic application.

First, you add two new methods to the PRJUSROBJECT DLL file. The first procedure (CheckRights) is the main routine that verifies the user's rights to an object. The second routine (LoadRights) is a support routine that is called by CheckRights. You also need to add some more code to the general declarations portion of the 4class module (see Listing 21.30). Place this right after the code you added for the Login/Logout features of the class.

TYPE **Listing 21.30. Adding code to the declarations section of the UsrObject class module.**

```
'
' user access verification vars
Private wsRights As Workspace
Private dbRights As Database
Private rsRights As Recordset
Private blnRightsLoaded As Boolean
'
Enum urLevel
    urNone = 0
    urReadOnly = 1
    urReadModify = 2
    urReadModAdd = 3
    urReadModAddDel = 4
    urextended = 5
End Enum
```

Now add the method that loads the dataset into local objects. Enter the code from Listing 21.31 into your project.

21

TYPE   **Listing 21.31. Adding the `LoadRights` function to the DLL.**

```
Private Sub LoadRights()
    '
    ' load user's rights collection
    '
    Dim strSQL As String
    '
    strSQL = "SELECT * FROM secAccess WHERE UserID='" & strUserIDProp & "'"
    '
    Set wsRights = DBEngine.CreateWorkspace("wsUser", "admin", "")
    Set dbRights = wsRights.OpenDatabase(strDBName)
    Set rsRights = dbRights.OpenRecordset(strSQL, dbOpenSnapshot)
    '
    blnRightsLoaded = True
    '
End Sub
```

Now add the routine to check the access rights for a particular secured object. Create a function called `CheckRights` and enter the segment of code in Listing 21.32.

TYPE   **Listing 21.32. Checking access rights for a secured object with `accRights`.**

```
Public Function CheckRights(strObject As String, urCheck As urLevel) As Boolean
    '
    ' see if user has proper rights
    '
    On Error GoTo LocalErr
    '
    If blnRightsLoaded = False Then
        LoadRights
    End If
    '
    CheckRights = False ' assume it's not good!
    '
    With rsRights
        .MoveLast
        If .RecordCount <> 0 Then
            .FindFirst "Object='" & strObject & "'"
            If .NoMatch = False Then
                CheckRights = (urCheck <= .Fields("[Level]"))
            End If
        End If
    End With
    '
    Exit Function
    '
LocalErr:
    Err.Raise Err.Number, App.EXEName & ".usrObject", Err.Description
    '
End Function
```

21

This function accepts two parameters (the object and requested rights level), and it returns TRUE or FALSE depending on whether the user has been granted the requested rights level. If no rights level is on file, this function returns zero (no access).

Now save the DLL project files. Next, you add code to the Test project that uses the access rights to limit user access to the system.

For this example, you check the user's login rights at the very start of the application. If they do not have the proper rights, they cannot see the first screen.

The code in Listing 21.33 shows how the Main method should now look. This version of Main checks the user's access rights to the user maintenance form before displaying it to the user.

TYPE   **Listing 21.33. Before the change in the Main procedure.**

```
Public Sub Main()
    '
    ' main entry for form-less project
    '
    Set objUser = New usrObject
    objUser.DBName = App.Path & "\..\..\data\security\security.mdb"
    '
    ' now try to start up
    If objUser.UserLogin = True Then
        If objUser.CheckRights("UserMaint", urReadModAdd) Then
            objUser.UsersForm
        Else
            MsgBox "You do not have rights to this application", vbExclamation,
"Login Failed"
        End If
        objUser.LogUser urLogOut
    End If
    '
    End
    '
End Sub
```

That's it! Now save and run the test project. This time, log into the application using MCA as the user and the password. This user does not have the proper rights to the User Maintenance data entry form. When you attempt to log in, you get a message telling you that you do not have rights to run the application (see Figure 21.10).

Figure 21.10.
Failing the rights validation test.

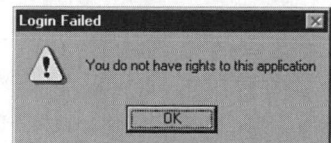

21

With this tool, you can create and manage any type of secured program object you like. You can create security levels that restrict user access to entire programs or to individual forms or reports, disable menu items or command buttons, and even disable or hide individual fields within a form. It is very easy to add these security features to all your Visual Basic programs.

Auditing User Actions

Now that you have a way to force users to log in and out of your application and a way to establish and restrict user access to program objects, you can allow users to create an *audit trail* for all the secured activity. Audit trails are very valuable tools for tracking application use. With good audit trails you can tell when users log in and out of your application and what kinds of program operations they perform. Audit trails can also provide vital information you can use to debug your applications. Often users are not able to remember just what it was they were doing when they received an error message. Good audit trails can tell you the exact date and time the user encountered the error.

Developing a User Audit System

Adding a user audit system to your applications is really very easy. You need only a few additional routines in your DLL library. First, you need a way to write information to an audit log file. Second, you need a way to trigger the creation of audit records. You can write audit information any time. Typically, you want to keep track of each time a user logs into and out of an application. You might also want to log each time a user performs any critical operation, such as printing a sensitive report or running a mass update routine. One of the most common uses for audit logs is to track any modifications made to database records. Let's look at how you can create detailed audit logs that show all the fields that were modified, including the old value and the new value for each field.

The Audit Log Library Routines

You need only a handful of properties and methods to implement an audit log class. First, add a new class module to the DLL project. Set its name to logObject and save it as logObject.cls.

Now add the code in Listing 21.34 to the general declarations section of the new class module.

Listing 21.34. Declaring class-level variables for the
`logObject` module.

`TYPE`

```
Option Explicit
'
' local storage
Private strFileName As String
Private intFileHandle As Integer
Private strHeader As String
'
```

Next, you need to create the `Property Let` and `Property Get` statements for the `logObject` properties. The code in Listing 21.35 shows you how to do this. Add this code to your `logObject` class module.

`TYPE` **Listing 21.35. Adding the Public properties of `logObject`.**

```
Public Property Get FileName() As Variant
    FileName = strFileName
End Property

Public Property Let FileName(ByVal vNewValue As Variant)
    strFileName = vNewValue
End Property

Public Property Get LogHeader() As Variant
    LogHeader = strHeader
End Property

Public Property Let LogHeader(ByVal vNewValue As Variant)
    strHeader = vNewValue
End Property
```

Finally, add the code from Listing 21.36 to the `Class_Initialize` and `Class_Terminate` events of the module. This handles all the initial setup and final cleanup of the `logObject` class.

Listing 21.36. Coding the `Class_Initialize` and `Class_Terminate`
events.

`TYPE`

```
Private Sub Class_Initialize()
    '
    ' init stuff
    '
    strFileName = App.EXEName & ".log"
```

21

continues

Listing 21.36. continued

```
        intFileHandle = -1
        strHeader = "Audit Log"
        '
End Sub

Private Sub Class_Terminate()
    '
    ' clean up loose ends
    '
    On Error Resume Next
    '
    Close #intFileHandle
    '
End Sub
```

The main method of the class is the WriteLog method. This method is the one you call to send
an audit line to the log. Add a new Public subroutine called WriteLog to your logObject class
and enter the code from Listing 21.37.

TYPE **Listing 21.37. Coding the WriteLog method.**

```
Public Sub WriteLog(ParamArray varParms() As Variant)
    '
    ' write a log entry
    '
    On Error GoTo LocalErr
    '
    Dim lngItems As Long
    Dim lngLoop As Long
    Dim strLine As String
    Dim vbQuote As String
    Dim strUser As String
    Dim strDate As String
    '
    vbQuote = Chr(34)
    '
    If intFileHandle = -1 Then
        OpenLogFile
    End If
    '
    If modUsrObject.strUserIDSaved = "" Then
        strUser = "NO_USER"
    Else
        strUser = modUsrObject.strUserIDSaved
    End If
    '
    ' basic stuff
    strLine = vbQuote & Format(Now(), "general date") & vbQuote & ","
    strLine = strLine & vbQuote & strUser & vbQuote & ","
    '
    ' stuff from caller
    lngItems = UBound(varParms)
    For lngLoop = 0 To lngItems
```

```
            strLine = strLine & vbQuote & varParms(lngLoop) & vbQuote & ","
    Next
    strLine = Left(strLine, Len(strLine) - 1) ' drop last comma
    '
    ' send it out
    Print #intFileHandle, strLine
    '
    Exit Sub
    '
LocalErr:
    Err.Raise Err.Number, App.EXEName & ".logObject", Err.Description
    '
End Sub
```

> **TIP**
>
> Notice that you are enclosing all items in quotation marks. This makes it easier for you to convert this file into a database in the future (if you want to) because most conversion tools expect strings in quotations.

Notice that there is only one parameter sent to the WriteLog method. This parameter is actually an array of parameters. By using the ParamArray keyword, you are telling Visual Basic to put all parameters sent to this method into a single variant array. Now, whether the caller sends you 1 or 100 items in the call, you can access them all through this array.

Now you can add the two Private support routines OpenLogFile and WriteHeader. These are called as needed from the WriteLog method (see Listing 21.38).

TYPE   **Listing 21.38. Coding the OpenLogFile method.**

```
Private Sub OpenLogFile()
    '
    ' open the file for output
    '
    On Error Resume Next
    '
    ' see if the file exists
    intFileHandle = FreeFile
    Open strFileName For Input As intFileHandle
    '
    ' if missing, make a new one
    If Err.Number <> 0 Then
        Open strFileName For Output As intFileHandle
        WriteHeader
    End If
    Close #intFileHandle
    '
```

21

continues

Listing 21.38. continued

```
     ' open existing file
     Open strFileName For Append As intFileHandle
     '
End Sub

Private Sub WriteHeader()
     '
     ' send out standard header
     '
     Print #intFileHandle, String(60, "*")
     Print #intFileHandle, strHeader
     Print #intFileHandle, "Created: " & Format(Now(), "general date")
     Print #intFileHandle, String(60, "*")
     Print #intFileHandle, ""
     '
End Sub
```

Notice that the OpenLogFile method first checks to see whether the file exists. If it does not, a new one is created and a log header is written to the new file.

Now add the final routine, ClearLog. This one allows you to clear an existing log file and start out fresh. Add the code from Listing 21.39 to your class module.

TYPE **Listing 21.39. Coding the ClearLog method.**

```
Public Sub ClearLog()
     '
     ' clear all records from the log
     '
     On Error GoTo LocalErr
     '
     Dim intFile As Integer
     '
     intFile = FreeFile
     '
     Open strFileName For Output As intFile
     WriteHeader
     Close #intFile
     '
     Exit Sub
     '
LocalErr:
     Err.Raise Err.Number, App.EXEName & ".logObject", Err.Description
     '
End Sub
```

Now save the DLL project again. You have created all the routines you need in order to add detailed audit trails to any Visual Basic project. This is the last of the modifications to the prjUsrObject DLL library. But before going on to the next section, let's make a final modification to the test project to verify that the audit routines are working.

Recording User Activity in an Audit File

The next step is to add code to the current project that records each time a user logs in or out of the application. You need to modify the general declarations section to add a module-level object variable for the logging object:

```
Option Explicit
'
' project-level vars
'
Public objUser As Object
Public objLog As Object ' <<< new line
```

You also need to modify the Main routine to include the initialization of the log object and writes to the log file. Listing 21.40 shows how your Main routine should look now.

Listing 21.40. Adding audit logging to the Main routine in

TYPE **the test project.**

```
Public Sub Main()
    '
    ' main entry for form-less project
    '
    Set objUser = New usrObject
    objUser.DBName = App.Path & "\..\..\data\security\security.mdb"
    '
    Set objLog = New logObject
    objLog.filename = App.Path & "\" & App.EXEName & ".log"
    objLog.LogHeader = App.EXEName & " Audit Log"
    '
    ' now try to start up
    If objUser.UserLogin = True Then
        objLog.WriteLog "UserLogin", "Main"
        If objUser.CheckRights("UserMaint", urReadModAdd) Then
            objLog.WriteLog "UserMaint", "Main", "StartForm"
            objUser.UsersForm
            objLog.WriteLog "UserMaint", "Main", "ExitForm"
        Else
            MsgBox "You do not have rights to this application", vbExclamation,
"Login Failed"
        End If
        objUser.LogUser urLogOut
        objLog.WriteLog "UserLogOut", "Main"
    End If
    '
    End
    '
End Sub
```

21

Now save and run the test project. Log into the application with default as the User ID and Password and then log back out. You have just created an audit file called PRJUSRTEST.LOG in the same directory as the test project. Open the file using Notepad and review its contents. You see the login record, the start of the form, the end of the form, and the log out record. The results of a similar run are included in the following lines:

```
***************************************************************
prjTest Audit Log
Created: 19-Feb-97 12:39:19 AM
***************************************************************

"19-Feb-97 6:04:59 AM","default","UserLogin","Main"
"19-Feb-97 6:04:59 AM","default","UserMaint","Main","StartForm"
"19-Feb-97 6:06:22 AM","default","UserMaint","Main","ExitForm"
"19-Feb-97 6:06:27 AM","default","UserLogOut","Main"
```

Once you confirm that your objects are working properly, compile the ActiveX DLL and close the project. You're now ready to create a short data entry application that uses all the features of your new security library.

Adding Security to a Data Entry Form

In this final example, you build a quick data entry form using data-bound controls, and add user login, access rights, and audit logging to the form. This shows how you can provide tight security even in simple data-bound forms.

WARNING

You need to run the SecTest.SQV script using the SQLVB5 interpreter to create the proper tables and entries in the BOOKS5.MDB that is used by this exercise. You can find this SQV script in the Chap21 folder on the CD. See Appendix A for more information on running SQLVB5.

First, start a new Visual Basic 5 Standard EXE project and select Project | References... to load the new Security library (prjUsrObject.dll) to your project (see Figure 21.11).

Refer to Table 21.6 and Figure 21.12 to lay out the new data entry form.

WARNING

The command buttons on this form are in a control array. You must pay close attention to how they are arranged on the form in order for the security features to work properly.

Figure 21.11.

Loading the new security library into a Visual Basic project.

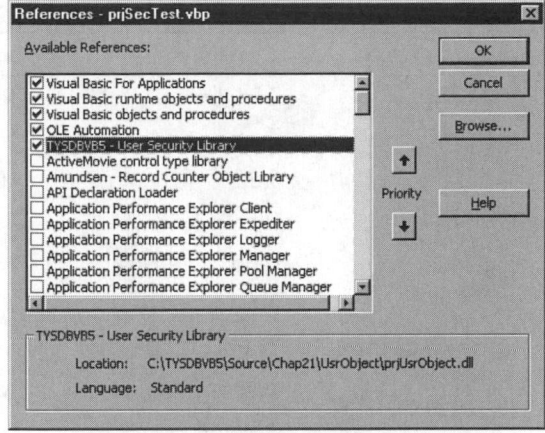

Figure 21.12.

Laying out the new data entry form.

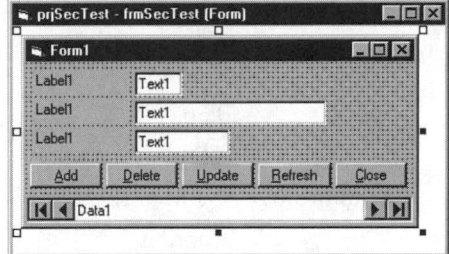

Table 21.6. Controls for the Data Entry form.

Control	Property	Setting
VB.Form	Name	frmSecTest
	Caption	"Form1"
	ClientHeight	2010
	ClientLeft	60
	ClientTop	345
	ClientWidth	4890
	LinkTopic	"Form1"
	ScaleHeight	2010
	ScaleWidth	4890
	StartUpPosition	3 'Windows Default
VB.CommandButton	Name	cmdBtn
	Caption	"&Delete"

21

continues

Table 21.6. continued

Control	Property	Setting
	Height	300
	Index	4
	Left	1020
	TabIndex	7
	Top	1260
	Width	900
VB.CommandButton	Name	cmdBtn
	Caption	"&Add"
	Height	300
	Index	3
	Left	60
	TabIndex	6
	Top	1260
	Width	900
VB.CommandButton	Name	cmdBtn
	Caption	"&Update"
	Height	300
	Index	2
	Left	1980
	TabIndex	5
	Top	1260
	Width	900
VB.CommandButton	Name	cmdBtn
	Caption	"&Refresh"
	Height	300
	Index	1
	Left	2940
	TabIndex	4
	Top	1260
	Width	900

Control	Property	Setting
VB.CommandButton	Name	cmdBtn
	Caption	"&Close"
	Height	300
	Index	0
	Left	3900
	TabIndex	3
	Top	1260
	Width	900
VB.TextBox	Name	txtField
	DataSource	"Data1"
	Height	300
	Index	2
	Left	1380
	TabIndex	2
	Text	"Text1"
	Top	840
	Width	1200
VB.TextBox	Name	txtField
	DataSource	"Data1"
	Height	300
	Index	1
	Left	1380
	TabIndex	1
	Text	"Text1"
	Top	480
	Width	2400
VB.TextBox	Name	txtField
	DataSource	"Data1"
	Height	300
	Index	0
	Left	1380
	TabIndex	0

21

continues

Table 21.6. continued

Control	Property	Setting
	Text	"Text1"
	Top	120
	Width	600
VB.Data	Name	Data1
	Align	2 'Align Bottom
	Caption	"Data1"
	Connect	"Access"
	DatabaseName	""
	DefaultCursorType=	'DefaultCursor
	DefaultType	2 'UseODBC
	Exclusive	0 'False
	Height	345
	Left	0
	Options	0
	ReadOnly	0 'False
	RecordsetType	1 'Dynaset
	RecordSource	""
	Top	1665
	Width	4890
VB.Label	Name	lblPrompt
	Caption	"Label1"
	Height	300
	Index	2
	Left	120
	TabIndex	10
	Top	840
	Width	1200
VB.Label	Name	lblPrompt
	Caption	"Label1"
	Height	300

Control	Property	Setting
	Index	1
	Left	120
	TabIndex	9
	Top	480
	Width	1200
VB.Label	Name	lblPrompt
	Caption	"Label1"
	Height	300
	Index	0
	Left	120
	TabIndex	8
	Top	120
	Width	1200

Save this new project as PRJSECTEST.VBP and save the form as FRMSECTEST.FRM.

Next you need to add code to the form. Listing 21.41 shows the code for the general declarations area and the Form_Load event.

TYPE | **Listing 21.41. Coding the declarations and the Form_Load event.**

```
Option Explicit
'
Dim objUser As Object
Dim objLog As Object

Private Sub Form_Load()
    '
    SetForm ' set up form
    SetLog ' set up log stuff
    SetUser ' set up user stuff
    '
End Sub
```

Now add the code for the three support routines called from Form_Load. The SetForm routine binds the input controls to the data fields, sets the form captions, and fills the data control with live records (see Listing 21.42).

21

TYPE **Listing 21.42. Coding the SetForm method.**

```
Public Sub SetForm()
    '
    ' set up form controls
    '
    Me.Caption = "Security Test Form"
    '
    lblPrompt(0).Caption = "Author ID"
    lblPrompt(1).Caption = "Name"
    lblPrompt(2).Caption = "DOB"
    '
    txtField(0).DataField = "AUID"
    txtField(1).DataField = "Name"
    txtField(2).DataField = "DOB"
    '
    Data1.BOFAction = vbMoveFirst
    Data1.EOFAction = vbMoveLast
    Data1.DatabaseName = App.Path & "\..\..\data\books5.mdb"
    Data1.RecordSource = "Authors"
    Data1.Refresh
    '
End Sub
```

The SetLog method simply initializes the logObject and sets its properties in preparation for writing audit log entries (see Listing 21.43).

TYPE **Listing 21.43. Coding the SetLog method.**

```
Public Sub SetLog()
    '
    ' setup logging
    '
    Set objLog = New logObject
    objLog.filename = App.Path & "\" & App.EXEName & ".log"
    objLog.LogHeader = App.EXEName & " Audit Log"
    '
End Sub
```

Finally, the SetUser method initializes the user object, then lets the user login. If the login is successful, the row of command buttons is enabled, based on the user's rights for each item (see Listing 21.44).

TYPE **Listing 21.44. Coding the** `SetUser` **method.**

```
Public Sub SetUser()
    '
    ' set up user details
    '
    Dim ctlTemp As Control
    '
    ' create object & set properties
    Set objUser = New usrObject
    objUser.DBName = Data1.DatabaseName
    objUser.LoginTitle = "Security Test Form"
    '
    ' login and set up rights
    If objUser.UserLogin = True Then
        objLog.WriteLog "LogIn", objUser.UserID
        For Each ctlTemp In Controls
            If TypeOf ctlTemp Is CommandButton Then
                ctlTemp.Enabled = objUser.CheckRights(ctlTemp.Caption,
ctlTemp.Index)
            End If
        Next
    Else
        End ' reject user
    End If
    '
End Sub
```

Notice that the control array index was used to actually indicate the rights level for each button. The Close button is index 0 (no rights needed), but the Delete button is index 4 (Read/Mod/Add/Del rights). This is a very efficient way to gather rights data for a user. Note also that the audit log is written if the user is successful in logging into the form.

Now you can add the code for the button array. This allows users (if they have the proper rights) to add, edit, or delete records from the table. Add the code from Listing 21.45 to the `cdmBtn_Click` event.

TYPE **Listing 21.45. Adding code to the** `cmdBtn_Click` **event.**

```
Private Sub cmdBtn_Click(Index As Integer)
    '
    ' handle button clicks
    '
    On Error GoTo LocalErr
    '
    Select Case Index
        Case 0 ' close
            objLog.WriteLog "LogOut", objUser.UserID
            objUser.LogUser urLogOut
```

21

continues

Listing 21.45. continued

```
                Unload Me
        Case 1 ' refresh
            Data1.UpdateControls
        Case 2 ' update
            Data1_Validate vbDataActionUpdate, 1
            Data1.UpdateRecord
        Case 3 ' add
            Data1.Recordset.AddNew
            txtField(0).SetFocus
        Case 4 ' delete
            objLog.WriteLog "Delete", Data1.RecordSource, txtField(0).DataField,
txtField(0), ""
            objLog.WriteLog "Delete", Data1.RecordSource, txtField(1).DataField,
txtField(1), ""
            objLog.WriteLog "Delete", Data1.RecordSource, txtField(2).DataField,
txtField(2), ""
            Data1.Recordset.Delete
            Data1.Recordset.MovePrevious
    End Select
    '
    Exit Sub
    '
LocalErr:
    MsgBox Err.Description, vbExclamation, Err.Number
    '
End Sub
```

Note that there are steps to write deleted records to the audit file, but not to log edits or adds. These transactions are handled in the Validate event of the data control.

There is one support routine you need to add to the form. This routine is used to generate a "friendly name" for each of the action codes that occur in the Validate parameter list. Add the code in Listing 21.46 to your form.

TYPE **Listing 21.46. Coding the GetAction method.**

```
Public Function GetAction(intAction As Integer) As String
    '
    ' convert action constant into friendly name
    '
    Select Case intAction
        Case vbDataActionMoveFirst '1
            GetAction = "MoveFirst"
        Case vbDataActionMovePrevious '2
            GetAction = "MovePrevious"
        Case vbDataActionMoveNext '3
            GetAction = "MoveNext"
        Case vbDataActionMoveLast '4
            GetAction = "MoveLast"
```

```
        Case vbDataActionAddNew '5
            GetAction = "AddNew"
        Case vbDataActionUpdate '6
            GetAction = "Update"
        Case vbDataActionDelete '7
            GetAction = "Delete"
        Case vbDataActionFind '8
            GetAction = "Find"
        Case vbDataActionBookmark '9
            GetAction = "Bookmark"
        Case vbDataActionClose '10
            GetAction = "Close"
        Case vbDataActionUnload '11
            GetAction = "Unload"
    End Select
    '
End Function
```

Now you need to add one more set of code. Listing 21.47 shows the code you need to enter into the Data1_Validate event. This code checks to see if any of the columns have been altered. If so, an audit log is generated.

TYPE **Listing 21.47. Adding code to the Data1_Validate event.**

```
Private Sub Data1_Validate(Action As Integer, Save As Integer)
    '
    ' log any changes
    '
    Dim ctlTemp As Control
    '
    MousePointer = vbHourglass
    '
    ' check text boxes for changed data
    For Each ctlTemp In Controls
        If TypeOf ctlTemp Is TextBox Then
            If ctlTemp.DataChanged Then
                objLog.WriteLog GetAction(Action), Data1.RecordSource,
ctlTemp.DataField, Data1.Recordset.Fields(ctlTemp.DataField), ctlTemp
            End If
        End If
    Next
    '
    MousePointer = vbNormal
    '
End Sub
```

That's all there is to it. Now save the form as FRMSECTEST.FRM and the project as PRJSECTEST.VBP, and run it. If you log in as USERA, you have very limited access to the data (see Figure 21.13).

21

Figure 21.13.

Viewing the data
entry form with
limited access rights.

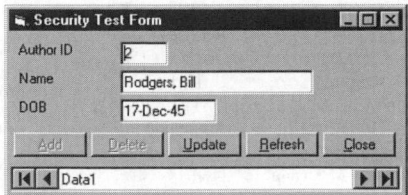

You now have a data-bound entry form with user login/logout, access checking, and field-level audit trails for any updated records. You can use this library on data bound forms, forms that use Microsoft DAO, or even other VBA-complaint applications that require auditing, user logins, or access rights management.

Summary

In today's lesson, you learned several methods you can use to increase the level of security for your Visual Basic database applications. You learned about the limitations of using the Microsoft Access SYSTEM security file and database encryption.

This lesson also showed you how you can add application-level security to your Visual Basic programs by adding user login/logout routines and creating a user access rights scheme for your applications. In this lesson, you designed and implemented a login screen that you can use for all your Visual Basic applications, and you created several screens for maintaining user lists and managing access rights for each user.

You also learned how to add an audit trail option to your programs. You added routines to a new OLE Server DLL library that logs all critical user activity to an audit trail file, including user logins, database modifications, and all critical program operations, such as running reports or processing mass database updates.

Best of all, the routines you built here can be used in all your future Visual Basic applications.

Quiz

1. What are the disadvantages and limitations of using the Microsoft Access SYSTEM.MDA file to secure a database?
2. What are the disadvantages of using data encryption to secure a database?
3. What is the difference between application security and database security?
4. What are the two main features of a good application security scheme?
5. Can application security schemes prevent unauthorized access to data by tools such as Visdata and Data Manager?

21

6. Why would you use an access rights security scheme in your application?

7. Why add audit trails to an application?

Exercise

Assume that you are a systems developer for a large corporation. Your company has had a problem keeping track of the fixed assets (desks, chairs, computers) in one of its divisions. Your manager has asked you to develop a system to help manage the tracking of these fixed assets.

These assets are a large portion of the net worth of this organization. Therefore, management wants to keep track of any changes made to the items in this database. You decide that the best way to assist them in their efforts is to place an audit log in your application.

Use the skills you developed in this chapter to modify project 20ABC01.VBP to construct a fixed asset tracking system. Follow these guidelines in the construction of this project:

☐ Use Data Manager to create a new database for fixed assets. Name this database CH20EX.MDB, and add a table called Assets. Include the following fields in this table:

Field	Type	Length
AssetID	TEXT	12
Description	TEXT	40
Cost	CURRENCY	
DateAcq	DATE/TIME	
SerialNo	TEXT	20
Department	TEXT	10

☐ Build a form to enter and edit the data records for this table. Use a data control to manage the records. Use the default (Text1, Text2, and so on) for text field's Name property. Set the Name property of the form to frmFixedAssets. Make this the first form displayed after the login process.

☐ Make your system write to an audit log any time a record is changed. Include Ch20ex.mdb.Assets as the name of the changed object, the user who made the change, and the AssetID of the changed record in the log. Use the same log as used by the login and logout routine. (Hint: Research the Data Changed event.)

21

WEEK 3

15

16

17

18

19

20

21

In Review

The third and final week of this book covered several very important topics. This week's work focused on database issues you encounter when you develop database applications for multiple users or multiple sites. You learned advanced SQL language for manipulating records within existing databases (DML). You also learned the five rules of data normalization and how applying those rules can improve the speed, accuracy, and integrity of your databases.

You learned about Visual Basic database locking schemes for the database, table, and page level. You also learned the advantages and limitations of adding cascading updates and deletes to your database relationship definitions. You learned how to use Visual Basic keywords `BeginTrans`, `CommitTrans`, and `Rollback` to improve database integrity and processing speed during mass updates.

You were introduced to the Remote Data Control and the Remote Data Objects. You learned to use these tools to attach to RDBMSs. You learned the properties, methods, and events of these useful tools.

You learned how to write data entry forms that use the ODBC API calls to link directly with the ODBC interface to access data in registered ODBC data sources. You also learned how to install the ODBC Administrator and how to create new ODBC data sources for your ODBC-enabled Visual Basic programs.

You learned how to distribute data across multiple sites by using database replication. You learned how to create a Design Master and replicas. You learned how to synchronize data changes to a member of a replica set. You also learned how *not* to distribute specified data tables during the synchronization process.

In the final lesson, you learned how to create application-level security schemes such as user login and logout, program-level access rights, and audit trails to keep track of critical application operations.

Day 15: Updating Databases with SQL

To start your final week of study, you learned how to add, delete, and edit data within tables using the DML (Data Manipulation Language) SQL keywords. You learned that by using DML statements you can quickly create test data for tables and load default values into startup tables. You also learned that DML statements—such as Append queries, Make Table queries, and Delete queries—can outperform equivalent Visual Basic code versions of the same operations.

You learned how to manage data within the tables using the following DML keywords:

☐ The INSERT INTO statement can be used to add new rows to the table using the VALUES clause.

☐ You can create an Append query by using the INSERT INTO_FROM syntax to copy data from one table to another. You can also copy data from one database to another using the IN clause on an INSERT INTO_FROM statement.

☐ You can create new tables by copying the structure and some of the data using the SELECT_INTO statement. This statement can incorporate WHERE, ORDER BY, GROUP BY, and HAVING clauses to limit the scope of the data used to populate the new table you create.

☐ You can use the DELETE FROM clause to remove one or more records from an existing table. You can even create customized views of the database using the JOIN clause, and remove only records that are the result of a JOIN statement.

Day 16: Database Normalization

In Day 16's lesson, you learned how to improve database integrity and access speed using the five rules of data normalization. You learned the following five rules:

☐ Rule 1: Eliminate repeating groups. If you have a set of fields that have the same name followed by a number (Skill1, Skill2, Skill3, and so forth), remove these repeating groups, create a new table for the repeating data, and relate it to the key field in the first table.

☐ Rule 2: Eliminate redundant data. Don't store the same data in two different locations. This can lead to update and delete errors. If equivalent data elements are entered in two fields, remove the second data element, create a new master table with the element and its partner as a key field, and then place the key field as a relationship in the locations that formerly held both data elements.

☐ Rule 3: Eliminate columns not dependent on keys. If you have data elements that are not directly related to the primary key of the table, these elements should be removed to their own data table. Only store data elements that are directly related to the primary key of the table. This particularly includes derived data or other calculations.

☐ Rule 4: Isolate independent multiple relationships. Use this rule to improve database design when you are dealing with more than one one-to-many relationship in the database. Before you add a new field to a table, ask yourself whether this field is really dependent upon the other fields in the table. If not, create a new table with the independent data.

☐ Rule 5: Isolate related multiple relationships. Use this rule to improve database design when you are dealing with more than one many-to-many relationship in the database. If you have database rules that require multiple references to the same field or sets of fields, isolate the fields into smaller tables and construct one or more link tables that contain the required constraints that enforce database integrity.

Day 17: Multiuser Considerations

On Day 17, you learned about the three important challenges that face every database programmer writing multiuser applications:

☐ Database locking schemes

☐ Using cascading updates and deletes to maintain database integrity

☐ Using database transactions to provide commit/rollback options for major updates to your database

You learned that there are three levels of locking available to Visual Basic programs:

☐ *The database level*—You can use the Exclusive property of the data control or the second parameter of the OpenDatabase method to lock the entire database. Use this option when you need to perform work that affects multiple database objects (such as tables, queries, indexes, relations, and so on).

☐ *The table level*—You can set the Options property of the data control to 3 or the third parameter of the OpenRecordset method to dbDenyRead+dbDenyWrite in order to lock the entire table for your use only. Use this option when you need to perform work that affects multiple records in a single table (for example, increasing the sales price on all items in the inventory table).

☐ *The page level*—Microsoft Jet automatically performs page-level locking whenever you use the data control to edit and save a record, or whenever you use Visual Basic code to perform the Edit/AddNew and Update/CancelUpdate methods. You can use the LockEdits property of the Recordset to set the page locking to pessimistic (to perform locking at edit time) or optimistic (to perform locking only at update time).

You learned how to use Visual Basic to enforce referential integrity and automatically perform cascading updates or deletes to related records. You learned that there are times when it is not advisable to establish cascading deletes (for example, do not use cascading deletes when the base table is a validation list and the foreign table is a master).

Finally, you learned how to use database transactions to protect your database during extended, multitable operations. You learned how to use the BeginTrans, CommitTrans, and Rollback methods of the workspace object. And you learned some of the advantages and limitations of transaction processing.

Day 18: Using the Remote Data Control and the Remote Data Objects

On Day 18, you learned about two alternate methods for accessing remote data. You learned that you can use the Remote Data control to create simple data entry forms with data-bound controls. You also learned to use the Remote Data Objects to create Visual Basic 5.0 programs that can access data from a remote RDBMS.

Along with the details of the Remote Data Control and the Remote Data objects, you also learned some of the basics of remote data access in general. You learned about:

☐ *Cursor drivers*—These are the tools that manage the location of the Recordset pointer in a dataset. You learned you can use client-side or server-side cursor drivers with RDC/RDO connections.

☐ *Dataset types*—You learned there are a number of dataset types available to you when you connect to remote data sources including ForwardOnly—ReadOnly sets, Static sets, Keysets, and Dynamic sets.

☐ *Lock types*—You learned there are several different lock types you can use when accessing data from your remote data source. You can use ConcurrentLock sets that perform locks as soon as you receive the data rows, or you can use several versions of optimistic locking that only attempt to lock the rows when you update them.

You also learned the details of the following Microsoft Remote Data Objects:

☐ The rdoEngine object—This is the top-level data engine used to access remote data.

☐ The rdoEnvironment object—This is the RDO equivalent of the Microsoft Jet Workspace object.

☐ The rdoConnection object—This is the RDO equivalent of the Microsoft Jet Database object.

☐ The rdoResultset object—This is the RDO equivalent of the Microsoft Jet Recordset object.

☐ The rdoTable object—This is the RDO version of the Microsoft Jet Table object.

☐ The rdoColumn object—This is the RDO version of the Microsoft Jet Field object.

☐ The rdoQuery object—This is the RDO version of the Microsoft Jet QueryDef object.

☐ The rdoParameters object—This is a special collection of query parameters for the rdoQuery object.

Day 19: ODBC Data Access via the ODBC API

On Day 19, you learned how to use the Open Database Connectivity (ODBC) API to directly link your Visual Basic program to target data sources through the ODBC interface. The ODBC interface is generally faster than Microsoft Jet when it comes to linking to ODBC-defined data sources.

You also learned how to install the ODBC interface on your workstation and how to use the ODBC Administrator program to install ODBC driver sets and define data sources for ODBC connections.

You learned how to build a program library that uses a minimum set of ODBC API calls along with several Visual Basic wrapper routines. This library set provides the basic functions necessary to read and write data to and from a defined ODBC data source. You can use these routines to create fully functional data entry forms for ODBC data sources.

Finally, you used the library routines to build a data entry form that opens a link to a defined ODBC data source and allows the user to read and write data records for the ODBC data source.

Day 20: Database Replication

Day 20 focused on database replication. In database replication terminology, the main or central database is referred to as the *Design Master*. A copy of the Design Master is referred to as the *replica*. The combination of the Design Master and all replicas is referred to as the *replica set*. Database replication is the process of synchronizing data so that it is the same across all members of the replica set.

Database replication is a good tool to use in the development of systems deployed across a WAN or to remote users. Replication can also be used to make copies of databases that cannot be shut down. Replication is also good for creating reporting databases and data marts.

Do not use database replication when a centralized data storage facility can be used, such as a Web-enabled application. Also, don't use replication in heavily transaction-oriented applications, or in applications where up-to-the minute accuracy is of paramount importance.

Tables, fields, and properties are added to a database when it is made a Design Master. The addition of these items is necessary to track changes to data and to facilitate the synchronization between members of the replica set. These additions, however, consume additional physical hard drive space.

Creating and changing the Replicable property of a database to T creates a Design Master. Once the Design Master is created, you can use the Make Replica method to make copies of it. Finally, you use the Synchronize method to replicate data changes to members of the replica set. Data synchronization is the act of copying data changes from one member of a replica set to another.

The Synchronize method can be used to import data changes, export data changes, perform "two-way" data changes, and even perform data exchanges over the Internet.

Synchronization errors occur when two members of a replica set try to synchronize records that both have changed. Errors may also occur during the synchronization process when design changes are made to a database that are violated by replicas prior to synchronization of the changes. Violation of referential integrity can be encountered by a replica that added records to its database that uses validation records deleted in another replica. Record locking in a multiuser environment can also cause synchronization errors.

There are four topologies for the synchronization of replicas. These are the star, linear, ring, and fully connected topologies. The star is the most common, but like all the other topologies it has certain strengths and weaknesses.

There may be times when you do not want to replicate objects contained in one database to other members of the replica set. If such is the case, use the KeepLocal method before you create the Design Master. This method keeps the object from being copied to other replica set members.

Day 21: Securing Your Database Applications

In your final lesson in this book, you learned several methods that can improve user and application-level security for your Visual Basic database applications. You learned about the limitations of using the Microsoft Access SYSTEM security file and database encryption.

This lesson also showed you how you can add application-level security to your Visual Basic programs by adding user login/logout routines and creating a user access rights scheme for your applications. In this lesson, you designed and implemented an OLE Server DLL library that you can use for all your Visual Basic applications, and you created several screens for maintaining user lists and managing access rights for each user.

You also learned how to add an audit trail option to your programs. You added routines to a new OLE Server DLL library that logs all critical user activity to an audit trail file, including user logins, database modifications, and all critical program operations, such as running reports or processing mass database updates.

APPENDIX

A

The SQL-VB5 Project

This appendix contains a step-by-step explanation of the creation of the SQL-VB5 Interpreter project. This program is already on the CD-ROM included with your copy of the book. The SQL-VB5 program in this lesson allows you to use an ASCII editor to create SQL scripts that SQL-VB5 can read and process. SQL-VB5 can handle fully commented, multiline SQL scripts. You'll find that SQL-VB5 is a very handy data management tool.

NOTE

> You do not need to construct this project from scratch. It is already on the CD-ROM. However, you may want to go through this chapter as an added tutorial in constructing SQL-enabled applications in Visual Basic.

The Benefits of SQL-VB5

You may often need to quickly generate sample database layouts for a programming project. You may even need to build some test data to run through data editing or reporting routines. The SQL-VB5 program enables you to do all that. The SQL-VB5 program is able to read SQL scripts you create with the Windows Notepad application (or any other ASCII editor). Listing A.1 is a sample SQL script that can be processed by SQL-VB5.

Listing A.1. A sample SQL script.

```
//
// load and read data tables
//


// open a database
dbOpen C:\TYSDBVB5\SQLVB5\SCRIPTS\BOOKS5.MDB

// open some tables to view
SELECT * FROM Authors;
SELECT * FROM Titles;
SELECT * FROM Publishers;
SELECT * FROM BookSales;
SELECT * FROM Buyers;
SELECT * FROM [Publisher Comments];

//
// eof
//
```

Listing A.1 opens a database and then displays several data tables on the screen. This same script could perform any valid SQL statement and show the results on the screen for the user to review or edit.

The advantage of generating database layouts using SQL-VB5 is that you have some documentation on the database structure that you can refer to in the future. You can also use SQL-VB5 to generate test SELECT queries and other SQL statements before you put them into your Visual Basic programs. Finally, SQL-VB5 is an excellent tool for exploring SQL and your databases.

Designing SQL-VB5

Before jumping into code mode, let's lay out some general design parameters for the SQL-VB5 project. SQL-VB5 should be able to do the following:

- ☐ Open an ASCII file that contains valid SQL script statements.
- ☐ Process the open file sequentially and perform all SQL statements in the file, including all SQL DDL and SQL DML keywords.
- ☐ Display any result sets created by the SQL statements (SELECT_FROM) in data grids that can be reviewed by the user. To keep the project relatively simple, allow users to only view the results of queries, not update them.
- ☐ Provide an MDI interface so that more than one result set can be viewed at a time.
- ☐ Provide a VBA-compliant object model interface so that SQL-VB5 can be called from within other programs.
- ☐ Provide the ability to read an MDB file and generate a valid SQL-VB5 script to re-create the database structure, including all tables, indexes, and relationships.
- ☐ Provide a simple About box to display program information.
- ☐ Provide direct access to editing SQL script files without having to exit the SQL-VB5 program.
- ☐ Allow users to add comment lines in the SQL-VB5 script for documentation purposes.
- ☐ Provide reasonable error trapping and reporting to aid in debugging SQL scripts.
- ☐ Allow users to open any Microsoft Jet-supported database format and allows users to create new Microsoft Jet-format databases.

That last item may be a surprise to some. Remember that Microsoft Access SQL has no keyword for opening, closing, or creating a database! You add your own script keywords to handle this.

To accomplish all this, you need three forms, three standard code modules, and one class module:

- ☐ SQLVBMain: An MDI form to enclose all activity.
- ☐ SQLVBChild: A child form that displays the result sets.
- ☐ SQLVBAbout: A simple form that displays the About box.
- ☐ SQLVBMOD: A Visual Basic code module that contains all the methods for interpreting an SQL-VB5 script.
- ☐ SQLVBGEN: A Visual Basic code module that contains all the methods for generating an SQL-VB5 script from the existing MDB.
- ☐ SQLVBCLASS: A Visual Basic code module that contains the primary startup routine (Main).
- ☐ Application: A Visual Basic class module that encapsulates the object model interface.

The SQLVBMain form needs some menu items and a CommonDialog control to handle the Open File dialog that runs the SQL scripts. The SQLVBChild form needs a Data control and a DBGrid control to handle the result sets. The SQLVBAbout needs a couple of Label controls and a single OK command button.

The SQLVBMOD code module needs three main routines and a host of supporting routines. The three main routines are

- ☐ SQLFileOpen: To open the ASCII file selected by the user.
- ☐ SQLFileProcess: To process the SQL commands in the file.
- ☐ SQLFileClose: To safely close the ASCII file upon completion.

The SQLVBMOD needs an error routine; some special routines to handle the database OPEN, CLOSE, and CREATE commands; a routine to handle the SQL DML commands (SELECT_FROM); and a routine to handle the SQL DDL commands (CREATE TABLE, for example). You can add these as you go along.

The SQLVBGEN module needs routines to read the selected MDB and then write out the SQL-Visual Basic code that represents the tables, fields, indexes, and relationships defined in the MDB. It also has a handful of routines to handle script headers and footers, comment lines, and saving the finished script to the disk.

The SQLVBCLASS module has a single Sub Main() used to start the application.

The application class module has the properties and methods needed to allow external VBA programs to access and run SQLVB methods. Other programs can create their own instance of SQL-VB5 and then run all the primary commands. The object model for SQL-VB5 is described in Figure A.1 and Table A.1.

Figure A.1.

The SQL-VB5 *object model.*

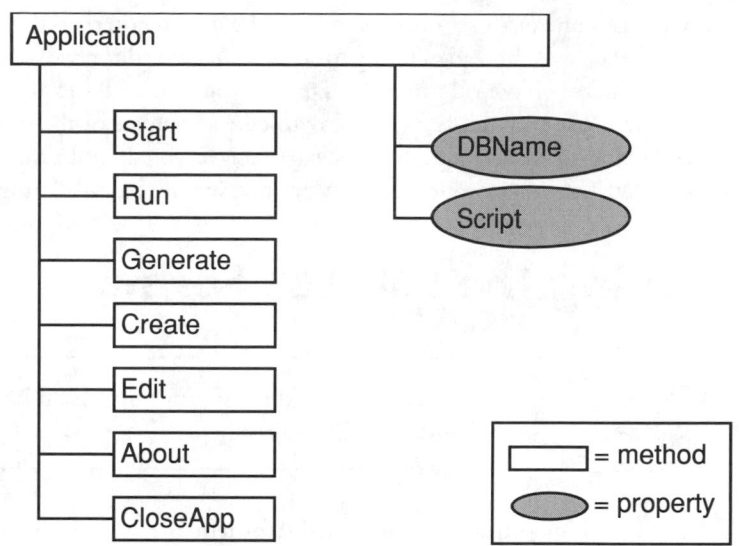

Table A.1. The SQL-VB5 object model.

Object Type	Name	Description
Properties	DBName	Name of the MDB database to open.
	Script	Name of the SQL-Visual Basic script to open.
Methods	Start	Starts SQL-VB5 in interactive mode. Same as launching the EXE from Explorer.
	CloseApp	Closes SQL-VB5 interactive session.
	Run	Runs the SQL-VB5 script found in the Script property.
	Generate	Generates an SQL-VB5 script from the MDB database found in DBName.
	Create	Starts SQL-VB5 text editor to create a new SQL-VB5 script using the name in the Script property.
	Edit	Starts the SQL-VB5 text editor to edit an existing script using the name in the Script property.

You need one other set of tools to meet the design criteria—the ability to edit scripts from within SQL-VB5. Instead of trying to create your own editor, we show you how you can include the Windows Notepad program as part of your Visual Basic project. This can be done with minimal effort, and it is a great way to take advantage of the software already available on users' desktops. This is perfectly legal as long as you do not provide users with a copy of the NOTEPAD.EXE program. Because all Windows systems have this program already, you're all set.

Creating the SQL-VB5 Forms

NOTE
If you haven't already done so, start up Visual Basic 5.0 and prepare a new Standard EXE project.

The first thing you do is define the MDI form for the project. This form provides the interface to the Notepad editor for managing script files. It also enables users to run existing scripts to see the results. Because it is a multidocument interface, you need to add some menu options to enable users to arrange the forms within the workspace. Finally, you add access to an About box through the menu.

SQLVBMain Form

Add an MDI form to your project by selecting Project | Add MDI Form from the Visual Basic main menu. This form contains a few controls that allow the user to open an ASCII file to edit or run, arrange the various child forms open within the SQLVBMain MDI form, and show the About box upon request. Use Table A.2 and Figure A.2 as guides as you build the form.

NOTE
In Table A.2, be sure to place the common dialog, label, and command button controls directly "on" the picture controls. Visual Basic does not allow standard controls to be placed directly on an MDI form. You can, however, place Picture controls on an MDI form, and then place your standard controls on the Picture controls.

Figure A.2.
*Laying out the
SQLVBMain MDI
form.*

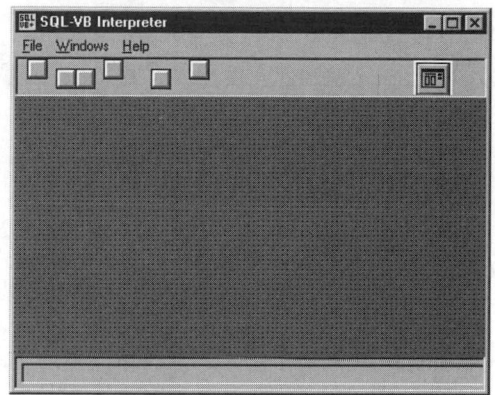

Table A.2. Visual Basic controls for the SQLVBMain MDI form.

Control	Property	Setting
VB.MDIForm	Name	SQLVBMain
	BackColor	&H8000000C&
	Caption	"SQL-VB Interpreter"
	ClientHeight	4140
	ClientLeft	1065
	ClientTop	1800
	ClientWidth	5910
	WindowState	2 'Maximized
VB.PictureBox	Name	Picture2
	Align	2 'Align Bottom
	Height	420
	Left	0
	Top	3720
	Width	5910
VB.Label	Name	lblProgress
	BorderStyle	1 'Fixed Single
	Height	255
	Left	60
	Top	60
	Width	9375

continues

Table A.2. continued

Control	Property	Setting
VB.PictureBox	Name	Picture1
	Align	1 'Align Top
	Height	495
	Left	0
	Top	0
	Width	5910
MSComDlg.CommonDialog	Name	CommonDialog1
	Left	4980
	Top	0
Threed.SSCommand	Name	cmdBtn
	Height	255
	Index	0
	Left	2160
	Top	0
	Width	255
	RoundedCorners	0 'False
Threed.SSCommand	Name	cmdBtn
	Height	255
	Index	1
	Left	120
	Top	0
	Width	255
	RoundedCorners	0 'False
Threed.SSCommand	Name	cmdBtn
	Height	255
	Index	2
	Left	1680
	Top	120
	Width	255
	RoundedCorners	0 'False

Control	Property	Setting
Threed.SSCommand	Name	cmdBtn
	Height	255
	Index	3
	Left	480
	Top	120
	Width	255
	RoundedCorners	0 'False
Threed.SSCommand	Name	cmdBtn
	Height	255
	Index	4
	Left	1080
	Top	0
	Width	255
	RoundedCorners	0 'False
Threed.SSCommand	Name	cmdBtn
	Height	255
	Index	5
	Left	720
	Top	120
	Width	255
	RoundedCorners	0 'False

Now that you have created the form, you need to add the menu. Table A.3 shows the hierarchy of the menu items you need for the SQLVBMain form.

Table A.3. Menu tree for the SQLVBMain MDI form.

Property	Name	Setting
Menu	Name	mnuFile
	Caption	"&File"
Menu	Name	mnuFileNew
	Caption	"&New..."

continues

Table A.3. continued

Property	Name	Setting
Menu	Name	mnuFileEdit
	Caption	"&Edit..."
Menu	Name	mnuFileClose
	Caption	"&Close"
Menu	Name	mnuFileSpc03
	Caption	"-"
Menu	Name	mnuFileAuto
	Caption	"&Generate..."
Menu	Name	mnuFileRun
	Caption	"&Run..."
Menu	Name	mnuFileSp01
	Caption	"-"
Menu	Name	mnuFileExit
	Caption	"E&xit"
Menu	Name	mnuWindows
	Caption	"&Windows"
	WindowList	-1 'True
Menu	Name	mnuWindowsItem
	Caption	"&Cascade"
	Index	0
Menu	Name	mnuWindowsItem
	Caption	"Tile &Horizontal"
	Index	1
Menu	Name	mnuWindowsItem
	Caption	"Tile &Vertical"
	Index	2
Menu	Name	mnuWindowsItem
	Caption	"&Arrange"
	Index	3

Property	Name	Setting
Menu	Name	mnuHelp
	Caption	"&Help"
Menu	Name	mnuHelpAbout
	Caption	"&About"

As you build the menu, you need to set two additional properties of the &Windows menu item. Set the Index property to zero and set the WindowList property to True. This forces Visual Basic to create a dynamic list of all the child forms open under the SQLVBMain MDI form window.

The final step in completing the SQLVBMain form is adding the Visual Basic code that activates the various menu options selected by the user. Because most of that code calls other routines you have not yet written, skip the Visual Basic code for now; you get back to it at the end of the project.

Before continuing with the lesson, save this form as SQLVBMAI.FRM and save the project as SQLVB5.VBP.

Creating the SQLVBChild Child Form

The SQLVBChild child form displays any result set created by SQL statements in the script being processed. You need two controls on this form—a data control and a data-bound grid control. Add a new form to your project by selecting Project | Add Form from the Visual Basic main menu. Use Table A.4 and Figure A.3 as guides for creating SQLVBChild.

Figure A.3.

Laying out the SQLVBChild form.

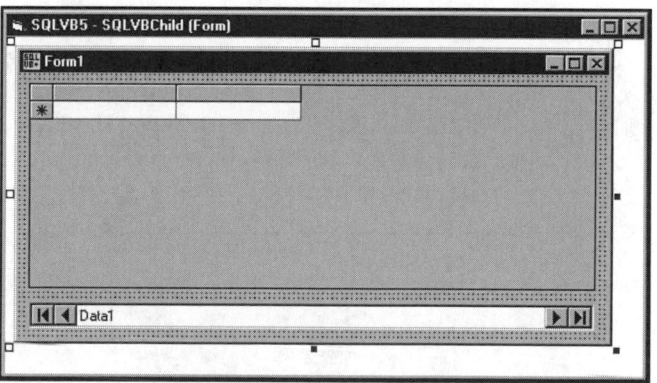

Table A.4. Visual Basic controls for the SQLVBChild child form.

Control	Property	Setting
Form	Name	SQLVBChild
	Height	3690
	Width	7485
	MDIChild	-1—True
Data	Name	Data1
	Height	300
	Left	120
	Top	2820
	Width	7095
	Visible	False
DBGrid	Name	DBGrid1
	Height	2535
	Left	120
	DataSource	Data1
	Top	120
	Width	7095

You need to add code in four locations within the SQLVBChild form: the Form_Load event, the Form_Activate event, the Form_Unload event, and the Form_Resize event.

TIP

> To add code to one of the form events, double-click any empty location of the form to bring up the Visual Basic code window for SQLVBChild. The first event you should see is the Form_Load event. You can use the drop-down list box on the right to locate other events for the form object.

Open the Visual Basic code window for the Form_Load event and add the Visual Basic program code in Listing A.2.

TYPE	**Listing A.2. Adding code to the `Form_Load` event.**

```
Private Sub Form_Load()
    '
    Me.Data1.Refresh
    DoEvents
    '
    ' set the captions
    Me.Caption = Trim(strGlobalSelect)
    Me.Data1.Caption = Trim(strGlobalSelect)
    Me.DBGrid1.Caption = Trim(strGlobalSelect)
    '
End Sub
```

The code in Listing A.2 first refreshes the data control and yields to let Windows catch up with any pending messages, then sets the Caption properties.

The `Form_Unload` event contains a single line of code. This line clears up the main (SQLVBMain) form's menu display.

```
Private Sub Form_Unload(Cancel As Integer)
    '
    SQLVBMain.mnuWindows.Visible = False
    '
End Sub
```

Next, add code to the `Form_Activate` event. This updates the MDI form menus and rebinds the data from the data control to the grid display.

```
Private Sub Form_Activate()
    '
    SQLVBMain.mnuWindows.Visible = True
    DBGrid1.ReBind
    '
End Sub
```

The last code piece needed for the SQLVBChild form is the code behind the `Form_Resize` event (see Listing A.3). This code automatically resizes the DBGrid and Data controls whenever the user resizes the form. Note the `If` test that occurs at the start of the routine. Whenever a form is minimized, the `Form_Resize` event occurs. Attempts to resize a minimized form result in Visual Basic errors, so check to make sure the form is *not* minimized before you continue with the routine.

TYPE Listing A.3. Adding code to the `Form_Resize` event.

```
Private Sub Form_Resize()
    '
    If Me.WindowState <> 1 Then
        With DBGrid1
            .Width = Me.ScaleWidth
            .Left = 1
            .Top = 1
            .Height = Me.ScaleHeight
        End With
    End If
    '
End Sub
```

After you have entered these pieces of code, save the form as `SQLVBCHI.FRM`. It's a good idea to save the project at this time, too.

Creating the SQLVBAbout Form

The last form you need for this project is the SQLVBAbout form. This is the form that lists the name and version of the program and its authors, and so on. Use Table A.5 and Figure A.4 as guides as you create this form for your project.

Figure A.4.

Laying out the SQLVBAbout form.

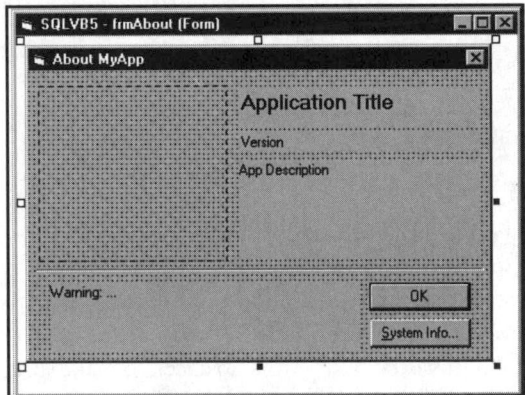

Table A.5. Visual Basic controls for the SQLVBAbout form.

Control	Property	Setting
VB.Form	Name	frmAbout
	BorderStyle	3 'Fixed Dialog
	Caption	"About MyApp"

Control	Property	Setting
	ClientHeight	3555
	ClientLeft	2340
	ClientTop	1935
	ClientWidth	5730
VB.CommandButton	Name	cmdOK
	Cancel	-1 'True
	Caption	"OK"
	Default	-1 'True
	Height	345
	Left	4245
	Top	2625
	Width	1260
VB.CommandButton	Name	cmdSysInfo
	Caption	"&System Info..."
	Height	345
	Left	4260
	Top	3075
	Width	1245
VB.Image	Name	Image1
	Height	2173
	Left	120
	Stretch	-1 'True
	Top	180
	Width	2343
VB.Line	Name	Line1
	BorderColor	&H00808080&
	BorderStyle	6 'Inside Solid
	Index	1
	X1	84.515
	X2	5309.398
	Y1	1687.583
	Y2	1687.583

continues

Table A.5. continued

Control	Property	Setting
VB.Label	Name	lblDescription
	Caption	"App Description"
	ForeColor	&H00000000&
	Height	1170
	Left	2610
	Top	1125
	Width	2985
VB.Label	Name	lblTitle
	Caption	"Application Title"
	Font	Name="MS Sans Serif"
		Size=12
	ForeColor	&H00000000&
	Height	480
	Left	2640
	Top	240
	Width	2985
VB.Line	Name	Line1
	BorderColor	&H00FFFFFF&
	BorderWidth	2
	Index	0
	X1	98.6
	X2	5309.398
	Y1	1697.936
	Y2	1697.936
VB.Label	Name	lblVersion
	Caption	"Version"
	Height	225
	Left	2640
	Top	780
	Width	2985

Control	Property	Setting
VB.Label	Name	lblDisclaimer
	Caption	"Warning: ..."
	ForeColor	&H00000000&
	Height	825
	Left	255
	Top	2625
	Width	3870

This version of the About box offers the user the ability to gather system information. This is done through a set of API calls that read and collate keys from the Registry. You need to add some APIs and code to perform the Registry lookups.

First, add the code from Listing A.4 to the general declarations section of the form.

TYPE Listing A.4. Coding the declarations for the SQLVBAbout form.

```
Option Explicit

' Reg Key Security Options...
Const READ_CONTROL = &H20000
Const KEY_QUERY_VALUE = &H1
Const KEY_SET_VALUE = &H2
Const KEY_CREATE_SUB_KEY = &H4
Const KEY_ENUMERATE_SUB_KEYS = &H8
Const KEY_NOTIFY = &H10
Const KEY_CREATE_LINK = &H20
Const KEY_ALL_ACCESS = KEY_QUERY_VALUE + KEY_SET_VALUE + _
                       KEY_CREATE_SUB_KEY + KEY_ENUMERATE_SUB_KEYS + _
                       KEY_NOTIFY + KEY_CREATE_LINK + READ_CONTROL

' Reg Key ROOT Types...
Const HKEY_LOCAL_MACHINE = &H80000002
Const ERROR_SUCCESS = 0
Const REG_SZ = 1                           ' Unicode nul terminated string
Const REG_DWORD = 4                        ' 32-bit number

Const gREGKEYSYSINFOLOC = "SOFTWARE\Microsoft\Shared Tools Location"
Const gREGVALSYSINFOLOC = "MSINFO"
Const gREGKEYSYSINFO = "SOFTWARE\Microsoft\Shared Tools\MSINFO"
Const gREGVALSYSINFO = "PATH"

Private Declare Function RegOpenKeyEx Lib "advapi32" Alias "RegOpenKeyExA"
(ByVal hKey As Long, ByVal lpSubKey As String, ByVal ulOptions As Long, ByVal
samDesired As Long, ByRef phkResult As Long) As Long
```

continues

Listing A.4. continued

```
Private Declare Function RegQueryValueEx Lib "advapi32" Alias "RegQueryValueExA"
(ByVal hKey As Long, ByVal lpValueName As String, ByVal lpReserved As Long,
ByRef lpType As Long, ByVal lpData As String, ByRef lpcbData As Long) As Long
Private Declare Function RegCloseKey Lib "advapi32" (ByVal hKey As Long) As Long
```

Note that you can place API declarations directly in a form as long as you precede these declaration lines with the `Private` keyword.

Next, create a new method called `GetKeyValue` to use these API calls and constants. Enter the code from Listing A.5 into the project.

TYPE Listing A.5. Coding the `GetKeyValue` function.

```
Public Function GetKeyValue(KeyRoot As Long, KeyName As String, SubKeyRef As
String, ByRef KeyVal As String) As Boolean
    Dim i As Long                                    ' Loop Counter
    Dim rc As Long                                   ' Return Code
    Dim hKey As Long                                 ' Handle To An Open
➥Registry Key
    Dim hDepth As Long                               '
    Dim KeyValType As Long                           ' Data Type Of A
➥Registry Key
    Dim tmpVal As String                             ' Tempory Storage
➥For A Registry Key Value
    Dim KeyValSize As Long                           ' Size Of Registry
➥Key Variable
    '------------------------------------------------------------
    ' Open RegKey Under KeyRoot {HKEY_LOCAL_MACHINE...}
    '------------------------------------------------------------
    rc = RegOpenKeyEx(KeyRoot, KeyName, 0, KEY_ALL_ACCESS, hKey) ' Open Registry
➥Key

    If (rc <> ERROR_SUCCESS) Then GoTo GetKeyError   ' Handle Error...

    tmpVal = String$(1024, 0)                        ' Allocate Variable
➥Space
    KeyValSize = 1024                                ' Mark Variable Size


    '------------------------------------------------------------
    ' Retrieve Registry Key Value...
    '------------------------------------------------------------
    rc = RegQueryValueEx(hKey, SubKeyRef, 0, _
                        KeyValType, tmpVal, KeyValSize)    ' Get/Create Key
➥Value

    If (rc <> ERROR_SUCCESS) Then GoTo GetKeyError   ' Handle Errors

    If (Asc(Mid(tmpVal, KeyValSize, 1)) = 0) Then    ' Win95 Adds Null
➥Terminated String...
        tmpVal = Left(tmpVal, KeyValSize - 1)        ' Null Found,
```

A

```
Extract From String
    Else                                        ' WinNT Does NOT
➥Null Terminate String...
        tmpVal = Left(tmpVal, KeyValSize)       ' Null Not Found,
➥Extract String Only
    End If
    '----------------------------------------------------------------
    ' Determine Key Value Type For Conversion...
    '----------------------------------------------------------------
    Select Case KeyValType                      ' Search Data
➥Types...
    Case REG_SZ                                 ' String Registry
➥Key Data Type
        KeyVal = tmpVal                         ' Copy String Value
    Case REG_DWORD                              ' Double Word
➥Registry Key Data Type
        For i = Len(tmpVal) To 1 Step -1        ' Convert Each Bit
            KeyVal = KeyVal + Hex(Asc(Mid(tmpVal, i, 1)))  ' Build Value Char.
➥By Char.
        Next
        KeyVal = Format$("&h" + KeyVal)         ' Convert Double
➥Word To String
    End Select

    GetKeyValue = True                          ' Return Success
    rc = RegCloseKey(hKey)                      ' Close Registry Key
    Exit Function                               ' Exit

GetKeyError:        ' Cleanup After An Error Has Occured...
    KeyVal = ""                                 ' Set Return Val To
➥Empty String
    GetKeyValue = False                         ' Return Failure
    rc = RegCloseKey(hKey)                      ' Close Registry Key
End Function
```

Now add one more new routine to call the GetKeyValue method. Add StartSysInfo to your project and enter the code in Listing A.6.

TYPE **Listing A.6. Coding the StartSysInfo subroutine.**

```
Public Sub StartSysInfo()
    On Error GoTo SysInfoErr

    Dim rc As Long
    Dim SysInfoPath As String

    ' Try To Get System Info Program Path\Name From Registry...
    If GetKeyValue(HKEY_LOCAL_MACHINE, gREGKEYSYSINFO, gREGVALSYSINFO,
SysInfoPath) Then
        ' Try To Get System Info Program Path Only From Registry...
    ElseIf GetKeyValue(HKEY_LOCAL_MACHINE, gREGKEYSYSINFOLOC, gREGVALSYSINFOLOC,
SysInfoPath) Then
```

continues

Listing A.6. continued

```
                ' Validate Existance Of Known 32 Bit File Version
                If (Dir(SysInfoPath & "\MSINFO32.EXE") <> "") Then
                    SysInfoPath = SysInfoPath & "\MSINFO32.EXE"

                ' Error - File Can Not Be Found...
                Else
                    GoTo SysInfoErr
                End If
        ' Error - Registry Entry Can Not Be Found...
        Else
            GoTo SysInfoErr
        End If

        Call Shell(SysInfoPath, vbNormalFocus)

        Exit Sub
SysInfoErr:
        MsgBox "System Information Is Unavailable At This Time", vbOKOnly
End Sub
```

Finally, Listing A.7 shows the code for the Form_Load event and the two command button click events. Add this to your form.

TYPE   **Listing A.7. Adding code to the `cmdSysInfo_Click` event.**

```
Private Sub cmdSysInfo_Click()
  Call StartSysInfo
End Sub

Private Sub cmdOK_Click()
  Unload Me
End Sub

Private Sub Form_Load()
    '
    Me.Caption = "About " & App.Title
    lblVersion.Caption = "Version " & App.Major & "." & App.Minor & "." &
➥App.Revision
    lblTitle.Caption = App.Title
    lblDescription = App.FileDescription
    Image1.Picture = SQLVBMain.Icon
    Me.Icon = SQLVBMain.Icon
    lblDisclaimer = ""
    '
End Sub
```

Now save the form as SQLVBABO.FRM and save the project.

Adding the SQLVBMain Code

Now that you have created all three forms, you can go back to SQLVBMain and add the code
behind the menu options. This is also the time when you add code that calls the Windows
Notepad program from within SQLVB.

First, add the code from Listing A.8. This arranges the command button bar on the top of
the form.

TYPE **Listing A.8. Coding the** `LoadCmdBtns` **subroutine.**

```
Public Sub LoadCmdBtns()
    '
    Dim Top As Integer
    Dim Left As Integer
    Dim Width As Integer
    Dim Height As Integer
    '
    Top = 45
    Height = Picture1.Height * 0.75
    Width = Height * 1.1
    '
    For x = 0 To 5
        cmdBtn(x).Top = Top
        cmdBtn(x).Left = (x * Width) + 45
        cmdBtn(x).Width = Width * 0.9
        cmdBtn(x).Height = Height
        cmdBtn(x).BevelWidth = 2
        cmdBtn(x).RoundedCorners = False
    Next
    '
    cmdBtn(0).Picture = LoadPicture(App.Path & "\pics\new.bmp")
    cmdBtn(1).Picture = LoadPicture(App.Path & "\pics\open.bmp")
    cmdBtn(2).Picture = LoadPicture(App.Path & "\pics\save.bmp")
    cmdBtn(3).Picture = LoadPicture(App.Path & "\pics\sum.bmp")
    cmdBtn(4).Picture = LoadPicture(App.Path & "\pics\camera.bmp")
    cmdBtn(5).Picture = LoadPicture(App.Path & "\pics\undo.bmp")
    '
    cmdBtn(0).ToolTipText = "New"
    cmdBtn(1).ToolTipText = "Edit"
    cmdBtn(2).ToolTipText = "Close"
    cmdBtn(3).ToolTipText = "Generate"
    cmdBtn(4).ToolTipText = "Run"
    cmdBtn(5).ToolTipText = "Exit"
    '
End Sub
```

Note that this routine sets the picture, tool tip, size, and actual position of each of the
command bar buttons.

Now add the following code to the Form_Load and Form_Unload events.

```
Private Sub MDIForm_Load()
    LoadCmdBtns ' set up buttons
End Sub

Private Sub MDIForm_Resize()
    LoadCmdBtns
    lblProgress.Width = Me.ScaleWidth * 0.98
End Sub
```

Next, add the code from Listing A.9 to the cmdBtns_Click event. This handles all the command button selections.

TYPE   **Listing A.9. Adding code to the cmdBtn_Click event.**

```
Private Sub cmdBtn_Click(Index As Integer)
    '
    Select Case Index
        Case Is = 0
            mnuFileNew_Click
        Case Is = 1
            mnuFileEdit_Click
        Case Is = 2
            mnuFileClose_Click
        Case Is = 3
            mnuFileAuto_Click
        Case Is = 4
            mnuFileRun_Click
        Case Is = 5
            mnuFileExit_Click
    End Select
    '
End Sub
```

Next, add the code for the File | Close menu selection.

```
Private Sub mnuFileClose_Click()
    '
    On Error Resume Next
    SQLFileClose
    InitApp
    '
End Sub
```

Add code behind the Help menu option that shows off the SQLVBAbout form. To open the code window for the About menu option, select Help | About. When the code window pops up, insert the following code:

```
Private Sub mnuHelpAbout_Click()
    frmAbout.Show vbModal
End Sub
```

Now add code that gives the user the ability to control the multiple child forms within the SQLVBMain MDI form. Select Windows | Cascade and insert the following code:

```
Private Sub mnuWindowsItem_Click(Index As Integer)
    '
    Me.Arrange Index
    '
End Sub
```

The Arrange method requires a single parameter. This value determines whether the windows are cascaded, tiled, arranged as icons, and so on. Because you built the menu as a control array (with indexes), the Index parameter passed to this menu tells Visual Basic which operation was requested. All you need to do is call the method and pass the parameter.

Now add the code behind the File | Exit menu option. This code safely closes down all open child windows before exiting to the operating system.

```
Private Sub mnuFileExit_Click()
    Unload Me
End Sub
```

Select File | Run and add the following code line. Notice that the code line starts with the comment character. This tells Visual Basic to treat this line as a comment, not as executable code. You have it "commented out" right now because you haven't created the SQLMain routine yet. You do that in the next section when you create the SQL-VB5 Main code module.

```
Private Sub mnuFileRun_Click()
    SQLMain     ' call main job w/o parm
End Sub
```

Now add the following code to the File | Generate menu item. This calls the routines that generate a new script from an existing MDB.

```
Private Sub mnuFileAuto_Click()
    AutoGen ' call routine to read MDB and create SQV
End Sub
```

The following two segments of code should be added behind the File | New and File | Edit menu options. The code calls a routine that you build in the SQL-VB5 Main module, so you have commented out the calls for now to prevent Visual Basic from reporting an error at compile time.

```
Private Sub mnuFileEdit_Click()
    LoadNotePadFile "Edit Existing SQLVB File"
End Sub

Private Sub mnuFileNew_Click()
    LoadNotePadFile "Create New SQLVB File"
End Sub
```

Now that all the code is added, save this form and save the project. As a test, you can run the project. You can't do much except view the About box and exit, but you can check for compile errors.

Creating the SQL-VB5 Main Module

The SQLVBMOD code module contains the major portion of the system. It's here that you add the routines that can read and execute the SQL statements found in the ASCII file. You also add routines to handle any errors that occur along the way. Even though this module does a lot, you have only slightly more than 10 routines to define before you complete the project.

Declaring Global Variables

First, you need to declare a set of variables to be used throughout the entire project. These variables contain information about the script being processed, any forms that are open, and so forth. Add a module to the project by selecting Project | Add Module from the Visual Basic main menu. Set its Name property to SQLVBMOD and enter the lines in Listing A.10 into the declarations section. The meaning and use of these variables becomes clearer as you build the various routines within the module.

TYPE   **Listing A.10. Adding the global variables.**

```
'
' general declarations
'
Global strSQLFile As String
Global intGlobalErr As Integer
Global intSQLFlag As Integer
Global intDBFlag As Integer
Global intSQLFileHandle As Integer
Global strSQLLine As String
Global intLine As Integer
Global strLine As String
Global strGlobalSelect As String
Global strGlobalDBName As String
Global db As Database
Global ws As Workspace
Global intForms As Integer
Global TblForms() As Form
Global strConnect As String
Global strVersion As String
Global blnSQLQuiet As Boolean
```

Creating SQLMain

The top-most routine in this module is the SQLMain routine. This routine has only three tasks: open the script file, process the script commands, and close the script file. Let's write a module that does all that. To add a new procedure to the module, select Tools | Add Procedure from the Visual Basic main menu. Enter SQLMain(cRunFile) as the name, select the Sub radio button, and select the Public radio button. Now enter the code in Listing A.11.

TYPE **Listing A.11. Coding the SQLMain routine.**

```
Sub SQLMain(Optional cRunFile As Variant)
    '
    ' main loop for interpreting SQL ASCII file
    '
    If IsMissing(cRunFile) = True Then
        cRunFile = ""
    End If
    '
    InitApp                 ' clean up environment
    SQLFileOpen CStr(cRunFile) ' open the script
    If intGlobalErr = False Then
        SQLFileProcess        ' process the script
    End If
    SQLFileClose            ' close the script
    '
    cRunFile = ""           ' clear passed parm
    'If intGlobalErr = False Then
    '   MsgBox "Script Completed", vbInformation
    'End If
End Sub
```

The routine in Listing A.11 does all the things mentioned earlier and adds two more actions. You perform some application initialization. You set an error condition during the SQLFileOpen routine in case something goes wrong when you open the file. Then you can check that error condition before you try to run the SQLFileProcess routine. Also, once the script processing is complete, you show the user a friendly little message box.

Creating SQLFileOpen

Let's start building the next level of routines. The first is the SQLFileOpen routine. Use the CommonDialog control to get the filename from the user. If a filename was selected, open that file for processing, and then return to SQLMain. Notice that you have built in an error trap to catch any problems that may occur during file selection and opening.

Select Tools | Add Procedure from the Visual Basic main menu and set the name to SQLFileOpen(cSQLFile). Make this a Public Sub procedure. Now enter the code in Listing A.12 in the procedure window.

Listing A.12. Coding the `SQLFileOpen` routine.

```
Sub SQLFileOpen(strSQLFile As String)
    '
    ' open the SQV script file
    '
    On Error GoTo SQLFileOpenErr
    '
    If Len(Trim(strSQLFile)) = 0 Then
        SQLVBMain.CommonDialog1.DialogTitle = "Load SQLVB File"
        SQLVBMain.CommonDialog1.DefaultExt = "SQV"
        SQLVBMain.CommonDialog1.Filter = "SQLVB File¦*.SQV"
        SQLVBMain.CommonDialog1.ShowOpen
        strSQLFile = SQLVBMain.CommonDialog1.filename
    End If
    '
    If Len(Trim(strSQLFile)) = 0 Then
        intGlobalErr = True
        intSQLFlag = False
        GoTo SQLFileOpenExit
    End If
    '
    intSQLFileHandle = FreeFile(0)
    Open strSQLFile For Input As intSQLFileHandle
    intGlobalErr = False
    intSQLFlag = True
    GoTo SQLFileOpenExit
    '
SQLFileOpenErr:
    If Err <> 32755 Then
        ErrMsg Err, Error$, intLine, strSQLFile, "SQLFileOpen"
    End If
    InitApp
    intGlobalErr = True
    '
SQLFileOpenExit:
    '
End Sub
```

Creating `SQLFileClose`

Let's skip over the `SQLProcess` routine and write the `SQLFileClose` routine next. The only task this routine has to complete is to safely close the script file upon completion. Create a `Public` `Sub` procedure called `SQLFileClose` and enter the code in Listing A.13.

Listing A.13. Coding the `SQLFileClose` routine.

```
Sub SQLFileClose()
    '
    ' close the SQV text file
```

```
        '
        On Error GoTo SQLFileCloseErr
        '
        If intGlobalErr = False Then
            If intSQLFileHandle <> 0 Then
                Close (intSQLFileHandle)
            End If
            intSQLFlag = False
        End If
        GoTo SQLFileCloseExit

SQLFileCloseErr:
        ErrMsg Err, Error$, intLine, strLine, "SQLFileClose"
        InitApp
        '
SQLFileCloseExit:
        '
End Sub
```

Creating SQLFileProcess

Now you get to the heart of the program—SQLFileProcess. This routine reads each line of the script file and performs whatever processing is necessary to build and execute the SQL statements in the script. You also add a few lines that show the user the script lines as they are processed. Also, remember that the script file has regular SQL statements, special database CONNECT, VERSION, QUIET, OPEN, CREATE, and CLOSE words, and comments. This processing routine has to handle each of these differently. Of course, you need an error handler, too.

Create a Public Sub procedure called SQLFileProcess and enter the code in Listing A.14. Don't be discouraged by the length of this piece of code—it won't take you long to enter it into the project.

TYPE **Listing A.14. Coding the SQLFileProcess routine.**

```
Sub SQLFileProcess()
    '
    ' main loop for processing ASCII file lines
    '
    On Error GoTo SQLFileProcessErr
    '
    Dim cToken As String
    '
    If intSQLFlag = False Then
        GoTo SQLFileProcessExit
    End If
    '
    strSQLLine = ""
    While Not EOF(intSQLFileHandle)
```

continues

Listing A.14. continued

```
            If intGlobalErr = True Then
                GoTo SQLFileProcessExit
            End If
            '
            Line Input #intSQLFileHandle, strLine
            intLine = intLine + 1
            strLine = Trim(strLine) + " "
            If Len(strLine) <> 0 Then
                cToken = GetToken(strLine)
                If Right(cToken, 1) = ";" Then
                    cToken = Left(cToken, Len(cToken) - 1)
                End If
                '
                SQLVBMain.lblProgress.Caption = strLine
                DoEvents
                Select Case UCase(cToken)
                    Case Is = "//"
                        ' no action - comment line
                    Case Is = "DBCONNECT"
                        SQLdbConnect
                    Case Is = "DBVERSION"
                        SQLdbVersion
                    Case Is = "DBOPEN"
                        SQLdbOpen
                    Case Is = "DBMAKE"
                        SQLdbMake
                    Case Is = "DBCLOSE"
                        SQLdbClose
                    Case Is = "DBQUIET"
                        SQLQuietFlag
                    Case Else
                        strSQLLine = strSQLLine + strLine
                        If Right(strLine, 2) = "; " Then
                            SQLDoCommand
                            strSQLLine = ""
                        End If
                End Select
            End If
        Wend
        GoTo SQLFileProcessExit
        '
SQLFileProcessErr:
    ErrMsg Err, Error$, intLine, strLine, "SQLFileProcess"
    InitApp
    '
SQLFileProcessExit:
    '
End Sub
```

Several things are happening in Listing A.14. Let's review the routine more closely. After setting up the error trap and initializing variables, the main While..Wend loop starts. This loop reads a line from the script file opened by SQLFileOpen, updates a line counter, removes any trailing or leading spaces from the line, and then adds a single space at the end of the line. This single space is added to help the GetToken function do its work.

The SQL-VB5 program processes each line of script word by word. The first word in each command line is used to determine how SQL-VB5 processes the line. The GetToken function returns the first word in the line (you learn more about GetToken a bit later). Next, you show the current script line to the user by updating SQLVBMain.lblProgress. Notice that you added the DoEvents command right after updating the label. This forces your program to pause a moment, and that allows Windows time to send the message that ultimately updates the SQLVBMain form.

Once the main form is updated, the program must handle the word it pulled from the script line. Usually, the word is an SQL keyword and SQL-VB5 can add it to the cSQLLine variable for eventual processing. However, there are several words that require special handling. These words are listed in Table A.6 along with comments about how they are handled.

Table A.6. Script words that require special handling.

Script Word	Handling Comments
//	This is the comment word. If a line begins with this keyword, ignore the rest of the line and get the next line in the script. You must leave at least one space between the // and the comment. For example, //comment would be rejected by SQL-VB5, but // comment is just fine.
DBCONNECT	This is the keyword that you can use to set the CONNECT property of the database. This allows you to open non-Microsoft Jet databases or even ODBC data sources. Consult the Microsoft Visual Basic documentation for valid syntax here. Basically, anything that works in Visual Basic's Connect property works here, too.
DBVERSION	This is the value that sets the version of database to be created. Valid values are 1.1, 2.0, and 3.0.
DBOPEN	This is the OpenDatabase word. If a line starts with this keyword, call a special routine (SQLdbOpen) that executes a Visual Basic OpenDatabase operation.

continues

Table A.6. continued

Script Word	Handling Comments
DBMAKE	This is the CreateDatabase word. If a line starts with this key-word, call a special routine (SQLdbMake) that executes a Visual Basic CreateDatabase operation.
DBQUIET	Use this keyword to suppress the display of SQL-VB5 when you call it from other programs (using the object model). If this value is set to True, no screens appear; only the script is processed.
DBCLOSE	This is the CloseDatabase word. If a line begins with this key-word, call a special routine (SQLdbClose) that executes a Visual Basic Close operation on a database object.

If the word found at the start of the line is not one of those listed in Table A.6, the program assumes that it is a valid SQL word and adds the entire line to the variable cSQLLine. After doing this, the routine checks to see whether the current line ends with a semicolon (;). If so, the program attempts to execute the SQL statement using the SQLDoCommand routine. After executing this routine, the cSQLLine variable is cleared in preparation for the next SQL statement.

This process is repeated until the program reaches the end of the script file. At that time, the routine exits SQLFileProcess and returns to the SQLMain routine.

Now would be a good time to save the SQLVBMOD code module and save the project. You can't run the program at this point because you added references to several routines that do not yet exist. You add those final routines in the next section.

Creating the Support Routines

Now that you have entered all the main routines, you need to add several support routines. Almost all these support routines are called directly from SQLFileProcess. You concentrate on those first and add others as needed.

The first routine called from SQLFileProcess is GetToken. This routine takes a line of script and returns the first word in the list. You use this word (often referred to as a *token*) as a way to determine how SQLFileProcess handles each line of script. Because GetToken returns a value, it is a *function*. To create a Visual Basic function, select Insert | Procedure. Enter the function name as GetToken(cString As String) As String and select the Function radio button. Now enter the code in Listing A.15 in the code window.

TYPE **Listing A.15. Coding the GetToken routine.**

```
Function GetToken(cString As String) As String
    '
    ' get a token from the input line
    '
    Dim intTemp As Integer
    '
    intTemp = InStr(cString, " ")
    If intTemp > 0 Then
       GetToken = Left(cString, intTemp - 1)
    Else
       GetToken = ""
    End If
    '
End Function
```

The comments in the code explain things pretty well. You use the Visual Basic InStr function to locate the first occurrence of a space within the script line, and then use that position to grab a copy of the first word in the line. If you can't find a word, you return an empty string.

Now let's add the three "setup" values you can use in your scripts: DBCONNECT, DBVERSION and DBQUIET. These three keywords do not actually execute any real actions, but they do set values used by the other action words DBOPEN and DBMAKE.

First, add the code for the DBCONNECT keyword from Listing A.16. This code just accepts the Connect string from the script and saves it to an internal variable.

TYPE **Listing A.16. Coding the SQLDBConnect method.**

```
Public Sub SQLdbConnect()
    '
    ' set global connect property
    '
    strConnect = strSQLLine
    '
End Sub
```

Now, add the code from Listing A.17 to handle the DBVERSION keyword.

TYPE **Listing A.17. Coding the SQLdbVersion subroutine.**

```
Public Sub SQLdbVersion()
    '
    ' set global version value
    '
```

continues

Listing A.17. continued

```
        Dim strTemp As String
        '
        strTemp = GetToken(strSQLLine)
        '
        Select Case UCase(strTemp)
            Case "1.0"
                strVersion = dbVersion10
            Case "1.1"
                strVersion = dbVersion11
            Case "2.0"
                strVersion = dbVersion20
            Case "3.0"
                strVersion = dbVersion30
        End Select
        '
    End Sub
```

Next, add the code for the DBQUIET keyword. This sets a value that can suppress form displays. This is handy for performing script runs where you do not want to see any GUI display. Enter the code from Listing A.18.

TYPE   **Listing A.18. Coding the SQLQuietFlag subroutine.**

```
Public Sub SQLQuietFlag()
    '
    Dim strTemp As String
    '
    strTemp = GetToken(strSQLLine)
    '
    If UCase(strTemp) = "YES" Then
        blnSQLQuiet = True
    Else
        blnSQLQuiet = False
    End If
    '
End Sub
```

The next three routines you add handle the DBOPEN, DBMAKE, and DBCLOSE script words. These are all non-SQL commands that you need in order to open, create, and close Microsoft Access Jet databases. The first one you add is the routine that handles opening a Microsoft Access Jet database. Use the Visual Basic menu to create a Public Sub routine named SQLdbOpen and enter the code in Listing A.19.

Listing A.19. Coding the SQLdbOpen routine.

```
Sub SQLdbOpen()
    '
    ' open an existing database
    '
    On Error GoTo SQldbOpenErr
    '
    Dim strOpen As String
    Dim intTemp As Integer
    '
    strLine = Trim(strLine)  ' drop any spaces
    intTemp = InStr(strLine, " ") ' locate first embedded space
    strOpen = Mid(strLine, intTemp + 1, 255) ' get rest of line
    '
    ' if line ends w/ ";", dump it!
    If Right(strOpen, 1) = ";" Then
        strOpen = Left(strOpen, Len(strOpen) - 1)
    End If
    '
    ' now try to open database
    Set ws = DBEngine.CreateWorkspace("wsSQLVB", "admin", "")
    Set db = ws.OpenDatabase(strOpen, False, False, strConnect)
    strGlobalDBName = strOpen
    intDBFlag = True
    GoTo SQldbOpenExit
    '
SQldbOpenErr:
    ErrMsg Err, Error$, intLine, strLine, "SQldbOpen"
    InitApp
    '
SQldbOpenExit:
    '
End Sub
```

Listing A.19 performs three tasks. First, it strips the DBOPEN keyword off the script line. Second, if a semicolon (;) appears at the end of the line, the routine drops it. What's left is the valid database filename in the variable cOpen. The routine then attempts to open this file using the stored Connect string. Once that's done, the routine returns to SQLFileProcess.

The next routine to add handles the DBCLOSE command. This is a simple routine. Its only job is to close the Microsoft Access Jet database. This routine also closes any open child forms and clears flag variables. Create a Public Sub called SQLdbClose and add the code in Listing A.20.

TYPE   **Listing A.20. Coding the `SQLdbClose` routine.**

```
Sub SQLdbClose()
    '
    ' close open database
    '
    On Error Resume Next ' ignore errors here
    '
    db.Close
    '
    For x = 0 To intForms
        Unload TblForms(x)
    Next x
    '
    intForms = 0
    intDBFlag = False
    '
End Sub
```

The final routine to handle special commands is the routine that processes the DBMAKE keyword to create new Microsoft Access Jet databases. This one works much like the DBOPEN routine except that there are a few additional chores when creating a new file. Create a Public Sub called SQLdbMake and enter the code in Listing A.21.

TYPE   **Listing A.21. Coding the `SQLdbMake` routine.**

```
Sub SQLdbMake()
    '
    ' make a new database
    '
    On Error GoTo SQLdbMakeErr
    '
    Dim strMake As String
    Dim intTemp As Integer
    '
    strLine = Trim(strLine)  ' drop any spaces
    intTemp = InStr(strLine, " ") ' locate first embedded space
    strMake = Mid(strLine, intTemp + 1, 255) ' get rest of line
    '
    ' if line ends w/ ";", dump it!
    If Right(strMake, 1) = ";" Then
        strMake = Left(strMake, Len(strMake) - 1)
    End If
    '
    ' try to open it (to see if it already exists)
    nSQLMakeHandle = FreeFile(0)
    Open strMake For Input As nSQLMakeHandle
    Close nSQLMakeHandle
    '
    nResult = MsgBox("ERASE [" + strMake + "]", vbYesNo + vbQuestion, "Database
➥Already Exists!")
    If nResult = vbYes Then
```

```
            Kill strMake
        Else
            ErrMsg 0, "Script Cancel - database already Exists", intLine, strLine,
    ⇒"SQLdbMake"
            InitApp
        End If
        '
        ' now try to make a new database
    SQLdbMake2:
        ' create a new db, close it, then open for use
        Set ws = DBEngine.CreateWorkspace("wsSQLVB2", "admin", "")
        Set db = ws.CreateDatabase(strMake, dbLangGeneral, strVersion)
        db.Close
        Set db = ws.OpenDatabase(strMake, False, False, strConnect)
        strGlobalDBName = strMake
        intDBFlag = True
        GoTo SQLdbMakeExit
        '
    SQLdbMakeErr:
        If Err = 53 Then
            Resume SQLdbMake2
        Else
            ErrMsg Err, Error$, intLine, strLine, "SQLdbMake"
            InitApp
        End If
        '
    SQLdbMakeExit:
        '
    End Sub
```

A few things in this routine deserve attention. First, the routine drops the first word from the script line (the DBMAKE word). Then it strips the semicolon off the end of the line, if necessary. Then, instead of performing the create operation, the routine first tries to open the file. This is done to see if it already exists. If it does, you can issue a warning before you clobber that multimegabyte database that the user has been nursing for the last few months. If no error occurs when you try to open the file, the routine sends out a message warning the user and asking if it's okay to erase the existing file. If the answer is Yes, the file is erased. If the answer is No, a message is displayed, and script processing is halted.

Now, if an error occurs during the attempt to open the file, you know that the file does not exist. The local error handler is invoked and the first thing it checks is whether the error was caused by an attempt to open a nonexistent file. If so, the error handler sends the routine to the file creation point without comment. If the error has another cause, the global error handler is called and the program is halted.

Finally, after all the file creation stuff is sorted out, the routine executes the Visual Basic CreateDatabase operation and returns to the SQLFileProcess routine. Notice that you declared two parameters during the CreateDatabase operation. The first parameter (vbLangGeneral) tells Visual Basic to use the general rules for sorting and collating data. The second parameter (strVersion) can be set by the user with the DBVERSION keyword.

The last routine called from `SQLFileProcess` handles the execution of SQL statements. Create a `Public Sub` called `SQLDoCommand` and enter the code in Listing A.22.

TYPE   **Listing A.22. Coding the `SQLDoCommand` routine.**

```
Sub SQLFileProcess()
    '
    ' main loop for processing ASCII file lines
    '
    On Error GoTo SQLFileProcessErr
    '
    Dim cToken As String
    '
    If intSQLFlag = False Then
        GoTo SQLFileProcessExit
    End If
    '
    strSQLLine = ""
    While Not EOF(intSQLFileHandle)
        If intGlobalErr = True Then
            GoTo SQLFileProcessExit
        End If
        '
        Line Input #intSQLFileHandle, strLine
        intLine = intLine + 1
        strLine = Trim(strLine) + " "
        If Len(strLine) <> 0 Then
            cToken = GetToken(strLine)
            If Right(cToken, 1) = ";" Then
                cToken = Left(cToken, Len(cToken) - 1)
            End If
            '
            SQLVBMain.lblProgress.Caption = strLine
            DoEvents
            Select Case UCase(cToken)
                Case Is = "//"
                    ' no action - comment line
                Case Is = "DBCONNECT"
                    SQLdbConnect
                Case Is = "DBVERSION"
                    SQLdbVersion
                Case Is = "DBOPEN"
                    SQLdbOpen
                Case Is = "DBMAKE"
                    SQLdbMake
                Case Is = "DBCLOSE"
                    SQLdbClose
                Case Is = "DBQUIET"
                    SQLQuietFlag
                Case Else
                    strSQLLine = strSQLLine + strLine
                    If Right(strLine, 2) = "; " Then
                        SQLDoCommand
                        strSQLLine = ""
```

A

```
                  End If
              End Select
          End If
      Wend
      GoTo SQLFileProcessExit
      '
SQLFileProcessErr:
      ErrMsg Err, Error$, intLine, strLine, "SQLFileProcess"
      InitApp
      '
SQLFileProcessExit:
      '
End Sub

Sub SQLDoCommand()
      '
      ' handle SQL Command
      '
      On Error GoTo SQLDoCommandErr    ' set error trap
      '
      Dim cTemp As String              ' holds token
      '
      ' skip errors if you're deleting objects
      cTemp = GetToken(Trim(strSQLLine)) ' get first word
      Select Case UCase(cTemp)
          Case Is = "DELETE"           ' don't report error
              On Error Resume Next
          Case Is = "DROP"             ' don't report error
              On Error Resume Next
          Case Is = "ALTER"            ' don't report error
              On Error Resume Next
      End Select
      '
      ' check for queries that return a view
      Select Case UCase(cTemp)
          Case Is = "TRANSFORM"
              ShowTable strSQLLine, strGlobalDBName       ' show view form
          Case Is = "SELECT"
              If InStr(UCase(strSQLLine), " INTO ") <> 0 Then
                  ws.BeginTrans
                  db.Execute strSQLLine, dbSeeChanges + dbFailOnError  ' execute make-
➥table SQL
                  ws.CommitTrans
                  db.Close
                  Set db = Nothing
                  Set db = ws.OpenDatabase(strGlobalDBName, False, False, strConnect)
              Else
                  db.Close
                  Set db = Nothing
                  ShowTable strSQLLine, strGlobalDBName   ' show view form
                  Set db = ws.OpenDatabase(strGlobalDBName, False, False, strConnect)
              End If
          Case Else
              ws.BeginTrans
              db.Execute strSQLLine, dbSeeChanges + dbFailOnError     ' execute SQL
              ws.CommitTrans
```

continues

Listing A.22. continued

```
        db.Close
        Set db = Nothing
        Set db = ws.OpenDatabase(strGlobalDBName, False, False, strConnect)
    End Select
   GoTo SQlDoCommandExit              ' exit routine
   '
   ' local error handler
SQLDoCommandErr:
   ErrMsg Err, Error$, intLine, strLine, "SQLDoCommand"
   On Error Resume Next
   ws.Rollback
   InitApp
   '
   ' routine exit
SQlDoCommandExit:
   '
End Sub
```

Even though it looks as though several things take place in this routine, only three tasks are being handled by SQLDoCommand. First, you get the first word in the script line, and then you have to make a couple of decisions on how to properly execute the SQL statement.

If the first word is DELETE, DROP, or ALTER, you turn off the local error handler. This is done for convenience. You want to be able to create scripts that can use the SQL words DELETE, DROP, and ALTER to remove table objects from the database. Because the objects may not exist, you could get errors that can halt the script processing. To make life simple, SQL-VB5 ignores these errors. Once you write a few SQL-VB5 scripts, you'll appreciate this feature.

Next, you have to check for the SQL keywords that can return result sets. These are TRANSFORM and SELECT. These keywords should be handled differently from SQL statements that do not return result sets. If you see TRANSFORM, you call the ShowTable routine to load and display the SQLVBChild child form on the screen. If you see SELECT, you make one additional check. If the line contains the INTO keyword, you have an SQL statement that creates a new table. Using the INTO keyword means that the SELECT statement does not return a result set. If there is no INTO in the SQL statement, you hand the statement off to the ShowTable routine. If the line starts with any other SQL keyword, you simply execute the command using the Visual Basic Execute method on the database.

The SQLDoCommand routine calls the ShowTable routine, so you need to add that routine to the project. This is a simple routine that updates some variables, creates a new instance of the SQLVBChild child form, and shows the new form. Create a Public Sub called ShowTable and enter the code in Listing A.23.

Listing A.23. Coding the ShowTable routine.

```
Sub ShowTable(cSQL As String, strDB As String)
    '
    ' show a selected table
    '
    strGlobalSelect = strSQLLine
    strGlobalDBName = strDB
    '
    intForms = intForms + 1
    ReDim Preserve TblForms(intForms) As Form
    Set TblForms(intForms) = New SQLVBChild
    Load TblForms(intForms)
    TblForms(intForms).Caption = CStr(intForms)
    TblForms(intForms).Data1.DatabaseName = strGlobalDBName
    TblForms(intForms).Data1.RecordSource = strGlobalSelect
    TblForms(intForms).Data1.Refresh
    TblForms(intForms).Show
    TblForms(intForms).WindowState = vbMinimized
    TblForms(intForms).WindowState = vbNormal
    '
End Sub
```

The only fancy stuff in this module involves the creation of new Form objects. Remember that you created a global array called TblForms in the declaration section of the module? This routine increases the size of the array by 1 each time it is invoked. Also, this routine uses the Visual Basic SET command to create a new *instance* of the SQLVBChild child form. This new instance is a *copy* of SQLVBChild that has its own "life" once it is created and loaded. By making copies in this way, you can create multiple, independent versions of the SQLVBChild form to display various datasets.

You need to add another support routine. This one handles the loading of the scripts into the Windows Notepad for editing. This is called from the SQLVBMain MDI form. Create a Public Sub called LoadNotePadFile(cLoadMsg As String) and enter the code in Listing A.24.

Listing A.24. Coding the LoadNotePadFile routine.

```
Sub LoadNotePadFile(cLoadMsg As String, Optional strScript As String)
    '
    ' load notepad as an editor
    '
    On Error GoTo LoadNotePadFileErr:
    '
    Dim cEditFile As String
    Dim nAppID As Long
    '
    If IsMissing(strScript) = False And strScript <> "" Then
        cEditFile = strScript
    Else
```

continues

Listing A.24. continued

```
            SQLVBMain.CommonDialog1.DialogTitle = cLoadMsg
            SQLVBMain.CommonDialog1.DefaultExt = "SQV"
            SQLVBMain.CommonDialog1.Filter = "SQLVB File¦*.SQV"
            SQLVBMain.CommonDialog1.ShowOpen
            cEditFile = SQLVBMain.CommonDialog1.filename
        End If

        If Len(cEditFile) <> 0 Then
            nAppID = Shell("NotePad " + cEditFile, 1)
            AppActivate (nAppID)
        End If
        GoTo LoadNotePadFileExit
        '
LoadNotePadFileErr:
        ErrMsg Err, Error$, 0, cEditFile, "LoadNotePadFile"
        InitApp
        '
LoadNotePadFileExit:
        '
End Sub
```

Most of this code should look familiar. The first part of the routine in Listing A.24 sets up and activates the CommonDialog object to allow the user to select an existing file or create a new file. Once this is done, the routine forces Windows to load a new instance of the Notepad application, and then gives that application the focus. Now the user sees the Notepad application (with the selected file loaded, too!). The SQL-VB5 application resumes processing once it gains the focus again.

The next routine you need to add to SQLVBMOD is the global error handler. This routine (shown in Listing A.25) simply displays the error messages and waits for the user to click the OK button before it returns to the calling routine. Create a Public Sub called ErrMsg and enter the code in Listing A.25.

TYPE Listing A.25. Coding the ErrMsg routine.

```
Sub ErrMsg(nErr As Integer, cError As String, intLine As Integer, strLine As
➥String, cModule As String)
    '
    ' report an error to user
    '
    Dim cMsg As String
    '
    cMsg = "ErrNo:" + Chr(9) + Str(nErr) + Chr(13)
    cMsg = cMsg + "ErrMsg: " + Chr(9) + cError + Chr(13)
    cMsg = cMsg + "LineNo:" + Chr(9) + Str(intLine) + Chr(13)
    cMsg = cMsg + "Text: " + Chr(9) + strLine
    '
```

```
      If blnSQLQuiet = False Then
          MsgBox cMsg, vbCritical, cModule
      End If
      '
  End Sub
```

No real magic in this routine. Listing A.25 is passed the Visual Basic error number and error message, the script line number and script line text, and the name of the SQL-VB5 routine that experienced the error. All this is formatted into a readable (if not entirely welcome) message that is displayed to the user. Notice that you used the tabs (Chr(9)) and carriage returns (Chr(13)) to make the information easier to read.

The routine in Listing A.26 handles all the initialization chores for the start of a script. It is also called whenever an error is reported and when the program is exited. Create a Public Sub procedure called InitApp and enter the code in Listing A.26.

TYPE   **Listing A.26. Coding the InitApp routine.**

```
Sub InitApp()
    '
    ' set up app values
    '
    On Error Resume Next ' ignore any errors here
    '
    ' close all child forms
    For x = 0 To intForms
        Unload TblForms(x)
        Set TblForms(x) = Nothing
    Next x
    '
    ' close open database
    If intDBFlag = True Then
        db.Close
        Set db = Nothing
        Set ws = Nothing
    End If
    '
    ' close open script file
    If intSQLFlag = True Then
        Close (intSQLFileHandle)
    End If
    '
    ' reset flags & stuff
    nSQLFile = ""
    intSQLFlag = False
    intDBFlag = False
    nGlobalErr = False
    blnSQLQuiet = False
    intLine = 0
    strConnect = "" ' "Access;"
```

continues

Listing A.26. continued

```
        strVersion = dbVersion30
        '
End Sub
```

Adding the Sub Main Routine

There is one final routine you need to add to the project to make SQL-VB5 start. It's the sub Main method. This starts the entire application, instead of the SQLVBMain form. Add another code module to your project and set its Name property to SQLVBClass. Now add the following code to the module:

```
Public Sub Main()
    '
    Dim strCmd As String
    strCmd = Command$
    '
    ' ignore system commands
    If Left(strCmd, 1) = "-" Then
        Exit Sub
    End If
    '
    ' see if user passed a file
    If Trim(strCmd) <> "" Then
        SQLMain strCmd
    Else
        SQLVBMain.Show
    End If
    '
End Sub
```

This routine allows you to send a script file on the command line when you start the program. First, SQL-VB5 checks to see if the first character of the command is a hyphen (-). This designates a system command and is ignored by SQL-VB5. For example, when you start SQL-VB5 from the OLE request, the -Embedded command is passed to SQL-VB5 by the operating system. This lets you write special code that executes the first time someone attempts to reference the application.

Next, if there is a valid command on the line, it is passed to the script processor for immediate attention. Otherwise, the MDI form is shown to the user.

Now you need to change the Startup property of the project. Select Project | Properties and set the Startup Form to Sub Main. Save the project before continuing.

> **WARNING**
>
> It is very important that you set the Startup Form to Sub Main. If you forget to do this, your code runs just fine as a standalone application, but does not accept command-line parameters and cannot run as an OLE Server object.

That's the last routine in the SQLVBMOD code module. Save this module and save the project before you continue. In the next section, you add the code that reads an existing MDB and generates a valid SQL-Visual Basic script.

Creating the SQLVBGEN Module

Because you have the entire Microsoft DAO at your disposal, it is possible to read an existing MDB and generate a valid SQL-Visual Basic script that can be used to re-create the database structure. This can be done by walking through all the collections of table, index, relationship, and field objects. In this section you create the code that does just that.

First, add a new BAS module to your project. Set its Name property to SQLVBGEN. Then add the code from Listing A.27 to the general declarations section of the module.

TYPE | **Listing A.27. Coding the general declaration section of SQLVBGEN.**

```
Option Explicit

Dim cDBName As String
Dim cWrLine As String
Dim cWrFile As String
Dim objDB As Database
Dim nWrFile As Integer
Dim EOL As String
Dim INDENT As Integer
```

These are the only module-level variables you need for this section.

Coding the AutoGen Method

The top-level routine (called AutoGen) is used to create the entire script. It accepts two parameters: the MDB name and the SQL script name. Add the code in Listing A.28 to your module.

TYPE   **Listing A.28. Coding the AutoGen subroutine.**

```
Public Sub AutoGen(Optional cDB As Variant, Optional cSQV As Variant)
    '
    ' =======================================================
    ' inputs:
    '    cDB        database name to read
    '    cSQV       script name to write
    '
    ' outputs:
    '    produces script file
    '
    ' processing:
    '    Ask for database to load and file to save results.
    '    Enum all tables, fields, indexes and relations
    ' =======================================================
    '
    ' some local vars
    EOL = Chr(13) + Chr(10)
    INDENT = 3
    intGlobalErr = False
    '
    ' handle missing parms
    If IsMissing(cDB) = True Then
        cDB = ""
    End If
    If IsMissing(cSQV) = True Then
        cSQV = ""
    End If
    '
    ' we can run silent
    If cDB <> "" And cSQV <> "" Then
        SQLVBMain.Visible = False
    End If
    '
    AutoGenDBOpen cDB        ' get mdb file
    '
    If intGlobalErr = False Then
        AutoGenSQVOpen cSQV       ' get sqv file
    End If
    '
    If intGlobalErr = False Then
        CreateScript     ' create script
    End If
    '
    ' let'em know it's done
    If intGlobalErr = False Then
        If SQLVBMain.Visible = True Then
            MsgBox cWrFile + " Script Created", vbInformation
        End If
    End If
    '
    ' clean up
    Close (nWrFile)
    nWrFile = 0
    cWrFile = ""
```

```
        cDBName = ""
        cDB = ""
        cSQV = ""
        intGlobalErr = False ' reset
        '
End Sub
```

Most of the code is self-explanatory. Notice that there is logic to determine whether the user should see any visual displays. This is here because you may want to run this generator as part of the OLE object model and do not need to see the SQLVBMain form.

The AutoGenDBOpen Method

Next, add the AutoGenDBOpen routine from Listing A.29. This opens the MDB.

TYPE   **Listing A.29. Coding the AutoGenDBOpen subroutine.**

```
Public Sub AutoGenDBOpen(Optional cDB As Variant)
    On Error GoTo AutoGenDBOpenErr
    '
    If IsMissing(cDB) = True Or Len(cDB) = 0 Then
        SQLVBMain.CommonDialog1.DialogTitle = "Load MDB File"
        SQLVBMain.CommonDialog1.DefaultExt = "MDB"
        SQLVBMain.CommonDialog1.Filter = "MS Jet Database File¦*.MDB"
        SQLVBMain.CommonDialog1.Flags = cdlOFNFileMustExist
        SQLVBMain.CommonDialog1.CancelError = True
        SQLVBMain.CommonDialog1.ShowOpen
        cDBName = SQLVBMain.CommonDialog1.filename
    Else
        cDBName = cDB
    End If
    '
    If Len(cDBName) = 0 Then
        intGlobalErr = True
    Else
        cDBName = Trim(cDBName)
        Set objDB = OpenDatabase(cDBName)
    End If
    GoTo AutoGenDBOpenExit
    '
AutoGenDBOpenErr:
    If Err <> 32755 Then
        ErrMsg Err, Error$, intLine, strLine, "AutoGenDBOpen"
    End If
    intGlobalErr = True
    '
AutoGenDBOpenExit:
End Sub
```

The `AutoGenSQVOpen` method

Now add the `AutoGenSQVOpen` subroutine from Listing A.30. Notice that, if no name is supplied for the script, `SQL-VB5` invents one based on the MDB name.

TYPE **Listing A.30. Coding the `AutoGenSQVOpen` subroutine.**

```
Public Sub AutoGenSQVOpen(Optional cSQV As Variant)
    On Error GoTo AutoGenSQVOpenErr
    '
    Dim intTemp As Integer
    '
    If IsMissing(cSQV) = True Or Len(cSQV) = 0 Then
        cWrFile = cDBName
    Else
        cWrFile = cSQV
    End If
    '
    intTemp = InStr(cWrFile, ".")
    If intTemp > 0 Then
        cWrFile = Mid(cWrFile, 1, intTemp - 1)
    End If
    cWrFile = cWrFile + ".sqv"
    '
    If IsMissing(cSQV) = True Or Len(cSQV) = 0 Then
        SQLVBMain.CommonDialog1.DialogTitle = "Create SQV File"
        SQLVBMain.CommonDialog1.DefaultExt = "SQV"
        SQLVBMain.CommonDialog1.Filter = "SQV Script File¦*.SQV"
        SQLVBMain.CommonDialog1.filename = cWrFile
        SQLVBMain.CommonDialog1.Flags = cdlOFNCreatePrompt Or
➥cdlOFNOverwritePrompt
        SQLVBMain.CommonDialog1.CancelError = True
        SQLVBMain.CommonDialog1.ShowOpen
        cWrFile = SQLVBMain.CommonDialog1.filename
    End If
    '
    If Len(cWrFile) = 0 Then
        intGlobalErr = True
    Else
        nWrFile = FreeFile
        Open cWrFile For Output As nWrFile
    End If
    GoTo AutoGenSQVOpenExit
    '
AutoGenSQVOpenErr:
    If Err <> 32755 Then
        ErrMsg Err, Error$, intLine, strLine, "AutoGenDBOpen"
    End If
    intGlobalErr = True
    '
AutoGenSQVOpenExit:
    '
End Sub
```

The `CreateScript` method

Now you're ready for the fun stuff. The next method is the one that actually creates the script. Add the code from Listing A.31 to the module.

TYPE **Listing A.31. Coding the `CreateScript` subroutine.**

```
Public Sub CreateScript()
    '
    ' walk through database objects and produce text file
    '
    On Error Resume Next
    '
    Dim objTableDef As TableDef
    Dim objIndex As Index
    Dim objRelation As Relation
    '
    ' add script header
    cWrLine = WrScriptHeader(cDBName)
    Print #nWrFile, cWrLine
    '
    ' add database create code
    cWrLine = WrCreateDB(cDBName)
    Print #nWrFile, cWrLine
    '
    ' add table create code
    For Each objTableDef In objDB.TableDefs
        cWrLine = WrCreateTable(objTableDef)
        If Len(cWrLine) > 0 Then
            Print #nWrFile, cWrLine
        End If
        '
        For Each objIndex In objTableDef.Indexes
            cWrLine = WrCreateIndex(objIndex, objTableDef.Name)
            If Len(cWrLine) > 0 Then
                Print #nWrFile, cWrLine
            End If
        Next
    Next
    '
    ' add relation create code
    For Each objRelation In objDB.Relations
        cWrLine = wrCreateRelation(objRelation)
        If Len(cWrLine) > 0 Then
            Print #nWrFile, cWrLine
        End If
    Next
    '
    ' add script footer
    cWrLine = WrScriptFooter
    Print #nWrFile, cWrLine
    '
    SQLVBMain.lblProgress = ""
End Sub
```

Although it looks a bit long, CreateScript is actually a pretty simple routine. First, it creates a script header, then the database, then all the tables, then the relationships, and finally, it writes a script footer. Simple, right? Now let's get into the subprocesses called from this method.

The WrScriptHeader and WrScriptFooter Methods

You need to add some code comments at the start and end of all your scripts. Add the WrScriptHeader and WrScriptFooter routines from Listing A.32.

TYPE **Listing A.32. Coding the WrScriptHeader function.**

```
Public Function WrScriptHeader(cMDB) As String
    '
    ' write header for text file
    '
    Dim cTemp As String
    '
    cTemp = "// " + String(60, "*") + EOL
    cTemp = cTemp + "// DATABASE CREATE SCRIPT FOR [" + cMDB + "]" + EOL
    cTemp = cTemp + "// " + String(60, "*") + EOL
    cTemp = cTemp + "// SQLGEN Version 5.0 - 03/97(MCA)" + EOL
    cTemp = cTemp + "// " + EOL
    cTemp = cTemp + "// For use with SQL-VB Interpreter" + EOL
    cTemp = cTemp + "//" + EOL
    cTemp = cTemp + "// CREATED: " + Format(Date, "General Date") + EOL
    cTemp = cTemp + "//" + EOL
    cTemp = cTemp + "// " + String(60, "*") + EOL
    '
    WrScriptHeader = cTemp
    '
End Function

Public Function WrScriptFooter()
    '
    ' create end of script footer
    '
    Dim cTemp As String
    '
    cTemp = "// " + String(60, "*") + EOL
    cTemp = cTemp + "// " + "END OF FILE" + EOL
    cTemp = cTemp + "// " + String(60, "*") + EOL
    '
    WrScriptFooter = cTemp
    '
End Function
```

The `WrCreateDB` Method

Next, add the `wrCreateDB` method from Listing A.33.

TYPE **Listing A.33. Coding the `WrCreateDB` function.**

```
Public Function WrCreateDB(cMDB) As String
    '
    ' write the create db line
    '
    Dim cTemp As String

    SQLVBMain.lblProgress = "Creating Script Header..."
    DoEvents

    cTemp = EOL
    cTemp = cTemp + "// Create new database" + EOL
    cTemp = cTemp + "dbMake " + cDBName + ";"
    cTemp = cTemp + EOL
    '
    WrCreateDB = cTemp
    '
End Function
```

The `WrCreateTable` method

The next step is to create each table definition. This is actually a two-step process. First, you need to create the table and its fields. Then you need to create the indexes that belong to the table. The code in Listing A.34 creates the table itself and calls the function to create the field definitions.

TYPE **Listing A.34. Coding the `WrCreateTable` function.**

```
Public Function WrCreateTable(tblObject As TableDef) As String
    '
    ' create a write table SQL statement
    '
    Dim cTemp As String
    Dim cTable As String
    Dim objField As Field
    '
    ' ignore system tables
    cTable = tblObject.Name
    If UCase(Left(cTable, 4)) = "MSYS" Then
        WrCreateTable = ""
        Exit Function
```

continues

Listing A.34. continued

```
End If
'
' ignore non-native MDB tables
If tblObject.Attributes <> 0 Then
    WrCreateTable = ""
    Exit Function
End If
'
SQLVBMain.lblProgress = "Creating Tables..."
DoEvents
'
' if it contains spaces, enclose in braces
If InStr(cTable, " ") <> 0 Then
    cTable = "[" + cTable + "]"
End If
'
' start SQL line
cTemp = "// Create " + cTable + EOL
cTemp = cTemp + "CREATE TABLE " + cTable + EOL
cTemp = cTemp + Space(INDENT) + "(" + EOL
'
' add each field
For Each objField In tblObject.Fields
    cTemp = cTemp + Space(INDENT) + WrCreateField(objField)
    cTemp = cTemp + "," + EOL
Next
'
' fix up end of line
If Right(cTemp, Len(EOL) + 1) = "," + EOL Then
    cTemp = Left(cTemp, Len(cTemp) - (Len(EOL) + 1)) ' strip last EOL and
➥comma
    End If
    cTemp = cTemp + EOL
    cTemp = cTemp + Space(INDENT) + ");" + EOL ' add final paren and semi-colon
'
    WrCreateTable = cTemp ' return result to caller
End Function
```

Note that the WrCreateTable method skips any tables that start with "MSYS" or that have their attributes set. This eliminates all non-Jet and all Microsoft system tables from the definition set.

The WrCreateField and FieldTypeName Methods

Now build the WrCreateField routine from Listing A.35.

TYPE **Listing A.35. Coding the WrCreateField function.**

```
Public Function WrCreateField(fldObject As Field) As String
    '
    ' create a field line
    '
    Dim cTemp As String
    '
    ' get field from collection
    cTemp = fldObject.Name
    '
    ' if it has a space, enclose in braces
    If InStr(cTemp, " ") <> 0 Then
        cTemp = "[" + cTemp + "]"
    End If
    '
    ' add a spacer
    cTemp = cTemp + " "
    '
    ' add the field type
    cTemp = cTemp + FieldTypeName(fldObject)
    '
    ' if it's a text field, add the length
    If fldObject.Type = dbText Then
        cTemp = cTemp + "(" + CStr(fldObject.Size) + ")"
    End If
    '
    ' return results
    WrCreateField = cTemp
    '
End Function
```

This routine calls the FieldTypeName function to convert the integer type value into a printable data type name. Add the FieldTypeName function from Listing A.36 to your project.

TYPE **Listing A.36. Coding the FieldTypeName function.**

```
Public Function FieldTypeName(fldObject As Field) As String
    '
    ' get field type value
    ' return field string name
    '
    Select Case fldObject.Type
        Case Is = dbDate
            FieldTypeName = "DATE"
        Case Is = dbText
            FieldTypeName = "TEXT"
        Case Is = dbMemo
            FieldTypeName = "MEMO"
        Case Is = dbBoolean
            FieldTypeName = "BOOLEAN"
```

continues

Listing A.36. continued

```
            Case Is = dbInteger
                FieldTypeName = "INTEGER"
            Case Is = dbLong
                FieldTypeName = "LONG"
            Case Is = dbCurrency
                FieldTypeName = "CURRENCY"
            Case Is = dbSingle
                FieldTypeName = "SINGLE"
            Case Is = dbDouble
                FieldTypeName = "DOUBLE"
            Case Is = dbByte
                FieldTypeName = "BYTE"
            Case Is = dbLongBinary
                FieldTypeName = "LONGBINARY"
            Case Else
                FieldTypeName = "UNKNOWN"
    End Select
    '
    If fldObject.Attributes And dbAutoIncrField Then
        FieldTypeName = "COUNTER"
    End If

End Function
```

The `WrCreateIndex` method

Now that all the field work is done, it's time to build the indexes. Listing A.37 shows the code for the `WrCreateIndex` method.

TYPE   Listing A.37. Coding the `WrCreateIndex` function.

```
Public Function WrCreateIndex(idxObject As Index, cTable As String) As String
    '
    ' create index code line
    '
    Dim cTemp As String
    Dim cIndex As String
    Dim fldObject As Field
    '
    ' ignore system table indexes
    If UCase(Left(cTable, 4)) = "MSYS" Then
        WrCreateIndex = ""
        Exit Function
    End If
    '
    If InStr(cTable, " ") <> 0 And Left(cTable, 1) <> "[" Then
        cTable = "[" + cTable + "]"
    End If
```

```
'
' ignore indexes for foreign keys
If idxObject.Foreign = True Then
    WrCreateIndex = ""
    Exit Function
End If
'
' start SQL line
cTemp = "// Index " + idxObject.Name + EOL
If idxObject.Unique = True Then
    cTemp = cTemp + "CREATE UNIQUE INDEX "
Else
    cTemp = cTemp + "CREATE INDEX "
End If
'
' if name has spaces, add braces
cIndex = idxObject.Name
If InStr(cIndex, " ") <> 0 Then
    cIndex = "[" + cIndex + "]"
End If
cTemp = cTemp + cIndex
'
' prepare to add fields
cTemp = cTemp + " ON " + cTable + EOL
cTemp = cTemp + Space(INDENT) + "("
'
' get each field in index
For Each fldObject In idxObject.Fields
    cTemp = cTemp + fldObject.Name
    If fldObject.Attributes = dbDescending Then
        cTemp = cTemp + " DESC"
    Else
        cTemp = cTemp + " ASC"
    End If
    cTemp = cTemp + ","
Next
'
' fix up end of field list
If Right(cTemp, 1) = "," Then
    cTemp = Left(cTemp, Len(cTemp) - 1)
End If
cTemp = cTemp + ")"
'
' handle index attributes
If idxObject.Primary = True Then
    cTemp = cTemp + " WITH PRIMARY" ' primary key
End If
'
If idxObject.IgnoreNulls = True Then
    cTemp = cTemp + " WITH IGNORE NULL" ' ignore nulls
End If
If idxObject.Required = True And idxObject.Primary = False Then
    cTemp = cTemp + " WITH DISALLOW NULL" ' disallow nulls
End If
'
' last bit here!
```

continues

Listing A.37. continued

```
        cTemp = cTemp + ";" + EOL
        '
        WrCreateIndex = cTemp
        '
End Function
```

The code for the WrCreateIndex method is a bit involved. First, this routine ignores any index that starts with "MSYS." This is assumed to be one of the Microsoft reserved system indexes. Next, all indexes are built to support foreign keys. They are handled later in the Relationships collection. Next, the Fields collection is built (including the ascending/descending attributes) and added to the definition. Finally, the attribute bits are checked for things like primary key, ignore nulls, and other settings.

The wrCreateRelation Method

Now it's time to add the wrCreateRelation routine. This builds any relationship definitions into the script. Add the code from Listing A.38 to your module.

TYPE   **Listing A.38. Coding the wrCreateRelation function.**

```
Public Function wrCreateRelation(relObject As Relation) As String
    '
    ' create relation/constraint code
    '
    Dim cTemp As String
    Dim fldObject As Field
    Dim cTable As String
    Dim cForgTable As String
    Dim cFields() As String
    Dim x As Integer
    Dim z As Integer
    '
    cTable = relObject.Table
    cForgTable = relObject.ForeignTable
    '
    ' ignore system tables
    If UCase(Left(cTable, 4)) = "MSYS" Then
        wrCreateRelation = ""
        Exit Function
    End If
    If UCase(Left(cForgTable, 4)) = "MSYS" Then
        wrCreateRelation = ""
        Exit Function
    End If
    '
```

```
    SQLVBMain.lblProgress = "Creating Relations..."
    DoEvents
    '
    ' if it has spaces, add braces
    If InStr(cTable, " ") <> 0 Then
        cTable = "[" + cTable + "]"
    End If
    If InStr(cForgTable, " ") <> 0 Then
        cForgTable = "[" + cForgTable + "]"
    End If
    '
    ' create array of field name/foriegn names
    x = 0
    For Each fldObject In relObject.Fields
        ReDim Preserve cFields(x + 1, 2) As String
        cFields(x, 1) = fldObject.Name
        cFields(x, 2) = fldObject.ForeignName
        x = x + 1
    Next
    '
    cTemp = "// create relation " + relObject.Name + EOL
    cTemp = cTemp + "ALTER TABLE " + cForgTable
    cTemp = cTemp + " ADD CONSTRAINT " + relObject.Name + EOL
    '
    ' write out local table fields
    cTemp = cTemp + Space(INDENT) + "FOREIGN KEY ("
    For z = 0 To x - 1
        cTemp = cTemp + cFields(z, 2) + ","
    Next
    cTemp = Left(cTemp, Len(cTemp) - 1) + ") "
    '
    ' write out foreign table/fields
    cTemp = cTemp + "REFERENCES " + cTable + "("
    For z = 0 To x - 1
        cTemp = cTemp + cFields(z, 1) + ","
    Next
    cTemp = Left(cTemp, Len(cTemp) - 1) + ");" + EOL
    '
    wrCreateRelation = cTemp
    '
End Function
```

This is much like the index routine. Any definition that has "MSYS" as part of either table (left or right) is ignored. Notice that the Fields collection must be traversed for relation objects, too.

That's the end of the generate portion of the script. Next you add the object interface for use as an OLE Server.

Compiling and Testing SQL-VB5

All you need to do now is compile the program as an executable and you're done. But first, let's run a test script through the system to make sure all is working properly. You run this test by starting SQL-VB5 from within Visual Basic. If all goes well, you create a final compiled version that runs faster.

Go ahead and run the application. The first test script is called SQLVB01.SQV. You can find it in the ChapXA\Scripts folder on the CD. This script contains a set of lines that open a database and then create several result sets to display. Before you run the first script, you should load it for editing and make sure the drive letter and path are correct for your desktop setup. To load the SQL script file, select File | Edit. This brings up the Open File dialog. Locate the SQLVB01.SQV script file in the TYSDBVB\SQLVB directory on your machine (see Figure A.5).

Figure A.5.

Testing the
SQLVB01.SQV
script.

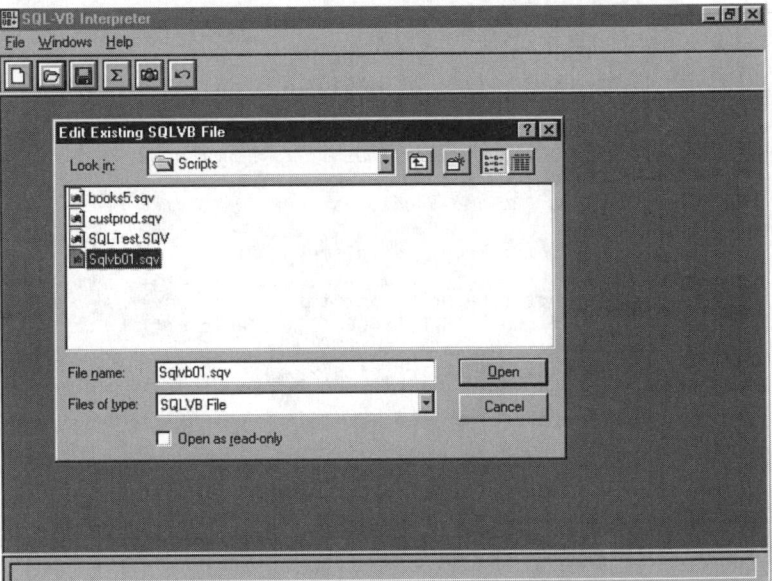

When the file is loaded into Notepad, inspect the script line that opens the database file. Make sure the path and drive letters match your desktop setup (see Figure A.6).

Make any changes needed and exit Notepad. Make sure you save the script if you made any updates. Now you are ready to run the script.

To run the script, select File | Run and use the File Open dialog box to locate the SQLVB01.SQV script file. Once you select the file, the program automatically begins processing the script. The line at the bottom of the screen shows the script lines as they are processed. The

SQLVB01.SQV script opens a database and creates six result set forms. Figure A.7 shows these six forms after they have been rearranged on the screen.

Figure A.6.

Editing the script.

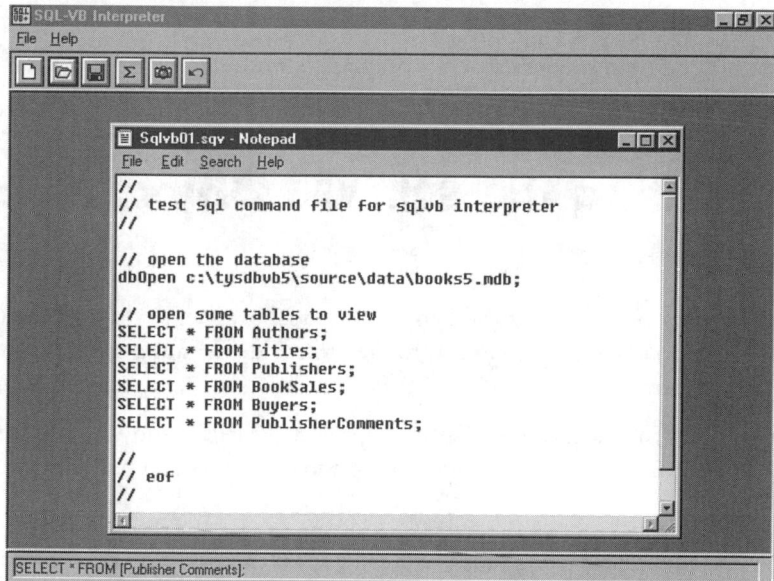

Figure A.7.

Viewing the results of SQLVB01.SQV.

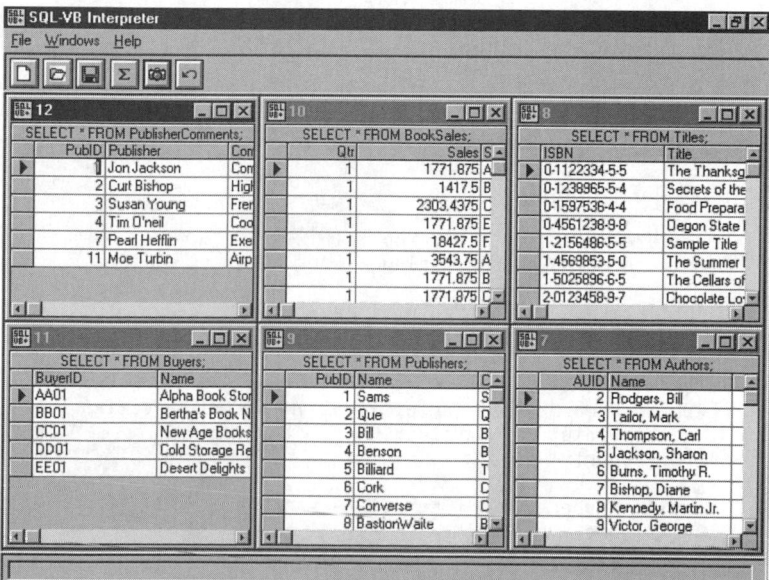

If you have problems with the script, review the SQLVB01.SQV file for errors. You may also have to review the Visual Basic code to check for program errors. If the script ran without errors, you can check out other aspects of the program, including the Windows menu and resizing the grid forms.

When you are sure that the program is working properly, you can continue with the next section of the chapter.

Creating the SQL-VB5 Object Model Interface

Now you're ready to add an object model wrapper to the SQL-VB5 Interpreter. All you need to do is add a class module to the project, define some methods and properties, and you're all set.

First, add a class module to the project (Project | Add Class Module) and set its Name to Application. Now you're ready to add properties and methods to the class.

Adding Properties to the Object Model

You need two properties: DBName and Script. Listing A.40 shows the Property Let and Property Get code for both items. Be sure to add the Private variables in the general declaration section, too.

TYPE   **Listing A.40. Adding properties to the Application class.**

```
Option Explicit

Private strScript As String
Private strDBName As String

Public Property Get Script() As Variant
    Script = strScript
End Property

Public Property Let Script(ByVal vNewValue As Variant)
    strScript = vNewValue
End Property

Public Property Get DBName() As Variant
    DBName = strDBName
End Property
```

```
Public Property Let DBName(ByVal vNewValue As Variant)
    strDBName = vNewValue
End Property
```

A

Adding Methods to the Object Model

Now that you have some properties built, you're ready to add some methods to the model. You can execute these methods from within other Visual Basic-compliant applications.

First add the Start and CloseApp methods. You can use these to start an instance of SQL-VB5 and close it when you're done (see Listing A.41).

TYPE **Listing A.41. Coding the Start and CloseApp subroutines.**

```
Public Sub Start()
    '
    ' starts interactive mode
    '
    SQLVBMain.Show
    '
End Sub

Public Sub CloseApp()
    '
    ' end instance of application
    '
    Dim frmTemp As Form
    '
    For Each frmTemp In Forms
        Unload frmTemp
    Next
    End
    '
End Sub
```

The Run method can be used to run SQL-VB5 against the name in the Script property.

```
Public Sub Run()
    '
    ' calls Run routine
    '
    If Trim(strScript) <> "" Then
        SQLMain strScript
    Else
        SQLMain
    End If
    '
End Sub
```

The Generate method can read the MDB in the DBName property and create a script with the name in the Script property.

```
Public Sub Generate()
    '
    ' calls autogen routine
    '
    If Trim(strDBName) <> "" And Trim(strScript) <> "" Then
        AutoGen strDBName, strScript
    Else
        AutoGen
    End If
    '
End Sub
```

You can also add the Edit and Create methods to allow external programs to start the SQL-VB5 editor to edit or build new scripts.

```
Public Sub Edit()
    '
    ' call edit routine
    '
    If Trim(strScript) <> "" Then
        LoadNotePadFile "", strScript
    Else
        LoadNotePadFile "Select Script to Edit"
    End If
    '
End Sub

Public Sub Create()
    '
    ' calls new file routine
    '
    If Trim(strScript) <> "" Then
        LoadNotePadFile "", strScript
    Else
        LoadNotePadFile "Enter Name of New Script"
    End If
    '
End Sub
```

Finally, what interface would be complete if it didn't allow external calls to the About box?

```
Public Sub About()
    '
    ' calls about box
    '
    frmAbout.Show vbModal
    '
End Sub
```

That's it for the object model. Save and compile the program. In the next step you build a quick Visual Basic application to test the object model.

Testing the Object Model

Start a new Visual Basic 5.0 Standard EXE, and add a single control array of five command buttons to the project. Refer to Figure A.8 for captions, size, and location of the buttons.

Figure A.8.

A test form for the SQL-VB5 object model.

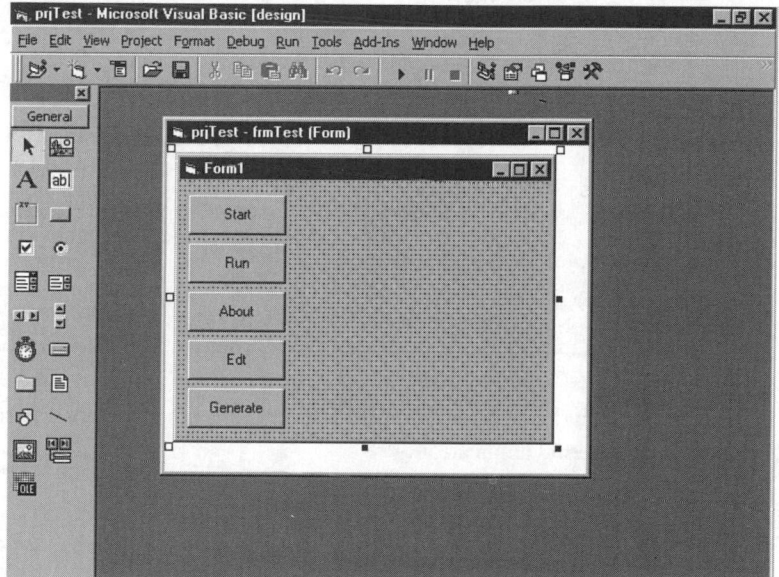

To create an instance of SQL-VB5, you need an object variable and you need to set that variable to reference the application class of SQL-VB5. To do this, first add a form-level variable to the general declaration section of the form.

```
Option Explicit
'
Dim objSQLVB5 As Object
```

Next, you need to add the following code to the Form_Load event. This code makes the object variable refer to the application class of your compiled SQL-VB5.

```
Private Sub Form_Load()
'
    Set objSQLVB5 = CreateObject("SQLVB5.Application")
'
End Sub
```

Now you need to add code to the command1_Click event of the form. This contains all the code you need to test the SQL-VB5 object model. Enter the code in Listing A.42 into the Command1_Click event.

TYPE **Listing A.42. Adding code to the `Command1_Click` event.**

```
Private Sub Command1_Click(Index As Integer)
    '
    Select Case Index
        Case 0 ' start
            objSQLVB5.Start
        Case 1 ' run
            objSQLVB5.Run
        Case 2 ' about
            objSQLVB5.About
        Case 3 ' edit
            objSQLVB5.Script = "c:\tysdbvb5\source\chapxa\scripts\sqltest.sqv"
            objSQLVB5.Edit
        Case 4 ' generate
            objSQLVB5.DBName = "c:\tysdbvb5\source\data\books5.mdb"
            objSQLVB5.Script = "c:\tysdbvb5\source\chapxa\scripts\books5.sqv"
            objSQLVB5.Generate
    End Select
    '
End Sub
```

Save and run the project. You can now test the various buttons and see how SQL-VB5 responds to your external application.

Modifying SQL-VB5

You now have a very valuable tool to add to your database programming tool kit. You can use SQL-VB5 to generate database layouts for all your projects in the future. You can also use SQL-VB5 to test data integrity options, load test data into existing tables, and even create simple data backup and replication scripts.

You could even add more options to the project. Here are some additional features that you might want to consider:

☐ Add the ability to create non-Microsoft Jet database files such as dBASE, FoxPro, and Paradox. To do this, you need to add additional parameters to the dbMake script line along with corresponding code in the SQLdbMake routine to handle the added information.

☐ Add the ability to edit data within the grids that appear in the main form. You need to review the DBGrid control and set some additional parameters before you launch the SQLVBChild form.

☐ Make SQL-VB5 an Add-In application. This involves adding a class module to the project and declaring an SQL-VB5 class with at least one method that loads and processes a script. Check the Visual Basic documentation on creating OLE-enabled applications for more information on how to create a Visual Basic Add-In.

Appendix

B

Preparing Online Help for Your Database Application

Today you will learn how to build help applications for your Visual Basic 5 database application. You will create help files in a standard word processor and attach them to your application. You will then see an application that can facilitate much of the work encountered in the creation of a help file.

To perform the exercises in this chapter, you will need a word processor that can save your data files in rich text format (RTF). Microsoft Word is an example of such a program. You will also need the help compiler HCW.EXE. This file ships on the Visual Basic 5 CD. The setup file for this program can be found in the \\TOOLS\HCW directory on the CD. If you haven't done so, go to the TOOLS\HCW directory and install this application.

An Overview of Developing a Help System for Your Application

Including online help with your Visual Basic database application is important for several reasons. First, online help makes your application look "finished." The user gains greater confidence in your application if there is an online resource that he or she can turn to for assistance.

Second, online help makes a system easier to use. Users don't have to search for printed manuals for answers to their questions. Researching information online is faster and easier than leafing through printed manuals. Users don't have to leaf through a table of contents or an index to get the appropriate answer. Instead, users can use the search feature of the online help.

Third, online help can be customized. For instance, users can enter their own comments using the Annotation function. This helps to inform others of policy decisions and system uses. It also helps in the use of the system across different functional areas.

You should also understand the drawbacks of using online help. Many users have not accepted the paradigm of searching for information online. Some users like to take manuals home with them on the weekend. Others like to write important notes in the margins of their manuals. Others find it a strain on their eyes to read long descriptions of information on-screen. Also, if the online help is poorly designed, users can get trapped in endless loops and not find the information they expect.

Overall, the benefits of attaching an online help file to your application far outweigh the drawbacks. Help of any sort, even if it is the name and phone number of the program developer, should be included with any application you develop.

Steps in Creating a Help File

You should follow these steps in order to build a help file for your application. (This lesson focuses on each step in detail.)

1. Write a topic file. This is the word processing document that contains the text and codes of the help file.
2. Save the topic file in rich text format.
3. Create a project file to tell the help compiler how to build the help file.
4. Compile your project using HCW.EXE.
5. Attach help to your Visual Basic application.
6. Test and revise as needed.

Creating Topic Files

The first step in creating your online documentation is to create a topic file. The topic file contains the text that the user sees when he or she presses F1 in your application. This file also contains codes in the form of footnotes that the WinHelp program uses to determine how the system is to function.

We used Microsoft Word 7 in the development of this lesson's examples to create the topic file. If you are not using Word, make sure your word processor supports the following capabilities:

- Saving text in rich text format
- Adding custom footnote markings
- Working with hidden text

Before starting, make sure that your default system options are set so that you can view hidden text. In Word, select Options... from the Tools menu. Next, select the View tab. Then, under Non-printing Characters, check the Hidden Text checkbox.

You might also want to select the Print tab and then check the Hidden Text checkbox in the Include with Document section. This allows you to print any hidden text codes entered into your document.

As with good programming, it is important that you design your help file before you build it. The following exercises cover the design of the help file at the end. You will be much better at designing the help file after you have learned how it is built. Now let's build the topic file.

Writing the Text

To start the project today, begin by building a text file that contains the information the user reads when help is requested. You will build a file to attach to the Company Master application you started in Week One.

Let's keep the text file short and enter only information for the three sections of the application: Company Information, Contact Information, and Other Information. Although you enter a small amount of information, it provides you with the skills you need to build help files of any size.

You should now enter into your word processor the text shown in Figure B.1. You can find this text in the TOPICS.DOC file found in the \TYSDBVB5\SOURCE\APPXB\HELP directory on the CD that ships with this book. You could also import TOPICS.RTF into your word processing package if you are using a word processor other than Word.

Figure B.1.

The text for your sample help file.

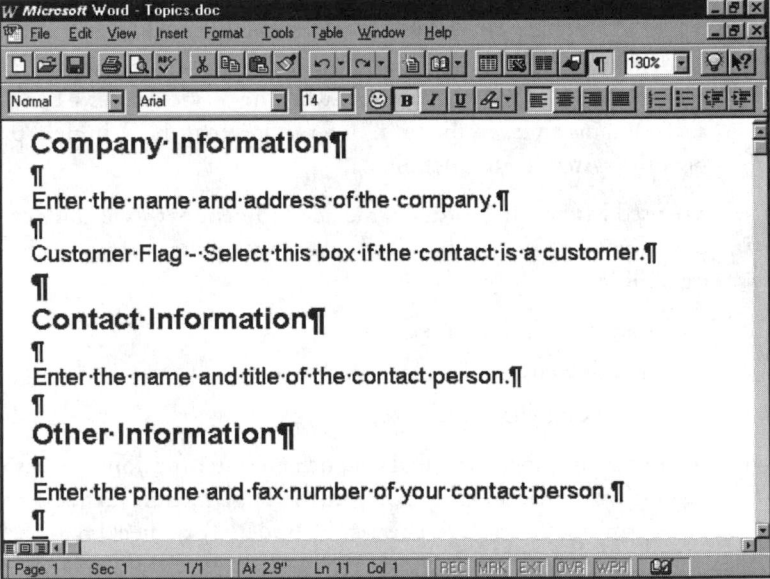

Separate Topics with Hard Page Breaks

Each topic in your text file must be separated with a hard page break. In Word, you enter hard page breaks by pressing Ctrl+Enter. Now do this between each topic. Your file should look like the one shown in Figure B.2.

Figure B.2.

The text file with page breaks between the topics.

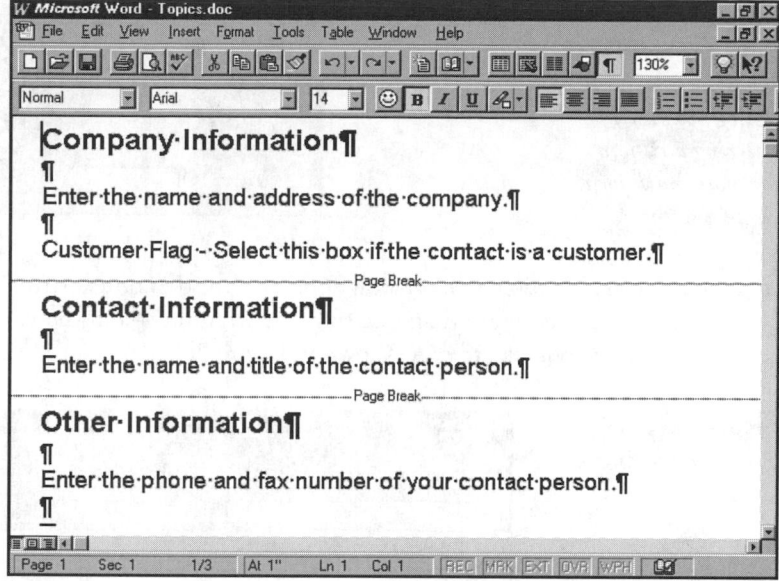

Now that the text entry is complete, you can start entering the format codes. These codes inform the help compiler what to do with this text.

Entering the Context String

The context string is the unique identifier for a topic and serves as the unique key for the help system. Users do not see this code; it is only used by the WinHelp program for ordering the topics.

You need to insert a footnote to designate a context string for a topic. The footnote is marked with a pound sign (#). To insert a footnote, follow these steps:

1. Move the cursor in front of the title for the topic but after the page break for the previous topic. For the first topic in the exercise, place the cursor to the left of the C in the first topic heading, Company Information.

2. Select Footnote... from the Insert menu. The Footnote and Endnote dialog box appears. (See Figure B.3.)

3. Select the Footnote radio button (if not already checked) in the dialog that appears.

4. In the Numbering section of the Footnote dialog box, click the Custom Mark button and enter #.

5. Select OK.

Figure B.3.

The Microsoft Word Footnote and Endnote dialog box, used for entering a custom footnote mark for a context string.

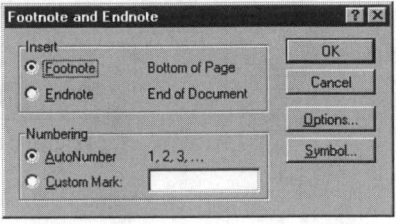

The footnote section of Word now appears. Type the context string CompanyInformation. Be sure you have no more than one space between the # and the context string. Your screen should now look like the one shown in Figure B.4.

Figure B.4.

Entering the context string.

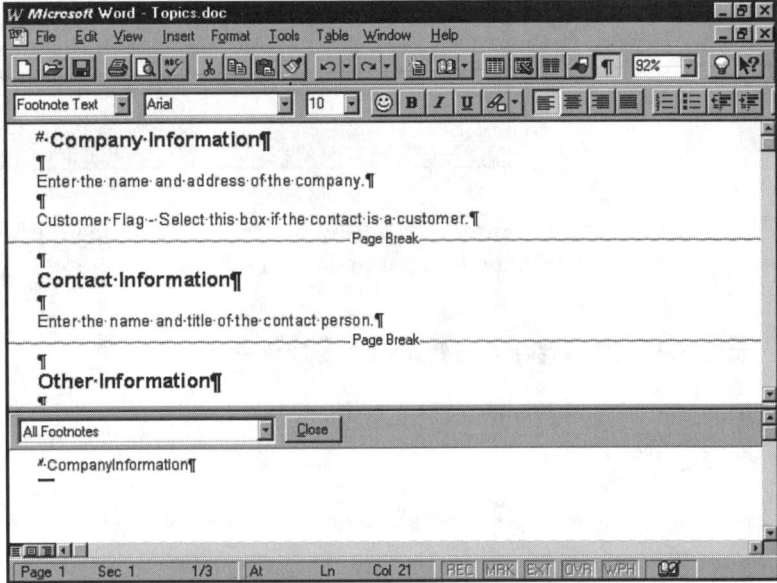

When building the context string, it is important not to leave any spaces in your text. Entering Company Information (with a space) results in a compile error. It is also a good practice to match the context string as closely as possible to the heading you place on each topic. This prevents confusion when dealing with a large number of context strings.

The context string is the only required footnote for each topic. The following sections discuss optional help file footnotes that you should also include with each topic.

Entering the Title

Now that you have entered the context string for the first topic, it is time to enter the title footnote. The title is displayed as the topic in the Help Topics Find tabbed dialog box of the help system. (See Figure B.5.) It's a good practice to use the topic heading from the topics file as the title of the text for this footnote.

Figure B.5.

The Windows 95 Help Topics Find tabbed dialog box.

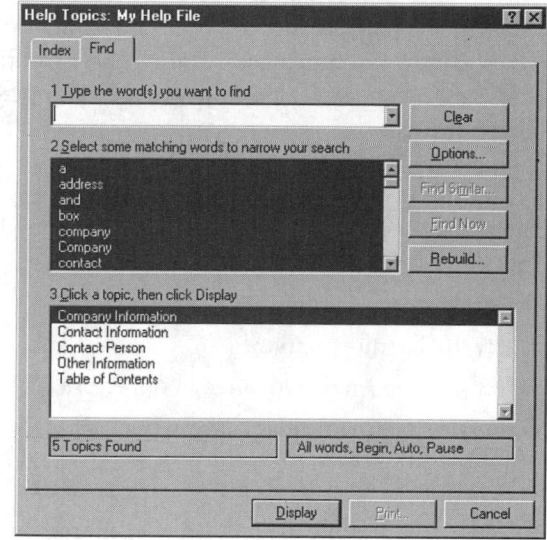

Entering the title is similar to entering the context string. However, the title footnote can include spaces between the words and is designated by the dollar sign ($) custom footnote mark rather than the pound sign (#).

Follow these steps in order to insert a title for the Company Information topic:

1. Move your cursor to the left of the letter C in Company Information. Footnotes can appear in any order, just as long as they are located before the topic heading and after the page break for the previous topic.

2. Select Insert | Footnote.

3. Click the Footnote button.

4. Click the Custom Mark button and then enter the dollar sign ($) as the custom mark. Click OK.

5. Type the title Company Information.

You can find help topics in the Help Topics dialog box by typing a keyword for a topic and then clicking the Display button. Determining which keywords apply to a specific topic is the focus of the next section.

Entering Keywords

Keywords are used in the WinHelp Help Topics Find tab to find topics. You use the same techniques for entering keyword footnotes as you did for entering context strings and titles. However, there are two differences: You can have multiple keywords for each topic (each keyword separated by a semicolon), and you use the uppercase letter K as the custom footnote mark for the topic.

Follow these steps in order to define a keyword for the first topic:

1. Insert the cursor before the letter C in Company Information and after the $ title footnote marker.

2. Select Footnote... from the Insert menu.

3. Select the Footnote option.

4. Select Custom Mark and enter an uppercase *K*.

5. Select OK and then enter the keyword Company in the footnote.

NOTE   It is possible to enter keywords for a topic and not a title. This results in an >>Untitled Topic<< message appearing in the Topics section of the Help Topics Find tab. To avoid this, always include a title if you use a keyword.

Entering the Browse Sequence

The last code to enter is the browse sequence. The *browse sequence* defines the order in which you can move through help screens by pressing the forward (>>) and reverse (<<) buttons at the top of your help screen. This footnote is defined by the plus sign (+), and it uses the following syntax:

```
group name:sequence
```

In this line, the group name is followed by a colon and then by the order in which the topic appears in the group. The group allows you to connect all related topics in the help file so that users can move forward and backward in order to review any related information. The sequence is the position of the topic within the group.

For this exercise, let's add a browse sequence for Company Information.

1. Insert the cursor before the C in Company Information and after the K footnote mark.
2. Select Footnote... from the Insert menu.
3. Check the Footnote option.
4. Select the Custom Mark option and enter a plus sign (+). Press OK.
5. Enter Company:1 as the footnote. Make sure to leave no more than one space between the footnote mark and the C.

You have entered all the necessary footnotes for the first topic. Your screen should now look like the one shown in Figure B.6.

Figure B.6.

All the footnotes for the Company Information topic.

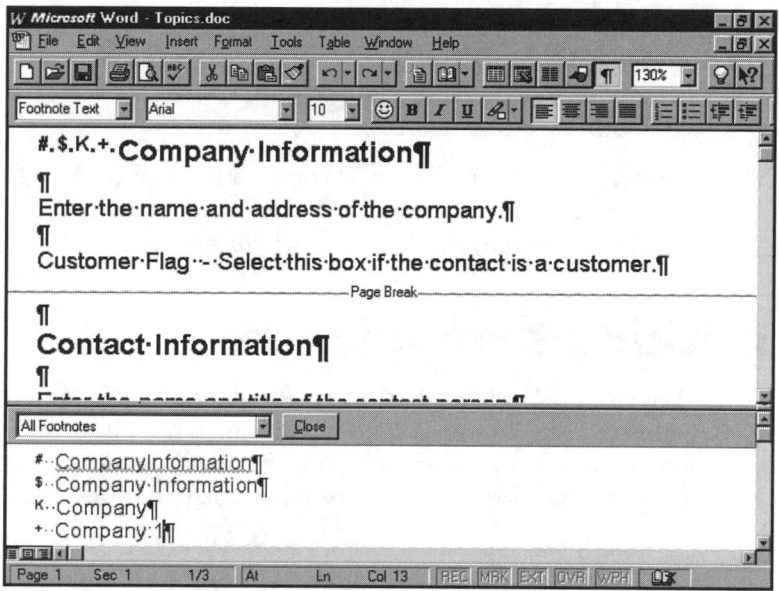

Continue this exercise by entering the footnotes for the other two topics in your file. Use Table B.1 as a guide.

Table B.1. Footnote information for the contact information and other information topics.

Topic	Footnote Type	Code	Footnote Text
Contact Information	Context string	#	ContactInformation
	Title	$	Contact Information

continues

Table B.1. continued

Topic	Footnote Type	Code	Footnote Text
	Keyword	K	Contact
	Browse sequence	+	Company:2
Other Information	Context string	#	OtherInformation
	Title	$	Other Information
	Keyword	K	Other
	Browse Sequence	+	Other:1

Saving the File

You should now save all of the information that you have entered into your topic file. First, save the information as a Word 6 document. To do this, select Save from the File menu. Save your information as TOPICS.DOC.

Now save the file as an RTF file. Do this by selecting Save As... from the File menu. Open the Save File As Type combo box and select Rich Text Format. Enter TOPICS.RTF in the File Name box. Then, execute the save by selecting Save.

Tracking the Topic Files

When creating large help files, keeping track of the different footnotes can become quite cumbersome. For instance, all the context strings must be unique and the browse sequence must follow an order within each group. For just three topics, this is not a hard task. But for 50, 100, or 1000 topics, this task becomes much more difficult.

Therefore, it's recommended that you keep track of all the footnotes you enter for each topic in a spreadsheet. This helps you in establishing the browse sequence and ensures that each context string is unique. For each topic, keep the heading from the topics file as well as details on each footnote that you enter.

A tracking file also helps you build the project file, which is the subject of the next section.

Creating the Project File

When you have entered your help text in a document, inserted the appropriate footnotes, and saved the document as an RTF file, you are ready to build the project file. The *project file* tells the help compiler how to create a help file (HLP) from the topic file (the RTF).

The project file is very similar to an INI file. Enter information in sections, which each have a heading enclosed in square brackets ([ ]). These files can be created in a text editor and must be saved as unformatted ASCII text. Now open the Notepad accessory in Windows to create the project file.

Enter the following text to create the project file. Save your file into the same directory as your `TOPICS.RTF` file and name it `PROJECT.HPJ`.

```
; Project file for the Company Master Help
;
[Options]
Title=My Help File  ;Title to Appear on the Help Title Bar
ErrorLog = Error.TXT  ;File to store compile errors
[Files]
Topics.RTF  ;Name of the file containing the topics
[Config]
BrowseButtons()  ;Macro to place browse buttons on the help screens
[Map]; section to define context string parameters
CompanyInformation                          1
ContactInformation                          2
OtherInformation                            3
```

Components of the Project File

The first section of the project file is the [Options] section. This section, if used, should always be the first section of the topic file. Although it is not required that you use this section, it is highly recommended. This is where you identify the title that appears on your help title bar as well as the name of the file that is used to collect compilation errors.

Here is the syntax to follow when entering an [Options] section:

```
[Options]
Title=My Help File  ;Title to Appear on the Help Title Bar
ErrorLog = Error.TXT  ;File to store compile errors
```

The second section is the Titles section. This section is required in all project files. It contains the name of the topic file (the TOPICS.RTF file in this exercise) from which the help file is created. You entered only one line in this section:

```
[Files]
Topics.RTF  ;Name of the file containing the topics
```

The third section is the [Config] section. This section lets you declare macros to be executed when your finished help file is compiled. In the [Config] section you have entered a macro name that places browse buttons at the top of the help screen to aid you in moving through the defined browse sequences. For this section, enter the following:

```
[Config]
BrowseButtons()  ;Macro to place browse buttons on the help screens
```

The final section in the exercise is the [Map] section. In this section, you enter numeric references to the context strings that you entered into the RTF file. Be very careful when building this section. Your context strings must be identical to the context strings entered in the RTF file. Enter the following:

```
[Map]; section to define context string parameters
CompanyInformation                          1
ContactInformation                          2
OtherInformation                            3
```

There are several other sections you can place in your project file. The [Buildtags] section, for instance, allows you to designate the topics in the RTF file that are to be compiled. There is also a [Windows] section where you can set parameters for the sizing, background colors, and locations of your help file.

You can also place an [Alias] section in your project file. Aliases allow you to assign multiple context strings to the same topic. This is useful when you delete topics in your RTF file. See the VB 5 Books Online, *The Microsoft Help Compiler Guide*, for a complete discussion on each of these sections.

Now that you have created your project file, it is time to compile your help application.

Compiling Your Help Project

You should now start the Microsoft Help Workshop application to compile your project. Please note that you have to install this application from the Visual Basic 5 CD if you have not already done so. The SETUP.EXE file for the Help Workshop can be found in the \\TOOLS\HCW directory of the Visual Basic 5 CD.

Once you start the Help Workshop, select File | Open... and find the PROJECT.HPJ file you created in the preceding exercise. Enter the name of PROJECT.HLP in the Help File box at the top of the screen. Your screen should look similar to Figure B.7.

Now select File | Compile. This brings up the Compile a Help File dialog box. Select the Browse... button and find the PROJECT.HPJ file you created previously. Select the Compile button to begin the compilation of your help file. The result is a PROJECT.HLP file that can be accessed directly from the Windows Explorer, or by selecting File | Run Winhelp... in Help Workshop.

You are prompted for any compilation errors that are written to the error file ERROR.TXT. Review any error messages you receive and then edit the project and topic file as needed. Then you can recompile your project.

Figure B.7.

The Help Workshop application.

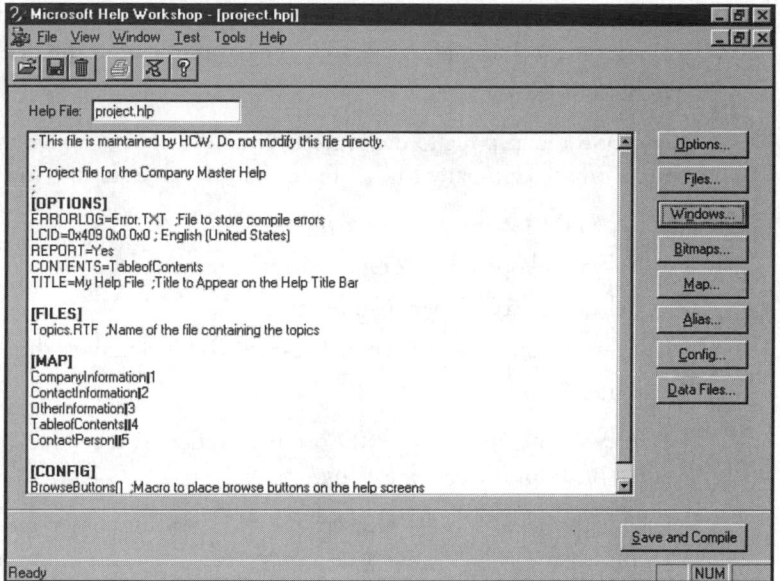

Linking Help to Your Visual Basic Database Application

When the PROJECT.HLP file is created, it is ready to be attached to your Visual Basic database application. Before attaching it, however, let's first review the file. To do this, open the Windows Explorer, and then double-click the file PROJECT.HLP. The first topic, Company Information, should now appear.

You now attach the help file to the Company Master application that you've been working on in this book. To do this, you first attach help information by setting Visual Basic 5 control properties. After that, you use code to assign help definitions. When you have completed that, you add menu applications to the application that automatically bring up the Contents, Search, Help on Help, and About Help information.

Using Properties to Attach Help Information

Follow these steps to attach a help file to your project:

1. Select Project | Properties… from the Visual Basic 5 Projects menu. Then select the General tab.

2. Select Help File and then enter the name of the help file (PROJECT.HLP), including its path. You can also click the _ box at the right of the field to Search for the file.

3. Select OK.

This assigns the help file to the project. You now need to assign the help context ID to the controls on the Company Master form. Follow these steps to make the attachments:

1. Open the Company Master project.

2. Select and open the Company Master form.

3. Select the txtCompanyName control.

4. Press F4 and move to the HelpContextID property in the Properties window.

5. Enter 1.

The entry in the HelpContextID property refers to the value you set in the project file (PROJECT.HPJ) for the context string.

Save your form and run the project. Click in the Company Name field and press F1. You should now see the help you wrote for the Company Information topic.

Now exit help and return to form design mode. Assign the remaining input fields within the Company Information frame to HelpContextID 1. Assign 2 to the HelpContextID property for all the fields in the Contact Information frame, and assign 3 to all the input fields in the Other Information frame.

Run the project and select any field on the form. Press F1 to bring up help. Select the Index button and then the Find tab. Notice that the keywords appear in the middle box and the titles appear in the lower box.

You can use the >> button in the Company Information topic to move to the Contact Information topic. This happens as a result of setting the browse sequence for both topics to the same group. Notice that Company Information comes first within this browse sequence. This is due to the browse sequence of Company:1 for the Company Information topic and Company:2 for the Contact Information topic.

While in help, select the Contents button. Company information should now be displayed. The Contents button displays the first topic in your help file if you do not declare a contents topic in your project file. Declaring this topic and building a contents page is the subject of the next lesson.

Building the Contents Page, Adding Jumps, and Modifying the Project File

To build the contents page, you need to build a topic, assign footnotes, create jumps to the underlying topics, and modify the project file. When you have done this, you then need to recompile the project.

Reopen your topics file (TOPICS.DOC) and enter the following information for the contents page. Make sure that you insert a page break between the Other Information topic and your new topic.

```
Table of Contents
This is the page we will use for our Table of Contents.
_Select the topic you would like to view.
Company Information
Contact Information
Other Information
```

You now add a jump to each of the three sections in the contents page. To do this, follow these steps:

1. Use your mouse to select Company Information in the Table of Contents topic.

2. Double-underline this text. In Word, this can be done by selecting Format | Font... and then selecting Double from the Underline combo box.

3. Add the context string of the topic to which you would like to jump immediately after the double-underlined text (the context string itself should not be double-underlined). For example, your first jump should appear as this:

   ```
   Company InformationCompanyInformation
   ```

4. Assign the hidden text attribute to the context string you just added. This can be done by selecting CompanyInformation. Next, select Format | Fonts..., and then check the Hidden Effect checkbox.

5. Now double-underline the other two jumps, and insert the context strings of the desired topics. For Contact Information, the context string is ContactInformation. For Other Information, the context string is OtherInformation. Make sure these context strings have the hidden text effect.

Use the following information to insert the footnotes for the Table of Contents topic:

Footnote Type	Code	Footnote Text
Context string	#	TableofContents
Title	$	Table of Contents
Keyword	K	Contents;Table of Contents

Adding Pop-Ups

Let's add one more feature to your topic file—a pop-up. A *pop-up* is a box of text that displays on top of the active help topic. It is commonly used to provide term definitions without requiring the user to select a jump to a different topic. A jump should therefore be used to elaborate on the current topic, not to serve as a topic itself. See Figure B.8 for an example.

Figure B.8.

A pop-up.

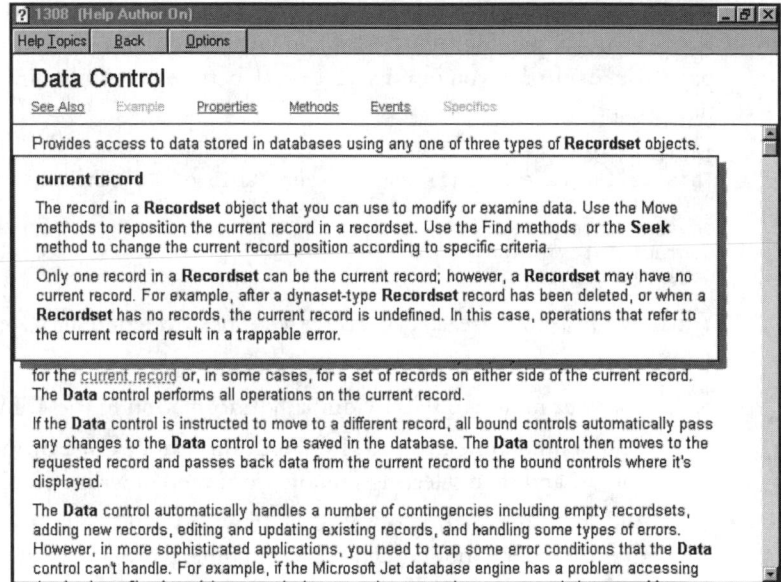

Adding a pop-up to your help topic is the same as adding a jump, except that you use a single underline for the pop-up text rather than the double underline used for the jump text. Follow these steps to add a jump:

1. Create a new topic for your pop-up text. In this exercise, you enter the definition of Contact Person in the Contact Information topic. Enter the following text and footnotes for this topic:

```
Contact Person
The person to whom we send monthly statements.
```

Footnote Type	Code	Footnote Text
Context string	#	ContactPerson
Title	$	Contact Person
Keyword	K	Contact

2. Single-underline Contact Person in the Contact Information topic.

3. Insert the context string `ContactPerson` immediately after the single-underlined text Contact Person.

   ```
   Contact PersonContactPerson
   ```

4. Assign the hidden text effect to the `ContactPerson` context string added in the previous step.

5. The text added to call the pop-up should be similar to the text displayed in Figure B.9.

Figure B.9.

Adding a pop-up.

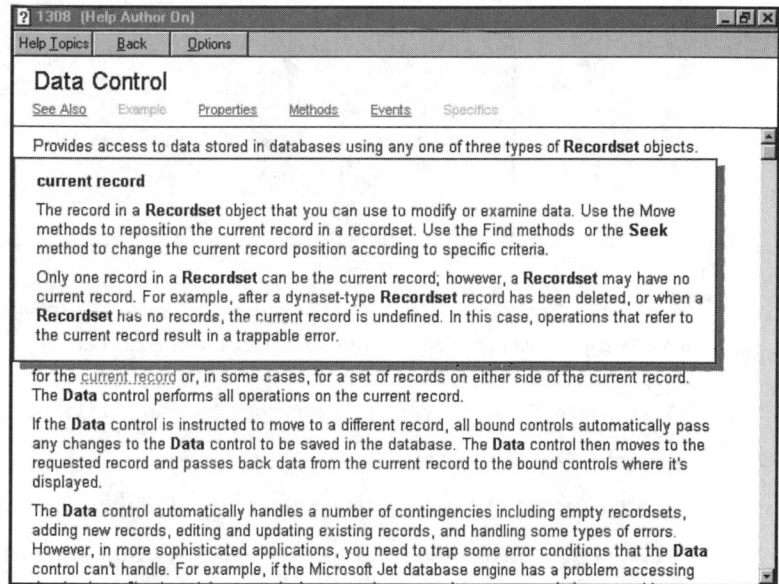

You have now completed the revisions to the topic document. Save this document in RTF format. Also, save the document a second time in your word processor's normal format.

Changing the Project File

You now need to make some changes to the project file. Remember that you created this file earlier in the Notepad application and gave it the name PROJECT.HPJ. Bring up Notepad and open this file. This file should look like the one shown in Figure B.10.

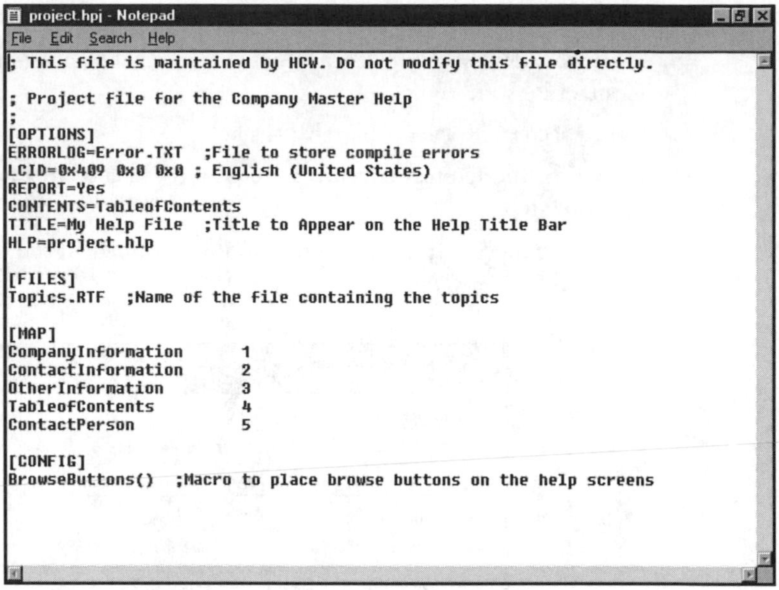

Figure B.10.

PROJECT.HPJ, *the*
Project file.

```
project.hpj - Notepad                                            _ 8 X
File  Edit  Search  Help
; This file is maintained by HCW. Do not modify this file directly.

; Project File for the Company Master Help
;
[OPTIONS]
ERRORLOG=Error.TXT  ;File to store compile errors
LCID=0x409 0x0 0x0 ; English (United States)
REPORT=Yes
CONTENTS=TableofContents
TITLE=My Help File  ;Title to Appear on the Help Title Bar
HLP=project.hlp

[FILES]
Topics.RTF  ;Name of the file containing the topics

[MAP]
CompanyInformation       1
ContactInformation       2
OtherInformation         3
TableofContents          4
ContactPerson            5

[CONFIG]
BrowseButtons()  ;Macro to place browse buttons on the help screens
```

You first need to edit the [Options] section to identify the topic you want to use as your contents topic. Modify this section so that it looks like this:

```
[Options]
Title=My Help File  ;Title to Appear on the Help Title Bar
ErrorLog = Error.TXT  ;File to store compile errors
Contents = TableofContents
```

TableofContents is the context string you assigned in the earlier exercise.

You also need to modify the [Map] section for the new topics you added. Change this section of PROJECT.HPJ so that it looks like the following:

```
[Map]; section to define context string parameters
CompanyInformation                         1
ContactInformation                         2
OtherInformation                           3
TableofContents                            4
ContactPerson                              5
```

You do not add a context string for the pop-up because you will not reference it from a Visual Basic control.

Save your changes to this file, and exit to the Microsoft Help Workshop, and then compile your help file.

When the file is successfully compiled, return to Visual Basic and run the Company Master application. Select a control in the Contact Information frame and press F1. Select the underlined phrase Contact Person. Your definition now appears (see Figure B.11).

Figure B.11.
A pop-up definition.

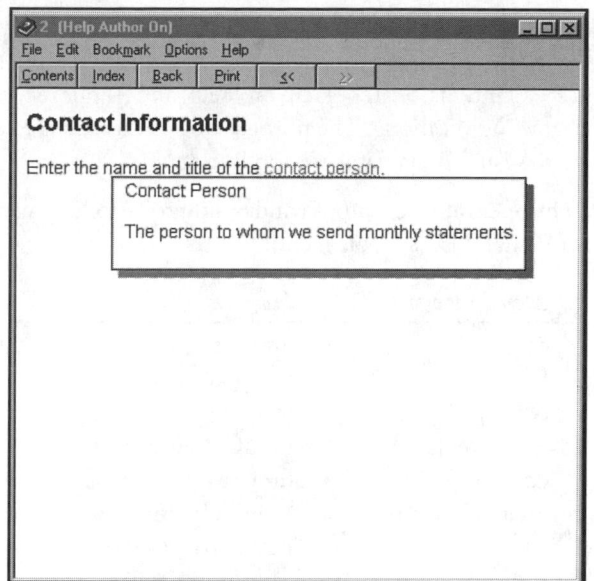

Next, select the Contents button to display the Table of Contents topic. Select any of the underlined items to jump to their topic. When you're in the topic, select the Back or Contents button and return to the original screen.

Using Code to Set the Help File Project Option and the HelpContextID Property

In the previous exercise, you attached the help filename by entering it in the Project Options section and setting the HelpContextID in each control's properties. You can also set these values at runtime. Just enter the following code in the Form_Load procedure to open the help file and set help context IDs:

```
Sub Form_Load ()
'assign the help file
   App.HelpFile = "C:\TYSDBVB5\SOURCE\APPXB\HELP\PROJECT.HLP"
'set the help context id for a control
   txtName.HelpContextID = 1
End
```

You need to set a HelpContextID for each control to which you want to add help. Be forewarned that this can be a very time-consuming chore if you have a large number of controls or a large number of forms in your Visual Basic database application.

Adding Help Functions to Menus

You see Contents, Search, Help on Help, and About menu items on the Help menu of most Windows applications. The purpose of this exercise is to show you how to add these items to your Visual Basic database application.

Start by opening a new project and building the following menu by choosing Menu Editor... from Visual Basic's Tools menu:

Menu Item	Name
&File	mnuFile
E&xit	mnuExit
&Help	mnuHelp
&Contents	mnuContents
&Search	mnuSearch
Help&onHelp	mnuHelponHelp
—	mnuSep1
&About	mnuAbout

Save this form as HELPMENU.FRM and the project as HELPMENU.VBP.

 **NOTE**

> The code in this example can either be entered manually or taken from the CD that ships with this book.

Now enter the following code in the Form_Load procedure of your HELPMENU.FRM file:

```
Private Sub Form_Load ()
'assign the help file to use (insert your path)
   App.HelpFile = "C:\TYSDBVB5\SOURCE\APPXB\HELP\PROJECT.HLP"
End Sub
```

The line App.HelpFile = "C:\TYSDBVB5\SOURCE\APPXB\HELP\PROJECT.HLP defines the help file for the project.

Next, create a new module by selecting Add Module from the Project menu, name it PRCHELP.BAS, and insert the following code inside the general declaration section:

```
Option Explicit
#If Win16 Then
    Declare Function WinHelp Lib "User" (ByVal hwnd As Integer,
    _ ByVal lpHelpFile As String, ByVal wCommand As Integer,
    _ ByVal dwData As Any) As Integer
    Declare Sub ShellAbout Lib "shell.dll" (ByVal hWindOwner As Integer,
    _ ByVal lpszAppName As String, ByVal lpszMoreInfo As String,
    _ ByVal hIcon As Integer)
```

```
#Else
    Declare Function WinHelp Lib "user32" Alias "WinHelpA" (ByVal hwnd As Long,
    _ By Val lpHelpFile As String, ByVal wCommand As Long,
    _ ByVal dwData As Any) As Long
    Declare Function ShellAbout Lib "shell32.dll" Alias "ShellAboutA"
    _ (ByVal hwnd As Long,
    _ ByVal szApp As String, ByVal szOtherStuff As String,
    _ ByVal hIcon As Long) As Long

#End If
Global Const HELP_QUIT = 2
Global Const HELP_INDEX = 3
Global Const HELP_HELPONHELP = 4
Global Const HELP_PARTIALKEY = &H105
```

Insert a new procedure by selecting Procedure from the Insert menu, name it HelpFile, and insert the following code:

```
Sub HelpFile (frmForm As Form, nHelpCmd As Integer)
    Dim i As Integer
    Dim nFlag As Integer
    Dim aData As Variant
    '
'Test for the naming of a help file
    If Len(LTrim(RTrim(App.HelpFile))) = 0 Then
        MsgBox "No Help File Available"
        GoTo HelpFile_Exit
    End If
'Set a text flag
    Select Case nHelpCmd
        Case Is = HELP_QUIT
            nFlag = True
        Case Is = HELP_INDEX
            nFlag = True
        Case Is = HELP_HELPONHELP
            nFlag = True
        Case Is = HELP_PARTIALKEY
            nFlag = True
        Case Else
            nFlag = False 'invalid command!
    End Select
'Pass parameters to the DLL call
    If nFlag = True Then
        If nHelpCmd = HELP_PARTIALKEY Then
            i = WinHelp(frmForm.hWnd, App.HelpFile, nHelpCmd, "")
        Else
            i = WinHelp(frmForm.hWnd, App.HelpFile, nHelpCmd, 0&)
        End If
    Else
        MsgBox "Invalid Help Command Value"
    End If
    '
HelpFile_Exit:
End Sub
```

Adding the About Box to Your Application

Create a new procedure by selecting Insert | Procedure and entering the following code:

```
Sub WinAboutPage (frm As Form)
   Dim MoreInfo$
   '
   MoreInfo$ = "Copyright " + Chr$(169) + " 1994 Software Company, Inc."
   MoreInfo$ = MoreInfo$ + Chr$(13) + "Technical Support: 800-555-7777"
   '
   Call ShellAbout(frm.hWnd, app.Title, MoreInfo$, frm.Icon)
End Sub
```

Entering Code in the Menu Events

First, enter the following code in the mnuContents_Click event:

```
Private Sub mnuContents_Click ()
   Helpfile Me, Help_index
End Sub
```

Second, enter the following code in the mnuSearch_Click event:

```
Private Sub mnuSearch_Click ()
   HelpFile Me, Help_PartialKey
End Sub
```

Third, enter the following code in the mnuHelponHelp_Click event:

```
Private Sub mnuHelponHelp_Click ()
HelpFile Me, Help_HelponHelp
End Sub
```

Fourth, enter the following code in the mnuAbout_Click event:

```
Private Sub mnuAbout_Click ()
   WinAboutPage Me
End Sub
```

Fifth, enter the following code inside the mnuExit_Click event:

```
Private Sub mnuExit_Click()
   Unload Me
End Sub
```

And finally, enter the following code inside the Unload event for your form:

```
Private Sub Form_Unload (Cancel As Integer)
   HelpFile Me, Help_Quit
End Sub
```

Save your form and project. Run the project and select each of the menu items. Notice that Help | Contents displays the Contents page of the help file you created earlier today and declared in the Form_Load event. Selecting Help | Search displays a listing of topics from the same help file. The menu selection Help | Help on Help displays a screen similar to

Figure B.12, which shows the Win 95 help topics. Selecting Help | About displays a dialog similar to Figure B.13, which contains information about your program. Finally, selecting Exit from the File menu stops the execution of the program.

Figure B.12.
Help on Help.

Figure B.13.
The About box.

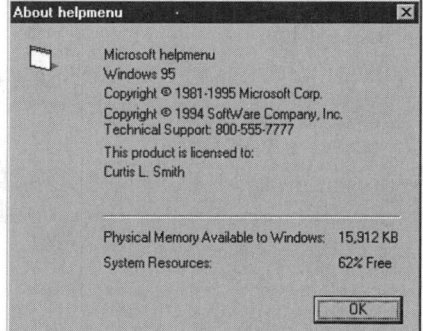

How This Program Works

You first began this project by entering code in the general declaration section for two API calls. The first call was made to the Windows help system to display the Help on Help, Search, and Contents information. The second call is solely for the About box:

```
#If Win16 Then
    Declare Function WinHelp Lib "User" (ByVal hwnd As Integer,
    _ ByVal lpHelpFile As String, ByVal wCommand As Integer,
    _ ByVal dwData As Any) As Integer
```

```
   Declare Sub ShellAbout Lib "shell.dll" (ByVal hWindOwner As Integer,
   _ ByVal lpszAppName As String, ByVal lpszMoreInfo As String,
   _ ByVal hIcon As Integer)
#Else
   Declare Function WinHelp Lib "user32" Alias "WinHelpA" (ByVal hwnd As Long,
   _ ByVal lpHelpFile As String, ByVal wCommand As Long,
   _ ByVal dwData As Any) As Long
   Declare Function ShellAbout Lib "shell32.dll"
   _ Alias "ShellAboutA" (ByVal hwnd As Long,
   _ ByVal szApp As String, ByVal szOtherStuff As String,
   _ ByVal hIcon As Long) As Long

#End If
```

Notice that you used the compilation directive (#if) to insert the code so that this application runs under the 16-bit version of Visual Basic 4. You then used the #Else directive to insert the 32-bit version. By doing this, the application runs under either version of Visual Basic (16- or 32-bit), or Visual Basic 5.

The final entries into the general declaration section are to define the constants that are called by the Help menu items:

```
Global Const HELP_QUIT = 2
Global Const HELP_INDEX = 3
Global Const HELP_HELPONHELP = 4
Global Const HELP_PARTIALKEY = &H105
```

The HelpFile procedure performs the following tasks:

☐ It declares variables:

```
Sub HelpFile (frmForm As Form, nHelpCmd As Integer)
   Dim i As Integer
   Dim nFlag As Integer
   Dim aData As Variant
```

☐ It tests for the declaration of a help file and returns a message if none is declared:

```
If Len(LTrim(RTrim(App.HelpFile))) = 0 Then
   MsgBox "No Help File Available"
   GoTo HelpFile_Exit
End If
```

☐ It flips a switch depending upon which value has been selected. This switch is set to True if a valid case is passed:

```
Select Case nHelpCmd
   Case Is = HELP_QUIT
      nFlag = True
   Case Is = HELP_INDEX
      nFlag = True
   Case Is = HELP_HELPONHELP
      nFlag = True
   Case Is = HELP_PARTIALKEY
      nFlag = True
   Case Else
      nFlag = False 'invalid command!
End Select
```

☐ It makes the API call depending upon the value passed:

```
If nFlag = True Then
    If nHelpCmd = HELP_PARTIALKEY Then
        i = WinHelp(frmForm.hWnd, App.HelpFile, nHelpCmd, "")
    Else
        i = WinHelp(frmForm.hWnd, App.HelpFile, nHelpCmd, 0&)
    End If
Else
    MsgBox "Invalid Help Command Value"
End If
HelpFile_Exit:
End Sub
```

The WinAboutPage procedure makes an API call to display an About box. Parameters are passed for a company name and a technical support number:

```
Sub WinAboutPage (frm As Form)
    Dim MoreInfo$
    '
    MoreInfo$ = "Copyright " + Chr$(169) + " 1994 Software Company, Inc."
    MoreInfo$ = MoreInfo$ + Chr$(13) + "Technical Support: 800-555-7777"
    '
    Call ShellAbout(frm.hWnd, app.Title, MoreInfo$, frm.Icon)
End Sub
```

The Click events for the menu items are defined to call the HelpFile procedure and pass the appropriate parameters:

```
Sub mnuContents_Click ()
    Helpfile Me, Help_index
End Sub

Sub mnuSearch_Click ()
    HelpFile Me, Help_PartialKey
End Sub

Sub mnuHelponHelp_Click ()
HelpFile Me, Help_HelponHelp
End Sub

Sub mnuAbout_Click ()
    WinAboutPage Me
End Sub

Sub mnuExit.Click()
    Unload Me
End Sub
```

Finally, when the form unloads, housekeeping should be performed and any help screens that have been left open should be closed. This is the role of the Form_Unload event.

```
Sub Form_Unload (Cancel As Integer)
    HelpFile Me, Help_Quit
End Sub
```

Please note that Unload Me was used in the Exit menu item rather than End. Using the End command would stop execution of the program without triggering the Unload event.

B

Using Help Authoring Tools to Create Your Help File

There are commercial products available that greatly reduce the time required for developing a help file. These products automate the process by which footnotes are entered, context strings are mapped, project files are built, and the help file is compiled. In addition, these programs can "strip" footnotes from your topic file so that you can use it for your printed documentation.

There is a tradeoff that you should be aware of when using an authoring tool. Any tool undoubtedly makes you more efficient in the creation of topic files; but if it takes you more time to install and learn the product than you save by using it, you are better off producing the file manually.

The ultimate determinant in whether or not to purchase a help authoring tool is based upon the size of your projects. Simple one- or two-screen applications are probably best documented manually. More complex, multiscreen applications will best be documented with the assistance of a help authoring tool.

There are numerous authoring tools available. They range in price from approximately $100 to $500. Many of these products must be purchased directly from their authors. It is hard for us to recommend one specific help authoring tool over another because your own personal working habits dictate which tool is best for you and your project. Please consult the advertising found in the back of trade publications to obtain the distributors, pricing, and titles of the latest authoring tools.

In order to learn how these tools operate, you might preview an intriguing authoring tool available free of charge from Microsoft. It is called WHAT6.EXE. This file can be obtained from the Microsoft Web site, CompuServe, and America Online services. This tool is actually a Word document template that contains a series of macros that assist in the building of topic files. It is unsupported by Microsoft, which means you have no one to turn to if you have a problem or a question. Weigh this factor very carefully before you decide to utilize this tool on a live project.

Designing Your Help System

Let's turn to the design of your help application. As demonstrated in the exercises for this lesson, your help topic file contains the information that users depend upon to operate your application. An effective help system must be designed properly to meet the users' needs.

Make sure you understand who will be using your system. For instance, you would design and write one type of help topic file for highly sophisticated users and another for novice users.

Different levels of users have different technical needs and viewpoints concerning the use of computers as productivity tools. Meet the expectations of your users, both technically and emotionally.

Always plan what you will include in your help system. Don't begin writing until you have given consideration to the detail you want to provide and the browse sequences you want the user to see. Plan your topics to be no more than a few pages long. The topics should also be more than a sentence or two in length. You will find it better to use one topic that is two pages long in order to describe every field on a report, rather than writing many short topics in order to explain each control.

Keep the design of your help system simple. Also, be sure to use jumps judiciously: You don't want your users jumping through page after page of information. It is better to duplicate help information rather than have the user continually jumping from screen to screen in order to find the answer to a simple question.

Don't try to model your users' business practices when building the topic file. Your system should be designed to be versatile, allowing for changing environments. Your help system should follow the same thought processes. Don't dictate how the system should be used optimally, but rather show the users how to do what they need to do. You will be surprised by the clever ways in which a well-designed system can be used.

Don't burden the users of your system with the obvious. For example, don't tell the users to enter a phone number in a field with a label Phone Number and an input mask of (###) ###-####. Everyone knows that this means to enter a phone number. Not everyone will know, however, where this number is used throughout the system or on what reports it appears. Be informative and follow through to the end. Don't stop your explanation when only 75 percent of the process has been defined.

It is best to write your online documentation as you build your system. Help files should be read and reviewed for suitability as part of the testing cycle. Writing the topic file as you code keeps you from forgetting key features of your design. Functionality is best documented when it is fresh in your mind.

Remember to budget time in your system design plan to write your online documentation. Writing is hard work and requires patience, perseverance, and attention to detail. Allow time for numerous rewrites and edits. Many experienced technical writers estimate that it takes approximately one hour to type a page of text. Make estimates based upon this rate and then adjust it according to the speed at which you work. Double the result that you get to allow sufficient time if you run into any problems.

Do not release a programming project that has not been properly documented. It is a mistake to think that you can provide quality documentation at a future date if you can't provide it at the ship date. A help system is needed most when users are new to the system and just beginning to learn it. Everyday work demands can distract you from the "less important" and routine responsibilities of your job. Always remember that creating a new project is exciting, but writing about a new project is often quite tedious. Discipline on your part is required in order to get the job done.

If you are managing a team of developers, allow them the time needed to develop documentation. There are no shortcuts in system development or documentation. Items that are not finished when they should have been always come back to haunt you to an even greater extent some time in the future.

Know your writing abilities and seek assistance when needed. Many system programmers find it difficult to write. Their expertise lies with system design and coding, not with writing. This is not a bad thing in itself, as long as you are honest with yourself and are not ashamed to seek out technical writers for assistance.

Determine whether you will have both written and online documentation. You should provide both forms of documentation. It is easier to write the online documentation first and then use it as the starting point for your printed documentation. The online documentation follows the natural flow of the system.

Remember that users depend on your documentation to enable them to understand how to operate the systems that help them perform their jobs. You have a great responsibility to properly document your system and to make it easy to use and quick to learn.

Summary

Every application should have a help file attached. A help file ensures that the system is used as it was intended. It also gives the application a more "finished" look and feel.

The following key points were covered in this lesson:

1. You need to create a topic file and a project file in order to build a help file.

2. The topic file you create includes all the text and footnotes for the help system. It is written in rich text format (RTF).

3. You insert footnotes to define each topic. Insert a # footnote to declare a context string, a $ footnote to denote a title, an uppercase K to denote a keyword, and a plus sign (+) to denote the browse sequence.

4. The project file contains the codes that inform the compiler how to build the help file from the topics file. It is saved as ASCII text and must have an .HPJ extension.

5. You declare your project's help file by setting its path and name in the Project Options section. You declare your topic for a control by setting its HelpContextID property.

6. Jumps can be added to your help file by double-underlining your jump text and immediately inserting the context string of the topic to which the user will jump. This context string is then formatted as hidden text.

7. You can create a pop-up window the same way you create a jump; but you use single-underlined text rather than double-underlined text.

8. You can add help menu items to your application by making an API call to WinHelp.

9. There are several programs known as authoring tools that are available commercially. These programs can assist you in creating help files. The size of your application dictates whether an authoring tool is worth the time and financial investment.

10. Plan your help file before writing it. Remember to write your online help first. Also, prepare your documentation as you develop your application rather than after the project is completely coded. Always keep your system simple, while making sure that all the information the user expects to find in your documentation is indeed there.

Quiz

1. What custom footnote mark do you insert for a context string? Can you put spaces in the text of this footnote?

2. What custom footnote mark do you insert for a title? Can you use spaces in this footnote?

3. Where will keywords be used in your help application? What separator do you use if you want to insert multiple keywords for a topic?

4. In what format(s) should you save your topic file? In what format(s) should you save your project file?

5. How do you declare a contents page in your help file?

6. What control property do you set in order to identify the help topic to display when the control has focus and F1 is pressed? Where does this value come from?

7. How much time should you budget to produce one typed page of documentation?

Exercises

1. Build a browse sequence that makes a topic the third topic to appear in a group called Processing.

2. Build a jump for the text "Creating a New Project" that opens a topic titled Creating a New Project with the context string `NewProject`.

3. Build a pop-up rather than a jump for the topic discussed in Exercise 2.

4. Add a topic to the help file created in this lesson to describe the Company Master form. Recompile your project and attach help to the form. (Hint: Be sure to modify the [Map] section of your project file for the context string.)

APPENDIX
C

Answers to Quizzes and Exercises

Day 1

Answers to Day 1 Quiz

1. The two data control properties you must set when you link a form to a database are the DatabaseName property and the RecordSource property.

2. Set the Caption property of the data control to display a meaningful name between the record pointer arrows.

3. You must set the DataSource property of the input control to the data table and the DataField property of the input control to the field name in the data table.

4. You only need one line of Visual Basic code (not including the `Sub...End Sub` statements) to add delete functionality to a data entry form when using the Visual Basic data control. An example of this code is

```
datTitles.Recordset.Delete   ' delete the current record
```

5. Select either the Save Changes or Prompt to Save Changes option from the Program Starts environmental variable option group. This can be found by selecting the menu option Tools | Options and then selecting the Environment tab. Once one of these choices is selected, you save, or will be prompted to save, your project each time you run it.

Answers to Day 1 Exercises

1. While in design mode, select the form by clicking anywhere on the form that doesn't have a control. Press F4 and select the Caption property. Type "The Titles Program" and press Enter. Note that the title appears on the title bar of the form as you type.

2. Complete the following steps to build an Exit button:

   ☐ Double-click the Command Button control on the Visual Basic toolbox to add a new button to the form.

   ☐ Set the Name property to cmdExit for the new button.

   ☐ Drag the new button to align it with the Add and Delete buttons.

   ☐ Set the Caption property to E&xit.

   ☐ Enter the following code in the `cmdExit_Click` procedure:
   ```
   Private Sub cmdExit_Click()
       End
   End Sub
   ```

   ☐ Save your changes and execute your program.

   ☐ Click the Exit button to stop the program.

3. Modify the `cmdAdd_Click` procedure as shown below to set the focus on the ISBN field when the Add button is pressed.

```
Private Sub cmdAdd_Click()
    datTitles.Recordset.AddNew  ' Add a new record to the table
    txtISBN.SetFocus  ' Set the focus to the txtISBN control
End Sub
```

Day 2

Answers to Day 2 Quiz

1. The three main building blocks of relational databases are data fields, data records, and data tables.

2. The smallest building block in a relational database is the data field.

3. A data record is a collection of related data fields.

4. The main role of a primary key in a data table is to maintain the internal integrity of a data table.

5. A data table can have any number of foreign keys defined. It can, however, have only one primary key defined.

6. There are only two values that can be stored in a BOOLEAN data field: −1 (true) and 0 (false).

7. The highest value that can be stored in a BYTE field is 255. Visual Basic allows users to enter up to 32767 without reporting an error, but any value higher than 255 is truncated to a single-byte value.

8. Any attempt to edit and update a counter field results in a Visual Basic error.

9. The CURRENCY data type can store up to four places to the right of the decimal. Any data beyond the fourth place is truncated by Visual Basic without reporting an error.

10. You can use the International applet from the Windows Control Panel to determine the display format of DATE data fields.

Answers to Day 2 Exercises

1. There are three records in the table.

2. The SSN (Social Security Number) would make an excellent primary key for this table because it would be unique for all records entered.

C

3. The answer to part C appears in the following table:

Field	Data Type	Visual Basic Type
SSNo	Text	String
Last	Text	String
First	Text	String
Age	Byte	Integer
City	Text	String
St	Text	String
Comments	Memo	String

4. Perform the following steps to add the checkbox: First, double-click the checkbox control. Second, position the checkbox in an aesthetically pleasing position on the form. Third, set these properties:

Property	Setting
DataSource	datFieldTypes
DataField	BOOLEAN
Name	chkBoolean

Run your program and check the BOOLEAN box. Notice that nothing happens to the BOOLEAN text field. Now move to the subsequent record, and then return. You should see –1 displayed in the BOOLEAN text field.

This example shows how to use a checkbox to enter values into fields. Your program can now reference this field and get the value as –1 (yes) or 0 (no), which are the only two values that can be in a BOOLEAN type data field.

Day 3

Answers to Day 3 Quiz

1. Visual Basic database objects are dataset-oriented. You work with a set of records at one time, not one record at a time as you would with a record-oriented database.

2. The Dynaset is the most common Visual Basic data object. It is the object created when you open a form with a data control.

3. Dynasets use minimal RAM resources. Visual Basic stores only the pointers to the records in the underlying table, not the actual data.

4. Weaknesses of using Dynasets include the following:

   ☐ You can't specify an index with a Dynaset. Dynasets are only a portion of the underlying table, whereas indexes are for the entire table.

☐ You can't use the Seek method with Dynasets.

☐ Errors can occur if records in the underlying table have been altered or deleted between the time that the Dynaset is created and the time that a record is updated.

5. Table data objects allow you to use indexes and the Seek method.

6. You do not use the Refresh method with the Table data object because this object is the underlying data.

7. You must use code to open a Table object in Visual Basic.

8. A Snapshot stores all the data in the workstation's memory, whereas the Dynaset stores only pointers to the data. The Snapshot is also read-only and can't be updated. A Dynaset can be updated.

9. You use the Database data object to extract field and table names from a database.

Answers to Day 3 Exercises

1. You use the Dynaset data object because it is the only data object that can update an ODBC data source. Your code might look like this:

```
Sub Form_Load()

'Create a database and dynaset object
Dim Dat as Database
Dim rsDyn as Recordset

'Declare standard variables
Dim cDBN ame as String
Dim cTable as String

'Initialize variables
cDBName = "c:\DATAS\ACCTPAY.MDB"
cTable = "Vendors"

'Set values
set Dat = OpenDatabase(cDBName)
Set rsDyn = Dat.OpenRecordset(cTable,dbOpenDynaset)

End Sub
```

2. The Snapshot data object should be used for this purpose because it does not change after it is created. This prevents the data used in your report from being updated while your report is generating.

Your code might look like this:

```
Sub Form_Load()

'Create a database and snapshot object
Dim Dat as Database
Dim rsSnap as Recordset
```

```
'Declare standard variables
Dim cDBName as String
Dim cTable as String

'Initialize variables
cDBName = "c:\DATAS\ACCTPAY.MDB"
cTable = "Vendors"

'Set values
set Dat = OpenDatabase(cDBName)
Set rsSnap = Dat.OpenRecordset(cTable,dbOpenSnapshot)

End Sub
```

3. You use the Table data object because it gives you instant information when records are changed. Your code might look like this:

```
Sub Form_Load()

'Create a database and table object
Dim Dat as Database
Dim tblObject as Recordset

'Declare standard variables
Dim cDBName as String
Dim cTable as String

'Initialize variables
cDBName = "c:\DATAS\ACCTPAY.MDB"
cTable = "Vendors"

'Set values
set Dat = OpenDatabase(cDBName)
Set tblObject = Dat.OpenRecordset(cTable,dbOpenTable)

End Sub
```

Day 4

Answers to Day 4 Quiz

1. You can establish a database for a data control by setting the DatabaseName property of the data control to the name of the database (including the path), or to a defined variable that points to the database. For example, to attach the data control Data1 to a Microsoft Access database C:\DATAPATH\XYZ.MDB, you can enter the following:

```
Data1.DatabaseName = "C:\DATAPATH\XYZ.MDB"
```

2. You use the RecordSource property to establish the name of a table for a data control in Visual Basic. For example, to set the data control Data1 to a table of vendors in an accounts payable application, you can type the following:

```
Data1.RecordSource = "Vendors"
```

It is better form, however, to assign the RecordSource to a variable that has been defined and points to the data table. Here's an example:

```
Dim cTable as String' Declare the variable
cTable = "Vendors" ' Establish the name of the table
Data1.RecordSource = cTable ' Set the data control
Data1.Refresh ' Update the data control
```

3. The `UpdateControls` method takes information from the underlying database table and places it in the form controls; whereas the `UpdateRecord` method takes information entered into the form controls and updates the attached table.

4. Checkboxes should only be bound to Boolean fields and can only produce values of 0 (No or False) and −1 (Yes or True).

5. You use the DataField property to bind a control to a table field.

6. The standard color for a Windows 95 form is light gray. Input areas are white. Display-only controls are light gray. Labels are left-aligned.

Answers to Day 4 Exercises

1. You should enter the following code as a new procedure in the general declarations section:

```
Sub OpenDB()
'Declare the variable for the name of the database
Dim cDBName as String
'Assign the variable to a database, including the path
cdbName = App.Path + " \Students.MDB"
'Set the name of the database used by the data control
Data1.DatabaseName = cDBName
'Refresh and update the data control
Data1.Refresh
End Sub
```

2. Your code should look like this:

```
Sub OpenDB()
  'Declare the variable for the name of the database
Dim cDBName as String
'Declare the variable for the table
Dim cTable as String
'Assign the variable to a database, including the path
cdbName = App.Path + "\Students.MDB"
'Assign the variable to the appropriate table
cTable = "Addresses"
'Set the name of the database used by the data control
Data1.DatabaseName = cDBName
'Set the name of the table used by the data control
Data1.RecordSource = cTable
'Refresh and update the data control
Data1.Refresh
End Sub
```

C

3. Your code should look like this:

```
Sub OpenDB()
Dim cDBName as String
Dim cTable as String
Dim cField1 as String
Dim cField2 as String
Dim cField3 as String
Dim cField4 as String
Dim cField5 as String
'Assign variables
cdbName = App.Path + "\Students.MDB"
cTable = "Addresses"
cField1 = "StudentID"
cField2 = "Address"
cField3 = "City"
cField4 = "State"
cField5 = "Zip"
'Set the data control properties
Data1.DatabaseName = cDBName
Data1.RecordSource = cTable
'Bind the text fields
txtStudentID.DataField = cField1
txtAddress.DataField = cField2
txtCity.DataField = cField3
txtState.DataField = cField4
txtZip.DataField = cField5
'Refresh and update the data control
Data1.Refresh
End Sub
```

Day 5

Answers to Day 5 Quiz

1. Input validation occurs as the data is entered, whereas error trapping occurs after the data is entered. Input validation is used to guarantee uniformity in the data that is saved.

2. Subtracting 32 from the lowercase value returns the uppercase value.

3. The KeyPress event occurs whenever a key is pressed.

4. No, a validation list can be entered in any order.

5. The txtUpper field is being trimmed of spaces and then tested to see whether the length is anything other than zero. This code is used to test whether any values are entered into a field. The Trim command is used to remove any spaces entered into the field either intentionally or inadvertently.

6. Conditional field validation should be performed at the form level. Users may skip around on the form using the mouse, thus making field-level validation impractical.

7. Validation lists should be loaded by the `Form_Load` procedure.

8. The first section is the format of a positive number. The second section is the format of a negative number. The third section is the format of zero. Each section is separated by a semicolon (;).

Answers to Day 5 Exercises

1. Enter the following code inside your field's `KeyPress` event:

```
Sub FieldName_KeyPress(KeyAscii as Integer)
    If KeyAscii >26 then 'If anything other than a control code
        If Chr(KeyAscii) >= "a" and Chr(KeyAscii) <= "z" Then
            KeyAscii = KeyAscii - 32 ' Capitalize small letters
        Else
            KeyAscii = 0 ' No input from keyboard
        End if
    End if
End Sub
```

2. `#,##0.00;-#,##0.00`

3. Enter the following code into the `cmdOK_Click` event:

```
Sub cmdOK_Click ()

    Dim nOK as Integer ' Declare a test variable

    nOK = True

    If Len(Trim(txtDate)) = 0 then ' Check for entry (exclusive of spaces)
        MsgBox "Input is required in the txtDate field before this record
            _can be saved" ' Issue a message if no data is entered
        nOK = False 'Set test variable to False
        txtDate.SetFocus ' Place cursor in txtDate
    End if

    If nOK = True then
        Unload Me ' Exit form if data is entered
    End if
End sub
```

4. Enter the following code in the `Form_Load` event:

```
Sub Form_Load()

    'Load the combo box
    cboEmployees.AddItem "Smith"
    cboEmployees.AddItem "Andersen"
    cboEmployees.AddItem "Jones"
    cboEmployees.AddItem "Jackson"

End sub
```

You set the Sorted property of the combo box to True to alphabetically sort the information displayed in the combo box. This property can only be set at design time.

C

Day 6

Answers to Day 6 Quiz

1. The three bands are the header, footer, and detail bands. The header is used to insert information that displays on the top of each page of the report. The footer band inserts information on the bottom of each page of the report. The detail band displays the actual information.

2. Crystal Reports Pro can attach to any database type recognized by Visual Basic 5. This includes Microsoft Access, dBASE, FoxPro, Btrieve, Paradox, and any ODBC data source.

3. You can type text directly on a form in Crystal Reports Pro, but remember that it cannot be moved or resized (you can, however, change the font size and appearance). The more versatile way to enter text is with the Text Field option from the Insert menu.

4. You can produce mailing labels in Crystal Reports Pro by selecting File | New and then selecting the Mail Label item.

5. You can browse data in a database by choosing a field on the report during design time and selecting Browse Field Data from the Edit menu.

6. Yes, you can add selection criteria to your Crystal Reports Pro report by choosing the Select Records Expert from the Report menu and then entering your criteria.

7. You can join tables in Crystal Reports Pro by selecting Visual Linking Expert from the Database menu option.

Answers to Day 6 Exercises

1. Here is the formula:

   `Count({NameLast})`

2. `IsNull({EmployerID})`

3. Perform the following steps to build the report:

   ☐ Start Crystal Reports Pro and select New from the File menu. Select the `BOOKS5.MDB` database.

   ☐ Double-click the PubID field in the PublisherComments table and drop the field in the detail band of the form. Do the same for the Publisher and Comments fields.

   ☐ Choose Printer Setup from the File menu and then select the Landscape option.

- [ ] Drop the Name field in the detail band. Next, select Database | Visual Linking Expert. Create the link between the Publisher Comments and the Publishers tables on the PubID field, if it is not already done.

- [ ] Select Sort Records from the Report menu. Double-click the Name field and set the sort direction to descending.

- [ ] Select Text Field from the Insert menu. Enter Comments on Publishers as the title text and then select Accept. Drop the field in the middle of the page header band. Select Format | Font and then select Arial, 14 point bold, and press OK.

- [ ] To insert the count of the records, select the PubID field and then choose Grand Total from the Insert menu. Select Count from the combo box that appears and then press OK.

- [ ] Select Insert | Special Field | Page Number Field and drop the field in the page footer band of the report.

- [ ] Select Special Field | Print Date Field from the Insert menu. Drop the field in the page footer band of the report.

- [ ] Print the report by selecting Print | Printer from the File menu.

- [ ] Print the report definition by selecting Print | Report Definition from the File menu.

Day 7

Answers to Day 7 Quiz

1. The Visdata project can be found in the Samples\Visdata subdirectory of Visual Basic 5.

2. To copy a table, simply select the table from the Table/Queries window, press the alternate mouse button, and select Copy Structure.

3. You need to Refresh the Tables/Queries window each time you enter an SQL statement to create a new table.

4. You can open and edit Excel spreadsheets in Visdata.

5. The Properties object in the Database window shows the complete name and path of the database, the version of the database engine in use, the connect property, the login time-out, the Microsoft Access version, the replica ID, and several other update settings.

6. You compact databases to remove empty spaces where deleted records used to reside, and to reorganize any defined indexes that are stored in the database.

7. You can compact a database onto itself with the File | Compact MDB command. This action is not advisable, however, as problems can occur during the compacting process.

8. You cannot modify a table's structure once data has been entered. You must delete all records before you can modify the structure.

9. You can save queries in Visdata for future use. You do this by building a query with the Query Builder and saving the results, or by entering an SQL statement and saving its result set.

10. Visdata can export data in the following formats:
    - ☐ Microsoft Access (Jet)
    - ☐ dBASE IV, III
    - ☐ FoxPro 2.6, 2.5, 2.0
    - ☐ Paradox 4.x, 3.x
    - ☐ Btrieve
    - ☐ Excel 5, 4, 3
    - ☐ Text
    - ☐ ODBC

11. You can use the Files | Compact Database option to convert existing Microsoft Access 2.0 databases to newer versions by selecting the new data format at the Compact Database submenu. Do not do this, however, as this is not the same converter used by Microsoft Access, and some objects in the database will be unusable by Access after the conversion.

Answers to Day 7 Exercises

1. To create the new database, select File | New | Microsoft Access | Version 7.0 MDB. Next, enter the path and the name of the database, and save.

2. Click the alternate mouse button in the Database window and select New from the menu that appears to build the new table. Insert the name tblCustomers in the Table Name field. Next, select Add to insert the fields. Enter the name, type, and size for each field, clicking OK after you complete each one. When all fields are entered, select Close. When you return to the Table Structure form, select Build Table.

3. To build the primary key, first make sure that tblCustomers is highlighted in the DatabaseQueries window, and select Design from the menu that appears when you click the alternate mouse button in the Database window. Select the Add Index

button from the Table Structure window. Enter the name of the primary key (PKtblCustomers), and click the ID field in the Available Fields list box. Make sure that the Primary and Unique checkboxes have been checked. Finally, click OK to build the primary key index.

4. Select the tblCustomers table from the Database window and click the alternate mouse button. Select Design from the menu that appears. Next, select Print Structure in the bottom right corner of the Table Structure window.

5. To enter records, first double-click tblCustomers. You can enter data in any Form type you want; however, you can only to enter Notes data in the Grid form.

6. To copy a table structure, highlight the table, click the alternate mouse button, and select Copy Structure. Leave the Target Connect String empty and make sure that neither the Copy Indexes, nor the Copy Data checkboxes are checked. Enter the table name tblVendors when prompted for the name of the new table. Select the OK button to create the table.

   Once the table is copied, you should then go into the table design and add a primary key. Build this index the same way you built the primary key for the tblCustomers table.

7. To export, select File | Import/Export. Select the tblCustomers table and then press Export Table(s). Next choose the text format as the data source, and click OK. You are then prompted to enter a path and a name. Select Save, and the file is created.

   Review the file. Notice that empty fields in a record are denoted by the use of two commas (,,).

Day 8

Answers to Day 8 Quiz

1. SQL stands for Structured Query Language. You pronounce SQL by saying the three individual letters (ess-que-ell). It is *not* pronounced *sequel.*

2. Use the SELECT_FROM statement to select information from table fields.

3. Use the asterisk (*) in a SELECT_FROM statement to select all the fields in a data table. For example, to select all fields in a table of customers, you can enter the following SQL statement:

```
SELECT * FROM Customers
```

4. Use the ORDER BY clause to sort the data you display. For example, to sort the data from quiz answer 3 by a field contained within the table, CustomerID, you would enter the following:

```
SELECT * FROM Customers ORDER BY CustomerID
```

5. A WHERE clause can be used to limit the records that are selected by the SQL statement, as well as to link two or more tables in a result set.

6. Use the AS clause to rename a field heading. For example, issue the following SQL statement to rename the field CustomerID in the Customers table to Customer.

   ```
   SELECT CustomerID AS Customer FROM Customers
   ```

7. SQL aggregate functions are a core set of functions available in all SQL-compliant systems used to return computed results on numeric data fields. The functions available through Jet include AVG, COUNT, SUM, MAX, and MIN.

8. Chief among the drawbacks of using Visual Basic functions in your SQL statement is the loss of portability to other database engines. There is also a slight performance reduction when Visual Basic functions are used in your SQL statement.

9. Both the DISTINCT and DISTINCTROW clauses extract unique records. The DISTINCTROW command looks at the entire record, whereas DISTINCT looks at the fields you associate with it.

10. You should always use the ORDER BY clause when you use the TOP n or TOP n PERCENT clauses. The ORDER BY clause ensures that your data is sorted appropriately to allow the TOP n clauses to select the appropriate data.

11. The three types of joins found in Microsoft Access Jet SQL are INNER, LEFT, and RIGHT. An INNER JOIN is used to create updatable result sets whose records have an exact match in both tables. The LEFT JOIN is used to return an updatable result set that returns all records in the first table in your SQL statement, and any records in the second table that have matching column values. The RIGHT JOIN is just the opposite of the LEFT JOIN; it returns all records in the second table of your SQL statement and any records in the first table that have matching column values.

12. UNION queries are used to join tables that contain similar information but are not linked through a foreign key. An example of a UNION query would be listing all of your company's customers and suppliers located in the state of Iowa. There won't be any foreign key relationships between a data table of supplier's information and a table of customer's information. Both tables will, however, contain fields for names, addresses, and phone numbers. This information can be joined through a UNION query and displayed as one result.

Answers to Day 8 Exercises

1. SELECT * FROM CustomerMaster

2. SELECT InvoiceNo, CustomerID AS Account, Description, Amount FROM OpenInvoice

3. SELECT InvoiceNo, CustomerID AS Account, Description, Amount FROM OpenInvoice ORDER BY CustomerID, InvoiceNo

4. SELECT * FROM Suppliers WHERE City LIKE ("New York *") and State = "NY"

5. SELECT CustomerMaster.CustomerType, CustomerMaster.Name, CustomerMaster.Address, CustomerMaster.City, CustomerMaster.State, CustomerMaster.Zip FROM CustomerMaster WHERE CustomerMaster.CustomerType = "ABC"

6. SELECT CustomerID, Name FROM CustomerMaster WHERE Left(Name,3) = "AME"

7. SELECT DISTINCT OpenInvoice.CustomerID, CustomerMaster.Name FROM OpenInvoice INNER JOIN CustomerMaster ON OpenInvoice.CustomerID = CustomerMaster.CustomerID ORDER BY OpenInvoice.CustomerID

8. SELECT TOP 5 * FROM OpenInvoice ORDER BY Amount Desc

9. SELECT Name, Phone FROM CustomerMaster WHERE State = "OHIO" UNION SELECT Name, Phone FROM Suppliers WHERE State = "Ohio"

Day 9

Answers to Day 9 Quiz

1. A property is data within an object that describes its characteristics, whereas a method is a procedure that can be performed upon an object. You set a property, and invoke a method.

2. The top level DAO is the DBEngine.

3. You use the RepairDatabase method to repair a database. This command uses the following syntax:

   DBEngine.RepairDatabase DatabaseName

4. The syntax for the CompactDatabase method is

   DBEngine.CompactDatabase oldDatabase, newDatabase, locale, options

   Please note that oldDatabase and newDatabase require the database name and path.

5. Visual Basic creates a default Workspace if you fail to identify one when you open a database.

6. The OpenRecordset method can open data from a data source as a Table, a Dynaset, or a Snapshot.

7. The CreateTableDef method builds a table in a database. The syntax of this statement is

   Database.CreateTableDef(table name)

8. Use the Type property of the Field object to display the data type of a table column.

9. The Index data object can be used to contain information on Microsoft Jet databases only.

10. The QueryDef object stores Structure Query Language (SQL) statements. A QueryDef is faster than an actual SQL statement because Visual Basic has to perform an additional preprocessing step for an SQL statement, which it does not need to perform for the QueryDef.

Answer to Day 9 Exercise

Drop a command button onto a form, name it cmdCreate, and enter the following code:

```
Private Sub cmdCreate_Click()

    On Error Resume Next

    'Define Variables
    Dim dbFile As DATABASE
    Dim cDBName As String
    Dim tdTemp As TableDef
    Dim fldTemp As Field
    Dim idxTemp As Index
    Dim relTemp As Relation
    Dim ctblCustomers As String
    Dim ctblCustomerTypes As String
    Dim cidxCustomers As String
    Dim cidxCustomerTypes As String
    Dim crelName As String

    'Set variables
    cDBName = App.Path + "\10ABCEX.MDB"
    ctblCustomers = "Customers"
    ctblCustomerTypes = "CustomerTypes"
    cidxCustomers = "PKCustomers"
    cidxCustomerTypes = "PKCustomerTypes"
    crelName = "relCustomerType"

    'Delete the database if it already exists
    Kill cDBName

    'Create the database
    Set dbFile = CreateDatabase(cDBName, dbLangGeneral, dbVersion20)

    'Create the Customers table
    Set tdTemp = dbFile.CreateTableDef(ctblCustomers)

    'Insert fields into the Customers table
    Set fldTemp = tdTemp.CreateField("CustomerID", dbText, 10)
    tdTemp.Fields.Append fldTemp
    Set fldTemp = tdTemp.CreateField("Name", dbText, 50)
    tdTemp.Fields.Append fldTemp
    Set fldTemp = tdTemp.CreateField("Address1", dbText, 50)
    tdTemp.Fields.Append fldTemp
    Set fldTemp = tdTemp.CreateField("Address2", dbText, 50)
    tdTemp.Fields.Append fldTemp
```

```
        Set fldTemp = tdTemp.CreateField("City", dbText, 25)
        tdTemp.Fields.Append fldTemp
        Set fldTemp = tdTemp.CreateField("StateProv", dbText, 25)
        tdTemp.Fields.Append fldTemp
        Set fldTemp = tdTemp.CreateField("Zip", dbText, 10)
        tdTemp.Fields.Append fldTemp
        Set fldTemp = tdTemp.CreateField("Phone", dbText, 14)
        tdTemp.Fields.Append fldTemp
        Set fldTemp = tdTemp.CreateField("CustomerType", dbText, 10)
        tdTemp.Fields.Append fldTemp

        'Build the Primary Key index to the Customers table
        Set idxTemp = tdTemp.CREATEINDEX(cidxCustomers)
        idxTemp.PRIMARY = True
        idxTemp.Required = True
        Set fldTemp = tdTemp.CreateField("CustomerID")
        idxTemp.Fields.Append fldTemp
        tdTemp.Indexes.Append idxTemp

        'Add the Customers table to the databases
        dbFile.TableDefs.Append tdTemp

        'Create the Customer Types table
        Set tdTemp = dbFile.CreateTableDef(ctblCustomerTypes)

        'Insert fields into the Customer Types table
        Set fldTemp = tdTemp.CreateField("CustomerType", dbText, 10)
        tdTemp.Fields.Append fldTemp
        Set fldTemp = tdTemp.CreateField("Description", dbText, 10)
        tdTemp.Fields.Append fldTemp

        'Build the Primary Key index for the Customer Types table
        Set idxTemp = tdTemp.CREATEINDEX(cidxCustomerTypes)
        idxTemp.PRIMARY = True
        idxTemp.Required = True
        Set fldTemp = tdTemp.CreateField("CustomerType")
        idxTemp.Fields.Append fldTemp
        tdTemp.Indexes.Append idxTemp

        'Add the CustomerTypes table to the database
        dbFile.TableDefs.Append tdTemp

        'Create the relationship
        Set relTemp = dbFile.CreateRelation(crelName)
        relTemp.TABLE = ctblCustomerTypes
        _' The table that contains the validation information
        relTemp.ForeignTable = ctblCustomers
        _' The table that utilizes the validation table
        Set fldTemp = relTemp.CreateField("CustomerType")
        fldTemp.ForeignName = "CustomerType"
        relTemp.Fields.Append fldTemp
        dbFile.Relations.Append relTemp

        'Issue a message when the procedure is completed
        MsgBox "Database build is complete"

End Sub
```

Day 10

Answers to Day 10 Quiz

1. The chief advantage of using the Data Control is that you can quickly build a Visual Basic database application without the use of much code. The disadvantages of using the Data Control include the following:

   ☐ The project will be more difficult to maintain.

   ☐ Data entry forms will not be as easily utilized in other database applications.

2. The chief advantage of using code to build Visual Basic data entry forms is that you have complete control of the process. Code can also be used in other Visual Basic projects to quickly build forms.

3. The `Find` method most resembles the SQL `WHERE` clause.

4. The `Seek` method can be used only on Recordsets opened as tables. `Seek` cannot be used on Dynasets or Snapshots.

5. The four `Move` methods that can be applied to the Recordset object are `MoveFirst`, `MovePrevious`, `MoveNext`, and `MoveLast`.

6. The `FindFirst` method starts its search from the beginning of the Recordset. The `FindLast` method starts its search from the end of the Recordset.

7. You use the Bookmark to remember a specific location in a dataset.

8. The `Seek` method is the fastest way to locate a record in a dataset.

9. You create a control array in Visual Basic by copying and pasting a control on a form and answering Yes when prompted to create a control array by Visual Basic.

10. You must invoke the `Edit` or `AddNew` method prior to writing to a dataset with the `Update` method.

Answers to Day 10 Exercise

Perform the following steps to complete the addition of the ZipCity form:

1. Open Visdata and create the new table ZipCity. Add a field for ZIP code (Zip) and for city (City).

2. Modify the menu on the Company Master form by adding mnuListZip with a caption of &Zip/City.

3. Add the following code to the `mnuListZip_Click` event:

```
Private Sub mnuListZip_Click()

    'Open the ZipCity form
    frmZipCity.Show 1

End Sub
```

4. Create a new form (frmZipCity) and add a field for ZIP code and a field for City. Set the Tag property of these two textboxes to ZIP and City, respectively.

5. Add a control array to this form. Do this by adding a command button, naming it cmdBtn, and then copying and pasting it seven times.

6. Make the following variable declarations in the General Declaration of your form:

```
Option Explicit

Dim dbFile As DATABASE
Dim cDBName As String
Dim rsFile As Recordset
Dim cRSName As String
Dim nBtnAlign As Integer
Dim nResult As Integer
```

7. Add the following procedure to your form:

```
Sub StartProc()
    '
    ' open db and rs
    '
    ' on error goto StartProcErr
    '
    cDBName = App.Path + "\master.mdb"
    cRSName = "ZipCity"
    '
    nResult = RSOpen(cDBName, cRSName, dbOpenDynaset, dbFile, rsFile)
    If nResult = recOK Then
        nResult = RecInit(Me)
    End If
    '
    If nResult = recOK Then
        nResult = RecRead(Me, rsFile)
    End If
    '
    GoTo StartProcExit
    '
StartProcErr:
    RecError Err, Error$, "StartProc"
    GoTo StartProcExit
    '
StartProcExit:
    '
End Sub
```

8. Add the following to the frmZipCity Form_Load event:

```
Private Sub Form_Load()

    ' initialize and start up
    '
    StartProc ' open files
    nResult = RecEnable(Me, False)   ' turn off controls
    nBtnAlign = btnAlignBottom       ' set alignment var
    BtnBarInit Me, nBtnAlign         ' create button set
    BtnBarEnable Me, "11111111"      ' enable all buttons

End Sub
```

9. Add the following to the `Form_Resize` event:

```
Private Sub Form_Resize()
    BtnBarInit Me, nBtnAlign    ' repaint buttons
End Sub
```

10. Add the following to the `Form_Unload` event:

```
Private Sub Form_Unload(Cancel As Integer)
    dbFile.Close    ' safe close
End Sub
```

From this point, save your work and run the project. Please note that most of this code can be copied directly from the `StateProv` example.

Day 11

Answers to Day 11 Quiz

1. The use of graphics in your Visual Basic database applications offers the following advantages:

   ☐ Visual representation of data is easier to understand than tables or lists.

   ☐ Graphics offer a different view of the data.

   ☐ Graphics give your application a polished appearance.

2. The NumSets property determines how many groups of data will be plotted. The NumPoints property shows how many points will be plotted in the group.

3. No, `graphBar3D` should be `gphBar3D`.

4. The Tab character, `Chr(9)`, separates data points in a series. The carriage return/line feed combination—`Chr(13) + Chr(10)`—separates datasets for QuickData.

5. Yes, GraphTitle is a valid property.

6. `gphBlit` sets the graph control to bitmap mode.

   `gphCopy` copies the graph to the Windows Clipboard.

   `gphDraw` draws the graph on-screen.

7. The Variant data type must be used for all optional arguments.

8. The following code moves the data pointer to the end of a dataset and counts the total number of records in the set:

```
Dim nPoints as Integer
Dim rsData as Recordset

rsData.Movelast
nPoints = rsData.RecordCount
```

Answers to Day 11 Exercises

You can complete this project by performing the following steps:

1. Create the database in Visdata. Build the table, add the fields, and enter the data.

2. Start Visual Basic and begin a new project. Insert LIBGRAPH.BAS and FRMGRAPH.FRM into your project.

3. Build the new form by adding the command buttons. Insert the following code behind each button:

```
Private Sub cmdPie_Click()

    Dim rsFile As Recordset
    Dim dbFile As DATABASE
    Dim cSQL As String
    Dim cField As String
    Dim cTitle As String
    Dim cLegend As String
    Dim cLabel As String
    Dim dbName As String

    cSQL = "Select * from Activity WHERE month =1"
    cField = "Passengers"
    cLegend = ""
    cLabel = "Airline"
    cTitle = "Market Share for January"
    dbName = "c:\abc\ch12\12abcex.mdb"

    Set dbFile = DBEngine.OpenDatabase(dbName)
    Set rsFile = dbFile.OpenRecordset(cSQL, dbOpenSnapshot)

    ShowGraph gphPie3D, rsFile, cField, cTitle,
    _cFldLegend:=cLegend, cFldLabel:=cLabel

End Sub

Private Sub cmdLine_Click()

    Dim rsFile As Recordset
    Dim dbFile As DATABASE
    Dim cSQL As String
    Dim cField As String
    Dim cTitle As String
    Dim cLegend As String
    Dim cLabel As String
    Dim dbName As String

    cSQL = "Select Month, Sum(Passengers) as TotPassengers from
    _Activity Group by Month;"
    cField = "TotPassengers"
    cLegend = ""
    cLabel = "Month"
    cTitle = "Total Activity"
    dbName = "c:\abc\ch12\12abcex.mdb"
```

```
        Set dbFile = DBEngine.OpenDatabase(dbName)
        Set rsFile = dbFile.OpenRecordset(cSQL, dbOpenSnapshot)

        ShowGraph gphLine, rsFile, cField, cTitle, _
        _cFldLegend:=cLegend, cFldLabel:=cLabel, _
        _cLeftTitle:="Passengers", cBottomTitle:="Month"

    End Sub

    Private Sub cmdBar_Click()
        Dim rsFile As Recordset
        Dim dbFile As DATABASE
        Dim cSQL As String
        Dim cField As String
        Dim cTitle As String
        Dim cLegend As String
        Dim cLabel As String
        Dim dbName As String

        cSQL = "Select * from Activity WHERE Airline='ABC';"
        cField = "Passengers"
        cLegend = ""
        cLabel = "Month"
        cTitle = "ABC Airlines Annual Activity"
        dbName = "c:\abc\ch12\12abcex.mdb"

        Set dbFile = DBEngine.OpenDatabase(dbName)
        Set rsFile = dbFile.OpenRecordset(cSQL, dbOpenSnapshot)

        ShowGraph gphBar3D, rsFile, cField, cTitle, _
        _cFldLegend:=cLegend, cFldLabel:=cLabel, _
        _cLeftTitle:="Passengers", cBottomTitle:="Month"

    End Sub
```

Day 12

Answers to Day 12 Quiz

1. Using a data-bound list or combo box increases the speed of data entry, gives you added control over data validation, and provides suggested values to use for entry.

2. You set the RowSource property to identify the data source for the list box.

3. The BoundColumn property sets the column that is saved in the new data record. Put another way, it's the field that is extracted from the source and placed in the destination. Remember that the bound column does not have to equal the ListField property of the control.

4. You set the DataSource property to the name of the dataset that should be updated by the contents of the data-bound list/combo box. You set the DataField property

to identify the field in the dataset determined by the DataSource property that will be updated.

5. You must set the AllowAddNew property to `True` to permit users to add records. You must set the AllowDelete property to `True` to permit removal of records.

6. Use the `BeforeDelete` event to confirm deletion of records.

7. The column-level events of the data-bound grid control provide field-level validation functionality.

8. You would use the data-bound combo box, rather than the data-bound list box, when you want to allow the user to type the entry or when space on the data entry form is limited.

9. You use the `ReBind` method to refresh a data-bound grid.

10. Subforms are typically used to display data from two different data tables that are linked through a common key. For example, subforms can display invoice detail of a customer linked by customer ID, or work orders that have been performed on a fixed asset linked by asset ID.

Answers to Day 12 Exercises

Complete the following steps to build this form:

1. Add a data control (Data1) and a data-bound list box to a new form.

2. Set the following properties of Data1:

DatabaseName   `C:\VB4\BIBLIO.MDB` (include appropriate path)
RecordSource   Publishers

3. Set the DataSource property to Data1 and the ListField property to Name for the data-bound list.

4. Add a second data control (Data2) and set its Database property to `BIBLIO.MDB` and its RecordSource property to Publishers.

5. Add text fields in an array to the form. Set their DataSource properties to Data2 and their DataField properties to their respective fields.

6. Add a third data control to the form. Set its DatabaseName to `BIBLIO.MDB` (include path) and its RecordSource property to Titles.

7. Set the Visible property of all three data controls to `False`.

8. Add a data-bound grid to the form. Set its DataSource property to Data3.

9. Load the dataset column names into the grid by selecting Retrieve Fields from the context menu of the DBGrid. Then select Properties from the context menu of the DBGrid and click the Columns tab. Make sure that the Visible checkbox is selected only for the Title, Year Published, and ISBN columns.

10. Use the context menu again on the DBGrid and select Edit. Resize the columns as needed.

11. Set the BoundColumn property of the data-bound list control to PubID. Blank out the DataField and DataSource properties.

12. Enter the following code in the `DBList1_click` event:

```
Private Sub DBList1_Click()

    Dim cFind As String

    cFind = "PubID=" + Trim(DBList1.BoundText)
    Data2.Recordset.FindFirst cFind

End Sub
```

13. Enter the following code in the `Data2_Reposition` event:

```
Private Sub Data2_Reposition()

    Dim cSQL As String

    cSQL = "Select * from Titles WHERE PubID=" + Trim(Text1(0))

    Data3.RecordSource = cSQL ' filter the data set
    Data3.Refresh ' refresh the data control
    DBGrid1.ReBind ' refresh the data grid

End Sub
```

14. Save and execute your program.

Day 13

Answers to Day 13 Quiz

1. These are the benefits of using SQL to create and manage data tables:

    ☐ SQL statements can serve as documentation for your table layouts.

    ☐ It's easy to produce test or sample data tables with SQL statements.

    ☐ You can easily load test data into new tables with SQL statements.

    ☐ You can utilize SQL for multiple data platforms.

2. The syntax is

```
CREATE TABLE TableName (Field1 TYPE(SIZE), Field2 TYPE(SIZE), _);
```

You first enter CREATE TABLE, followed by the name of the table, and then the fields in parentheses. The field types and sizes (sizes apply to TEXT columns only) are entered after each field.

3. The default size of a Microsoft Jet TEXT field is 255 bytes.

4. You use the ALTER TABLE_ADD COLUMN statement to add a column to a table. The ALTER TABLE_ADD COLUMN statement uses the following format:

```
ALTER TABLE <Name of Table> ADD COLUMN <Name of column> <Type> <Size>;
```

5. You use the DROP TABLE statement to remove a table from a database. The DROP TABLE statement uses the following format:

```
DROP TABLE <Table Name>;
```

6. You create indexes to data tables with the CREATE INDEX SQL statement.

7. The following are the three forms of the CONSTRAINT clause:

- ☐ PRIMARY KEY
- ☐ UNIQUE
- ☐ FOREIGN KEY

C

Answer to Day 13 Exercise

Enter the following code to build the CustomerType and Customers tables. Please note that the CustomerType table must be built before the Customers table, because of the foreign key constraint on CustomerType in the Customers table.

```
// Create the database
dbmake C:\CUSTOMER\CH13EX.MDB;
// Build the Customer Types Table
CREATE TABLE CustomerType(
    CustomerType TEXT(6) CONSTRAINT PKCustomerType PRIMARY KEY,
    Description TEXT(30));
// Build the Customers table
CREATE TABLE Customers(
    CustomerID TEXT(10) Constraint PKCustomerID PRIMARY KEY,
    Name TEXT(30),
    CustomerType TEXT(6) CONSTRAINT FKCustomerType
      _REFERENCES CustomerType(CustomerType),
    Address TEXT(30),
    City TEXT(30),
    State TEXT(30),
    Zip TEXT(10),
    Phone TEXT(14),
    Fax TEXT(14));
// Build the index on Zip
CREATE INDEX SKZip on Customers(Zip);
//Display the results
SELECT * FROM CustomerType;
SELECT * FROM Customers;
```

Day 14

Answers to Day 14 Quiz

1. These are the three main parts of error handlers in Visual Basic:

   ☐ The On Error Goto statement

   ☐ The error handler code

   ☐ The Exit statement

2. The four ways to exit an error handler routine are

   ☐ Resume: Returns to execute the code that caused the error.

   ☐ Resume Next: Resumes execution of the Visual Basic code at the line immediately following the line that created the error.

   ☐ Resume label: Resumes execution at a specified location in the program that caused the error.

   ☐ EXIT SUB or EXIT function: Exits the routine in which the error occurred. You could also use END to exit the program completely.

3. You use Resume to exit an error handler when users have done something that they can easily correct. For example, a user may have forgotten to insert a disk in drive A or close the drive door.

4. You would use Resume Next to exit an error handler when the program runs properly even though an error has been reported, or if code within the program corrects the problem.

5. You use Resume label to exit an error handler when you want the program to return to a portion of code that allows for correction of the invalid entry. For example, if the user enters numeric data that yields improper results (division by zero, for example) you may want the code to redisplay the input screen so that entry can be corrected.

6. You would use the EXIT command or the END command to terminate the program when there is no good way to return to the program once the error has occurred. This might happen if the user forgot to log onto a network or if there is insufficient memory to run the program.

7. The following are the four types of Visual Basic errors:

   ☐ General file errors: Errors that occur when you try to open, read, or write file information.

   ☐ Database errors: Errors that occur during database operations such as reads, writes, or data object creation or deletion.

☐ Physical media errors: Errors that are caused by physical devices, such as printers and disk drives.

☐ Program code errors: Errors that result from improper coding.

8. You should not use error trapping for the Visual Basic Data Control because it provides its own error trapping.

9. It is a good idea to open a data table with the FORM LOAD event. This allows you to capture most database-related errors prior to any data entry.

10. The advantage of a global error handler is that it enables you to create a single module that handles all expected errors. The major disadvantage of a global error handler is that you are not able to resume processing at the point at which the error occurs. To be able to resume processing at the point of an error, you need to use Resume, Resume Next, or Resume label in a local error handler.

11. The Err.Raise method allows you to create your own error message and confirm to the Visual Basic standard, including the ability to "post" a message to another application through the OLE object model interface.

Answers to Day 14 Exercises

1. Insert a command button on a new form, and then double-click that button and enter the following code:

```
Private Sub Command1_Click()
    On Error GoTo Command1Clickerr
    Dim cMsg As String ' Declare string
    Open "C:\ABC.TXT" For Input As 1 'Open file
    GoTo Command1ClickExit
'Error handler
Command1Clickerr:
    If Err.Number = 53 Then
        cMsg = "Unable to open ABC.TXT" + Chr(13)
        MsgBox cMsg, vbCritical, "Command1Click"
        Unload Me
        End
    Else
        MsgBox CStr(Err.Number) & " - " & Err.Description, vbCritical,
"Command1Click"
        Resume Next
    End If
'Routine exit
Command1ClickExit:
End Sub
```

2. You first need to place a common dialog on your form. Then place a command button and add the following code to it:

```
Private Sub Command2_Click()
    On Error GoTo Command2ClickErr
    'Declare variables
```

```
        Dim cFile As String
        Dim cMsg As String
        Dim nReturn As Integer
        'Define the file to open
        cFile = "C:\ABC.TXT"
        'Open the file
        Open cFile For Input As 1
        MsgBox "ABC.TXT has been opened."
        GoTo Command2ClickExit
    'Error handler
    Command2ClickErr:
        If Err = 53 Then
            cMsg = "Unable to open ABC.TXT!" + Chr(13)
            cMsg = cMsg + "Select OK to locate this file. "
            cMsg = cMsg + "Select CANCEL to exit this program." + Chr(13)
            nReturn = MsgBox(cMsg, vbCritical + vbOKCancel, "Command2Click")
            If nReturn = vbOK Then
                CommonDialog1.filename = cFile
                CommonDialog1.DefaultExt = ".txt"
                CommonDialog1.ShowOpen
                Resume
            Else
                Unload Me
            End If
        Else
            MsgBox CStr(Err.Number) & " - " & Err.Description
            Resume Next
        End If
    'Routine exit
    Command2ClickExit:
    End Sub
```

Day 15

Answers to Day 15 Quiz

1. You use the INSERT statement to insert data into tables. The basic form of this statement is

   ```
   INSERT INTO TableName(field1, field2,...) VALUES(value1, value2,...);
   ```

2. You use the INSERT INTO_FROM statement to insert multiple records into a data table. The format of this statement is

   ```
   INSERT INTO TargetTable SELECT field1, field2 FROM SourceTable;
   ```

3. You use the UPDATE_SET statement to modify existing data. This statement uses the following form:

   ```
   UPDATE <table name> SET <field to update> = <New Value>;
   ```

4. You use the SELECT_INTO_FROM SQL statement to create new tables and insert existing data from other tables. The format of this statement is

```
SELECT field1, field2 INTO DestinationTable FROM SourceTable;
```

In this statement, field1 and field2 represent the field names in the source table.

5. You use the DELETE_FROM statement to remove records from a data table. The form of this statement is

```
DELETE FROM TableName WHERE field = value;
```

Answers to Day 15 Exercises

1. Enter the following INSERT_INTO statements after your CREATE INDEX statement to insert the data.

```
INSERT INTO CustomerType VALUES('INDV', 'Individual');
INSERT INTO CustomerType VALUES('BUS', 'Business - Non-corporate');
INSERT INTO CustomerType VALUES('CORP', 'Corporate Entity');
INSERT INTO Customers VALUES('SMITHJ', 'John Smith', 'INDV',
    '160 Main Street', 'Dublin', 'Ohio', '45621',
    '614-569-8975', '614-569-5580');
INSERT INTO Customers VALUES('JONEST', 'Jones Taxi', 'BUS',
    '421 Shoe St.', 'Milford', 'Rhode Island', '03215',
    '401-737-4528', '401-667-8900');
INSERT INTO Customers VALUES('JACKSONT', 'Thomas Jackson', 'INDV',
    '123 Walnut Street', 'Oxford', 'Maine', '05896',
    '546-897-8596', '546-897-8500');
```

2. Your script should now look like this:

```
// Create the database
dbmake C:\CUSTOMER\CH15EX.MDB;
// Build the Customer Types Table
CREATE TABLE CustomerType(
    CustomerType TEXT(6) CONSTRAINT PKCustomerType PRIMARY KEY,
    Description TEXT(30));
// Build the Customers table
CREATE TABLE Customers(
    CustomerID TEXT(10) Constraint PKCustomerID PRIMARY KEY,
    Name TEXT(30),
    CustomerType TEXT(6) CONSTRAINT FKCustomerType REFERENCES
     _CustomerType(CustomerType),
    Address TEXT(30),
    City TEXT(30),
    State TEXT(30),
    Zip TEXT(10),
    Phone TEXT(14),
    Fax TEXT(14));
// Build the index on Zip
CREATE INDEX SKZip on Customers(Zip);
// Insert Data
INSERT INTO CustomerType VALUES('INDV', 'Individual');
INSERT INTO CustomerType VALUES('BUS', 'Business - Non-corporate');
INSERT INTO CustomerType VALUES('CORP', 'Corporate Entity');
```

C

```
INSERT INTO Customers Values('SMITHJ', 'John Smith', 'INDV',
    '160 Main Street', 'Dublin', 'Ohio', '45621',
    '614-569-8975', '614-569-5580');
INSERT INTO Customers Values('JONEST', 'Jones Taxi', 'BUS',
    '421 Shoe St.', 'Milford', 'Rhode Island', '03215',
    '401-737-4528', '401-667-8900');
INSERT INTO Customers Values('JACKSONT', 'Thomas Jackson', 'INDV',
    '123 Walnut Street', 'Oxford', 'Maine', '05896',
    '546-897-8596', '546-897-8500');
// Copy data into the localities table
SELECT CustomerID, City, State INTO Localities FROM Customers;
// Display the results
SELECT * FROM CustomerType;
SELECT * FROM Customers;
SELECT * FROM Localities;
```

3. You would issue the following SQL statement to delete the SMITHJ record from the Customers table:

```
DELETE FROM Customers WHERE CustomerID = 'SMITHJ';
```

You would use the DROP TABLE command to delete an entire table. To delete the Customers table, you would issue the following statement:

```
DROP TABLE Customers;
```

Day 16

Answers to Day 16 Quiz

1. It is not necessarily a good idea to look at database optimization strictly from the point of view of processing performance. Other factors such as data integrity are also important. The role of data normalization is to strike a balance between speed and integrity.

2. If the term "First Normal Form" is applied to a database, it means that the first rule of data normalization—eliminate repeating groups—has been achieved.

3. The first rule of data normalization is to delete repeating groups, whereas the second rule of normalization requires the deletion of redundant data. Rule one requires the separation of fields that contain multiple occurrences of similar data into separate tables. Rule two requires that fields that must maintain constant relationships with other fields (for example, the name of a customer as associated with the customer ID) should be placed in a separate table.

4. Do not include calculated fields in a data table. Not only does the calculated data take up disk space, but problems can arise if one of the fields used in the calculation is deleted or changed. Calculations are best saved for forms and reports. Placing a calculated field in your data table violates the third rule of data normalization—eliminate columns not dependent on keys.

5. You invoke the fourth rule of data normalization if you have multiple independent one-to-many relationships within the same table. You need to use this rule when you unwittingly create relationships that do not necessarily exist. For example, if you included educational degree in the Employee skills table in the examples used in this lesson, you mistakenly aligned skills with degrees that do not necessarily match.

6. You invoke the fifth rule of data normalization if you have multiple dependent many-to-many relationships. To resolve any potential conflict under this rule, you might need to break the different components of the relationships into separate tables and link them through another table.

Answers to Day 16 Exercises

1. To achieve First Normal Form, you must delete repeating groups. In this exercise, this includes the fields for the multiple automobiles (VehicleType1, Make1, Model1, Color1, Odometer1, VehicleType2, Make2, Model2, Color2, Odometer2). This requires that you create two tables. The first tracks the customers (Customers), and the second tracks their vehicles (Vehicles).

Customers Table	Vehicles Table
CustomerID (primary key)	SerialNumber (primary key)
CustomerName	CustomerID (foreign key)
License	VehicleType
Address	Make
City	Model
State	Color
Zip	Odometer
Phone	

Please note that by separating the VehicleTypes into a separate table, you can have any number of vehicles for a customer. Also note that SerialNumber makes a better primary key than License because the serial number of an automobile does change, whereas a license plate can change on an annual basis.

Next, you need to reach Second Normal Form. This requires you to take the Customer and Vehicle tables and remove any redundant data. There is no redundant data in the Customers table. The Vehicles table, on the other hand, has redundant data describing the VehicleType. You should move the type information into a separate table to yield the following structure:

Customers	Vehicles	VehicleTypes
CustomerID (Primary Key)	SerialNumber (Primary Key)	VehicleType (Primary Key)
CustomerName	CustomerID	Make (Foreign Key)
Address	License	Model
City		VehicleType (Foreign Key)
State	Color	
Zip	Odometer	
Phone		

To reach Third Normal Form, you must delete any fields that do not describe the primary key. A review of all fields shows that you have already eliminated any fields that do not describe the entire primary key.

To achieve Fourth Normal Form, you need to separate any independent one-to-many relationships that can potentially produce unusual answers when you query the data. The Vehicles table does have several one-to-many relationships with the CustomerID and the VehicleType fields. The combination of these two fields in the same table would not, however, lead to misleading results further down the line. Therefore, you do not need to make any changes to reach Fourth Normal Form.

Similarly, no changes need to be made to reach Fifth Normal Form because you have no dependent many-to-many relationships in your tables. Most data structures do not require you to use the fourth and fifth rules of normalization to optimize your structure.

As a final point, you might want to add a Comments field to each table. This allows users to store any miscellaneous data they choose to track. Adding a memo field to track comments is a good idea in almost every table, because memo fields do not take up room when empty, and they provide great flexibility to your system.

2. The following SQL code builds these tables:

 **NOTE**

> Please note that you need to create the VehicleTypes table before the Vehicles table. This is required because the Vehicles table has a foreign key constraint to the VehicleTypes table. In such situations, the foreign key must be defined prior to its use in another table, or an error occurs.

```
Create Table Customers
  (CustomerID TEXT (10),
   CustomerName TEXT (40),
```

```
        Address TEXT (40),
        City TEXT (40),
        State TEXT (20),
        Zip TEXT (10),
        Phone TEXT (14),
        Comments MEMO,
        CONSTRAINT PKCustomers Primary Key (CustomerID));
Create Table VehicleTypes
    (VehicleType TEXT (10),
        Make TEXT (25),
        Model TEXT (25),
        Comments MEMO,
        CONSTRAINT PKVehicleTypes Primary Key (VehicleType));
Create Table Vehicles
    (SerialNumber INTEGER,
        CustomerID TEXT (10),
        License TEXT (10),
        VehicleType TEXT (10),
        Color TEXT (15),
        Odometer INTEGER,
        Comments MEMO,
        CONSTRAINT PKVehicles Primary Key (SerialNumber),
        CONSTRAINT FKCustomer Foreign Key (CustomerID)
        _REFERENCES  Customers(CustomerID),
        CONSTRAINT FKType Foreign Key (VehicleType)
        _REFERENCES VehicleTypes(VehicleType));
```

Day 17

Answers to Day 17 Quiz

1. The Microsoft Jet database engine provides three levels of locking: database locking, which locks the entire database for exclusive use; table locking, which locks a table for exclusive use; and page locking, which locks data pages 2KB in size.

2. You want to use database locking when compacting a database because compacting affects all the objects in a database.

3. You want to use table locking when doing a mass update of a single table. You want exclusive use of the data to be changed, but you do not necessarily have to have exclusive use of the entire database when performing field update functions.

4. You use the LockEdits property of a recordset to control how page locking is handled by your application. Setting this property to True means you have pessimistic locking. Setting this property to False means you have optimistic locking.

5. Pessimistic locking prohibits two users from opening a data page at the same time (that is, when the Edit or AddNew method is invoked). Optimistic locking permits two users to open the same page but only allows updates to be saved by the first user to make the changes.

6. You *cannot* use pessimistic locks on an ODBC data source. ODBC data sources use optimistic locking only.

7. When cascading deletes are used in a relationship, each time a base table element is deleted, all foreign table records that contain that element are deleted.

8. You use transaction management in your applications to provide an opportunity to reverse a series of database updates if your program fails to complete all requested data changes. This is particularly useful if you have processes that affect multiple tables within the database. Failure to fully complete such a transaction could lead to a database that has lost or inaccurate data. This can also result in a database that is difficult or impossible to repair.

9. The limitations of transactions include the following:

   ☐ Some database formats do not support transactions.

   ☐ Datasets that are the result of some SQL JOIN or WHERE clause, and datasets that contain data from attached tables do not support transactions.

   ☐ Transaction operations are kept on the local workstations, which could lead to errors if the process runs out of space in the TEMP directory.

10. Declaring a unique workspace object is not required; however, it is highly recommended that you do so because transactions apply to an *entire* workspace.

Answers to Day 17 Exercises

1. Enter the following code to load a database exclusively when you bring up a form:

```
Private Sub Form_Load()

    Dim DB As Database
    Dim dbName As String

    On Error GoTo FormLoadErr

    dbName = App.Path + "\abc.mdb"
    Set DB = DBEngine.OpenDatabase(dbName, True) ' Open database exclusive
    MsgBox "Database opened successfully"
    GoTo FormLoadExit

FormLoadErr:
    MsgBox "Unable to load database ABC.MDB"
    GoTo FormLoadExit

FormLoadExit:
    Unload Me

End Sub
```

2. Enter the following code in the Form_Load event to load a table exclusively:

```
Private Sub Form_Load()

    Dim db As Database
```

```
        Dim rs As Recordset
        Dim dbName As String
        Dim tabName As String

        dbName = App.Path + "\abc.mdb"
        tabName = "Customers"

        On Error GoTo FormLoadErr

        Set db = DBEngine.OpenDatabase(dbName)
        Set rs = db.OpenRecordset(tabName, dbOpenTable,
        _dbDenyRead + dbDenyWrite) ' table opened exclusively
        MsgBox "Table opened exclusively"
        GoTo FormLoadExit

    FormLoadErr:
        MsgBox "Unable to load table exclusively"
        GoTo FormLoadExit

    FormLoadExit:
        Unload Me

    End Sub
```

3. To start the project, insert the following code into the general declarations section:

```
Option Explicit

'Declaration of global variables
Dim DB As Database
Dim wsUpdate As Workspace
Dim nErrFlag As Integer
```

Next, start a new procedure and insert the following code. This code creates a workspace and opens the database.

```
Public Sub OpenDB()

    On Error GoTo OpenDBErr

    Dim dbName As String

    nErrFlag = 0 'Reset the error flag
    dbName = App.Path + "\abc.mdb"

    'Open the workspace and database
    Set wsUpdate = DBEngine.CreateWorkspace("WSUpdate", "admin", "")
    Set DB = wsUpdate.OpenDatabase(dbName, True)
    GoTo OpenDBExit

OpenDBErr:
    MsgBox Trim(Str(Err)) + " " + Error$(Err), vbCritical, "OpenDB"
    nErrFlag = Err

OpenDBExit:

End Sub
```

Now build the following procedure to perform the posting:

```
Public Sub Post()

    On Error GoTo PostErr

    Dim cSQL As String

    wsUpdate.BeginTrans

    'Create the SQL statement to insert the records.
    _'Note that we do not use the TransNo field
    _'as it is a counter field necessary only
    _'for the Transactions table
    cSQL = "INSERT INTO History Select CustID, InvoiceNo,
    _Amount FROM Transactions"
    DB.Execute cSQL

    'Delete the temporary transactions data
    cSQL = "DELETE FROM Transactions"
    DB.Execute cSQL

    'Commit the transactions
    wsUpdate.CommitTrans
    MsgBox "Transactions have been committed"

    'Set the error flag and exit the program
    nErrFlag = 0
    GoTo PostExit

PostErr:
    'Display the error and rollback the transactions
    MsgBox Trim(Str(Err)) + " " + Error$(Err), vbCritical, "Post"
    wsUpdate.Rollback
    MsgBox "Post routine has been aborted"

PostExit:

End Sub
```

Finally, insert the following code into the cmdPost_Click event:

```
Private Sub cmdPost_Click()

    OpenDB
    If nErrFlag = 0 Then
        Post
    End If

    If nErrFlag <> 0 Then
        MsgBox "Error Reported", vbCritical, "cmdPost"
    End If

    Unload Me

End Sub
```

You can test this program by building the database in Visdata or Data Manager and then inserting some sample records into the Transactions table.

Day 18

Answers to Day 18 Quiz

1. The Standard Data control uses the Microsoft Jet database engine to connect to databases. The Remote Data control uses a different data engine designed to connect to remote database management systems (RDBMSs).

2. Cursor drivers are the tools that manage the location of the recordset pointer in a dataset. RDO/RDC connections can use client-side or server-side cursors.

3. The four dataset types available when using RDO/RDC connections are:

   ☐ rdOpenForwardOnly—Creates a read-only, scroll-forward-only dataset. This is the default option.

   ☐ rdOpenStatic—Creates an updatable dataset that has non-changing membership.

   ☐ rdOpenDynamic—Creates an updatable dataset that has changing membership. Record keys are not used.

   ☐ rdOpenKeyset—Creates an updatable dataset that has changing membership. Record keys (the key set) are created to point to all members of the set. This enables you to use bookmarks with the dataset.

The five lock types you can use with RDO/RDC are:

☐ rdConcurReadOnly—Provides no row-level locking. This is the default option.

☐ rdConcurLock—Provides pessimistic locking for the entire row set. The lock occurs as soon as the data is accessed—not when an edit operation begins.

☐ rdConcurRowver—Provides optimistic locking based on internal row ID values (usually, the TimeStamp column).

☐ rdConcurValues—Provides optimistic locking based on a column-by-column check of the data in each row.

☐ rdConcurBatch—Provides optimistic locking based on the value in the UpdateCriteria property when using Batch Update mode. Not supported by all RDBMSs.

The Microsoft equivalent of the rdoResultset object is the Recordset object. The rdoResultset and the Microsoft Jet Recordset object both contain the actual collection of data records for display or update.

The RDO/RDC equivalent of the Microsoft Jet Workspace object is the rdoEnvironment object. You can use the rdoEnvironment object and the Workspace object to manage connections to multiple databases and to control transaction management.

Answer to Day 18 Exercise

To complete this assignment, you need to create a data form that has two buttons, and a list box. You use RDO for this project, so be sure to add the RDO library from the Project | Components menu.

1. Start a new Visual Basic 5 Standard EXE project.

2. Add two command buttons (cmdTables and cmdClear) and a list box (List1) to the form.

3. Add the following code to the form (this is all the code you need).

```
Private Sub cmdTables_Click()
    '
    ' get rdo table collection
    '
    On Error GoTo LocalErr
    '
    Dim rdoEnv As rdoEnvironment
    Dim rdoCon As rdoConnection
    Dim rdoTbl As rdoTable
    '
    ' set env/con
    Set rdoEnv = rdoEngine.rdoCreateEnvironment("rdoTEMP", "admin", "")
    Set rdoCon = rdoEnv.OpenConnection("")
    '
    ' update the tables collection
    rdoCon.rdoTables.Refresh
    '
    ' show table properties
    List1.Clear
    For Each rdoTbl In rdoCon.rdoTables
        List1.List(List1.ListIndex) = rdoTbl.Name & " [" & rdoTbl.Type
➥& "]"
    Next
    '
    rdoCon.Close
    rdoEnv.Close
    Set rdoTbl = Nothing
    Set rdoCon = Nothing
    Set rdoEnv = Nothing
    '
    Exit Sub
    '
LocalErr:
    MsgBox Err.Description, vbExclamation, "RDOTables"
    '
End Sub

Private Sub cmdClear_Click()
    List1.Clear
End Sub

Private Sub Form_Load()
    '
```

```
        Me.Caption = "RDBMS Tables Lister"
    '
    End Sub
```

4. Save and run the project.

Day 19

Answers to Day 19 Quiz

1. The letters "ODBC" stand for Open Database Connectivity.

2. When you use the Microsoft Jet interface to connect to an ODBC data source, your Visual Basic program must first communicate with Microsoft Jet, which communicates to the ODBC front end. When you use the ODBC API, your Visual Basic program communicates directly with the ODBC front-end, skipping the Microsoft Jet layer entirely.

3. When you use the ODBC API to link to your data, you are actually creating a static, snapshot-type dataset. You must collect a set of data and bring it back to your workstation. You might also be limited by the amount of memory available on the workstation.

4. You use the ODBC Administrator to define or modify ODBC data sources. This program is part of the Windows Control Panel.

5. You can use the ODBC interface to connect to Excel spreadsheets and event text files, as long as an ODBC driver is installed on your system to handle the data format. There is no restriction to the type of data that you can access from an ODBC data source (as long as the driver exists for that format).

6. Before you can pass an SQL SELECT statement to a new ODBC data source, you must complete the following four preliminary steps:

   □ Allocate an environment handle (SQLAllocEnv) to create a unique identifier for this ODBC session.

   □ Allocate a connection handle (SQLAllocConnect) to create a unique identifier for this ODBC connection.

   □ Connect to the ODBC data source (SQLConnect) using the data source name, user login, and password.

   □ Allocate a statement handle (SQLAllocStmt) to create a unique identifier for passing data and SQL statements back and forth.

Answer to Day 19 Exercise

To complete this assignment, you must first register a new ODBC data source on your workstation. To do this:

1. Call up the ODBC Administrator from the Windows Control Panel.

2. Press the Add button, and select Microsoft Access as the database driver.

3. Set the DSN name to Exer19 and then press the Database button to select the target database (C:\TYSDBVB5\SOURCE\CHAP19\EXERCISE\EXER19.MDB).

4. Select OK to save the new ODBC definition.

Next you need to create a Visual Basic 5.0 Standard EXE project that is almost identical to the prjSQLTest project you built in this chapter. If you want, you can copy that project to a new directory and make the following changes:

1. Copy the prjSQLTest project to a new directory.

2. Load the prjSQLTest project.

3. Modify the StartDB method to match the following code:

```
Public Sub StartDB()
    '
    ' handle chores of connecting and getting data
    '

    ' create reference to ODBC object
    Set objSQL = New objODBC
    '
    ' populate properties
    objSQL.DataSource = "Exer19" ' <<< modified line
    objSQL.UserID = "admin"
    objSQL.Password = ""
    objSQL.SQL = "SELECT * FROM SampleTable" ' <<< modified line
    objSQL.Table = "SampleTable" ' <<< modified line
    objSQL.Key = "Name"
    objSQL.ResultSetType = sqlStatic
    objSQL.CursorDriver = sqlUseODBC
    objSQL.LockType = sqlValues
    '
    ' do real work
    objSQL.Connect ' establish connection
    objSQL.Refresh ' build dataset
    objSQL.MoveFirst Me ' display first row
    '
End Sub
```

4. Modify the screen to contain three input boxes and three label controls. Set the label control captions to: Name, Address, and Phone.

5. Save and run the project.

Day 20

Answers to Day 20 Quiz

1. Database replication refers to the act of creating a master database (the Design Master) and copies of the master (replicas), and synchronizing data contained in all members of the replica set (the Design Master and all replicas).

2. You may want to use database replication in systems deployed on a wide area network or to remote users. Replication can also be useful for making backups of databases that cannot be shut down to make a copy. Replication is also good for building datasets that must be "frozen," which is a reason for building static databases and reporting systems.

3. You do not want to use replication in an application that can be better deployed as an intranet application. Also, replication should not be considered in systems that are heavily transaction-orientated (such as reservation systems), or where data accuracy and timeliness are of the utmost importance (such as emergency response systems).

4. Three fields are added to each table when a database is turned into a Design Master. The first field, s_Generation, identifies records that changed during data entry. The second, s_GUID, serves as a unique identifier for each record. The third field, s_Lineage, stores the name of the last replica set to update the record.

5. The Replicable and the ReplicableBool properties are added to the database during creation of the Design Master to indicate that replicas can be made of the Design Master.

6. A replicable database consumes an additional 28 bytes per record, plus the space required to accommodate the additional system tables added when the database is made replicable.

7. An AutoNumber field stops incrementing by 1 and starts inserting random numbers for each new record added to a table. This is but one reason why AutoNumber data types should not be used in your application.

8. You use the MakeReplica method to create a copy of the Design Master. You can also use the MakeReplica method to create a copy of any member of the replica set (that is, you can use a replica other than the Design Master). In fact, you are better off using a copy of a replica set member as a backup of the Design Master than you are using a tape backup.

9. In a synchronization conflict, the Microsoft Jet engine takes the record that has been changed the greatest number of times. In the case of a tie, the Microsoft Jet engine takes the record from the replica set member with the lowest ReplicaID.

C

10. You can use the star, linear, ring, and fully connected topology synchronization schemes. The star is the most commonly used.

11. Use the KeepLocal method to keep database objects from replicating to other members of the replica set. This method must be used *before* the Design Master is created.

Answers to Day 20 Exercise

You should keep the Design Master at your Cincinnati office. Distribute all tables, except for the SalaryInfo table, to the Los Angeles, Chicago, and New York offices.

For backup, each office should synchronize often with the Cincinnati Office. The Chicago office, given its size, should synchronize more often than the other two remote offices. In case of failure of the Cincinnati database, the Chicago database is probably the best choice to use as a backup. Do not keep a tape backup of the Cincinnati database. The use of a backup copy of the Design Master could be disastrous for the entire replica set.

You should use the star topology in your synchronization strategy. This is the easiest to understand and use, as well as being the most logical because the order in which databases synchronize is unimportant.

The following code can be attached to a command button (in this case cmdKeepLocal) to keep the SalaryInfo table from replicating. It then goes on to turn the EMPLOYEE.MDB database into a Design Master, and creates a replica named COPYCHI.MDB.

```
Private Sub cmdKeepLocal_Click()

    Dim dbMaster As Database
    Dim LocalProperty As Property
    Dim KeepTab As Object
    Dim repProperty As Property


    'Open the database in exclusive mode
    Set dbMaster = OpenDatabase("c:\tysdbvb5\source\data\employee.mdb", True)

    Set KeepTab = dbMaster.TableDefs("SalaryInfo")
    Set LocalProperty = dbMaster.CreateProperty("KeepLocal", dbText, "T")
    KeepTab.Properties.Append LocalProperty
    KeepTab.Properties("Keeplocal") = "T"

    MsgBox "The SalaryInfo table is set to not replicate"

    'Create and set the replicable property
    Set repProperty = dbMaster.CreateProperty("Replicable", dbText, "T")
    dbMaster.Properties.Append repProperty
    dbMaster.Properties("Replicable") = "T"

    'Display a message box
```

```
    MsgBox "You have created a Design Master out of EMPLOYEE.MDB!"

    dbMaster.MakeReplica "c:\tysdbvb5\source\data\copychi.mdb", "Replica of " &
"dbMaster"

    dbMaster.Close

    MsgBox "You have created a copy of EMPLOYEE.MDB"

End Sub
```

Use the following code from the Click event of a command button (cmdSynch) to synchronize the Chicago and the Cincinnati databases:

```
Private Sub cmdSynch_Click()
    Dim dbMaster As Database

    'Open the database
    Set dbMaster = OpenDatabase("c:\tysdbvb5\source\data\employee.mdb")

    dbMaster.Synchronize "c:\tysdbvb5\source\data\copychi.mdb"

    MsgBox "The synchronization is complete."

End Sub
```

Day 21

Answers to Day 21 Quiz

1. The disadvantages and limitations of using the Microsoft Access SYSTEM file to secure a database include:

   ☐ You must own Microsoft Access to create a SYSTEM security file. You can't use a Visual Basic 5 utility to create a SYSTEM file.

   ☐ It is possible to have multiple SYSTEM files, which could lead to problems if the wrong file is used.

   ☐ SYSTEM file security can be removed by simply deleting the SYSTEM file itself.

   ☐ Some applications do not recognize the SYSTEM file. It is possible for these applications to skirt the security implemented within the SYSTEM file.

2. The disadvantages of using data encryption to secure a database include:

   ☐ Encryption affects an entire database and cannot be applied only to critical tables.

   ☐ Encrypted databases can't be read by other programs. This makes distribution of data more difficult.

   ☐ Encrypted databases cannot be replicated using the Microsoft Replication Manager tools.

3. Application security focuses on processes, not just the underlying data. Application security allows you to grant permissions for forms, reports, and procedures. Database security, on the other hand, focuses strictly on the data and the database.

4. There are the two main features of any good application security scheme:

   ☐ It must have a process that allows users to log into the application using stored passwords.

   ☐ It must have an access rights scheme that limits the functions that users can perform within the system.

5. Application security schemes can't prevent unauthorized use of your data by tools such as the Visual Data Manager. Application security only works within an application. Therefore, you should not rely on it as the only means of securing your application or your data.

6. Access rights security schemes build an added level of security into your application. This type of security allows you to define a set of secured operations within your application and then define access rights for each of the operations on a user-by-user basis.

7. You add audit trails for these reasons:

   ☐ To track when users log into and out of applications.

   ☐ To provide detail as to the status of the application when a system error occurs.

   ☐ To keep a record of major user activities, such as data table updates and the running of key reports or processes.

Answers to Day 21 Exercise

You can complete this assignment by using the SecTest project as a guide.

1. Start SQL-VB5 and build the Assets table in a database called EXER21.MDB. Be sure to add the secUsers and secAccess tables in the database definition. Use the SQL-Visual Basic code in the secTest.SQV script as a guide.

2. Add some records to the Assets, secUsers, and secAccess tables in the new database. You can do this with SQL-VB5 or with the Visual Data Manager.

3. Now start a new Visual Basic 5.0 Standard EXE project. Create a form with six input textboxes and size label prompts (use control arrays). Add a five-item command button array and a data control to the form.

4. Add a reference to the new security objects library. Select Project | Components from the main menu and locate and select the library you built in Chapter 21.

5. Add the following code to the form. This is all the code you need for the form. (You can copy most of this from the SecTest project).

```vb
Option Explicit
'
Dim objUser As Object
Dim objLog As Object

Private Sub cmdBtn_Click(Index As Integer)
    '
    ' handle button clicks
    '
    Dim X As Integer

    On Error GoTo LocalErr
    '
    Select Case Index
        Case 0 ' close
            objLog.WriteLog "LogOut", objUser.UserID
            objUser.LogUser urLogOut
            Unload Me
        Case 1 ' refresh
            Data1.UpdateControls
        Case 2 ' update
            Data1_Validate vbDataActionUpdate, 1
            Data1.UpdateRecord
        Case 3 ' add
            Data1.Recordset.AddNew
            txtField(0).SetFocus
        Case 4 ' delete
            For X = 0 To 5
                objLog.WriteLog "Delete", Data1.RecordSource, _
txtField(X).DataField, txtField(X), ""
            Next X
            Data1.Recordset.Delete
            Data1.Recordset.MovePrevious
    End Select
    '
    Exit Sub
    '
LocalErr:
    MsgBox Err.Description, vbExclamation, Err.Number
    '
End Sub

Private Sub Data1_Validate(Action As Integer, Save As Integer)
    '
    ' log any changes
    '
    Dim ctlTemp As Control
    '
    MousePointer = vbHourglass
    '
    ' check text boxes for changed data
    For Each ctlTemp In Controls
        If TypeOf ctlTemp Is TextBox Then
            If ctlTemp.DataChanged Then
                objLog.WriteLog GetAction(Action), Data1.RecordSource, _
ctlTemp.DataField, Data1.Recordset.Fields(ctlTemp.DataField), ctlTemp
```

```
                    End If
                End If
        Next
        '
        MousePointer = vbNormal
        '
End Sub

Private Sub Form_Load()
    '
    SetForm ' set up form
    SetLog ' set up log stuff
    SetUser ' set up user stuff
    '
End Sub

Public Sub SetLog()
    '
    ' setup logging
    '
    Set objLog = New logObject
    objLog.filename = App.Path & "\" & App.EXEName & ".log"
    objLog.LogHeader = App.EXEName & " Audit Log"
    '
End Sub

Public Sub SetUser()
    '
    ' set up user details
    '
    Dim ctlTemp As Control
    '
    ' create object & set properties
    Set objUser = New usrObject
    objUser.DBName = Data1.DatabaseName
    objUser.LoginTitle = "Assets Login"
    '
    ' login and set up rights
    If objUser.UserLogin = True Then
        objLog.WriteLog "LogIn", objUser.UserID
        For Each ctlTemp In Controls
            If TypeOf ctlTemp Is CommandButton Then
                ctlTemp.Enabled = objUser.CheckRights(ctlTemp.Caption,
ctlTemp.Index)
            End If
        Next
    Else
        End ' reject user
    End If
    '
End Sub
    '
Public Sub SetForm()
    '
    ' set up form controls
    '
    '
```

```
    Me.Caption = "Assets Login"
    '
    lblPrompt(0).Caption = "AssetID"
    lblPrompt(1).Caption = "Description"
    lblPrompt(2).Caption = "Cost"
    lblPrompt(3).Caption = "DateAcq"
    lblPrompt(4).Caption = "SerialNbr"
    lblPrompt(5).Caption = "Department"
    '
    txtField(0).DataField = "assetid"
    txtField(1).DataField = "description"
    txtField(2).DataField = "cost"
    txtField(3).DataField = "dateacq"
    txtField(4).DataField = "serialnbr"
    txtField(5).DataField = "department"
    '
    Data1.BOFAction = vbMoveFirst
    Data1.EOFAction = vbMoveLast
    Data1.DatabaseName = App.Path & "\exer21.mdb"
    Data1.RecordSource = "Assets"
    Data1.Refresh
    '
End Sub

Public Function GetAction(intAction As Integer) As String
    '
    ' convert action constant into friendly name
    '
    Select Case intAction
        Case vbDataActionMoveFirst '1
            GetAction = "MoveFirst"
        Case vbDataActionMovePrevious '2
            GetAction = "MovePrevious"
        Case vbDataActionMoveNext '3
            GetAction = "MoveNext"
        Case vbDataActionMoveLast '4
            GetAction = "MoveLast"
        Case vbDataActionAddNew '5
            GetAction = "AddNew"
        Case vbDataActionUpdate '6
            GetAction = "Update"
        Case vbDataActionDelete '7
            GetAction = "Delete"
        Case vbDataActionFind '8
            GetAction = "Find"
        Case vbDataActionBookmark '9
            GetAction = "Bookmark"
        Case vbDataActionClose '10
            GetAction = "Close"
        Case vbDataActionUnload '11
            GetAction = "Unload"
    End Select
    '
End Function
```

6. Save and run the project.

Appendix B

Answers to Appendix B Quiz

1. You use the pound sign (#) for a context string. You cannot put spaces in the context string footnote.

2. You insert the dollar sign ($) as the custom mark for a title footnote. These footnotes can include spaces.

3. Keywords will be used in the Search box of your help application. You use the semicolon (;) to separate multiple keywords in a topic.

4. You should save your topic file in rich text format *and* in your word processor's normal file format (in case you need to make subsequent revisions). Your project file should be saved in ASCII text and given an .HPJ extension.

5. The contents page of your help file is declared in the [Options] section of the project file by making the following entry:

```
Contents = ContextString
```

In this entry, the context string is the topic you want displayed as the contents page. The first topic of your help file becomes the contents page by default if none is declared.

6. You set the HelpContextID property to identify the help file that appears when the control has focus and F1 is pressed. The numeric value for this field is determined in the [Map] section of the project file.

7. Allow approximately one hour for each typed page of documentation. Adjust this figure for your personal writing style.

Answers to Appendix B Exercises

1. `+ Processing:3`

2. <u>Creating a New Project</u>NewProject

   Note that the jump text is double-underlined. Also note that the context string, NewProject, should be formatted as hidden text.

3. Just change the double-underlined text to single-underlined text and the jump becomes a pop-up.

4. You perform the following steps in order to complete this exercise:

   ☐ Open your topic file.

   ☐ Enter text for a new topic. Give the topic a descriptive heading such as The Company Master Form.

☐ Insert footnotes for the context string, title, and keywords.

☐ Save the file in RTF format.

☐ Add the context string to the [Map] section of the project file.

☐ Compile your project.

☐ Set the HelpContextID of the form to the number you have assigned the context string in the project file.

☐ Execute your program and press F1.

C

INDEX

MACMILLAN COMPUTER PUBLISHING USA

A VIACOM COMPANY

Technical --- Support:

If you need assistance with the information in this book or with a CD/Disk accompanying the book, please access the Knowledge Base on our Web site at **http://www.superlibrary.com/general/support**. Our most Frequently Asked Questions are answered there. If you do not find the answer to your questions on our Web site, you may contact Macmillan Technical Support **(317) 581-3833** or e-mail us at **support@mcp.com**.

Teach Yourself Visual Basic 5 in 21 Days, Fourth Edition

Nathan Gurewich & Ori Gurewich   *Covers Visual Basic 5*

Using a logical, easy-to-follow approach, this international best-seller teaches readers the fundamentals of developing programs. It starts with the basics of writing a program and then moves on to adding voice, music, sound, and graphics.

This book uses shaded syntax boxes, techniques, as well as Q&A, Do/Don't, and workshop sections to highlight key points and reinforce learning.

$29.99 USA $42.95 CDN   *New—Casual*
0-672-30978-5   *1,000 pp.*

Teach Yourself Database Programming with Visual J++ in 21 Days

John Fronckowiak and Gordon McMillan, et al.   *Covers Visual J++*

Using a step-by-step, easy-to-follow format, this complete resource takes users beyond the basic product information and guides them through database integration and interface development. This book highlights new technologies, including JavaBeans, JDBC, DAO Object Library, RDO Object Library, ActiveX, and COM.

$39.99 USA $56.95 CDN   *New—Casual—Accomplished*
1-57521-262-5   *750 pp.*

Access 97 Unleashed, Second Edition

Dwayne Gifford, et al.   *Covers Access*

Access has become one of the most accepted standards of database management for personal computers. The *Unleashed* format for this book allows current and new users to quickly and easily find the information they need on the new features. It also serves as a complete reference for database programmers new to Access. Readers learn advanced techniques for working with tables, queries, forms, and data. This book shows how to program Access and how to integrate the database with the Internet.

$49.99 USA $70.95 CDN   *Accomplished—Expert*
0-672-30983-1   *1,100 pp.*

Alison Balter's Mastering Access 97 Development, Second Premier Edition

Alison Balter   *Covers Access 97*

One of the premier corporate database applications, Access is a powerful application that can be programmed and customized. This book shows users how to develop simple and complex applications for Access 97 and how to create tables, forms, queries, reports, and objects. It also teaches how to program Access applications for a client/server environment. The CD-ROM includes source code, reusable functions, forms, and reports.

$49.99 USA $70.95 CDN   *Accomplished—Expert*
0-672-30999-8   *1,100 pp.*

Developing Personal Oracle7 for Windows 95 Applications, Second Edition

David Lockman   *Covers Personal Oracle7 for Windows 3.1 and Windows 95*

An update to the successful first edition, this comprehensive reference takes users through the process of developing powerful applications while teaching them how to effectively use Personal Oracle7. The CD-ROM includes current versions of Personal Oracle7 for Windows 3.1 and Windows 95.

$49.99 USA $70.95 CDN   *New—Casual*
0-672-31025-2   *800 pp.*

Add to Your Sams Library Today with the Best Books for Programming, Operating Systems, and New Technologies

The easiest way to order is to pick up the phone and call

1-800-428-5331

between 9:00 a.m. and 5:00 p.m. EST.
For faster service please have your credit card available.

ISBN	Quantity	Description of Item	Unit Cost	Total Cost
0-672-30978-5		Teach Yourself Visual Basic 5 in 21 Days, Fourth Edition	$29.99	
1-57521-262-5		Teach Yourself Database Programming with Visual J++ in 21 Days (Book/CD-ROM)	$39.99	
1-57521-174-2		Web Programming with Visual J++ (Book/CD-ROM)	$39.99	
0-672-30983-1		Access 97 Unleashed, Second Edition (Book/CD-ROM)	$49.99	
0-672-30999-8		Alison Balter's Mastering Access 97 Development, Second Premier Edition (Book/CD-ROM)	$49.99	
1-57521-213-7		Designing and Implementing Microsoft Proxy Server	$39.99	
1-57521-212-9		Designing and Implementing Microsoft Index Server	$39.99	
0-672-31025-2		Developing Personal Oracle7 for Windows 95 Applications, Second Edition (Book/CD-ROM)	$49.99	
❏ 3 ½" Disk		Shipping and Handling: See information below.		
❏ 5 ¼" Disk		TOTAL		

Shipping and Handling: $4.00 for the first book, and $1.75 for each additional book. Floppy disk: add $1.75 for shipping and handling. If you need to have it NOW, we can ship product to you in 24 hours for an additional charge of approximately $18.00, and you will receive your item overnight or in two days. Overseas shipping and handling adds $2.00 per book and $8.00 for up to three disks. Prices subject to change. Call for availability and pricing information on latest editions.

201 W. 103rd Street, Indianapolis, Indiana 46290

1-800-428-5331 — Orders   1-800-835-3202 — FAX   1-800-858-7674 — Customer Service

Book ISBN 0-672-31018-X

Installing the CD-ROM

The companion CD-ROM contains all the source code and project files developed by the authors, plus an assortment of evaluation versions of third-party products. To install this material, please follow these steps.

Windows 95 / NT 4 Installation Instructions

1. Insert the CD-ROM into your CD-ROM drive.
2. From the Windows 95 or NT 4 desktop, double-click the My Computer icon.
3. Double-click the icon representing your CD-ROM drive.
4. Double-click the icon labeled `setup.exe` to run the CD-ROM installation program.

   This program creates a Program group with icons for running the programs on the CD-ROM. No files are copied to your hard drive during this installation.

 **NOTE** If you are running Windows 95 and the Autoplay feature is enabled, the `setup.exe` program executes automatically after you insert the CD-ROM into the drive.

Windows NT 3.51 Installation Instructions

1. Insert the CD-ROM into your CD-ROM drive.
2. From the File Manager or Program Manager, choose Run from the File menu.
3. Type `<drive>\setup.exe` and press Enter, where `<drive>` corresponds to the drive letter of your CD-ROM drive. For example, if your CD-ROM drive is `d:`, type `d:\setup.exe` and press Enter.

The installation process creates a program group containing the icons necessary to browse the CD-ROM.